MW01362937

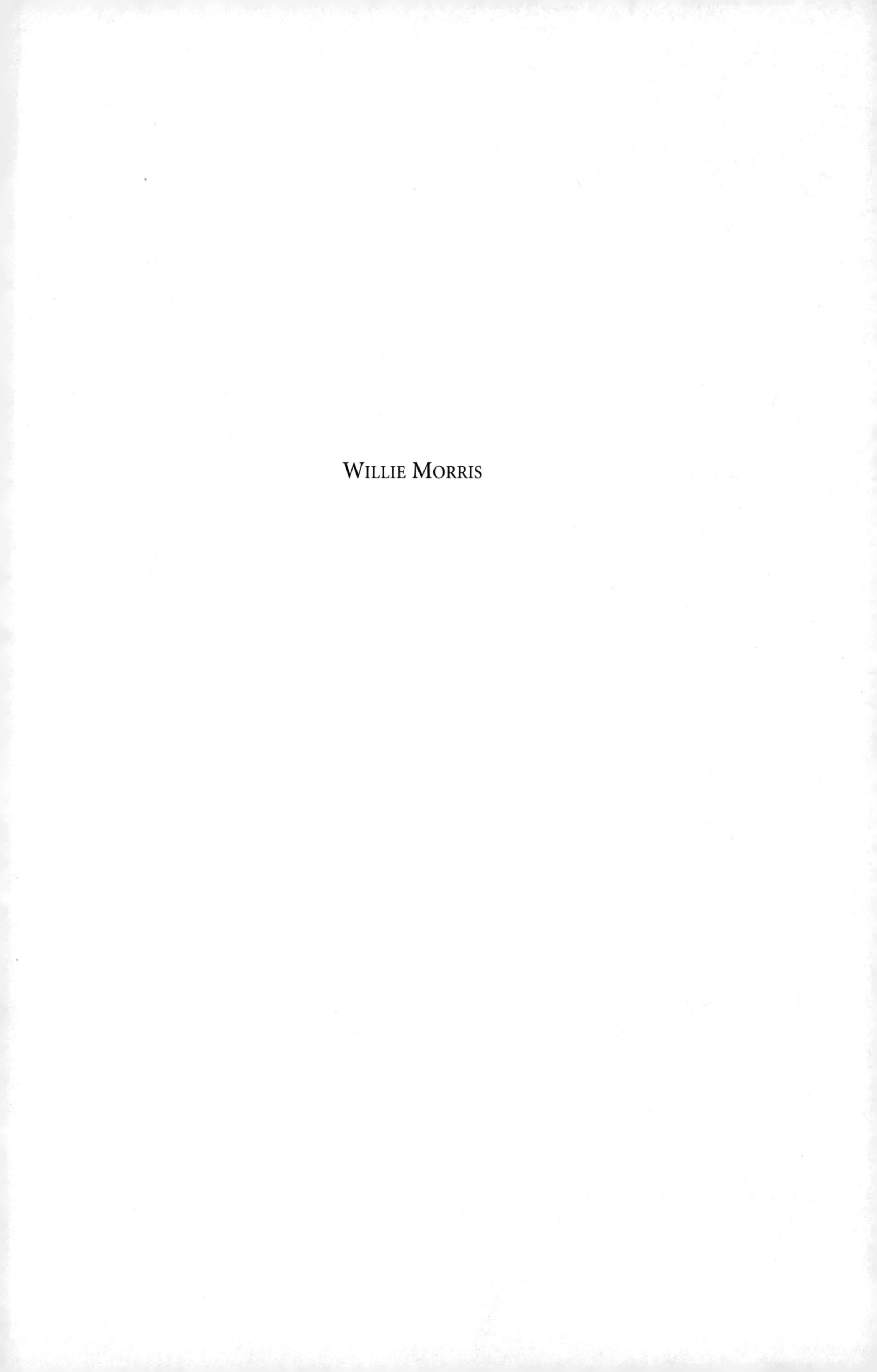

WILLIE MORRIS

Willie Morris

An Exhaustive Annotated Bibliography and a Biography

Jack Bales

Foreword by Rick Bragg

McFarland & Company, Inc., Publishers
Jefferson, North Carolina, and London

LIBRARY OF CONGRESS CATALOGUING-IN-PUBLICATION DATA

Bales, Jack.
Willie Morris : an exhaustive annotated
bibliography and a biography / Jack Bales ;
foreword by Rick Bragg.
p. cm.
Includes bibliographical references and index.

ISBN 0-7864-2478-8 (illustrated case binding : 50# alkaline paper) 

1. Morris, Willie — Bio-bibliography.
2. Authors, American — 20th century — Biography.
3. Mississippi — Biography.
I. Title.
PS3563.O8745Z63 2006 821'.8 — dc22 2006007710

British Library cataloguing data are available

©2006 Jack Bales. All rights reserved

No part of this book may be reproduced or transmitted in any form or by any means, electronic or mechanical, including photocopying or recording, or by any information storage and retrieval system, without permission in writing from the publisher.

On the cover: Willie Morris and his dog Pete,
Oxford, Mississippi, January 1982

Manufactured in the United States of America

McFarland & Company, Inc., Publishers
Box 611, Jefferson, North Carolina 28640
www.mcfarlandpub.com

For Beth Perkins and Carla Bailey,

who have lived through them all.

Table of Contents

PART III
Published Writings About Willie Morris

Foreword

Rick Bragg

Before the funeral, he lay in state in the Old Capitol, in a rotunda that smelled of floor wax and flowers and rich, sad, tortured history. I stood on the sidewalk, waiting my turn, and watched the procession trickle inside. There were best-selling authors and quietly respected ones, men and women who called him mentor and friend, and people who had gotten drunk with him and saved the world, only to find that, once they sobered, the world was still in pretty sorry shape. There were pillars of society in respectable gray suits and sensible heels, lawyers and doctors and at least one governor, a man who had never pandered to the mob, and found a mirror in the dead man's ideals. There were reverent English teachers who had taught his works to half-dazed high school seniors, and aspiring writers who would have given anything to write just one day with his humanity and elegance. There were intellectuals and poets and Sweet Potato Queens, and people who had never written anything except a grocery list, but loved to read writing that by God made them feel something. And here there were the black folks of Mississippi, men and women who filed past his coffin in respect, because they knew that he had used his talents to try and chip away at the injustices of his state and time.

I talked to the mourners one by one, gathering string. I learned that, when he had been a young, hotshot magazine editor in New York, he had held court in a Chinese restaurant. He had not cared for the food, but had so loved the cocktails. I met old men who told me, "You know ol' so-and-so in that book? Well, that was ME." And they would say it with fierce pride, knowing, perhaps, that because of him a ragtag gaggle of barefoot boys would never vanish into time, but would be stamped into pages of immortality. I talked to men who remembered being with him when he played "Taps" at the Yazoo cemetery at the burials of soldiers, chatted with women and men who had known, personally, a dog named Skip and a cat named Spit McGee.

The night before, I had spoken with a great writer, another Southerner, about the passing. We had talked about how fine it was that his Mississippi had allowed this man to lie in state, a generosity usually granted only politicians.

"The State of Mississippi knows how to treat a writer," said Pat Conroy, from the other end of the telephone line. "The State of South Carolina will throw my body in a dumpster. And the State of Alabama will drag you behind a Buick."

But the man in the coffin would suffer no indignities. Death grinds away all burs, and the day of the viewing mourners passed the coffin and buffed his memory, smiling and even laughing as soon as they stepped outside. All of them had received, one book at a time, the gift of his talents, his intellect, and some had even been given pieces of his time and heart. I stood there, in line, and thought of what Willie Morris had given me.

* * *

It had been just a few years before his death. I was in Jackson, signing books in Lemuria, one of the great book stores of the South. On the back cover was an endorsement from Willie, words of great kindness. But I was still surprised when I looked up and saw him there in line with his wife, JoAnne Prichard, a heavy bag of books in his hand. He had me sign them, one by one, to his friends. I still have a picture of it, Willie leaning over the table, telling me to say this and that, me writing as fast as I could, on fire with pride and, as my own Momma would have said, pretty full of my little self. But that was not his gift.

Sometime later, we had gone out with a group of friends to eat fried catfish and French fries and fried dill pickles, grease and salt, a reason to live. I listened to Willie talk about politics and history and life as he knew it, about cemeteries and restless spirits, about martyrs and murderers and a state apparatus that had for so long refused to cull the killers from the general population. I expected, as he talked, to see the ghost of Medgar Evers scratching at the glass. He talked and talked, loose as a brown-bag bottle could get him, until we teetered to the car. Later, in his study, he talked on, until the visitors had slipped away, leaving just me and him, and the stories.

I told him I believed the South produced so many writers because, as a people, we grew up on stories, stories of loss and pain and fury and regret. He nodded and said that might be so.

I was getting ready to politely take my leave when he reached for a copy of my first book, opened it to the first page, and began to read aloud. I thought he was just being kind again, but he read on and on and on, page after page after page. The introduction vanished into the first chapter, and then on, and ... then he snapped the book closed.

To this day, it was one of the nicest things that has ever happened to me in my life. I cannot say exactly why, but to sit there and hear my words read aloud in his voice, in a voice that seemed to magically understand where I meant emphasis to be, where I meant pauses to come, was like air itself. I fed on it, sucked it in, and it made me want to do more of it, and more and more.

"You say it's the story," Willie said, "but I say it's the language."

* * *

I would learn, only at his graveside, that he was just that kind with others. I wasn't special, after all. But he was, in his generosity. The more I learned about him, the more I understood that. In the pages of this book are pieces of Willie's voice, pieces of paper that, stacked high enough, formed a life. He seemed to write everything as a writer, not only as communication, but something better, warmer, something — I don't know — important. I wish, sometimes, I could have read his grocery list.

* * *

At his house, after the funeral, the table seemed to strain under good food. Southern cooks had laden it with fried chicken and casseroles, and someone had brought a plate of tomato sandwiches on white bread with mayonnaise. Because it was a wake, of sorts, someone had cut off the crusts. There was banana puddin', and pound cake. I ate standing up, more than enough to be polite. Banana puddin' at a funeral is still banana puddin'. As I wandered around I came to his study, to the chair where he had sat that night, the night he made me feel like I belonged in his craft. I did not stand there long. I do not believe in ghosts as strongly as Willie did, and what I felt there, mostly, was emptiness.

But I will never hear the word "language" quite the same again.

Rick Bragg, author of the critically acclaimed memoir All Over but the Shoutin', *won the 1996 Pulitzer Prize in Feature Writing for his "elegantly written stories about contemporary America." He is a Professor of Writing in the Journalism Department at the University of Alabama in Tuscaloosa.*

Preface

I began researching this book in the summer of 1995, although I did not realize it at the time. I had recently read Willie Morris's *North Toward Home* and *My Dog Skip*, and I wrote the author to compliment him on his books and to ask a few questions. My letter arrived at an opportune moment, for I had caught him between writing projects, and he was able to respond with a long handwritten letter. (I found out later that Morris preferred felt-tip pens to computers. His wife, JoAnne, said he "closed his eyes" while walking by hers.) I wrote once more, asking additional questions about his many books and articles, and thereupon began a correspondence and friendship that would last literally until the day before his untimely death on August 2, 1999.

Although Morris's reputation rests largely on his books of nonfiction, particularly his first memoir, *North Toward Home*, he also received widespread recognition as a journalist, news commentator, novelist, editor, and essayist. Critics have often singled out his perceptive understanding of and deep affection for the South as well as his passionate convictions about the importance of race relations in America. As Peter Applebome observes in his *New York Times* obituary, "Rather than merely a vivid interpreter of Southern life, Mr. Morris's legacy is as someone who was ahead of his time in exploring the confluence of region and nation, and how much the South's distinctive experience of race, family and history was so deeply a part of the nation's experience as well."

Morris's own roots grew just as deep. The seventh-generation Mississippian enjoyed driving around his ancestral town of Raymond (his maternal grandmother, born in Raymond, was the grandniece of the first territorial governor of the state and the niece of another governor and United States senator). He also loved to take friends on tours of the Delta, particularly his hometown of Yazoo City. During one of my several visits to Mississippi, Morris drove me along virtually every street and road in his childhood community, talking about his formative years, reminiscing about his family, and pointing out sites both personal and historic. As our conversation turned to an article he was working on, I commented on how fulfilling his life as an author must be. "Well, Jack," he nodded, "I couldn't live without writing, and I have no alternative to words. "Besides," he shrugged, "I can't do anything else."

But he *did*, as the first part of the present book attests. "North Toward Home to Mississippi: The Life and Works of Willie Morris" provides an in-depth literary biography largely based on hundreds of primary sources, such as letters, newspaper articles, and interviews. Its first chapter, "Early Years (1934–1952)," chronicles Morris's youth in Yazoo City. "College Days and Controversy (1952–1956)" covers his four years at the University of Texas, focusing on his confrontation with the school's Board of Regents over editorial policy of the campus newspaper, the *Daily Texan*. After graduation, Morris studied in England as a

Rhodes scholar, as detailed in "An American Abroad (1956–1960)." The fourth chapter, "Crusading Journalist (1960–1971)," explores his editorial career, first with the *Texas Observer* and then with *Harper's Magazine*. After Morris resigned from *Harper's* in 1971 following a bitter dispute with the magazine's publisher and owner, he sequestered himself in Bridgehampton, New York, as described in "Adrift on Long Island (1971–1979)." In the next section, "South Toward Home (1979–1999)," I examine both the circumstances behind his return to his native state and the last years of his life. My "Epilogue" contains reminiscences by some of Morris's friends, summaries of the author's works that were published posthumously, and observations about his artistic achievements and literary reputation. Extensive endnotes document my research and amplify my conclusions. More than fifty photographs, some never before published, are interspersed throughout the book and capture Morris at various stages of his life.

The second and third parts of the present volume, annotated bibliographies of works both by and about Morris, grew from my biographical research. Soon after I discovered the author's works in 1995, I began tracking down his many articles and essays, even going so far as to page through the hundreds of issues of the *Daily Texan* and *Texas Observer* to which he had contributed pieces. I located invaluable primary and secondary documents and bibliographic citations by poring over his 17,000 papers at the University of Mississippi. I also consulted hundreds of reference volumes, indexes, databases, and books relating to southern literature and history.

Morris immediately became interested in my research, and I began sending him copies of many of the works I found, particularly decades-old articles he had written. As he related the circumstances behind his writings, he would suggest other avenues of research. "Sometime when we're together," he wrote in August 1996, "let's sit down and I'll prod my memory on magazine pieces I've written over the years which you may not know about." During one conversation, he reminded me that in 1976 he had spent several months in Washington, D.C., as writer-in-residence at the *Washington Star*. I went through the back files of the paper for copies of all the articles he wrote. Three of them, which recount the tour of Civil War battlefields he took with his son and writer James Jones and his son, are reprinted herein as Part IV.

The numbered bibliographies in Part II (items 1 to 964) and Part III (items 965 to 2109) are divided into broad categories and are limited to English-language publications. Entries within each category are arranged chronologically. Works published on the same date in Part II are sub-organized alphabetically by title, though if more than one Morris book was published in a given year, the title that was released first is listed first. Works published on the same date in Part III are subarranged alphabetically by author, and if no author is listed, then by title. The annotations in the bibliographies provide summaries of the works cited.

I added cross references (that is, citation numbers) in the annotations where appropriate. They are particularly useful in noting revisions and reprintings of Morris's works in Part II. For example, in 1976 Morris wrote "Another CIA Story Still Lurks in a Shopping Bag" for the *Washington Star* (item 812). It was republished as "Memoir of a Legendary Spy" in *Newsday* (item 813) and as "8" of "Vignettes of Washington" in his collection of essays, *Terrains of the Heart and Other Essays on Home* (item 16-H). Years later he revised the article for inclusion in chapter 2 of his memoir *New York Days*.

The annotation of each original piece contains the work's full publication history. To avoid repetition (the author's *North Toward Home*, for example, is cited numerous times in the bibliographies) and because Morris's book titles are easily located in my table of contents, I do not include the item numbers when referring to the titles of his books.

I often cite two or more component parts of one work, such as the individual essays in Morris's collections of essays. In these instances, the full bibliographic information for the book is listed only once; citations to the essays or component pieces include cross references back to the parent volume. For instance, Morris's *Homecomings* is documented in item 40, and its six essays are listed and annotated in items 41 to 46.

Primary and secondary works are generally listed separately in their respective sections, Part II and Part III. For example, Morris's articles and editorials concerning his views on *Daily Texan* editorial policy are noted in Part II, while the assorted secondary works about the controversy that his views generated in the *Texan* are recorded in Part III. If a letter to the editor, however (either by or about Morris), is in direct response to a cited literary work, the reference to the correspondence follows the citation to that work. For instance, the bibliographic reference to a letter from a reader objecting to one of Morris's articles in the *Daily Texan* (item 280-A) appears after the citation to the article itself (item 280). Morris's response to an editor's comments about his memoir *New York Days* (item 1206-C) is listed after the citation to the published criticism (item 1206-B). Morris's letter is also documented as item 963 in the "Letters to the Editor" section of Part II.

After excerpts from Morris's *North Toward Home* appeared in the *Saturday Evening Post* (item 729), various readers in the author's hometown wrote letters to the *Yazoo City Herald*. Because the correspondence was not published in the *Post*, however, I did not list the letters alongside Morris's work but instead included them with other newspaper citations in Part III (for example, see items 1547 to 1551).

Like all bibliographers, I had to make arbitrary decisions. For instance, as a boy, Morris often went by the names "William Morris" or "William Weaks Morris." Occasionally he was addressed as "Willie Weaks." By the end of his sophomore year in college, he consistently wrote under "Willie Morris," and in the interest of consistency I use that name throughout.

I chose to place citations to articles about Morris appearing in newspaper magazines that are identified with their parent papers (such as the *New York Times Magazine*, the *New York Times Book Review*, and the *Washington Post Book World*) in the newspaper section of Part III. Morris wrote several articles for *Parade* magazine, but because the newspaper supplement is not identified with a corresponding newspaper title, I placed these references in the magazine section of Part II.

Although the *Texas Observer* is today published as a magazine, it was a newspaper when Morris wrote for it; in fact, back then the masthead proclaimed that each issue was "an independent-liberal weekly newspaper." Morris's numerous contributions are listed in a section devoted to the *Texas Observer*, and secondary articles are cited in the newspaper section of Part III.

Some of the book reviews annotated in Part III were published not under individual titles, but with other reviews under collective titles such as "Non-Fiction," "Fiction," or "Book Reviews." If the collective heading appears on the same page as the cited review, I adopted this heading, with quotation marks, as the title in the bibliographic reference. If the collective title does not appear on the same page as the review, I simply used the word Review, with no quotation marks, in place of the title.

A few other explanations about titles are necessary. Magazine and newspaper title changes always frustrate bibliographers, and I relied heavily upon Library of Congress authority records. For example, *Harper's Magazine* became *Harper's* in 1976 (and went back to *Harper's Magazine* in 1987). In 1973, the *Austin American* changed its name to the *Austin American-Statesman*, the title under which it had been publishing its weekend editions. Citations to works from magazines or newspapers include the publication titles in use at those particular times.

In newspaper citations that do not include the names of cities, I added the identifying localities in parentheses, such as the *(Baltimore) Sun* and the *(Memphis) Commercial Appeal*. For newspaper citations not nationally well known, I noted identifying states in parentheses, for instance, the *Hinds County (Miss.) Gazette* and the *(Greenville, Miss.) Delta Democrat-Times*. I omitted in my citations, however, the parenthetical identifiers to a few publications that I cite numerous times. These are the *Clarion-Ledger* and *Jackson Daily News* of Jackson, Mississippi; the Yazoo,

Mississippi *Yazoo Herald*, *Yazoo City Herald*, and *Yazoo Daily Herald*; the Austin-based *Texas Observer*; and the University of Texas *Daily Texan* (called the *Summer Texan* during the summers).

I examined every one of the more than 2,000 items in the two bibliographies. With the exception of a few newspaper articles for which I could not determine pagination at the Library of Congress (it does not own, for example, the *Oxford [Miss.] Eagle*), I provided bibliographic information for each. To prevent Part III from becoming unwieldy, I did not cite every published work on the author and his writings that I located. I omitted several dozen book reviews from small-town newspapers because they were similar to reviews from national periodicals I had already documented. In my research I also came across some primary and secondary works for which I could not verify publication details, and these, too, were not included in my book.

Library databases, particularly full-text ones, are invaluable to students and scholars. I have noticed, however, that database citations do not always include the pagination of magazine and newspaper articles. Whenever I had questions, I verified publication information at the Library of Congress or other libraries.

An index appears at the end of the book. Numbers preceded by a lower-case "p" refer to page numbers throughout the book. Numbers without a "p" denote item numbers in the bibliographies.

Like most researchers, I owe an enormous debt to the many people who assisted me. I am especially grateful to my colleagues at the University of Mary Washington in Fredericksburg, Virginia. Beth Perkins, a native Mississippian like Willie Morris, read this book in manuscript form, checking for errors and inconsistencies. Her encouragement was crucial as I struggled with countless details and seemingly insurmountable bibliographic problems. Carla Bailey located numerous items through interlibrary loan and made sense of citations on which I had given up. Library Director Roy Strohl always offered greatly appreciated support and camaraderie. Tim Newman worked miracles with his computer expertise. I also want to thank my fellow colleagues at the Reference Desk, especially Ron Comer, to whom I often turned for guidance on writing and literary matters.

William M. Anderson Jr., President of the University of Mary Washington, has been interested in my various writing projects since I started working in the campus library in 1980. Without his generosity this book could not have been written.

I am grateful for the friendship of Willie Morris's family. His widow, JoAnne Prichard Morris, suggested many editorial improvements. His son, David Rae Morris, provided one of the photographs. Both responded promptly to all of my many questions and allowed me to quote from unpublished correspondence.

I owe much to many individuals in Mississippi who knew Willie Morris. In the early 1950s, Morris's friend Ralph Atkinson was the photographer for the Yazoo High School newspaper, the *Flashlight*. Ralph spent hours sifting through hundreds of photographs, and his contributions appear throughout my book. Hunter Cole gave me much editorial advice and sent me several photographs of Morris he had taken over the years. John E. Ellzey, the long-time reference librarian at the Ricks Memorial Library in Yazoo City, verified the bibliographic information for dozens of articles in the *Yazoo Herald* and supplied details about the history of the town. When asked if I could use her photograph of Morris at William Faulkner's grave in Oxford, Kay Holloway immediately gave her permission. Michelle Hudson, the reference librarian at the Eudora Welty Library in Jackson, immediately replied to numerous questions and verified citations in the *Clarion-Ledger*. Mary Jones and Burke Jones scanned and printed a photograph from Morris's high school yearbook, the *Mingo Chito*. Norman A. Mott Jr. readily granted me permission to use the photograph of Morris he took in 1967 for the dust jacket of *North Toward Home* (and just as quickly addressed my questions about Morris and the town in which the author grew up). Vernon Sikes of the *Yazoo Herald* took a photo of Morris's footstone especially for this book. Chris Todd sent me many photographs from the files of the *Clarion-Ledger* in Jackson.

Larry Wells, the dean of Morris scholars, patiently and at great length replied to dozens of questions. Some of Morris's childhood friends graciously consented to be interviewed, including Daisye Love Askew, Jimmy Ball, B. Barrier, and Marsha Williams.

My twin brother, Dick Bales, has been a comrade and confidant for as long as I can remember. He never failed to come through with a few supportive words when I needed them (and blunt literary criticism when I needed that). Rick Bragg has often remarked on how much Willie Morris meant to him, both professionally and personally, and I am pleased that he was able to contribute his fine foreword to my book. Caralinn Cole of Houston spent hours looking up citations for me. Steven L. Davis, assistant curator of the Southwestern Writers Collection at Texas State University-San Marcos, checked many citations in the *Texas Observer*. Donald R. Eldred has shared his love for literature — and wise counsel — with me for decades. Jennifer Ford, Head of Archives and Special Collections at the J. D. Williams Library, University of Mississippi, promptly replied to dozens of letters and queries. For years Larry L. King, Morris's former colleague at *Harper's Magazine*, has given advice, answered questions, and been a good friend (and no one can park a car like "Lawyer Blaine"). Antoinette Parker scanned and printed many photographs for me. Beverley Shelesky obtained dozens of needed books. When I first started my Morris research, archivist Lisa K. Speer enthusiastically tracked down citations, pored over documents, and assisted me on numerous occasions. I met Richard Sturges in Yazoo City during a "Remembering Willie" celebration, and I am grateful for his photographic expertise. Edwin M. Yoder Jr. and Willie Morris became friends as Rhodes scholars on the *Flandre* bound for England. Ed provided many details of Morris's life as well as advice and support as I worked on this book. I originally wrote my Willie Morris chronology for *Conversations with Willie Morris* (Jackson: University Press of Mississippi, 2000). It is updated here with permission of the University Press of Mississippi, which also allowed me to use a few sentences from that book and my *Shifting Interludes: Selected Essays* (2002).

I also wish to thank Jennifer Aronson (Curator of Visual Collections, J. D. Williams Library, University of Mississippi), Bob Bailey, Phyllis Bales, Neal Biggers, Porter Blakemore, Charles Bolton (Director of the Center for Oral History and Cultural Heritage at the University of Southern Mississippi), Todd Breyfogle (Editor, *American Oxonian*), Burt Britton, Fred Brown, The Center for American History at the University of Texas at Austin, the *Clarion-Ledger* of Jackson, Mississippi, William B. Crawley Jr., James E. Davis, John Evans, Claudine Ferrell, Susan Garcia, Lara George (of the *Texas Observer*), Bob Grattan, Mary Grattan, Matthew Guderian, Berna Heyman, Mike Hill, Orley Hood, Mary Ann Keith (Publisher / Editor of the *Hinds County Gazette*), Harold Kelly, Kevin Kelly, Harriet DeCell Kuykendall, Lucius Lampton, Kathy Lawrence (Director of Student Publications, University of Texas at Austin), Ron Lindsey, Louis J. Lyell, Vay Gregory McGraw, Nan McMurry, Jon Meacham, Frances Mitchell, John Mosqueda, Sam Olden (President, Yazoo Historical Society), Beth Bales Olson, Linda Peterson, Mike Quinn, Susan Reid, Sid Salter, David Sansing, Seetha Srinivasan (Director, University Press of Mississippi), A. Truman Schwartz, John Spong, Jack Stevens, Steve Stewart, William Styron; Roscoe "Rocky" Suddarth; Richard D. Sylvester, Jim Tarwater, Sam Ulmschneider, John E. Wallace (Principal, Yazoo City High School), Jack Walsdorf, Paulette Watson, Linton Weeks, Curtis Wilkie, Charles Reagan Wilson (Director, Center for the Study of Southern Culture), Yazoo City High School, and the *Yazoo Herald* of Yazoo City, Mississippi.

I am especially grateful to Laura Bales and Patrick Bales, who are a constant, marvelous presence in my life.

Jack Bales
Simpson Library,
University of Mary Washington
Spring 2006

Chronology

1934 .... William Weaks Morris born on November 29 in Jackson, Mississippi, the only child of Henry Rae Morris (1899–1958) and Marion (Weaks) Morris (1904–1977); family moves to Yazoo City, Mississippi, six months later

1946 .... Begins writing sports stories for the *Yazoo Herald* newspaper

1951–1952 .... Editor of Yazoo High School newspaper, the *Flashlight*, during senior year

1952 .... Graduates class valedictorian in May and is voted "most likely to succeed" by classmates; enters University of Texas in Austin that fall and joins staff of student newspaper, the *Daily Texan*

1955 .... Elected to membership in Phi Beta Kappa honor society

1955–1956 .... Editor-in-chief of *Daily Texan* during senior year

1956 .... Publishes first article for a national magazine, "Mississippi Rebel on a Texas Campus," in the March 24 *Nation*; graduates from University of Texas in June with a B.A. degree in English; in October matriculates at Oxford University's New College as a Rhodes scholar

1957 .... Pet dog Skip dies in the spring

1958 .... Studies history at Oxford University; associate editor of *Texas Observer* in the summer; marries Celia Ann Buchan on August 30; father dies on September 2

1959 .... Receives B.A. degree in modern history from Oxford University; son David Rae Morris born in England on November 1

1959–1960 .... Takes graduate courses in American and British history at Oxford University; returns to *Texas Observer* as associate editor in July 1960

1961–1962 .... Editor-in-chief and general manager of *Texas Observer* from March 1961 to November 1962

1962–1963 .... Sits in on graduate courses at Stanford University in Palo Alto, California

1963–1965 .... Associate editor, *Harper's* magazine

1965 .... *The South Today: 100 Years After Appomattox* (editor)

1965–1967 .... Executive editor, *Harper's* magazine

1966 .... M.A., Oxford University

1967 .... Awarded honorary Ph.D. from Grinnell College; first book, *North Toward Home*, is published (which received the "Houghton Mifflin Literary Fellowship Award for Non-fiction"); appointed editor-in-chief of *Harper's* magazine in May; excerpts 45,000 words from William Styron's *The Confessions of Nat Turner* in September issue

1968 .... Elected to the Texas Institute of Letters; receives Carr P. Collins Award from Texas Institute of Letters for *North Toward Home*, which recognizes the best nonfiction book by a Texas author or about Texas; publishes Norman Mailer's "The Steps of the Pentagon" in March *Harper's*; awarded honorary Ph.D. from Gettysburg College

1969 .... Willie and Celia Morris divorce

1970 .... Publishes Seymour M. Hersh's "My Lai 4: A Report on the Massacre and Its Aftermath" in May *Harper's*

1971 .... Publishes Norman Mailer's "The Prisoner of Sex" in March *Harper's*; resigns from *Harper's* that month (along with most of the contributing editors) and moves to Bridgehampton, New York; *Yazoo: Integration in a Deep-Southern Town*; *Good Old Boy: A Delta Boyhood*

1972 .... Receives Steck-Vaughn Award from Texas Institute of Letters for *Good Old Boy*, which recognizes the best book for children by a Texas author or about Texas

1973 .... *The Last of the Southern Girls*

1975 .... *A Southern Album: Recollections of Some People and Places and Times Gone By*

1976 .... Writer-in-residence at the *Washington Star* newspaper from January to March

1977 .... Mother dies on April 15; friend James Jones dies on May 9 and Morris completes last several chapters of *Whistle* (1978), final volume of Jones's World War II trilogy

1978 .... *James Jones: A Friendship*

1979–1980.... Returns to Mississippi in December 1979 to accept position as visiting lecturer in University of Mississippi's English Department. Begins teaching courses in creative writing and the American novel when classes start in January

1981 .... *Terrains of the Heart and Other Essays on Home*. Transfers to Journalism Department at University of Mississippi in the fall as lecturer and writer-in-residence

1983 .... Pet dog Pete dies on February 1; *The Courting of Marcus Dupree*; *Always Stand In Against the Curve and Other Sports Stories*

1984 .... Receives a Christopher Award for *The Courting of Marcus Dupree*, which recognizes those "who have achieved artistic excellence in films, books, and television specials affirming the highest values of the human spirit"

1988 .... Multimedia Entertainment, Inc. films *Good Old Boy* in Natchez, Mississippi, and The Disney Channel broadcasts motion picture in the fall

1989 .... Public Broadcasting System televises *Good Old Boy* as part of its *Wonderworks* series; *Good Old Boy and the Witch of Yazoo*; *Homecomings*

1990 .... *Faulkner's Mississippi*; Mississippi Library Association selects *Homecomings* as best Mississippi nonfiction book of the year; marries JoAnne Shirley Prichard on September 14 and moves to Jackson, Mississippi

1991 .... Resigns in February as writer-in-residence from University of Mississippi, effective the end of the academic semester

1992 .... *After All, It's Only a Game*

1993 . . . . *New York Days*

1994 . . . . Receives Governor's Award for Excellence in the Arts from the Mississippi Arts Commission; Mississippi Institute of Arts and Letters selects *New York Days* as best nonfiction book of the year

1995 . . . . *My Dog Skip*; *A Prayer for the Opening of the Little League Season*

1996 . . . . Awarded third annual Richard Wright Medal for Literary Excellence at Natchez Literary Festival; "A Prayer Before the Feast," introductory essay to *Centennial Olympic Games: Official Souvenir Program, July 19–August 4, 1996*

1998 . . . . *The Ghosts of Medgar Evers: A Tale of Race, Murder, Mississippi, and Hollywood*; Alcon Entertainment begins filming *My Dog Skip* in the spring

1999 . . . . In mid-year named to the national advisory board of the First Amendment Center at Vanderbilt University in Nashville. Dies on August 2 of cardiomyopathy after suffering a heart attack and is buried in Yazoo City, Mississippi; *My Cat Spit McGee* published posthumously; Warner Bros. releases motion picture *My Dog Skip*

2000 . . . . *My Mississippi*

2001 . . . . *Taps: A Novel*

2002 . . . . *Shifting Interludes: Selected Essays*

2004 . . . . Posthumously elected to the Texas Intercollegiate Press Association Hall of Fame

PART I

North Toward Home to Mississippi: The Life and Works of Willie Morris

Early Years (1934–1952)

"Tell me about where you come from," a friend once said to me, and I could do no better than this: I love the South because it helps me remember. It helps me know who I am. When I am there, it haunts me that all my people— my great-grandparents, my grandfather and grandmother, my aunts and uncles, my father— lie close by in the dark earth. Be with me, *my father whispered to me when he was dying. I am aware that I am among them and that they will always be with me.*[1]— Willie Morris, *A Southern Album* (1975)

William Weaks Morris was defined in large measure by his southern roots, his respect of the past, and his loyalty to family, friends, and home. He was born on November 29, 1934, in Jackson, Mississippi, but grew up in Yazoo City, a small town located, he writes in the opening chapter of *North Toward Home*, "on the edge of the delta, straddling that memorable divide where the hills end and the flat land begins." During his youth he acquired a strong sense of history, place, and family. "We had a closeness to the earth," he reminisced in 1996, "and we were so *isolated*, although I do not think we knew that then. We sat barefoot on the porches in the summer nights and listened to the stories of the old people."[2]

Intensely proud of his southern heritage, he often wrote about his ancestors. His mother's relations included Cowles Mead, his great-great-great uncle who served as the acting territorial governor of Mississippi from 1806 to 1807. Morris's "true family hero," however, was Henry S. Foote, his great-great uncle and a United States senator from 1847 to 1852. An "erratic, courageous bantam of a man" and a political moderate who opposed secession, Foote drew a pistol on Missouri Senator Thomas Hart Benton in April 1850 during a stormy political debate, "but a colleague managed to snatch the gun away while Benton was inviting my uncle to go ahead and shoot." Foote continued to fight secession after he was elected governor of Mississippi in 1851. When the southern states broke with the Union, he remained with the Confederacy, "trapped in it along with so many other Southern moderates," and served in the Confederate Congress.[3]

Top: **Willie Morris was born in Jackson, Mississippi, in 1934 but grew up in Yazoo City, a small town some forty miles north of the state capital. In 1937 the Morris family moved into this frame house on Grand Avenue, one of the town's main thoroughfares. Daisye Love Rainer Askew, a school friend of Morris and the 1951 Yazoo City High School Homecoming Queen, remembers that the high school boys "always liked to play football at Willie's house because it was right on Grand Avenue where everybody would drive up and down. I can remember Willie's dog Skip running back and forth along the street. The girls would all drive by, honk the car horn, and wave at the boys" (courtesy R. H. Sturges).** ***Bottom:*** **The first grade class taught by Miss Bass at Main Street Elementary School in Yazoo City, Mississippi, in 1941. Willie Morris is in the front row, third from left, wearing the striped shirt (courtesy Ralph Atkinson).**

Morris was particularly close to his maternal grandmother, Mamie, who was descended from the Harper family of Raymond, Mississippi. "All my people came from Raymond; they founded Raymond," Morris often remarked. Born in 1878, shortly after the Northern army withdrew its troops from Mississippi, Mamie was the "repository of those vanished times" for Morris and often told him vivid stories of his forebears.[4] His great-grandfather George W. Harper of Raymond founded and edited the *Hinds County Gazette*, one of the oldest extant newspapers in the state. He was elected mayor of the town, served as major of the local militia, and continued to edit the newspaper until May 12, 1863. As Sherman's army marched through town on its way to burn Jackson, soldiers, acting on orders from General Grant, destroyed his printing presses

Main Street Elementary School's second grade class, taught by Mrs. Page (standing behind the class) in 1942. Willie Morris is the boy kneeling on the far right side of the first row (courtesy Ralph Atkinson).

by dumping them in the town well. In an essay about his great-grandfather, Morris wrote that his ancestral home was used as a hospital during the Civil War:

> My great-grandmother helped nurse the wounded of both sides in the family house. She took down a letter, my grandmother Mamie would tell me years later, from a dying twenty-year old soldier from Illinois to his mother, and made sure the Federal officers sent it up through the lines. The house, I was told, ran with blood, which dripped down the rain gulleys. As I was reminded over and over as a boy, the family cow soon disappeared. My great-grandmother, with several mouths to feed, went to the captain of the Federal troops and complained that his soldiers had stolen their cow. "Find this lady a cow," the captain ordered his staff, and then graciously escorted her home. "Mama said he was such a nice man," Mamie and my great-aunts would say to me as late as the 1940s sitting in the parlor on North Jefferson in Jackson, "such a nice honest man who cared," but when the original cow wandered home the next day, and the herd increased to two, Yankee chivalry was not rewarded with the return of the merchandise.[5]

Morris's father, on the other hand, sprang from a pedigree not nearly as genteel. "He was

The "Safety Club" at Main Street Elementary School in Yazoo City, Mississippi, included, front row, left to right: Marion ("Pee Wee" or "Sonny") Baskin, Vanjon Ward, and Willie Morris. Second row, left to right: Ralph Atkinson and Edwin "Honest Ed" Upton. Safety Club members were street crossing helpers to the policeman. All five boys were in the second grade (courtesy Ralph Atkinson).

Top: **As a second-grader, Willie Morris (left) was the groom in a "Tom Thumb wedding," presented by students in the lower elementary grades. His good friend Ralph Atkinson (center) was the minister and Vanjon Ward (right) was the best man. The group of about twenty-five students performed matinee and evening performances at the Dixie Theater in Yazoo City and went on the road to Jackson for a matinee performance at the capital city's Lamar Theater. The three members of the mock wedding party are standing in front of the Ricks Memorial Library in Yazoo City in 1942. The widely publicized marriage of midget Charles S. Stratton (also known as General Tom Thumb) to Lavinia Warren, another midget, in 1863 inspired many American communities to stage Tom Thumb weddings, which featured children in elaborate wedding attire (courtesy Ralph Atkinson).** ***Bottom:*** **Willie Morris and his classmates took part in a "Hindpaw and Bailhay Circus," presented in the high school gymnasium in 1942 for the benefit of the American Red Cross. Among the hundred or so students participating were (standing fourth and fifth from left) second graders Willie Morris and Ralph Atkinson dressed as cowboys and riding stick horses. This event likely supported the nation's war efforts in the early days of World War II (courtesy Ralph Atkinson).**

country," Morris reminisced in 1984. "I doubt if he gave much thought to the Confederacy, or the aristocratic South of my maternal forebears." Henry Rae Morris came from Camden, Tennessee — one hundred miles west of Nashville — the son of Tennessee state senator William Morris and his wife Nancy (Stegall) Morris. Orphaned as a small boy, Rae, as he was called, was raised by relatives. After high school he enlisted in the Army, and he was waiting along with other Tennessee boys in New York City for a troop ship to take them to Europe when the Armistice was signed. He then moved to the Deep South to find a job and went to work for the Standard Oil Company in Jackson.

In the late 1920s he met Marion Harper Weaks, the daughter of Edmund Percy and Marion "Mamie" (Harper) Weaks. The two married on May 16, 1929, in Jackson but moved the forty-two miles north to Yazoo City in 1935 when Willie, their only child, was about six months old.[6]

Willie Morris reported in *North Toward Home* that his mother cried over having to leave the big city for a "bedraggled place" like Yazoo City (population 5,579 in 1930), where residents still found the Great Flood of 1927 a lively topic of conversation. As a graduate of Millsaps College and a student at the American Conservatory of Music in Chicago, the accomplished pianist saw little in the unpaved streets and cramped homes to attract her. At first the Morris family occupied a small frame house with an "ancient old lady" they called "Aunt Tish," but in 1937 they moved to Grand Avenue and a larger house, where Willie Morris lived until he went away to college. Rae Morris owned a Cities Service gas station on Main Street and later worked as a bookkeeper for the Goyer Wholesale Grocery Company.[7] Years later Morris remembered that his father, a tall, "thin and gaunt" man, worked long hours to support his family:

A birthday party for Ralph Atkinson (standing in back row, far right) in October 1944. Willie Morris is standing in the back row, far left, waving to the camera (courtesy Ralph Atkinson).

> He would deliver gasoline and fuel out to the farmers in the hills and in the Delta, and the scenes of poverty that I would see in that farm country are still etched in my memory. He never really made much money. My mother was teaching piano so we got through all right. There were only three of us, but it was a very tough time there in those farm communities of the Deep South during the Depression.[8]

One pastime that helped young Morris get through those tough years was sports. His father had played semi-pro baseball in western Tennessee and was nicknamed "Hooks" for the way he could hook-slide with "willowy grace." Willie's earliest childhood memory, in fact, was of his father teaching him the rudiments of baseball. "I guess I was about three years old, and my father and I were alone in the old Goose Egg Park in Yazoo City, and he mapped out a miniature baseball diamond with pieces of cardboard for the bases and home plate." When his father, an outdoorsman and "indomitable country athlete," played ball with his own baseball club, the man let young Willie — who was too small to swing a bat — try his hand at bunting a ball.[9]

Willie soon added basketball and football to his athletic interests. Perhaps due to his father's Tennessee roots, he enthusiastically supported the Volunteers of the University of Tennessee's football team. According to childhood friend Ralph Atkinson, "Willie was stuck to the radio on Saturdays as he listened to announcer Bill Stern's play-by-play de-

After school sandlot football games in the fall always drew Willie Morris and his friends, many of whom would later show up in *Good Old Boy* and his other books. The photograph, taken when the "good old boys" were in junior high school (grades 6–8) includes (front row, left to right): Clifton "Bo" Collins, Jimmy Lawson, Leslie Coody, Clifton Sanders, and an unidentified boy. Standing from left to right are: Bobby Tackett, Willie Morris (who always called the plays), Billy "Muttonhead" Shepherd, and Charles "Big Boy" Wilkinson (courtesy Ralph Atkinson).

As a youngster, Morris carved "Willie M." into the trunk of this magnolia tree in his grandparents' yard on North Jefferson Street in Jackson. The house has since been torn down, and the site is now an asphalt parking lot. According to *A Cook's Tour of Mississippi*, in which this photo appears, "During the summer of 1980, a vandal cut the name from the tree, although the tree still stands." It was still living in the summer of 2005 (courtesy the *Clarion-Ledger*).

scriptions of the Volunteers' games, especially when they faced their national nemesis, the Wildcats of the University of Kentucky."[10]

Although Rae Morris had aspirations that his son become a professional baseball player, Marion — a pianist, organist, teacher, and an "aggressive artistic mother" — preferred that her son develop a taste for the fine arts. She insisted that he learn how to play the piano and scolded him when he rebelled against her lessons at age nine. Her husband, however, sided with Willie. "Let him alone to grow," he admonished her.

This rebuke was apparently one of the few times that Rae Morris crossed his wife. "My mother relentlessly criticized him," the author wrote in a profile of his father, and she badgered him about social niceties such as wearing a coat and tie or attending men's Bible classes in town. Pulitzer Prize-winning author Edwin M. Yoder Jr., who knew Morris for over forty years, remembered Mrs. Morris as "very high strung, obviously worried about Willie, fretful, but loving. She clearly crowded Willie, from childhood on." Little wonder that the author's posthumously published novel *Taps* features a young protagonist with no father and an overbearing, domineering mother.[11]

Although Morris viewed his father as a "passive parent," he grew to recognize that the man did indeed worry about him and inwardly hoped his son would reach goals he never managed to accomplish. "It never occurred to me," Morris wrote, "to question the dislocations he must have suffered marrying into a volatile, proper Mississippi family rooted in its lost, dispossessed past." Morris eventually realized that their mutual love of baseball gave them a special bond that his mother could neither control nor share. Even as a child his father took him to games out in rural Yazoo County or in Jackson, and almost every afternoon during the summer the two would go to an old baseball field where his father would hit flies or line drives. Years later, Morris looked back on those carefree days: "It was a dreamy, suspended state, those late afternoons, thinking of nothing but outfield flies as the world drifted lazily by on Jackson

Members of the Yazoo Junior High School basketball team in 1948 included (front row, seated from left to right): Edwin "Honest Ed" Upton, Willie Morris, Billy "Muttonhead" Shepherd, Robert Pugh, Hilary "Bubba" Barrier, Charles "Big Boy" Wilkinson, and Clifton Sanders. Standing in the center of the back row is Coach Louis Thornton. In school Morris also played on the baseball team (courtesy Ralph Atkinson).

Willie Morris and other junior high ensemble winners who had won "superior ratings" at the senior high level in the State Band Contest played at their eighth grade graduation in 1948. Standing from left to right: Willie Morris, Ralph Atkinson, and Wilson "Henjie" Henick. Seated left to right: Natoma Woodruff, unidentified girl, Benny Kern, Ina Rae Aven, and Nancy Kay King (courtesy Ralph Atkinson).

Avenue. I learned to judge what a ball would do by instinct, heading the way it went as if I owned it, and I knew in my heart I could make the big time."

According to his high school coach, Harold "Hardwood" Kelly, Morris was indeed a good bunter and center fielder. "Willie was in charge of the outfield," declared Kelly, recalling one game in which Morris moved his teammates around when a particular batter came up, telling the coach (correctly, as it turned out) that he knew where the opposing batter would hit the ball. Morris also excelled in basketball, and he would usually make four out of five shots. The opposing team, said Kelly, "had to guard him very carefully, and this is why we won so many games, be-

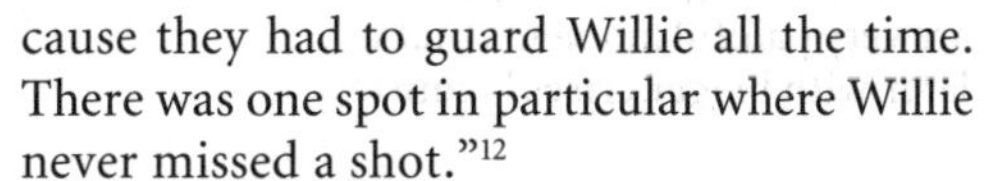

cause they had to guard Willie all the time. There was one spot in particular where Willie never missed a shot."[12]

But Morris's achievements were not limited to the baseball field or the basketball court. Omie Parker, his favorite high school teacher, was interviewed in 1980 upon the publication of a new edition of *Good Old Boy* that he dedicated to her. She recalled that even at an early age her protégé was "a born leader" and an ambitious boy with a "creative mind." He began working on the school newspaper, the Yazoo High School *Flashlight*, in the sixth grade, running errands and covering the Pee Wee League sports teams. At age fourteen he was an editorial writer for the paper, and by 1950 he was writing a column, "The Sports Closet." His name (and face, with photographs by Ralph Atkinson) soon became a fixture in the *Flashlight*. Front-page articles in the April 25, 1951, issue, for example, note

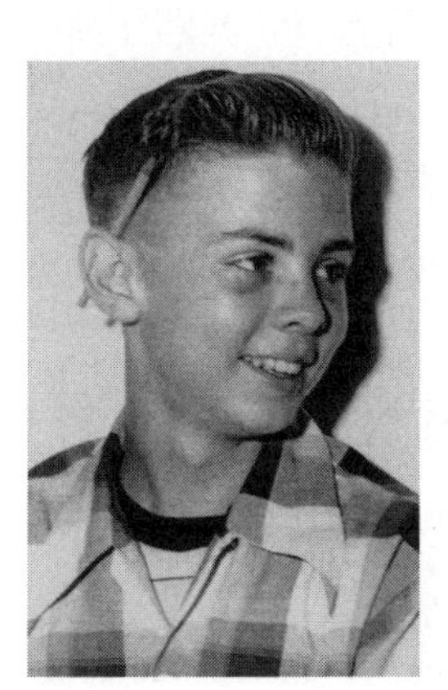

Willie Morris in "editor" pose. This photograph accompanied his 1950 sports column, "The Sports Closet," in the Yazoo High School newspaper, the *Flashlight*. In *North Toward Home*, Morris writes: "At fourteen I was an editorial writer for the Yazoo High *Flashlight*.... Later I worked my way up to the editorship, where my *Flashlight* prose resounded to strange, esoteric rhythms, supplemented with ambitious, unheard-of-words" (courtesy Ralph Atkinson).

The Yazoo High School Indians basketball team in 1950. Willie Morris is number 15, standing in the back row next to the last player on the right side. In 1997, Morris recalled his days as a high school athlete: "I got through a lot of painful adolescent periods as I was playing sports.... After you miss a free throw or a couple of free throws with half a second to play that would have won the game for you, you can't go hide. When you're growing up, especially when you're an adolescent, these are very painful moments that you chalk up to experience. They help you later with bigger crises" (courtesy Ralph Atkinson).

that Morris was elected to the National Honor Society, the National Athletic Scholarship Society, and the Quill and Scroll, the local honorary journalism society. Another article informs readers that the "brilliant young playwright, William Morris, local junior," wrote a play, *Mystery in Mexico*, for the Yazoo High School annual Spanish class assembly. At the annual convention of the Mississippi High School Press Institute, Morris was elected vice president "for the ensuing year," and in a state solo and ensemble contest in Jackson, Morris and other members of a cornet trio—his friends Ralph Atkinson and Wilson "Henjie" Henick—took "superior ratings."[13]

In the early 1950s, as war raged in Korea, the three youths regrettably had to display their musical prowess outside of high school band classes and ensemble contests. Many units in the Dixie Division of the National Guard (which covered several states in the Deep South) were activated during the conflict. Local youths were sent overseas, and some began returning far too early. "They started sending the corpses home," Morris said a quarter of a century later, "and Henjie Henick and Ralph Atkinson and I were the only three boys in town that could play the trumpet fairly well. We found ourselves for a period of many months being called out of school and playing 'Taps' on our trumpets for these military funerals."

Atkinson remarked in the spring of 2005 that they performed "Taps" for about twenty of the area soldiers who died in the Korean Conflict. "None of the 'good ole boys' in Willie's childhood served in the military," he added, as "they were too young or too old for the wars and 'armed conflicts' of their early lives." But in Yazoo City's Glenwood Cemetery, he and his two friends still performed a valuable service for their country, and Morris would spend years pondering its significance as he worked on a novel based on these boyhood experiences.[14]

In the meantime, the fledgling journalist wrote about other events in his hometown. When he was twelve years old, his father, knowing that Willie wanted to contribute sports stories to the city newspaper, gave him a second-hand portable Smith-Corona typewriter for Christmas. With that present, his destiny was ordained, according to his mother. "I could hear the typewriter in your room when you were twelve years old—always scribbling on the typewriter," she told him decades later. "I knew you were going to be a writer even then." In the summer of 1997 he recounted that for his first bylined article in the *Yazoo Herald*, he covered a baseball game between Yazoo City and Satartia high schools. The boy was so excited, however, that he forgot to include at least one significant detail in his story. "Lo and behold, the article came

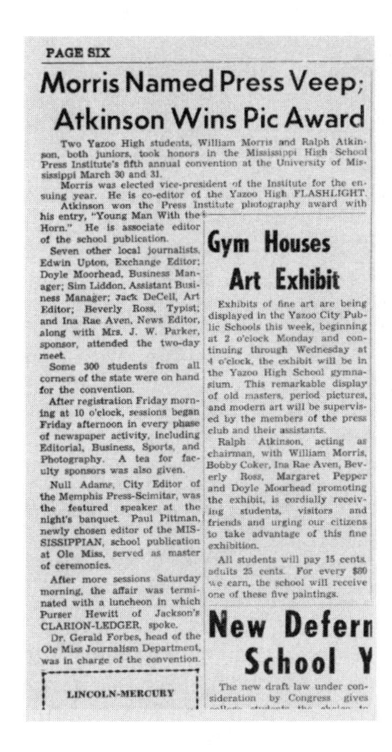

PAGE SIX

Morris Named Press Veep; Atkinson Wins Pic Award

Two Yazoo High students, William Morris and Ralph Atkinson, both juniors, took honors in the Mississippi High School Press Institute's fifth annual convention at the University of Mississippi March 30 and 31.

Morris was elected vice-president of the Institute for the ensuing year. He is co-editor of the Yazoo High FLASHLIGHT.

Atkinson won the Press Institute photography award with his entry, "Young Man With the Horn." He is associate editor of the school publication.

Seven other local journalists, Edwin Upton, Exchange Editor; Doyle Moorhead, Business Manager; Sim Liddon, Assistant Business Manager; Jack DeCell, Art Editor; Beverly Ross, Typist; and Ina Rae Aven, News Editor, along with Mrs. J. W. Parker, sponsor, attended the two-day meet.

Some 300 students from all corners of the state were on hand for the convention.

After registration Friday morning at 10 o'clock, sessions began Friday afternoon in every phase of newspaper activity, including Editorial, Business, Sports, and Photography. A tea for faculty sponsors was also given.

Null Adams, City Editor of the Memphis Press-Scimitar, was the featured speaker at the night's banquet. Paul Pittman, newly chosen editor of the MISSISSIPPIAN, school publication at Ole Miss, served as master of ceremonies.

After more sessions Saturday morning, the affair was terminated with a luncheon in which Purser Hewitt of Jackson's CLARION-LEDGER, spoke.

Dr. Gerald Forbes, head of the Ole Miss Journalism Department, was in charge of the convention.

LINCOLN-MERCURY

Gym Houses Art Exhibit

Exhibits of fine art are being displayed in the Yazoo City Public Schools this week, beginning at 2 o'clock Monday and continuing through Wednesday at 4 o'clock, the exhibit will be in the Yazoo High School gymnasium. This remarkable display of old masters, period pictures, and modern art will be supervised by the members of the press club and their assistants.

Ralph Atkinson, acting as chairman, with William Morris, Bobby Coker, Ina Rae Aven, Beverly Ross, Margaret Pepper and Doyle Moorhead promoting the exhibit, is cordially receiving students, visitors and friends and urging our citizens to take advantage of this fine exhibition.

All students will pay 15 cents, adults 25 cents. For every $80 we earn, the school will receive one of these five paintings.

New Defern School Y

The new draft law under consideration by Congress gives

Willie Morris and his friend Ralph Atkinson, juniors at Yazoo High School, "took honors in the Mississippi High School Press Institute's fifth annual convention" in March 1951, according to this article in the Yazoo High *Flashlight.* Morris served as co-editor of the student newspaper his junior year, and was editor-in-chief his senior year (1951–52). Atkinson was the *Flashlight* photographer (courtesy Willie Morris).

Staffers for the 1951 Yazoo High School yearbook, *Mingo Chito*, included (front row, left to right): Bernard Hitt, Ronnie Osborne (who as a Marine recruit died in Korea later that year), and Flint Liddon. Back row, left to right: Willie Morris, Berry Reece, and Ralph Atkinson (courtesy Ralph Atkinson).

out, and I discovered that I had neglected to provide the final score. It was quite a debut." He later worked part-time as a disc jockey, sports announcer, and news analyst for WAZF, a 500-watt local radio station.[15]

Naturally, Morris's boyhood also revolved around his friends, and he was well-known and popular among his classmates. "Willie was the all–American boy," Daisye Love Askew reminisced a few years after the author's death. "He had this infectious smile and was just so cute and so funny and everybody loved him." Marsha Williams recounted similar memories of the gregarious Morris. "He was very outgoing and he was *so funny*. He always had some sort of prank going on."

Morris's sense of humor was legendary, and it is not surprising that even as a boy he was playing jokes on both his friends and town residents. Williams recalled the occasion when Willie convinced a local woman that he was a Hollywood movie scout. "He said he was going to send her a contract from Walt Disney, who was very interested in a song she had written, 'The Billy Goat Song.' She just didn't catch on. She played the song and he acted so interested. She went up and down Main Street telling the story that she had been interviewed by this wonderful man from Hollywood."[16]

Both Askew and Benjamin "B." Barrier, younger brother of Morris's close friend Hilary "Bubba" Barrier, vividly remembered the small wireless AM transmitter with microphone that enabled Morris to broadcast over nearby radios. Unsuspecting townspeople would be listening to music when suddenly their radios would blare announcements such as "Russia is bombing the United States" or "This is the Superintendent of Yazoo City Schools. There will be no school tomorrow, as we must make emergency repairs."

"Willie just loved to play pranks," laughed Barrier. "He was a big prankster." And some of his most memorable jokes involved his dog Skip, a smooth-haired English fox terrier his parents bought for him when the boy was nine years old. "Skip is a strong player in almost any memory that I have of Willie," Ralph Atkinson told National Public Radio's Noah Adams soon after the release of *My Dog Skip*, the motion picture based on

Willie Morris (disguised as Sir Whoopin Tom Lipscott) holds his faithful dog Skip, an English smooth-haired fox terrier featured in several of Morris's works, including the popular memoir ***My Dog Skip.*** This photograph accompanied a humorous 1951 Yazoo High School newspaper article by Ralph Atkinson titled "Noted English Lecturer Views Blimy YHS Campus." The first paragraph reads: "'I, Lord Whoopin Tom Lipscott of Catfish on the Muddybank in London, England, was superlatively impressed by the cordiality and hospitality YHS students extended me upon my arrival here,' stated the renowned English lecturer during a recent visit to Yazoo High campus" (courtesy Ralph Atkinson).

Playwright Willie Morris (lower right) hams it up with "detectives" and Yazoo High School friends Arthur Davis (left, with cigar) and Ralph Atkinson in the Spanish class play. This photograph accompanied an article in the April 25, 1951, school ***Flashlight*** headlined "Spanish Group to Stage 5-Act Mystery Friday." One wonders if editor Morris had a hand in writing this favorable report: "Written by the brilliant young playwright, William Morris, local junior, the play centers around the baffling murder of Hose Perro (Tom Sanders), a well-to-do Mexican rancher. Suspect after suspect is drawn into the plot, and not until the very finish is the killer's identity disclosed. Ralph Atkinson, as the incomparable Ricardo Tracee, plays a chief role in the melodrama" as an investigator who "finds difficulty in solving his first case. Arthur Davis, as Arturo Watson, is Tracee's assistant" (courtesy Ralph Atkinson).

A 1951 Yazoo High School faculty committee meeting included, seated left to right: Frances Oakley, Harold Kelly, Omie (Mrs. John W.) Parker, and Eleanor Lester. Standing: Frances Barlow (far left) and Harold Moody. Morris wrote affectionately of both Harold "Hardwood" Kelly, the head basketball and baseball coach and assistant football coach at Yazoo High School, and Omie Parker, his favorite and most influential high school teacher (courtesy Ralph Atkinson).

Majorettes for the 1952 Yazoo High School band were (left to right): Shirley Walne, Dee Phillips, Betty Farish, Sandra Seward, Betty Lou Rogers, and Wilma Blakemore. Dee Phillips was the "blond majorette" whom Willie Morris mentioned in *North Toward Home*: "But that summer brought a felicitous change, for I fell deeply in love, with a fifteen-year-old blond beauty from the upper end of the county. I gave her my senior class ring, and I was filled with pride when she marched in front of the forty-eight piece high school band as a majorette, twirling her baton and strutting in her tight satin uniform" (courtesy Ralph Atkinson).

Morris's book of the same name. Memorable scenes in both the book and the movie depict Morris's canine companion with his paws on the steering wheel of a car, apparently driving down the street all by himself. "That is absolutely true," affirmed Atkinson. "Of course, Skip was not actually driving, but Willie had slouched down where he could just barely see over the dashboard.... People would stand on the street and say, 'Did you see that? That was a dog driving that car.'"

Marsha Williams recalled that Morris's "love of Skip was so well known, as was his riding around with Skip." She added that "Willie was always up to something. He was so much fun to be with, and he was interested in so many things." Said Daisye Love Askew: "We all knew Willie was destined for great things because he was so clever."[17]

This destiny certainly seemed assured even as early as his sophomore year. In January 1950 Morris "overwhelmed all opposition" as he won the election for Yazoo High

Trio of trumpeters in 1952: Ralph Atkinson, Willie Morris, and Wilson "Henjie" Henick. These three played "Taps" for the Yazoo City veterans killed in Korea, which Morris describes in *North Toward Home* and around which he develops his posthumously published novel *Taps*. According to Atkinson, they actually played cornets, not trumpets, and Morris probably borrowed a trumpet for this photograph, which ran in the 1952 high school yearbook. From *North Toward Home*: "One day in the summer, an official in the local American Legion telephoned me. He told me he had heard I could play the trumpet, and wanted to know who else could play. I told him Ralph Atkinson was the best of us at the trumpet, and Henjie Henick was almost as good... . As they began sending back the hometown soldiers who were being killed at the front lines in Korea, the three of us played for more funerals than we could keep count of" (courtesy Ralph Atkinson and Yazoo City High School).

WILLIAM MORRIS
Wit and wisdom is born with a man.
Nat'l. Hon. Soc. 3, 4; Ath. Sch. 3, 4; Quill and Scroll 3, 4; Y-Club 4; Class Pres. 1; V. Pres. 4; S. C. 2, 3, 4, Sec. and Treas. 2, V. Pres. 4; Who's Who 2, 3; Press Club 1, 2, 3, 4, Asst. Ed. 3, Ed. 4; Annual Staff 2, 3, 4; Band 1, 2, 3, 4; Basketball 2, 3, 4; Baseball 2, 3, 4; Boys' State 3; Glee Club 2, 3; Hi-Y 1.

Left: **Willie Morris and his achievements as they appear in *Mingo Chito*, the 1952 Yazoo High School yearbook. Morris and his friend Hilary "Bubba" Barrier were co-vice presidents of the senior class (courtesy Mary Jones, Burke Jones, and Yazoo City High School). *Right:* William "Red" Milner (left) and Willie Morris were outfielders on the 1952 Yazoo High School Indians baseball team. In 1951, Morris led the team in batting with a .300 average, followed by Milner's .262 average. Morris also played on the 1950 Yazoo American Legion state championship team. "That fall they gave us shiny blue jackets," he writes in *North Toward Home*, "with 'Miss. State Champions' written on the back; I was so happy with that jacket I almost wore it out" (courtesy Ralph Atkinson).**

School Student Council secretary-treasurer. Co-editor of the *Flashlight* his junior year (1950–51), he was editor-in-chief of the newspaper his senior year, co-vice president of the senior class, and class valedictorian. Moreover, his fellow students voted him "most versatile boy," "wittiest boy," and "senior boy most likely to succeed."[18]

But succeeding in what profession? That was still an open-ended question. Morris recounted in *North Toward Home* that after his high school graduation in the spring of 1952, he was prepared to attend the University of Mississippi, marry his high school sweetheart, and settle down on her father's huge cotton plantation as part of the state's educated landed gentry. His own father, however, realizing the lack of economic opportu-

Morris and friends pose in the French Quarter of New Orleans on the Class of 1952's senior trip, including (kneeling, left to right): Willie Morris and Ralph Atkinson. (Standing, left to right): Hilary "Bubba" Barrier, Billy "Muttonhead" Shepherd, Bobby Rhodes, and Vernon Netherland. According to one senior, the students enjoyed their visit to New Orleans so much that the staff at the Monteleone Hotel declined to let the Class of 1953 stay there (courtesy Ralph Atkinson).

The formal 1952 yearbook photograph of Willie Morris. The students of Yazoo High School voted him "Most Versatile Boy," "Wittiest Boy," and "Senior Boy Most Likely to Succeed." Morris also served as valedictorian of his class (courtesy Ralph Atkinson and Yazoo City High School).

Among the graduating seniors of Yazoo High School's class of 1952 were (front row, seated left to right): Willie Morris, Billy "Muttonhead" Shepherd, and Billy Rhodes. Standing, second row, left to right: Daisye Love Rainer, James Boatner, and Martin Shumacher. Standing, back rows, left to right: Robert Pugh, Jimmy Lawson, Chet Gean, Ralph Atkinson, and Melvin Upchurch. Morris and good friend Daisye Love Rainer wrote the class prophecy of the fifty-two member graduating class (courtesy Ralph Atkinson).

nity in his native state, urged him instead to "get the hell out of Mississippi." His mother, too, undoubtedly wanted him to expand his horizons a bit, for as Ralph Atkinson pointed out, she helped "shape Willie's vision of the world and the opportunities that awaited him beyond Yazoo City." So "one cold, dark morning in the early fall," he said good-by to Skip and his parents ("my mother, as the story always goes, cried, and my father looked thin as death"). As he boarded a Southern Trailways bus headed for Austin, Texas, he also said good-by to his familiar Mississippi Delta. "Memories of pleasant days and pleasant associations in the halls of YHS will always linger with you," he recalled the commencement speaker telling him and the other members of his Yazoo High School class. "These memories make up a happy part of your life, a part that you are now leaving for another life."[19]

Willie Morris was setting off for just that new life. In a few days he would enroll in the University of Texas.

COLLEGE DAYS AND CONTROVERSY (1952–1956)

I shall never forget that moment the bus pulled away from the old hometown. I looked back at my mother and dad on the platform. "We are investing our future years in you," she had said. "Make us proud." A hush seemed to fall on the town as I rode away, and it, too, along with the years that pas[sed], seemed to challenge me.... I have made my way from one life into another, and now I am ready to lick this old world.[20]—Willie Morris, *Daily Texan*, 17 September 1952

Willie Morris first intended to "lick this old world" by entering the radio and television profession. In high school he had enjoyed working for station WAZF, which broadcast, as he intoned during station breaks, "'high above the Taylor and Roberts Feed and Seed Store, in downtown Yazoo City, the Gateway to the Delta.'" As a freshman at the University of Texas, he had even taken classes in the school's radio and television program; in fact, at the end of that year he was offered a job as a play-by-play announcer for a minor league baseball team in Austin. By then, however, Morris was becoming interested in print rather than electronic media, and he turned the position down, though as he admitted years later, "I was certainly tempted."[21]

Tempting, too, were the sports programs at the University of Texas. Rae Morris knew that the school was not only one of the best universities in the South, but it also boasted an excellent baseball team with a nationally renowned coach. Shortly before Willie graduated from high school, the elder Morris took a bus to Austin to visit the campus for himself. He returned to Yazoo City extolling the university's virtues. "That's the goddamndest thing you ever saw," he exclaimed to his son, adding that the main campus building was thirty stories high, the baseball field was carved out of native rock, and the daily student newspaper was "bigger than the *Yazoo Herald* that comes out only once a week." No school in Mississippi could compare to it, he said, and Willie, heeding his father's advice, applied for admission.[22]

Morris (back left) and several of his boyhood friends served as groomsmen in the 1955 wedding of Joan Jackson and Ralph Atkinson in the First Baptist Church of Yazoo City. Standing beside Morris is Pastor Wilmer C. Fields. At the time of the wedding, Morris was a student at the University of Texas in Austin (courtesy Ralph Atkinson).

The teenager realized that the University of Texas was "certainly the biggest state university in the South," and it was, for good reason, often referred to as the "Forty Acres." He did not know a single one of its fourteen thousand students, and the "sprawling campus" seemed much bigger than the entire city of Memphis, where his father had occasionally taken him to see Ole Miss football games or watch the Memphis Chicks play baseball. It was all "heady stuff" for a seventeen-year-old boy from Mississippi, he told an interviewer in 1975, and "I just became immersed in this huge — what to me seemed huge — campus and the luxury of the fraternity and sorority houses and just the bigness of the place, and this frenetic over-organization that existed there."

Morris, sensing that the key to success lay in campus activities, soon joined some of these organizations, including the Freshman Council, student government, the Reserve Officers Training Corps Band, intramural sports, the freshman baseball team, and Delta Tau Delta fraternity. He soon wearied, however, of the "ritualized childishness and grasping narcissism of the fraternity life" and gradually ceased participating in society activities.[23]

Morris's other interests quickly occupied his time, particularly reporting and writing for the student newspaper. Anne Chambers, the *Daily Texan* editor during Morris's first year, recalled in May 1953 that one rainy day the previous September, a "young freshman peeked his sunshiny face around the corner of the office and introduced himself. Dear Willie (Yazoo City) Morris ... has been a bright sparkle in our sometimes over-cynical staff crowd."[24]

Morris's sparkle first gleamed that same September when Chambers and the other "tolerant seniors" who edited the paper allowed him write a weekly column. "Neighboring News" was his "personal insight on what's happening in other colleges," and he soon displayed a knack for humorously summarizing and reporting news items that he read each week in campus newspapers from around the country. For example, in an October 1952 column he wrote that "a forest is currently being planted in honor of the eminent professor, Albert Einstein, at Stamford, Connecticut. The big enigma is: will all the trees have square roots?" And from a column the following month: "The subject for a recent debate between two representatives of the freshman class and a pair of upperclassmen at Oklahoma University was 'Should blue jeans be worn in the quadrangle center?' Perhaps it will clear up the overall situation."[25]

Though old-fashioned by today's standards, "Neighboring News" proved to be a popular feature of the Eisenhower-era *Daily*

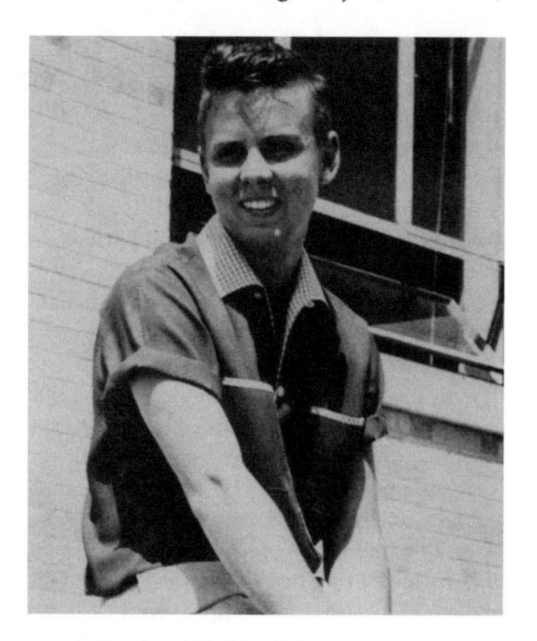

Willie Morris at the University of Texas in Austin. Soon after he arrived on campus his freshman year, he made his way to the offices of the campus newspaper, the *Daily Texan*, and introduced himself. The "tolerant seniors" who edited the paper "were bemused enough to give me a weekly column in my first semester," he recounted in *North Toward Home*, and his "Neighboring News" debuted on September 18, 1952 (courtesy of the Center for American History, the University of Texas at Austin, CN Number 02431).

Texan, and Morris regularly contributed the column until mid–January 1953, when his writing career moved in a new direction. Texas journalist Sam Blair was a veteran sports staffer for the *Daily Texan* during the 1952–53 academic year, and almost fifty years later he remembered when Morris first walked into the sports office: "He had a cherubic face, eyes bright with wonder and curiosity, and a drawl that sounded mighty slow even to a bunch of ol' Texas Boys." Coincidentally, shortly before he met Morris, Blair and other sports staff members had passed around a letter of recommendation from Omie Parker, Morris's high school English and journalism teacher, to the sports editor. In glowing terms she commented on "her brightest, most gifted student." She noted, Blair recalled, that Morris "was as industrious as he was friendly, and asked that this unknown newcomer just be given a chance."

As a second-semester freshman, Morris had that chance: covering intramural sports. Morris ruefully observed a few months after he accepted the assignment that to pacify "a frightful bevy of fraternities, clubs, co-ops, and every other organization mentionable on these Forty Acres," the journalist reporting on intramurals must be tactful, impartial, and "a statesman of the rarest quality." With this assessment, no wonder the sports staffers thought Morris's job was, as Blair put it, "the lowliest beat in the department." Morris acted, however, as if "he had been handed a plane ticket to Cuba and told to go interview Hemingway," and beginning in February 1953, readers frequently saw "Texan Intramural Coordinator" below his byline.[26]

In spite of all his new duties, he continued to read college newspapers from around the country. Slowly he became cognizant of ideas and issues not usually discussed in Yazoo City, such as integration and academic freedom. The high standards and values of Frank Lyell, his freshman English professor and a close friend of southern author Eudora Welty, inspired him to write and read more purposefully. Inspiration also came during a notable evening he spent with a young graduate student and his wife in their apartment. As Morris gazed at their many books—"more books than I had ever seen before in a private dwelling"—she asked him what he wanted to do after college. He immediately replied that he wanted to be a writer, though he blurted the words before he really thought much about them. "Stirred by the conversation and by all the books I had seen," Morris began making regular visits to the campus library. "I started reading books in a kind of systematic way for the first time in my life," he recalled some twenty years later, "and for the first time, at the age of seventeen or eighteen, I gradually started becoming aware of something. For lack of a better phrase, something beyond myself, which I suppose is a good part of what education, good education, is."[27]

Morris's articles in the *Daily Texan* gradually reflected this new awakening. In the fall of his sophomore year he began a regular column of "anecdotes and campus philosophy" that he called "The Round-Up," which he wrote in addition to his sports articles. But mixed in with the athletic highlights and campus gossip were articles decidedly more thoughtful in tone and literary in nature. In his "Round-Up" of January 13, 1954, for example, he offered a historical look at the wartime university of January 1944, observing that students then "considered their chance at education a rare privilege." A month later he wrote about a walk across the campus, where he found himself "absorbed in sunshine and the flow of Life and Time." The following week Morris asked twenty-five persons to name the five individuals, living or dead, with whom they would most like to talk. He printed their replies, including his own response at the bottom of the list: "W. Morris, a hapless soul trying to escape the throes of ignorance: Christ, my great grandfather, Robert E. Lee, Whitman, the Unk[n]own Soldier."[28]

As a sophomore English major who was taking "a lot of hours in journalism," the ambitious Morris began contemplating the possibility of editing the *Daily Texan* his senior year. As a junior, he served as the paper's sports editor and provided full coverage of all Texas Longhorn athletic events. His other articles featured essays and commentaries rather than the campus anecdotes and stories that students had read with amusement the year before. Pieces in October 1954, for instance, included his "thoughts on turning 20," a review of the United Nations' nine-year record of accomplishments and failures, and a history of the university's "stoic, stately, enduring" Tower. His essay "Here's What to Do When a Tornado Hits," published in March 1955, was the winner of the annual Clarence E. Gilmore award "for the best editorial or interpretative article written by a University of Texas student on some phase of safety."[29]

A month later, Morris filed as a candidate for editor of the *Daily Texan*. The student offices were decided by campus-wide elections, and on April 27 Morris "glided to landslide victor[y]"—3,357 votes over his competitor's 1,914—as he pledged "fair, hard-hitting editorials" and a "conscious desire to prevent an inert, indifferent University populace." Students soon saw that he kept his word with both promises; in his first editorial less than two months after he won the election, he told them that "we have been appalled by the tragic shroud of indifference which cloaks our undergraduate. This student apathy, this disregard o[f] all save the most material, is a thing of the mid–Twentieth Century. If we do not kill it now, here and on a thousand campuses, it will eventually kill us...."[30]

Morris often railed against complacency and conformity, for he strongly felt that healthy discussion — even controversy — led to intellectual stimulation and were part of the learning process. Dismayed and frustrated as he was by the apathy on the University of Texas campus, he could not have been particularly astonished. As a *Daily Texan* colleague recalled a decade later, the 1950s were "those largely uninspiring years of McCarthy, Shivers, and Eisenhower." Texas Governor Allan Shivers was a rigorously conservative politician who admired and followed Senator Joseph McCarthy. The Board of Regents then administering the university was composed of cattle ranchers, corporation lawyers, and men in the oil and natural gas industries, who to Morris represented "the most uncivilized wealth in America." The "twin d[ei]ties" gas and oil controlled the state, and because the University of Texas depended on state tax revenue from the oil industry and natural gas producers, Governor Shivers, the regents, and University President Logan Wilson all believed that change on campus was neither necessary nor desirable. "It was a stolid and unimaginative time," Morris recalled in his autobiography, "and few were those to take a dare."[31]

Morris, however, was one of those few. Just two months after the campus election, on "a viciously hot Texas afternoon in June," he moved into the editor's office of the student newspaper. Adding "Daily Texan Editor" after his name for perhaps the first time, he wrote that the university's Board of Regents, in the wake of *Brown v. Board of Education of Topeka*, would soon "define the path the University will follow on undergraduate integration." *Daily Texan* readers were probably not surprised by Morris's front-page news story or subsequent articles that supported campus desegregation; in a student "stump speaking" rally during the election campaign, he told the crowd that the University of Texas was "ready for integration." Nonetheless, by October he was responding in "The Round-Up" to readers who felt that the newspaper's liberal stance did not represent the views of the student body. Confirming what high school teacher Omie Parker noticed years ago — that Morris "could stand alone for what he thought was right" — he stated that although "we encourage conflicting views ... we are not afraid to voice our own views, regardless of the majority's.... A university ideally is a community where prejudices and class hatred ebb low, and eventually, through the perpetual hourglass of social change, fade into the realm of nonexistence."[32]

Willie Morris in front of the University of Texas Tower, circa 1955. He paid tribute to the Tower in an October 1954 article for the *Daily Texan*. "This is the Tower," he wrote. "A towering mass of granite, 308 feet high; an architect's miracle, rising high above our petty worldly dealings" (courtesy the Center for American History, the University of Texas at Austin, CN Number 11899).

As significant as this issue was during the mid–1950s in the largest university in the South, it was his aggressive stand on freedom of the press, not integration, that would define Morris's editorship. During a February 4, 1956, breakfast meeting of the university Student-Regent Liaison Committee, the discussion turned to the editorial practices of the *Daily Texan*. Committee members questioned Morris's policies, feeling that he did not present the opinions of the "majority of the student body" and did not print "both sides of every story." The regents consequently directed the Texas Student Publications (TSP) Board, an independent corporation that directs campus publications, to enforce and interpret strictly the rules in the TSP *Handbook*.[33] Morris promptly responded to this decision with a boxed editorial on page 1 of the newspaper. One paragraph summarized his beliefs:

> The editor feels that to submit to a stricter interpretation of the TSP Handbook will take away The Texan's power to comment editorially on state issues. He sees this point of view as a further step toward censorship. He feels to comply would seriously weaken The Texan's tradition, would set a dangerous precedent for future Texan editors, would violate the University student body's trust in the editor and in The Texan, and would immeasurably injure the cause of college journalism. He feels he cannot submit to what appears to be suppression. He must point out that the Regents, in the final analysis, not only have complete control over what goes into The Texan, but over the life of The Texan as well.[34]

Morris immediately tested this new "stricter interpretation" of the TSP *Handbook*. During the Board's meeting on February 4, the regents stated that because the university is funded by the state, the *Daily Texan* should not criticize state administrators, nor should it discuss sensitive state and national matters that affect the university. Two days later, on Monday morning, Morris submitted several editorials for publication, including a "guest editorial" from the *New York Times* that was critical of the Fulbright-Harris natural gas bill. This piece of legislation, then pending in Congress, would exempt natural gas producers from federal price controls and regulations. Harrell Lee, editorial director of the Texas Student Publications Board, rejected the editorial "on the grounds that material on the other side of the issue had not been presented to balance." After Dr. DeWitt C. Reddick, acting director of the university's School of Journalism, concurred with Lee, Morris requested a meeting of the TSP Board to appeal the decision. The board approved the "banned" editorials, but Morris nonetheless pressed on, arguing the larger censorship question. During the five-hour session that afternoon and evening, Morris told Lee and Reddick that their strict interpretations of the TSP *Handbook* "would take away all rights of the editor." Lee replied, "It is my opinion, the Regents don't

Nancy McMeans, Willie Morris (center), and Jimmie McKinley at a *Daily Texan* party, circa 1955. Morris filed as a candidate for editor of the University of Texas newspaper in April his junior year. After a campus-wide election, the paper reported that he coasted to a "landslide" victory, with 3,357 votes over his competitor's 1,914 (courtesy the Center for American History, the University of Texas at Austin, CN Number 11898).

feel the Texan is being edited with the zeal which would bring favorable feelings toward the University."[35]

With these two opening salvos, a "legacy of defiance" began that "laid the foundation for generations of [*Daily Texan*] editors to emulate." When one of Morris's pieces was withheld from publication, he would retaliate by running outlandish, long-winded editorials under titles such as "Don't Walk on Grass" or "Let's Water the Pansies." Occasionally readers would turn to the editorial page and find a huge heading proclaiming "This Editorial Censored" or "This Editorial Withheld" in the middle of white space where the editorial would normally have been published. The regents "hit the ceiling!" Morris exclaimed years later. "God, they hit the ceiling over that. They had more high-level meetings on that."[36]

Fortunately, Morris had supporters who believed he had the right to express his opinions in the *Daily Texan*. On February 8, Texas writer and folklorist J. Frank Dobie sent a letter to the paper stating, "I rejoice at the resistance of the editors of The Daily Texan to the tyranny of censorship. I have never heard of a censor who was not a flunkey to some form of power fearful of having daylight let in on its privileges and operations." Readers were not allowed to finish the letter, however, for after Morris finished editing the February 9 issue and went home to bed, a faculty-appointed newspaper supervisor quickly removed offending portions of Dobie's fiery blast, including the often-quoted observation that the Texas Regents "are as much concerned with free intellectual enterprise as a razorback sow would be with Keats's 'Ode on a Grecian Urn.'" After the liberal *Texas Observer* obtained a copy of the original letter, the paper published it under the title "Dobie Unexpurgated," with the previously deleted sentences highlighted in italics.[37]

Ronnie Dugger, founder and editor of the free-speaking *Observer*, continually backed Morris in his fight to preserve civil liberties for the *Daily Texan*. On February 15 Dugger editorially urged the University of Texas Regents to resign, accusing them of "inquisitorial arrogance," and the next week he praised the young editor in a lengthy profile. And media coverage was not limited to Texas. "Texas U. Editor Pushes Crusade," reported the *New York Times* on February 19. Associated Press and United Press International also picked up the story, and popular television host Dave Garroway "mentioned the controversy" on the *Today* show in New York City. Morris's parents, understandably upset, telephoned from Mississippi asking, "Son, you in trouble? They won't kick you out of school so close to graduation, will they?"

Morris would indeed receive his diploma, for by spring "there was a loosening up" and the furor began to die down. The Board of Regents had passed more directives in attempts to limit his free speech (one member, rancher-oilman Claude Voyles, explained to a newspaper reporter that "We're just trying to hold Willie to a college yell"), but Morris and his staff "held to our prerogatives" to publish what they wished. "They underestimated the interest of the student body," he told Dugger, and the regents "underestimated the stubborn resistance of the Texan staff. And they didn't count on the discussion in the state and national press outside. Now they see what they've done, and we hope we can maintain our free status as a newspaper."[38]

Morris battled hard all year to maintain that free status. Although he was proud of his successes (and to this day he is regarded as "a hero" among *Daily Texan* staff members), he implied in his last issue that the year ended in a Pyrrhic victory at best. The paper had sustained "a telling blow" during the long struggle, one that would severely constrict the rights of next year's editor. In April the TSP Board sanctioned new editorial policies, one of which required a journalism professor to approve all *Texan* editorials and news stories before publication. Another stipulated that the paper could no longer discuss "personalities," only analyze "issues."[39]

In subsequent years, Morris occasionally wondered if he would change anything if he could go back and relive that long spring semester. In his memoir he wrote that "there could have been more subtle and practical ways of dealing with the problem," but in college he was too young "for this kind of personal diplomacy." During a 1997 interview, he speculated that he could have used satire and "more humor in little things." In May 1956, without the benefit of hindsight, he mused that during his editorship he may have "succumbed to the overexuberance of a naive idealism," acting like an "articulate Quixote in search of windmills." At the same time, he added, youth is by nature "overexuberant and naively idealistic," and in his case the winds that operated the windmills "were tornadic, and played for keeps."[40]

Just as Morris reflected on his editorship over the years, so have some of his friends and colleagues. In 1980, professor of journalism emeritus DeWitt C. Reddick was asked about Morris, with whom he clashed on so many issues. "I kind of felt like he always wrote and felt from the heart," Reddick replied, "but his experience on The Texan taught him to write from the head." Nearly twenty years later, Jim Roach, professor of government emeritus at the university, remembered Morris as "quite an immature young guy from a little Mississippi town. He was bright and clever and determined. He made friends with everybody. He was a good student. He ended up in one of my classes, which were much smaller then, and we became friends." Before Carol Hatfield returned to her alma mater as editor of *Discovery* magazine, she worked with Morris on the *Texan*. "He was a great editor, asking questions at a time when questions needed to be asked. He didn't like authority. He was always chafing at authority. He wanted you to write against the institutional or authoritarian view."[41]

As *Daily Texan* editor, Morris lambasted the institutional view even at the end of his term. A writer's final "30" column is usually reserved for emotional retrospection. In "The Last Round-Up," iconoclast Morris chose to steer clear of "the meaningless sent[i]mentalism of most farewells" and instead decry Americans' "principle of acquisition" and their "frigid disdain of thought and emotion, of all things intangible and irrelevant." Perhaps still smarting from his duels with the Board of Regents, he criticized campus administrators for "submitting to those who relish the corporate purse." Although the university "was constructed on the nobility of the human spirit," it now "bows obsequiously for the legislative penny. It condones the tyranny of the majority, and it encourages in its students sedate complacency...."[42]

Two weeks after the article's publication, on June 3, 1956, Morris received his bachelor of arts degree in English, graduating magna cum laude and a member of Phi Beta Kappa. In keeping with the convictions he championed in "The Last Round-Up" and other articles, he did not plan to marry immediately after graduation, ease into a comfortable job and lifestyle, have children—"two boys and a girl"—and then get "bogged down in dullness, complacency, and the corporate mentality" like some of his classmates. Rather, in the fall he would be bound for England—Oxford University in particular—where he would study as a Rhodes scholar.[43]

An American Abroad (1956–1960)

I think it was my sophomore year at the University of Texas. I was sitting in a big chemistry class and I was reading the Daily Texan, and I saw a story on the front page about [how] they were taking applications for the Rhodes scholarships, for the Rhodes competition. They listed what the Rhodes scholarships were, the criteria and so forth. I read this and I said, "God, I sure would like to get one of those someday." I started asking around, people who knew about it, and I concluded that I was going to apply in my senior year. And I did.[44]—Willie Morris, during a 1975 interview

Fortunately for Morris, the Rhodes scholar application process took place during the fall of his senior year at the University of Texas, well before he became embroiled with the regents over his editorship of the *Daily Texan*. He did not need any distractions, for the scholarship competition that would enable a select few to study at Oxford University for at least two years was, as he remembered years later, "tough and grueling." That was the intent of British statesman and award founder Cecil John Rhodes, who demanded "the best men for the world's fight" (women were not eligible until 1976). He also insisted that winners of the international fellowships "should not be mere bookworms, but should have those qualities of character and personality which would lead them to take an effective concern in public interest."[45]

These winners were selected after a three-stage competition that included both oral interviews and written essays. After tests at the University of Texas, Morris advanced to the state finals in Houston. Two men from each state were chosen to proceed to eight regional competitions. During this third stage, the southern finals in New Orleans, the interviewing committee of former Rhodes scholars hosted a cocktail party for Morris and the eleven other applicants. After Morris talked with the young men, he was not particularly sanguine about his chances:

> When I met the others, most of whom came from the best Eastern schools, in their carefully tailored suits and their button-down collars, I thought they were the smoothest people I had ever encountered, for they could talk with an easy grace about everything from the book publishing business to the stock market to all the nuances of the objective correlative. One of them was talking to me about the latest plays in New York, and in my discomfort I looked down at the cuff of my trousers and noticed a big cigarette hole! The rest of the evening I stood there with one leg crazily crossed on the other, scratching at myself and wondering how I had ever got into such a situation.[46]

The competition, Morris recalled, "brought out who you were and what you knew and felt." During the final formal interview in early December 1955, he found himself discussing a broad range of subjects, "from American foreign policy to Eisenhower's farm program to the modern novel." After it was over, the committee deliberated for an hour, called all twelve candidates into a room, and announced the four winners. "'Did I hear right?' I asked Woods, the Mississippi candidate. 'Did *I*?' he said."[47]

Morris later learned that he was the first Rhodes scholarship winner from the University of Texas in ten years. His father, upon hearing the news, told him, "Well, you will never have to worry about a job again." A person with a somewhat different reaction to his accomplishment was Celia Ann Buchan, a junior from Houston. She had met Morris in the spring of 1955 and had gone out with him, she remembered years later, "now and again." She wrote in her memoir that he had "caught my attention" during his stand against the University Board of Regents, and now that he had won a scholarship to study at Oxford "I began to look at Willie a little more attentively."[48]

In the summer of 1956 while en route to New York City to visit friends, Buchan stopped overnight in Yazoo City to visit Morris, "where his mother treated me like Queen Elizabeth — or Princess Margaret at the very least — and Willie tantalized us with his upcoming departure for England." Morris was all set to sail in October, and prior to boarding the *Flandre* he enjoyed three days in Washington and a week in New York City. He told his former English professor Frank Lyell (who had written a letter of recommendation in support of his Rhodes application), that his sightseeing trip around New York "can indeed be likened to a small young lad with his first bottle of Mississippi Jack Daniel." As Morris chronicled in a travel piece for the *Daily Texan*, he met comedian Steve Allen, who "seemed informed and inquisitive about our late lamented University of Texas press controversy. There were a profitable two hours with John Fischer, the Texas-born editor of *Harper's Magazine*, a kind, affable ex–Rhodes Scholar who offered wholesale bits of advice on the Oxford curriculum." On the day before

University of Texas student Celia Ann Buchan met Willie Morris in the spring of 1955. In her memoir, she wrote that he had "caught my attention" with the controversial articles he wrote during his senior year as editor of the *Daily Texan*, and they were married in her hometown of Houston on August 30, 1958. Wrote Morris in *New York Days*: "The two of us were important on the campus in those languid Eisenhower years. I was editor of the student daily; she was a Phi Beta Kappa and was even elected 'Sweetheart of the University'; five thousand students sang 'The Eyes of Texas' to her in the school gymnasium." This photograph originally appeared in the 1956 UT yearbook, *The Cactus*, as part of a two-page tribute to Buchan as the "Sweetheart of The University of Texas" (courtesy of Texas Student Publications, the University of Texas at Austin).

Pictured in the 1956 University of Texas yearbook is Willie Morris at his desk in the offices of the *Daily Texan*. In a brief essay published with his photo, Morris summarized the campus newspaper's accomplishments during his senior year as editor. The first paragraph reads: "This was an unusually noteworthy year for a liberal, hard-hitting Daily Texan. A heated controversy with the Board of Regents concerning editorial policies made national headlines. The 1955–56 Texan seemed to pioneer what it called 'a new concept of college journalism,' by presenting penetrating editorial comment on controversial state and national issues, as well as salient campus developments" (courtesy Texas Student Publications, the University of Texas at Austin).

he left for England, Morris took a "hurried train trip" to Swarthmore, Pennsylvania. At a reception given by Dr. Courtney Smith, president of Swarthmore College, "I tested my first cup of hot tea, and met the Rhodes men I shall live with during these next two years. It was a grand experience, and the Scholars were precisely as I had expected: purposeful intellectuals with a gloss of the all–American, well-informed, friendly, and sensitive."[49]

The next day Morris and the other Rhodes scholars, representing thirty states and twenty-three colleges and universities, met on the French Line pier and prepared to board the *Flandre*:

> There were photographers, champagne toasts, smeared lipstick, a twinge or two of abrupt sadness. As we sailed away from the harbor, the 3[2] Rhodes Scholars gathered in the cold rain watching the Statue [of Liberty] fade into the mist. "So long, old girl," laughed Ed Yoder, my friend from North Carolina. The towering skyscrapers of Manhattan soon seemed like toys on a sandy beach. When we returned to the deck later, the rain had become a moist breeze, and the continent had given way to a placid sea.[50]

Morris used the time on board the *Flandre* to get acquainted with the men with whom he would be spending the next two

Willie Morris (fourth from left, front row) and his fellow Rhodes scholars aboard the *Flandre*, bound for England. The photograph was taken by Georges Gratiet on October 7, 1956, between New York and Plymouth. The Rhodes scholars and other Americans sailing to Oxford included (left to right sitting): Fred Myers, Russ McCormmach, Steven Brush, Willie Morris, Maurice Tenn, Ed Selig, A. Truman Schwartz, Dick Baker, Art Siler, Dave Maxwell, Ham Richardson. Left to right standing: Paul (Dick) Burgess, John Sadler, Van Ooms, Bob Picken, Paul Carter, Gary Christianson, Neil Rudenstine, Conn Anderson, Mark Ball, Reg Stanton, Richard D. Sylvester, Oliver Johns, Mike Hammond, John D'Arms, Jess Woods, Roscoe (Rocky) Suddarth, Edwin M. Yoder Jr., Ron Rebholz. Staircase: Don Sniegowski, Carey Parker, Davis Bobrow, Vince Larson (courtesy Richard D. Sylvester. The photo and names of the 1956 sailing party appeared in the Fall 2003 *American Oxonian*).

years. They "are fine as they can be," he wrote his parents from the ship, and "are the best group of boys I have ever seen." He enthusiastically told Frank Lyell that "the Rhodes men are just as I expected: well-groomed, sensitive, remarkably intelligent and well-informed. My cabin-mates are delightful fellows. One is from Reed College, [Oregon]; the other from St. Peter's College, New Jersey. Ed Yoder & I seem to be the only genuine Southerners in the outfit, and you can imagine some of the arguments we have prompted."[51]

The *Flandre* reached Plymouth on Wednesday, October 10, from which the students boarded a train for Oxford. On his first day at the university, "a chilled misty October forenoon touched with the teasing Oxford rain," he and the approximately fourteen other first-year students at New College who had signed up for the Philosophy of Politics and Economics curriculum each met privately with the head tutor. The Oxford education was based on the tutorial system, in which students, after intensive reading, wrote weekly

WILLIAM WEEKS MORRIS
Scholar. Son of Mr. and Mrs. H. R. Morris. Public schooling in Yazoo City where graduated with distinction in 1952. Was member of National Honor Society and National Athletic Scholarship Society. Graduated Magna Cum Laude University of Texas, June, 1956. Awarded Jesse Jones journalism scholarship two consecutive years at university and elected Phi Beta Kappa. Elected Rhodes Scholar in 1956 and studied at New College University of Oxford in England. President of the Oxford American Association and member of Oxford University varsity basketball team.

***Yazoo County Story*, a pictorial history of the county published in 1958, featured Willie Morris among its "Famous Yazooians," with a brief biography (note misspelled middle name) and his senior class photo from the 1956 University of Texas yearbook. He was twenty-four years old. Morris was so well known in Yazoo City, even as a young man, that newspaper articles about him sometimes included only his first name in the headlines. For instance, after he was elected editor of the *Daily Texan* in 1955, the *Yazoo City Herald* ran a profile titled "'Willie' Reaches High Rung in His Ladder of Success" (courtesy the Yazoo Historical Society). See item 1879.**

or twice-weekly essays and discussed them privately with their college tutors, called dons. Morris soon found British linguistic philosophy (part of his "P-P-E" curriculum) "a lot of gobbledygook," and after being assigned to write a paper on "What Is Real?" switched to history.[52] "I think history is much better than P-P-E," Morris wrote his parents and grandmother in the spring of 1957:

> I am thoroughly enjoying history, and like my tutor very much. I have done two essays for him this term, and he says he is highly pleased with my work. I am doing English history right now, beginning with th[e] first century and working straight on up. Later, I will do a term or two on general European history from 1789 to 1870, a term on political theory, three terms on English constitutional history, and two terms and a thesis on a special topic. I think from the list I will choose slavery and s[ec]ession in the US, from 1850 to 1862.[53]

Morris took an intensive course in American history that covered this decade before the Civil War, which "awakened me to the history of my own country." In 1959 he received his bachelor of arts degree in modern history, an era that "began in the year zero and ended in 1900. Everything after that was considered journalism." From 1959 to 1960 he did graduate work in American-British diplomacy during the ten or fifteen years prior to World War II.[54]

But Morris spent his time on other activities besides reading and tutorials. Soon after the term started, he wrote his parents and grandmother that "the lectures here are pretty good" but admitted that "few people go" as attendance was optional. Comprehensive examinations were given at the end of three years, and with the only formal requirement being the regular essay, a student could do very much as he pleased. Morris was not at Oxford a month before he tried out for the varsity basketball team. He knew he would face some tough competition; the player-coach, for example, had been captain at the University of North Carolina, and the guard had played at Princeton. "Nonetheless it was to my astonishment that I not only was named to the team —compliments to [coach] Hardwood Kelly and the Yazoo High Indians— but was the sixth man, sharing point-guard duties with Schork of Massachusetts. And when Schork hurt his ankle in the third or fourth game, I was in the starting lineup." In a mid–November game, he wrote his parents, he "made 19 points against an RAF base." At the end of the season he earned a "half-blue," a dark blue-and-white necktie that was the equivalent of a varsity letter, by playing in the traditional yearly match against Cambridge University.[55]

As he did in Yazoo High School, Morris also balanced academics with writing and other activities. In spring 1957 he wrote his parents and grandmother Mamie that "the journalism bug has bitten me, and I have done two article[s] for the magazines here. I am enclosing the first one, in Isis." Morris followed "Eisenhower," his assessment of the president published in the February 27 issue of Oxford University's publication, with an article on Adlai Stevenson that he co-authored with his friend Ed Yoder. Stevenson's visit was sponsored by the American Students Association, an organization that "mainly existed to bring in illustrious speakers," and Morris served as its president.[56]

In August 1958, Morris's mother telephoned him to say that his father was near death. He flew home to see him one last time, then drove to Houston to marry Celia Buchan. A few days later, on the voyage back to England with his new wife, Morris learned that his father had died. He recalled years later that during his final visit with Rae Morris, "I tried to work up my nerve to say, 'If I ever have a boy, I'll name him after you,'" but he could not say it. Morris did, however, keep his word. His and Celia's son, David Rae Morris, was born in Oxford on November 1, 1959. Under socialized medicine, Morris told his friends on numerous occasions, David "cost us student parents 82 cents, and they never sent the bill."[57]

As Willie studied American and British history at Oxford, Celia not only took care of David but also delved into Greek tragedy and Shakespeare with a don from New College. In the spring of 1960, however, both parents realized that it was time to leave Oxford. Celia faced "the practical problems of caring for David in a third-floor walk-up with no conveniences," and Willie felt "waterlogged with the past." At about that time he received a letter from his friend and mentor Ronnie Dugger, editor of the *Texas Observer*. Dugger also needed a change — a respite from the grind of putting out a weekly publication virtually all by himself. Would Morris take over for awhile? He "accepted with alacrity," thrilled at the challenge of stamping his own mark on the *Texas Observer* just as he had done with the *Daily Texan*. Willie and Celia packed their belongings, said good-bye to friends, and when David was about a half-year old, the Morris family sailed into New York harbor aboard the *Île de France*. From there they would drive to Austin.[58]

More than three decades would pass before Morris returned to Oxford, "the old, brave, magnificent town" that was "forever imbued in my memory with an uncommon maze of emotions." He regarded the three-and-one-half years of "relatively quiet time" there as a "marvelous antidote" to the stress of his last year at the University of Texas. Furthermore, because the Oxford terms were roughly six months long, the lengthy vacations afforded him — and most American students— the opportunity to travel all over Europe, "which was right there on the doorstep anyway."

He did not, curiously, write much about this significant period. When critics questioned why he seemed to gloss over these years in his first memoir, he responded that "I was simply not ready to write about Oxford." He had been back in the United States for less than a decade before he started *North Toward Home*, and he was just beginning to comprehend this "most exotic time of my life," an adventure that was both exhilarating and intimidating.[59]

Perhaps, as Edwin M. Yoder Jr. suggested, the "clue to Willie's reticence about Oxford" can be found in "My Two Oxfords," an essay Morris contributed to his 1989 book *Homecomings*. The author lists "a mere sampling" of famous Oxonians and asks readers to "imagine the oppressiveness of their footfalls as their spirits stalked a callow young American there a generation ago." Morris and "others among the Americans of our time," wrote Yoder, "held Oxford in awe," and "he was haunted in that special way of his by the ghosts of the great figures who had preceded us."[60]

Morris was also overwhelmed by the beauty and sheer magnitude of Oxford University. He once told a reporter who had asked about his experience abroad that "I've always had a difficult time trying to relate it to the stream of my whole life." A number of colleges make up the larger university, and he observed in "My Two Oxfords" that New College, his college, "was new in 1379" and that his stay there "was the first and last time I would ever live in a museum." The college's "spires and cupolas and quadrangles," he continued, "its towers and gables and oriels and hieroglyphs, its ancient walls with the shards of glass embedded on top, its chimes and bells resounding in the swirling mists, made home seem distant and unreal." As he wondered in 1991, several decades after he returned to the United States: "How did an American boy fit into *that*?" Yazoo City certainly did not prepare him for it; indeed, while sailing on the *Flandre* he wrote Frank Lyell that "I really feel as if all this has been too much for a provincial to take."[61]

At first, other students also wondered if it would be too much for him. As the Rhodes scholars and other Americans going to Oxford intermingled aboard the *Flandre*, they "examined one another warily." One of them was Roscoe Suddarth, a student from Yale University who thirty years later would serve as the American ambassador to Jordan. As the New College students were led through the university's medieval labyrinth of passages the night of their arrival, Suddarth noticed the "wonder and perplexity" in Morris's eyes. "I remember saying to myself, 'This kid from Mississippi is going to have a real problem here. Is he going to be able to handle the great difference between Mississippi and Oxford?'"

But he soon saw a different side of "this kid from Mississippi." In the mid–1960s, Morris began writing a novel set in Oxford, *The Chimes at Midnight*, and he asked Suddarth and other close friends for their recollections of those years in England. Suddarth told him:

> I think I was right in my impression that you would not be able to make the leap that Oxford required in terms of separation from your past and from your own experience. But little did I realize that what you would do would make Oxford accept you on *your* terms. As the year went along it became quite obvious that Willie Morris was a unique personality and that the people of Oxford came more and more to realize it.... But I hope you won't underestimate, Willie, in your novel if it comes out that way, the incredible fascination that people had for you and had for the Mississippi that you had grown up in. Your way of almost creating your own imaginary Faulknerian universe, with Bubba Barrier, RC Colas, big Moon Pies, and the stories of the baseball games, and your grandmother, and the [high] school, and the colored folks around town and all that. Really, Yazoo, as you remember, became one of the principal ramparts of the scene while we were at Oxford.[62]

Others have had similar recollections about Morris. A student who met him on the *Flandre*, for instance, found him "the most fascinating guy in the whole bunch." A classmate, A. Truman Schwartz, said that "he was, of course, brilliant, but he didn't wear his learning on his sleeve, as did some of our Ivy League brethren. He was not above mocking the stuffiness of that tradition and the even stuffier style of Oxford. I think that irreverence attracted acolytes." Edwin M. Yoder Jr. contended in a thoughtful and perceptive essay included in his 2004 memoir that "Willie was easily the most celebrated and charismatic American Oxonian of his years and — with the possible exceptions of Pete Dawkins and Bill Bradley — of his era."

Morris himself looked back on his classmates in his article "Were We the Best?," in which he discussed what the Rhodes scholarships meant to him and others in the Class of 1956. He believed that their years abroad "expanded our universe" and enabled them to find a "continuity with the best historical, literary and intellectual tradition of the Western world." He concluded by summarizing the "values" inherent in the awards and advising "we Americans" never to surrender "to hopelessness or cynicism in the face of callousness and entrenched greed."[63]

Morris would need strong values when he got back to Texas. As editor of the *Texas Observer* he would be facing this darker side of human nature.

CRUSADING JOURNALIST (1960–1971)

The Observer was a muckraking paper in the sense that we used investigative reporting, which Lord knows Texas needed, and still does.... There were aspects of Texas that repelled my Mississippi soul: the terrible extremes of poverty and wealth and the callousness of the oil and gas culture would offend any Southern boy from the Delta, believe me. It was a rapacious society.[64]— Willie Morris, during a 1980 interview

These aspects of Texas repelled others besides Morris; they drove twenty-four-year-old Ronnie Dugger to launch the first issue of the feisty *Texas Observer*—"an independent liberal weekly newspaper"— on December 13, 1954. Dugger was a 1951 graduate of the University of Texas and former editor of the *Daily Texan*, who early in his tenure of the college paper laid out his hard-hitting editorial policy: "The Texan is liberal. It will temper its ideals with realism. But it will never swerve from equal opportunity for all, special privilege for none."[65]

Dugger carried this ideological platform to the Austin-based *Texas Observer*. The eight-page newspaper was not interested in supermarket openings, drug store sales, sports scores, or the Texas society news that other papers covered. To focus attention on the state's abysmal commitment to racial and economic fairness, Dugger and his small staff instead championed liberal causes, thereby placing the *Texas Observer* squarely in the middle of political and intellectual controversy. Covering events that the mainstream press seldom mentioned, the muckraking publication reported on the abominable conditions of mental hospitals and nursing homes ("A Dismal Study — The Aged in Texas" blazoned one headline), rural sharecroppers, illiteracy, fanatical right-wing organizations, the slums in major Texas cities, book censorship, academic freedom, the social ineffectiveness of the death penalty, racial injustice, and the various and sundry political shenanigans in the state legislature. Although the readership in the 1950s and 1960s seldom went above 6,000, Morris proudly noted in a ten-year anniversary article that "by the sheer force of its ardor and its talent, it began to be read by everyone in the state whose opinions had authority."[66]

Dugger, of course, was well familiar with the plainspoken Morris and his articles in the *Daily Texan*. The *Texas Observer* had backed the young editor in his disputes with the University of Texas Regents, and Dugger had sent him a letter at the end of his term congratulating him for "refus[ing] to be embarrassed in the act of confessing that you believe in high principles." Morris had occasionally contributed articles to the *Texas Observer* while he was a student; during his junior year he reported that Mississippi voters, in an attempt to forestall integration of the state's school system, ratified a constitutional amendment approving "full equalization and adequate financing of Mississippi's segregated public schools."[67]

Morris wrote many more pieces for the *Texas Observer* during the summer of 1958 when he was home from Oxford between terms. As associate editor, he covered political rallies and fundraisers, detailed the shortcomings of the Texas school system, and produced lively profiles of small-town newspaper editors. One day he drove to the small (population 2,000) community of Boerne, Texas, and talked to black and white residents for his piece about a referendum that would allow two Negro children to attend a white school. In his riveting article, as Dugger recalled two years later, "You did not learn until the last paragraph [that] liberalism had lost."[68]

With all this experience, Morris knew what to expect when the *Texas Observer* editor asked him if he would like to come back to the newspaper. At about that time, coincidentally, Morris was "trying to figure out what I was going to do when I got home" and was contemplating journalism as a career. He had even written a letter to Hodding Carter, editor and publisher of Greenville, Mississippi's

Delta Democrat-Times, whom he had met when the older man spoke at the University of Texas. Morris asked him if he had any job openings, but Carter replied that his son, Hodding Carter III, was going to join him at the paper. Recalled Morris in 1997: "Unfortunately, there were no alternatives then. If you were liberal and did not go to work for Hodding Carter in Mississippi as a newspaperman in the late fifties, there was nothing. So I went back out to Texas, as Dugger was leaving the *Observer* and he wanted me to take over."[69]

Morris returned to the paper as associate editor in July 1960 and became editor and general manager in March 1961. He felt a sense of "wonderful freedom" as he drove "all around the State of Texas, from El Paso to Texarkana, writing long stories about things happening in small communities that no one ever heard of." He traveled to McAllen, Texas, to meet a woman accused of being a Communist simply because she disagreed with the beliefs of the House Un-American Activities Committee. He drove six hundred miles to El Paso to present a talk on "Communism: A Threat to the Liberal Position," which he summarized for the *Texas Observer*. While in El Paso he interviewed painter and writer Tom Lea for a newspaper profile. He publicized the Texas lawmakers who wanted to require every public school and college teacher to take an oath acknowledging a "Supreme Being." Morris interviewed students, faculty, and administrators for a lengthy October 1960 front-page story on how the University of Texas was handling integration (the article's subtitle concluded: "On-Campus Services Open; Housing, Sports Segregated"). Another article featured on page 1 described his "cloak and dagger" infiltration of the John Birch Society.[70]

The newspaper was covering the upcoming presidential election in the summer and fall of 1960. Soon after he arrived in Austin, Morris and his wife drove to Blanco, Texas, for "Lyndon Johnson Day." He followed Kennedy and Johnson's campaign all over the state, and in September he observed that "the presidential candidate is New England to the core. Through the densest crowds, under a burning sun, he sits cool, comfortable, and unruffled. His smile is warm and friendly. Johnson is more colorful and more folksy. His big frame seems to straddle a convertible. He looks very much like a county sheriff in a local centennial parade."[71]

The *Observer* was known not only for its political and social concerns but also for its cultural interests, and the paper featured book reviews, literary essays, and art news. Morris occasionally veered off from straight reportage and contributed descriptive, lyrical impressions of Texas and Mississippi. In "Precisely at 70" he wrote of the "sad, brutal, empty loneliness" of driving across the vast terrain of Texas, and he contemplated his own mortality in "Journey to Recognition." In "The Rain Fell Noiselessly," he recounted a trip to Yazoo City to visit family and a close friend:

> There wasn't much light left and the rain was settling in for the night when Bubba came by in his pick-up and asked me to ride out and see his cotton. We drove up Washington, past the Courthouse, over the hill onto the Vicksburg highway, and there it was, the delta, spreading out before us miles and miles as far as you could see — perfectly flat, jungle green, it went on and on to the rim of the sky, ending there like a phantom in the rising grey mists. Just below the road the Yazoo River, dark, sluggish, bended and straightened and moved on toward the Mississippi, and far out to the west, far out in that alluvial flatness, there was a strip of orange, holding out stubbornly against the clouds and the night. Sometimes the sky exploded with lightning and thunder, and it rained hard.[72]

Celia Morris astutely observed in her memoir that the years in Oxford were now "paying off" for her husband. "His weekly tutorials had taught him something about the way politics works and what it takes to shift power from one group to another. The year he'd steeped himself in American history had given him a context for what was and was not happening in Texas. And the hundreds of essays he'd read had tuned his ear to English prose at its best, with fine results for his own writing."

Nevertheless, looming deadlines, constant travel, and exhausting nights without sleep eventually took their toll. By 1962, Morris, like Dugger before him, had "run out of gas," and he began making plans to leave the *Texas Observer*. One regular reader of the newspaper was John Fischer, editor-in-chief of *Harper's Magazine* and a former Rhodes scholar whom Morris had met in 1956 before his own trip to Oxford. Morris had recently written an article for *Harper's* on the "Superpatriots" of Houston, and in early 1962, Fischer asked him to consider joining the staff as associate editor. The older man was looking forward to retirement, and the offer came with the understanding that if the arrangement worked out, Morris would succeed him as editor.[73]

Morris did not accept immediately. His wife had applied to several graduate schools and had accepted a Woodrow Wilson Fellowship to Stanford University. Because the "bone-wearying work" at the *Texas Observer* had caught up with him, he thought he might relax for a while in California. Fischer agreed, advising him to "go out there" and "read, reflect." The Morrises left Texas for Palo Alto, and while she studied English, he sat in on some graduate history classes and started writing a memoir. He thought about working on a doctoral degree in history at Stanford, but abandoned the idea when he was not awarded a fellowship.

In the spring of 1963, Morris took a Greyhound bus to New York City to talk to John Fischer. At about the time he returned home, enthusiastic about *Harper's* and New York and ready to pull up stakes immediately, Celia decided that she would finish her graduate studies at the City University of New York. Their futures settled — at least for the moment — the Morris family moved east, and with the publication of the July 1963 issue, Morris's name was on the masthead of *Harper's*. He quickly rose through the magazine's ranks and became editor-in-chief in 1967, shortly before Houghton Mifflin brought out his memoir *North Toward Home*.[74]

In 1967 the editor of the *Yazoo City Herald*, Norman A. Mott Jr., took this photograph for the dust jacket of *North Toward Home*. Willie Morris's house on Grand Avenue is in the background (courtesy of Norman A. Mott Jr. and the *Yazoo Herald*).

Morris began the book as a novel but soon felt "I was making a mistake," and he decided to write a nonfiction work instead. He divided it into the three principal localities of his life: Mississippi, Texas, and New York. Although he knew that it might seem presumptuous for a thirty-year-old man to write his life history, "I did feel quite strongly that I had a story to tell about myself that would be a reflection of many of the realities of my generation, especially, but not exclusively, my generation of Southerners." In his "autobiography in mid-passage," the southern expatriate explains that numerous members of his generation — Mississippians who reached maturity in the early 1950s—felt "alienated

Upon its publication in 1967, *North Toward Home* was both a critical and popular success. Here Willie Morris signs a copy of his "autobiography in mid-passage" at a book-signing party (courtesy of the Center for American History, the University of Texas at Austin, CN Number 02516).

from home yet forever drawn back to it, seeking some form of personal liberty elsewhere yet obsessed with the texture and the complexity of the place from which they had departed." As Morris challenges the social, political, and cultural issues that polarized the nation from the 1940s through the 1960s, he struggles to understand his regional identity.[75]

His dilemmas are reflected in the book's title. As he recalled in a 1986 interview, during his early years in Mississippi "there was only one issue and that was race, the albatross of race." Morris and his friends played baseball and football with blacks, but underlying this friendliness was always an undercurrent of violence. Whites would often torment blacks and play cruel tricks on them, for "they were ours, to do with as we wished."

Morris relates in *North Toward Home* that he began to question the "Mississippi Way of Life" while a student at the University of Texas. By talking to people and reading history and great literature, he slowly acquired a new perspective, an understanding of the complexity of race relations and other social conditions. On a visit home the summer before his senior year, he and a friend attended an organizational meeting of a local chapter of the White Citizens Council. As he listened to the mob—"for it *was* a mob"—he realized how much he had changed morally and intellectually. "I was not the same person I had been three years before.... I knew ... that a mere three years in Texas had taken me irrevocably, even without my recognizing it, from home."

As Morris moved on to New York City and *Harper's*, he eventually regarded North as home, albeit reluctantly. He would always love Mississippi, but he and other ambitious "young people from the provinces" also felt an "ineluctable pull of the cultural capital." They came to New York "because we *had* to," he contends in his book. While he disparages the city—the "Big Cave" he calls it—for its snobbery and the "isolated callousness of the city-dweller," he simultaneously finds Manhattan comforting to the mind and exhilarating to the spirit as he pores over manuscripts in the offices of *Harper's Magazine*.[76]

North Toward Home received the prestigious Houghton Mifflin Literary Fellowship Award for nonfiction, the Francis Parkman Prize from the Texas Institute of Letters, and the Carr P. Collins Award for "the best nonfiction book of the year by a Texan." A selection of the Literary Guild, it was widely praised by critics and prompted the reviewer for *America* to exclaim, "*Harper's* is indeed in good hands."[77]

As the youngest editor-in-chief in the 117-year history of the nation's oldest magazine, Morris aggressively set out to transform the stodgy, patriarchal *Harper's* into one of the country's most exciting and influential periodicals, attracting contributions from well-known writers such as William Styron, Robert Penn Warren, Arthur Miller, James Dickey, Gay Talese, Norman Mailer, Truman Capote, Ralph Ellison, Philip Roth, and Walker Percy. "A lot of distinguished magazines have folded over the years," Morris remarked soon after he was appointed editor. "They were venerable institutions but they did not move with the times.... The idea is to be relevant, and we fully intend to be that."

Morris's desire to create a relevant magazine with a truly national focus, one that

"I came to the city and it changed my life," Willie Morris wrote in the opening chapter of *New York Days.* He joined the staff of *Harper's* in 1963 and four years later became the youngest editor-in-chief in the 117-year history of the nation's oldest magazine. He resigned in March 1971 after becoming embroiled in editorial as well as financial disputes with the periodical's owner and publisher. According to his friend Edwin M. Yoder Jr., Morris often remarked after leaving New York City that "I was once editor of a high school newspaper called the *Flashlight.* The publishers of *Harper's* took away my batteries." This picture of Morris on the streets of New York City originally appeared in *A Pictorial History of Yazoo County* (courtesy of the *Yazoo Herald*).

would reflect the issues of the times and the diversity of the country, spurred him to hire young but already well-established writers, whom he called "contributing editors." These included Larry L. King, Marshall Frady, John Corry, and David Halberstam, each of whom was responsible for writing a certain number of articles per year. Morris directed them to cover "real events" and "capture something of the feeling of the country right now." In return, he said he would "set the tone and character of the magazine. You can't run a magazine as if it had a personality of its own. You have to have a purpose."[78]

The publication of nearly book-length — and often controversial — articles was a hallmark of Morris's years as editor. Soon after he moved into the editor-in-chief's office at *Harper's*, he excerpted 45,000 words from William Styron's *The Confessions of Nat Turner* for the September 1967 issue. Styron's best-selling novel went on to win the 1968 Pulitzer Prize. (He had earlier written about his fascination with Nat Turner for "The South Today," the special supplement to the April 1965 issue of *Harper's*). According to Morris, the article that "evoked the most intense response among readers" was Seymour M. Hersh's cover story in the May 1970 issue on Vietnam's My Lai massacre and its aftermath. At 90,000 words, Norman Mailer's article about his experiences during the massive October 1967 peace demonstration in Washington, D.C., "The Steps of the Pentagon," took up virtually the entire March 1968 issue. When the corresponding book came out in 1968 under the title *The Armies of the Night*, it won the Pulitzer Prize and the National Book Award. David Halberstam contributed his scathing political profiles of "the best and the brightest" decision-makers responsible for the quagmire in Vietnam. Years before Bill Moyers earned his reputation as one of the country's most highly respected broadcast journalists, he wrote for Willie Morris, whom he first met during their student days at the University of Texas. Moyers's 45,000-word cover story for the December 1970 issue, titled "Listening to America," became a best-seller when it was published in 1971 by Harper's Magazine Press.[79]

As contributing editor Larry L. King recalled years later, these were energizing, animated years, for "you could hardly pick up the news mags or the newspapers or turn on a talk show without everyone saying what great things were happening at *Harper's*." He gave Morris much of the credit for this success: "He believed in giving the writer a free reign in search of his own voice; he was not afraid of innovation, bold language, or outrageously divergent points of view published cheek to jowl." Furthermore, "His editing hand was so intuitive that often the writer would be abashed he hadn't written it exactly that way in the first place." Bill Moyers echoed King's opinion. Upon receiving his *Harper's* assignment that would develop into the popular "Listening to America," he said, "Willie has no hang-ups about style, tradition, length — no preconceived ideas of shaping a writer. He is much more interested in me and what I might have to say than in his own idea of what I should say." Even Robert Manning, editor of rival publication *Atlantic Monthly*, conceded that Morris "turned the magazine for a brief time into what Madison Avenue liked to call a 'hot book.'"[80]

Manning was correct in that the glory days of *Harper's* were meteoric but fleeting. Rising postal costs, inflation, and a decline in circulation ate away at the magazine's profits, as did advertising revenues lost to television and special-interest publications (as one publisher succinctly put it, "If you're Head Ski Company, you advertise in the top ski magazine").[81]

Adding to Morris's concerns were his serious philosophical differences with *Harper's* publisher William S. Blair and owner John Cowles Jr. (whose family owned the Minneapolis Star and Tribune Company). The liberal and outspoken *Harper's* may have been "hot" on Madison Avenue, but Blair and Cowles felt that the assessment was not nearly so positive west of the Hudson River. In January 1971, Blair wrote Morris a confidential memo that addressed both his concerns and his ideas for improving the magazine's profit margin. For example, he thought that circulation would increase if the periodical focused on a specialized hobby or interest, in the way that *Golf Digest* appealed to golfers. The publisher followed this six-page memo with a report more than three times as long that he read aloud several weeks later at an executive board meeting in Minneapolis. During the tense three-and-a-half-hour session, he told Morris that he believed the staff writers were paid too much for too few articles and that the magazine "had caught on only with 'Eastern communicators.'" A businessmen on the board chimed in: "No wonder it's such a failure. Who are you editing this magazine for? A bunch of hippies?"[82]

Morris defended *Harper's* and his staff both verbally and in correspondence. He suggested that money could be saved if both his salary of $37,500 and Blair's of $54,000 be trimmed by one-third (Blair refused). In a confidential, six-page memo to the publisher, Morris pointed out that the contributing editors were not overpaid; in fact, they made more money writing for other magazines than they did for *Harper's*. He added that in his travels around the country, he talked to many people who read and admired the monthly.

> We have generated more national publicity in the last three years than we had in the previous fifteen or twenty. (The Press sections of the current *Time* and *Newsweek* are cases in point.) I know the responsible newspaper people all over the country admire *Harper's* considerably. It is a Magazine that is getting people aroused, interested, and engaged as never before, and it breaks my heart that we have not found the means to capitalize on all this and to bring our deficits down.[83]

But as Morris recounted years later, he now realized that "these were waning days." Unwilling to change the periodical's focus and content, the independent-minded editor quit in March 1971, explaining in a press release that "it all boiled down to the money men and the literary men. And, as always, the money men won." His drastic step immediately prompted the mass resignations of most of the contributing editors, who, along with Norman Mailer and William Styron, vowed never again to write for *Harper's*. Although the magazine has subsequently solicited a few of these writers, all have kept that promise.[84]

The abrupt loss of his high-profile position was just one of Morris's mounting list of troubles. His "waning days" actually began in 1969, when he and his wife divorced after months of bitter quarrels and periods of angry silence. "I had come out of a ten-year marriage with most of my illusions shattered and a withering sense of loss and waste," Celia Morris wrote in her memoir, "but also with a son I loved...." David stayed with his mother, while Morris moved into an apartment and became a weekend father. After turning in his resignation from *Harper's*, he left New York City for Bridgehampton, a small town on the east end of Long Island. Though lonely and "feeling very sorrowful," as he remembered two years later, he was determined not to work for anyone but instead earn his living as a full-time writer. Never again would he edit another magazine.[85]

Adrift on Long Island (1971–1979)

I discovered this area by accident, from the back of a chartered bus a few years ago, with advertising salesmen from Harper's going to Montauk for a conference. In a lethargy that day, I glanced out my window; things flickering obliquely before my eyes brought me awake: lush potato fields on the flat land, village greens, old graveyards, shingled houses, ancient elms along the streets, and far in the distance the blue Atlantic breakers. It was the unfolding of one's profoundest dreams, and I knew then I would come back here someday for a long time.[86]—Willie Morris, "Bridgehampton: The Sounds and the Silences" (1974)

Morris returned sooner than he expected. His destination after leaving *Harper's Magazine* in March 1971 was the small, solitary town of Bridgehampton, New York, whose flat land with its "haunting, brooding quality" reminded him of the Mississippi Delta. The area, he also thought, "is a land that enlists loneliness," so the location seemed appropriate to him. He had told publisher William S. Blair in February that he would "fight to the last for the survival of *Harper's* as an enduring American institution," and in defeat he now fled miles from New York where he could nurse his wounds in a self-imposed literary exile. Before cleaning out his office, however, he penned a farewell note to the members of the *Harper's* staff (except Blair) and thanked them for their "loyalty and hard work on our magazine." He concluded his letter by relating how "Abe Lincoln told the story of the boy who stubbed his big toe on an old tree trunk. The boy said it hurt too much to laugh, but he was too big to cry."[87]

Although "clearly downhearted, if not depressed," as one friend recalled, Morris was not at a loss for either emotional solace or material resources during this bleak period. He and his contributing editors received literally hundreds of letters after they resigned, which expressed "support, encouragement, regret, and anger," as Morris noted in a form letter of appreciation mailed to each correspondent. Many wrote to cancel their subscriptions to *Harper's*, telling him that they did not wish to read the magazine now that he was no longer its editor. Publisher Alfred Knopf Jr. stated that he was shocked at the news, for *Harper's* was the most outstanding periodical in the country. Author Robert Penn Warren, who had enjoyed writing for Morris, felt that the editor's resignation was a disaster, both for him personally and for the publishing field in general. One letter was especially poignant: "I will never forget how good you were to me to take time out to see me twice in New York, when I was coming from and going to Oxford," wrote Bill Clinton. "I hope you will find some purpose and peace of mind. Know that a lot of us who can't even scrawl an intelligent sentence are grateful for the work you have done at *Harper's*."[88]

Morris's resignation on March 1 and its aftermath dominated literary news for weeks. Arthur Miller, William Styron, Arthur M. Schlesinger Jr., James Jones, John Kenneth Galbraith, and Gay Talese all signed an "appeal" to John Cowles Jr., asking that he rehire the former editor. George Frazier of the *Boston Globe* wrote Morris to tell him to watch for his forthcoming column. In "The Lit'ry Life," Frazier declared that during the four years of Morris's editorship, "he converted a moribund, stuffy, utterly humorless Harper's into one of the very best magazines ever published in America."[89]

Along with the personal letters and newspaper tributes came job opportunities. "People were calling every 10 minutes to offer contracts and deals," recalled Edwin M. Yoder Jr. One of the first was from Sargent Shriver. Shriver was then involved in Senator Edmund Muskie's campaign for the Democratic nomination for president, and he wanted Morris to work for Muskie as his speechwriter. The College of Communication at Ohio University in Athens invited him to join the faculty as a visiting lecturer. The managing editor of

Sports Illustrated asked him to write an occasional article for the magazine. The American Association of State Colleges and Universities wanted him to do an in-depth analysis of campus newspapers, while an editor at *Family Circle* told Morris's agent the magazine would pay $3,000 for an interview with Mrs. Lyndon Johnson. The *New York Times* interviewed the former editor after Duke University President Terry Sanford offered him a visiting professorship "for a week, a month, a year, as long as I like." Morris refused them all. "I've been working pretty much steadily as an editor since I was 15," he remarked soon after he left *Harper's*, "and I think it's time to take a rest. If I can make a living, I don't want to work for anybody for a while."[90]

Heeding his own words, Morris began to concentrate on his writing. *Yazoo: Integration in a Deep-Southern Town* (much of which originally appeared in the June 1970 *Harper's*) was published only a few months after he left New York City. Because many southern states had ignored the mandates of the 1954 United States Supreme Court decision, *Brown vs. Board of Education of Topeka*, the Supreme Court in October 1969 ordered thirty Mississippi districts, including Yazoo City, to integrate their schools immediately and completely by January 7, 1970. Morris happened to see a "brief wire service story" in the *New York Times* about the federal order, and in 1969 and 1970 he made six trips back to his hometown to observe how it handled the court-ordered desegregation. He interviewed young, middle-aged, and elderly people of both races in the midst of this rapid social change. By around noon on January 7, with the national press watching, "it was quite apparent that Yazoo City had indeed integrated its schools calmly and deliberately." Morris believed that this was due to the "remarkably strong" leadership of whites and blacks who helped convince town residents that integration would preserve the public school system, not destroy it. "An immense facade was beginning to crack, barely perceptible at first, but to a writer and a son of Mississippi, it was the little things which were gradually enclosing and symbolizing the promise and the magnitude of what might be taking place here."

The numerous reflections of Yazoo City residents are not the only observations that Morris records in his book. The author acknowledges that he initially did not want to revisit his hometown, even at this critical juncture in Mississippi's tumultuous history. He eventually, however, confronts his past as "a son of that bedeviled and mystifying and exasperating region" and gains a new perspective on his present and a sense of guarded optimism for the future.[91]

Morris includes vivid reminiscences about his hometown in several of his other books. "If there is anything that makes southerners distinctive from the main body of Americans," he told an interviewer in 1975, "it is a certain burden of memory and a burden of history.... I think sensitive southerners have this in their bones, this profound awareness of the past...." Morris warmly recounts his rich heritage in *Good Old Boy*, which he wrote for his son, David Rae, who had asked him what it was like to grow up in the Deep South. This delightful celebration of Morris's youth, complete with practical jokes, boyish misadventures, a malevolent witch, giant Indians, and a daring rescue in a haunted house, received the Steck-Vaughn Award from the Texas Institute of Letters in 1972 as the "best book for children" by a Texan.[92]

Over the years, *Good Old Boy* has become a staple among students in Mississippi, and for the rest of his life, Morris regularly received fan mail from devoted readers. In June 1997 I visited Morris and his wife, JoAnne, and one evening in a restaurant, several diners stopped by our table to meet Morris and ask for his autograph. They all mentioned *Good Old Boy*, with one man fervently telling him, "It's the only book I ever read in school that I liked." (Later that evening, JoAnne told me that such ringing public endorsements of the book "happen all the time.") After students at a Vicksburg, Mississippi, elementary school enjoyed it in 2003, local resident Jimmy Ball, who as a boy lived across the street from Morris, was asked to talk to the class. "I went down there and I was treated like a rock star," Ball said. "They had me sign autographs and asked me questions just like a celebrity."[93]

Why have southern readers remained so fascinated with *Good Old Boy*? Morris's intricate weaving of reminiscences and folklore certainly contributes to the volume's popularity, as does his story about the Witch of Yazoo. According to the author, an "exceptionally mean and ugly woman" was chased by the town sheriff into the swamps by the Yazoo River, where she was trapped in quicksand. Just before her "ghastly, pockmarked head" disappeared from view, she vowed, "I will break out of my grave and burn down the whole town on the morning of May 25, 1904!" The town residents retrieved her body, and after they buried her in the cemetery, "around her grave they put the heaviest chain they could find — some thirty strong and solid links." On May 25, 1904, Yazoo City did indeed burn down, and the next day, "after the murderous flames had consumed themselves," wrote Morris, residents went to the cemetery, where they discovered that "the chain around the grave had been broken in two."[94]

Although the fire was reportedly begun by a boy playing with matches in his home on Mound Street, the legend of the witch's grave has been a part of Yazoo City history for decades. Jimmy Ball affirmed in 2005 that he, Morris, and their friends used to play in Glenwood Cemetery, and "I certainly remember that story. We all knew it as we were growing up." Long-time Yazoo City reference librarian John E. Ellzey said a year earlier that library patrons often ask about the witch. "Newspaper accounts after the fire, of course, don't mention it. The Yazoo history books make no mention of it, but believe me, people knew about the grave and the witch legend long before *Good Old Boy*." Ellzey added that although records do not indicate who, if anyone, is buried at the spot, local funeral home director Vay Gregory McGraw "thinks the grave may hold someone who was an Odd Fellow," as chains are an Odd Fellow symbol. The Gregory Funeral Home has been operating in Yazoo for over one hundred years, and McGraw believes that her family buried the person in the Witch's Grave. This cannot be proved, however, as the funeral home's files all burned in the 1904 fire.[95]

Readers of *Good Old Boy* (as well as of Morris's other works) regularly travel to Yazoo City's Glenwood Cemetery to seek out the grave, which is still encircled by a chain with a missing link. In 1996 a large stone marker was placed at the site in honor of the sexton who for years guided visitors to the burial place. The volume has, as the monument indicates, "brought national renown to this vengeful woman and her shameful deed," for the legend has been widely publicized in books and articles, including Morris's 1989 sequel, *Good Old Boy and the Witch of Yazoo*. The author himself always found the enormous popularity of *Good Old Boy* "kind of a phenomenon," admitting that while he was writing the affectionate memoir about his hometown and boyhood, "I never for a moment thought ... that it would have such a fantastic effect on kids.[96]

Morris's acute awareness of the past and his roots are also evident in his books of essays. He is a master stylist in this genre; the award-winning *Homecomings*, with its original artwork, particularly illustrates his precision and eloquence in crafting short works of fiction and nonfiction. Other volumes of essays include *Terrains of the Heart and Other Essays on Home*, *Always Stand In Against the Curve and Other Sports Stories*, *After All, It's Only a Game*, and the posthumously published *Shifting Interludes*. His lengthy narrative, "My Own Private Album: The Burden and Resonance of My Memory," introduces *A Southern Album*.

Dozens of reviewers and critics have praised Morris's expertise at explaining the South — particularly its past — to the rest of the nation. "We have few writers more capable than Morris of making childhood believable, of re-creating the small-town South in which he himself grew up a generation ago," wrote Jonathan Yardley in a review of Morris's first novel, *The Last of the Southern Girls*. The story traces the successes and failures of Carol Hollywell, a bright, beautiful, and ambitious Arkansas debutante from Ole Miss who comes to Washington, D.C., and becomes the belle of Capitol Hill. While Yardley and other critics generally extol those parts of the novel recounting Carol's southern girlhood, they are, however, considerably less favorable in their assessments of the rest of the book.[97]

Morris explains in the introduction to a 1994 edition of *The Last of the Southern Girls* that he wrote the novel one dreary winter soon after he left *Harper's*—"my crowning ambition at the time"—and that consequently "I was severely discombobulated." His dog Ichabod Crane had just died, and "my relationship with a beautiful, complex, Washington, D.C., celebrity whom I loved had culminated, too."

Morris's friend, socialite Barbara Howar, apparently played a pivotal role in the writing of his novel. Many Washington-area readers and reviewers saw similarities between her and the fictitious Carol Hollywell. In addition, the plot of *The Last of the Southern Girls* resembled the narrative of Howar's memoir, *Laughing All the Way*, which was published at about the same time as Morris's book. Both works featured prominent and ambitious women from the South who had disastrous affairs with Washington, D.C., politicians before suffering equally miserable, though wealthy, marriages.[98]

The two books were often reviewed together (hers usually more favorably than his), and talk show hosts clamored for interviews with the two authors. Reporters bombarded each with annoying questions about the other, all of which produced "a considerable strain to their relationship." When asked if his book was a *roman à clef*, Morris hedged: "Just to survive, a writer has to draw on the experience of his fellow human beings, quite often on those he loves the most.... Carol Hollywell is not Barbara Howar. Carol Hollywell is me, Willie Morris." The irreverent Howar kept the gossip press buzzing with her waggish response to the same question: "He has his heroine involved with a Congressman. Honey, I've never taken up with a Congressman in my life. I'm such a snob I've never gone below the Senate."[99]

At the height of this literary embarrassment, Morris acknowledged in a signed statement that although he wrote his novel "as an independent effort," he could "also understand in retrospect that I was also feeding on another being too closely." This "feeding" is perhaps understandable, given his attachment to both Howar and his first work of fiction. While working on the book, he excitedly wrote his friend and confidant Edwin M. Yoder Jr. about his progress: "A year ago today was the *Harper's* business, and I just finished the first draft of *The Last of the Southern Girls*.... It's set in Washington, D.C. and Long Island, with flashes to certain places in the South, and the protagonist is a woman. I'm afraid I've fallen in love with her...."[100]

The Last of the Southern Girls was clearly a disappointment to Morris's readers; the book's reception and reviews were disheartening as well to its author, who was attempting to capture the mood of 1960s Washington in a serious work of fiction. "Much has changed in my life in the past year," he wrote his literary agent while working on the book. "It has been very hard to master a new form, to live alone far removed from all the sources of my old ambitions, and to exist from day to day in a web of financial insecurity." Faced with looming child support payments and still coming to terms with his divorce, Morris found living "day to day" to be a constant struggle. Little wonder that David Rae Morris recalled in 2005 that these "early years at Bridgehampton right after [my father] left *Harper's* I think were probably pretty rough.... *Southern Girls* came out and he was having a hard time."[101]

But Morris's frame of mind gradually improved. During an interview for the *Washington Post* soon after the publication of his novel, he admitted that when he left *Harper's* "I was scared at first.... It was like getting over a marriage or a love affair, but now I feel I'm a much better, free soul." What seemed to help was the small, hospitable village of Bridgehampton, which reminded him of Yazoo City. He and some friends organized a softball team of "bartenders, potato farmers, writers, and teen-agers" called the Golden Nematodes (named after the bug that attacks young potato plants), which regularly played on "languid Sunday afternoons" during the summer. In an op-ed piece for the *New York Times*, "Bridgehampton: The Sounds and the Silences," he declared that the town had "the most beautiful terrain in America," and he grew to depend upon year-round residents and fellow writers such as Truman Capote, John Knowles, Joseph Heller, Peter Matthiessen, and James Jones for companionship and lively conversation.[102]

Bobby Van, owner of Bobby Van's "legendary literary watering hole" where Morris and his friends congregated in Bridgehampton, looked back on those years two decades later: "We were all running away from something. I had come back from Vietnam and was starting my life over. Willie Morris had left *Harper's*. Jim Jones was looking for a home in the country, for privacy. In a sense, we all had something in common." Morris loved not only the solitude for writing that Bridgehampton afforded him but also the conviviality at Bobby Van's. Bridgehampton, he told an interviewer in 1976, is a "damned good place to work. And you have people that you can talk to at night when you put your work aside."[103]

Morris was particularly close to James Jones, whose World War II experiences provided much of the background for the celebrated novels *From Here to Eternity* and *The Thin Red Line*. In February 1976, during Morris's two-month stint as writer-in-residence for the *Washington Star* newspaper, Jones drove his and Morris's teenage sons to Washington, D.C., for a two-week stay. Besides sightseeing around the nation's capital, the four tourists also visited several Civil War battlefields. Both men were intense students of the war, and their wanderings around these sites, "haunted ground where the toll of death had been so monumental," emotionally shook them. "It's incredibly sad," Jones observed at Antietam. "It breaks my heart. You wonder why it was necessary, why human beings have to do that to each other." The two talked of the "spiritual, mystical weight" of the Civil War on the American people, and the trip became one of Morris's most treasured memories.[104]

In April the following year, Morris's mother in Yazoo City died. Family friends there could not locate him by telephone, so they called Jones, who broke the news to his friend. "Come on home with me for a while," he told him. "You shouldn't be alone." Morris had barely cleaned out the family house and put it up for sale when Jones, who had long suffered from congestive heart failure, died in May. Fifteen years older than Morris, he had been a mentor and "like a brother to me." He had been struggling to finish *Whistle*, the final volume of his World War II trilogy, and the two writers had arranged for Morris to use Jones's notes and tape-recorded material to complete the novel's last several chapters. Morris followed this book in 1978 with his own *James Jones: A Friendship*, a combination biography and affectionate memoir. "He was a man of deep moral principle [and] ultimate bedrock integrity," Morris wrote with heartfelt emotion. "He was a prop, a pillar. He knew about character because he had character."[105]

Following the publication of his tribute to his close friend, Morris left Bridgehampton. As local resident and author Winston Groom remembered a few years later, "After Jim Jones died, the Hamptons didn't mean as much to Willie." Morris was an only child with no living family members except for his son. Now that both of his parents were dead, he realized that "out of blood and belonging" he needed to come home again — that it was necessary for him to have some proximity with his roots and the touchstones of his past. The world had taken a couple of turns by late 1979, and it was time for Morris to go south toward home.[106]

South Toward Home (1979–1999)

It was in the East that I grew to middle age. I cared for it, but it was not mine. I had lived nearly 20 years there, watching all the while from afar as my home suffered its

> *agonies, loving and hating it across the distance, returning constantly on visits or assignments. The funerals kept apace, "Abide with Me" reverberating from the pipe organs of the churches, until one day I awoke to the comprehension that all my people were gone. As if in a dream, where every gesture is attenuated, it grew upon me that a man had best be coming on back to where his strongest feelings lay.*[107]— Willie Morris, "Coming on Back" (1981)

Willie Morris experienced a few pangs of homesickness in the spring of 1978. He was in Greenwood, Mississippi, to speak at an art festival and soon began asking about old friends and wandering around the area. "I'm so attuned to this land," he told a local reporter interviewing him. "You never get it out of your blood. You have all these memories associated with it."[108]

He also noticed that the political situation in Mississippi was changing. The civil rights movement had made significant progress in easing racial tensions, and he started thinking that it might be time to return to his native state. "Truman Capote told me once that all Southerners go home sooner or later," he often remarked in succeeding years, "even if it's in a box. Well, I didn't want to wait that long." He asked his friend Larry Wells, who with his wife, Dean Faulkner Wells, owned Yoknapatawpha Press in Oxford, to explore the possibility of his coming to teach at the University of Mississippi. The Ole Miss chancellor was "all for it," Wells recalled, "but the English Department budget lacked funding." Consequently, public and private donors around the state were contacted to help raise money for Morris's salary and the expenses for visiting speakers.[109]

Morris came down to Oxford from Bridgehampton in 1979 to see the campus and the community and to meet some of the residents. It was a beautiful October weekend, and Wells and others had planned several social gatherings so Morris would be sure to enjoy himself. Sid Graves, the director of the

Willie Morris and his dog Pete, a black Labrador, outside Oxford, Mississippi, in January 1982. The Associated Press covered Pete's death in February 1983, noting that Morris and Pete "found each other" in Bridgehampton, New York, in the mid–1970s: "'My heart's been cut out because he was my brother,' said Morris, a former editor of *Harper's* magazine and now a journalist-in-residence at the University of Mississippi. 'I'm an only child. I'll get a wife before I get another dog.'" Later that year, Morris told author Studs Terkel during an interview that "we buried Pete up in the town cemetery in Oxford. The mayor got him up there very close to the Faulkner plot" (©1982 David Rae Morris. All Rights Reserved).

public library in Clarksdale, Mississippi, and a fan of Morris's books, had set up a lecture that helped pay for his trip. Following the author's speech, a cocktail party, and dinner, his hosts drove Morris to Rowan Oak, William Faulkner's home. It was about one o'clock in the morning, Wells remembered, and the moon was bright:

> We walked around the house, and it was one of those enchanted moments. The next evening we gave a dinner party for Willie and invited people we thought he'd like, a mixture of academic people and people from town. The next day was the football game, which is a big ritual here. We had a picnic on the campus in a tree-lined grove, then went to the game.... After that weekend Willie felt that Oxford would be congenial to him, not just the people but the life-style.[110]

Willie Morris by the grave of William Faulkner in St. Peter's Cemetery, Oxford, Mississippi, circa mid–1980s. Morris returned to his native Mississippi in late 1979 after decades of self-imposed exile, and in 1981 he told a reporter for the New Orleans *Times-Picayune*: "In this town you have the pervasive spirit of Mr. Bill Faulkner. As a Mississippi writer, I don't think I could have lived in Faulkner's hometown twenty years ago — the place he spent a lifetime writing about. The shadow effect would have been too much. But now I get a strange sustenance from his spiritual presence. It's a kind of emotional support for me" (courtesy of Kay Holloway).

By December, Morris was comfortably settled in a "modest one-story house with white shingles" on Faculty Row, which curves uphill into the University of Mississippi campus. The spring semester of 1980 found him teaching courses in creative writing and the American novel. He emphasized contemporary American fiction in his novel class, and had, as he told his students, "a rather eclectic reading list, designed in part to accommodate several of the authors of these books who will come to Ole Miss to talk with you." Students soon packed one of the largest lecture rooms at the university to hear John Knowles speak on *A Separate Peace*, James Dickey read his poetry, William Styron discuss *The Confessions of Nat Turner* and his newly published *Sophie's Choice*, Gloria Jones talk about her late husband's *From Here to Eternity*, and other writers converse about their works. "He had people *running* to that class; he had people crowding into that lecture hall," exclaimed Larry Wells. "It would hold about eighty — he had 120 in the class. The aisles were filled, and I've never seen that kind of excitement over literature."[111]

Morris's first year as a visiting lecturer was a "resounding success," according to a University of Mississippi fund raising letter. Despite his popularity, however, Morris did not enjoy teaching, nor did he like grading assignments, short answer quizzes, and term papers. In the fall of 1981, he left the English faculty for a position as lecturer and writer-in-residence with the Journalism Department. Although he still had papers to grade, he did not have to spend as much time on class preparations as he did before. He was also able to teach magazine feature writing, and in October he and his students published the first issue of the *Ole Miss Magazine*. The professionally produced, twenty-four-page "independent expression of both the noteworthy and casual things here" featured works by students and faculty. The contributions of advisor Morris included not only his article about a recent visit to the University of Texas, "The Search for Billy Goat Hill," but also his editorial skills. "I saw him edit their papers with his sure hand and it was magic," remembered Larry Wells. "He could turn the mundane into the profound with a few strokes of his pen."[112]

Morris took pains to encourage these aspiring young authors, particularly when he recognized exceptional talent. For example, after reading a short story by freshman Donna Tartt, he urged her to enroll in a graduate short story course taught by Barry Hannah, also a writer-in-residence. She soon outshone the other students, and following her first year transferred to Bennington College in Vermont, where she began writing a novel. A publishers' bidding war culminated in Alfred A. Knopf, Inc. paying her $450,000 for *A Secret History*. In another instance, a University of Mississippi law student who had sat in on some of Morris's classes began writing his first novel and asked him for advice, which was generously given. Subsequently Morris wrote a blurb for the book's dust jacket, praising John Grisham's *A Time to Kill* as "a powerful courtroom drama" and "a compelling tale of a small southern town searching for itself."[113]

Willie Morris in "The Grove" on the University of Mississippi in Oxford, mid–1980s. Morris began teaching classes at Ole Miss in 1980, and he soon became a popular figure both on campus and around the town. In 1984, a newspaper reporter observed: "In the Warehouse [an Oxford pub], Willie holds forth after class, swapping stories with the students, memorizing sensations and quotes for his own future writing, but mainly giving of himself to them in a way they are unused to receiving from one of their parents' or professors' generation. In his old navy windbreaker, the padding of his middle years below the still-smooth round face lends Willie the appearance of an amiable bear. Or a friendly lion" (courtesy of the Keating Collection, Southern Media Archive, University of Mississippi Special Collections).

As Morris offered literary counsel to fledgling authors, he did not forget his own career. For years he had been working on *Taps*, a novel set during the Korean War, but as he told one of the many reporters who interviewed him shortly after he arrived at Ole Miss, "I've sort of put my novel aside while I'm here." Larry Wells and Yoknapatawpha Press reissued *Good Old Boy* in 1980, and a year later Morris's first book of essays appeared, *Terrains of the Heart and Other Essays on Home*, also by Yoknapatawpha Press. Although he had not written a large work of nonfiction since *North Toward Home*, his intense interest in history and a chance conversation with a former colleague would lead him to a project that would take nearly two years to complete.[114]

While on a magazine assignment in Mississippi, David Halberstam visited Morris in Oxford. The two men's conversation turned to sports, particularly to Marcus Dupree, an outstanding black high school football player from the little town of Philadelphia, Mississippi. He had received national media attention as one of the best running backs in the country, and both black and white residents of the town cheered for him on game days. Philadelphia and Neshoba County were also widely recognized, however, as the scene of one of the state's most brutal crimes: the 1964 murders of civil rights workers James Earl

In May 1987, Willie Morris was one of the speakers at the dedication of new grave markers — including that of his great-grandfather, Major George W. Harper — in the Confederate section of the Raymond, Mississippi, city cemetery. Morris's maternal grandparents are also buried in this cemetery. Here he kneels beside the gravestone of his grandmother, Marion "Mamie" Harper Weaks (courtesy of the Raymond, Mississippi *Hinds County Gazette*).

Chaney, Andrew Goodman, and Michael Schwerner.[115]

At Halberstam's suggestion, Morris began working on an article about the football player, but as he spent days talking to Dupree, his family, and his friends, he began to perceive the young man's life as a metaphor for the changing South. "The more I got into it, the more I saw accumulating ironies," Morris recalled. For instance, Dupree was born "one month less a day" before the civil rights workers were slain. His high school graduating class was the first in Philadelphia in which both white and black students had attended all twelve grades together in integrated schools. The project slowly evolved into an entire book, *The Courting of Marcus Dupree*, which won the thirty-fifth annual Christopher Award for "artistic excellence in books, films or television specials that affirm the highest values of the human spirit."[116]

This multilayered work is not merely a football book, nor is it a biography. Morris instead interweaves civil rights history, the story of Dupree's "courting" by major football powers, and his own autobiography, drawing comparisons between his life and Dupree's. "This narrative, much as an act of the subconscious, has really become a book about two small-town Mississippi boys — a seventeen-year-old black and a middle-aged white, and the young black's odyssey into the greater world would coincide, or almost did, with the middle-aged white's return from a long exile.... Each of the two sprang from a most radically different heritage — yet from a mutual one, too."[117]

This combination of sports, autobiography, and history was always one of Morris's favorite books. Although some reviews were glowing ("your writing, your impressions, even just your phrases are deeply moving," social historian Studs Terkel told him), many were unfavorable, even brutally cutting. One of the earliest notices appeared in the Memphis *Commercial Appeal*. A staff writer for the newspaper wrote that the book was "not particularly enlightening on the subject of college football recruiting," and he suggested that Morris quit writing about Mississippi and "bid goodbye to the ghosts of Yazoo and Mr. Bill [Faulkner] ... and move on to new territory." On the day Morris's friends in Oxford read the review, they knew he would be despondent when they saw him that evening. "Willie will be brooding tonight," warned the town mayor, John Leslie. "He'll be down, I guarantee you. He's real sensitive...."[118]

Morris's sensitivity and broodiness — as well as his fondness for bourbon — were well known among his friends. A born night owl who once wrote in the *Daily Texan* that "the day is cringing and artificial," he especially craved companionship in a favorite bar late in the evenings. Ultimately, however, the drinking buddies would have to go home, and he would be left by himself. "It's Sunday nights in a small town that get to me," he sighed late one night shortly after *The Courting of Marcus Dupree* was published. "The loneliness."[119]

Morris also was thin-skinned, and he too

often dwelled upon slight affronts (real or imagined). The many negative reviews of a complex work on which he had spent months researching and writing sent him into a deep depression, and he neglected most of his responsibilities, including those at the University of Mississippi. "He really became Mr. Hyde more than Dr. Jekyll," observed a companion of the time. Said another, "Willie's drinking is not a healthy thing. He has not done the work he should have done." Although Morris wrote a few articles for magazines and newspapers and fiddled with *Taps* on occasion, he would publish no books for six long years.[120]

But then he got reacquainted with an old friend. Her name was JoAnne Prichard, a senior editor at the University Press of Mississippi in Jackson. They first met in the spring of 1967, when he came to Yazoo City during National Library Week to talk to students at the local high schools. "That was my first year of teaching," she recalled in 2005. Prichard taught eleventh grade English in Yazoo City, and over the years "Willie spoke to my classes a couple of times." She also team-taught a humanities course with algebra teacher Harriet DeCell, and after the two women wrote a history of Yazoo County, Morris contributed the introduction. He and Prichard would see one another casually at social occasions, but that was all. She was married at the time, and later on, "even when I was not married and he would visit Yazoo City, we didn't get together."[121]

That all changed in 1988. Prichard wrote in March to tell him that the University Press of Mississippi was publishing a new series of books in the fall, the Author and Artist Series, "which will bring together works of Mississippi writers and visual artists." The first volume, she said, would feature stories by Eudora Welty, and "we are very hopeful that you will agree to write the second volume in the series."

Their literary collaboration on *Homecomings*, which included the art of Morris's friend William Dunlap, would eventually lead to a more personal relationship. Recalled Prichard: "I went to Oxford to do an interview with Willie and Bill, then I just found I was going back to Oxford more and more." Soon after their marriage on September 14, 1990, Morris resigned his position at Ole Miss and moved to Jackson.[122]

All of Morris's friends emphatically agree that his wife helped him put his life and career back together. He became more at peace with himself and his surroundings, and he enjoyed relaxing at home. "Willie told me that JoAnne had 'saved his life' and also was giving him 'the best years of his life,'" affirms Larry L. King, his colleague from *Harper's*. Says another friend of several decades, "There was another warm body in the house, so Willie was not alone — the thing he feared most." She eased him into a comfortable, domestic lifestyle, with family, friends, and regular meals. "I love being in Jackson," Morris exclaimed a few years after his marriage. "I have dinner twice a month with Eudora Welty. It's just a short ride to Yazoo City or on up to Greenville to Doe's Eat Place. I love my wife, and I have five great cats."[123]

She also encouraged him in his writing, even early in their relationship. In 1989, *National Geographic* published his cover story on William Faulkner and Oxford, Mississippi. In March the following year, he wrote his son that he had been concentrating hard on revising and expanding the piece, which would be published in book form as *Faulkner's Mississippi*. "Am very pleased with the work.... JoAnne and I are very close, may get married soon."[124]

Now that Morris was content in a spacious house, he dusted off his bound volumes of *Harper's* and began work on a sequel to *North Toward Home*, which would cover his years as the magazine's editor. *New York Days* is a romantic look at New York City in the late 1960s as viewed by a wide-eyed young provincial suddenly immersed in its glamour and drama. But like his first book, it's more than just an autobiography, as he also tried to capture what was transpiring in America at that time. "Our magazine was right in the middle of the '60s storm, in every sense," he told an interviewer upon the book's publication. "So while I've tried to reflect my own experiences, and something of the communal flavor of Manhattan,... I've tried also to reflect the temper of the times."[125]

When Willie Morris and JoAnne Prichard married in September 1990, he moved into her house on Northside Drive in Jackson. Here Morris (left) and author William Styron relax on the deck (circa 1990). The two men met in the mid–1960s, after Morris invited Styron to contribute an essay to a special *Harper's Magazine* supplement on the South. More than three decades later, Styron delivered one of the eulogies at Morris's funeral service (courtesy of Hunter Cole).

Although *New York Days* received numerous favorable reviews— including a warm front-page tribute in the *New York Times Book Review*— some readers thought the memoir was too nostalgic, devoid of juicy anecdotes and score-settling. Their argument has some validity, though Morris was unapologetic and shrugged off all criticism. The memories were his, no one else's, and he wrote them down as he remembered them (wearing out 180 felt-tip pens in the process). He often remarked that the book took him two-and-one-half years "plus a lifetime" to write, as he deliberately waited twenty years before tackling it to let hard feelings subside. "I had tried to make peace with the period earlier, and I felt that bitterness would be self-destructive. I wanted the book to be generous in spirit."[126]

Perhaps he was too generous, but at nearly sixty years old, Morris was no longer the Young Turk of old, the David who challenged the Goliaths of the Texas Board of Regents, the Texas legislature, and *Harper's Magazine* with steely resolve and searing prose. When a national magazine offered him the "very lucrative assignment" of writing a cover story on a prominent figure, he turned it down as "I felt no human chemistry with him, indeed could not abide him nor anything he stood for." He admitted that in his thirties he would have enthusiastically accepted the proposal, but at this stage of his life he did not wish to be adversarial, tough, and critical. As he wrote in an essay about growing older and more tolerant, "What I really wish to do now is write about people and places and things that intrigue me, that I admire."

At the top of this list were home and his childhood experiences, which figured in many of his works. After completing the emotionally draining *New York Days*, he wanted to take a break and write something just for pleasure, just for fun. He did not have far to look for a suitable topic. "What's more fun," he reminisced to a reporter, "than the dog of your boyhood?"[127]

The dog of Morris's boyhood was Skip, given to him when he was in the third grade. Although his family had owned several dogs before, none was as talented as Skip. He could play football, go on errands, run the 100-yard dash in 7.8 seconds, and even drive a car (with a little help). Morris transferred these memories to the pages of *My Dog Skip*, a poignant, bittersweet tribute to the canine companion of his youth. "It was a lazy town," he wrote of Yazoo City, "all stretched out on its hills and its flat streets, and over the years Skip also grew to know almost every house, tree, street, and alley. Occasionally he wandered around the town by himself, and everybody of any consequence knew who he was."[128]

Morris readily admitted that growing up

Willie Morris on Bell Road near Yazoo City, Easter Sunday, 1991. An ancient Indian trail, Bell Road is a narrow sunken roadway with high dirt sides. Its name came from the bells located on treacherous curves, which travelers rang to warn approaching traffic. Morris and his wife, JoAnne, loved to explore Mississippi by driving down two-lane roads and little-traveled byways (courtesy of Hunter Cole).

in Yazoo City was not as idyllic as it seemed to him at the time; moreover, he knew that others had far different experiences. "Mississippi," he remarked during a lengthy interview in 1997, "has changed since my boyhood time, and for the better. It could not have been any worse than in the fifties and sixties. It was for black people essentially a police state...." His next book, *The Ghosts of Medgar Evers: A Tale of Race, Murder, Mississippi, and Hollywood*, is in large part an odyssey back to this racist past, particularly June 1963 when thirty-seven-year-old civil rights activist Medgar Evers was shot in the back and killed in front of his wife and children at their home in Jackson. White supremacist and Ku Klux Klan member Byron De La Beckwith was charged with the slaying, but despite such overwhelming evidence as eyewitnesses and his fingerprint on the assassin's rifle, he was freed after the all-white juries in two trials deadlocked.[129]

Murder, however, has no statute of limitations. When the Hinds County, Mississippi, assistant district attorney, Bobby DeLaughter, reopened the case in 1990, Beckwith was prosecuted once more and convicted four years later. Morris covered the third trial for the magazine *New Choices for Retirement Living* and was spellbound by its proceedings. Impressed by the historical significance of the event and fascinated with the intricate story of how DeLaughter, Evers's wife Myrlie, and others relentlessly pushed for justice, Morris convinced friend and movie producer Frederick Zollo (*Quiz Show*, *The Paper*, *Mississippi Burning*) that he should make a motion picture based on the murder case. Zollo agreed and secured Rob Reiner (*A Few Good Men*, *When Harry Met Sally*, *Stand by Me*) to direct the film.[130]

Morris served as a consultant for this 1996 production, *Ghosts of Mississippi*. (Sharp-eyed moviegoers, in fact, can catch a glimpse of the author's *North Toward Home* as Peggy DeLaughter, the wife of Beckwith's prosecutor, reads it in bed.) "It's a story about redemption, really," he explained to a *New York Times* interviewer during the movie's filming. And for Morris, confronting once again the paradoxical and complicated past of his native state, with its history of guilt and meanness and tragedy, but also of grace and courage and solicitude, the filming was truly both painful and redeeming. "We all love Mississippi," he often told Yankee visitors, "but sometimes she doesn't love us back. She is a difficult and ardent mistress."[131]

Ghosts of Mississippi went on to lose millions at the box office; moreover, it was pilloried by reviewers who believed that the film should have focused not on the district attorney and the trial of Byron De La Beckwith, but instead on the saga of the courageous man whom Beckwith murdered. Born in 1926 in the small town of Decatur, Mississippi, Medgar Evers spent years traveling throughout the state helping to fight segregation, and he served as the first Mississippi field secretary of the National Association for the Advancement of Colored People.

Morris chronicles the remarkable story of this inspiring leader in *The Ghosts of Medgar Evers*, in which he once again effectively juxtaposes and intertwines history with autobiography. Tempering nostalgia with harsh reality, he retraces both his and Evers's lives as descendants of two vastly

Willie Morris greets his friend Bill Clinton (right) during a 1992 campaign rally in Jackson, at which presidential candidate Clinton spoke and Morris emceed. Morris gave his fellow Rhodes scholar a copy of his limited edition book, *My Two Oxfords*. Morris later recalled: "He saw me and came up and hugged me, and I had a copy of that book and I gave it to him. He immediately turned to an assistant and said, 'Put this in the briefcase. I want to read it.' And Bill Clinton whispered to me then, shortly before the election when he was holding on in the polls, 'Willie, it's going to be a tough few weeks, but I *think* we're going to make it'" (courtesy of the *Clarion-Ledger*).

In March 1994, Willie and JoAnne Morris moved to a large house on Brookdale Street in Jackson. Morris adopted this huge room on the second floor as his study, or "work room," as he called it. He wrote with a felt-tip pen, not a computer, organizing his thoughts on note cards before putting any words down on paper. "Then when he got ready to write," said his wife, JoAnne, during an interview, "he would stack the note cards into categories, and those were his chapters" (Spring 1997, courtesy Fred Brown).

different Mississippis while he simultaneously details the history of the movie and his own experiences as a consultant. "Hollywood was the last place in the world I might have expected to raise certain questions and to learn certain truths about Mississippi and Mississippians and America and Americans. The filming of this movie would turn out to be as delicate and multilayered as the final Beckwith trial itself and all that had gone before, for *Ghosts* [*of Mississippi*] would represent nothing if not a stark reliving of an unquenchable past."[132]

Willie Morris by the grave of the Witch of Yazoo, the legendary character he embellished and immortalized in his memoir *Good Old Boy*. As children, Morris and his friends often played in Glenwood Cemetery, where an unmarked grave bordered by a large chain with a missing link indicated, according to local lore, the burial site of a witch who had burned down much of the city in 1904. Readers of *Good Old Boy* (as well as of Morris's other books) regularly travel to Yazoo City's Glenwood Cemetery to seek out the grave, which is still surrounded by a chain with a missing link. A large stone marker placed at the site in 1997 reads (in all capital letters): "According to local legend ... On May 25, 1904, the Witch of Yazoo City broke out of these curious chain links surrounding her grave and burned down Yazoo City. Writer Willie Morris's classic 'Good Old Boy' brought national renown to this vengeful woman and her shameful deed."

Morris clearly enjoyed his behind-the-scenes role in a major motion picture, and he was gratified when Hollywood beckoned again upon the publication of his memoir recounting his youth in Yazoo City with canine companion Skip and girlfriend Rivers Applewhite. After film director Jay Russell turned the last page of the author's memoir *My Dog Skip*, he said that "I first had to dry my eyes from crying and the second thing I did was call Willie Morris to inquire whether the rights were available." Russell already knew Morris; he had interviewed him while filming the documentary *Highway 61*, the first of a five-part PBS series on famous American highways titled *Great Drives*. Soon he secured not only the necessary permission from the author but also the assistance of screenwriter/filmmaker John Lee Hancock, screenwriter Gail Gilchriest, and Academy Award–winning producer Mark Johnson.[133]

A relatively new production company, Alcon Entertainment, began filming in 1998. Although Yazoo City had changed so much over the years that much of the motion picture was filmed in less-developed Canton, Mississippi, Morris was pleased with the results and found shooting to be especially poignant. "Observing the actors depicting my long-departed kin was a déjà vu of the most impressive kind," he remarked on more than one occasion. Film veterans Kevin Bacon (*Mystic River*, *Apollo 13*, *A Few Good Men*, *Footloose*) and Diane Lane (*Under the Tuscan Sun*, *The Perfect Storm*, *Murder at 1600*, *Judge Dredd*) starred as his mother and father, while Frankie Muniz — who a year later would be featured in the television program *Malcolm in the Middle*— played young Willie. More than a half dozen Jack Russell terriers were used in the title role, one of which was the well-known "Eddie" on the NBC sitcom *Frasier*.[134]

Although *My Dog Skip* was shown to selected audiences in 1999, Warner Bros. did not release it for general distribution until early 2000. The reviews were nearly all positive, and the filmmakers found themselves in the enviable position of producing a motion picture that made more money its second week than it did the first. Gene Shalit on the *Today* show singled out Frankie Muniz for turning in "as splendid a performance by a youngster as I have ever seen." He added that the film was not just for children: "Don't be put off by this title. This is a grown-up movie for adults that young people will also cherish."[135]

Willie Morris leaves his handprints in a block of wet cement in downtown Canton, Mississippi. The concrete marker was made in June 1998 to commemorate the filming of the motion picture *My Dog Skip* in Canton that spring. Standing next to Morris are Wayni Terrill (center) and Janet White (right) of the Canton Convention and Visitors Bureau (courtesy of the *Clarion-Ledger*).

At a birthday party for Eudora Welty in 1998, fellow Mississippi writers Willie Morris (clasping Miss Welty's hand), Ellen Douglas (rear center), and Margaret Walker (seated at right) join University Press of Mississippi Associate Director Seetha Srinivasan (right rear) in congratulating the Pulitzer Prize–winning author. The celebration was held in Lemuria bookstore in Jackson (courtesy of the *Clarion-Ledger*).

Morris himself also reveled in the film, though he did not see its final version. During the last week of July 1999, he and JoAnne flew to New York City to view a preliminary screening. "Just returned from New York," he exuberantly wrote a friend on July 30. "The movie *My Dog Skip* is an absolute classic! It's a work of rare beauty. Everything comes together: acting, photography, script, music. You're going to love it."[136]

As Morris eagerly awaited the release of the motion picture, he started planning his next work, a memoir about his father and baseball. As JoAnne got up on the morning of August 2, her husband opened his eyes long enough to

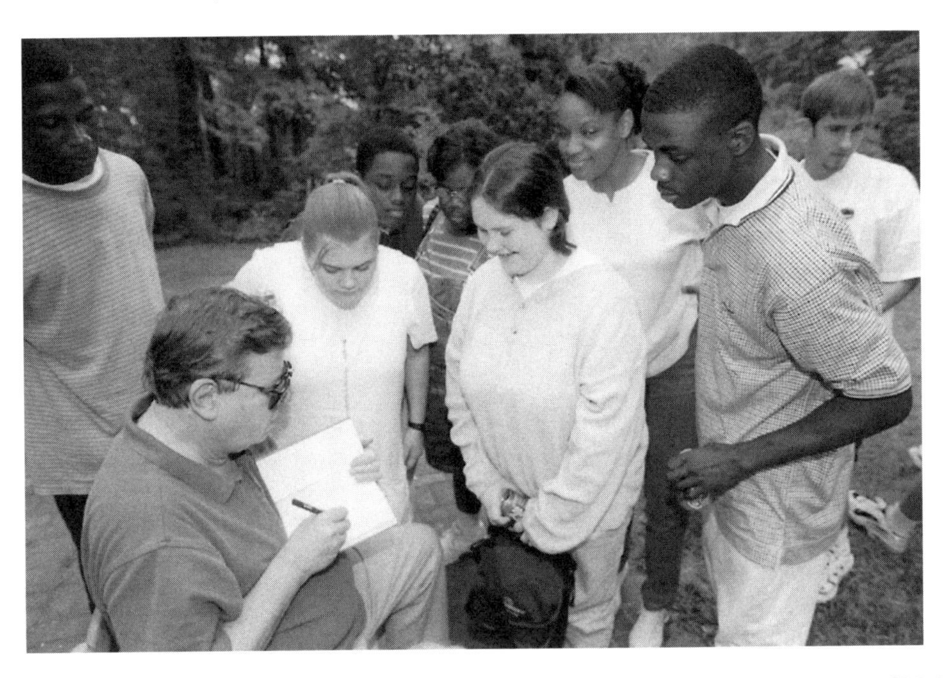

Pearl, Mississippi, students gather around Willie Morris in his back yard as he signs a copy of *My Dog Skip* for Leah Davis (directly in front of Morris, with bag). To help the students recover from a tragic shooting in the school, their ninth-grade English teacher assigned *Good Old Boy*. They liked it so much she invited the author to discuss his work in her class. He proposed that the class visit him instead. "We'll have Coca-Colas and Moon Pies and talk about books," he said (April 1998, courtesy of the *Clarion-Ledger*). See item 1791.

comment on his baseball book and to ask her about some stationery and postcards he needed. She assured him that everything was taken care of, and he went back to sleep. At about 11:30 in the morning, as she talked to two friends in her downstairs office about a proposed volume for the University Press of Mississippi, she heard him call her name. "Seconds later," JoAnne recalled, "he yelled again, and it was urgent. So I left the room and went upstairs to the bedroom and he was saying, 'I can't breathe, I can't breathe.' And he was sweating, just dripping wet."

She called for an ambulance, and while one friend went outside to wait and flag it down, the other helped her get Morris's shirt off. "He was panicking," JoAnne remembered. "He talked to me about getting *Taps* together. He said, 'After I'm gone, don't grieve.' And then he added, 'Well, yes, grieve a little. I do want you to grieve a little. But I want you to be happy and fulfilled. You're the best wife I ever had.'"

The ambulance arrived and JoAnne rode with him to St. Dominic Hospital in Jackson. "Willie wanted me to invite everyone to the premiere of *My Dog Skip*. He kept trying to talk, so they gave him morphine so he would keep the oxygen mask on. Then they took him upstairs. At no time did I get a sense it was as bad as it was."

As JoAnne waited, a nurse came to tell her that it was indeed serious. Some friends came to the hospital to be with her, and she called her stepson in New Orleans, David Rae Morris. "It all just hit me. The last thing I heard was that they were going to clear his lungs." A doctor told her late in the afternoon that her husband was unconscious, and that even if he lived, he had lost so much oxygen that he would not function as a normal person. "How would you know?" JoAnne shot back. "You don't know how smart he was to begin with."[137]

At 6:21 that evening, sixty-four-year-old Willie Morris died. "There's just this big, damned black hole," JoAnne tearfully told a friend who had driven to Jackson from New

Orleans after he had heard the news. The official cause of death was cardiomyopathy, but as one mourner theorized, “He gave so much of his heart away he didn’t have any reserves left when he needed them.”[138]

Those recipients, however, had not forgotten their friend. Many of them would soon be gathering in Mississippi to thank him one final time.

EPILOGUE

The ghosts are all around me, of those I loved now across the divide; I have learned the silence of the grave. Is death, too, merely part of the adventure? I have a recurring dream, a strange reverie, of entering a favorite place I once knew, a dimly lit restaurant on the great Eastern littoral with Tiffany lamps and a mahogany bar. As I come in, the dozens of people there turn and see me. They are all people I have cared for who are dead, not a living person among them, and they greet me one by one with warmth and affection, as in Fellini's dance of mortality.[139]— Willie Morris, "'Now That I Am Fifty'" (1985)

Following Willie Morris's death in the early evening of August 2, 1999, obituaries across the country recalled his literary accomplishments, engaging personal characteristics, and affection for the South. Particularly moving among the many memorial tributes were the reminiscences of friends and former colleagues. John Evans, owner of Lemuria bookstore in Jackson, remembered the encouragement and literary advice Morris gave young writers. "'Whether it was journalists or blues writers or whatever, Willie was supportive of anyone who was involved in creative aspects,' Evans said." David Halberstam contributed many penetrating articles to Morris's *Harper's* and recalled the editor's unique literary skills. "He was an enormously gifted editor and an enormously gifted writer himself," declared the Pulitzer Prize–winning author. "I always thought he was the best writer in the bunch." Author William Styron, another Pulitzer Prize winner, agreed. "He was a brilliant editor and a great companion and a wonderful friend, and I always thought he was one of the best editors America ever produced in the magazine field." Morris met Bill Clinton in 1968 when the future president was in New York, preparing to sail for England where he would study as a Rhodes scholar. After Morris died, Clinton reminisced about *North Toward Home*, which he deemed a "beautifully written, evocative portrait of one person's love for the South who had profound regret over the racial situation.... He showed us how we could love a place and want to change it at the same time. It was really an important thing he did for me. He showed us we could go home."[140]

Morris himself left Long Island, New York, for home in late 1979. Larry Wells, who was instrumental in the author being hired by the University of Mississippi, remembered that his presence was felt immediately on campus: "Students were sitting in the aisles and they were smiling. I sat in on some of his classes and it was like going to the LSU [Louisiana State University] game. The classes were so happy." David Sansing, Professor Emeritus of History at Ole Miss, stressed his friend's positive influence on others. "'The one amazing thing about Willie was that he could get people to believe in themselves,' Sansing said. 'He could inspire you and had the ability to make you think you were the most important person in the world.'" John Leslie was town mayor during those Oxford years and looked back on all the writers Morris brought to campus. "When he came here our national publicity changed just because of him and the friends he brought here."[141]

Although they did indeed bring publicity to Oxford, Morris's own reputation as a spokesman for the South had a much broader impact. As former Mississippi Governor William F. Winter observed after his friend's death, Morris's legacy is that of a "storyteller who was an interpreter of life in the state and this part of the country for the rest of [the] country and the rest of the world." For example, in the fall of 1982, *Time* magazine asked the author "to examine changes at Ole Miss" during the twenty years since September 30, 1962, the day "the campus of the University of Mississippi was shattered by riots protesting the admission of the first black student," James Meredith. Morris had his journalism class publish a special issue of *Ole Miss Mag-*

Pallbearers carry the casket of Willie Morris from First United Methodist Church in Yazoo City after his funeral service on August 5, 1999. At left of casket, front to back: David Sansing (near center of photograph), Rick Cleveland, Charles Henry, and John Evans. On the right, front to back: Richard Howorth, Malcolm White, Peyton Prospere, and Bob Yarbrough. The two persons on the front and back of the casket are from the funeral home. Wearing glasses (front, center) is Morris's friend from Yazoo City, Sam Olden. At the extreme right is William Styron and just beneath him (with hat) is minister Will Campbell. Styron's wife, Rose, is talking to Campbell (courtesy of the *Clarion-Ledger*).

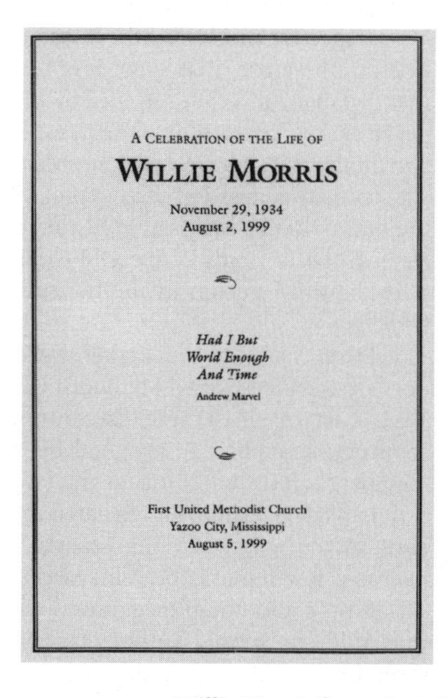

A CELEBRATION OF THE LIFE OF

WILLIE MORRIS

November 29, 1934
August 2, 1999

Had I But
World Enough
And Time
Andrew Marvel

First United Methodist Church
Yazoo City, Mississippi
August 5, 1999

A Celebration of the Life of Willie Morris

Organ Prelude	Hannah Kelly
Opening Remarks	Will D. Campbell
New Testament Lesson	The Reverend Larry Speed
Prayer	
"In The Garden"	First United Methodist Choir
Old Testament Lesson	The Reverend Larry Speed
Reading from Canon Henry Scott Holland	Will D. Campbell
"Amazing Grace"	Jewell Bass
Remarks	Will D. Campbell
Organ Interlude	Hannah Kelly
Eulogies from Willie's World	William Styron David Halberstam Mike Espy Josephine Ayres Haxton William F. Winter
"Abide With Me"	First United Methodist Choir

Graveside Service

Music *"Darkness on the Delta"* *"Brokedown Palace"* *"We'll Meet Again"*	Raphael Semmes, Duff Dorrough and Jim "Fish" Michie
Remarks	Jill Conner Browne
Remarks and Reading from *North Toward Home*	Winston Groom
Committal from the *Book of Common Prayer*	Will D. Campbell
TAPS	Bob Davidson Hogan Allen

Willie Morris funeral service program, August 5, 1999.

azine to commemorate the historic occasion. Allison Brown, the editor of that issue, noted that "Willie recognized that most of us knew little about the events that led to the Meredith crisis. And that was all the more reason for us, students at the University of Mississippi 20 years later, to learn about, write about and gather information about something we had not seen first hand."[142]

Morris acknowledged another twenty-year anniversary in August 1997. He explained in an article for *USA Today* two decades after the death of Elvis Presley why the native Mississippian and "his mythology have endured in the national imagination." Earlier that year, in *George* magazine's "Back to Mississippi," he chronicled the filming of a Hollywood motion picture about the murder of Mississippi civil rights activist Medgar Evers and reflected on the state's racist and "virulent" past.[143]

In the mid–1980s, broadcast journalist Bill Moyers commented on Morris's kindliness and affability, prophetically remarking that "in the end it will be the quality of his life that is the real contribution Willie ... made to our times." As others did after Morris died, Richard Howorth, owner of Oxford's bookstore Square Books, recalled the same attributes. "With Willie, what you saw was what you got. He was extremely influential, generous, and open to all students and all others not in the University scene. The one quality that stands out the most is his generosity. He would try to do what he could in all situations." Newspaper editor Sid Salter met Morris "and his beloved black Labrador retriever, Pete," along the football sidelines at the Philadelphia, Mississippi, high school in 1981 when Morris was working on *The Courting of Marcus Dupree*. In Salter's published tribute, he wrote that although the author was "a mentor, a friend and a guiding force in my own life and work, Willie remained from his childhood days in Yazoo City a gentle Southern man particularly predisposed to kindness to the elderly, to children and to animals—a good ole boy."[144]

The small footstone (with Willie Morris's incorrect birth date) was placed by a local organization at Morris's grave in Yazoo City's Glenwood Cemetery. Visitors to the site occasionally leave books, flowers, trinkets, and other gifts as memorials. The marker was replaced in March 2006 with a black slate stone bearing this epitaph: "Even across the divide of death, friendship remains an echo forever in the heart. Willie Morris." The carved lettering on a large slab behind the stone reads "Willie Morris" and "William Weaks Morris / November 29, 1934–August 2, 1999" (courtesy of Vernon Sikes).

What with his expansive, outgoing nature and his refusal to recognize any class or economic distinctions, Mississippi's "good ole boy" had a far-reaching circle of friends and admirers. ("He didn't cull nobody" was the succinct observation of one old farmer). He spoke as earnestly with grade school students who asked about the Witch of Yazoo as he did with politicians and journalists who wanted his perspective on the South. It was not surprising, therefore, that some seven hundred men, women, and children filed by his closed pecan casket, covered in white lilies, during a two-hour visitation in Jackson on August 5. The seventh-generation Mississippian became the first writer in Mississippi history to lie in state in the Rotunda of the Old Capitol and only the third person in the twentieth century.[145]

From Jackson the casket was driven north to the First United Methodist Church in Yazoo City, in which more than four hundred mourners assembled to say good-bye and remember their friend. Minister and civil rights activist Will D. Campbell officiated at "A Celebration of the Life of Willie Morris." He delivered a few remarks on "this sweet soul,... this simple and complex genius," while author William Styron, author David Halberstam, former U.S. Agriculture Secretary Mike Espy, author Josephine Ayres Haxton (pen

David Rae Morris chats with Alice DeCell Wise at the burial site of his father. He placed the rubber snake atop the grave of the Witch of Yazoo as a tribute to his father's love of practical jokes. David Rae Morris received his bachelor's degree from Hampshire College (1982) and his master's from the University of Minnesota (1991). A resident of New Orleans, he is a photojournalist and documentary photographer whose photos have appeared in *Newsweek*, *Time*, *USA Today*, the *New York Times*, and many other newspapers and magazines. He is currently working on an exhibit for the Ogden Museum of Southern Art in New Orleans featuring portraits he made of his father and excerpts from his father's letters (courtesy of the *Clarion-Ledger*).

name Ellen Douglas), former Governor William F. Winter, and Morris's high school algebra teacher, Harriet DeCell Kuykendall, presented "Eulogies from Willie's World." At the conclusion of the funeral service, Reverend Campbell addressed the packed church: "His life was a speech for 64 years. A good speech deserves a good hand. Will you join me in a standing ovation?" The crowd rose, and for twenty-eight seconds they loudly applauded, recognizing not only the man they respected but also his books that entertained, informed, and inspired.[146]

Morris was buried just thirteen paces from the grave of the Witch of Yazoo in the old section of Yazoo City's Glenwood Cemetery, which dates to the 1840s. "Willie had always said to me that he wanted to be buried in the old part of the cemetery he loved so much," said his friend Sam Olden. Added Morris's son, David Rae, "The closer Willie is to the witch, the more at home he'll be." At the graveside, two members of a Jackson band concluded the service by playing "Taps," honoring Morris just as he used to pay tribute to fallen soldiers more than four decades earlier.[147]

Works both by and about Willie Morris have appeared since his sudden death at age sixty-four. The University Press of Mississippi, which had published his *Homecomings* and *After All, It's Only a Game*, brought out a new cloth edition of *North Toward Home* on the sixth-fifth anniversary of his birth. The press also published *Remembering Willie*, a compilation of the eulogies given at his funeral and some of the many tributes published after his death; *Conversations with Willie Morris*, a collection of twenty-five incisive profiles and interviews; and *Shifting Interludes*, an anthology of thirty-two Morris essays and articles.

Other Morris works were also published posthumously. Released just three months after his passing, *My Cat Spit McGee* is a warm and funny account of the author's conversion from a longtime "dog man" to an unabashed cat lover who delighted in serving as his feline companion's "valet, butler, and menial, daily and in perpetuity."[148]

After Morris finished this sequel to *My Dog Skip*, he and his son, photojournalist David Rae Morris, began discussing a joint project that would explore Mississippi's complex history through both words and photographs. In *My Mississippi*, literally a historical portrait of his beloved native state, Willie Morris examines the "snarled confluence of [Mississippi's] past and present" as well as its promise for the future. David Rae Morris's full-color photographic narrative, "Look Away," is his provocative challenge to confront the past and not merely understand it. He said in an interview shortly after the book's publication that "I have tried to strike a careful balance between the history and tragedy of Mississippi and the beauty and magic of the land and the people. It can be a great burden, but it is something my father spent his life and his work dealing with. My responsibility is to carry on his legacy."[149]

Willie Morris completed a draft manuscript of *My Mississippi* in July 1999. By then he was already taking notes for his next book and talking about getting back to a novel he had been tinkering with for over a decade. Regrettably, neither would get much of his attention. He wrote to a friend on July 3 that the new book would "go into my relationship with my father in detail when I was growing up: how baseball and dogs were our strongest bond. The title will be *One for My Daddy*, with a subtitle something like *A Personal Memoir of Baseball* or some such. Then back to *Taps*!!"[150]

Morris drew a great deal upon his boyhood memories while writing *Taps*, and the novel's title reflects both the book's nonfictional aspects and its motif. Throughout his life he often reminisced about how he and his high school friends Ralph Atkinson and Henjie Henick played "Taps" at the funerals of local servicemen killed overseas. For instance, in December 1978 a reporter asked about his current book project. "'It's called "Taps,"' he replied, 'and the thread of it is sort of autobiographical.... You might say it's a book about growing up during the Korean War.'"[151]

JoAnne Prichard Morris displays a copy of her late husband's *Taps*, which she edited for posthumous publication. Inspecting its cover is family cat Spit McGee, whose story is chronicled in Morris's *My Cat Spit McGee*, published shortly after the author's death in 1999. Mrs. Morris, an editor and writer, lives in Jackson (April 2001, courtesy of the *Clarion-Ledger*).

In *Taps*, Morris returns to the Yazoo City of his boyhood in the guise of teenager Swayze Barksdale of the sleepy Delta town Fisk's Landing. Like their real-life counterparts, Swayze and his friend Arch Kidd are introduced to the realities of war when they play "Taps" on their trumpets at the funerals of the Korean War dead. Many other episodes and characters from Morris's past reappear in the novel. Just as Morris and his friends used to do, Swayze and Arch flip coins to decide who plays "Taps" at the graves and who plays it off in the distance as the echo. Morris's mother bears more than just a coincidental resemblance to the obsessive mother of young Swayze. David Rae Morris observed in a 2005 interview: "The mother is so thinly veiled. So she's not a piano teacher [like the author's mother], but a dance teacher. It hit home pretty hard for me, at least on an emotional level, that this was all the truth. I learned more about my father by reading *Taps* than I learned from reading anything he had written before."[152]

Morris wrote *Taps* over much of his thirty-year literary career, beginning it even before he published his classic *North Toward Home* in 1967 while editor of *Harper's* magazine. He worked on the novel sporadically while living in New York, but in the 1980s, after he returned to Mississippi, he completed a solid working draft.

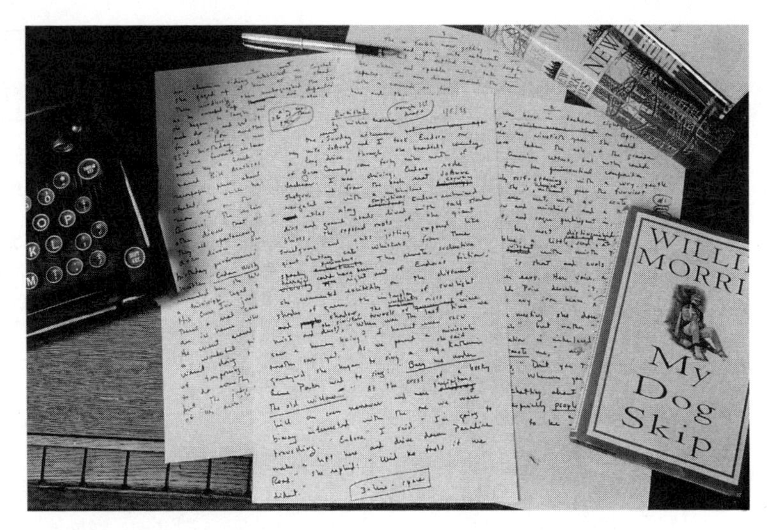

The original manuscript of "Mississippi Queen," Willie Morris's profile of author Eudora Welty, published in the May 1999 issue of *Vanity Fair* (manuscript from the collection of Jack Bales; photograph courtesy R. H. Sturges).

He still, however, wanted to rewrite portions of it. From time to time he read passages aloud to his wife, JoAnne, and the two would discuss possible changes while he polished a sentence here or tightened a paragraph there. Among his final words to her after his heart attack was the request to "get *Taps* together." Fortunately, the book already *was* together, though in the months after his death JoAnne went over the manuscript carefully, checking facts and spellings and making the few changes that he had indicated in the margins of the pages. But that was all. As she said in an interview after the novel's publication, "I didn't write any new material unless it was a transition sentence.... 'Taps' is absolutely Willie's book."[153]

Morris always believed that this novel would be his defining volume. "*Taps* is my baby. It's my life's work," he often commented. In it he captured the ideas and beliefs that touched (no, *consumed*) him all his life: loyalty to family and friends, the importance of the past, the allegiance to a place and the power of land, the unquestioning love of a dog, the glory and disappointment of sports, the meanness and tragedy of racial injustices, and the fragility of human life.[154]

After reviewing Willie Morris's *Homecomings* in early 1990, a *Boston Globe* writer concluded: "There's damn fine life left in this man's prose." Some ten years later, readers of Jackson's *Clarion-Ledger* agreed, selecting Morris as Mississippi's favorite nonfiction author of the millennium. Belying the words of one of the favorite authors of his youth, Thomas Wolfe, he clearly showed in the last decade of his life that, both literally and metaphorically, you *can* go home again.[155]

David Halberstam recognized Morris's journey south toward home in his eulogy, pointing out that "he loved good writing and good books, but what he loved best was this region and this country." Although Morris decried the racism of the Old South and acknowledged the need for constructive social change, he also deeply cared for the area's rich history and traditions. And whether he was examining the significance of home and family, considering the role of sports in society, reflecting on the stormy 1960s, or exploring the paradoxical and complicated past of his native state, his writing personified his enduring love for this region.[156]

Notes

The following abbreviations are used throughout the Notes:

Clarion-Ledger	*(Jackson, Miss.) Clarion-Ledger*
DT	University of Texas *Daily Texan*
ST	University of Texas *Summer Texan*
TO	*Texas Observer*
WM	Willie Morris
Yazoo City Herald	*Yazoo City (Miss.) Herald*
Yazoo Herald	*Yazoo (Yazoo City, Miss.) Herald*

Early Years (1934–1952)

1. WM, *A Southern Album: Recollections of Some People and Places and Times Gone By* (Birmingham, Ala: Oxmoor House, 1975), n. pag.

2. WM, *North Toward Home* (Boston: Houghton Mifflin Co., 1967), p. 4; WM, "Going Home with Mark Twain," *American Heritage* 47 (October 1996), p. 68.

3. WM, *North Toward Home*, pp. 10–11 (WM misspells Mead's name as "Meade"); WM and William Dunlap, "Dialogue: The Author and the Artist," in *Homecomings* (Jackson: University Press of Mississippi, 1989), p. xviii; "Mead, Cowles," in *Biographical Directory of the United States Congress, 1774–1989, the Continental Congress, September 5, 1774, to October 21, 1788, and the Congress of the United States, from the First Through the One Hundredth Congresses, March 4, 1789, to January 3, 1989, Inclusive*, ed. Kathryn Allamong Jacob and Bruce A. Ragsdale, bicentennial ed. (Washington, D.C.: United States Government Printing Office, 1989), p. 1486; "Mead, Cowles," in *Who Was Who in America: Historical Volume, 1607–1896* (Chicago: Marquis-Who's Who, 1963), pp. 351–52; Donald C. Bacon, "Foote, Henry S.," in *The Encyclopedia of the United States Congress*, ed. Donald C. Bacon, Roger H. Davidson, and Morton Keller (New York: Simon & Schuster, 1995), vol. 2, p. 856; John Edmond Gonzales, "Foote, Henry Stuart," in *The Encyclopedia of Southern History*, ed. David C. Roller and Robert W. Twyman (Baton Rouge: Louisiana State University Press, 1979), pp. 464–65. Meadville, Mississippi, was named for Cowles Mead. Foote served as state governor from 1852 to 1854.

4. Melissa Baumann, "Willie Morris: 'I Will Forever Consider This My Home,'" *Clarion-Ledger / Jackson Daily News*, 8 October 1978, sec. G, p. 1; WM, *A Southern Album*, n. pag.

5. WM, "My Great-Grandfather," in *Homecomings*, pp. 14–15. Harpers Ferry, Virginia (now part of West Virginia), was founded by WM's maternal ancestors. "The man who originally ran the ferry, from which the town got its name, was a great-great-great uncle and I have been to Harpers Ferry many times with my son, David" (WM, interview by Orley B. Caudill, 28 May 1975, transcript, Mississippi Oral History Program of the University of Southern Mississippi, Hattiesburg, p. 1). WM notes in his interview that "most of my people lost almost everything in the Civil War, so there is none of that land that has remained within the family, certainly [none] that I know of" (p. 3).

6. WM, "What It Takes for a Son to Understand a Father," *Parade*, 26 August 1984, p. 16; WM interview by Caudill, p. 4; Frank O'Beirne, *The Harpers of Virginia, West Virginia, and Mississippi* (Arlington, Va.: privately printed, 1982), pp. 28, 37–38, 53; John Griffin Jones, "Willie Morris," in *Mississippi Writers Talking* (Jackson: University Press of Mississippi, 1983), vol. 2, pp. 77–79; WM to Robert Loomis, 12 July 1999, from the collection of Jack Bales; WM, *North Toward Home*, p. 14.

7. WM, *North Toward Home*, pp. 14–17; *Mississippi Statistical Summary of Population, 1800–1980* (Jackson: Mississippi Power and Light Company, 1983), n. pag. (by 1940 the population had climbed to 7,258); Ellen Johnson, "Family, Music, Antiques—Marion's Loves," *Yazoo City Herald*, 9 March 1972, sec. B, p. 4; WM, "Going Home with Mark Twain," p. 69; John Carr, "Down Home: Willie Morris," in *Kite-Flying and Other Irrational Acts: Conversations with Twelve Southern Writers*, ed. John Carr (Baton Rouge: Louisiana State University Press, 1972), pp. 98–99; WM, *After All, It's Only a Game* (Jackson: University Press of Mississippi, 1992), p. 9. WM's boyhood home was originally numbered 607 Grand Avenue, but "due to the official renumbering of all the streets" in the early 1960s, it is now 615. See *Mullin-Kille and Chamber of Commerce Yazoo City, Mississippi Telephone Street Guide and Householders' Directory* (Dallas, Tex.: Mullin-Kille, 1963), pp. 123, 141.

8. WM, *North Toward Home*, p. 9; WM interview by Caudill, pp. 12–13.

9. WM, "What It Takes for a Son to Understand a Father," p. 16; WM, *North Toward Home*, p. 9; WM to Loomis; Omie Parker, letter to author, 17 January 1997.

10. Ralph Atkinson, email to author, 13 May 2005. See also WM, "Always Stand In Against the Curve," in *Always Stand In Against the Curve and Other Sports Stories* (Oxford, Miss.: Yoknapatawpha Press, 1983), pp. 51–62.

11. WM to Loomis; WM, "What It Takes for a Son to Understand a Father," pp. 16–17; Edwin M. Yoder Jr., email to author, 3 May 2005.

12. WM to Loomis; Morris, "What It Takes for a Son to Understand a Father," p. 16; WM, *North Toward Home*, p. 103; Harold Kelly, conversation with author, Yazoo City, Miss., 12 June 1997.

13. "Former School Teacher Reminisces About Willie," *Yazoo Herald*, 8 November 1980, sec. B, p. 1; Parker to Bales; WM, *North Toward Home*, p. 130; WM, "The Sports Closet," Yazoo High School *Flashlight*, 23 January 1950, p. 4. According to articles in the 25 April 1951 issue of the *Flashlight*: "The National Honor Society holds high

membership requirements of scholarship, service, character and leadership. The student in order to be eligible for nomination must stand in the upper one-third scholastic division of his class." Candidates for the National Athletic Scholarship Society "are chosen on the basis of character, scholastic ability, leadership and not on athletic ability alone. The attitude of the individual boy toward the game, his team mates, and associates, figures greatly in the nomination nod." Quill and Scroll is an honorary journalism society. A nominated student "must be in the upper division of his class and must do noteworthy work on the individual publication." WM wrote in his "notebook" (a sort of diary) that in 1948 he won the American Legion "medal." According to *North Toward Home* (page 144) this was a "Citizenship Award."

14. WM interview by Caudill, p. 28; Ralph Atkinson, email to author, 30 May 2005; *North Toward Home*, pp. 91–101. According to Ralph Atkinson, the boys actually played cornets, not trumpets.

15. WM, preface to *After All, It's Only a Game*, p. 9; WM, *James Jones: A Friendship* (Garden City, N.Y.: Doubleday & Co., 1978), p. 17; Jack Bales, "A Conversation with Willie Morris," in *Conversations with Willie Morris*, ed. Jack Bales (Jackson: University Press of Mississippi, 2000), p. 163; WM, *North Toward Home*, pp. 103–104, 131.

16. Daisye Love Askew, telephone conversation with author, 17 May 2005; Marsha Williams, telephone conversation with author, 14 May 2005.

17. Askew, telephone conversation; Benjamin "B." Barrier, telephone conversation with author, 17 May 2005; Ralph Atkinson, interview by Noah Adams, *All Things Considered*, National Public Radio, 3 March 2000; Williams, telephone conversation.

18. "Jerry Barrier Takes Prexy in Primary; Morris, Faulkner Win," Yazoo High School *Flashlight*, 23 January 1950, p. 1; *Mingo Chito*, 1952 [yearbook of Yazoo High School] (Dallas: Taylor Publishing Co., 1952), n. pag.

19. WM, *North Toward Home*, pp. 140–45; Carr, "Down Home: Willie Morris," p. 99; Atkinson-Adams interview; WM, "Well, Here I Am: Stiff Upperlip Helps Freshmen Survive Test," *DT*, 17 September 1952, p. 4.

College Days and Controversy (1952–1956)

20. WM, "Well, Here I Am," p. 4.

21. WM, *North Toward Home*, p. 131; Bales, "A Conversation with Willie Morris," pp. 166–67.

22. Carr, "Down Home: Willie Morris," p. 99. See also WM, *North Toward Home*, pp. 143–45.

23. WM, *North Toward Home*, pp. 143, 153–55; WM, "Aggie Season Opens As Spirit Blazes High," *DT*, 24 November 1953, p. 1; WM, *James Jones*, p. 51; WM interview by Caudill, p. 21; "Friars Select Four New Members," *DT*, 6 November 1955, p. 1. WM occasionally wrote a column for the *Daily Texan* titled "Assignment Forty Acres." Despite WM's disdain for fraternity life, he maintained close friendships with some of its members, who in 2002 dedicated a room in the Delta Tau Delta house in his honor. See Marshall Maher, "In Memory of Willie Morris," *DT*, 15 April 2002, p. 4.

24. Anne Chambers, "'30' on Last 'Notes' Marks End for This Texan Editor," *DT*, 17 May 1953, p. 4.

25. WM, *North Toward Home*, p. 162; WM, "Neighboring News: $6,500 Is Chickenfeed to Our Aggie Friends," *DT*, 18 September 1952, p. 4; WM, "Neighboring News: Cops Cost Oklahoma Gift of Rare Books," *DT*, 30 October 1952, p. 4; WM, "Neighboring News: 'Mental' Delegates Listen to Napoleon," *DT*, 19 November 1952, p. 4.

26. Sam Blair, "Willie Morris' Brilliance Proved in UT Days: Author and Editor Took on Regents, Earned Admiration at College Paper," *Dallas Morning News*, 4 August 1999, sec. A, p. 31; WM, "Assignment Forty Acres: Co-ordinator Wears Smile Despite Sneers, Enemies," *DT*, 30 April 1953, p. 4.

27. WM, *North Toward Home*, pp. 162–65; Celia Morris, *Finding Celia's Place* (College Station: Texas A&M University Press), p. 86; WM interview by Caudill, pp. 21–22.

28. WM, "The Round-Up," *DT*, 23 September 1953, p. 1; WM, "The Round-Up," *DT*, 13 January 1954, p. 1; WM, "The Round-Up," *DT*, 11 February 1954, p. 1; WM, "The Round-Up," *DT*, 18 February 1954, p. 1.

29. WM interview by Caudill, p. 26; Marjorie Hoffman, "Willie Morris Comes Home Again," *Austin American*, 25 May 1973, p. 4; WM, *North Toward Home*, p. 175; WM, "The Round-Up," *DT*, 20 October 1954, p. 1; WM, "Triumph, Tragedy Give New Concept," *DT*, 17 October 1954, p. 4; WM, "A Symbol: Stoic, Stately, Enduring," *DT*, 1 October 1954, p. 10; WM, "Here's What to Do When a Tornado Hits," *DT*, 9 March 1955, p. 3.

30. "Morris, Watkins File for Editor of Texan," *DT*, 21 April 1955, p. 1; Carl Burgen, "UT Voters Put Farabee, Morris, Siegel, Holder, Richards In; Yell Leader Run-Off," *DT*, Election Extra, 27 April 1955, p. 1; WM, "Don't Skip This Editorial: A New Year for the Texan—We'll Play Hard and Clean," *ST*, 7 June 1955, p. 4.

31. WM, "The Editor's Notebook: Coercive Conformity," *DT*, 8 January 1956, p. 4; WM, "A Special Report on UT and Its Students—Overwhelming Conformity May Kill Us Yet," *DT*, 16 March 1956, p. 4; WM, "The Last Round-Up," *DT*, 20 May 1956, p. 4; G[reg] O[lds], "Willie Morris in Texas," *TO*, 24 November 1967, p. 9; WM interview by Caudill, p. 29; WM, *North Toward Home*, pp. 169–70, 186.

32. WM, *North Toward Home*, pp. 175–76, 180; WM, "Regents to Discuss Court Decision Soon," *ST*, 7 June 1955, p. 1; J. C. Goulden, "Candidates Want Desegregated UT," *DT*, 27 April 1955, p. 1; "Former School Teacher Reminisces About Willie," p. 1; WM, "The Round-Up," *DT*, 21 October 1955, p. 3.

33. Doyle Harvill and Vaden Smith, "'Banned' Editorials Accepted After Five-Hour TSP Meeting," *DT*, 7 February 1956, p. 1; [WM], "Daily Texan Press Freedom—It Involves Every UT Student: An Editorial," *DT*, 7 February 1956, p. 1. Members of the TSP Board included six students and five faculty members. See "Students Lead on TSP by 6–5," *DT*, 7 February 1956, p. 3.

34. WM, "Daily Texan Press Freedom," p. 1. See also WM, "Mississippi Rebel on a Texas Campus," *Nation* 182 (24 March 1956), pp. 232–234.

35. WM, "Daily Texan Press Freedom," p. 1; Harvill and Smith, p. 1. See also "Gas Issue Stirs Texas U. Dispute," *New York Times*, 10 February 1956, p. 3; "Gas Editorial Ban Ordered at Texas U," *New York Times*, 29 February 1956, p. 16. Supporters of the gas bill argued that it was needed "to free thousands of producers from redtape regulations and provide an incentive for exploring and developing new gas reserves." Critics said that passage of the bill would "add $600 million to $900 million a year to gas bills of consumers and to give a windfall worth billions to big oil companies owning most of the gas" ("Senate Passes Natural Gas Bill," *Daily Texan*, 7

February 1956, p. 1). In a February 7 interview, University of Texas Regent Claude Voyles told a reporter, "'We feel *The Daily Texan* is going out of bounds to discuss the Fulbright-Harris gas bill when 66 percent of Texas tax money comes from oil and gas'" (Tara Copp and Robert L. Rogers, *The Daily Texan: The First 100 Years* (Austin: Eakin Press, 1999), p. 71).

36. Maher, "In Memory of Willie Morris," p. 4; [WM], "Don't Walk on Grass," *DT*, 8 February 1956, p. 4; "This Editorial Censored," *DT*, 26 February 1956, p. 3; "This Editorial Withheld," *DT*, 28 February, 1956, p. 4; WM interview by Caudill, p. 31; WM, *North Toward Home*, pp. 186–92. During a 1975 interview, WM said: "I remember I got a call from old Jonathan Daniels, bless his soul, the editor of the *Raleigh News & Observer* in North Carolina, just out of the blue one day, and I had never met him before. And he said, 'Brother Morris, I hear you are having trouble down there.' I said, 'Yes, sir!' He said, 'Well, I want you to know that anytime that they hold back an editorial and you have to run that white space, you just send it up to me and I will publish it.' And he did. He published quite a few of my editorials in the *Raleigh News & Observer*" (WM interview by Caudill, p. 31).

37. "Dobie Blasts Regents," *DT*, 9 February 1956, p. 1; J. Frank Dobie, "Dobie Unexpurgated," *TO*, 15 February 1956, p. 3; WM, *North Toward Home*, p. 190. In an editorial note preceding Dobie's letter, Ronnie Dugger wrote that after the bowdlerized version appeared in the *Daily Texan*, the newspaper supervisor, Barbara Liggett, "was criticized the next day for running even as much of it as she did without consulting the editorial director, Harrell Lee."

38. [Ronnie Dugger], "Regents Should Resign," *TO*, 15 February 1956, p. 2; R[onnie] [D]ugger, "Willie and the College Yell," *TO*, 22 February 1956, p. 6; Vaden Smith, "Dahlin Calls Friday Meeting of TSP Board for Analysis," *DT*, 9 February 1956, p. 1; WM, *North Toward Home*, pp. 190–91; "Texas U. Editor Pushes Crusade," *New York Times*, 19 February 1956, p. 60.

39. Copp and Rogers, p. vi; WM, "There Will Be Similar Moments: A Word in Closing," *DT*, 20 May 1956, p. 4; WM, "Toward Absolute Control: Subtle Paralysis," *DT*, 10 April 1956, p. 4; WM, *North Toward Home*, p. 191.

40. WM, *North Toward Home*, pp. 192–93; Bales, "A Conversation with Willie Morris," pp. 167–68; Morris, "There Will Be Similar Moments," p. 4. In October 1956, WM wrote from his home in Yazoo City to the *Texas Observer*: "After a summer here I know we of the Texan sponsored our cause to an extreme, leaned too hard on the prerogatives of the college press, were too zealous and emphatic. Yet I am prouder now than ever of the principles we defended and nourished, even if it was with immoderation" (WM, "Letter from Yazoo City," *TO*, 10 October 1956, p. 3).

41. Elizabeth Bennett, "The Daily Texan: A Look at the Workings of a Campus Paper and Its Editors," *Houston Post*, 13 January 1980, sec. BB, p. 4; Mike Kelley and Anne Morris, "Legendary Editor Took on the Texas Establishment: Willie Morris, 1934–1999," *Austin American-Statesman*, 4 August 1999, sec. A, p. 1.

42. WM, "The Last Round-Up," *DT*, 20 May 1956, p. 4.

43. "William Morris Graduates with Highest Honors," *Yazoo City Herald*, 7 June 1956, p. 3; "Morris Is to Edit Continuing Observer," *TO*, 16 December 1960, p. 1; WM, "Special Report on UT and Its Students," p. 4; WM, "The Editor's Notebook: Coercive Conformity," p. 4; WM, *North Toward Home*, pp. 185–86; "Morris to Enter Oxford Next Fall," *DT*, 4 January 1956, p. 6.

An American Abroad (1956–1960)

44. WM interview by Caudill, p. 39.

45. WM, "Were We the Best?," *Parade*, 18 August 1985, pp. 16–17; WM, *New York Days* (Boston: Little, Brown and Co., 1993), p. 40; "Morris to Enter Oxford Next Fall," p. 6.

46. WM, *North Toward Home*, pp. 181–82.

47. WM, "Were We the Best?," p. 17; WM, *North Toward Home*, pp. 182–83. See also "Morris Selected Rhodes Scholar in Region Finals," *DT*, 11 December 1955, p. 1.

48. WM, *North Toward Home*, p. 183; WM interview by Caudill, p. 12; Celia Morris, *Finding Celia's Place* (College Station: Texas A&M University Press, 2000), pp. 68, 75.

49. Morris, *Finding Celia's Place*, p. 77; WM to Frank H. Lyell, 6 October 1956, Willie Morris Papers, Department of Archives and Special Collections, John Davis Williams Library, University of Mississippi; Frank H. Lyell to Emmett L. Hudspeth, 13 October 1955, Willie Morris Papers, Department of Archives and Special Collections, John Davis Williams Library, University of Mississippi; WM, "Southerner in an Old World: Former Editor Explores One Isle Before Embarking for Another," *DT*, 24 October 1956, p. 2. WM said during an interview that "I almost went to work for Lyndon Johnson when I was twenty-one, on my way to school in Oxford. I talked to Walter Jenkins in Washington, and they wanted me to come back and go to work for Johnson in the summers. I'm glad that I didn't now, but I came close to it. Then I got all wrapped up in Europe" (WM interview by Caudill, p. 37).

50. "Morris to Enter Oxford Next Fall," p. 6; WM, "Southerner in an Old World," p. 2.

51. WM to Henry Rae and Marion Morris, Tuesday afternoon [9 October 1956], Willie Morris Papers, Department of Archives and Special Collections, John Davis Williams Library, University of Mississippi; WM to Frank H. Lyell.

52. WM, "Remembering Dennis Potter, 1935–1994: The Moviegoer," *Village Voice*, 21 June 1994, p. 32; WM interview by Caudill, pp. 41–42; WM, "A Texan at Oxford," *Texas Quarterly* 3 (Winter 1960), pp. 21–22.

53. WM to Henry Rae Morris, Marion Morris, and Marion Weaks, Friday [March-April 1957], Willie Morris Papers, Department of Archives and Special Collections, John Davis Williams Library, University of Mississippi. In this undated letter to his parents and grandmother (internal evidence indicates he wrote it in either March or April 1957), WM mentions a recent phone call from home informing him that his dog Skip had died. "I imagine things are lonesome without Skipper. I sure will miss him."

54. Jones, "Willie Morris," pp. 86–87; "Morris Is to Edit Continuing Observer," p. 1. WM received a second-class degree at Oxford. "After two weeks of essay exams (six hours a day) and an oral, overall grades were given as 1st (class), 2nd, 3rd, 4th, pass, and fail. I got a Second, the equivalent of a B+. (Most American Rhodes Scholars got this.) I *thought* I had a First, which is another story. The B.A. by tradition became an M.A. after a few years, six or seven I believe. The formal degree is B.A., M.A., Oxon" (WM, letter to author, 28 December 1997). See also Morris, *Finding Celia's Place*, pp. 95–96.

55. WM to Henry Rae Morris, Marion Morris, and Marion Weaks, Thursday [November 1956?, indicated by

internal evidence], Willie Morris Papers, Department of Archives and Special Collections, John Davis Williams Library, University of Mississippi; WM, "My Two Oxfords," in *Homecomings*, p. 66; WM interview by Caudill, p. 42; WM, "Always Stand In Against the Curve," pp. 78–79, 89–90; WM to Henry Rae Morris, Marion Morris, and Marion Weaks, Thursday [postmarked 15 November 1956], Willie Morris Papers, Department of Archives and Special Collections, John Davis Williams Library, University of Mississippi.

56. WM to Henry Rae Morris, Marion Morris, and Marion Weaks, Friday [March-April 1957, indicated by internal evidence], Willie Morris Papers, Department of Archives and Special Collections, John Davis Williams Library, University of Mississippi; WM, "Eisenhower," Oxford University *Isis*, no. 1292 (27 February 1957), p. 20; WM and Ed Yoder, "Down South We Fry Them on the Sidewalks," Oxford University *Isis*, no. 1298 (22 May 1957), p. 8; WM, letter to author, 28 December 1997.

57. WM, *North Toward Home*, p. 196; WM, "What It Takes for a Son to Understand a Father," p. 17; Morris, *Finding Celia's Place*, p. 101; WM, "Free Enterprise Wins, $51 to 82 Cents," *TO*, 2 September 1960, p. 5.

58. Morris, *Finding Celia's Place*, pp. 92, 103–105; WM, *North Toward Home*, p. 197, WM interview by Caudill, p. 47.

59. WM, "In a Shifting Interlude," *American Way* 24 (15 September 1991), p. 62; WM interview by Caudill, pp. 40, 43; Bales, "A Conversation with Willie Morris," pp. 168–69.

60. Edwin M. Yoder Jr., "Willie Morris," in *Telling Others What to Think: Recollections of a Pundit* (Baton Rouge: Louisiana State University Press, 2004), p. 205; WM, "My Two Oxfords," p. 64.

61. William Delaney, "Willie Morris: Fiction Still Alive in U.S.," *Washington Star*, 19 March 1976, sec. F, p. 12; WM, "My Two Oxfords," pp. 63, 65; WM, "In a Shifting Interlude," p. 148; WM, letter to Frank H. Lyell.

62. WM, "Were We the Best?," p. 16; Roscoe Suddarth, email to author, 5 June 2005; Roscoe Suddarth to WM, tape recording, Willie Morris Papers, Department of Archives and Special Collections, John Davis Williams Library, University of Mississippi; Delaney, "Willie Morris," p. 12. WM never completed *The Chimes at Midnight*; the unfinished manuscript is among his papers at the University of Mississippi.

63. Morris, *Finding Celia's Place*, p. 68; A. Truman Schwartz, email to author, 6 June 2005; Yoder, "Willie Morris," p. 205; WM, "Were We the Best?," pp. 16–17. Bill Bradley, a star basketball player at Princeton, entered Oxford University in the fall of 1965. In 1978 he was elected to the United States Senate. Pete Dawkins received the Heisman football trophy at West Point, where he was captain of the football team and president of his class. After graduating from the military academy in 1959, he began his studies at Oxford.

Crusading Journalist (1960–1971)

64. Jones, "Willie Morris," pp. 88–89.

65. Richard Ray Cole, "A Journal of Free Voices: The History of *The Texas Observer,*" Master's thesis, University of Texas at Austin, 1966, pp. 61–62, 69–70.

66. WM, "A Dismal Study — The Aged in Texas," *TO*, 26 August 1960, pp. 1–3; WM, "Serious Thought and Writing by Concerned Young Men," *TO*, 11 December 1964, p. 3. See also Cole, p. 3.

67. Ronnie Dugger, "The Firing Line: A Student Voice," *DT*, 20 May 1956, p. 4; WM, "Mississippian[s] Would Improve but Maintain Separate Schools," *TO*, 10 January 1955, p. 3.

68. WM, "Blakley's Campaign Turns on Union Leaders," *TO*, 27 June 1958, pp. 1, 5; WM, "Daniel Gets Going." *TO*, 4 July 1958, pp. 1, 8; WM, "Henry's Unorganized Organization," *TO*, 11 July 1958, p. 3; WM, "A Symbol of Past on Texas Stump," *TO*, 11 July 1958, pp. 1, 5; WM, "Schools Need Teachers, Books," *TO*, 4 July 1958, pp. 1, 4; WM, "'A Function to Perform': Ray Bailey of the Luling Newsboy," *TO*, 22 August 1958, p. 8; WM, "Integration in Boerne: Two Children in a One-Room School," *TO*, 8 August 1958, pp. 1, 6, 7; Ronnie Dugger, "Outgoing, Incoming Editors Talk: Ronnie Dugger," *TO*, 16 December 1960, p. 5.

69. Bales, "A Conversation with Willie Morris," pp. 169–70; [WM], "Editor Carter Talks Tonight," *DT*, 1 March 1956, p. 1; Jones, "Willie Morris," p. 83.

70. WM interview by Caudill, p. 48; WM, "A Public Apology: Whispers, Dissent in a Valley Town," *TO*, 17 November 1961, pp. 1, 3; WM, "A Texas Liberal's View: The Threats and Challenges of Communism," *TO*, 29 December 1961, pp. 1, 3–4; WM, "El Paso's Tom Lea: A Desert and Ranch Man," *TO*, 13 January 1962, pp. 1, 6; WM, "Angry Atheist Hunt: Red Threat Also Cited in Hearing," *TO*, 11 March 1961, pp. 1, 3; WM, "Integration at U. T.: On-Campus Services Open; Housing, Sports Segregated," *TO*, 21 October 1960, pp. 1–3; WM, "Spy Adventure in Austin: An Intruder in Cell 772," *TO*, 6 May 1961, pp. 1–3. See also Jones, "Willie Morris," pp. 91–92; WM, *North Toward Home*, pp. 255–56.

71. WM, "Johnson's 'Homecoming': Barbecue in Blanco," *TO*, 5 August 1960, pp. 1, 3; WM, *North Toward Home*, p. 233–36, 252–54; WM, "Two Views of a Campaign Tour: Sights, Sounds from a Truck," *TO*, 16 September 1960, p. 2.

72. Bales, "A Conversation with Willie Morris," p. 168; WM, *North Toward Home*, p. 199; Jones, "Willie Morris," p. 88; WM, "Precisely at 70," *TO*, 27 June 1958, p. 2; WM, "Journey to Recognition," *TO*, 9 September 1960, p. 6; WM, "The Rain Fell Noiselessly," *TO*, 22 August 1958, p. 6.

73. Morris, *Finding Celia's Place*, p. 106; WM, *North Toward Home*, pp. 201–202, 310; WM, *New York Days*, pp. 15–16, 36; WM, "Houston's Superpatriots," *Harper's Magazine* 223 (October 1961), pp. 48–56; WM interview by Caudill, p. 57.

74. Morris, *Finding Celia's Place*, pp. 121–22, 128. WM, *New York Days*, p. 18; Jones, "Willie Morris," pp. 84–85. Morris published the first part of *North Toward Home* that he wrote in California as "Memoirs of a Short-Wave Prophet" in the *New Yorker* of 30 November 1963. See Bales, "A Conversation with Willie Morris," pp. 170–71.

75. "Willie Morris: *The Last of the Southern Girls,*" *Library Journal* 98 (1 February 1973), p. 442; Carr, "Down Home: Willie Morris," p. 97; WM, *North Toward Home*, pp. 319–20. "Autobiography in mid-passage" appears on the dust jacket flap of *North Toward Home.*

76. David Rae Morris, "Photographer's Note," in *My Mississippi*, by WM, photographs by David Rae Morris (Jackson: University Press of Mississippi, 2000), p. 105; WM, *North Toward Home*, pp. 78, 131, 179–80, 318, 336.

77. Carol Whitcraft, "Harper's Editor Willie Morris Due 'Roundup' Honors," *Austin American*, 16 November 1968, p. 33; "Harper's Editor Cites U.S. Role," *Dallas*

Times Herald, 24 March 1968; "Morris, Willie 1934- ," in *Contemporary Authors: A Bio-Bibliographical Guide to Current Writers in Fiction, General Nonfiction, Poetry, Journalism, Drama, Motion Pictures, Television, and Other Fields*, ed. Linda Metzger, New Revision Series, vol. 13 (Detroit: Gale Research Co., 1984), p. 378; *Awards, Honors & Prizes*, 22d ed. (Detroit: Gale Group, 2004), vol. 1, p. 1020; Edward P. J. Corbett, "Book Reviews," *America* 117 (9 December 1967), p. 720.

78. "A Spur for Harper's," *Newsweek* 69 (22 May 1967), p. 71; Larry L. King, "Looking Back on the Crime, or Rememberin' Willie and Them," in *The Old Man and Lesser Mortals* (New York: Viking Press, 1974), p. 285; Richard Cohen, "*Harper's* Willie Morris," *Women's Wear Daily: The Retailer's Daily Newspaper*, 19 August 1969, p. 38.

79. WM interview by Caudill, pp. 61–62; Jones, "Willie Morris," pp. 94–96; King, "Looking Back on the Crime," pp. 286–87; Stuart Little, "What Happened at 'Harper's,'" *Saturday Review* 54 (10 April 1971), p. 45; Rebecca Bain, "An Interview with Willie Morris," in *Conversations with Willie Morris*, p. 188.

80. John Carr, "Honkies, Editors, & Other Dirty Stories: Larry L. King," in *Kite-Flying and Other Irrational Acts*, p. 145; King, "Looking Back on the Crime," pp. 285, 287; "South Toward Home," *Time* 95 (1 June 1970), p. 77; Robert Manning, *The Swamp Root Chronicle: Adventures in the Word Trade* (New York: W. W. Norton & Co., 1992), pp. 360–61.

81. King, "Looking Back on the Crime," p. 297; John Tebbel and Mary Ellen Zuckerman, *The Magazine in America, 1741–1990* (New York: Oxford University Press, 1991), p. 320.

82. WM, *New York Days*, pp. 341–43, 355; Bill Blair to WM, 19 January 1971, Larry L. King Archives, Southwestern Writers Collection, Alkek Library, Texas State University-San Marcos. In 1993, WM published *New York Days*, a first-person account of his years at *Harper's*. After it received a highly complimentary, front-page review in the September 5, 1993, issue of the *New York Times Book Review*, Blair and others wrote letters to the editor criticizing both the book and WM's editorship. One of the decisions made at the February 1971 board meeting was to trim the magazine's budget. Blair stated in his letter that this decision "was not taken suddenly." For WM "to present it as a willful and precipitate decision of a few narrow-minded Midwesterners, rather than the final outcome of an experiment lasting two years and costing several hundred thousand dollars, is, to say the least, misleading... . It is sad to see that this disdain for fact in favor of fantasy, which was the root cause of his problems at Harper's, continues to this day." See William S. Blair, "'New York Days,'" *New York Times Book Review*, 10 October 1993, p. 35; Lewis Lapham, "Advertisements for Themselves: A Letter from Lewis Lapham," *New York Times Book Review*, 24 October 1993, pp. 3, 39; Willie Morris, "The Battle Over 'New York Days,'" *New York Times Book Review*, 19 December 1993, p. 31.

83. WM, *New York Days*, p. 342; WM to William S. Blair, 17 February 1971, Willie Morris Papers, Department of Archives and Special Collections, John Davis Williams Library, University of Mississippi.

84. WM to John Cowles Jr., 1 March 1971, Willie Morris Papers, Department of Archives and Special Collections, John Davis Williams Library, University of Mississippi; WM, *New York Days*, pp. 344, 355–56; Alden Whitman, "Morris Resigns in Harper's Dispute," *New York Times*, 5 March 1971, p. 37; Larry L. King, *None But a Blockhead: On Being a Writer* (New York: Viking, 1986), pp. 145–46. In his press release, Morris singled out Mailer's "The Prisoner of Sex" as having "deeply disturbed the magazine's owners." Several persons intimately involved with the situation, however, denied that this was a factor, and even Morris, years later, admitted in *New York Days* that the article was "less at that moment substantive than symbolic" (p. 356). Stuart Little's "What Happened at 'Harper's'" details Morris's final days at *Harper's*. See also Michael Shnayerson, "He'll Always Have Elaine's," *Vanity Fair* 56 (October 1993), pp. 130+. In Larry L. King's essay, "Looking Back on the Crime," he pinpointed several significant issues: "Willie Morris, never very patient with office politics and not excelling in the field, may have abdicated owner Cowles's ear to his in-house enemies at great expense; the rest of us, occupied with our own books and other out-of-house assignments, perhaps took too much for granted in failing to learn what transpired at all those tense Minneapolis meetings between Willie Morris, his detractors, and the harassed owners" (pp. 297–98).

85. Morris, *Finding Celia's Place*, p. 156; WM, *New York Days*, pp. 250, 281; "Willie Morris: *The Last of the Southern Girls*," *Library Journal* 98 (1 February 1973), p. 442. WM missed the perquisites of power after he left *Harper's*: "All of a sudden, the phone was not ringing. It was wintertime and it was snowing and there was a great silence out there. I talked to Bill Moyers and he said, 'Well, you're only 37 and you've still got a typewriter'" (Philip Martin, "Like Bourbon Through Silk: The Flowing Cadences of Willie Morris Reflect the South's Stubborn Persistence," *(Little Rock) Arkansas Democrat-Gazette*, 17 February 1995, sec. E, p. 8).

Adrift on Long Island (1971–1979)

86. WM, "Bridgehampton: The Sounds and the Silences," *New York Times*, 1 March 1974, p. 29.

87. Mary Cummings, "*Hampton Life* Interviews Willie Morris," *Hampton Life* 4 (October 1978), p. 11; WM, "Bridgehampton," p. 29; WM, *New York Days*, pp. 288–89; WM interview by Caudill, p. 80; WM to Blair; WM to *Harper's* staff, 8 March 1971, Willie Morris Papers, Department of Archives and Special Collections, John Davis Williams Library, University of Mississippi. According to Edwin M. Yoder Jr., WM often remarked after leaving New York City that "I was once editor of a high school newspaper called the *Flashlight*. The publishers of *Harper's* took away my batteries." Edwin M. Yoder Jr., email to author, 15 May 2005.

88. Edwin M. Yoder Jr., email to author, 3 May 2005; WM to "Friend," 18 September 1971, Willie Morris Papers, Department of Archives and Special Collections, John Davis Williams Library, University of Mississippi; Alfred Knopf Jr. to WM, 5 March 1971, Willie Morris Papers, Department of Archives and Special Collections, John Davis Williams Library, University of Mississippi; Robert Penn Warren to WM, 6 March 1971, Willie Morris Papers, Department of Archives and Special Collections, John Davis Williams Library, University of Mississippi; Bill Clinton to WM, 5 March 1971, Willie Morris Papers, Department of Archives and Special Collections, John Davis Williams Library, University of Mississippi. The quoted excerpt from the Clinton letter appears in Larry L. King, "The Book on Willie Morris," *Texas Monthly* 29 (May 2001), p. 172.

89. "3 Pulitzer Winners Make Harper's Plea," *New York Times*, 10 March 1971, p. 40; George Frazier to WM, 5 March 1971, Willie Morris Papers, Department of Archives and Special Collections, John Davis Williams Library, University of Mississippi; George Frazier, "The Lit'ry Life," *Boston Globe*, 6 March 1971, sec. 1, p. 6.

90. Shnayerson, "He'll Always Have Elaine's," p. 140; Bales, "A Conversation with Willie Morris," p. 173; John R. Wilhelm to WM, 27 April 1971, Willie Morris Papers, Department of Archives and Special Collections, John Davis Williams Library, University of Mississippi; Ray Cave to WM, 10 May 1971, Willie Morris Papers, Department of Archives and Special Collections, John Davis Williams Library, University of Mississippi; Darrell Holmes to WM, 15 July 1971, Willie Morris Papers, Department of Archives and Special Collections, John Davis Williams Library, University of Mississippi; Babette Ashby to Joan Daves, 27 April 1973, Willie Morris Papers, Department of Archives and Special Collections, John Davis Williams Library, University of Mississippi; "Notes on People," *New York Times*, 6 May 1971, p. 48; D[ouglas] N. M[ount], "Authors & Editors: Willie Morris," *Publishers' Weekly* 199 (14 June 1971), p. 16. Shortly after WM resigned from *Harper's*, Yoder and his family visited him in Bridgehampton, where he was "saturating himself nightly in Mahalia Jackson gospel songs and a recorded recitation of General Lee's farewell to his troops" (Yoder, "Willie Morris," p. 198).

91. WM, *Yazoo: Integration in a Deep-Southern Town* (New York: Harper's Magazine Press, 1971), pp. 28, 42, 44, 107, 133, 177; WM, *The Courting of Marcus Dupree*, Garden City, N.Y.: Doubleday & Co., 1983, pp. 238–39; Jones, "Willie Morris," pp. 109–110.

92. WM interview by Caudill, pp. 20–21; Metzger, *Contemporary Authors*, p. 378; *Awards, Honors & Prizes*, p. 1020.

93. Jimmy Ball, telephone conversation with author, 7 June 2005. Ball added: "I was asked to do it this year, but I could not be there on the date they wanted." The Willie Morris papers in the Department of Archives and Special Collections at the University of Mississippi contain hundreds of letters from readers of *Good Old Boy*, dating from the early 1970s to the 1990s.

94. WM, *Good Old Boy: A Delta Boyhood* (New York: Harper & Row, 1971), pp. 3–7.

95. The *Yazoo Herald, A Pictorial History of Yazoo County* ([Lincoln Center, Mass.]: Heritage House Publishing, 1996), p. 18; Ball, telephone conversation; John E. Ellzey, emails to author, 30 August 2004 and 11 July 2005. In 1988, Morris served as an on-site consultant when *Good Old Boy* was filmed by Multimedia Entertainment, Inc. in Natchez, Mississippi. The Disney Channel broadcast the movie that fall and in 1994 Vidmark Entertainment made it available on videocassette under the title *The River Pirates*.

96. For example, the tale of the Witch of Yazoo appears in Michael Norman and Beth Scott, "The Witch's Curse," in *Historic Haunted America* (New York: Tor, 1995), pp. 188–90; "Festival Overcomes Heat, Humidity," *Yazoo Herald*, 22 May 1996, sec. A, pp. 1, 12; Bales, "A Conversation with Willie Morris," p. 174.

97. Jonathan Yardley, "Yen for Power," *New Republic* 168 (19 May 1973), p. 29.

98. WM, "Author's Note," in *The Last of the Southern Girls* (Baton Rouge: Louisiana State University Press, 1994), n. pag.; Bret Watson, "Having Headed South Toward Home, Willie Morris Brings a New Book North," *Avenue* 8 (December-January 1984), p. 142.

99. Myra MacPherson, "Belle, Books and Scandal," *Washington Post*, 13 May 1973, sec. K, pp. 1, 3; Edmund Fuller, "Gadding About Washington with a Southern Lady," *Wall Street Journal*, 5 July 1973, p. 6.

100. WM to whom it may concern, 7 May 1973, Willie Morris Papers, Department of Archives and Special Collections, John Davis Williams Library, University of Mississippi; WM to Edwin M. Yoder Jr., 1 March 1972, from the collection of Edwin M. Yoder Jr.

101. WM to Joan Daves, 12 October 1972, Willie Morris Papers, Department of Archives and Special Collections, John Davis Williams Library, University of Mississippi; David Rae Morris, telephone conversation with author, 27 June 2005.

102. MacPherson, "Belle, Books and Scandal," sec. K, p. 3; WM, *James Jones*, pp. 165, 181; "Bridgehampton: The Sounds and the Silences," p. 29; Lawrence Wells, "The Days of Wine and Letters," *Southwest Airlines Magazine* 30 (October 2000), pp. 67–69, 143; WM, *New York Days*, p. 292.

103. Wells, "The Days of Wine and Letters," pp. 67, 143; Delaney, "Willie Morris," p. 12.

104. WM, *James Jones*, pp. 224–34; WM, "The Fields of War Become a Cold Companion," *Washington Star*, 22 February 1976, sec. H, p. 4; Jones, "Willie Morris," p. 97.

105. WM, *James Jones*, pp. 13–14, 29–30, 244–47; Delaney, "Willie Morris," p. 12.

106. Watson, "Having Headed South Toward Home," p. 144; Wells, "The Days of Wine and Letters," p. 69; WM, *New York Days*, p. 368; J. Michael Kennedy, "It's a Dog's Life," *Los Angeles Times*, 29 June 1995, sec. E, p. 5. Winston Groom moved to Bridgehampton in 1975 to write his first novel, *Better Times Than These*. He would achieve literary fame in 1986 with *Forrest Gump*.

South Toward Home (1979–1999)

107. WM, "Coming on Back," *Life* 4 (June 1981), p. 110.

108. William Thomas, "Willie Morris, Home Again," *(Memphis) Commercial Appeal*, "Mid-South" section, 2 March 1980, p. 8; James Dickerson, "Willie Morris Comes Home Again to the Delta," *Greenwood (Miss.) Commonwealth*, 4 April 1978, p. 2.

109. Dickerson, "Willie Morris Comes Home Again to the Delta," p. 2; David Rae Morris, telephone conversation with author, 27 June 2005; Elizabeth Mullener, "Like Other Mississippi Exiles, Writer Willie Morris Comes Home," *(New Orleans) Times-Picayune*, 15 March 1981, sec. 3, p. 10; Larry Wells, email to author, 11 June 2004; James Conaway, "Willie Morris in the Land of Faulkner," *Washington Post*, 28 December 1982, sec. C, pp. 1, 3; Randy Williamson, "Willie Morris: Author Joins UM Staff," University of Mississippi *Daily Mississippian*, 16 October 1979, p. 3. In 1984, Morris told a reporter who came to Oxford, Mississippi, to interview him: "The state has changed in 20 years, enough to make it bearable. Race is no longer obsessive — the albatross around the necks of both whites and blacks" (Mary Lynn Kotz, "Willie Morris Is Home Again at Ole Miss," *St. Petersburg (Fla.) Times*, 22 July 1984, sec. D, p. 8.

110. Larry Wells, email to author, 5 July 2005; Watson, "Having Headed South Toward Home," p. 144.

111. Watson, "Having Headed South Toward Home," p. 136; Williamson, "Willie Morris," p. 3; WM, untitled

notes for American novel class, Willie Morris Papers, Department of Archives and Special Collections, John Davis Williams Library, University of Mississippi; "South Toward Home," *Washington Post Book World*, 29 November 1981, p. 15; "William Styron to Speak at UM," *Oxford (Miss.) Eagle*, 2 April 1981; Charles Chappell, "Lawrence Wells of Oxford: An Interview," *Mississippi Quarterly: The Journal of Southern Culture* 48 (Spring 1995), pp. 334–35. WM lived on 16 Faculty Row in Oxford.

112. "The Willie Morris Visiting Lectureship at the University of Mississippi," undated fundraising letter from the University of Mississippi Foundation, Willie Morris Papers, Department of Archives and Special Collections, John Davis Williams Library, University of Mississippi; Bales, "A Conversation with Willie Morris," p. 177; Chappell, "Lawrence Wells of Oxford," p. 335; "Welcome," *Ole Miss Magazine* 1 (October 1981), p. 2; WM, "The Search for Billy Goat Hill," *Ole Miss Magazine* 1 (October 1981), pp. 12–14; Larry Wells, email to author, 5 March 2005. Other issues of the *Ole Miss Magazine* are dated December 1981, spring 1982, and September 30, 1982.

113. WM, *New York Days*, p. 369; Shnayerson, "He'll Always Have Elaine's," p. 144; Elizabeth Devereaux, "Willie Morris's New York Memoir," *Publishers Weekly* 240 (7 June 1993), p. 18; Chappell, "Lawrence Wells of Oxford," p. 334; WM, "Memoir," in *Grisham: An Exhibition*, by Thomas M. Verich and the Department of Archives and Special Collections, University of Mississippi (University: University of Mississippi Libraries, 1994), p. 7.

114. Thomas, "Willie Morris, Home Again," p. 6.

115. WM, preface to *The Courting of Marcus Dupree* (Jackson: University Press of Mississippi, 1992), pp. 11–12. With the exception of WM's preface and a sports reporter's postscript, which are unique to this edition, the pagination of the reissue is identical to that of the Doubleday original.

116. Garland Reeves, "Mississippi Writer, Athlete Have Deep Ties," *Clarion-Ledger*, 15 November 1983, sec. B, p. 3; WM, *The Courting of Marcus Dupree* (Garden City, N.Y.: Doubleday & Co., 1983), pp. 15–19, 41; Kotz, "Willie Morris Is Home Again at Ole Miss," sec. D, p. 8; *Awards, Honors & Prizes*, p. 416.

117. WM, *The Courting of Marcus Dupree*, p. 236.

118. WM, conversation with the author, 11 November 1998; Studs Terkel, "An Interview with Willie Morris," in *Conversations with Willie Morris*, p. 102; John Branston, "Tales of Dupree, Oxford and Philadelphia," *(Memphis) Commercial Appeal*, 16 October 1983, sec. G, p. 3; Watson, "Having Headed South Toward Home," p. 148.

119. WM, "The Round-Up," *DT*, 6 April 1955, p. 1; Watson, "Having Headed South Toward Home," p. 140. In his memoir, Edwin M. Yoder Jr. writes of a conversation Morris had with him and his wife: "'They say I have a bourbon problem,' Willie remarked to Jane and me one night, in one of his more reckless moods. 'Hell, I don't have a problem at all. I can get all the bourbon I want'" (Yoder, "Willie Morris," p. 199). Peter Applebome notes in his obituary of Morris: "Mr. Morris drank too much bourbon and red wine, smoked too many Viceroys, stayed up too late and caroused too much" (Peter Applebome, "Willie Morris, 64, Writer on the Southern Experience," *New York Times*, 3 August 1999, sec. A, p. 13).

120. WM, "As the Years Go By, Do We Grow ... Crankier — Or More Tolerant?," *New Choices: Living Even Better After 50* 36 (April 1996), pp. 34–36; King, "The Book on Willie Morris," p. 198; Watson, "Having Headed South Toward Home," p. 142.

121. JoAnne Prichard Morris, telephone conversation with author, 5 July 2005; Noel Workman, "An Interview with JoAnne Prichard Morris," *Delta Magazine* 3 (July/August 2005), pp. 28–29; WM, introduction to *Yazoo: Its Legends and Legacies*, by Harriet DeCell and JoAnne Prichard (N.p.: Yazoo Delta Press, 1976), pp. xi-xii.

122. JoAnne Prichard to WM, 16 March 1988, Willie Morris Papers, Department of Archives and Special Collections, John Davis Williams Library, University of Mississippi; Joe Rogers, "Notable Nuptials," *Clarion-Ledger*, 14 September 1990, sec. E, p. 4; WM to Gerald Turner, 2 February 1991, Willie Morris Papers, Department of Archives and Special Collections, John Davis Williams Library, University of Mississippi.

123. Larry L. King, email to author, 1 July 2005; Yoder, "Willie Morris," p. 199; Shnayerson, "He'll Always Have Elaine's," p. 144; Rheta Grimsley Johnson, "A Very 'Happy Puppy' Writes in Jackson, Miss.," *Atlanta Journal / The Atlanta Constitution*, 2 April 1995, sec. B, p. 1. David Rae Morris wrote in *My Mississippi* that his father's second marriage helped transform him "into a happier and mellower person" (David Rae Morris, "Photographer's Note," p. 106). In mid-2005, an interviewer told Prichard Morris: "Some say you turned him [WM] around... ." She replied: "People give me a lot more credit than is due. I think he just needed a wife — a confidant — somebody who was non-judgmental and always looked out for his best interests, and, well, somebody who was always there" (Workman, "An Interview with JoAnne Prichard Morris," p. 28).

124. WM, "Faulkner's Mississippi," *National Geographic* 175 (March 1989), pp. 313–39; WM to David Rae Morris, 18 March 1990, Willie Morris Papers, Department of Archives and Special Collections, John Davis Williams Library, University of Mississippi.

125. Charlie Rose, "An Interview with Willie Morris," in *Conversations with Willie Morris*, pp. 130–31; Devereaux, "Willie Morris's New York Memoir," p. 18.

126. Elizabeth Hardwick, "'I Had Had My Pinnacle,'" *New York Times Book Review*, 5 September 1993, pp. 1, 13–15; Martin, "Like Bourbon Through Silk," sec. E, p. 8; Leslie R. Myers, "New York Dazed," *Clarion-Ledger*, 25 August 1993, sec. D, p. 1; Tim Warren, "Willie Morris' Return to His Legendary, Literary Past," *(Baltimore) Sun*, 22 September 1993, sec. C, p. 8.

127. WM, "As the Years Go By," p. 36; Charlie Rose, "An Interview with Willie Morris," in *Conversations with Willie Morris*, p. 144; J. Michael Kennedy, "It's a Dog's Life," *Los Angeles Times*, 29 June 1995, sec. E, p. 5.

128. WM, *My Dog Skip* (New York: Random House, 1995), pp. 5, 8, 9–10, 11–12, 20–21. WM told an interviewer in 1995: "'After struggling so much with *New York Days*, I decided I wanted to do a book that would be fun to write. And what better to write a book about than my dog,' he says. 'The memories came back in a rush'" (Craig Wilson, "Willie Morris' Pet Project Evokes Mississippi Memories," *USA Today*, 20 April 1995, sec. D, p. 4).

129. Bales, "A Conversation with Willie Morris," p. 155; WM, *The Ghosts of Medgar Evers: A Tale of Race, Murder, Mississippi, and Hollywood* (New York: Random House, 1998), pp. 5–6, 41–59. See also Maryanne Vollers, *Ghosts of Mississippi: The Murder of Medgar Evers, The Trials of Byron De La Beckwith, And the Haunting of the New South* (Boston: Little, Brown and Co., 1995).

130. WM, "Justice, Justice at Last," *New Choices for Retirement Living* 34 (June 1994), pp. 42–46; WM, "Back to Mississippi," *George* 2 (January 1997), pp. 68–71, 88–90.

131. Rick Bragg, "To Bind up a Nation's Wound with

Celluloid," *New York Times*, 16 June 1996, sec. 2, p. 36; Julia Cass, "Willie Morris Stays Home: Author Finds Write Stuff in Mississippi," *Chicago Tribune*, 2 January 1984, sec. 5, p. 2.

132. WM, *The Ghosts of Medgar Evers*, pp. 5, 14–20, 62–63, 240–60.

133. *My Dog Skip: Production Information* (Burbank: Warner Bros. Pictures, 1999?), p. 3 (part of a Warner Bros. production packet for the motion picture *My Dog Skip*); Ron Wolfe, "A Man and His Dog: Arkansan Makes a Movie About a Boy's Best Friend," *(Little Rock) Arkansas Democrat-Gazette*, 5 March 2000, sec. E, pp. 1–2. The fictional Rivers Applewhite of Morris's *My Dog Skip* was a composite based on several school friends, including Werdna Dee Phillips (who went by Dee), Nettie Taylor Livingston, and Barbara Hollowell (JoAnne Prichard Morris, emails to author, 11 & 15 August 2005).

134. *My Dog Skip: Production Information*, pp. 5, 8. "Willie Morris," in *Three Minutes or Less: Life Lessons from America's Greatest Writers*, by the PEN/Faulkner Foundation (New York: Bloomsbury, 2000), p. 323.

135. Claudia Eller and James Bates, "FedEx Chief Banks on Film-Making Package," *Los Angeles Times*, 14 March 2000, sec. C, p. 1; "'My Dog Skip,'" *Today*, 31 January 2000, National Broadcasting Co., Inc., NBC News Transcripts, http://web.lexis-nexis.com/universe (accessed 1 February 2000).

136. WM, letter to author, 30 July 1999.

137. JoAnne Prichard Morris, telephone conversation with author, 5 July 2005.

138. Sherry Lucas, "Author Morris Dies at Age 64," *Clarion-Ledger*, 3 August 1999, sec. A, pp. 1, 5; Curtis Wilkie, *Dixie: A Personal Odyssey Through Events That Shaped the Modern South* (New York: Scribner, 2001), pp. 331–32; Raad Cawthon, "Eloquent in Voicing His Roots, Humanity," *Philadelphia Inquirer*, 5 August 1999, sec. D, p. 3.

Epilogue

139. WM, "'Now That I Am Fifty,'" *Parade*, 21 April 1985, p. 17.

140. Billy Watkins, "Willie Morris: A Few Last Words," *Clarion-Ledger*, 4 August 1999, sec. E, p. 1; Sherry Lucas, "Friends Can't Imag[in]e State Without Morris," *Clarion-Ledger*, 3 August 1999, sec. A, p. 5; Bill Clinton, "Eulogy," *Time* 154 (16 August 1999), p. 21.

141. Jim Dees, "Oxford Remembers Willie Morris," *Oxford (Miss.) Eagle*, 3 August 1999, p. 1; Diala S. Husni, "Ole Miss, Oxford Remember Morris," University of Mississippi *Daily Mississippian*, 4 August 1999, p. 8.

142. Gina Holland, "Southern Writer Willie Morris Dies," *Chicago Sun-Times*, 4 August 1999, p. 51; WM, "At Ole Miss: Echoes of a Civil War's Last Battle," *Time* 120 (4 October 1982), p. 8; Allison Brown, "Reflections from the Editor," *Ole Miss Magazine* 2 (30 September 1982), p. 3.

143. WM, "20 Years Later, The King Reigns," *USA Today*, 13 August 1997, sec. A, p. 13; WM, "Back to Mississippi," p. 71.

144. Watson, "Having Headed South Toward Home," p. 148; Husni, "Ole Miss, Oxford Remember Morris," p. 8; Sid Salter, email to author, 29 April 2005; Sid Salter, "Up in 'Willie's Heaven,' Morris Will Be Telling Mississippi Stories That God Will Want to Hear," *Scott County (Miss.) Times*, 4 August 1999.

145. Sherry Lucas, "'Power Crowd' Celebrates Author's Life," *Clarion-Ledger*, 6 August 1999, sec. A, p. 7; Billy Watkins, "'Good Old Boy' Goes Out Like a Statesman," *Clarion-Ledger*, 6 August 1999, sec, A, p. 1; WM, introduction to *My Mississippi*, p. xvi; Rick Bragg, "To a Beloved Native Son, A Mississippi Farewell," *New York Times*, 6 August 1999, sec. A, p. 10. The other two Mississippians were former Governor James P. Coleman, who died in 1991, and former U.S. Senator John C. Stennis, who died in 1995. Following Morris's death, his widow and son donated his corneas, which restored the sight of two Mississippians. See Cesar G. Soriano, "Gift of Sight Adds to Author's Legacy," *USA Today*, 18 August 1999, sec. D, p. 2.

146. Lucas, "'Power Crowd' Celebrates Author's Life," sec. A, p. 1; *A Celebration of the Life of Willie Morris*, funeral service program, First United Methodist Church, Yazoo City, Mississippi, 5 August 1999; Vernon Sikes, "Willie Makes Final Trip Home," *Yazoo Herald*, 7 August 1999, p. 1; "Reverend Will D. Campbell," in *Remembering Willie* (Jackson: University Press of Mississippi, 2000), p. 12. Pallbearers at WM's funeral were Homer Best, Rick Cleveland, John Evans, Charles Henry, Richard Howorth, Peyton Prospere, David Sansing, Malcolm White, and Bob Yarbrough.

147. Sherry Lucas, "Willie Morris to Be Buried Near Witch's Grave," *Clarion-Ledger*, 5 August 1999, sec. A, p. 1; Sikes, "Willie Makes Final Trip Home," p. 14. WM played in Yazoo City's Glenwood Cemetery as a boy, and when he moved to Jackson he often visited it. In February 1983 he scrawled this epitaph: "Willie Morris, 1934—19—, American writer and editor who, from his earliest childhood as a Yazoo boy, loved as no man can this beautiful cemetery and the county and state in which it is located" (Willie Morris Papers, Department of Archives and Special Collections, John Davis Williams Library, University of Mississippi).

148. WM, *North Toward Home* (Jackson: University Press of Mississippi, 1999); *Remembering Willie*; *Conversations with Willie Morris*; WM, *Shifting Interludes: Selected Essays*, ed. Jack Bales (Jackson: University Press of Mississippi, 2002); WM, *My Cat Spit McGee* (New York: Random House, 1999), p. 4.

149. WM, introduction to *My Mississippi*, p. xv; "An Interview with David Rae Morris," University Press of Mississippi Online Catalog, http://www.upress.state.ms.us/inside/my_mississippi/ask.html (accessed 30 July 2005).

150. "Publisher's Note," in *My Mississippi*, p. ix; WM, letter to author, 3 July 1999.

151. Phil Thomas, "Willie Morris Pays Tribute to His Friend James Jones," *(New Orleans) Times-Picayune*, 17 December 1978, sec. 3, p. 10.

152. WM, *Taps: A Novel* (Boston: Houghton Mifflin Co., 2001), pp. 6, 36; David Rae Morris, telephone conversation with author, 27 June 2005.

153. Judith Rosen, "Fond Farewell: 'Taps' for Willie Morris," *Publishers Weekly* 248 (2 April 2001), p. 19; Don O'Briant, "Mississippi Author Plays His 'Taps' from the Grave," *Atlanta Journal-Constitution*, 8 April 2001, sec. C, p. 1.

154. WM, letter to author, 19 June 1999; O'Briant, "Mississippi Author Plays His 'Taps' from the Grave," sec. C, p. 1.

155. Gail Caldwell, "Willie Morris' Southern Fire Is Still Burning," *Boston Globe*, 10 January 1990, p. 69; Billy Watkins, "Mississippi's Favorite Writers," *Clarion-Ledger*, 14 June 1999, sec. D, pp. 1–2.

156. "David Halberstam," in *Remembering Willie*, p. 20; Charles Reagan Wilson, "Director's Column," *Southern Register* (Spring 2004), p. 2.

PART II
Published Writings by Willie Morris

CONTENTS

Books

1 *The South Today: 100 Years After Appomattox.* Edited by Willie Morris. New York: Harper & Row, 1965.

In April 1965, the centennial of General Robert E. Lee's surrender to General Ulysses S. Grant, *Harper's Magazine* published a special supplement, "The South Today," in which nine of these eleven essays ("now revised and extended") were first published (see item 725). Morris writes in the foreword to his book that "this collection of essays, while placing the last hundred years in their historical perspective, has as its main emphasis the South as it has become — the present relationship between South and North, between Southern white and Southern Negro, the moods and fears of the Southern people, the changing faces of the land and the cities." All the contributors, except for one, are native southerners, and they "were encouraged to draw upon their own experiences in describing the changes they have witnessed and the kind of future they foresee." Although these historians, journalists, and other writers address problems in the contemporary American South, for the most part they also express hope for the future of the region and its people. Conservative James J. Kilpatrick, for example, predicts that blacks "will find in the emerging South a certain receptivity and maturity that promise for both races a better time ahead."

The South Today includes: "Foreword" by Morris, pp. vii–ix (a revision of his *Harper's* foreword); "From the First Reconstruction to the Second" by C. Vann Woodward, pp. 1–14; "This Quiet Dust" by William Styron, pp. 15–38; "The Impending Crisis of the Deep South" by D. W. Brogan, pp. 39–49; "Georgia Boy Goes Home" by Louis E. Lomax, pp. 50–65; "Mississippi: The Fallen Paradise" by Walker Percy, pp. 66–79; "A Conservative Prophecy: Peace Below, Tumult Above" by James Jackson Kilpatrick, pp. 80–88; "W. J. Cash After a Quarter Century" by Edwin M. Yoder, pp. 89–99; "A Vanishing Era" by Whitney M. Young Jr., pp. 100–101; "Why I Returned" by Arna Bontemps, pp. 102–114; "The Ever-Ever Land" by Jonathan Daniels, pp. 115–25; and "The Unexpected Dividend" by Philip M. Stern, pp. 126–41. Yoder's and Stern's works do not appear in the *Harper's Magazine* collection; also, the supplement includes four works that are not republished in Morris's book: "Black Bourgeoisie" by LeRoi Jones (poem), "Voices from the South" by Robert Coles (quotations), "Notes on the Literary Scene: Their Own Language" by Louis D. Rubin Jr. (essay) and "Long View: Negro" by Langston Hughes (poem).

2 *North Toward Home.* Boston: Houghton Mifflin Co., 1967.

An "autobiography in mid-passage" in which Morris traces his life from his boyhood in segregated Mississippi to his college and post-college years in Texas, and to New York City, where in 1967 he became the youngest editor-in-chief of *Harper's*, America's oldest magazine. As a young southern liberal, he grew hostile towards his native state. After settling in the East, Morris realized that despite this antagonism, he (as well as other southern expatriates of his generation) would always feel the deep pull of home. "For a long time in my life, I had been ashamed of my Mississippi origins. Yet shame was too simple and debilitating an emotion, too easy and predictable — like bitterness. It was more difficult to *understand* one's origins, to discover what was distinctive and meaningful in them, to compare them with the origins of others, to give shape to them for the sake of some broader understanding of place and experience" (page 386). Throughout his memoir, Morris struggles to come to terms with his regional identity as he challenges the complex and emotionally charged issues that confronted Americans during the mid-twentieth century.

Excerpted in *Terrains of the Heart* (item 10), *Always Stand In Against the Curve* (item 33), *After All, It's Only a Game* (item 51), the *New Yorker* (item 720), *Commentary* (item 726), *Harper's Magazine* (items 727–28), the *Saturday Evening Post* (item 729), *Southern Exposure* (item 765), *As Up They Grew* (item 865), *Love, Capitalism, Violence, and Other Topics* (item 866), *An Anthology of Mississippi Writers* (item 868), *Baseball Diamonds* (item 871), *Mississippi Writers: Reflections of Childhood and Youth* (item 876), *Elements of Literature* (item 881), *Mississippi Writers: An Anthology* (item 885), *The Yankees Reader* (item 886), *Joy in Mudville* (item 887), *The Oxford Book of the American South* (item 901), *Southern Selves* (item 908), *Voices in Our Blood* (item 918), *Baseball: A Literary Anthology* (item 919), *American Decades, 1960–1969* (item 1367), and the *Hinds County (Miss.) Gazette* (item 1680). Yoknapatawpha Press reissued *North Toward Home* in 1982 with an introduction by Edwin M. Yoder Jr. written especially for this new edition.

3 *Yazoo: Integration in a Deep-Southern Town.* New York: Harper's Magazine Press, 1971.

A chronicle of the efforts of Morris's hometown to comply with Supreme Court–ordered school integration. Drawing upon the author's personal observations gleaned during six trips to the area in 1969 and 1970, *Yazoo* movingly explores how the forced integration of the public schools affected this deep-southern town on the edge of the Mississippi Delta. With sensitivity, yet with blunt honesty and objectivity, Morris describes the emotional conflicts, the painful realities, and the growing sense of pride experienced by the residents of Yazoo as they resolve in 1969 to accomplish with dignity the task that they could not bring themselves to undertake by edict of the *Brown v. Board of Education of Topeka* decision fifteen years earlier. "Since my town is the place which shaped me, for better or worse, into the creature I now am, since it nurtured me and gave me much of whatever sensibility I now possess, since it is a small Deep-Southern place where the land and the remembered places have changed very little,... I knew, as I had known for some time, that going back for me ... would bring the most intense emotional pain.... I finally went home because the urge to be there during Yazoo's most critical moment was too elemental to resist, and because I would have been ashamed of myself if I had not" (pages 11–13). Excerpted in *Terrains of the Heart* (item 11) and *Harper's Magazine* (item 731).

4 *Good Old Boy: A Delta Boyhood*. New York: Harper & Row, 1971.

A memoir of Morris's adventurous youth, which he wrote to tell his son "what I was doing when I was your age" in a small southern town that "was a very special place for me" (page x). Part fact, part elaborate fiction and folklore, *Good Old Boy* features an evil witch, giant Indians, a haunted house, and a boy straight out of *Huckleberry Finn* who lives in the swamps outside Yazoo City. Morris retells some of the anecdotes from the "Mississippi" section of *North Toward Home*. "There was terror for me in that school. Miss Abbott was my fourth grade teacher, and for the first time my grades were bad and my conduct report worse. Miss Abbott had a pink nose and came from a small town in South Mississippi. The only book she ever read through and through, she told us, was the Bible, and you lived to believe her, and to feel bad about the day she got hold of that book.... Miss Abbott's religion was one of fear and terror — it got you by the hind end and never let go. It was a thing of long, crazy speeches; she wanted you to believe she herself was in telephone contact with the Lord, and had hung the moon for Him on day number four" (pages 22–23). Excerpted in *Families* (item 758), *Mississippi Writers: Reflections of Childhood and Youth* (item 875), *Mississippi Writers: An Anthology* (item 884), *Where the Red Fern Grows* (item 913), and on the web page *Yazoo: Gateway to the Delta* (item 1999). Yoknapatawpha Press reissued *Good Old Boy* in 1980 with both Morris's original foreword and a "foreword to the 1980 edition."

5 *The Last of the Southern Girls*. New York: Alfred A. Knopf, 1973.

In Morris's first novel, he follows the Washington, D.C., career of Carol Hollywell, debutante from De Soto Point, Arkansas, and beauty queen of Ole Miss. The starry-eyed — but ambitious — southern belle takes a job in 1957 as a congressional aide and eventually rises to the top of Capitol Hill's power and social circles. She becomes so absorbed in her "ultimate pursuit" of the political life, however, that she sacrifices much that she once held dear just so she can stay in Washington, including her integrity, her marriage, and in the end, her fiancé, a congressman whose unforgivable sin is his failure to win a Senate election. Upon its publication, Morris's novel was widely criticized as a thinly disguised account of the life of his friend and lover, Washington socialite Barbara Howar. "That was how Carol started coming to Jack Winter's quarters on the Hill. She arrived unannounced one Monday morning at nine, and by the end of the week, since she knew better than most that even on this level power is as power does, residing as it must in whosoever occupies the avenues of access to the leader, she had made friends with his administrative assistant and displaced, in authority if not in name, the elderly Southern widow who managed his office. After a few days she had straightened out the correspondence and the flow of telephone calls, advised him to replace three or four inefficient souls on his small staff, and interviewed applicants for the vacated jobs. All of this harkened back to her youthful days with the senior Senator from Kentucky, the years dissolving for her as a stream slips again into older contours, and from time to time she experienced the sharpest *déjà vu*'s" (pages 57, 188–89). Excerpted in *Ladies' Home Journal* (item 732). Louisiana State University Press reissued *The Last of the Southern Girls* in 1994 with an author's note by Morris written especially for this new edition.

6 *A Southern Album: Recollections of Some People and Places and Times Gone By*. Edited by Irwin Glusker; narrative by Willie Morris. Birmingham, Ala: Oxmoor House, 1975.

Morris's introductory narrative to a collection of photographs depicting the heritage of the South is his personal testimony as to what it means for him to be a Mississippian and a southerner. In "My Own Private Album: The Burden and Resonance of My Memory," he also reflects on how his roots touch upon his career as a writer and how urban sprawl is changing the landscape. Opposite and complementing the pictures are passages from some of the South's best-known writers, including Flannery O'Connor, William Faulkner, John Crowe Ransom, Eudora Welty, James Agee, Carson McCullers, William Styron, Robert Penn Warren, Harper Lee, and Thomas Wolfe. Many of the seventy-one photographs are in color, and some photos are spread across two pages. Glusker was the original art director of *American Heritage* and the former art director of *Life* magazine. Oxmoor House is the book division of the magazine *Southern Living*. "Could my generation be the last to have known, and lived, the old warring impulses to be both Southern and American? Before the great television culture, before *Brown v. Board of Education*, before the federal expressways and suburban sprawls which so disfigured and reshaped the land we had once known, the South of my youth was more closely akin, physically and in spirit, to the 1920s and 1930s than to the 1960s and 1970s. In its driftlessness and isolation and vanity it was a pause, a halfway point; it had a patina of time, as poignant and fragile as an old photograph" (n. pag.). Excerpted in *Southern Living* (item 735), the *(Memphis) Commercial Appeal* (item 811), and the *Houston Post* (item 811).

7 *James Jones: A Friendship*. Garden City, N.Y.: Doubleday & Co., 1978.

An affectionate biography and memoir of Morris's Long Island neighbor and celebrated author of *From Here to Eternity* and *The Thin Red Line*. Morris explains in an introductory note that the book is not a critical, scholarly study of Jones's life and works but is rather an "illumination of a friend, and perhaps of myself and others of us, and I hope it tells something about writing, especially about being a writer in America." As Morris discusses their relationship, he also talks about his own life and career since he resigned from *Harper's* in 1971. Morris met Jones in New York City in the late 1960s, and they became close friends after the older author and his family left Paris in 1974 and returned to the United States. Relying on his own recollections and those of Jones's family and friends, Morris traces the man's personal life and writing career. In the final section of this anecdotal portrait, he movingly recounts Jones's struggle with congestive heart failure and his friend's determination to finish *Whistle*, the final volume in his World War II trilogy, before he dies. "I was to learn over the years that beneath the rough exterior was a profoundly cultured and sophisticated man, a student of literature, history, art, and music. He ... had, too, an almost religious dedication to his work. Up until two days before he died he would be talking into a tape recorder about his novel. Even with the final collapse of his body he was the sanest man I ever knew. He was, in the truest and best sense, an old-fashioned man. He and his work were all of a piece; I never knew anyone who was more like his own writing, so attuned to the deep, informing spirit of it" (page 26). Excerpted in *Terrains of the Heart* (item 17) and *Atlantic Monthly* (item 739). The University of Illinois Press reissued *James Jones: A Friendship* in 2000 with a foreword by Winston Groom written especially for this new edition.

8 *Terrains of the Heart and Other Essays on Home*. Oxford, Miss.: Yoknapatawpha Press, 1981.

A collection of essays and short pieces—most of them previously published—on the themes of home and homecoming. Morris comments in the foreword that while he was working on this book and rereading the numerous articles he had written over the years, "I was astonished by how many times I had used the word 'home.' As I perused these many thousands of words, some of which I myself had forgotten, this chord of homecoming seemed to be one of the very threads of my existence as a Southern-American of the Twentieth Century." The volume comprises the following essays (items 9 through 29):

9 "Coming on Back." In *Terrains of the Heart*, pp. 3–38 (see item 8).

A revision of an essay published in *Life* magazine (item 750). Excerpted in *A Place Called Mississippi* (item 900).

10 "An Old House on a Hill." In *Terrains of the Heart*, pp. 39–58 (see item 8).

Chapters 8 and 10 of the "New York" section of *North Toward Home* (not from the August 1967 issue of *Harper's Magazine* as indicated in the bibliographic reference, nor from the June and July 1967 issues that serialized the book). In the first part of the piece, Morris describes commuting to New York from a "big old farmhouse sitting on a hill overlooking a valley seventy miles north of the city."

11 "Loving and Hating It." In *Terrains of the Heart*, pp. 59–75 (see item 8).

Excerpts from *Yazoo: Integration in a Deep-Southern Town* (not from the May 1970 issue of *Harper's Magazine* as indicated in the bibliographic reference, nor from the June 1970 issue that excerpted the book). Includes much of chapter 1 of Part 1, chapter 2 of Part 1, chapter 2 of Part 3, and much of chapter 3 of Part 3.

12 "Where Does the South End?" In *Terrains of the Heart*, pp. 76–78 (see item 8).

An essay originally published as "Observer Notebook" in the *Texas Observer* (item 644).

13 "The Other Oxford." In *Terrains of the Heart*, pp. 79–89 (see item 8).

An essay originally published as "A Texan at Oxford" in the *Texas Quarterly* (item 713).

14 "Weep No More, My Lady." In *Terrains of the Heart*, pp. 90–94 (see item 8).

An essay originally published in *Reader's Digest* (item 734).

15 "Christmases Gone." In *Terrains of the Heart*, pp. 95–97 (see item 8).

A revision of "Christmases Gone in Mississippi," published in *Newsday* (item 839). Further revised as "A Return to Christmases Gone" for *Mississippi* (item 772).

16 "Vignettes of Washington." In *Terrains of the Heart*, pp. 98–153 (see item 8).

From January to March 1976, Morris contributed three articles a week to Washington D.C.'s *Washington Star* as the newspaper's writer-in-residence (see item 1617). Eleven of his articles, with consecutive numbers as titles, appeared in *Terrains of the Heart* under the collective title "Vignettes of Washington" (items 16-A through 16-K):

A "1." In *Terrains of the Heart*, pp. 98–104 (see item 8).

An essay originally published as "What About the Girl Who Stays Here?" in the *Washington Star* (item 818).

B "2." In *Terrains of the Heart*, pp. 104–108 (see item 8).

An essay originally published as "When Your House Is 8 Feet Wide, You Get Visited" in the *Washington Star* (item 833).

C "3." In *Terrains of the Heart*, pp. 108–112 (see item 8).

An essay originally published as "A Down-Home Pilgrim's Progress" in the *Washington Star* (item 816).

D "4." In *Terrains of the Heart*, pp. 112–15 (see item 8).

An essay originally published as "The Real Meaning of Washington" in the *Washington Star* (item 831).

E "5." In *Terrains of the Heart*, pp. 115–121 (see item 8).

An essay originally published as "'It's the Last Gentleman Thing in This Town'" in the *Washington Star* (item 822).

F "6." In *Terrains of the Heart*, pp. 121–24 (see item 8).

An essay originally published as "'The Past Is Never Dead,' And Violence Goes On" in the *Washington Star* (item 814).

G "7." In *Terrains of the Heart*, pp. 124–28 (see item 8).

A revision of "Honeymoon and Stars at Harpers Ferry," published in the *Washington Star* (item 824).

H "8." In *Terrains of the Heart*, pp. 128–33 (see item 8).

An essay originally published as "Another CIA Story Still Lurks in a Shopping Bag" in the *Washington Star* (item 812).

I "9." In *Terrains of the Heart*, pp. 133–39 (see item 8).

An essay originally published as "Girl from Silver Spring with Songs of Lament" in the *Washington Star* (item 820).

J "10." In *Terrains of the Heart*, pp. 140–48 (see item 8).

An essay originally published as "A Long Visit with a Country Lawyer" in the *Washington Star* (item 834).

K "11." In *Terrains of the Heart*, pp. 148–53 (see item 8).

An essay originally published as "'I've Found My La Belle Aurore'" in the *Washington Star* (item 828).

17 "I Am Not Resigned." In *Terrains of the Heart*, pp. 154–73 (see item 8).

Excerpts from chapters 1, 11, and 13 of *James Jones* (not from the March 1978 issue of *Atlantic*

Monthly as indicated in the bibliographic reference, nor from the June 1978 issue that excerpted the book).

18 "The Day the President Left Yazoo." In *Terrains of the Heart*, pp. 174–81 (see item 8).
An essay originally published in *Jackson: The Mississippi Magazine* (item 742).

19 "The Lending Library of Love." In *Terrains of the Heart*, pp. 182–85 (see item 8).
An essay originally published in *Newsweek* (item 733).

20 "Good Friends ... Dogs, Sons and Others." In *Terrains of the Heart*, pp. 186–89 (see item 8).
An essay originally published in *Parade* (item 747). Excerpted in *Mosaic I* (item 882).

21 "A Girl I Once Knew." In *Terrains of the Heart*, pp. 190–92 (see item 8).
Morris reminisces about Annie, a woman he "should have married" when he was living on Long Island. "The love we had was never destroyed; it was merely the dwindling of circumstance. How does one give up Annie? Only through loneliness and fear, fear of old loves lost and of love renewed — only those things, that's all."

22 "Legacies." In *Terrains of the Heart*, pp. 193–95 (see item 8).
As essay originally published as the introduction to *Yazoo: Its Legends and Legacies* (item 924).

23 "Different Terrains." In *Terrains of the Heart*, pp. 196–98 (see item 8).
An essay originally published as "Different Terrains of the Heart: Willie Morris; Ole Miss vs. Long Island" in the *Bridgehampton Sun* (item 841).

24 "Stingo and Bilbo in the Mansion." In *Terrains of the Heart*, pp. 199–216 (see item 8).
Morris recollects a stay at the Governor's Mansion in Jackson, Mississippi, with his son, David, author William Styron, and Styron's wife, Rose. He also discusses his longtime friendship with Styron and briefly profiles Governor William Winter. "But here, suddenly, on Capitol Street, the Governor's Mansion loomed before us, a cherished and familiar place amidst the dwindling of dreams. As Rose and Bill and David and I sighted it from our car in a soft dusk of springtime, it had a touch of lost moments for me when I walked barefoot on the sidewalk and looked upward toward its curtained windows and wondered what monumental events might be transpiring in there."

25 "A Cook's Tour." In *Terrains of the Heart*, pp. 217–22 (see item 8).
Excerpts from the introduction to *A Cook's Tour of Mississippi* (item 926).

26 "A Man for All Seasons." In *Terrains of the Heart*, pp. 223–29 (see item 8).
An essay originally published in the University of Mississippi's *Daily Mississippian* (item 842).

27 "The Stable." In *Terrains of the Heart*, pp. 230–35 (see item 8).
Morris revises an essay published in *American Bookseller* (item 748) by adding a few of his experiences working with Larry Wells, owner of Yoknapatawpha Press, and his wife, Dean Faulkner Wells. One evening, shortly after the publishing company reprinted his *Good Old Boy*, "I found myself with Dean and Larry putting dust jackets on the books until the late hours, cutting the shrink wrappage, and handling the telephone calls.... I told them I had never had such assignments from my various Eastern publishers."

28 "The Americanization of Mississippi." In *Terrains of the Heart*, pp. 236–43 (see item 8).
Excerpts from a symposium keynote address that was published in the *Southern Quarterly* (item 743) and *Sense of Place: Mississippi* (item 870).

29 "The Ghosts of Ole Miss." In *Terrains of the Heart*, pp. 244–65 (see item 8).
A revision of an essay published in *Inside Sports* (item 746). See also item 1118.

30 *The Courting of Marcus Dupree*. Garden City, N.Y.: Doubleday & Co., 1983.
Marcus Dupree was born in Philadelphia, Mississippi, in 1964, the same year that civil rights workers Andrew Goodman, Michael Schwerner, and James Earl Chaney were murdered outside the small town. Seventeen years later, Dupree, a black member of Philadelphia's first high school senior class that has been racially integrated since first grade, is "the most sought-after and acclaimed high school football player in America" (page 15). Among his numerous friends is the son of the white deputy sheriff implicated in the killings. On one level, this complex work is a skillful combination of sports reporting, historical

analysis, and biography, in which Morris recounts the madness surrounding the college recruitment of the best high school running back in the country. On another, it is a story of racial changes and civil rights, particularly in small Mississippi towns. On a third level, as the author draws parallels between his own life and Dupree's, the book is an autobiography akin to *North Toward Home.* "In the seats between the twenty-yard lines, I noticed, the white and black townspeople sat together, and the rows where the students sat was a sea of white and black, but as the concrete grandstand curved toward the south end zone, the patrons were almost entirely black people.... As I sat there in my solitude, I was suddenly overwhelmed with memories of my own high school days—the cheerleaders and majorettes, the yellow school buses, the little boys in the end zone, the parents sitting on cushions in the grandstand, the snare drums and trumpets, the heat mirages shimmering from the grass, the squeaky public-address system. I could have closed my eyes and been sixteen again, in Crump Stadium in the Yazoo of the Korean War years" (page 77).

Excerpted in the *Clarion-Ledger / Jackson Daily News* (items 844, 846, and 847), the *Atlanta Journal and Constitution* (item 845), *Mississippi Writers: Reflections of Childhood and Youth* (item 877), and *A Century of Heroes* (item 891). A revised excerpt from chapter 10 published as "Cheerleaders vs. Baton Twirlers" in *After All, It's Only a Game* (item 54). A revised excerpt from chapter 16 published as "Willie Morris—Misty, Water-Colored Memory of My First College Football Game" in *Southern Living* (item 759). The University Press of Mississippi reissued *The Courting of Marcus Dupree* in 1992 with a preface by Morris written especially for this new edition and a postscript by sports reporter Billy Watkins.

31 *Always Stand In Against the Curve and Other Sports Stories.* Oxford, Miss.: Yoknapatawpha Press, 1983.

A collection of seven sports-related works that includes one short story ("The Fumble") and six autobiographical essays; five of the seven pieces have never before been published. Morris, who participated in athletics both in high school and college, views sports as a metaphor for life itself. As he writes in the foreword: "For many of us, especially from what was the small-town South, sports was a nexus for much that was meaningful to us: dexterity, fulfillment, radiant well-being—and pain and struggle and disappointment." The volume comprises the following pieces (items 32 through 38):

32 "The Fumble." In *Always Stand In Against the Curve*, pp. 1–33 (see item 31).

A high school football story set in the Deep South, in which the Choctaws of "a poor little town of undistinguished facades" in the Mississippi Delta take on the undefeated Central High Tigers of Jackson, "a brisk metropolis of well over 100,000 citizens" and the capital of the state. The "majestic school buildings" of Central High "were right around the corner from the Capitol and the Governor's Mansion and covered an entire block, self-assured and expansive as any university.... Our school, given its size, could barely get thirty boys together and played in the lowly Delta Valley Conference against other little towns out in the flat cotton country." Republished in *After All, It's Only a Game* (item 55). See also items 1155, 1158, and 1663.

33 "The Phantom of Yazoo." In *Always Stand In Against the Curve*, pp. 35–50 (see item 31).

An excerpt from chapter 8 of the "Mississippi" section of *North Toward Home.* Republished in *After All, It's Only a Game* (item 51). See also items 720 and 881.

34 "Always Stand In Against the Curve." In *Always Stand In Against the Curve*, pp. 51–62 (see item 31).

Morris recalls that after he and his Yazoo City High School teammates won the 1950 state championship baseball title, they traveled to Baton Rouge, Louisiana, to compete in the "Southern finals." The first game in the playoffs "exists for me now in a curious blur, every movement attenuated. Our all-state shortstop dropped two pop flies. Our left-hander mishandled a casual line drive.... In the second inning with no one on base, a towering fly came out in my direction. For one terrifying moment I lost it in the lights, then caught it with a desperate hand-over-heels lunge." Republished in *A Modern Southern Reader* (item 895).

35 "Bevo Goes to Notre Dame." In *Always Stand In Against the Curve*, pp. 63–69 (see item 31).

In the fall of 1954, while Morris was a student at the University of Texas, he and a friend drove to South Bend, Indiana, for the UT–Notre Dame football game with "the official Texas mascot, a 1,500-pound longhorn steer by the name of Bevo V." Bevo, Morris remembers, "was one mean creature. He was the fifth in the succession of heralded longhorns who reigned in Austin, making his ceremonial appearance at all the games...." See also items 232, 234, and 235.

36 "Bringing Basketball to England." In *Always Stand In Against the Curve*, pp. 71–91 (see item 31).

Morris's recollections of playing basketball at Oxford University in the mid–1950s. He comments that after he tried out for — and much to his "astonishment" was named to — the varsity team, "I returned to my histories and British Constitutional documents with a vigor I thought I had lost forever. The secret lanes and river walks and time-imbued quads and gardens of the magic town assumed an unexpected luster."

37 "One for My Daddy." In *Always Stand In Against the Curve*, pp. 93–99 (see item 31).

When Morris lived in Bridgehampton, New York, in the 1970s, he played on a softball team called the Golden Nematodes, "after the insects which attacked the young potato plants without succour or mercy." He fondly recalls the game in which he hit a home run in the bottom of the ninth inning to win the game for his team. "Every August for many years the writers who lived in the Hamptons had played the artists and actors in a benefit softball game. The twenty-fifth renewal of this event was to take place on the diamond in East Hampton. It was a fund-raiser, if memory correctly serves me, for George McGovern's Presidential campaign, which in itself may have suggested something of doom."

38 "The Search for Billy Goat Hill." In *Always Stand In Against the Curve*, pp. 101–116 (see item 31).

A revision of an essay published in *Ole Miss Magazine* (item 754).

39 *Good Old Boy and the Witch of Yazoo*. Oxford, Miss.: Yoknapatawpha Press, 1989.

A children's novel and sequel to *Good Old Boy*. After young Willie Morris of Yazoo City, Mississippi, and his friends come across a bucket of blood in the local slaughterhouse, they mischievously paint witches' signs on a deserted house. The boys are surprised when additional signs appear in town, and waves of hysteria and rumors of devil worshipers sweep the area. The prime suspect behind the supposed witchcraft and cult activity is the great-granddaughter of the Witch of Yazoo. "Bubba was referring to Yazoo's infamous Witch, who on May 25, 1904, was widely reputed to have escaped from the grave to burn the whole town down. The chains over her grave were discovered broken on that fateful day. 'Miss Eddie Mack' was Edwina McBride, a descendant of the legendary witch and a pretty suspicious person herself" (pages 15–16). A revised excerpt from chapter 7 published as "Me and Ollie" in *After All, It's Only a Game* (item 52).

40 *Homecomings*. With the art of William Dunlap. Author and Artist Series. Jackson: University Press of Mississippi, 1989.

A collection of six essays (two previously published) on the themes of remembrance and home. William Dunlap's paintings, which complement Morris's writings rather than illustrate them, are reproduced on color plates while black-and-white details of the artwork introduce the individual essays. In "Dialogue: The Author and Artist," the two friends and native Mississippians talk about memory, the land, shared experiences, and their own homecomings. Morris tells Dunlap that during his formative years in Yazoo City, Mississippi, "I was suffused with words all around me, people telling stories and telling them with immense flamboyance and sorrow, graphic stories. And as you said, there was the landscape — the nine shades of green everywhere, the kudzu vines, the flat land. The whole phenomenon of memory and how memory relates to the landscape itself and to the people around you, I think, probably pushed me along as a writer more than anything else." The volume comprises the following essays (items 41 through 46):

41 "My Great-Grandfather." In *Homecomings*, pp. 3–25 (see item 40).

Morris profiles his great-grandfather on his mother's side, George W. Harper. Harper was founder and editor of the *Hinds County Gazette* in Raymond, Mississippi, and served as town mayor and major of the local militia. "By all accounts, Major Harper grew to be regarded as one of the most prominent and respected men of his time in Mississippi, a man of integrity and one of the South's best editors, noted not only for his vivid prose but, in the tradition of the day, as an effective speaker as well."

42 "Anybody's Children." In *Homecomings*, pp. 27–39 (see item 40).

In May 1986, the small town of Oxford, Mississippi, struggled with the harsh realities of urban crime after a "beautiful Ole Miss graduate student" was found brutally murdered. Morris chronicles the trial of the Ole Miss student and "scion of big inherited wealth" arrested for the slaying. "My merchant friends around the square reported that business was down thirty percent during the trial. I saw no reason to disbelieve them. The courtroom was so crowded, with people standing two-deep along the walls, that the jury—eight women, four men, including one black man—complained at one point of being distracted."

43 "Mitch and the Infield Fly Rule." In *Homecomings*, pp. 41–47 (see item 40).

Morris, writer-in-residence at the University of Mississippi, humorously admits to a bout of middle-age infatuation with a young woman in his modern American novel class. "Ole Miss has forever been noted for its beautiful coeds. It has had several Miss Americas, and I will confess there were quite a few lovely girls in that class. They served to encourage the Socratic method.... The most beautiful of all was a willowy, full-breasted blond Chi Omega, twenty-one years old, tall and slender and lithesome with a throaty Bacall voice, wry and irreverent and whimsical, a fount of good cheer. And a straight-A student!" Republished in *Shifting Interludes* (item 92).

44 "Capote Remembered." In *Homecomings*, pp. 49–59 (see item 40).

A revision of "The Capote Chronicles," published in *Southern Magazine* (item 773). Republished in *Shifting Interludes* (item 72).

45 "My Two Oxfords." In *Homecomings*, pp. 61–77 (see item 40).

Morris observes that two Oxfords have figured prominently in his life: Oxford, England, where he studied as a Rhodes scholar at New College; and Oxford, Mississippi, where he served as writer-in-residence at the University of Mississippi. "Ultimately, one supposes now, I was only an interloper in the English Oxford. When the moment came, I collected my paraphernalia, mostly books, and returned home again to America.... As for the Mississippi Oxford, it lurks forever now in my heart. For it is the heart which shapes my affection for my two Oxfords, and across the years brings them ineluct[a]bly together for me." Republished as *My Two Oxfords* and as the foreword to *They Write Among Us* (item 944).

46 "A Return to Christmases Gone." In *Homecomings*, pp. 79–89 (see item 40).

A memoir republished from *Mississippi* (item 772). Republished as "Christmases Gone Revisited" in *Christmas Stories from Mississippi* (item 917). See also item 839.

47 *Faulkner's Mississippi*. Text by Willie Morris; photographs by William Eggleston. Birmingham, Ala: Oxmoor House, 1990.

A revision of a work published as a cover story in *National Geographic* (item 775).

48 *My Two Oxfords*. Wood engravings by John DePol. Council Bluffs, Iowa: Yellow Barn Press, 1992.

An essay originally published in *Homecomings* (item 45). This edition of *My Two Oxfords* comprises 210 numbered copies signed by the author and by the artist. Reprinted in 1993 by Blackwell North America (Lake Oswego, Oregon) in an edition of 1,200 copies.

49 *After All, It's Only a Game*. With art by Lynn Green Root. Author and Artist Series. Jackson: University Press of Mississippi, 1992.

A collection of six sports stories and brief memoirs organized under the headings Basketball (the first piece), Baseball (the next two), and Football (the last three). "The Blood Blister" is previously unpublished and "North Toward Starkville" has never appeared in book form. Rick Cleveland, a sports reporter for the Jackson, Mississippi, *Clarion-Ledger*, contributes a foreword (pp. 7–8) that offers his perceptions about Morris's love of athletics. He writes that the stories and essays show Morris's "love and devotion to sports" and "an unmistakable understanding of the essence of sports and the emotions our games evoke." *After All, It's Only a Game* also features Morris's preface, titled "My Father and Sports," and Lynn Green Root's lively color illustrations and line drawings. The volume comprises the following works (items 50 through 55):

50 "The Blood Blister." In *After All, It's Only a Game*, pp. 13–27 (see item 49).

A teenage basketball player wakes up one morning with a blood blister on his foot. His coach treats it, and the young man plays in a championship game against Lutherville. "Right at the final buzzer I ran into the wall after a loose ball and was sitting against it on the floor. The game was done, and the Lutherville people were rushing onto the court to cut down the nets, their cheerleaders performing one somersault after another on the hardwood. Blood was oozing a little from my shoe and my mouth felt full of cotton." A story republished in *Full Court* (item 897) and revised as "Asphalt" for the *Oxford American* (item 782).

51 "The Phantom of Yazoo." In *After All, It's Only a Game*, pp. 31–44 (see item 49).

An excerpt from chapter 8 of the "Mississippi" section of *North Toward Home* that was first reprinted in *Always Stand In Against the Curve* (item 33). See also items 720 and 881.

52 "Me and Ollie." In *After All, It's Only a Game*, pp. 45–49 (see item 49).

A revised excerpt from chapter 7 of *Good Old Boy and the Witch of Yazoo*. A group of white youngsters play a game of baseball with some black children. "Everybody got busy setting up a baseball diamond. The black kids had one more player than we did, not counting the little brothers and sisters who sat near the sideline silently watching us in all our gyrations, but that didn't matter. We agreed that their extra player would catch for both sides. They could bat first and use our gloves when we were at bat."

53 "North Toward Starkville." In *After All, It's Only a Game*, pp. 53–57 (see item 49).

A revision of an essay published in the *Clarion-Ledger* (item 850). See also item 849.

54 "Cheerleaders vs. Baton Twirlers." In *After All, It's Only a Game*, pp. 59–64 (see item 49).

A revised excerpt from chapter 10 of *The Courting of Marcus Dupree*. As Morris watches Mississippi high school athlete Marcus Dupree play in a football game, he also observes the two teams' cheerleaders. He compares high school cheerleaders with baton twirlers. "The twirlers would be quieter, more sedate. But there were other differences as well, almost existential in substance." See also items 845 and 847.

55 "The Fumble." In *After All, It's Only a Game*, pp. 65–95 (see item 49).

A story originally published in *Always Stand In Against the Curve* (item 32).

56 *New York Days*. Boston: Little, Brown and Co., 1993.

In this sequel to *North Toward Home*—and in a reportorial style similar to his first book—Morris reflects not only on his exhilarating years at *Harper's* but how that period mirrored the tumultuous 1960s. Relying on his own notes, friends' recollections, and back issues of the magazine, he lyrically chronicles his successes and failures in the epicenter of literary New York, where he hobnobbed with the leading intellectual, political, and entertainment figures of the time. With passion, candor, and occasional self-reproach, yet with an absence of rancor made possible by only the passage of time, he also traces how his youthful idealism ultimately proved disastrous for him and his colleagues. "There were eight million telephone numbers in the Manhattan directory, and every one of them would have returned my calls. I knew the writers, the poets, the intellectuals, the editors, the actresses, the tycoons, the homicide detectives, the athletes, the *belle figure*, and not a few *fakirs* and reprobates and charlatans. I wined with Sinatra and eavesdropped in the *trattorias* on the Mob. I sat next to DiMaggio in the Garden ringside seats and addressed literary matrons in hats in the Waldorf-Astoria. I danced with Scarlett O'Hara's younger sister and Scott Fitzgerald's only daughter" (page 4).

Excerpted in *Esquire* (item 777), *New York* (item 785), *American Way* (item 786), the *Los Angeles Times* (item 853), the *New York Times Book Review* (item 854), the *Washington Post* (item 855), *Magazine Article Writing* (item 889), *Leaving New York* (item 894) and *Booklist* (item 1435).

57 *My Dog Skip*. New York: Random House, 1995.

Elaborating on some of the episodes in the "Mississippi" section of *North Toward Home*, Morris reminisces about growing up in a small southern town with his dog Skip, a smooth-haired English fox terrier. They played baseball and football, got into "mutual mischief" (page 13), and fell in love with the same girl. *My Dog Skip* is a sentimental tribute to a boy's canine companion as well as a memoir of a bygone era of Saturday morning matinees, Nehi sodas, swimming holes, and Fourth-of-July political rallies. "All this was before the big supermarkets and shopping centers and affluent subdivisions with no sidewalks and the monster highways and the innocence lost.... We would sit out on our front porches in the hot, serene nights and say hello to everyone who walked by. If the fire truck came past, we all got in our cars to follow it, and Skip was always the first to want to go" (page 7). Excerpted in *At Random* (item 792) and *Biography and Autobiography* (item 912).

58 *A Prayer for the Opening of the Little League Season*. Illustrated by Barry Moser. San Diego: Harcourt Brace & Co., 1995.

A revision of a tongue-in-cheek prayer, published in the *Clarion-Ledger* (item 852), which asks "Almighty God" for His blessings on "all the baseball children of the earth." Morris, a longtime baseball player and fan, singles out youthful infielders, catchers, outfielders, pitchers, and rookies, as well as umpires, grandparents, "faithful mothers," "little brothers and sisters," and others associated with the sport. Each verse appears on a right-hand page while the matching left-hand page features an appropriate illustration by prize-winning artist Barry Moser. Morris himself is a character in one painting, while a bearded Moser sits in the bleachers in another. "Impart faith to the rookies whose toil is to wait in the bullpens, where their labor is anonymous, as it has been through mortal time, that they, too, shall inherit the earth, for theirs is a lonely calling" (n. pag.).

59 *The Ghosts of Medgar Evers: A Tale of Race, Murder, Mississippi, and Hollywood.* New York: Random House, 1998.

In 1996 Morris served as a historical consultant for the motion picture *Ghosts of Mississippi,* which recounts the story of the 1963 slaying of civil rights leader Medgar Evers and the trial and conviction three decades later of his murderer, Byron De La Beckwith. The movie lost millions at the box office, and numerous hostile reviewers (as well as the film's real-life protagonists) questioned director Rob Reiner's decision to focus on Beckwith and his trial rather than the courageous Evers. In *The Ghosts of Medgar Evers,* Morris weaves his experiences as a seventh-generation Mississippian with dramatic episodes from Evers's life, describes (at times with superfluous details) the making of the motion picture and his experiences on the movie sets, and ruminates on the South and racial healing. "I never met Medgar Evers and was living in New York at the time of his death. I wrote a book on the massive integration of the Mississippi public schools in 1970 and sensed the gradual softening of my home state's more virulent strains of racism. Federal legislation and court decisions were central to the salubrious changes that took place. But in Mississippi the outcroppings of the past are forever with us.... The confluence of past and present, the day-to-day mingling of the dark ghosts and the better angels of our nature, graphically evoked for me on the sets of the movie, was strange and often painful but emotionally redemptive at the same time" (pages 7–8).

60 *My Cat Spit McGee.* New York: Random House, 1999.

In this moving sequel to *My Dog Skip,* Morris describes how he had been a dog lover and "cat misanthrope" (page 11) all his life until his fiancée received a kitten for Christmas. He slowly begins to notice "a vulnerability to [the kitten], a warmth that I had never thought possible with cats" (pages 38–39). After it grows up and gives birth to a white kitten whom the author names Spit McGee, after a character in his book *Good Old Boy,* he became "against all past injunctions a cat-watcher, observing his curious development from a kitten on" (page 46). The author comments on feline traits and furnishes stories about his and Spit McGee's bond and friendship. When an eleven-year-old girl in his neighborhood asks him what he has learned from cats, he replies: "I've learned to care for them on their own terms. And that I know they care for us a lot. And don't try to figure them out too much" (page 139).

61 *My Mississippi.* Photographs by David Rae Morris. Jackson: University Press of Mississippi, 2000.

Morris and his son, photojournalist David Rae, offer their interpretations of modern-day Mississippi in a work published one year after the author's death. Although Willie Morris was a staunch defender of his native state, he was not unaware of its problems or its violent past. In a five-part, balanced essay he examines the land and its people, recognizing the state's virtues and acknowledging its faults. He also notes Mississippi's "contrasts and contradictions" as it enters a new century. For instance, it "remains at the bottom in the whole of the great American republic in social and educational and human services," but he believes it is near the top "in creativity and imagination and artistic accomplishment" (pages xi and 101). David Rae Morris explains that with his photographic narrative, "Look Away," he has "attempted to portray the places and the people of Mississippi as they have been shaped by history." He, a generation removed from his father, looks at Mississippi today and imagines "where it should be." Consequently, he presents "not a book of pretty pictures," but photographs that he hopes are challenging as well as appealing. "Indeed there are images in this collection that are neither pretty nor complimentary. But then, neither is the past. The land and the people are always witness to history, and to understand this can be a great burden. It is a lifelong challenge and one of the greatest lessons I have learned from my father" (page 108).

62 *Taps: A Novel.* Boston: Houghton Mifflin Co., 2001.

In this coming-of-age story set in Fisk's Landing, Mississippi (clearly Yazoo City), sixteen-year-old Swayze Barksdale plays patriotic marching songs on his trumpet as the town's young men leave for service in Korea. When some are killed fighting overseas and return home in coffins, Swayze and his best friend Arch Kidd play "Taps" at their funerals. With each funeral, Swayze grows more mature as he, his girlfriend Georgia, Arch, and their other friends learn worldly lessons about love, sacrifice, patriotism, and grief. Ultimately, Swayze and Arch also understand the deep significance of "Taps" as they confront the same loss and anguish felt by all the mourners who heard them play that haunting and melancholy tune. Morris fashioned many of the characters and incidents in *Taps* after those from his own life. "I knew the place better then than I did my own heart — every bend in the road and the cracks in every sidewalk. It was not in my soul then, only in my pores, yet as familiar to me as water or grass or sunlight. The town was poor one year and rich the next, and everything pertained to the land — labor and usury, mortgage and debt. We lived and died by nature, Anglos and Africans bound together in the whims of the timeless clouds. Our people played seven-card stud against God" (page 1). Excerpted in the *(Memphis) Commercial Appeal* (item 1843).

63 *Shifting Interludes: Selected Essays.* Edited by Jack Bales. Jackson: University Press of Mississippi, 2002.

Bales writes in his introduction that this anthology of thirty-two short compositions "is fashioned around several of the images that [Morris] often returned to in his literary works: people, places, and memories.... The varied works encompass biographical profiles, newspaper opinion / editorials, humor sketches, political analyses, travel pieces, a book review, sports commentaries, and, of course, his thoughts— both critical and affectionate — about his beloved Mississippi." The pieces span the years 1955 to 1999 and include the previously unpublished "A Long-Ago Rendezvous with Alger Hiss" and the first article Morris ever wrote for a national publication, "Mississippi Rebel on a Texas Campus." The volume comprises the following essays (items 64 through 95):

64 "Eisenhower." In *Shifting Interludes*, pp. 3–6 (see item 63).

An essay originally published in the Oxford University *Isis* (item 711).

65 "Down South We Fry Them on the Sidewalks." In *Shifting Interludes*, pp. 7–9 (see item 63).

An essay originally published in the Oxford University *Isis* (item 712).

66 "Southern Comforter." In *Shifting Interludes*, pp. 10–12 (see item 63).

An op-ed piece originally published in the *New York Times* (item 809).

67 "Weep No More, My Lady." In *Shifting Interludes*, pp. 13–17 (see item 63).

An essay originally published in *Reader's Digest* (item 734).

68 "It Took More Than Good Men to Win the War." In *Shifting Interludes*, pp. 18–22 (see item 63).

An essay originally published in the *Washington Star* (item 821).

69 "Of Northern Fears, Southern Realities, and Jimmy Carter." In *Shifting Interludes*, pp. 23–27 (see item 63).

An op-ed piece originally published in the *New York Times* (item 835).

70 "My Friend Marcus Dupree." In *Shifting Interludes*, pp. 28–32 (see item 63).

An essay originally published in *Parade* (item 761).

71 "What It Takes for a Son to Understand a Father." In *Shifting Interludes*, pp. 33–38 (see item 63).

An essay originally published in *Parade* (item 763).

72 "Capote Remembered." In *Shifting Interludes*, pp. 39–45 (see item 63).

An essay originally published in *Homecomings* (item 44). See also item 773.

73 "The Epistolary Soldier." In *Shifting Interludes*, pp. 46–51 (see item 63).

A book review originally published in the *Texas Observer* (item 958).

74 "In the Spirit of the Game." In *Shifting Interludes*, pp. 52–58 (see item 63).

An essay republished from *Southern Living* (item 778). See also item 883.

75 "My Friend Forrest Gump." In *Shifting Interludes*, pp. 59–69 (see item 63).

An essay originally published in the *Oxford American* (item 791).

76 "A Long-Ago Rendezvous with Alger Hiss." In *Shifting Interludes*, pp. 70–72 (see item 63).

In a previously unpublished essay, Morris recounts a quiet evening he spent in a New York City restaurant with accused Communist spy Alger Hiss. "I longed, out of old reportorial instincts on that pleasant yet vaguely discomfiting evening in that Village trattoria, to ask him if

Whittaker Chambers really had such bad teeth, as everyone said he did, and if Chambers had really hidden in a pumpkin the microfilm he said Hiss had given him.... In my deepest being, in fact, I yearned suddenly to inquire: 'Mr. Hiss, did you *do* it, or did you *not* do it?' On a social evening of pasta and Chianti even in that elusive faubourg, the quintessential things are often left unsaid."

77 "Mississippi Queen." In *Shifting Interludes*, pp. 73–86 (see item 63).

An essay originally published in *Vanity Fair* (item 803).

78 "The Round-Up." In *Shifting Interludes*, pp. 89–91 (see item 63).

An essay originally published in the *Daily Texan* (item 280).

79 "The Round-Up." In *Shifting Interludes*, pp. 92–93 (see item 63).

An essay originally published in the *Summer Texan* (item 319).

80 "Mississippi Rebel on a Texas Campus." In *Shifting Interludes*, pp. 94–99 (see item 63).

An essay originally published in the *Nation* (item 710).

81 "The Rain Fell Noiselessly." In *Shifting Interludes*, pp. 100–101 (see item 63).

An essay originally published in the *Texas Observer* (item 528).

82 "Despair in Mississippi; Hope in Texas." In *Shifting Interludes*, pp. 102–110 (see item 63).

An essay originally published in *Dissent* (item 719).

83 "Bridgehampton: The Sounds and the Silences." In *Shifting Interludes*, pp. 111–15 (see item 63).

An op-ed piece originally published in the *New York Times* (item 810).

84 "Prelude to Setting Off in a Camper to History." In *Shifting Interludes*, pp. 116–18 (see item 63).

An essay originally published in the *Washington Star* (item 823). Republished in *Willie Morris: An Exhaustive Annotated Bibliography and a Biography*.

85 "The South and Welcome to It: Does It Still Exist?" In *Shifting Interludes*, pp. 119–26 (see item 63).

An essay originally published in *Southern Magazine* (item 771).

86 "In a Shifting Interlude." In *Shifting Interludes*, pp. 127–43 (see item 63).

An essay originally published in *American Way* (item 781).

87 "The Day I Followed the Mayor Around Town." In *Shifting Interludes*, pp. 147–54 (see item 63).

Morris recounts a day he spent following his dog Pete around Bridgehampton, a village on eastern Long Island. Because Pete "would wander up and down Main Street all day greeting the people," he came to be known as "The Mayor of Bridgehampton." Pete "brings to me my boyhood, all the long-ago things I miss— my father's footsteps on the porch, my mother playing a hymn on the piano, all the boys and girls I once knew, and the smells of a new spring morning in Mississippi.... Dogs give continuity to a man's life; they help hold the fractured pieces of it together. When Pete the Mayor came to live with me, he reaffirmed the contours of my own existence." Morris wrote this essay in 1978; the original typescript is in the Willie Morris Collection, Department of Archives and Special Collections, John Davis Williams Library, University of Mississippi. He revised the article as "Pete, 'The Mayor of Bridgehampton'" for *Reader's Digest* (item 740).

88 "Coming on Back." In *Shifting Interludes*, pp. 155–71 (see item 63).

An essay originally published in *Life* magazine (item 750).

89 "A Love That Transcends Sadness." In *Shifting Interludes*, pp. 172–75 (see item 63).

An essay originally published in *Parade* (item 752).

90 "At Ole Miss: Echoes of a Civil War's Last Battle." In *Shifting Interludes*, pp. 176–80 (see item 63).

An essay originally published in *Time* (item 760).

91 "Now That I Am Fifty." In *Shifting Interludes*, pp. 181–83 (see item 63).

An essay originally published in *Parade* (item 767).

92 "Mitch and the Infield Fly Rule." In *Shifting Interludes*, pp. 184–87 (see item 63).

An essay originally published in *Homecomings* (item 43).

93 "Here Lies My Heart." In *Shifting Interludes*, pp. 188–96 (see item 63).

An essay originally published in *Esquire* (item 777).

94 "The John Foster Dulles." In *Shifting Interludes*, pp. 197–99 (see item 63).

An essay originally published in *Car and Driver* (item 784).

95 "As the Years Go By, Do We Grow Crankier — Or More Tolerant?" In *Shifting Interludes*, pp. 200–204 (see item 63).

An essay originally published in *New Choices* (item 797).

Articles in the Daily Texan

Readers of Willie Morris's works may never know the full extent of his contributions to the *Daily Texan*, the campus newspaper of the University of Texas. One problem is that the paper often featured unsigned editorials ranging in length from just a brief paragraph to more than a column. In addition, as Tara Copp and Robert L. Rogers point out on page 60 of their centennial history, *The Daily Texan: The First 100 Years* (item 1942), "All the 1950s editors wrote front-page news," but "the majority of *Texan* articles were published without bylines." This anonymity poses difficulties for researchers; although Morris as editor may have been responsible for the majority or perhaps even all of the pieces, a bibliographer cannot grant a writer unqualified authorship to hundreds of unsigned items without documentation.

In some cases, however, the works themselves provide such internal evidence. For instance, Morris occasionally referred to himself as "the editor" (items 317 and 409) and quoted from articles he had previously published under his byline (item 345). Also, given his well-known appreciation for the novels of Thomas Wolfe and William Faulkner, it is reasonable to assume that works praising these two authors can be attributed to him (items 316 and 455). Furthermore, the sentiments and wording of some of his impassioned editorials, such as the ones opposing the censorship of the *Daily Texan*, point to Morris (items 438, 442, and 450). After Chicago teenager Emmett Till was brutally murdered in Mississippi, several *Daily Texan* editorials protested northerners' blanket condemnation of all Mississippians (items 366, 372, and 427). Because Morris often proclaimed his affection for his native state, readers of the paper undoubtedly knew that he was the author of the Emmett Till editorials—as well as any other pieces about Mississippi (items 404 and 468). These articles published without bylines are identified in citations by a leading "[Unsigned]."

Daily Texan is abbreviated in citations as *DT*. During the summer, the newspaper was published semi-weekly as the *Summer Texan*; this title is abbreviated as *ST* in citations. (In the early 1970s, publication increased to four days a week, and the name *Daily Texan* was used year round.) University of Texas is frequently abbreviated in annotations as UT.

As a freshman and sophomore journalist at the University of Texas, Morris often changed his *Daily Texan* byline. He generally used "William" or "Willie," but occasionally he adopted "Bill" or even "William (Willie)." By the end of his sophomore year, he consistently wrote under "Willie," a practice he was to continue, with few exceptions, for the rest of his life.

96 "Well, Here I Am: Stiff Upperlip Helps Freshmen Survive Test." *DT*, 17 September 1952, p. 4.

In Morris's first article for the *Daily Texan*, he acknowledges that he is slightly homesick, as "it's hard to break yourself away from lifetime ties and a happy environment." He is "awed" by the challenges that await him, "yet, through it all, I remain hopeful, for I know that soon the spirit of the University of Texas will overcome me.... In time I will be as important as the next fellow. I will realize then that, pushed forward by UT, I will make my way, confident and unafraid, into the world."

97 "Neighboring News: $6,500 Is Chickenfeed to Our Aggie Friends." *DT*, 18 September 1952, p. 4.

Morris begins writing a regular column, which he calls "Neighboring News." Although "I may sink or swim, I think we should get better acquainted while the opportunity presents itself. I'm just a homespun Mississippi lad.... I come from a wonderful place, Yazoo City, (Ya-zoo r[h]ymes with sez-who) home of the most beautiful girls, the friendliest people, and the most intelligent dogs in Mississippi.... My job, as long as it lasts, is to give you, the reader, a personal insight on what's happening in other colleges." Students at Harvard University, for example, are using illegal stills to brew "moonshine." Sixty-five hundred dollars have "been appropriated to the poultry department" at Texas A&M University. Morris also provides news reports "on what's happening" at Kansas State University and the University of Oklahoma.

98 "Neighboring News: Politics Invades College Campuses." *DT*, 25 September 1952, p. 4.

Asserts that "politics are thrusting to the forefront. College campuses throughout the land are reacting with lively enthusiasm to the tempo of the day's issues.... In short, the current state of things signifies that college youth of today are not only becoming interested, but active in national affairs." Morris adds that parts of the "Solid South" will vote Republican "for the first time in many decades," and he publishes a political anecdote that in later years he would often repeat. A stranger in a Mississippi Delta town walks up to a resident and asks if he can settle there. "At which time the other drawled, 'If you're a Yankee, the state will protect you. If you're a Republican, the game laws will protect you.'" In Morris's "news from other schools," he mentions Kansas University, Kansas State College, and Texas A&M.

99 "Neighboring News: Cramming Gives Indigestion, Say Massachusetts Profs." *DT*, 30 September 1952, p. 3.

Beginning in this issue, Morris follows his byline with the title "Texan Exchange Editor." His "neighboring news" about other colleges includes a statement that professors at Boston University have determined that "cramming for exams proves very harmful, not only to the student['s] academic standing, but his health also, in much the same manner that overeating causes sickness. Since we consider cramming a very necessary evil, there's but one answer—you've got to eat sometimes." Morris also prints news accounts about the University of Southern California, Kansas State University, and Henderson State Teachers College.

100 "Neighboring News: Oklahoma Aggies Have Sidewalk Problem, Too." *DT*, 7 October 1952, p. 4.

"News from the outside world today is highlighted to some degree by the dispute taking shape at Oklahoma A&M. Students there have presented concrete evidence that sidewalks in Aggieland have become a dire necessity." After a rainstorm, the area by "several class buildings, as yet unenhanced with sidewalks, was left in such a muddy condition that hosts of Aggies were forced to remove their shoes to reach their destinations." Those who want sidewalks built "can easily argue that their opponents have no ground whatsoever to walk on." Morris's other feature stories come from Oregon University, the University of Oklahoma, and Marshall College.

101 "Aggieland Is No Longer Restricted to Just Cows." *DT*, 9 October 1952, p. 4.

"Doggonit!" Morris exclaims. Just as UT students have become accustomed to referring to Texas A&M as the Land of the Contented Cows, "we catch sight of a want-ad in the Aggie Battalion. It states: 'Three philosophical Scotties, Three dashing Dachshunds. Registered. Priced right.' 'Scuse us Aggs, we've been barking up the wrong tree." At the University of Alabama, students are being encouraged to have chest x-rays taken. "TB or not TB, that is the question. And at Alabama, they're finding the answer." Morris also publishes news from Kansas State University, Millsaps College, the University of Oklahoma, and the University of Southern California.

102 "Neighboring News: Hair-Raising Accident Befalls Miami Student." *DT*, 14 October 1952, p. 4.

Morris's column comprises "neighboring news" about students and faculty at nine universities and colleges. A student at Miami University reported that a local drug store "confused two prescription labels, causing him for the past year to rub stomach medicine on his scalp and drink his hair tonic. Ruined him for life, he accused. Why argue, Mac, when you have the healthiest scalp and the flattest stomach in Florida?"

103 "Studying Koloquy? Kansas U's for You." *DT*, 16 October 1952, p. 4.

News accounts from Southern Methodist University, Kansas University, Oklahoma A&M, and Louisiana State University. Among the courses offered at Kansas University, writes Morris, are Otorhinolaryngology, Complex Orthogonal Functions, Finite Dimensional Vector Space, and Koloquy. "Gone are the days of the Three R's."

104 "Neighboring News: Dancing Californians Have 'Grave' Problems." *DT*, 21 October 1952, p. 4.

Relates that police "rounded up" twenty-three students in a "California college town" for dancing in a local cemetery. "It's reached the point now where a poor fellow can't even dig up a date." Morris names Miami (Ohio) University, Southwestern University, the University of Arkansas, the University of Southern California, and Southern Methodist University in his other write-ups.

105 "Neighboring News: Please Do Not Throw Animals at Spectators." *DT*, 23 October 1952, p. 4.

Students at Baylor University are complaining because as they walk by the biology building, "time and time again [they] have narrowly escaped being hit by cat livers or other internal parts of dissected cats tossed from classrooms." A department head has warned the biologists not to dispose of the animal organs this way. "Yet many students shake their heads doubtfully and wonder, for they know that if the biologists have the guts, they'll do it again." Other college stories come from Tulane University and the University of Southern California.

106 "Neighboring News: Cops Cost Oklahoma Gift of Rare Books." *DT*, 30 October 1952, p. 4.

Morris singles out seven institutions in his "Neighboring News" column. An alumnus of the University of Oklahoma "paid a visit to the library to donate a part of his rare book collection. While the customary arrangements were being made, time expired on the man's parking meter," and he received a ticket. "The alum hastily checked out for the Controller's office, finding it closed. Disgusted with life in general, he took his books and left."

107 "'52 Campaign Leaves Nation, Campus Limp." *DT*, 6 November 1952, p. 4.

Commentary on the end of the 1952 presidential campaign. "The husky voice of a weary, heartbroken, yet proud Adlai Stevenson echoed through the radio across the landscape, as groups of students joined with the rest of America in hearing a plea for unity.... One could perceive the drama of that moment, which brought to a fitting climax a campaign marked from start to finish with keen competitiveness and crucial issues."

108 "Neighboring News: Shy Males Are Just Sitting Dear." *DT*, 11 November 1952, p. 4.

The editor of *Varsity*, the Cambridge University newspaper, "has hit the male on the head in answer to a shy fellow's request for advice. He consoled: 'The shy need never give up hope ... a woman out gunning never ignores a sitting shot.' But then, girls, have you ever had a sitting shot at a real deer?" Morris also refers to the University of Pennsylvania, Oklahoma City University, Purdue, and Texas A&M in his news briefs.

109 "Neighboring News: Some School Regulations Just Don't Hold Water." *DT*, 14 November 1952, p. 6.

Morris's reports, "typical of hundreds of others involving college students throughout the nation," mention eight academic institutions. "Authorities at Mississippi State College used to flub the tub back in the late 1800's. An excerpt from the state newspaper in the good ole days stated: 'Students are requested to take only one bath a week. They may have two if their roommate doesn't take his turn.' The plan never actually held too much water, and besides that the students raised too big a stink."

110 "Neighboring News: 'Mental' Delegates Listen to Napoleon." *DT*, 19 November 1952, p. 4.

"A workshop on aspects of mental health drew over 200 delegates to the College of the Pacific campus earlier this month. Participants came from far and near—farmers out of their fields, businessmen out of their offices, mineralogists out of their mines. Chief speaker was Napoleon Bonaparte." Morris's other news summaries encompass five colleges and universities.

111 "Neighboring News: Refinements Heck; Let's Go Italian." *DT*, 21 November 1952, p. 3.

Morris's column focuses on Stanford, Akron, Michigan State, Tulane, Kansas State, and Drake universities. An Italian restaurant in Stanford, California, has been unable to get permission "from the City Commission to enlarge its premises. The reason: As an agitated neighbor says, Stanford students have been staying out until 1:30 every morning, screaming, hollering, building bonfires, and raising the usual. 'They just like the spaghetti,' the proprietor said. But then, Stanfordites always have been the Roman kind."

112 [Unsigned]. "Neighboring News: Three Jacks Know It's a Mighty Little World." *DT*, 25 November 1952, 4.

"Here at UT, be specific when you speak of the Little Man on the Campus, particularly when he goes by Jack. Confusion reaps a harvest in this category," for three Jack Littles are enrolled at the University of Texas. "Yessir, son, this is a little world." In addition to his own school, Morris includes Selmer College, the University of Southern California, the University of Oregon, the University of Wisconsin, and a "Massachusetts Theatre Group" in the news paragraphs for his usual column.

113 "Ya Heard the One About the Aggie?" *DT*, 27 November 1952, p. 4.

Morris quotes from past articles in the *Daily Texan* in an attempt to define an "Aggie," a college student at UT's rival institution, Texas A&M University. "Or we could tell the story of the Aggie who, in the course of a chemistry class, was asked in what three states matter rests— and answered Mississippi, Louisiana, and Arkansas.... But this is a definition without end, without description, without need. Hook 'em, Horns!"

114 "Neighboring News: Key to Popularity Has Four Wheels." *DT*, 5 December 1952, p. 4.

"We have recently completed" a personal survey so extensive "that we can now enumerate the basic rules for popularity in colleges throughout the land. They are: 1. Be congenial; 2. Have a car; 3. Be a sport; 4. Have a car; 5. Be considerate; 6. Have a car; 7. Be dependable; 8. Have a car." Morris's brief column also contains a report from Olympic Junior College in California.

115 "Neighboring News: Dying Cost Keeps Pace with Soaring Living Fee." *DT*, 11 December 1952, p. 4.

Morris features news from nine institutions, including the University of Southern California. A writer for the school's *Daily Trojan*, after researching the high cost of funerals, "has deemed the burial problem very grave indeed. Claiming that prices connected with dying are much too expensive," the reporter is planning "to be buried in his own back yard. We advise, sir, that you try the lay-away plan. After all, funeral homes these days are exceptionally dependable, and they'll certainly be the last to let you down."

116 "Neighboring News." *DT*, 17 December 1952, p. 4.

"Noticing the careless manner in which petitions were being signed by students," a reporter at the University of Pittsburgh "conceived the idea for a new kind of Gallup Poll. He hastily drew up a petition stating: 'We the undersigned fully admit to being first-class jackasses.'" Twenty-four out of twenty-seven students signed the document. "Which will it be at Pitt? Yea or Neigh?" Morris also prints a story about students at Mississippi State College.

117 "Neighboring News: Kansas State Dislikes What Goes in Who's Who." *DT*, 18 December 1952, p. 4.

"Christmas is in the air," Morris observes in his "Neighboring News" column, "and campuses all over the country are contributing to the yuletide season." Among the seven schools Morris singles out is Kansas State University, where "folks ... can't tell who's who. College officials have decided to outlaw the nation-wide Who's Who selections from the K-State campus, because, so the administration says, there is a lack of uniformity in the system. In other words, according to K-State, Who's Who doesn't know what's what."

118 "Neighboring News: A New Year's Resolution; Let's Get Pinned in '53." *DT*, 6 January 1953, p. 4.

Besides providing news accounts from five colleges and universities, Morris contributes his listing of possible student New Year's resolutions. "It's resolution time once again and the wise college student who plans to follow those do's an[d] don't's may find the rigors of campus life much less unbearable. The average list will probably read something like this: 1. Get pinned. 2. Write home. 3. Keep my roommate sober. 4. Send the dean a valentine. 5. Make Phi Beta Kappa. 6. Bring the car back second semester. 7. Help some poor Aggie."

119 "Neighboring News: 'No-Doz Ode' Adds Pre-Exam Sparkle." *DT*, 11 January 1953, p. 4.

News from the University of Oklahoma, UCLA, Kansas State University, and Center Hill Stone College is preceded by Morris's "Ode to No-Doz," a tribute to the caffeine pill that helps students stay awake at night. The first and last few lines read: "There comes an exam time in every man's life, / When college is rugged — a struggle, a strife, / ... You spare us, you save us, you lessen our throes. Here's hats off to you, dear little No-Doz."

120 "Neighboring News: Mary Lous Deal Trouble to Prospective Suitors." *DT*, 15 January 1953, p. 4.

"A couple of Kansas State coeds ... have attracted a great deal of interest. The two frosh, both named Mary Lou Deal, caused a state of confusion throughout the entire school when they became roommates. The poor fellows who call up for dates have a problem. How do they know they'll get the right deal?" Morris's final "Neighboring News" column also includes remarks about students at five other colleges and universities.

121 "'Mural Basketball to Return to Scene." *DT*, 3 February 1953, p. 3.

Morris begins to cover intramural sports at the University of Texas, and the title "Texan Intramural Co-ordinator" follows his byline. "Basketball, king of Intramural sports, will commence its month-and-a-half domination of the local scene beginning Wednesday night, and simultaneously push second semester 'mural play into motion." One hundred seventy teams will compete. "Prognosticating the possible winners will undoubtedly be as futile as trying to kill an acre of East Texas johnson grass, and equally as foolish since the entry list includes a bevy of star-studded teams."

122 "'Mural Basketball Starts Wednesday." *DT*, 4 February 1953, p. 2.

"A basketball campaign which might generate into one of the most hectic in intramural history gets underway in Gregory Gym Wednesday night." Morris lists the "leading contenders" in the nine Class A leagues.

123 "SPE, Blomquist Sparkle in 'Mural Cage Openers." *DT*, 5 February 1953, p. 2.

"The lid was lifted on a boiler pot of intramural basketball at Gregory Gym Wednesday night, as 30 Class A and ten Class B aggregations moved into action." Morris writes up "the story behind what happened."

124 "Kappa Sig-SPE Tilt to Highlight Murals." *DT*, 8 February 1953, p. 3.

"Intramural basketball's yet young scramble moves into its third night Monday, with competition concentrated on Class A fraternity, Class B club and independent, and Mullet League contentions." Morris relates the highlights of the various "skirmishes."

125 "Five Frat Teams Win 'Mural Battles." *DT*, 10 February 1953, p. 2.

"A quintet of Class A fraternity kingpins became two-time winners Monday night in intramurals' smoldering basketball battle." Includes coverage of the games and scores.

126 "Roberts, Fijis Shine in 'Mural Battles." *DT*, 12 February 1953, p. 2.

"A previously untested Sigma Alpha Mu quint eked past Delta Kappa Epsilon, 25–23, in the featured game of Wednesday night's 19-game intramural cage list.... The 'mural basketball battle [is] still in its unforecastable stages but [is] materializing rapidly...." Includes coverage of the games and scores.

127 "Dorm B, Grove, PEM Powers in Class B." *DT*, 15 February 1953, p. 2.

"Four Class B crews— Dorm B, Oak Grove, Pem Club, and TLOK — established themselves as principal contenders for the B title as a result of action Friday night in the intramural cage race." Includes coverage of the games and scores.

128 "'Mural Musings: 'Fustest [sic], Mostest' Key to Cage Race." *DT*, 17 February 1953, p. 2.

"He who gets there 'fustest with the mostest,' advocated General Albert S. Johnston, wins the battles. Apply this tenet to a white-hot intramural cage race, and you've got the one ingredient that should make this campaign the most unforecastable in 'mural history." Morris lists the top basketball "powers" and adds that "entry dates for two other top intramural drawing attractions, table tennis and water polo, are near at hand."

129 "'Mural Fives Face Big Games Tonight." *DT*, 18 February 1953, p. 2.

"It's now-or-never night at Gregory Gym. That, simply speaking, is the story Wednesday night as 24 Class A crews swing into action in intramural basketball. Desperation will quite definitely be the keynote, for each of the teams has already dropped one decision." Morris explains how the "Class A race shapes up" and surveys the contests in the various leagues.

130 "AIME, Theleme Win in 'Mural Cage Play." *DT*, 20 February 1953, p. 2.

"A threesome of Class A aggregations— Theleme Co-op, TLOK, and AIME — emerged victorious in the intramural cage race, but only one, AIME, assumes an advantageous position as a result." Includes coverage of the games and scores.

131 "'Mural Basketball Will Reach Crucial Stage Monday Night." *DT*, 22 February 1953, p. 2.

"Intramural basketball, to now content with sparring blows and harmless clinches, reaches its first big crucial stage Monday. Inside track in five Class A loops, plus plenty of prestige, will be at stake Monday night when 10 of intramurals' mightiest unbeaten powers swing into action." Morris examines the principal matches and reports on games played two days earlier.

132 "Phi Psi, UCC Fives Pull 'Mural Upsets." *DT*, 24 February 1953, p. 2.

"An intramural basketball season, once as confused as Canal Street on New Year's Eve, has materialized into something definite.... Sigma Alpha Epsilon, Phi Gamma Delta, Phi Kappa Psi, Campus Guild, Blomquist, UCC, and AFROTC are now leading the keenly-competitive Class A flock, positions they assumed as aftermaths of Monday's play." Includes coverage of the games and scores.

133 "Winner's Bracket Complete in 'Murals." *DT*, 25 February 1953, p. 2.

"When nine Class B aggregations swept to their respective league finals Tuesday night, only the final chapter in 9 Class A and 12 Class B loops remained unwritten. And from current indications, it'll be a dramatic one." Morris describes how the "overall league-by-league picture shapes up."

134 "15 More Eliminated in 'Mural Basketball." *DT*, 26 February 1953, p. 2.

"Fifteen more basketball outfits ... found themselves rudely transported from intramural basketball's rapidly diminishing circle Wednesday night. Their abrupt adieu came as a result of losses sustained in the do-or-die losers' bracket, that group which has already suffered one defeat each and needs only one more for automatic elimination." Includes coverage of the games and scores.

135 "'Mural Basketball Champs Due Soon." *DT*, 27 February 1953, p. 2.

Intramural basketball "has given the old heave-ho to all but 27 Class A entries. Thirty-three crews have outlived Class B's battle for survival. But one thing's for sure — both numbers will dwindle before next week's play reaches its end." Morris lists the leading league teams.

136 "Monday's Games to Be Last for 9 Class A 'Mural Clubs." *DT*, 1 March 1953, p. 3.

"Going ... going ... gone. Monday night's 'mural basketball play will decide which nine Class A losers' bracket teams are still going, and which nine are gone. The survivors of Monday night's work must challenge the nine Class A crews yet to absorb defeat, in intramural affairs slated Tuesday and Wednesday nights." Morris reviews the principal matches and reports on recently played games.

137 "Phi Gams, SAE, and AIME Win Class A 'Mural Titles." *DT*, 5 March 1953, p. 2.

"A torrid intramural cager contention, to date as wild as Saturday night in the Congo, continued its unforecastable pattern Wednesday night. The stage is now ready for the culmination point, reserved for next week." Morris provides "the story" on the various games.

138 "BSU, Delts, Grove Win 'Mural Battles." *DT*, 10 March 1953, p. 2.

"Six more Class A league titlists and five Class B loop champs were produced Monday in intramural basketball's last regular-season session." Morris relates "what happened" during the matchups.

139 "Phi Psi's, SAE's, Grove, AFROTC in Finals." *DT*, 11 March 1953, p. 2.

"Phi Kappa Psi challenges Sigma Alpha Epsilon and Oak Grove tackles AFROTC at Gregory Gym Wednesday night in the Class A divisional race for supremacy." Morris surveys the forthcoming competitions and reports on recently played games.

140 "'Mural 'Kings' Ready for Final Playoffs." *DT*, 12 March 1953, p. 2.

"Intramurals' white-hot basketball scramble, as colorful in its four-weeks' existence as a chartreuse tuxedo, is down to the wire." Morris summarizes the completed games and explains "what will happen" during next week's contests in the "'mural race."

141 "'Mural Sports Nite Set for March 23." *DT*, 13 March 1953, p. 3.

"Sports Nite, long the granddaddy of intramural sports events, is little more than one week away.... Included on this year's agenda: all–University basketball clash between the two A finalists; a gymnastics bout between Texas and the University of Mississippi; volleyball between Texas and Baylor; wrestling, and table tennis." Morris also reports on "a pair of intramurals' top drawing attractions," the competitions in handball and table tennis.

142 "Gymnastics Heads Sports Nite Meet." *DT*, 18 March 1953, p. 2.

"When gymnastics teams representing Texas and Mississippi Southern clash in one of the manyfold events of twenty-third annual Sports Nite, sports enthusiasts who didn't give a flip for the ancient sport may have an abrupt change of opinion." Morris outlines the "events in the Sports Nite gymnastic competition," and he also comments briefly on the intramural basketball competitions.

143 "Grove, Kappa Sigs Move to A, B Finals." *DT*, 20 March 1953, p. 2.

Morris writes that during Thursday night's intramural basketball competitions, "The two victors were Kappa Sigma, who picked up the all–

University Class B crown at the expense of Oak Grove's Bees, and Oak Grove's A aggregate, who blasted Blomquist's Swedes to move into the campus finals. Thus the stage is all set for the grand finale on Sports Nite, matching Oak Grove and Sigma Alpha Epsilon for the Class A title." He also reports on water polo and softball competitions.

144 "Sports Nite Olympics Open in Gym Monday." *DT*, 22 March 1953, p. 3.

"Sports Nite—that rare combination of a six-ring circus and a miniature Olympics—makes its twenty-third appearance Monday night in Gregory Gym, and some 4,000 Texas sports enthusiasts should show up to welcome its return." Morris observes that Sports Nite features not only the Oak Grove and Sigma Alpha Epsilon championship basketball game but also volleyball, wrestling, gymnastics, and table tennis matches.

145 "University Entries Win Two Sports Nite Events." *DT*, 24 March 1953, p. 2.

"Two all–University intramural championships were decided at Gregory Gym Monday night, amidst the color and spectacularity of Sports Nite. The twenty-third annual affair also featured some of Texas' most adept volleyball, gymnastics, wrestling, and table tennis performers, vying in a quartet of exhibition titles." Morris provides coverage of the principal contests.

146 "Three Intramural Playoffs Set in Water Polo Thursday." *DT*, 25 March 1953, p. 2.

"Three loop championships are in the records, and another threesome flung into sudden-death playoffs, in intramurals' sizzling water polo race Tuesday." Morris tells "what happened" during both the water polo competitions and the intramural softball games.

147 "Theta Chi's, Phi Delts Rank High in Softball." *DT*, 29 March 1953, p. 3.

"Will they wilt in the stretch? Oft used as a judging point amongst major leaguers, the question is also appli[c]able to the current 'mural softball battle. More specifically it's applicable to Class A nines representing the SPE's, the Theta Chi's, and the Phi Delts, and the Class B Phi Delts, AEPi's, and Dekes. These are intramurals' only unwhipped fraternity teams." Morris outlines how the "'53 conflict shapes up" in the intramural softball fraternity division.

148 "Sigma Nu, LXA Top Intramural Action." *DT*, 31 March 1953, p. 4.

"A battling school of Sigma Nu's slithered like greased tadpoles past Kappa Sigma, 5–0, to steal the show in water polo fraternity playoffs Monday, and establish themselves as favorites in the all–University homestretch." Morris furnishes highlights of both water polo and softball intramural contests.

149 "Campus Sidelights: Brackenridge 'Refugees' Not Thirsty These Days." *DT*, 1 April 1953, p. 3.

An editor's note reports that "this is the first in a series of columns Willie Morris will write for the Texan dealing with everyday life at the University." Morris describes the "soul-stirring" chaos in his dormitory, Brackenridge Hall, that resulted when some unknown person or persons tore a water pipe from a wall. "Water was everywhere—on the patio, in the hallway—and produced a replica of Niagara Falls as it swept down three flights of stairs. Had the Ancient Mariner been there, he would've found a paradise.... A toilet pipe had broken loose up on the third floor, and poor 'B' section was in the process of being inundated by the water supply of the entire tri-dorm area."

150 "Assignment Forty Acres: Russian Planes Attack Strategic US Bases." *DT*, 8 April 1953, p. 4.

The first article in an occasional column, "Assignment Forty Acres," named for the size of the UT campus. In a prank reminiscent of Orson Welles's famous "War of the Worlds" hoax of 1938, Morris and several friends use a tape recorder and a portable radio to play a "sly stunt" on members of the university baseball team. "We began by recording some music. Then we interrupted, reporting inauthentically that Russian planes had just bombed out bases at several strategic spots on the globe. Two minutes later, the 'announcer' substantiated the report." The students hid the tape recorder under a bed, strategically placed a radio near it, and led "our guinea pigs" to the room. One of the athletes "fell on the bed and started moaning." Two others "took it all standing up, and turned white—a ghostly, pale, stunned white." A fourth left the room and "started a mild riot" when he returned to his fraternity house. When the "victims" discovered the truth, they were too relieved and "too happy to do anything drastic to us instigators." See also item 221.

151 "Water Polo Finals Set Thursday at 7." *DT*, 8 April 1953, p. 2.

"Sigma Nu, an outfit that gets better all the time, faces steady and sturdy Oak Grove for the 'mural water polo crown Thursday night. The squabble, set for Gregory pool at 7 p.m., shapes up to be as unpredictable as an East Texas thunderstorm, and is generally rated a tossup by pre-game odd[s]makers." Morris also reports on "'mural softball play" and "two of intramurals' top spring drawing cards, tennis doubles and horseshoe pitching."

152 "Sigma Nu Captures Water Polo Crown." *DT*, 10 April 1953, p. 2.

"Sigma Nu emblaz[o]ned their way into 'mural annals Thursday night and left a golden-tinted imprint on the records in the process. When Oak Grove fell 5–0 in the all–University water polo finals, intramural sports enthusiasts went home knowing they'd seen one of the best crews in 'mural history." Includes coverage of the game.

153 "Softball Race Led by Six Darkhorses." *DT*, 12 April 1953, p. 2.

"Six darkhorses, all on the comeback trail, are now firmly entrenched in the Class A 'mural softball battle as of Friday night. The sextet includes Campus Guild, AIEE, Reluctant, Oak Grove, Kappa Alpha, and Sigma Alpha Epsilon, who roared from the brink of elimination with impressive victories Friday." Includes coverage of recently played games and scores.

154 "Once-Beaten Clubs Pace Softball Play." *DT*, 14 April 1953, p. 2.

"Army ROTC, Campus Guild, and Brunette House, once-beaten and tottering on the brink of elimination, blasted their way to three league finals in intramurals' hot softball race Monday, but took completely different routes in so doing." Includes coverage of the games and scores.

155 "League Finals Wednesday in Class A 'Mural Softball." *DT*, 15 April 1953, p. 2.

"It's giant vs. giant-killer in intramurals' sizzling softball scramble Wednesday, as the class A race moves into its homestretch. Eight of the nine class A loop titles are in positions to be decided, for a triumph by an unbeaten team over a once-whipped squad at Whitaker Field Wednesday would automatically terminate league play." Morris summarizes the competitions in the various leagues and also remarks briefly on intramural golf matches.

156 "Assignment Forty Acres: 60 Per Cent of Students Spend Sleepless Nights." *DT*, 16 April 1953, p. 4.

Morris and some friends stay up all night studying. "Enraptured by the desire for learning, and armed with myriads of No-Doz[,] a quart of coffee, and a package of lemon drops, we prepare ourselves for our nocturnal sojourn, an extremely crucial hour quiz in How to Rid A Dog of Fleas 312 awaiting us on the morrow." At three o'clock in the morning, "as we take a breathing spell from the job at hand to get a breath of air from the window, the UT campus looks almost ethereal in its solitude — not an object moving, only the mist encircling the Tower, not a sound, except for the occasional sound of the chimes or a car in the distance."

157 "Five Softball Clubs in Divisional Finals." *DT*, 16 April 1953, p. 2.

"A quintet of star-sprinkled outfits shoved their way to intramurals' Class A divisional softball finals at Whitaker Field Wednesday, as competition in eight of nine leagues reached a showdown." Morris also reports on the "deciding clashes in each of the nine Class B leagues."

158 "'Mural Track Prelims Start Monday at 4." *DT*, 19 April 1953, p. 2.

"Competition in track and field, intramurals' most bitterly contested sport, commences Monday afternoon at Memorial Stadium, and you can bet your bottom dollar enthusiasm will run at a terrifically high pitch." Morris explains that "several organizations are battling it tooth 'n nail for the all-year cup, and their battle is going right down to the wire." Morris surveys the upcoming athletic contests, adding that "the culmination of track activity, the annual Intramural Championship Meet, takes place on Monday, April 27."

159 "Sewell Takes Title in 'Mural Shot Put." *DT*, 21 April 1953, p. 2.

"Phi Kappa Psi, SAE, Kappa Sigma, Oak Grove, Theleme, and McCracken maneuvered into intramurals' track and field spotlight Monday, and clearly indicated they'd be in the thick of the championship scramble that materializes next week." Morris reviews the principal contests.

160 "Divisional Finals Slated Wednesday." *DT*, 22 April 1953, p. 2.

"One of the finest aggregates of softball outfits in 'mural history assemble Wednesday as divisional playoffs get underway." Morris summarizes the competitions in the Class A and Class B divisions.

161 "SPE, Theta Chi in A Finals." *DT*, 23 April 1953, p. 2.

C. B. Sumrall "twirled his Sigma Phi Epsilon mates into intramurals' Class A fraternity finals Wednesday. The aged vet whiffed three batsmen with the potential tying runs on the paths in the last frame, as the SPE's edged powerful Phi Gamma Delta, 2–0." Morris relates "the story behind" the Class A and Class B softball divisional playoff games.

162 "Assignment Forty Acres: Texas Voters Like Yogi Berra, Tripod." *DT*, 24 April 1953, p. 6.

A humorous account of UT's election day. Although the election of student officers on April 22 seemed "devoid of its usual excitement, there was still plenty of the traditional Election Day color everywhere on the campus." For instance, there was an "impressive slate of write-in votes unearthed by the talliers. Yogi Berra, Cymbeline, and Abe Lincoln, all received write-in votes for president. Tripod, dog-about-the-campus, garnered a pair of votes for Cactus Associate Editor."

163 "Kappa Sigma, Oak Grove Dominate 'Mural Track." *DT*, 24 April 1953," p. 3.

"Kappa Sigma, McCracken, and Oak Grove dominated practically at every turn Thursday, and copped the '53 intramural divisional track titles at Memorial Stadium with relative ease." Includes coverage of the various events and "divisional point totals."

164 "Kappa Sigma Wins 'Mural Track Title." *DT*, 28 April 1953, p. 2.

"Spectacularity was the keynote in intramurals' traditional running of the all–University Track Meet at Memorial Stadium Monday.... High-flying Kappa Sigma, defending titlist and pre-meet favorite, virtually staged a runaway with the campus championship, tallying 26 points in so doing." Includes "summaries" of the competitions.

165 "Softball Playoffs Postponed by Rain." *DT*, 29 April 1953, p. 2.

"Old man weather put in an unwelcome visit to the Forty Acres Tuesday, and effected the postponement of a pair of all–University playoff skirmishes." Morris reports that the two softball games have been rescheduled and also reminds swimmers that "Wednesday is the final filing date for entries in the annual 'mural swimming meet."

166 "All-Star Water Polo Team Is Announced." *DT*, 30 April 1953, p. 2.

"It's all over but the reminiscing, but the '53 intramural water polo scramble will long be remembered as one of the most bitterly-contested ever." Morris names the twelve members of the "annual all–University water polo squad."

167 "Assignment Forty Acres: Co-ordinator Wears Smile Despite Sneers, Enemies." *DT*, 30 April 1953, p. 4.

Morris, writing about himself in the third person, laments that although the *Daily Texan* "Intramural Co-ordinator" tries to be "tactful" and "impartial," he is viewed as "lazy, no good, corrupt, incompetent, [and] irresponsible." However, "There is a smile upon his face, and there can be but one reason for it.... He knows that, without something to loosen its pent-up emotions upon, to dump the blame on, society would go stark raving mad."

168 "Sumrall vs. Conoley in Tonight's Finals." *DT*, 1 May 1953, p. 2.

"Newman Club, always a threat in 'mural circles, Friday finds itself in a position to produce the impossible. The impossible, purely and simply, is a clean sweep in all–University softball play." Morris reports on a recently played Newman Club victory, and he surveys the upcoming match between Newman and Sigma Alpha Epsilon in which the two teams will "square away for Class A honors."

169 "SPE Wins Crown; Swim Finals Set." *DT*, 3 May 1953, p. 2.

"A triple by catcher Joe Rohm with one on and two away in the last inning gave Sigma Phi Epsilon its second consecutive 'mural softball title (Class A) Friday night over mighty Newman Club." Includes coverage of both the game and the forthcoming swimming competitions.

170 "Delts, Sigma Chi's Swimming Champs." *DT*, 5 May 1953, p. 2.

"A perennial winner and a virtual newcomer in the always-ruggedly-contested field of intramural swimming almost produced a clean sweep in the fraternity swimming preliminaries at Gregory Gym Monday. Delta Tau Delta, defending co-titlists, and Sigma Chi, dominated practically at every turn in the six-event affair, meriting them an inside track in the Divisional Meet Thursday." Morris lists the qualifiers in the various events.

171 "Assignment Forty Acres: Mohairs Make UT History 'Victorious' in VC Defeat." *DT*, 7 May 1953, p. 3.

Two male students, costumed as Siamese twins Lotta and Notta Mohair, fail to be chosen queens of the Varsity Carnival. "Pitifully enough, the Twins were disqualified for serenading past 11 p.m. It came as a deflating blow to those many who backed the charming duo."

172 "AROTC, Grove Tie for Swimming Lead." *DT*, 8 May 1953, p. 2.

"Swimming machines representing Army ROTC and Oak Grove battled for upwards of an hour at Gregory Gym Thursday night, and finally finished in a 19–19 deadlock for intramural swimming supremacy, club division." Includes highlights of the principal competitions.

173 "Delts Take Crown in 'Mural Swimming." *DT*, 12 May 1953, p. 2.

"Delta Tau Delta's whirlwind swimming team posted one of intramurals' most stunning victories in years at Gregory Gym Monday night, and snared all–University swim honors with points to spare." Includes coverage of the matches and "tabulated results."

174 "Excitement, Upsets Highlight 1952–53 Intramural Year." *DT*, 14 May 1953, p. 2.

Morris reviews the high points of the 1952–1953 intramural year. "Intramurals, as tremendously important a phase in student life here at Texas as sunshine and rain winter and summer, has closed its books on another year — a year seasoned with its usual thrills, enlivened with a more than occasional upset, charged with its usual hard-luck stories, and dominated by a traditional presence of powerhouses."

175 "McCracken, SAE's, Grove Cop Awards." *DT*, 17 May 1953, p. 3.

"Oak Grove, Sigma Alpha Epsilon, and McCracken brought home intramurals' most prized awards, the annual All-Year Trophies, presented amidst the acclaim of some 150 colleagues Friday night." Morris reports on these and other awards "given for excellence in the vast 'mural setup."

176 "Blanket Tax Steal Favors Purchaser." *DT*, 17 September 1953, p. 1.

In Morris's first article of his sophomore year, he describes the advantages of the University of Texas Blanket Tax, "the biggest steal east of the setting sun." It "offers the buyer approximately $79.20 in entertainment for only $16.50 in actual cash. It is practically a 'must' for the UT student seeking the proverbial well-rounded education."

177 "The Round-Up." *DT*, 23 September 1953, p. 1.

An editor's note announces that "this new Texan feature, 'The Roundup,' will be initiated as a weekly column, and if reader reaction is favorable, will later appear twice a week." It will contain "anecdotes and campus philosophy," and readers are invited to send "contributions" to Morris. In his first "Round-Up" column (accompanied by his photograph), Morris writes that on campus there is a "virtually untapped reservoir of human experience and human interest. Out of this reservoir, a column is born, yours and mine, dedicated to life here at the University of Texas, to college days in all their once-in-a-lifetime color, to their solemnity, and, most of all, to their laughs." Morris follows his introductory remarks with three campus anecdotes. An editorial in this issue of the *Daily Texan* wishes him luck with his "ambitious undertaking" (item 1464).

178 "Sweltering Crowd Enjoys Sweet Longhorn Victory." *DT*, 27 September 1953, pp. 1–2.

Morris reports on the first UT football game of the academic year. "Thy favorite sport made its 1953 debut Saturday afternoon, and despite several tense moments to the contrary, ended sweet, but sweltering."

179 "The Round-Up." *DT*, 30 September 1953, p. 1.

Campus news and anecdotes collected by Morris. For example, a male student "told me this episode, which seems to be quite characteristic of pledge lines and the sort. Standers-by at the Tri-Delt pledge line last year heard this introduction: 'Bud Wiser, meet Barbara Booz.'" In addition, Morris gives humorous advice to freshmen on the "basic fundamentals" of coping with "problems" at the University of Texas. "These problems may be categorized into three classes: parking, girls, and professors. Upperclassmen generally disagree as to which is exactly the most vexing, but the campus parking problem has reached such dire extremes that only one thing remains to be done — blow up Ye Old Main Building to make room for a parking lot."

180 "The Round-Up." *DT*, 7 October 1953, p. 1.

Campus news and anecdotes collected by Morris. For example, "In the old days, UT lassies used to blush at naughty jokes. Nowadays, says Charlie, the boy down the hall, they try to memorize 'em."

181 "The Round-Up." *DT*, 14 October 1953, p. 1.

Among other campus news, Morris gives the results of a poll he conducted two days earlier of twenty-eight freshman beauty contest semi-finalists. Asked to comment on the UT males, "The lovelies deliberated for a few moments, then announced their decisions.... Seven of the lassies put UT gentlemen in the 'heavenly' class, sixteen dumped them into the average league, three judged them worthy of the mediocre (probably-kind-to-pets) division, and two placed them in the don't-see-their-dentists-twice-a-year category."

182 "The Round-Up." *DT*, 21 October 1953, p. 1.

As Election Day at the University of Texas approaches, Morris emphasizes the seriousness and "great challenge" of student government by profiling the fictitious "Stewfish Stout," a "congenial sort of fellow" who runs for and wins a position on the Student Assembly. "Assemblyman Stewfish must delve into the tangible problems of campus life. In investigating the complexities of the parking, telephone, Blanket Tax, Union, and a bevy of other questions he must recognize that the power of recommendation — in many instances the only power of student government — is influential and result-producing."

183 "The Round-Up." *DT*, 28 October 1953, p. 1.

Campus news and anecdotes collected by Morris. For instance, a popular Spanish professor "always gets a kick out of a question asked of him in a Spanish 407 class last year. A female member of the class raised her hand and asked, 'Dr. Tyler, I've been wondering a long time — do you think in Spanish or do you think in English?'" Also, on today, Election Day, Morris urges students to go to the polls. "Let's vote, shall we?"

184 "The Round-Up." *DT*, 4 November 1953, p. 1.

Campus news and anecdotes collected by Morris. A student "woke up Sunday morning in his dorm room and, to his astonishment, found the door to his room gone. He searched for a good half hour, and finally came across the door two floors down, under the staircase. Somebody had removed it as a Halloween prank." Morris also reports that students are excited about the upcoming football game against Baylor University. "Enlarged 'Beat Baylor' signs decorate greenboards in scores of classrooms."

185 "The Round-Up." *DT*, 11 November 1953, p. 1.

A character sketch of Dr. W. J. Battle, the "grand old man" of the University of Texas. Battle, who will celebrate his eighty-third birthday this month, came to the university in 1893 and has served not only as professor of classical languages but also as acting president (1914 to 1916) and dean of the faculty (1920 to 1948). "Through the years he has descended from [his office] to serve as pallbearer at a Negro coachman's funeral, design the seal of the University, teach the girls in Grace Hall to chant, and draw plans of almost every new building on the campus."

186 "Branch Gets Praise for 60-Minute Play." *DT*, 14 November 1953, p. 2.

Morris profiles Phil Branch, a UT football player. "Branch, a six-foot, 205-pound guard, has performed near-60-minute service in the Steer line this campaign. His three conversions in the scintillating tilt with Baylor last Saturday sent 13,000 Texas students home happy, and re-emphasized Phil's versatility."

187 "The Round-Up." *DT*, 18 November 1953, p. 1.

A plea for contributions to Campus Chest, a university charity. "If [all university students] could see the face of their best friend when he has been told his mother has cancer, they'd respect the Cancer Society.... If they could talk to a boy who loses all his belongings in a co-op fire, has a sick dad back home, and doesn't quite know what to do, they'd see the Contingency Fund as a wonderful thing.... So reap the benefits of a Campus Chest."

188 "Aggie Season Opens As Spirit Blazes High." *DT*, 24 November 1953, p. 1.

A page-1, headlined article reports that the UT football team will be playing its arch-rival, Texas A&M University, on Thanksgiving Day. Morris lists the upcoming festivities and declares that "anti–Aggie fervor, peren[n]ially the year's most intense manifestation of UT spirit, is gripping this sprawling campus of 14,000 like some boney-fingered sea demon, as the traditional game of games approaches. School spirit is flaming at a white-hot pace."

189 "The Round-Up." *DT*, 25 November 1953, p. 1.

As the UT Longhorns prepare to meet the Aggies of Texas A&M University on the football field, Morris pretends to eavesdrop on the conversations of "loyal spirits of long-departed Longhorns." A "general yarn-swapping period ensued.

Straining my ears, I heard several dismembered phrases—talks of grid immortals.... 'There ain't but one good kind of Aggie,' someone suddenly offered. 'That's beat Aggie. A badly beat Aggie.'"

190 "The Round-Up." *DT*, 2 December 1953, p. 1.

Campus news and anecdotes collected by Morris. For example, "He's savin' his Confederate money, boys.... His name is Robert E. Lee. He's a freshman from Temple, and he lives in Robert E. Lee Hall."

191 "The Round-Up." *DT*, 9 December 1953, p. 1.

Campus news and anecdotes collected by Morris. For instance, a recent article on smoking "asserted that a cigarette will lessen one's life span by ten minutes or thereabouts. The boys down the hall did a little figuring the other night and found out they should've been dead ten years ago."

192 "The Round-Up." *DT*, 16 December 1953, p. 1.

Morris imagines Santa Claus using a "jet-engined sleigh" on Christmas Eve. When Rudolph begs Santa, "Don't use the jet. I can lead the reindeer," Santa replies: "You're smart and you have promise but, well—you don't have you[r] BA degree yet, and you haven't so much as thought about your thesis. Prancer and Comet have two PhD's, and Dasher was a Rhodes Scholar."

193 "The Round-Up." *DT*, 6 January 1954, p. 1.

Campus news and anecdotes collected by Morris. For example, "Louise Phillips of Houston writes: 'I am very confused. It's the older generation. They tell us to keep shoulders to the wheel, our backs to the wall, our feet on the ground, our ears to the ground, and our heads out of the clouds. Yes, I'm very confused.' Want advice, Louise? Don't let it worry you. Keep your nose to the grindstone and relax."

194 "Lon Morris Edges Shorthorns, 73–72." *DT*, 10 January 1954, p. 2.

Coverage of a University of Texas–Lon Morris College basketball game. "A lanky young gentleman generally conceded to be Little all-America, coupled with a free throw of quite crucial proportions, spelt disaster for Texas' unwhipped Yearlings here Saturday night, as speedy Lon Morris squeaked by with a nail-gnawing 73–72'er in Gregory Gym."

195 "The Round-Up." *DT*, 13 January 1954, p. 1.

As students begin "settling down to exams," Morris describes the wartime UT campus of 12 January 1944. He observes that for students back then, a college education "was an essential part of the home effort. Even the V-12's [students in a US Navy officer training program], who were required to wear uniforms to class and to remain within three blocks of the campus, considered their chance at education a rare privilege.... In short, the populace of the University of Texas in 1944 was mature and grown up." Morris adds that much can transpire in ten years. "On January 12, 1954, our attitude toward education, just as toward many other things, has changed—today, I believe, we have no attitude. But we're searching."

196 "The Round-Up." *DT*, 3 February 1954, p. 1.

Campus news and anecdotes collected by Morris. For instance, "Latest Houston jargon: Sound him on the hose: (translated) phone him. Deep pocket lad: grown man. Eyes for the pad: sleepy, going to bed."

197 "The Round-Up." *DT*, 11 February 1954, p. 1.

Morris walks around the campus "absorbed in sunshine and the flow of Life and Time." Life in all its forms, from the ignorant to the indifferent to the ambitious, "flows on and on, tempered always to reality and the things at hand by the prodigious hands of Time on the Tower." Morris watches students, "within arm's length of me," typifying tragedy, loneliness, ambition, happiness, disappointment, vanity, hatred, and envy. "In this flow of Life, as one of 14,000 souls absorbed in the burning enthusiasm of a great center of knowledge and ambition, lurking on the threshold of something new, I am humbled by the insignificance of myself."

198 "1899 Valentine Conceals Child's Poignant Story." *DT*, 12 February 1954, p. 6.

Reports that the author William Sidney Porter, "who became more widely known as O. Henry," lived in Austin for twelve years. After he moved to Houston in the mid–1890s, he was charged with embezzling money from the Austin bank in which he worked, and he served a three-year prison term. His "prolific writing career" began after he settled in New York in 1902, though it was in Austin "that he developed the unique literary style destined to win for him immortality." Not long after Porter died, he was cleared of the embezzlement charges. "This, however, plagued his entire lifetime, and gave it a fiction-like poignancy." His Austin home is now operated as the O. Henry Museum.

199 "Jumping Jim: Richardson's Happy He Chose Basketball." *DT*, 16 February 1954, p. 2.

A profile of basketball player Jim Richardson, "one of the most highly-regarded clutch performers in the Southwest.... His sharp backboard work and uncanny jumping ability have prompted many Orange observers to dub him the most underrated member of the squad."

200 "Opera Preparation Just Like Circus." *DT*, 16 February 1954, p. 3.

Morris views the backstage preparations for the opera *Madame Butterfly*, which will be performed in the university gymnasium. "Gregory Gym presented itself as one seeming mass of humanity — humanity mobilized on trapezes, perched crazily atop 40-foot ladders, involved in the rather ticklish task of transforming a basketball court into a moonlit garden."

201 "The Round-Up." *DT*, 18 February 1954, p. 1.

Morris asks twenty-five persons around the campus this question: "If you had the opportunity to talk for an hour with any five people who ever lived, which five would you choose?" At the bottom of the list of responses is his own answer. "W. Morris, a hapless soul trying to escape the throes of ignorance: Christ, my great grandfather, Robert E. Lee, Whitman, the Unk[n]own Soldier." Morris poses the same question in his 30 March 1955 "Round-Up" (item 301).

202 "Longhorns 'Floor' Bears in Rough Game, 78–63." *DT*, 21 February 1954, pp. 1–2.

Coverage of a University of Texas-Baylor University basketball game. "Texas' temperamental Orange Ogres taught Baylor a bruising lesson in the fundamentals of liberal basketball Saturday evening, and proceeded with convincing finality to granulate the Bears, 78–63, before 7,000 or so irate fans."

203 "Tumblers of Good Will: Gymnast Falls for US." *DT*, 21 February 1954, p. 1.

Members of Sweden's Olympic gymnastics team, "on a leg of their fabulous 10,000-mile tour," display their skills during a performance at the University of Texas. Morris interviews Eric Linden, "commonly known in Europe as the father of Swedish gymnastics."

204 "The Round-Up." *DT*, 25 February 1954, p. 1.

Morris compares characteristics of a college "Ivy League man" with those of a "Teasip." The Ivy League student is "tradition-conscious. His great-great-grandfather studied the humanities at Ivy U. He's there now to carry on that intellectual tradition.... The Teasip doesn't give a whit for traditions. Sure, he has his Old B Halls, his Treaty Oak, but traditions and the present don't mix, and he lives solidly in the present."

205 "Wary Steer Cagers Visit Hogs Tonight." *DT*, 26 February 1954, p. 2.

Does not think the UT basketball team has much of a chance against the University of Arkansas. "Fourteen determined Texas gentlemen invade alien Ozark sod Friday, wary of the danger that lurks in their mountainous wake. The Steers challenge Arkansas' redoubtable Hogs in Fayetteville, and — let's be frank — the odds are asserting that Texas won't be stop[ping] the SWC [Southwest Conference] cage heap when it's over."

206 "Greatest Pivot?: Ellis Just Needs Confidence." *DT*, 3 March 1954, p. 2.

Although UT basketball player Ellis Olmstead looks "awkward" and "overly-slow" on the court, "his improvement has been steady and satisfying. He's big, of course, which compensates for his slowness.... But more than anything, it's his wide room for more self-assurance, sure to come with experience, which leaves anti–Longhorns worried."

207 "Steer Locker Room Happy but Quiet — Danger Ahead." *DT*, 3 March 1954, p. 2.

"The home dressing room was unusually quiet this Independence Day evening, filled with a subtle and demanding undertone of things to come." Although members of the UT basketball team "had just consumed an enjoyable evening" beating Texas Christian University, they "dwelt but a few seconds on the victory. Then, in sudden afterthought, they accepted the sudden-death showdown with Rice [University] as a grim reality of life."

208 "The Round-Up." *DT*, 5 March 1954, p. 1.

Pays tribute to Morris Williams Jr. Williams, a star golfer at the University of Texas, enlisted in the Air Force soon after graduation and died when his jet crashed on 16 September 1953. He "was recognized by sports experts as one of the best young golfers in history, and the most promising in the nation." Morris believes that in the light of Williams's death and "his unrealized hopes," members of the campus community should "re-evaluate ourselves" and "re-define our aims in life." For instance, "The athlete would do well to be a bit more cognizant of worthier goals, the scientist to exhibit more faith in purely human things, the journalist to be more tolerant, the professor to be more kindly toward young aspiration."

209 "Steers Open Playoff in Houston Tonight." *DT*, 5 March 1954, p. 3.

The UT basketball team plays Rice University this evening. "The prevailing issue these days—who's heir to the gilded [Southwest Conference] cage throne—bares itself in Houston Friday, as sturdy Texas and speedy Rice clash in the first of a scheduled two-of-three game showdown."

210 "Owls' Last-Second Goal Beats Longhorns, 72–71." *DT*, 9 March 1954, pp. 1, 3.

Reports that the Rice University Owls beat the UT Longhorns in basketball last week, 72–71. "Owl guard Sam Beavers ... provided the here-all and end-all. With 7,500 rather electrified Gregory [Gymnasium] witnesses making strange little crowd noises, Beavers doused a southpaw hook-shot in the last one-tenth second, and that—save for the split-second silence tha[t] ensued—was that."

211 "Opener in 5 Days: Linker Only Starter As Falk Continues Hunt for Hurlers." *DT*, 14 March 1954, p. 2.

The UT baseball season begins in less than a week, and Coach Bibb Falk "concedes one perplexing fact: only Boyd Linker, a righthander with blood'n fire on his fast one, is reliable as a starter.... 'It's pitching that's hurting us now,' moans Falk, whose crying towel is yet moist from March's gone by. 'One starter won't do the trick.'"

212 "The Round-Up." *DT*, 16 March 1954, p. 1.

Campus news and anecdotes collected by Morris. For example, "After weeks of anxiety, it's finally hit the campus. Last week, the Snak Shak upped coffee to ten cents." Also, "The classic remark, from a Prather Hall counselor to a roomer: 'What do you want for twenty bucks a month, running water?'"

213 "Longhorn '9' to Open Against OU Today at 3." *DT*, 19 March 1954, p. 1.

"Staunch in spots but conspicuously shallow in others, Texas' baseball team opens a new season at Clark Field Friday afternoon, and, as always, the perennial cloud of doubt hangs heavy. The Steers engage veteran Oklahoma in a two-game series here Friday and Saturday...." UT Coach Bibb Falk, "who's faced problems before, though seldom in such doleful magnitudes, finds himself thoroughly lacking in seasoned performers."

214 "Just Over-Herd: Towery's Had Enough 'Needling' for Season." *DT*, 26 March 1954, p. 2.

Brief sports stories featuring UT athletes. "Bob Towery, Texas' second baseman, is a bit dubious these days about vaccinations and such. The Fort Worth senior has been confined to the Health Center for the past week, a casualty of ROTC typhoid shots."

215 "The Round-Up." *DT*, 26 March 1954, p. 1.

Morris celebrates spring—the season in which "minds are 10,000 miles away" and "term assignments are April Fool jokes"—with a collection of campus anecdotes. "The mark of an educated man: learning to yawn with one's mouth closed in Government 610."

216 "Baseball Controversy Now Looms in Big 'H.'" *DT*, 31 March 1954, p. 2.

UT's baseball team faces Rice University today in Houston. "As Texas tries to extend its win skein to four Wednesday, there is sure to be a mild but very demanding undercurrent of experiment. [Coach Bibb] Falk will have an eye toward subversiveness in his pitching department, which has been the most vulnerable point on a rapidly brightening scene thus far."

217 "The Round-Up." *DT*, 1 April 1954, p. 1.

Campus news and anecdotes collected by Morris. For instance, "John Baker ... tells of a rainy, Spillanish April 1 back in '49. Someone led a cow into Hogg Auditorium and left her there. That night, as the thunder thundered and the rain rained, the caretaker of the auditorium had occasion to enter. Halfway down the aisle, in total darkness, he bumped into Bossie. 'Only human stampede in history caused by a milk cow,' says Baker."

218 "Mohr's Big Stick Powers UT Past Froggies, 13–3." *DT*, 11 April 1954, pp. 1–2.

Coverage of a UT-Texas Christian University baseball game in Austin. "The Longhorns discarded the wraps of a five-game hitting stupor to thump erratic TCU, 13–3, before some 2,000 Clark Field loyals."

219 "The Round-Up." *DT*, 13 April 1954, p. 1.

Early one morning, an "owl-eyed frosh" accidentally comes across a sack "on which a poem was written and a note attached: 'I have found in Texas an unrhymed poem. I dedicate this to all of you. Walt Whitman.'" The five-stanza poem, titled "The Poet of UT," ends with these lines: "Bound together to thousands, / By only a school song, a oneness of purpose, / Hating college on days when spirits are low, / Knowing well its faults, its shame, / Yet loving it still for what it is and as the writer says, / Loving not so much for, but despite, / Not for its virtues, but despite its faults." Morris often quoted variations of the last two lines, a passage by William Faulkner, when writing of his affection for Mississippi. Interestingly enough, at the end of his narrative in *My Mississippi*, he implies that he was in college "when I first came across these words." Slightly revised for the *Daily Texan* of 16 March 1955 (item 292).

220 "'Horns, Huskies Collide in Doubleheader Today." *DT*, 15 April 1954, p. 2.

"A pair of bigtime baseball monarchs, Texas and Nebraska, collide in a twin bill at Clark Field [in Austin] Thursday, to test—for the time being, at least—the reputed purity of the Southwest baseball strain."

221 "The Round-Up." *DT*, 23 April 1954, p. 1.

Morris and "a sprinkling of well-rehearsed stooges" use a tape recorder, a portable radio, and "the workings of an unusually sordid imagination" to play a hoax on some fellow students. Morris and his friends "began by recording music. Then we interrupted, reporting that the Russians had just declared war, and dropped a bevy of A-bombs at strategic points in the Pacific." The students then reported that "Congress had declared war, and various announcers, pundits, and correspondents (disguised voices all) began to relate the awesome news." The pranksters had concealed the tape recorder under a bed and had placed a radio near the bed so sound would seem to come from the radio, not the tape recorder. One "victim" who entered the room "turned a sickly white." Another "fled for the corner and lay on his stomach." A third "sprinted from the building before anyone could catch him." After it was revealed that "the thing was a complete hoax," one of the "guinea pigs" summarized the "goings-on in a spirit thoroughly out of tune with the times. 'You know,' he said, 'fear can sometimes be pretty funny. Even in this day and time.'" See also item 150.

222 "UT Faces Waco Hex, Baylor Bears Today." *DT*, 27 April 1954, p. 2.

"A gripping plate lethargy and the menace of a Waco hex notwithstanding, [Coach] Bibb Falk's Texas Steers go against Baylor in Waco Tuesday afternoon, their eyes trained toward an early Southwest Conference baseball crown."

223 "Bears, 'Horns Blast Away in 13–13 Draw." *DT*, 28 April 1954, p. 2.

Coverage of a UT–Baylor University baseball game. "Only a good reliable extra point kicker was absent at Katy Field [in Waco] Tuesday as Texas and Baylor huffed and puffed through three and a half hours of baseball pandemonium. The [Southwest Conference] embroilment ended at 13–13...."

224 "The Round-Up." *DT*, 30 April 1954, p. 1.

Campus news and anecdotes collected by Morris. For example, a student who works part time at a local service station "reports that a carload of high school boys from Grand Prairie came to Austin Saturday to visit an old high school chum now enrolled in the University. The car stopped at the station, and the driver asked: 'Can you please tell us how to get to the schoolhouse?'"

225 "Ags Invade Clark Field at 3." *DT*, 6 May 1954, p. 2.

"Dragging the wreckage of a rather disastrous baseball season, them [Texas A&M] Aggies come to town Thursday, the potential villain in Texas' bid for premature Southwest Conference laurels."

226 "Longhorns Squeeze by Pesky Ags, 3–2." *DT*, 7 May 1954, p. 3.

Coverage of a UT–Texas A&M baseball game. "A tight pitchers' feud for seven frames degenerated into a baseball surprise package at Clark Field [in Austin] Thursday, as Texas' Steers squeezed past the Aggies, 3–2."

227 "The Round-Up." *DT*, 7 May 1954, p. 1.

Campus news and anecdotes collected by Morris. For instance, "Larry Klein, junior from Dallas, has completed [a] rather comprehensive study on Argentina's political scene. In a letter to this column, Larry suggests that the Texan run an expose on dictator Juan Person. Title it 'Juan's Other Wife' he says."

228 "The Round-Up." *DT*, 14 May 1954, p. 1.

Profiles Ronnie Dugger, who edited the *Daily Texan* during the 1950-51 academic year. After Dugger, "tousle-headed and twenty," assumed his editorial duties, he "proceeded to infuse some impalpable force into the campus, a force that caused people to stop and read and think. Indeed, his surname became synonymous hereabouts with vitality of thought and freedom of expression."

229 "First Foe in NCAA Playoffs Unknown to Texas' Bibb Falk." *DT*, 16 May 1954, p. 3.

The University of Texas baseball team has "compiled a 14–5 record for the year" and qualifies for the National Collegiate Athletic Association playoffs. Coach Bibb Falk, "who's reputed to know more baseball than just about anybody, hasn't the faintest inkling who his Longhorns' first foe in the NCAA baseball playoffs will be. No one else has the answer either."

230 "International Students Want Americanizing." *DT*, 15 September 1954, p. 5.

Addresses the "problem of inadequate integration on the part of foreign students within the University framework." Morris names individuals and organizations that have "played salient roles in making the life of the foreign student here as pleasant as the circumstances deem possible." Among the "innumerable advantages" of knowing students from non–American cultures is that "in this era of permanent international tension, we may lend our rather cloistered outlooks a much broader and tolerant view."

231 "Bevo Balks, Steers Stampede, Tower Hue's OK." *DT*, 19 September 1954, p. 1.

The first football game of the season is marked by a "bull-headed" mascot, a UT victory, and temperatures in the mid-nineties. "A quaint autumn pastime called football made its 1954 campus debut here Saturday, and — despite several highly irregular moments to the contrary — ended sweet, but sweltering."

232 "Bevo Will Trek to ND to Spoil the Irish Jig." *DT*, 21 September 1954, p. 1.

The University of Texas mascot and his "caretakers" prepare to travel to South Bend, Indiana, for the UT–Notre Dame football game. "Bevo the Bull is spending his spare time packing these days. The 1,450-pound mascot, reputed nationally to be the most mammoth of all college mascots, embarks for South Bend, Ind., Wednesday afternoon. Mission: to serve as a one-steer ambassador for Saturday's grid clash." See also items 35, 234, and 235.

233 "The Round-Up." *DT*, 22 September 1954, p. 1.

Morris believes that the "real essence of life" lies in individuals and their "hopes, fears, loves, hates, desires, despairs, [and] vanities." As a journalist, he vows that "the Texan will try to understand people. As long as there is a 'Roundup,' there will be an attempt — however clumsy and immature — to ferret out the human elements and create a semblance of literature from this teeming hodge-podge of human nature." Morris also includes several campus news stories and anecdotes.

234 "Bevo Is Sensation on Midwest Jaunt." *DT*, 24 September 1954, p. 1

The University of Texas football team plays Notre Dame tomorrow, and Morris is traveling to South Bend, Indiana, with the UT mascot, a steer named Bevo. Morris writes from Springfield, Illinois: "Notes taken on safari in the Midwest: A trailer, a '53 Pontiac, three men, and a 1,500-pound slab of beef called Bevo V seemed to take Yankee-land somewhat aback Thursday." See also items 35, 232, 235, and 1465.

235 "The Round-Up." *DT*, 29 September 1954, p. 1.

Morris recounts his journey to South Bend, Indiana. "On 6 p.m. last Wednesday, three foolhardy young Texans harnessed a four-wheel trailer to the back of a Pontiac and embarked for a gilded place of storybook and sportspage fame called Notre Dame. Accompanying the threesome was one Bevo, 1,500-pound UT mascot, who was honor-guest-to-be at a certain battle of muscular skills.... It was quite an excursion, indeed, soon impressing upon one a realization that the best things in college are tuition-free...." See also items 35, 232, and 234.

236 "A Symbol: Stoic, Stately, Enduring." *DT*, 1 October 1954, p. 10.

Morris salutes the University of Texas Tower, completed in 1937 as "Austin's newest skyscraper, the 308-foot library and new main building." He also records "a few chapters" in its historic life. "This is the Tower. A towering mass of granite, 308 feet high; an architect's miracle, rising high above our petty worldly dealings: but more, a symbol of a magna[n]i[m]ous center of learning. Stoic, lonely, as it stands there it has somehow worked its way into the timeworn fiber of many lives."

237 "The Round-Up." *DT*, 6 October 1954, p. 1.
Morris includes a paragraph on the marital separation of actress Marilyn Monroe and baseball star Joe DiMaggio among other brief news stories and campus anecdotes. "This week's condolences: 11,023 UT gentlemen wish to extend their deepest sympathies to Mr. Marilyn Monroe in his hour of loss, with the one hope that the Yankees still love him."

238 "Townes Hall Law Students Aren't Aloof, Just Apart." *DT*, 7 October 1954, p. 3.
Morris addresses the campus community's misconceptions about law students and the law school building, Townes Hall. "To the average UT'er, the School of Law has always been pictured as a never-never land of dusty, yellowed volumes, inhabited by a species of natives mystically identified as Legal Minds.... And yet, recent studies have shown that the typical UT law student leads a wholesome, undiluted life these days."

239 "8,000 Students Make Exodus for Fall's Fabulous Weekend." *DT*, 8 October 1954, p. 1.
UT students get ready to "make the 200-mile jaunt" to Dallas so they can cheer on the Longhorns in a weekend football game against the University of Oklahoma Sooners. "An exodus much comparable to pioneer goldrush days begins early Friday, when the first waves of some 8,000 brash Texas students embark on a traditional week end of society and football. Dallas has braced its sprawling self for the collegiate influx...."

240 "The Round-Up." *DT*, 13 October 1954, p. 1.
Morris profiles "some people I know. If you've been here long, the odds are even-up you've seen them, talked to them, for ... they have contributed something fine and lasting to this University-city." The four individuals include the owner of a campus snack shop, an elevator operator, a dormitory porter, and the owner of a local drug store.

241 "Texas Loyals Wary, Poised for Porkers." *DT*, 16 October 1954, p. 1.
The University of Arkansas Razorbacks face off against the Texas Longhorns on the football field today in Austin. "University-town on the day of battle is poised, anxious, and a bit wary. For Saturday afternoon Mr. Bowden H. Wyatt brings a presumptuous band of Arkansas hill-folk into the city, whose intentions, it is rumored, won't altogether be to impress the ladies in Austin Sewing Circles Number Three and Four."

242 "Triumph, Tragedy Give New Concept." *DT*, 17 October 1954, p. 4.
The University of Texas is observing UN Week, and Morris "diagnose[s] the nine-year record" of the United Nations by reviewing the organization's accomplishments and failures. After discussing them, he asks: "Whence do they lead? The world has been thoroughly psychoanalyzed in the last nine years, to the end that the function of the UN in world affairs has taken on a new, more conservative concept." The "prospects" for the world parliament "appear rather bright, even when measured by a yardstick of modern common sense."

243 "The Round-Up." *DT*, 20 October 1954, p. 1.
Morris presents some "thoughts on turning 20." He admits that he and others who will soon "abandon our foolhardy teens for a world of men" will "greet adulthood with varying degrees of disillusion, cynicism, and apprehension." Among the people he blames for this loss of "boyish faith in people and things" are indifferent members of the campus community, instructors who fail "to offer a brief, passing word of encouragement" to a confused student, and "girls with pretty blue eyes" who have lost their "humility" because of the "warped 4–1" male/female student ratio. Consequently, "As we leave boyish things behind, we must nevertheless preserve the remnants of our boyish idealism, tempering it with a keen awareness of the ugly. Doing this, we shall see the sham in life become more and more insignificant while the beautiful in life becomes more and more significant — all at 20." Morris's column spurred two readers to contribute letters to the editor, with the second letter prompting a third person to write:

A Wright, Jim. "Please, Mr. Morris." *DT*, 21 October 1954, p. 3.
"Surly Jim Wright" objects to being misquoted in Morris's "scandal sheet."

B Fick, Will. "At Ease, Boy." *DT*, 29 October 1954, p. 3.
Sympathizes with Morris as he "blast[s] all manner of things," but finds his complaints to be "rebuttable." He concludes that "you're looking for Utopia — a 'brave new world.' It isn't available here, but what we have is pretty nice."

C Davidson, Bob. "Shame on You." *DT*, 3 November 1954, p. 3.

Takes Will Fick to task for criticizing Morris and his "fine" column (item 243-B). "Morris has hit upon something close to home for most of us. And, as one turning twenty, he has written for twenty-year-olds, not for men so experienced in the ways of the world as you, Mr. Fick."

244 "Longhorn Ace Linker to Be Pitching for US." *DT*, 21 October 1954, p. 2.

Baseball pitcher Boyd Linker, "the fellow who right-handed his way in the chief slot on Texas' mound staffs in '53 and '54, is exchanging his spikes for a pair of marching boots. He'll report to Oklahoma City next week for induction into the Army."

245 "4:30 Airport Rally to Send Steers South." *DT*, 22 October 1954, p. 1.

UT plays Rice University in football this weekend, and "some 4,000 Longhorn loyals [will] make a 160-mile jump southeastward to Houston Friday and Saturday."

246 "Bushbeaters, Ho! It's Election Time." *DT*, 24 October 1954, p. 1.

A summary of campus Election Week activities. "Bushbeating, speechmaking, and party caucusing are due to strike their shrillest notes between now and Wednesday morning, when UT's citizenry goes to the polls. Forty-five candidates will aspire for 25 Student Assembly seats."

247 "The Round-Up." *DT*, 27 October 1954, p. 1.

Morris predicts that today "will be a typical UT election day. Apathy among the masses, per usual, will be the prime feature." Nevertheless, the "UT election season, with all its ills and shortcomings, is indeed a tradition, one that perennially supplies the campus cynics with grumbles, the idealists with praises, and the groundkeepers with enough sweeping up to keep them away from the family for a month."

248 "Lady Jurors, GI Voters Hang in Balance Tuesday." *DT*, 31 October 1954, p. 6.

Reports that on November 2, Texans will vote on a number of state constitutional amendments. One proposal, which was "long since thrashed out by all states except five," would allow women to serve on juries. Another "would permit military personnel who entered the service in Texas to vote if they can satisfy certain conditions."

249 "Light Vote Expected Today As National Elections Begin." *DT*, 2 November 1954, p. 1.

"White-hot campaigns end in a brash flurry of political noisemaking Tuesday, as America settles herself to the task of choosing the party she will follow for the next two years." In Morris's election-eve news coverage, he observes that "the ultimate effect of Tuesday's voting may be condensed to the bluntness of one interrogative: Have the people of America been satisfied with the first two years of the Ike administration?"

250 "The Round-Up." *DT*, 3 November 1954, pp. 1, 6.

A fictitious narrative presumably fashioned from actual incidents at the University of Texas. "Many years ago in the land of Vanity, a kingdom of dwarf-like pygmies high in the clouds, there was a school for the young people called Whittle University. Here, from the farms and the teeming elites of Vanity, young pygmies convened for four long years to learn how to whittle." See also items 267, 290, 425, and 492.

251 "Symphonette Director Worked with Toscanini." *DT*, 5 November 1954, p. 6.

Summarizes the career of violinist and concertmaster Mishel Piastro, "who will direct the Longines Symphonette in Gregory Gym Monday."

252 "New Dorms to Help in Future Difficulties." *DT*, 7 November 1954, p. 3.

Morris announces that "three brand-new dorms will be opened next fall," but because the university population is "ballooning," he believes that "the housing picture is apt to go from bad to worse."

253 "Election Medley: They Still Like Ike, But Ike Did Not Run." *DT*, 9 November 1954, p. 4.

Reviews the results of the November 2 election races. "Tuesday's election turned out to be a political landslide, senior grade. For if the voting proved nothing else, it did prove this: Youth must be served by a cool, old-head Congress." This issue of the *Daily Texan* is incorrectly dated November 10.

254 "The Round-Up." *DT*, 10 November 1954, p. 1.

Morris details the early–1930s campus political career of Allan Shivers, who was "destined a decade and a half later" to become governor of Texas. "Those were the uncouth days of University politics, when ... Allan Shivers carried student voters in the palm of his hand." Morris observes that "as fate had it, the student president with the zest for controversy kept right on winning."

255 "The Round-Up." *DT*, 17 November 1954, p. 1.

Among Morris's campus news is his announcement that his dog Skip turns ten years old today. "Nine and a half years ago a Mississippi grammar school kid with an uncontrollable mop of hair and a black-and-white terrier with an uncontrollable left ear met for the first time. Not long after, their acquaintance blossomed into that rare man-animal friendship the poets love to talk about."

256 "Grid Holiday Petitions Grow; No Aggie Infiltration So Far." *DT*, 23 November 1954, p. 1.

The UT campus is preparing for its Thanksgiving-week festivities, which feature a pep rally and bonfire, a rally parade, and a football game with its arch rivals, the Aggies of Texas A&M University. "Some 500 more student signatures were affixed to Aggie-Holiday petitions Monday, upping to 1,500 those petitioning for a day off next week in event Texas whips A&M."

257 "The Round-Up." *DT*, 24 November 1954, p. 1.

Campus news and anecdotes collected by Morris. For example, "Munzer Khair and Sabri Malki, both seniors, resided all their lives on the same street in Damascus, Syria, a few blocks apart. They met for the first time at an International Students' meeting here at the University."

258 "6,000 Farmers Invading Austin." *DT*, 25 November 1954, p. 1.

Coverage of the "pre-game activities" that lead up to the Thanksgiving Day football game between UT and Texas A&M. "University-city's traditionally busiest day of them all materializes Thursday, with a quaint autumnal pastime called football due to take king-sized attention."

259 "The Round-Up." *DT*, 1 December 1954, pp. 1, 3.

Although many people think that students at UT are "unforgiveable [sic] wrong-doers" who are all "going to hell on a greased slide," Morris finds that "the University student body leans toward religion rather than away from it." He furnishes statistics on the high percentage of Methodist, Baptist, Catholic, and Presbyterian students, concluding that "today, more than ever before, the way is opening for the University to become one of the finest student religious centers in the nation." Revised as "Lies and Rumors: Digest Facts—Show These to the Folks" for the *Summer Texan* of 12 August 1955 (item 343).

260 "Best Solution Must Be Slow." *DT*, 5 December 1954, p. 5.

In the wake of the Supreme Court decision *Brown v. Board of Education of Topeka*, three juxtaposed columns address integration in the public schools. The first is preceded by "Now...," the second by "Tomorrow...," and the third — Morris's article — by "...Or Someday." Morris argues that hasty steps toward desegregation must be avoided, as "this question of actual equal political and social rights for Negroes involves such fundamental changes not only in superficial customs and manners, but in inbred ideas and ideals, that only a patient and comradely approach to the problem can be of permanent good." He believes that the "solution" will be found by "white and Negro leaders working in harmony."

261 "The Round-Up." *DT*, 8 December 1954, p. 1.

Among Morris's campus anecdotes and news stories are criticisms of higher education from Robert M. Hutchins, "the gentleman who has mashed a few staid academic toes in his lifetime." Hutchins contends that "'American universities are becoming high class flop houses where parents send their children to keep them off the labor market and out of their hair.'" Morris segues into a commentary on "this whole nightmare" of students' "rigorous schedules" and "sleepless nights." He insists that "someone must deal with one fundamental question: does our academic system insure a healthy — both physical and mental — atmosphere of learning?"

262 "Krekeler Says Germany Able, Not Happy About Re-Arming." *DT*, 10 December 1954, p. 1.

"The people of Germany are willing, able, and prepared — but not happy — to accept rearmament, Dr. Heinz L. Krekeler, West Germany's ambassador to the United States, told a standing-room-only crowd of 500 in Batts Hall Auditorium Thursday night." Morris provides coverage of the ambassador's speech.

263 "The Round-Up." *DT*, 15 December 1954, pp. 1, 6.

Narrates a Christmas story in which an angel came to earth to counsel Gregor Eastridge, a discouraged UT student. The young man told the angel that he was not going home for the holidays because "I'm all out of step, I guess. I don't understand things." As the angel spoke to Eastridge, all the other angels "listened anxiously. For they saw the boy as all youth that has ever lived and that ever will live,... and they saw his boyish cynicism as the cynicism of all ages and all creeds, and they saw his conflict between early idealism and cold fact diluted into the whole mysterious chemistry of growing up." When the angel finished speaking, "He looked the boy in the face and sighed. 'You must never, ever lose your faith in the innate goodness of everything.'" Eastridge walked back to his dormitory. "Somewhere he heard a radio playing 'White Christmas.' From under the bed he pulled out his battered old suitcase."

264 "Longhorns Meet Powerful Ponies in Southwest Conference Opener." *DT*, 4 January 1955, p. 2.

This evening the UT basketball team hosts the Mustangs of Southern Methodist University. "Texas peels the wraps off its 1955 Southwest cage season Tuesday night in Gregory [Gymnasium], but the new year promises very little indeed in the way of redemption for a drab December. With nine consecutive failures breathing down their battered young backs, the Steers make a go against SMU at 8 p.m."

265 "The Round-Up." *DT*, 5 January 1955, p. 1.

Morris offers "a few retrospective salutes and sour-faced side glances ... at the end of a cantankerous old year and the start of a brand-new one." For instance, "To Ronnie Dugger, a great editor of a potentially great newspaper, the Texas Observer." In Morris's later writings and speeches, he often would refer to television as "that great silencer of conversation." Here he writes: "To television, which is fast transforming us into a country of introverts and unsociables."

266 "Texas Falls to Mustangs, 74–51: Before Small Turnout Longhorns Drop Tenth." *DT*, 5 January 1955, p. 2.

"Lack-luster Texas passed and shot with slim success Tuesday night at Gregory Gym and muffed its [Southwest Conference] opener to hot-and-tepid SMU [Southern Methodist University], 74–51.... It was the tenth loss in a bloody row for the Steers...."

267 "The Round-Up." *DT*, 12 January 1955, pp. 1, 6.

A fictional story about Whittle University that is likely based on true events at the University of Texas. "'Twas indeed a proud place, this Whittle U. Its handsome corps of instructors were world authorities on, say, the backward whittle, and big toehold whittle." Slightly revised for "The Round-Up" of 11 January 1956 (item 425). See also items 250, 290, and 492.

268 "Just Over-Herd: Censure Wyatt, Senators Avow." *DT*, 13 January 1955, p. 2.

A compilation of brief sports-related news stories. Although football star Bowden C. Wyatt agreed to play for the University of Arkansas, he "inked a pact with his own Tennessee last week." Consequently, "The Arkansas Senate, or a portion thereof, put an official stamp of ill favor on Bowden.... In a resolution introduced by four senators, the lawmakers were asked to censure Wyatt for 'deliberately, intentionally and wholly repudiating his contract with the University of Arkansas.'"

269 "Morris Muses: The Texan Gives Semester Salute." *DT*, 1 February 1955, p. 2.

"At the end of a cantankerous old semester and the start of a new, our thoughts turn: To the sports loyalists at Texas University. With each of you the Texan hopes to share a spring filled with more than the usual share of sports activity." Additional "salutes" fill Morris's column, such as, "To Ted Williams, the man who shouldn't quit." A photograph of Morris, "Sports Editor of The Texan," accompanies his new column, which he titles "Morris Muses."

270 "Santee, DiMag, Doak: They Made the News." *DT*, 1 February 1955, p. 2.

A summary of "day-to-day" sports news from January 18 through January 29. "While 16,043 denizens of University-city disappeared into the nightmarish mire of final examinations, matched academic wits for two weeks, then folded their notebooks like PE majors and silently stole away, the world of sports stayed open for business."

271 "The Round-Up." *DT*, 2 February 1955, p. 1.

Campus news and anecdotes collected by Morris. For instance, "Sara Lynn of Dallas, University student now doing practice teaching, writes in about the time she allowed her third grade class, predominantly boys, to choose their own subject for a theme. They selected 'Why I Like Dogs Better Than Girls.'"

272 "Morris Muses: Texan to Answer 10 Big Questions." *DT*, 3 February 1955, p. 2.

The *Daily Texan* sportswriters "promise a crystal-clear picture of this spring's sport scene." In his "Morris Muses" column (see item 269), Morris lists ten questions concerning various sports and players that "we hope to answer, in varying degrees."

273 "Auburn Coach Charlie Waller May Fill Texas Grid Vacancy." *DT*, 4 February 1955, p. 1.

Announces that UT will likely hire "Charlie Waller, young grid assistant at Auburn," as its new backfield coach of the football team. "Negotiations with the 33-year-old Waller look 'very, very favorable,' authorities in the athletic department said late Thursday."

274 "Morris Muses: Texas Could Use This Guy Waller." *DT*, 4 February 1955, p. 2.

A compilation of brief sports-related news stories. "Charlie Waller, the precocious backfield strategist at Auburn, would indeed be a gold filling in the gap left by assistant coach Eck Curtis. And it looks as if he's on his way. We hope so."

275 "Morris Muses: Layne Enhances Inaugural Drills." *DT*, 8 February 1955, p. 2.

A few sports-related news stories. "It couldn't have been a better day for the opening of spring grid socials. The wind was brisk, the sky was clear, and the occasion was doubly enhanced by the presence of one Robert Layne, a blond-thatched connoisseur of the tossed football."

276 "The Round-Up." *DT*, 9 February 1955, p. 1.

Campus news and anecdotes collected by Morris. For example, "Dr. W. L. Brown, associate professor of psychology, tells his classes of the student who left UT for A&M, thereby raising the intelligence quotient of both institutions."

277 "Morris Muses: Reds Vacation in Afghanistan." *DT*, 10 February 1955, p. 2.

A compilation of brief sports-related news stories. "Pravda, Russian newspaper of sorts, reports the members of the Soviet Olympic squad are having an enjoyable time training in Afghanistan for the '56 games. We aren't surprised. For years, in fact, we've been scraping our funds to summer in north Afghanistan."

278 "Morris Muses: Grid Swap-Over Could Pay Off." *DT*, 11 February 1955, p. 3.

A compilation of brief sports-related news stories. "Sam Blair, last year's Texan sports editor, dropped us a line from Dallas Thursday. He's with the Dallas Morning News, turning out some good work — but last year's Texan readers probably won't be surprised." This article marks the last appearance of the author's "Morris Muses" column. Beginning in March he adopts a title he has used sporadically before, "Just Over-Herd" (see item 283).

279 "The Round-Up." *DT*, 16 February 1955, p. 1.

Campus news and anecdotes collected by Morris. For instance, friends of freshman Tubba Keesler "tell this story. Tubba was running the 880-yard event on the Grand Prairie High [School] track team in Dallas one afternoon.... Before the event started, the coach called him to one side: 'Keesler,' he said, 'I'm not going to let you run today. You'll throw us late getting home.'"

280 "The Round-Up." *DT*, 23 February 1955, p. 1.

Although Morris has tried "to become academic and urban and well-kept" at the University of Texas, he still misses his hometown. "And this is why the staunch old American pull of home affects me. It is born of many things, but mostly of loneliness and love, of people known and people forgotten, of a hillside cemetery and sweet-potato pie, of a country curve and a sweaty baseball suit,... of the dance band at midnight and the urgency of noon. All the lost and dead moments of youth and going-away have become a part of me, and I a part of them." Republished in *Shifting Interludes* (item 78) and as "Far-Away Student Writes Recollections of Home Town" in the *Yazoo City Herald* (item 806). Morris's column spurred a reader to write to the *Daily Texan*, and his remarks prompted another letter:

A Brown, Jack. "Just Ask Willie!" *DT*, 25 February 1955, p. 3.

Mocks the sentimentality of Morris's essay as well as the author's writing style. "Here are the country curve answers to those fundamental questions of life-on-earth, that life-and-death struggle. And written by a man (sic) born of loneliness and love, just as I was born of man and woman."

B Wiggins, Jack L. "To Willie." *DT*, 1 March 1955, p. 4.

Congratulates Morris on his "very exceptional" column and urges him "to stand fast against the critic who in his perverse glee will put the axe to any new-growing sprout of genius."

281 "4 Sophomores Chosen to Texan's Honor Five." *DT*, 25 February 1955, p. 2.

"Youth overshadowed experience in the first annual Daily Texan All–SWC [Southwest Conference] basketball quint selected Thursday. Four sophomores, all of whom swept across the 1955 Southwest cage scene with a common disrespect for age, acquired berths on the first squad."

282 "Orange Noses White but Fondren Shines." *DT*, 27 February 1955, p. 2.

UT football players compete against each other in a game. "An evasive young gentleman named Walter Fondren dominated all save the scoreboard timekeepers this muggy Saturday afternoon, as a veteran-guided Orange team outlasted the White, 40–35, in the spring football finale."

283 "Just Over-Herd: Souchak Prayed, Birdied, Got $6,000." *DT*, 1 March 1955, p. 2.

A compilation of brief sports-related news stories. Mike Souchak, "the ex–Duke gridder," won "$6,000 (24,000 beers) in the high-paying Houston Open this week end. That's $22 a stroke."

284 "The Round-Up." *DT*, 2 March 1955, p. 1.

Campus news and anecdotes collected by Morris. For example, "Thanks to Howard McCann, Houston freshman: 'Late to bed and / Early to rise, / Keeps your roommate / From using your ties.'"

285 "State Schoolboy Meet Opens This Morning." *DT*, 3 March 1955, p. 1.

The thirty-fifth annual University Interscholastic League State Tournament, "the kingfish of Texas' schoolboy cage industry," begins today, Thursday, in Gregory Gymnasium and will finish late Saturday. During the event, a "sizeable cross-section of the state's basketball loyalists" will have "consumed stacks of Gregory hotdogs [and] watched some 24 basketball games."

286 "3-A, 4-A Teams Open Tourney Slate Today." *DT*, 4 March 1955, p. 6.

Coverage of the University Interscholastic League State Tournament taking place at UT from March 3 through March 5. "Four Conference 3-A and four Conference 4-A quints open up in state [basketball] tourney activity Friday afternoon."

287 "Crozier Tech Wins 4-A; 3-A Goes to Victoria: Waco Bounced in Last Seconds." *DT*, 6 March 1955, pp. 1, 8.

Morris reports on a University Interscholastic League State Tournament championship game that was played in UT's Gregory Gymnasium. "Mammoth A. C. Black registered a tie-snapping jump shot in the last seventeen seconds Saturday night as Crozier Tech nipped Waco, 59–57, for 4-A schoolboy basketball supremacy."

288 "Sports Whirl." *DT*, 8 March 1955, p. 3.

A compilation of brief sports-related news stories. "Don't look now, but the Texas baseball lid-lifter is precisely ten days off. Clark Field reports have it that [Coach] Bibb Falk will start Clinton Irby, the San Antonio fireman, in the opener."

289 "Here's What to Do When a Tornado Hits." *DT*, 9 March 1955, p. 3.

Morris provides "several rudimentary facts about tornadoes" in an essay that was the 1955 winner of the annual Clarence E. Gilmore award "for the best editorial or interpretative article written by a University of Texas student on some phase of safety."

290 "The Round-Up." *DT*, 9 March 1955, p. 1, 4.

Another tale about Whittle University (see also items 250, 267, 425, and 492), whose story line is probably based upon factual circumstances at the University of Texas. For example, Whittle University's totem pole bears a resemblance to UT's Tower. "And arising upward from the geographic center of Whittle U ... was a totem pole, which stood as an immutable symbol of grandeur of this place."

291 "Steers, Okies Tangle in Inaugural Friday." *DT*, 13 March 1955, p. 2.

Reports that on March 18, UT will face the University of Oklahoma in the Longhorns' first baseball game of the season.

292 "The Round-Up." *DT*, 16 March 1955, pp. 1, 3.

A revision of the poem "The Poet of UT" from the 13 April 1954 issue of the *Daily Texan* (item 219). "This column's three readers, all fine, upstanding car-hops, have requested we reprint a bit of nonsense done last year. Owing two of them money and having just borrowed the other's bird dog, we hasten to comply."

293 "Just Over-Herd: Texas' Laugh-Man Uses Sound Effects." *DT*, 17 March 1955, p. 2.

A compilation of brief sports-related news stories. "Russell Boone, the artistic Sweeny center who passed up a Texas basketball scholarship at the last moment and enrolled at Tyler Junior College, was named to the all–American Junior College quint Wednesday."

294 "Pitcher Undecided on Eve of Opener." *DT*, 17 March 1955, p. 2.

States that UT will open its baseball season tomorrow in a home game against the University of Oklahoma, and "the salient question of the day hereabouts" is: who will be the starting pitcher? Coach Bibb Falk "was undecided at Wednesday practice sessions. In typical Falkian tradition, the starter won't be chosen 'till game time."

295 "Longhorn '9' to Open Against Sooners at 3." *DT*, 18 March 1955, p. 1, 2.

Today the University of Texas Longhorns "unravel their 1955 baseball slate against Oklahoma.... Some 3,000 Steer partisans are expected to turn up for Opening Day and 500 hundred [sic] or so more will be on hand Saturday when the same two squads get together."

296 "Steers Fall to Okies; Play Here Monday." *DT*, 20 March 1955, p. 1.

At UT's Clark Field on Saturday afternoon, March 19, "Oklahoma wrecked Texas' debut series hopes, 14–6, before 1,500 fans." The Steers also "dropped a 2–1 squeaker to the Sooners in Friday's inaugural" baseball game.

297 "The Round-Up." *DT*, 23 March 1955, p. 1.

Campus news and anecdotes collected by Morris. For instance, "some weeks ago" two students formed a petroleum corporation, and recently a Dallas company telephoned one of the young men, Tom LeBleu. "His roommate answered. 'We'd like to speak with Mr. LeBleu,' the official said. 'Is he in the office now?' 'No. He's in class,' the roommate answered."

298 "Just Over-Herd: Versatility Keynotes Pup's Performance." *DT*, 24 March 1955, p. 2.

A compilation of brief sports-related news stories. "The Castroville (pop. 950) Chamber of Commerce is doing neatly executed double somersaults this week. Reason: Tom Jungman and Ron Keller, Texas righthanders who have collected the Steers' first two wins, are hometown boys."

299 "Tough TCU Hosts Falks in 2 Games." *DT*, 25 March 1955, p. 2.

UT Coach Bibb Falk's Steers "launch their 1955 [Southwest Conference] slate" today against Texas Christian University at Fort Worth. "Texas, defending champ, enters the two-game set as the decided underdog, primarily because of a notoriously weak pitching corps."

300 "Longhorns Triumph, Tie in Twosome with Frogs." *DT*, 27 March 1955, pp. 1–2.

"Texas got the pitching it wasn't supposed to have here Saturday, and tripped TCU [Texas Christian University], 5–1, in a wintry Southwest Conference baseball inaugural. The nightcap, called after nine [innings] due to darkness, ended 1–1."

301 "The Round-Up." *DT*, 30 March 1955, pp. 1, 6.

Morris undertakes the same "experiment in humanity and the ages" that he wrote about in his column of 18 February 1954 (item 201). "We initially tried the thing last spring, and were surprised at the philosophical dust it kicked up.... We asked 50 people this question: If you had the opportunity to talk to any five persons who ever lived (regardless of nationality or age), for one hour each, whom would you choose?" Thirty-five persons "agreed to contribute" and Morris publishes their answers.

302 "Ponies Bump Steers; Play Again Today." *DT*, 31 March 1955, p. 2.

Southern Methodist University "got the pitching and the breaks at [UT's] Clark Field Wednesday, and crushed Texas, 5–3, before 3,000 sunny-day fans."

303 "Just Over-Herd: Wes Santee's Mile; A Once-in-a-Lifetime." *DT*, 3 April 1955, p. 3.

Morris's sports-related news items center on what was "seen and heard around the Memorial track Saturday afternoon: The way all eyes centered on Wes Santee, whose historic performance in the Jerry Thompson Mile will keep onlookers stocked in cinder talk for a long time."

304 "Wes Santee Runs Fastest American Mile in 4:00.5: Okie Aggies Garner Mythical Team Title." *DT*, 3 April 1955, p. 1.

"Wes Santee almost did it Saturday. The great Kansas miler established a new American record for the mile at the Texas Relays Saturday afternoon, but fell shy of the 4-minute mark by a flimsy one-half second."

305 "The Round-Up." *DT*, 6 April 1955, p. 1.
Morris believes that he, more "than any one person," has known "this University-city in the still void of the night." He describes the beauty of the night and why it appeals to him instead of the "cringing and artificial" day. "You are filled with a confidence that, here in the night, here in the solitude, here on the face of this strange city of books and formulas, you have found the very thing which you lost in the day — the promise, the dream and the hope, the strength, the way of life, and the wisdom."

306 "The Round-Up." *DT*, 13 April 1955, p. 1.
Campus news and anecdotes collected by Morris. For example, "Billy Rhodes of Houston writes in about the Texan who had such a poor memory he forgot the Alamo." (Rhodes grew up with Morris in Yazoo City, Mississippi.)

307 "Just Over-Herd: Don't Miss Sammy — He's Got a Future." *DT*, 14 April 1955, p. 2.
A compilation of sports-related news stories. "Jack Trench, frosh baseball coach, was with the Chicago Cubs at the age of 17."

308 "The Round-Up." *DT*, 20 April 1955, pp. 1, 5.
Morris prints the "main points borrowed in context from the far[e]well editorials of eight former Texan editors. I think they warrant a re-per[us]al, for they represent the greatest embodiment of each man's own personal philosophy as molded and re-molded by the people, places, and things of this University."

309 "Bibb a la Mode: Rome Didn't Know." *DT*, 26 April 1955, p. 3.
Anecdotes featuring UT baseball coach and "inimitable baseball strategist" Bibb Falk. As a sergeant during World War II, Falk was in charge of an Air Force base baseball team. The field was in poor shape, and he put a squad of soldiers "to the task of manicuring it into Triple A shape." Eight hours later, the men were still hard at work. "'Hey Sarge,' one of the soldiers finally said. 'How about easing up? Rome wasn't built in a day.' 'I know,' Falk replied. 'But I wasn't on that job.'"

310 "The Round-Up." *DT*, 6 May 1955, p. 1.
In response to a letter-writer who "requests a 'candid literary shot' of life in this University-city," Morris "bring[s] forth those few moments which serve — not to represent, but to beautify — three years of inexplicable academic living." His "recollections" include: "A night watchman whistling softly to himself in the night. A group of philosophy professors watching a baseball game and eating peanuts. And your wondering if a knuckleball fitted into their scheme of things.... A colored porter who sweeps rooms from 7:30 to 5 and sometimes talks to you — the child of the South — about books and football and sometimes segregation. And one day you realize he is your friend, and you are glad."

311 "The Round-Up." *DT*, 13 May 1955, p. 1.
Campus news and anecdotes collected by Morris. For instance, in an intramural track race, a student "finished eighth in a field of just that many. 'I didn't mind the man in the wheelchair passing me,' he commented later to observers. 'But the fellow with the crutches crowded me off the track.'"

312 "Criticism Began in Painter's Time." *DT*, 15 May 1955, p. 3.
Reports that in 1945, UT President T. S. Painter adopted the current faculty promotion system, a policy that "continues to draw critical volleys."

313 "Education, Politics in Regents' Work." *DT*, 19 May 1955, p. 4.
Morris explains the duties of the Board of Regents, "the official policy-making body of the University, and the governing board of the University system."

314 "The Round-Up." *DT*, 20 May 1955, p. 1.
Now that "the year has yawned away into the incorrigible ritual" of final examinations, Morris facetiously jots down "what we anticipate for next year." The bulleted listing includes: "The Regents will ban rollerskates" and "the Representative Party will hand out portable neon signs on Election Day." See also item 498.

315 "Don't Skip This Editorial: A New Year for the Texan — We'll Play Hard and Clean." *ST*, 7 June 1955, p. 4.
Morris, who is on campus editing the paper prior to his senior year, begins adding "Texan Editor" after his byline. In his inaugural editorial, he tells his readers that the *Daily Texan* "is bigger than any one man. We will protect it and its tradition with our youth and our strength and — if necessary — with our personal reputation and physical well-being.... You will hate us, but you will respect us. And when state demagogue or campus demagogue speaks slyly of press censorship, you will help us wage the fight." Republished

in the *Daily Texan* of 18 September 1955 (item 350).

316 [Unsigned]. "Hot, Green, Southern." *ST*, 7 June 1955, p. 5.

Morris editorially quotes a paragraph by the "great American novelist" Thomas Wolfe to describe UT's campus on "graduation day" the previous Saturday. "For once, Mr. Wolfe, the stone and asphalt face of this institution seemed almost human." See also item 344).

317 [Unsigned]. "An Open Invitation." *ST*, 7 June 1955, p. 5.

Morris editorially "encourage[s] contributions" to the *Daily Texan*'s "Firing Line," the newspaper's letters to the editor page. "Don't be afraid to tell us what you think ... nor to get downright hostile toward our editorial policy. For the true measure of any newspaper is its critics—and we want hard-hitting ones.... The editor will never alter the meaning of letters, but he retains the right to shorten them so that others may also be heard.... Them's the rules. Now fire away ... we promise not to duck."

318 "Regents to Discuss Court Decision Soon." *ST*, 7 June 1955, pp. 1, 15.

"The Board of Regents will define the path the University will follow on undergraduate integration at its July meeting, President Logan Wilson said Monday." Reports that last week the Supreme Court ordered "a 'prompt and reasonable start' toward integration on a local court enforcement basis."

319 "The Round-Up." *ST*, 7 June 1955, p. 5.

Morris's first "Round-Up" as editor of UT's student newspaper. He recognizes that "a newspaper is no schoolboy proposition," and he pledges that "every word we print, utter, or delete" is for the "better interests" of the men and women of UT. He adds several paragraphs about himself and his editorial philosophy. "What about the editor? You have a right to know something about the man who will provoke sneers and censures and perhaps a few smiles during the next twelve months. Most important, he is a strong believer in a free, unhindered press. The Yankees threw his great-grandfather's presses in the town well in 1863, and he hasn't forgotten it." Republished in *Shifting Interludes* (item 79). Slightly revised for Morris's "Round-Up" of 18 September 1955 (item 351). See also item 345.

320 "The Round-Up." *ST*, 10 June 1955, p. 4.

Campus news, anecdotes, and commentaries. For example, the UT Young Democrats "were out in force at registration Tuesday," but the Young Republicans were nowhere to be seen. "With an election year ensuing, the stage is seasoned for a pair of active political groups, each sincerely concerned with bringing forth the issues."

321 "The Round-Up." *ST*, 14 June 1955, pp. 4–5.

Morris comes to the defense of idealistic young men and women after the *Houston Post* criticized students as "radical" in an editorial. "Youth, we believe, was meant to be 'radical.' Within our fibre there is something which strains with angry, impetuous strength for the ideal. We daresay each new generation since time's beginnings has been called 'radical' by the generation preceding it. And the old heads who first saw the restlessness of democracy stirring young blood must have wondered what the universe was coming to."

322 "With Mom's Help: Lyndon Sidesteps Presidential Issue." *ST*, 14 June 1955, p. 1.

Discloses that Senator Lyndon Baines Johnson refused to talk to Texas reporters who asked about "his intentions in the upcoming presidential race."

323 "Mr. Farabee's Gotta Eat: Campus Waiting Uneasily — Appellate Court Must Act." *ST*, 17 June 1955, p. 4.

Reports that although Ray Farabee was elected president of the UT Students' Association in April, he has not been able to assume his office because of "a faulty Election Bill." Morris editorially urges the appropriate persons, "in the name of humanity," to resolve the issue.

324 "The Round-Up." *ST*, 17 June 1955, p. 5.

Morris supports the student president at the University of Southern California who believes that college students should "organize and protest" when they see fit. "Furthermore, a natural hostility should exist between students and administrators, not for hostility's sake certainly, but because — within the framework of a common educational purpose — the two conflicting philosophies nonetheless remain."

325 "In Texas: Press Must Speak Truth." *ST*, 21 June 1955, p. 1, 5.

Morris interviews Pulitzer Prize–winning editor Ken Towery of Cuero, Texas, speaker at a "Newspaper Reporters' Workshop" in Austin. Towery "thinks there should be a certain detachment between a newspaper and the governing and administrative bodies of a community." When told that the *Daily Texan* editor sits on the student president's cabinet, he replied that he "would back away" from this policy. "A newspaperman should be as independent as possible. Otherwise, he will be reluctant to criticize. And criticism is very important."

326 "The Round-Up." *ST*, 21 June 1955, p. 4.
Campus news, anecdotes, and commentaries. For instance, the *Daily Texan* "took a giant reportorial stride" yesterday when reporter Joel Kirkpatrick "was admitted to a Faculty Council meeting in the Union. Sessions in the past have been closed to Texan reporters. 'The general faculty has a right to know what's going on,' Kirkpatrick told Eugene Nelson, Council secretary, before the meeting."

327 "The Round-Up." *ST*, 24 June 1955, p. 5.
Campus news, anecdotes, and commentaries. For example, in response to accusations that he has "over-subscribed to the philosophies of certain former Texan editors, and one in particular," Morris sets forth his editorial convictions. "This newspaper will be imitative of no one. This newspaper will go strictly on its own. This newspaper will go out of its way to be individualistic." The one "particular" individual, though not named, was probably 1950–51 editor Ronnie Dugger.

328 "Student Officers Ousted; Regents May Set Election." *ST*, 28 June 1955, pp. 1, 7.
Announces that yesterday the appellate court removed from office the five student Representative Party candidates who had won positions in April's UT general election. The court did, however, append "a strong 'recommendation' the officers serve in their present positions until the general fall election.... The Regents will ultimately decide if the disqualified officers can retain their posts until the fall election."

329 "The Round-Up." *ST*, 28 June 1955, p. 4.
Morris urges the campus community to support a proposed constitutional amendment that "would broaden the investment base of the Permanent Fund and thereby bring in a considerably greater amount of cash than the current 2.7 average yield." See also item 364.

330 "The Round-Up." *ST*, 1 July 1955, p. 3.
Notes that earlier in the week the appellate court recommended that deposed Representative Party candidates who had won student offices in April's election may retain their positions until the fall election in October. Although the final decision rests with the Board of Regents, its members, according to Morris, will sanction the dean's "let-them-stay proposal with little thought and less bother."

331 "The Round-Up." *ST*, 6 July 1955, p. 3.
Campus news, anecdotes, and commentaries. For instance, Paul Kirton, the law assemblyman who defended "the deposed Representative Party candidates in the recent litigation, voiced an eloquent appeal to the Assembly in its Thursday meeting. Said Kirton: 'The chief fault of the Assembly in the past has been its hesitancy to stand up for our basic rights as students. I think we should understand and defend these rights at all times.' Agreed."

332 "The Round-Up." *ST*, 8 July 1955, p. 4.
Morris is "heartened" by the "announcement that Friday's Board of Regents meeting will be open to the public and the press. This is a clear departure from the traditional 'closed door' policy. It should be a permanent one. The people must have the opportunity to know.... Foremost on the agenda is the undergraduate segregation issue, which implicates the timeworn customs of a state and a nation and draws their political and philosophical eyes squarely upon the largest university in the South."

333 "Segregation Decision Due." *ST*, 8 July 1955, p. 1.
"Undergraduate desegregation and enrollment restriction, the University's two most marked questions, will be decided in a momentous Regents' meeting here Friday." Other items "scheduled for approval" include the UT budget and faculty promotions.

334 "The Round-Up." *ST*, 12 July 1955, pp. 4, 7.
Morris responds to the UT Board of Regents' decision on July 8 to desegregate the university. "Because the University has supposedly had the largest segregated school in the world, Friday's Regential verdict undoubtedly stands as the most significant action since the May 31 Supreme Court edict" (see item 318). The Regents' determination "promises to ease tensions everywhere."

335 "The Round-Up." *ST*, 19 July 1955, p. 4.
Campus news, anecdotes, and commentaries. For example, Barefoot Sanders, former UT student president, may run for the office of state

attorney general. "Where could any politician unearth a better label than Barefoot?... It's an old Scottish name, and, like the man who owns it, a vote producer of the fondest sort."

336 "The Round-Up." *ST*, 22 July 1955, p. 4.

Campus news, anecdotes, and commentaries. For instance, Morris lists the "ten greatest presidents of the United States" in the order suggested by historian Arthur Tourtellot. "Tourtellot says presidents reflecting the mood of a nation to a very high degree are poorly regarded by history. Coolidge was such a president, and so, he believes, is Eisenhower."

337 "The Round-Up." *ST*, 26 July 1955, p. 4.

Morris prints passages from a column by Lynn Landrum, "the salty old editorialist" of the *Dallas News*, and a letter published in the Memphis *Commercial Appeal* by William Faulkner, "the salty old novelist of Yoknapatawpha County." Landrum believes that integration can be accomplished by school systems having one set of school buildings for whites, another for blacks, and a third for both races. Faulkner attacks "a Mississippi plan to establish two separate public school systems."

338 "Crucial and Controversial: Progressive Policy." *ST*, 29 July 1955, p. 4.

Morris editorially praises political leaders from the United States and Russia, who, at the Summit in Geneva, Switzerland, "sat down to a conference table without sparring." He also commends the University of Texas, which "seemed to show progressive leadership, too. It was a month of crucial policy decisions and controversial questions, and, on the whole, they were handled well. The Regents opened Texas Western to undergraduate Negroes immediately, and set the Main University integration date at September, 1956."

339 "The Round-Up." *ST*, 2 August 1955, p. 4.

Morris objects to "State Auditor C. H. Cavness' proposed financial program for universities and schools" as it will use income from the institutions' public lands, but it will not impose taxes on the state's gas, oil, and sulphur interests. "The Cavness Plan, unintentionally but effectively, leaves Texas industry untaxed at the expense of exploiting our schools' capital."

340 "The New Old South: Time Transcended." *ST*, 5 August 1955, p. 3.

An editorial concerning the integration issue at UT. "One school of thought would close the University's academic doors to Negro undergraduates. The other would welcome him, seeking to encourage the self-improvement of a suppressed race.... The University stands in the middle. It is a community of the mature and open-minded, where young prejudice ebbs low. It is ready for desegregation. It represents what many refer to as the New South. We call it the New Old South."

341 "The Round-Up." *ST*, 5 August 1955, p. 3.

News and commentaries. For instance, "Our favorite neighbor back home ... remembers the lean lad from the clay hills who came through his fraternity's rush years ago. Name was J. P. Coleman and his socks didn't match. They [black] balled him. Tuesday Coleman reached the second primary in Mississippi's gubernatorial race."

342 "The Round-Up." *ST*, 9 August 1955, p. 3.

Campus news, anecdotes, and commentaries. For example, "The Dallas News Sunday reported William Faulkner would soon make an appearance in Dallas. The campus literary set should investigate. Perhaps Austin could bag him on the same trip."

343 "Lies and Rumors: Digest Facts—Show These to the Folks." *ST*, 12 August 1955, sec. 1, p. 4.

A revision of Morris's "Round-Up" from the 1 December 1954 issue of the *Daily Texan* (item 259). Morris adds that "the great bulk of anti–University feeling today stems from an incident known as the Rainey Controversy." In November 1944, the Board of Regents fired UT President Homer Price Rainey because he was "too liberal for the politicians." When Rainey unsuccessfully ran for governor in 1946, "his opponents relied primarily on a muddy campaign aimed at 'what goes on down at the University.'" See also items 385, 386 and 471.

344 "The Round-Up." *ST*, 12 August 1955, sec. 1, p. 4.

In a column "for the upperclassmen," Morris prints passages from Thomas Wolfe's *Look Homeward, Angel.* See also item 316.

345 [Unsigned]. "The Texan Tradition." *ST*, 12 August 1955, sec. 1, p. 4.

Declares that the "tradition" of the *Daily Texan* "is one which has never faded." The newspaper is primarily a student publication, "but in bad times for this institution it has risen to heights of journalistic integrity that do credit to the profession." In this editorial, Morris quotes from his "Round-Up" of 7 June 1955 (item 319).

346 "A Thought for Freshmen: Grow to Be a Thinker..." *ST*, 12 August 1955, sec. 1, p. 1.

Morris encourages all incoming freshmen and transfer students (who will be mailed this special issue of the *Summer Texan*) to "make the most" of their college years. "Grow to be a thinker, find your philosophy, search the universe for your place." Republished as "Grow to Be a Thinker ... A Thought for Freshmen" in the *American Oxonian* (item 804). See also item 1457.

347 "The Round-Up." *ST*, 16 August 1955, p. 3.

Campus news, anecdotes, and commentaries. For instance, "Congratulations to [the lecture series] Great Issues for snaring Adlai Stevenson. We don't like to play the part of pseudo-pedantic pessimist, but what if Mr. Stevenson announces for president between now and September 28? No 'political' speakers allowed you know." See also item 359.

348 "The Round-Up." *ST*, 19 August 1955, p. 4.

News and commentaries. For example, Morris believes that the Mobile County Board of Education in Alabama made a "sensible statement on desegregation" when it "decreed that schools would remain segregated next term 'to maintain scholastic standards and harmony with a minimum of potential violence, disorder, or friction.'"

349 "The Round-Up." *ST*, 23 August 1955, p. 4.

Warns voters not to be fooled by the "high-powered legal verbiage" of state Attorney General John Ben Shepperd, who plans on running for governor next year. To attract the support of anti-integrationists, Shepperd has announced that the Supreme Court rulings on desegregation do not apply to Texas because the Court has not specifically ruled against state laws that "still call for segregated schools." Morris opines that Shepperd's "assumption is ridiculous" and that "the point he has raised borders on a thin line between technicality and political expediency."

350 "A New Year for the Texan — We'll Play Hard and Clean." *DT*, 18 September 1955, p. 6.

Morris begins the academic year with an editorial originally published in the *Summer Texan* of 7 June 1955 (item 315). He adds to his "statement of policy" a paragraph of optimistic remarks on the state of the university.

351 "The Round-Up." *DT*, 18 September 1955, p. 6.

A revision of Morris's "Round-Up" from the *Summer Texan* of 7 June 1955 (item 319).

352 "The Round-Up." *DT*, 20 September 1955, p. 4.

Criticizes UT's Loyalty Oath, which all incoming students are supposed to sign, as a "standing joke" and a "prefabricated laugh." State schools in Texas "are among the few institutions of higher learning where an oath of loyalty is used to sift subversi[ve] elements out of the student body."

353 "The Texan Reports on Elections: UT Political Scene Superbly Muddled." *DT*, 20 September 1955, p. 4.

Summarizes "the story on student politics" at UT. "The election picture was already superbly muddled before Student President Ray Farabee ... announced his resignation. Now it approaches a rather ridiculous state of pseudo-anarchy."

354 "The Round-Up." *DT*, 21 September 1955, p. 4.

Reports on Presidential Assistant Harold E. Stassen's "realistic approach" to disarmament. Morris concludes that "the ambivalence of science has almost overnight created a dual image: on the one hand, universal destruction; on the other, universal prosperity."

355 "The Round-Up." *DT*, 22 September 1955, p. 4.

Profiles student Noel Hargrove, a leader of UT's Young Democrats organization, who "wants to translate national issues to a student perspective." Hargrove believes that college students "should know the issues of the forthcoming election," and "he wholeheartedly favors a series of public debates with the Young Republicans on salient issues, problems, and personalities."

356 "The Round-Up." *DT*, 23 September 1955, p. 4.

A commentary on former President Harry Truman. "His critics view him as meddlesome, hot-tempered, and untactful" while "his admirers view him as an unknown who made an approach to greatness.... In reality, the most fundamental and nearly irreproachable appraisal that could be made of Truman's Administration was that it operated with intelligence on the international scene and with unintelligence in domestic affairs."

357 "The Round-Up." *DT*, 27 September 1955, p. 4.

Responds to a student who "believes there should be a 'student lobby' to join other lobbyist groups during sessions of the Legislature.... Our only answer is that a student lobby (if that label is to be applied) would require the most careful and mature planning. It is common knowledge that relations between the University and the Legislature have always been rather delicate."

358 "The Round-Up." *DT*, 28 September 1955, p. 4.

Campus news and commentaries. For instance, "The acquittal of two Mississippi white men of the murder of Emmett Till, 14-year-old Chicago Negro, has worked the feelings of the North and the South raw." Many northern newspapers "are blaming all Southerners collectively. Such accusations, of course, are unfair and absurd.... The conduct of justice in Sumner, [Mississippi], feeble as it was, suffered further impediment from bloated newspaper play and warped propaganda moves. For in the end the trial of murder was turned into a trial of the Southern way of life."

359 "Clarification Needed." *DT*, 29 September 1955, p. 4.

Editorially notes that in the *Daily Texan* of September 28, a staff writer argued that UT should not have invited Adlai Stevenson to speak because the university prohibits political candidates making speeches on campus. Some readers believed that the columnist's opinion "was accepted as The Texan's official editorial stand. It was not.... The Texan this summer repeatedly upheld [the lecture series] Great Issues' right to invite Stevenson. We of The Texan, however, believe in a 'fighting balance.' Our columnists ... may air any view they please, within the bounds of ethics and decency. Censorship is a nasty instrument, and we would never violate the individual dignity of any journalist by dictating his personal beliefs." See also item 347.

360 "The Round-Up." *DT*, 29 September 1955, p. 4.

Campus news, anecdotes, and commentaries. For example, Morris wonders "what may have transpired" the evening of September 28 during a meeting between Lyndon Johnson and Adlai Stevenson at the Johnson ranch. "What, perforce, was said around the Senator's kitchen table?... Our generation will probably never know. But somehow, we feel, a passport to sit in on the night's conversation might well have been a passport to destiny."

361 "Upholds Trade and Aid." *DT*, 29 September 1955, p. 1.

Covers Adlai E. Stevenson's speech last night in a "packed Gregory Gym" on the UT campus. Stevenson, the "frontrunner for the 1956 Democratic presidential nomination," supported a "program of trade and aid on the one hand and criticized widespread American installment buying on the other. 'I wish people would take less interest in booms and more in stability,' he said."

362 "The Round-Up." *DT*, 30 September 1955, p. 4.

News and commentaries. For instance, "Saturday Review, the magazine most overlooked on American newsstands, has published a slate of twenty 'purposes of education.' Some of them, we believe, are worth remembering." Included in Morris's bulleted listing are: "To enable a person to look up important information when he needs it" and "to develop to the fullest whatever possibilities or potentialities a human being may have."

363 "The Round-Up." *DT*, 4 October 1955, p. 4.

A discussion of "liberalism" and "conservatism." Morris believes that the two "powerful terms with obviously powerful ramifications" are "leading us ... down a beautiful but tenuous road of meaningless generality. Conservative and liberal are modern labels applied to meet preconceived situations. And therein lies the whole labyrinthine pattern of confusion."

364 "The Round-Up." *DT*, 6 October 1955, p. 5.

Morris supports a proposed state constitutional amendment that will go before voters in November 1956. "The amendment would strengthen the investment base of the Permanent Fund, thereby bringing in a considerably greater amount of cash than the now average 2.7 yield." See also item 329.

365 "The Round-Up." *DT*, 7 October 1955, p. 4.

Campus news, anecdotes, and commentaries. "For a moderate facsimile of student politics on the Texas campus, get two television sets. Turn one to Channel 3, the other to Channel 7. Then go in the next room and turn on the vacuum cleaner."

366 [Unsigned]. "The Till Tragedy: Blanket Accusation Has Created Hatred." *DT*, 7 October 1955, p. 4.

"The trial of Emmett Till, 14-year-old Chicago Negro who was murdered in the Mississippi delta last month, has been exploited to the point of saturation. The case was indeed tragic.... The most regrettable and, unfortunately, lasting aspect of the whole case, however, was the blanket accusation made by Northerners and pressure groups of all decent Mississippians. For guilt, after all, is of an individual — not a collective — quantity." An editorial.

367 "Housing No. 1 Snag in Campus Integration." *DT*, 9 October 1955, p. 3.

Among the various news items in Morris's "campus cavalcade" is the announcement that the UT Desegregation Commission's report "showed no insurmountable barriers to social integration of Negro students on the University campus. It unearthed problems, however. Housing units seemed more wary of integration: only 11 of 131 favored a breakdown of segregation."

368 "Where Were We Going?: Return to Normalcy." *DT*, 9 October 1955, p. 3.

Morris summarizes news on campus and around the world after he asks: "Whither was the world going this week?" For example, "The University was moving toward a new kind of tolerance" as it prepared to integrate its campus. "The nation was slowly returning to a state of normalcy after President Eisenhower's heart attack two weeks ago."

369 "The Round-Up." *DT*, 12 October 1955, p. 4.

Dr. Walter W. Rostow, who speaks on campus today as part of the "Great Issues" program, is involved with a "challenging project" at the Massachusetts Institute of Technology. "Under a three-year grant from the Carnegie Foundation of New York, he is developing a new national portrait of the United States in a world setting." One of the questions he hopes to answer is: "How ... has our society responded to the challenge of its world-wide responsibilities over the last fifteen years?"

370 "The Round-Up." *DT*, 13 October 1955, p. 4.

Morris quotes from "an article of rare merit" by former Connecticut Senator William Benton, which appeared in the October 9 issue of *Family Week* magazine. Benton contends that Americans are living in an "Age of Conformity," and he tells them "don't be afraid to be different."

371 "The Spirit of Geneva — How Will It Affect Our Lives?" *DT*, 13 October 1955, p. 4.

An editorial on international relations and the "fluctuating world picture," published less than two weeks before the foreign ministers of the United States, the United Kingdom, France, and the Soviet Union meet in Geneva, Switzerland. "Some believe the 'spirit of Geneva' is but a masterful Soviet hoax. Indeed, the skeptics' argument is sound. East and West have fallen far shy of making any noticeable progress on the two major questions which will be on the Geneva docket — German reunification and global disarmament."

372 [Unsigned]. "All Too Typical." *DT*, 14 October 1955, p. 6.

The Chicago chapter of the National Association for the Advancement of Colored People "has passed a resolution calling for military occupation of Mississippi and the denial of the state's participation in federal affairs. The resolution arises from the tragic Emmett Till murder case, in which two Mississippi white men were acquitted for the alleged killing of a 14-year-old Chicago Negro last month." The organization's recommendation is "unfortunate," and "it is all too typical of the incendiary actions of extremists on both sides of the touchy segregation issue." An editorial.

373 "A Loss, A Beginning." *DT*, 16 October 1955, p. 5.

Morris follows a brief obituary of Dr. William J. Battle, "the last of the University's old guard," with highlights of campus and international news. Now that Pan-American Airways has contracted to purchase jet transport planes, "Our children, or perhaps our children's children, will think nothing of flying to Paris for a week end, or to London for a stage play. So it is, by minutes and weeks, the inexplicable patterns of our lives change."

374 "Sample's Registration Opens New UT Era." *DT*, 16 October 1955, p. 5.

A "campus cavalcade" of brief news stories, including a report that Thomas E. Sample's University of Texas registration letter, delivered last week to the campus registrar's office, "had sociological implications. It cracked all UT enrollment records, paving the way for what is sure to be a new chapter in University history."

375 "The Round-Up." *DT*, 18 October 1955, p. 4.

Comments on Henry Morton Robinson's argument in the November issue of *Holiday* magazine that "gentlemen who go to Ivy League colleges are 'naturally superior' to their less fortunate associates." Although Morris admits "it is painful, yet quite true, to acknowledge the legitimacy" of Robinson's line of reasoning, the *Daily Texan* editor adds "one cannot deny there is a certain amount of wholesomeness here that cannot be found at Yale or Princeton." See also item 376. Morris's column prompted a reader to respond in a letter to the editor:

A Wolf, R. "Ivy League Debunked." *DT*, 13 December 1955, p. 4.

"To hell with the Ivy League!... This is the Southwest, not New England. To be more specific, this is Texas, a state that has more tradition and a greater heritage than all the other 47 states put together. Perhaps you cannot grasp this feeling since you are not a Texan."

376 "The Round-Up." *DT*, 19 October 1955, p. 4.

Campus news, anecdotes, and commentaries. For instance, "Note from a reader who scanned Morton Robinson's article on the superiority of Ivy League Schools over state universities: 'The story was mighty saddening to one like me who missed schooling in the Ivy League. I almost cried out loud while driving my Cadillac to the bank.'" See also item 375.

377 "The Round-Up." *DT*, 21 October 1955, p. 3.

Morris responds to readers who disagree with the *Daily Texan*'s pro-integration stance and who believe it does not represent the attitudes of the student body. He asserts that "this newspaper has never feared dissenting opinions" and "we encourage conflicting views.... But we are not afraid to voice our own views, regardless of the majority's." Morris continues: "This bleeding heart and do-gooder understands the segregation problem, perhaps, as fully as any person at the University." The "Negro population" of his hometown is "roughly 70 per cent of the city's total," and "part of the sprawling colored section" of the city is near his house. "You can ride through this section at sundown, when the world is most still and humans most restive, and you are conquered by the ubiquity of the filth and poverty and ugliness. You find yourself asking a million why's...."

378 [Unsigned]. "The Till Case: Fact, Not Fancy, Required in Times of Transition." *DT*, 21 October 1955, p. 3.

Editorially maintains that the National Association for the Advancement of Colored People and northern magazines and newspapers "should take a long, cold look at the agitation caused by their exploitation of the Emmett Till murder case." Although the "Northern press" and "NAACP leaflets" portray Till's father as a "World War II hero who died fighting for his country," a newspaper in Mississippi states that he was "hanged in Italy ten years ago for the murder of one white woman and the rape of two others." The NAACP, as well as every publication that "continues to titillate emotion and aggrandize reason, should use fact, not fancy, at a time when social unrest lies just over the next hill."

379 "Geneva — Skeptical Hope." *DT*, 23 October 1955, p. 4.

A commentary on this week's Geneva Conference. "The hope and skepticism of a world, part and parcel of a new compound since Russia's milk-toast policy became the vogue, converges upon Geneva this week. Foreign ministers of the four Big Powers, John Foster Dulles of the United States, V. M. Molotov of Russia, Harold McMillan of Great Britain, and Eduard Pinay of France, will negotiate toward a so-called 'easing of world tensions.'"

380 "UT Election Fever Keyed to High Pitch." *DT*, 23 October 1955, p. 4.

Among the various news stories in Morris's "campus cavalcade" is a brief write-up about the upcoming UT elections. "Fervent campaigning entered the home stretch this week, midst a jungle of cardboard pretense and a stream of bold verbalizing. With elections but three days away, an unprecedented presidential race ... continued to attract speculation."

381 "The Round-Up." *DT*, 26 October 1955, p. 4.

The chair and secretary of the UT Faculty-Student Cabinet have compiled "a series of study groups." The ones "best received by Cabinet members will ultimately draw discussion and study." The topics are class attendance, extracurricular activities, classroom desegregation, improving the effectiveness of the Faculty-Student Cabinet, and registration.

382 "The Round-Up." *DT*, 27 October 1955, p. 4.

Attempts to answer the question: "Why the unbridgeable gulf between youth and age?" Morris believes older people "not only resent, but fear, new ideas," and "the suggestions and hopes of college students, even of the most intelligent and rational, are all too often shuttled away.... The challenge to the young man of today, as we see it, is to retain his powerful hopes, to battle the entrenched resentment of new ideas, and never surrender to shallow expediency or soul-destroying complacency."

383 "The Round-Up." *DT*, 28 October 1955, p. 4.

Interviews Bob Siegel, the "affable" and "articulate" vice-president of the UT Students' Association. "Siegel is naturally an easy man to know. He likes his work and he likes his leisure. Indeed, student government workers often accuse him of getting lost in his own enthusiasm."

384 "A Week Slips By..." *DT*, 30 October 1955, p. 5.

Highlights of last week's campus, national, and world news. "The Longhorns kept alive champagnet [sic] hopes of New Year's Eve in Dallas.... Princess Margaret's romance at last achieved the rank of an international issue, but was quite absent from the Geneva docket."

385 "The Round-Up." *DT*, 1 November 1955, p. 4.

Campus news, anecdotes, and commentaries. "Eleven years ago today, the UT Regents reconvened in Houston to consider the dismissal of [President] Homer Price Rainey. Their ultimate decision, so the story goes, precipitated one of the bitterest political fights in Texas history." See also items 343, 386, and 471.

386 "The Round-Up." *DT*, 2 November 1955, p. 4.

Recounts the events leading up to the dismissal of UT President Homer P. Rainey on 2 November 1944. "Our intention is not to dig up old bones, nor to arouse passions long since quietened. But this is well ingrained in the history of the University,... and may it serve to teach us that never again must education and politics become so inflamed." See also items 343, 385, and 471.

387 "The Round-Up." *DT*, 3 November 1955, p. 4.

Campus news and commentaries. "An important step has been taken toward giving every worthy American youngster the benefits of higher education. By gifts totaling $20 million, two of our largest private foundations have established the National Merit Scholarship Corporation."

388 "The Round-Up." *DT*, 4 November 1955, p. 4.

Campus news, anecdotes, and commentaries. "Ed, our traversing ex-roommate, writes from London: 'The English women are dull and tall. They like to talk, but you don't like to listen to them.... I am a long way from Austin, and most of all I miss the girls.' Knowing Ed, we would've guessed it."

389 "The Round-Up." *DT*, 5 November 1955, pp. 1, 6.

Encourages the UT Dads' Association to endorse a "crucial constitutional amendment," which will soon be presented before Texas voters. "The amendment, by strengthening the investment base of the University Permanent Fund, would solve building needs at all state-supported colleges and universities for the next twenty years without additional taxes."

390 "A Collegiate Week..." *DT*, 6 November 1955, p. 4.

Highlights of last week's campus, national, and world news. "University couples, per tradition, strolled across the autumnal campus, fell in love and perhaps out again, but Princess Margaret announced she would not marry Captain Peter Townsend."

391 "The Round-Up." *DT*, 8 November 1955, p. 4.

Urges the campus community to contribute to the UT charity Campus Chest. If students "could have seen the group of disabled veterans of a forgotten War watching the Round-Up Parade last spring, and known that Red Cross stands to benefit, they would probably place the Campus Chest drive in its proper place in the scale of things." The university is falling short of its goal, but "the true quota lies in the heart, the real challenge in simple human goodness."

392 "The Round-Up." *DT*, 9 November 1955, p. 4.

Campus news, anecdotes, and commentaries. "Tuesday's snow reminds us of the day four years ago it snowed for an hour and we got out of school for a week.... So the boys got together and shot basketball and played stud poker and read 'True Sports' for six solid days. And many were the lamentations of being sixteen and snowbound in the great Mississippi delta."

393 "The Round-Up." *DT*, 10 November 1955, p. 4.

News and commentaries. "Backward Mississippi, still smarting from the Emmett Till murder case, was conspicuously overlooked in the news last week. The occasion was the death of 'Blind Jim' Ivy, 75-year-old Negro, who was a favorite on the Ole Miss campus." Numerous white students attended his funeral, and monetary donations are earmarked for "Negro scholarships" in his honor. "This is the Mississippi of perverted racial passion—the same Mississippi that the nation's newspapers so thoroughly vilified in the Till tragedy."

394 [Unsigned]. "Looking Backward: Have We Reneged?" *DT*, 11 November 1955, p. 4.

Midway through the semester, Morris fears that "your student press" has "not approached doing justice to this campus, nor to the youth who endow it with life. We have done well on the crass exteriors: student elections, administrative policies, football games, Campus Chests, finances." However, "The true importance lies in the 17,535 [students], in preserving the integrity of their minds and the inviolability of their principles.... We can only pay tribute to all this by defending it...." The tone and wording of the remarks suggest that Morris wrote this unsigned editorial.

395 "The Round-Up." *DT*, 11 November 1955, p. 4.

Campus news and commentaries. The UT Bar Association "has taken action on a Texan proposal that law students speak of the main campus as 'down in the valley' rather than 'up on the hill.' The board of governors Wednesday night unanimously voted to refer to the campus as 'down in the pit.'"

396 "They Did Not Fail..." *DT*, 13 November 1955, p. 4.

Morris congratulates the UT students for their "institutional pride" and loyalty, which they displayed this past week by reaching "within a few hundred dollars" the goal of the charity Campus Chest. He cautions against complacency, however, for "there is much to be done" at the university. After rhetorically asking, "How can our unity be utilized?" he lists some of the "tasks at hand." For example, "It can be done by upholding student rights and privileges, and by defending the principle that controversy is often the essence of learning."

397 [Unsigned]. "On the Till Case." *DT*, 15 November 1955, p. 4.

Editorially regrets that a Mississippi grand jury did not indict the alleged murderers of Emmett Till, the "14-year-old Chicago Negro," on charges of kidnapping. "Those people who love and understand the South, such as the editor, can offer no rebuttal in this instance. They can only seek tolerance and good will among their fellow Southerners, and warn those who would seek exploitation through agitation of the current unrest that neither the time nor the situation warrants it."

398 "The Round-Up," *DT*, 15 November 1955, p. 4.

Campus news, anecdotes, and commentaries. "A troop of Brownie scouts strolled across the heart of the campus this afternoon, singing 'Davy Crockett' at the top of their lungs. This is too much sophistication. And snug in our ivory towers, we still herald the increase in crime."

399 "The Round-Up." *DT*, 16 November 1955, p. 4.

Profiles Henry Young McCown, UT's Dean of Student Services. "Dean McCown may be counted unique among University administrators. He is an Annapolis graduate. He has spent 35 years in the Navy. He has a son, age 21, now enrolled here; another, age 26, with a UT diploma; and a daughter, age 9, who is quite likely to follow in family footsteps."

400 "The Round-Up." *DT*, 17 November 1955, p. 4.

Outlines UT's plans to enlarge the student union and urges the Board of Regents to endorse the project. "To the Regents, we emphatically contend that expansion of the current Union represents the most aggravating of current building needs. Within the scope of common logic, it is indeed difficult to associate the South's largest and perhaps finest university with the structure we now have."

401 "Fifteen Hours to Anywhere: Dignity Should Grow As the World Shrinks." *DT*, 18 November 1955, p. 3.

The *Daily Texan* editorially pays tribute to the students from sixty foreign countries who attend UT. "If you have never known a foreign student, pick out somebody—from Italy or Afghanistan or Sweden or Iraq. Talk to him about his homeland and his loved ones, his hopes and his fears.... Search for understanding, and you shall find the common denominator."

402 "The Round-Up." *DT*, 18 November 1955, p. 3.

Morris denounces *Time* magazine for its "egregious partisanship under the physiognomy of objectivity," though he admires the breadth of its news coverage. "Time is undilutedly Republican. It is scurrilous in its treatment of left-wingers, yet staunchly favorable to racial desegregation." However, "Bias and all, Time is the only magazine that brings the news of the globe together so that the reader can own some sort of perspective on the happenings of the day."

403 "The Round-Up." *DT*, 23 November 1955, p. 4.

News and commentaries. "Robert Maynard Hutchins, the gentleman who has mashed more than a few staid academic toes, told a Canadian audience last week that graduates of liberal arts colleges 'provide the best defense for our free institutions.'" In his speech, he "criticized overspecialization in colleges."

404 [Unsigned]. "The Assembly Resolution: Students Must Preserve Basic American Liberty." *DT*, 29 November 1955, p. 4.

Editorially praises the *Mississippian*, the student newspaper at the University of Mississippi, for taking "a staunch stand on an issue involving the cause of human freedom. In spite of public pressure from the Citizens Councils, the quasi–Klan units that employ economic pressure to preserve segregation, and in the face of administrative hesitation, the student press went on record in support of the campus appearance of a Religious Emphasis Week speaker." The Citizens Councils "objected" to Ole Miss inviting Reverend Alvin Kershaw to speak after he won $32,000 on a television quiz show and pledged to donate part of the money to the National Association for the Advancement of Colored People.

405 "The Round-Up." *DT*, 29 November 1955, p. 4.

On his twenty-first birthday, Morris reflects on the past with gratitude and anticipates the future with cautious optimism. "It has been, in its prouder moments, a good life. We are happy for our deep–Southern upbringing [and] for the togetherness of a small town.... We marvel at the great unfolding of life here..., and the sense of joy in being a part of this unusual community is strong and real.... It is a marvelous time to be alive. We stand on the brink of a life of atomic power. We also stand in the midst of a disparaging bipolarity, and the image of nuclear warfare sharply intrudes, and the irony runs deep." Republished as "An Unexpected, Unimagined Thing" in the *American Oxonian* (item 805). See also item 1457.

406 "The Round-Up." *DT*, 30 November 1955, p. 4.

News and commentaries. "AEC Chairman Thomas Murray's idea that the American public be shown a hydrogen bomb blast is impractical. Nobody will lend him a stadium."

407 "The Editor's Notebook: The Battle Today." *DT*, 4 December 1955, p. 5.

Agrees with "historically oriented specialists" who suggest that the question of whether capitalism or communism will control the world in one hundred years "depends on how we counter the pressing problems in today's undeveloped areas. For communism, geared to crises and fastened to a dogma that capitalism will inevitably decay, is entering those regions with a savage intensity.... The battle today, cruel, unalterable, is for the mind of man. At stake are not the freedoms of this generation, but of our children's and those that follow."

408 "The Round-Up." *DT*, 6 December 1955, p. 4.

Campus news, anecdotes, and commentaries. James Hart, former UT chancellor and possible candidate for governor, writes in "The University As I See It" series that the University of Texas "'must be a beacon of enlightenment in a dark and troubled world. Here the free and courageous search for truth should go hand in hand with conscientious and inspiring teaching....' To state our concurrence would sound quite feeble."

409 [Unsigned]. "On Squares." *DT*, 7 December 1955, p. 3.

"The Editor, who usually doesn't do such things, was drinking milk down at the drugstore yesterday" when he heard students label a professor a "square" because "he lectures all period and grades like hell." The professor "in mention" is a well-respected scholar and teacher. "And ah, the irony doth run deep. For, thought we, the University can never reach greatness implicit in its philosophy with men of the drugstore strain around." An editorial.

410 "On College Football: Ed Price's Dilemma — We Hope He Stays." *DT*, 8 December 1955, p. 4.

Although "more than a few Texas partisans" want UT football coach Ed Price to resign, Morris hopes he stays. "Ed Price is a man among men. Some call him a humanitarian. Some say he is a great man and a poor coach. In this perverted profession [college football], the two qualities can, have been known to be, and usually are, separated." An editorial.

411 "City of 1,000 Secrets..." *DT*, 11 December 1955, p. 4.

Morris relates his impressions of New Orleans, where last week he competed for and won a Rhodes scholarship for study at Oxford University (see item 1478). "The Christmas lights are up, and the wind is harsh and cold. You can walk past Canal Street, arrogant in its newness, on to Bourbon, and you see the plump ladies in furs from New York browsing in the antique shops, and you see two old men, half-drunk from cheap whiskey and broke, crouched on the street corner speaking in low monotones, glancing upward with cold eyes."

412 "The Round-Up." *DT*, 13 December 1955, p. 4.

Morris prints passages from a letter by Terrell Guillory, who accuses him of being "mawkish as well as romantic," and "drunk on youth." Guillory asks: "Is it the task of the young man of talent to perfect a genuine instrument of communication, or to exhibit a mere flair for words or notes or paints and just eat up the ego juices silly people give him?" Morris regards the letter as a "personal affront," and although he "takes it in good heart," he wonders if other readers have similar feelings. "If so, we'd like to know. We feel that we have to."

413 "The Round-Up." *DT*, 14 December 1955, p. 3.

News and commentaries. "War on a major scale is outmoded, not because it is immoral but because it is suicidal. And that's unethical. This is the supreme fact of the century, and until we acknowledge its pragmatic existence, both diplomatically and personally, we will be operating in a precarious state of self-delusion."

414 [Unsigned]. "25% ... No More." *DT*, 14 December 1955, p. 3.

Editorially quotes from a passage by William Faulkner concerning "the whole white race today" that "should be taken to heart." White people make up only 25 percent of the world's population. "So, when will we learn that the white man can no longer afford, he simply does not dare, to commit acts which the other three-fourths of the human race can challenge him for, not because the acts are themselves criminal, but simply because the challengers of the acts are not white in pigment."

415 "The Round-Up." *DT*, 15 December 1955, p. 4.

Praises Adlai Stevenson, who "today commands more respect than any man in our politics save one." During the last three years, the presidential candidate "has devoted himself to deep thought, to reasonable and humane solutions to the world's more perplexing dilemmas." Morris reprints some of Stevenson's "more salient remarks" on significant national and world issues as quoted in the "elite but respectable" magazine *New Republic*.

416 "The Round-Up." *DT*, 16 December 1955, p. 4.

News and commentaries. "With a sweeping philanthropic move,... the Ford Foundation has effected far-reaching purposes. It has spearheaded a movement to raise teaching salaries at a critical time for American colleges, and it has given a substantial boost to American hospitals. It has given half a billion in aid to purposes closest to the national heart: education and health."

417 "The Editor's Note Book: It's Worth Preserving." *DT*, 18 December 1955, sec. A, p. 5.

Celebrates the "fathomless magic" of Christmas. "We know that there is much in this land worth preserving, and that Christmas, rich with its exuberance, brings out the best, which would outweigh the worst.... Let us find ways, morally, ethically, physically, to preserve our American Christmas, lest we lose it."

418 "The Round-Up." *DT*, 20 December 1955, p. 4.

Takes issue with Paul Wasserman, editor of the *Daily Trojan* at the University of Southern California, who editorially reproved southern college students for failing to support the integration of academic institutions. "To the contrary, the evolution away from fork-in-the-creek racism in Southern colleges and universities has been admirable and altogether fantastic. We regret Mr. Wasserman has not been near enough to this evolution to see it, and to reward it, as indeed it should be. It is in the colleges and universities of the South that the 'second class citizenship' of the Negro will initially be eradicated."

419 "The Round-Up." *DT*, 4 January 1956, p. 4.

Morris returns to UT from his Christmas vacation in Mississippi feeling both love for his native land and a "genuine sense of fear" as the state contends with court-ordered desegregation. "Never in our life have we been more attached to the people of Mississippi. Nor have we ever more clearly seen the danger it faces. Legally, segregation is a dead issue; the Court decision was inevitable. Practically, however, and within the stolid frame of day-to-day living, the problem has never been more real. For in Mississippi, the scapegoat of contemporary criticism, the past and the future converge into a turbulent present."

420 "The Round-Up." *DT*, 5 January 1956, p. 3.
Observations on President Eisenhower's upcoming State of the Union address. Sources in Eisenhower's administration "have indicated his requests will bear the stamp of a 'dynamic conservatism.' They will be heavily weighed in the direction of votes: social welfare legislation and domestic improvements calling for expenditures of billions of dollars."

421 "The Real 1956: What 1956 Will Bring." *DT*, 6 January 1956, p. 4.
Editorially surveys the "true" national, world, and campus issues of the forthcoming year. "Just as the President's [Eisenhower's] illness was the biggest news event of the old year, so is his unannounced intention clearly the dramatic political question of the new. The prof[f]erred decisions cover the full range of the elective horizon, and the Republican picture rests in a state of quiet inaction.... At the University, integration on an undergraduate level will take place in September...."

422 "The Editor's Notebook: Coercive Conformity." *DT*, 8 January 1956, p. 4.
Regrets that UT students' "desperate drive for security" results in a "treadmill education bare of all things save the most material, and unattended by either the letter or the spirit of intensity, feeling, and beauty." Morris believes that the students' "coercive conformity" is "integrally associated with the trend of the times: a trend that denies nonconformity while seeking a sense of certainty—this in an age where nothing, paradoxically, seems certain, and all is flux, and the shadow of the Bomb persists as an unconscious blot on happiness." See also item 502.

423 "The Round-Up." *DT*, 10 January 1956, p. 4.
Maintains that UT must recognize and encourage excellent classroom teaching among its faculty, as "the capstone of a great University lies in its caliber of undergraduate instruction." Faculty members have "moulded definite methods toward the recognition of worthy professors," and students will be asked to participate in "faculty evaluation."

424 [Unsigned]. "Latest Witch Hunt." *DT*, 11 January 1956, p. 4.
Editorially denounces the "latest Washington witch hunt: the Internal Security Subcommittee's investigation of supposed Communism within the nation's press. The latest inquiry, spearheaded by Mississippi's Senator [James] Eastland, who has never been one to inspire widespread confidence, could well develop into a fear-spawning hunt for journalistic witches."

425 "The Round-Up." *DT*, 11 January 1956, p. 4.
A revision of Morris's "Round-Up" article on Whittle University from the 12 January 1955 issue of the *Daily Texan* (item 267). See also items 250, 290, and 492.

426 "The Round-Up." *DT*, 12 January 1956, p. 3.
Details the "somewhat tawdry history" of the Texas-based "spurious insurance firm" US Trust and Guaranty. "The tangled web of Texas' latest scandal becomes progressively more intricate. The whole chronology of the explosive US Trust and Guaranty collapse reads like evasive fiction."

427 [Unsigned]. "Salt and Wounds." *DT*, 12 January 1956, p. 3.
Editorially scolds *Look* magazine for pouring "salt on old wounds in an article this week. As if the Emmett Till murder case has not already been sucked dry, author William Bradford Hule contributes a rather new and somewhat sensationalized slant to the whole chain of events which led to the murder of the young Chicago Negro. Hule's story represents a tragically perverted Northern attitude: namely, the people of Mississippi are collectively to blame for Till's death."

428 "On Grace Kelly." *DT*, 15 January 1956, p. 4.
Laments the forthcoming nuptials of Grace Kelly and Prince Rainier III of Monaco. "Acknowledging the frosty truth that we all cannot own kingdoms, several thousand University males this week turned to Emily Dickinson."

429 "The Tenuous Move." *DT*, 15 January 1956, p. 4.
Praises the "mature action" of the UT Student Assembly in approving two significant resolutions on January 12. One resolution will "strengthen underclass scholarship requirements" while the other supports "Congressional action in passage of the Korean GI Bill.... It would seem that the Assembly, encouragingly so, has recog-

nized its responsibility to consider and act upon state, national, and international issues bearing upon the lives of University students."

430 "Well-Preserved Victorianism." *DT*, 15 January 1956, p. 4.

Commentaries on several campus issues. Morris defends Dr. Bull Elkins, UT alumnus and president of the University of Maryland, for reportedly "pushing for more academic scholarships at the expense of athletic scholarships." If the newspaper stories "are true, and if Elkins is sponsoring the rather heretical movement for more scholarships for non-athletes, he deserves the moral backing of every university and college president and every reasonably rational college student in the nation."

431 "The Round-Up." *DT*, 17 January 1956, p. 4.

Ponders whether UT women today talk more openly about sex than did previous generations of female students. "A serious study of the existing campus situation is justified. We suggest that [various student groups] all make reports, and file them with the editor, who is interested in such things."

432 "The Round-Up." *DT*, 18 January 1956, p. 4.

News and commentaries. The University of Washington's School of Communications polled some of the country's "more respected journalists" about which newspapers ranked among the best in America. "There were no Texas papers on the entire slate. It might be well for Texans to ask themselves why this is so. Could it be that Texas newspapers are poor defenders of the people?"

433 "The Round-Up." *DT*, 31 January 1956, p. 3.

Summarizes and quotes from an article in the January issue of *Coronet* magazine by Tom Sutherland, director of the Texas Commission on Race Relations and a supporter of integration. "Sutherland sees two major stumbling blocks in the path of harmonious desegregation. One is the attitude 'of a few high public officials, who could have been key figures in preparing their people for a change that obviously is inevitable, but have chosen to fight it.' The other is 'a dangerous attitude cultivated by a newly-formed organization called Citizens Councils, which fans anti–Negro prejudice.' He predicts that the Councils will eventually be defeated."

434 [Unsigned]. "The Undeniable Trend: Toward Press Control." *DT*, 31 January 1956, p. 3.

Editorially warns that the "trend on American campuses, undeniably conspicuous, is toward absolute censorship of student newspapers." At Maryland University, "The former Student Government Association Publications Board, composed of six students and four faculty members, has been replaced by a committee of eight faculty members and two students. The change, in essence, implies that the student newspaper at Maryland is now a megaphone for the administration."

435 "The Round-Up." *DT*, 1 February 1956, p. 3.

Profiles Don McNiel, head of UT's Young Republicans. "This week, parenthetical to his academics but essential to his politics, he leads an accentuated GOP effort to recruit newcomers at registration. 'I believe every citizen should do something for his community and his country,' he says. 'My interest in the two-party system provides me an outlet to perform that duty.'"

436 "The Round-Up." *DT*, 2 February 1956, p. 3.

Relates that the co-editors of the *Daily Tar Heel* at the University of North Carolina in Chapel Hill angered many in the campus community when they "editorially deplored the hiring of head football coach Jim Tatum ... as the ultimate step toward an accentuated professionalism in Chapel Hill athletics." Students circulated a petition to hold a recall election later in the semester to remove the two editors from office. "We cite these developments, not because they are bizarre, but because they strike rather close to home: here and on a hundred campuses. To what extent, one might ask, are our American liberties being stifled at state universities?" One of the student editors, Ed Yoder, would join Morris at Oxford University in the fall as a Rhodes scholar, and the two would remain close friends until Morris's death in 1999. Yoder told Jack Bales in the summer of 2004 that "our mutual struggles as college editors were the initial inspiration of our friendship."

437 "The Round-Up." *DT*, 3 February 1956, p. 3.

Interviews Jack Maguire, the new executive secretary of the UT Ex-Students' Association. "Maguire is basically a newspaperman, with a journalistic reverence for independence, action, and prerogative. He wants a strong, active alumni organization, devoted to the best interests of the institution. 'Our only excuse for existence,' he believes, 'is to serve the University. How to best do that is the challenge facing us now.'"

438 [Unsigned]. "Daily Texan Press Freedom — It Involves Every UT Student: An Editorial." *DT*, 7 February 1956, p. 1.

Morris reports that the UT Board of Regents has ordered the Texas Student Publications (TSP) Board to enforce rigorously the policies in the Texas Student Publications *Handbook*. He thinks that a rigid interpretation of the "ambiguous" procedures in the *Handbook* may restrict the *Daily Texan*'s content, which needs to remain open for comment, criticism, and discussion. Those who oppose Morris's view argue that because the university depends upon state funds, the university's "student newspaper should not criticize state administrations or publications." Morris replies that "this is a state university, where freedom of discussion and expression should prevail, and that for the power of the purse to so coerce and trammel the old American right of a free press is to strike at the very core of our most fundamental liberties." An unsigned, boxed editorial that was initially rejected for publication by two UT administrators but was later approved by the TSP Board. See also item 1480.

439 "55-Year Daily Texan Tradition Endangered; Submission Would Injure Collegiate Press." *DT*, 7 February 1956, p. 3.

Morris explains his position on freedom of the press in an editorial that was rejected for publication by the editorial director of Texas Student Publications, Inc. (TSP) but was approved later by the TSP Board. "We look upon the Regents' pressure for a stricter interpretation of the Texas Student Publications Handbook and their order of 'closer scrutiny' on editorial matter as a fundamental threat to the 55-year Daily Texan tradition.... Freedom of inquiry, criticism, and nonconformity are guaranteed in our state and federal constitutions now almost 200 years old." Morris includes with his essay supporting quotations by famous writers and leaders (titled "Views on Freedom") and a quotation by Thomas Jefferson pertaining to "press freedom."

440 [Unsigned]. "Don't Walk on Grass." *DT*, 8 February 1956, p. 4.

"We feel it is high time that this newspaper reprimand students for walking on the grass. They do not realize what they do. A beautiful campus is one of the principles upon which this University was founded." A humorous editorial in protest of the UT Regents' attempts to censor the *Daily Texan*. In chapter 3, page 191, of the "Texas" section of *North Toward Home*, Morris writes: "Finally, after more troubles, after we ran blank spaces and editorials entitled 'Let's Water the Pansies,' or 'Don't Walk on the Grass' and held to our prerogatives to publish what we wished, there was a loosening up." See also items 443 and 1968.

441 [Unsigned]. "Regents' Latest Decision Would Kill Texan." *DT*, 8 February 1956, p. 4.

Editorially asserts that if UT adopts the decision in the Board of Regents' recently published statement (item 1483), the action "would kill" the campus newspaper. "By prohibiting The Texan's right to legitimate editorial comment on controversial state and national issues, it would destroy the press's basic freedom to take stands. Its implicit danger cannot be underestimated."

442 [Unsigned]. "Academic Freedom in Censorship Issue: An Editorial." *DT*, 9 February 1956, p. 1.

A boxed editorial strongly defending the *Daily Texan*'s "cause against Board of Regents censorship.... The Texan cannot yield. To do so would be to deny the principle of a campus free from coercion. Why should there be fear on the campus of a state university? Liberty of comment is the essence of education, and freedom of thought is the requisite to all integrity."

443 [Unsigned]. "Let's Water the Pansies." *DT*, 9 February 1956, p. 4.

"It is high time students took it upon themselves to water the pansies in front of the Union. It is a fundamental fact that pansies need watering." A humorous editorial in protest of the UT Regents' attempts to censor the *Daily Texan*. See also item 440.

444 [Unsigned]. "Prerogative of Dissent Defended by Texan: Student Support Overwhelming on Censorship Danger." *DT*, 9 February 1956, p. 4.

Editorially contends that "the prerogative of dissent against a political party, an elected official, or a legislative measure must never be dissolved.... In colleges and universities, the freedom to learn and to express unhampered by pressures, prejudices, and politics is essential, since without it, these institutions lose their reasons for existence. We are encouraged by the deep concern on the part of University students and faculty members on this new danger to an independent Texan."

445 "Regent Issue Involves University's Liberties: TSP Board Must Act Positively to Preserve Texan's Freedom." *DT*, 10 February 1956, p. 4.

As the Texas Student Publications Board prepares to scrutinize the editorial practices of the *Daily Texan*, editor Morris insists that the group "must be positive in its actions. Its obligation is to take into account the overwhelming manifestations of community support in The Texan's cause." The Board must also "set forth for all to see [its] convictions that a state university is a place of free inquiry and thought, and that University students must not be insulated from the events and trends of a highly changed world."

446 [Unsigned]. "Regents Didn't Foresee Censorship Implications." *DT*, 12 February 1956, p. 5.

Maintains that the *Daily Texan*'s right "to comment editorially ... must not be surrendered." The UT Regents "never foresaw the implications of their negative steps. They discounted, among other things, the stubborn resistance of The Texan staff, the sharp reaction of the students, and the genuine show of concerned public opinion off-campus." An editorial.

447 "The Round-Up." *DT*, 12 February 1956, p. 5.

Discovers that a warm day spent wandering around the hills of Austin, "far from the self-cancelling vacillation and doubt, renews one's faith in many things.... In these moments lies the heart of truth, the more-than-philosophical kind engraved on college stone. For the biggest story in our lives is not how to thwart the censors or dupe the Russians, but how to find ourselves, and in so finding, preserve the integrity of our own minds."

448 [Unsigned]. "Crux of the Controversy: Politics, Not Principles." *DT*, 14 February 1956, p. 4.

Trusts that in its meeting tonight, the Texas Student Publications Board "will take affirmative steps to strengthen The Texan's status as a student newspaper.... A student proposal states that out of the TSP sessions should come an assertion that The Texan is a student newspaper and that the editor is responsible to himself, and within broad areas to a student-dominated TSP Board. We think it should be reaffirmed." An editorial.

449 "The Round-Up." *DT*, 14 February 1956, p. 4.

Compares the *Daily Texan*'s disputes with UT's Board of Regents to the differences the young people of Spain have with Generalissimo Francisco Franco. "The question of how to handle Spain's discontented and assertive younger generation has almost pushed the Franco regime into a first-class crisis.... The educators who support Franco's propaganda-ridden rule are disturbed that students have been thinking for themselves, and in so doing have sensed the multiple wrongs of Franco's government."

450 [Unsigned]. "No Longer Mere Censorship: Regents' Legal Point; 'Terrifying Implications.'" *DT*, 15 February 1956, p. 4.

Relates that at their last meeting, the UT Regents unanimously ruled that the *Daily Texan* "could not comment on controversial state and national issues" because such actions violated Section 4, Article VI of House Bill 140. "The section says that state funds, whatever their source, shall not be used for 'influencing the outcome of any election, or the passage or defeat of any legislative measure.'" Bill Wright, UT Students' Association attorney general, "argued that, because of the 'terrifying implications' of the Regents' interpretation of the House Bill rider, any attempt to interpret the bill in this manner would threaten the freedom of every student on this campus and every member of the faculty." An editorial. See also item 461.

451 "The Round-Up." *DT*, 15 February 1956, p. 4.

Campus news and commentaries. Newspaper editor Hodding Carter, "who will speak here early in March, struck a blow for campus freedom in an editorial Thursday. His reference, though applied to the segregation trouble and to his state university, is rather universal. 'The rabid element in the state,' he wrote, 'by prohibiting freedom of discussion on college campuses, are admitting their fear of the "enemy" and branding their children as irresponsible will-o-the-wisps who don't have enough sense to make a choice when all facts are presented.'" See also items 468, 469, and 470.

452 [Unsigned]. "What's a Censored Paper?" *DT*, 15 February 1956, p. 4.

Editorially reports that the editorial director of the Texas Student Publications Board and the chair of the TSP Faculty Committee "rejected another editorial" yesterday. "This one was also on the Fulbright-Harris Natural Gas Bill, and was a reprint from The Christian Science Monitor, one of the nation's most respected and moderate dailies. Their argument was that publication of the editorial would add to the present 'crisis,' and that both sides of the issue had not been presented in editorials."

453 [Unsigned]. "At a Sister University: Freedom vs Coercion." *DT*, 16 February 1956, p. 4.

"Two professors, one at Mississippi State and another at Mississippi University, have resigned in protest to a neglect of free expression and academic freedom on the respective campuses." Morris lists the various "independent, although interrelated, situations" that led to the teachers' resignations. An editorial.

454 "The Round-Up." *DT*, 16 February 1956, p. 4.

Interviews UT Students' Association Attorney General Bill Wright, who has "strongly challenged" the Board of Regents' interpretation of a rider on an appropriations bill that prohibits the use of state funds to influence a legislative proposal or an election. The Board has cited the clause to declare that *Daily Texan* editorials on state political issues are illegal. "'The implications of the Board's legal interpretation extend far beyond college journalism,' Wright says. 'The house bill rider threatens the very existence of a free university committee.'"

455 [Unsigned]. "Hopeful Speculation." *DT*, 17 February 1956, p. 3.

Morris is pleased that UT is "trying to sponsor" William Faulkner's appearance on campus in the spring. "Faulkner, undoubtedly one of the century's great men, and perhaps the finest living American writer, would contribute a welcomed bit of nonconformity to a conforming campus." An editorial.

456 "The Round-Up." *DT*, 17 February 1956, p. 3.

Morris talks with Poul Vohra, the Indian Students' Association president, who "staunchly upholds peaceful coexistence as the supreme fact of our times. As his organization prepares to celebrate India's sixth year as a republic with a banquet Saturday, Vohra reports that 'democracy is there to stay.'"

457 [Unsigned]. "Texan Stand Defended." *DT*, 17 February 1956, p. 3.

"Four more college newspapers" have supported the *Daily Texan* "in its stand against Regental censorship.... And college journalists on a hundred campuses, long abused by similar political and economic coercion, have taken immediate note." An editorial.

458 "President's Duty: Clear and Wise for Nation." *DT*, 19 February 1956, p. 4.

Approves of President Eisenhower's veto of the natural gas exemption bill. "In view of the Senate's action in pushing through the Harris-Fulbright Bill under a smog of possible bribery, Mr. Eisenhower's decision was a wise one." The bill would have freed natural gas producers from federal price controls and regulation. Morris adds that the *Daily Texan* "has taken a stand against the Fulbright-Harris measure.... This stand, it is said, was one of the catalysts that provoked our trouble with the Board of Regents."

459 [Unsigned]. "Censorship via Censorship." *DT*, 21 February 1956, p. 3.

"Four more college newspapers ... have all editorialized against Regental interference with student press freedom. The support amongst our collegiate brethren is overwhelming, but not unexpected. College journalism, a misunderstood and overlooked craft, is knit together by the universality of aggravation." An editorial.

460 "The Round-Up." *DT*, 21 February 1956, p. 3.

News and commentaries. Reprints passages from an article in this month's *Harper's Magazine* by R. L. Bruckberger, the "French soldier-priest," who urges American intellectuals to explain the concepts of liberty and freedom to a "doubting and cynical world." Writes Bruckberger: "The American experiment tends to prove that freedom not only remains the best possible regime, but a necessary one for the continued existence of man as a thinking animal."

461 [Unsigned]. "Censorship, Interpretation, and House Bill 140: Legal Conference Urged on Controversial Rider." *DT*, 22 February 1956, p. 4.

"After six days, University administrators and attorneys have still taken no action on Student Attorney General Bill Wright's interpretation of House Bill 140. Immediate attention is warranted. The entire campus, students and faculty, are seriously concerned by the Regents' recent interpretation of the appropriations bill rider." An editorial. See also item 450.

462 "The Round-Up." *DT*, 22 February 1956, p. 4.

News and commentaries. Cites a "commendable" resolution "urging University of Alabama students 'to moderate their anti-integration activities.'" The resolution "seems representative of a trend among student senates on all campuses: a genuine concern for all issues touching upon the American college community."

463 [Unsigned]. "Letter to the Regents: Parts of Statement Deemed Encouraging." *DT*, 23 February 1956, p. 4.

The Texas Student Publications Board has sent a letter to the UT Regents that outlines what it feels are the rights and responsibilities of the editors of campus publications. Morris editorially lists several points in the letter that he finds "encouraging." For example, "The editors of the publications are requested to edit their respective publications so as to place primary emphasis upon on-campus affairs; yet student interest in state and national affairs is a recognized part of the educational objective of good citizenship, and it is quite natural and proper that this interest be reflected in student publications." He adds that these "points" are "fully consistent with the practices and principles of sound journalism."

464 "The Round-Up." *DT*, 23 February 1956, p. 4.

News and commentaries. Quotes from Adlai Stevenson's "philosophy" on desegregation, noting that it "coincides rather closely with President Eisenhower's." The presidential candidate "declares it the first duty of every citizen to work for freedom and equality for all. 'Freedom,' he says, 'means that every man may advance to the limit of his natural endowment without hindrance because of his race or religion.'"

465 "The Round-Up." *DT*, 24 February 1956, p. 3.

News and commentaries. "The Senate has investigated all sorts of things in recent years, but seldom has it been called upon to investigate its own integrity. This is the issue of the current [Albert] Gore investigation of accusations that funds were given the election coffers of senators for the purpose of influencing their votes."

466 "The Round-Up." *DT*, 28 February 1956, p. 4.

News and commentaries. "Thursday is a pivotal day in Texas politics. A foursome of gubernatorial presumptives, including one governor and one senator, have said they will reveal their intentions by then. The most dramatic disclosure will belong to Mr. [Allan] Shivers. The three-time governor, hoisting the states' rights banner via interposition, will televise his plans Thursday night."

467 [Unsigned]. "The Ugliness of Shame." *DT*, 28 February 1956, p. 4.

Six newspapers "editorialized last week in favor of campus press freedom.... The ugliness of a shameful situation continues.... This newspaper cannot bow so obsequiously to the intrusion of fear. As our judgment dictates, so shall we editorialize. And every inch of white editorial space superimposed by the label 'censored' or 'withheld' shall represent a grave affront to the dignity of the University, the continent, and the principle." An editorial.

468 [Unsigned]. "Editor Carter Talks Tonight." *DT*, 1 March 1956, p. 1.

Announces that newspaper editor Hodding Carter of Greenville, Mississippi, will speak on "The Legacy of the South" in the UT Union this evening. The Pulitzer Prize–winning editor of the *Delta Democrat-Times* is "noted for his stand on political and social problems." In Greenville he "accepted and started his crusade on a series of southern newspapers for a liberal approach to the South's Negro problem. His objective in his editorials and in his newspaper was 'to show non–Southerners what is good about us and Southerners what is bad about us.'" See also items 451, 469, and 470.

469 "The Round-Up." *DT*, 1 March 1956, p. 4.

Profiles Hodding Carter, crusading editor of the *Delta Democrat-Times* in Greenville, Mississippi, who is speaking tonight at UT. "Hodding Carter brings to Austin the warmth of the agrarian small-town, the courage of the nonconforming critic, and the hope of the troubled Southland. He is a man who has stood almost alone against an intolerance deeply ingrained in the social, economic, and political mores of a region." See also items 451, 468, and 470.

470 [Unsigned]. "Carter's Lecture." *DT*, 2 March 1956, p. 4.

"Hodding Carter, the fine editor who has sought enlightenment and good will in the South's stormy segregation dilemma,... translated our overwe[e]ning national fright to the segregation problem" in his speech yesterday evening. His warning was simple and explicit: that as a peoples [sic], we must not brand dissent and nonconformity as subversion and treachery." An editorial. See also items 451, 468, and 469.

471 "Twelve Years Later: A Visit with Dr. Rainey." *DT*, 6 March 1956, p. 3.

Interviews former UT President Homer P. Rainey, who was in Austin last week visiting friends. The Board of Regents fired him in 1944, but "he is still attached to the University, and deeply interested in what it is doing. 'Somehow I can't urge enough,' he said, 'that young people should think for themselves, formulate their own ideas and opinions, and find the courage to stand up for what they believe.'" See also items 343, 385, and 386.

472 "The Round-Up." *DT*, 7 March 1956, p. 4.

News and commentaries. Opines that Richard Nixon's "fate" within the Republican Party depends on the "attitude" of President Eisenhower. "If the President wants him as his running mate — so far he hasn't said, but his remarks have been suggestive — the dissident Republican factor will soon subside and probably accept him. If the President doesn't want him, the anti–Nixon sentiment is sure to burst forth in a move to nominate someone else.... To us it seems fully obvious that Eisenhower's decision to seek re-election brings with it a personal desire to have the same ticket as in '52."

473 "The Round-Up." *DT*, 8 March 1956, p. 4.

After "scanning the press," Morris reprints passages from the *Fort Worth Star-Telegram* and the Florida State University *Flambeaux*. The *Star-Telegram* reports that UT President Dr. Logan Wilson told a group of Texas officials last week that the university has adopted a "selective admission" policy. "The purpose is to keep the doors of the University open to every deserving youth desiring to enter them and at the same time avoid compromise on quality in education."

474 "The Round-Up." *DT*, 9 March 1956, p. 3.

Capsulizes an article in the March issue of *Harper's* by Jack Fischer, the magazine's editor. Fischer laments that "the modern conservative has long suffered from 'intellectual laryngitis,' which has proven particularly embarrassing because these same conservatives are up against an articulate, garrulous opposition." Although Democrats in recent months have written numerous books and articles, notable works by conservatives "are scarcer than Gutenberg Bibles."

475 "The Round-Up." *DT*, 13 March 1956, p. 4.

Morris reassesses the "censorship issue" at UT, which is "somewhat subdued now, but still quite real." Although the Texas Student Publications Board has announced that it will deliver its "reclarification" of the *Daily Texan*'s editorial policies to the Regents before their April meeting, the board members assigned to the task have accomplished little so far, and "there is grave doubt" that they will complete the revision by next month. Morris lists several "implications of the controversy." For instance, the case "proved that sup[p]ression cannot be justified by political differences. The Regents underestimated the reaction of students, state, national, and collegiate press, and The Texan itself." Morris records "negative results" as well. "A portion of the student body has been permanently alienated to The Texan. The action of the editors and staff has been attributed to opportunism, immaturity, and persecution." The newspaper's triumph, therefore, is perhaps a Pyrrhic victory, but "it is still victory. The Texan is still a student newspaper, and free conscience at this University has at least won for itself a stay of execution."

476 "The Round-Up." *DT*, 14 March 1956, p. 3.

News and commentaries. "Justice William O. Douglas is convinced the people of Russia want friendship with Americans. This is the sum of several personal convictions that emerged after Douglas' recent 8,000-mile trip through the Soviet Union.... 'Perhaps the Russian people always have wanted to be friendly with us,' he has written in Look Magazine. 'Under Stalin, they would not have felt free to open their homes as they do today.'"

477 "A Special Report on UT and Its Students—Overwhelming Conformity May Kill Us Yet." *DT*, 16 March 1956, p. 4.

Morris decries the "corruptive complacency" of UT in a lengthy essay. He is "discouraged" because at the university and across the country, "We have been prostituted by an overweening conformity which appears to have extracted from us not only the courage, but the desire, even the reflex, to do something about our loss of liberty." For instance, the U. S. Department of Justice continues to ignore the "constitutional guarantee that defendants are entitled to impartial juries." At UT, Morris "everywhere" sees a desire "to side with the majority, prompted partially by the smug complacency of modern America." There is a "stifling sort of conformity, and it exudes comfort, security, and silence." Students value little except the college degree, because it leads to an "easy and profitable job" with children, "a pretty wife," and two automobiles. Consequently, "The University of Texas is turning out accomplished nonentities, faultless and safe and more than able to appease the corporation or please the boss; but we are failing miserably in our output of entities, those individualists willing and competent to delve into ideas, to test new ones and criticize old ones, and to let the chips fall where they might." Morris "feels humble and honored" to be a part of the campus community, but he finds "no alternative save to consign it to a painful and suicidal national drift away from dignity and justice." See also item 502.

478 "The Round-Up." *DT*, 20 March 1956, p. 4.

News and commentaries. Believes that W. Lee "Pappy" O'Daniel's decision to enter the Texas governor's race "makes for more confusion. The man who hypnotized enough Texas voters in 1938 and again in 1940 to win the governorship in the first primary has conservatives ... somewhat worried. The large field will be to his liking, and his circus-like campaigns, full of vitriol and color, may even yet prove attractive to the state's rural electorate."

479 [Unsigned]. "Don't Ruffle Gentlemen with Bankbooks." *DT*, 22 March 1956, p. 4.

Announces that the Texas Student Publications (TSP) Board, assigned to "reclarify" the editorial policies of the *Daily Texan*, has begun revising the TSP *Handbook*. A board sub-committee has completed five pages of recommendations, which will be given to the Regents for their meeting in April. Morris finds parts of the report to be "highly dangerous." For example, "'It is recognized that criticism of legislators and other state officials, however justified such criticism may be to the editor or other Texan writers, is likely to create ill-will among those who exercise some measure of control over the University's appropriations. Criticism of this nature will be presented only when it seems, in extreme situations, to be in the best interests of the University.' Board approval of such a clause would constitute academic hypocrisy of the most discouraging breed." The *Texas Observer* singled out this unsigned editorial as Morris's work (item 1520).

480 "The Round-Up." *DT*, 22 March 1956, p. 4.

Observes that "Religious Emphasis Week was a success again this year. Visiting ministers spoke superbly, students signified a greater interest, and the entire mood seemed to underscore ours as a community of inquietude and faith." Morris cautions, however, that although the United States "is essentially a land of religious faith," spiritual beliefs "should never become coercive. Anything coercive, no matter how good, is bad, and the true test of our democracy lies with such things."

481 "The Round-Up." *DT*, 23 March 1956, p. 3.

"Novelist William Faulkner, interviewed in the recent issue of The Reporter on Southern segregation woes, again pronounced his 'go slow' warning. 'They should let us sweat in our own fears for a little while,' he said. 'If we are pushed by the government we shall become an underdog people fighting back because we can do nothing else.'" Morris provides the text of "some of his remarks." A letter by Faulkner published in *Life* magazine was reprinted in the 4 March 1956 issue of the *Daily Texan* under the title "Go Slow Now."

482 "The Round-Up." *DT*, 28 March 1956, p. 4.

News, anecdotes, and commentaries. "The Chinese Reds have added a new official sport: hand-grenade throwing. See where the first all–Conference team was named post-mortem."

483 "The Round-Up." *DT*, 4 April 1956, p. 4.

News and commentaries. Political analyst Walter Lippmann makes a number of "observations on the current disunity amongst the Democrats." Morris's listing includes: "At issue today is the deep question of Party strategy: is there to be a united Democratic front or are the Democrats to run, as under Truman in 1948, as a Northern party?"

484 [Unsigned]. "The University of Mississippi Controversy." *DT*, 4 April 1956, p. 4.

"Students at the University of Mississippi have begun a campaign to revoke a highly restrictive 'speakers' screen' contrived, per nationale, to discriminate against controversy." Last year the board of trustees at Ole Miss developed a policy "requiring that 'all speakers invited to the campus of all state institutions of higher learning be investigated and approved by the head of the institution involved.' ... One's first reaction to the Ole Miss campaign is borne of disillusion and a few archaic wounds: the story is so old. The selfsame ill, manifest on tens of campuses, has come to be an accepted way of doing things." An editorial.

485 [Unsigned]. "The Moral Sacrifice." *DT*, 6 April 1956, sec. A, p. 4.

Editorially berates the Texas Student Publications Board for its "'basic policies' on editorial practices" that it has sent to the UT Regents. The policy statement represents both a "moral sacrifice which robs this newspaper of another sizeable bit of its freedom" and a "serious denial of Texan independence." The new rules "deny the Texan the right to endorse candidates for state and national offices. They deny the Texan the right to discuss personalities in political campaigns.... Indeed, the entire tone, the very fabric, of the new set of rules is restrictive. The destiny of this newspaper rests upon them, and that destiny is endangered."

486 "The Round-Up." *DT*, 10 April 1956, p. 4.

Morris muses about his dog, who is old and in the "twilight of his years." Skip "is 12 now, and as dogs go that means almost 90.... He came to us at the age of three weeks. I was nine then, irascible, loud, desperately in need of an irascible and loud young fox terrier."

487 [Unsigned]. "Toward Absolute Control: Subtle Paralysis." *DT*, 10 April 1956, p. 4.

"Daily Texan editorial independence is being killed by a subtle creeping paralysis, borne of fright and appeasement." This week the UT Board of Regents "appointed a Regental subcommittee to study Texan editorial policies and principles" and "also put into effect the new editorial policies" prepared by the Texas Student Publications Board. "This trend toward absolute control, prompted some years ago, has never been so clear." An editorial.

488 "The Round-Up." *DT*, 12 April 1956, p. 4.

A tribute to Franklin D. Roosevelt, who died eleven years ago today. "His Presidency is being soberly appraised by history now. He was a man who molded history perhaps to a greater degree than any American President. The nation lay fallow for aggressive, positive leadership, and Roosevelt was an aggressive and positive leader whose greatest service to man consists in the fact that he proved it possible to be politically strong and yet humanitarian and liberal."

489 "The Round-Up." *DT*, 17 April 1956, p. 4.

News, anecdotes, and commentaries. "The chairman of English at Drake University has said he believes 'ain't I' is a proper and sensible phrase. 'Am I not,' he comments, 'is too hard to say, and doesn't sound a bit American.'"

490 "The Round-Up." *DT*, 19 April 1956, p. 4.

Summarizes an article in the *Manchester Guardian* by Swedish journalist Herbert Tingsten. Tingsten "analyzes the unique and much debated phenomenon of 'Americanism.' Describing its conforming pressures as 'aggressive, widespread, and influential,' Tingsten believes a corresponding national concept does not exist in other countries." He writes that although one may refer to a person in England as un–English or in Sweden as un–Sweden, "the idea of a particular kind of patriotism and a special feeling of unity does not exist."

491 "Skelton Urges Return to Honesty in Politics." *DT*, 19 April 1956, p. 1.

Reports that at a speech yesterday at the "University 'Y,'" Democratic Advisory Committee Chairman Byron Skelton "called for a return to honesty in partisan politics and slammed Governor Allan Shivers on a number of counts. 'I don't like to be too hard on our governor,' he said, 'but I have noticed that when someone is opposed to him, he resorts to smear tactics. Not long ago he was praising Lyndon Johnson. The case now seems to be different.'"

492 "The Round-Up." *DT*, 24 April 1956, pp. 1, 6.

Morris's final story in the *Daily Texan* about the mythical Whittle University (see also items 250, 267, 290, and 425). "It was an institution of suave and capable royalty, Prince Rainier von Dahlin and Queen Celee XIII, and of immensely penetrating and non-controversial rulership, Prime Minister Sir Log Wills." The circumstances in Morris's fictional essay are in all likelihood based upon true events at UT. For instance, Roland Dahlin is chairman of the Texas Student Publications Board, and Celia Buchan was crowned Sweetheart of the University of Texas earlier in April (see "Charmin' Celia Cradles Campus Crown." *DT*, 8 April 1956, p. 1). Morris would marry Buchan in 1958.

493 "The Round-Up." *DT*, 25 April 1956, p. 4.

News and commentaries. In a speech before the American Society of Newspaper Editors on April twenty-first, Adlai Stevenson "made a sober and penetrating appraisal of American foreign policy." He described it as "dreadfully in need of fresh ideas, and warned that unless we move rapidly to regain the initiative in the new era of world affairs now upon us, our leadership will suffer in the years ahead."

494 "The Round-Up." *DT*, 1 May 1956, p. 6.

Interviews Ray Farabee, who as vice-president in charge of UT student government affairs has visited over one hundred schools in thirty-five states "to counsel and advise." Farabee is convinced that many college administrators do not realize that "the student is the real center of education." Frequently "educators do little to help students divine any other purpose in higher education besides better paychecks on receipt of a degree or more desirable social positions. We need to think more in terms of what education can do to develop a philosophy of life."

495 "Johnson Forces Control Texas: The Fire Station Was Hot As Professors Led Liberals." *DT*, 6 May 1956, p. 1.

Relates that in a "jammed" UT-area precinct located atop a fire station, Democrats supporting both Senator Lyndon Johnson and Texas Governor Allan Shivers met to select delegates to a county convention. The Johnson backers won, and they picked "sixteen liberal-loyalists." The caucus "had been a rather strange admixture of mild hilarity and vociferous ill-temper. But only the most observant noticed Shivers forces had sat on the left, Johnson supporters on the right. And there was your paradox."

496 "Faculty Freedom: An Editorial." *DT*, 8 May 1956, pp. 1, 4.

Editorially denounces an "unusually vague" UT Faculty Council recommendation (see item 497) as "a remarkable bit of self-emasculation." If the university stipulates that a professor must refrain "'from open and public advocacy of, or opposition to, candidates for governor, lieutenant governor, and legislator,' it deprives the University of Texas teacher of his right to public advocacy,... a right enjoyed by all other segments of the population." See also item 506.

497 "Faculty Defeats 'Restrictive' Proposal: 'Political Advocacy' OK Approved Decisively." *DT*, 9 May 1956, pp. 1, 6.

Reports that a UT faculty voted down a recommendation from the Faculty Council suggesting that staff members "refrain from public advocacy of, or opposition to, the candidates for governor, lieutenant governor, and legislature." The faculty instead adopted a proposal, offered by Associate Professor of Economics Frederic Meyers, that "maintains the present rule 'as it has been interpreted in practice,' which 'includes the right publicly to support candidates for any public office.'" See also items 496 and 506.

498 "The Round-Up." *DT*, 10 May 1956, p. 4.

Morris recalls that in his "Round-Up" of 20 May 1955 (item 314), he "recorded rather presumptuously ... a haphazard congeries of forecasts for a year ensuing. Some, happily, turned out to be unerringly prognostic." He reprints the listing, of which the last item reads: "Then the Regents will ban the Round-Up." Morris ends his column with: "Which almost happened."

499 "The Round-Up." *DT*, 11 May 1956, p. 4.

Narrates how a staff writer for the University of Georgia student newspaper, "despite the vigilance of a corps of censors," exposed the university alumni society of arbitrarily changing "the traditional date of Alumni Day to accommodate the political plans of the current alumni president." Morris warns that next year's *Daily Texan* editors "inherit a beautifully-worded set of censorship clauses, a professorial censor, and a wretched trend toward complete TSP [Texas Student Publications] Board control."

500 "The Round-Up." *DT*, 15 May 1956, p. 4.

Campus news and anecdotes. The *Daily Texan* composing room foreman reminds Morris that the small printing plate which prints the stylized column heading "The Round-Up" has been a part of the newspaper nearly every day for three years. Although Morris first intended to take the "unobtrusive specimen of 2-by-2 inch domesticated steel" with him when he graduates, he announces that he will bury it instead. "If steel is endowed with human qualities, we are sure it is worn out, because it has spoken entirely too long; disillusioned too, having made quite its share of enemies. But it has served its purpose dutifully well, and ... it can at least take cheer in its old age in knowing that it existed, and that its voice — even if puny and sometimes rather inarticulate — has in its young brashness feared no man."

501 "The Round-Up." *DT*, 17 May 1956, p. 4.

Profiles Ronnie Dugger, editor of the *Texas Observer* and former editor of the *Daily Texan*. "In an era in which personal journalism has all but dwindled away, Dugger has transformed the somewhat rare independence of the Observer into a highly respectable little operation. He has quadrupled the weekly's circulation. Indeed, his paper has on occasion been likened in kind to the immensely influential Washington Post: it invariably reaches the offices of everyone who counts in Texas politics."

502 "The Last Round-Up." *DT*, 20 May 1956, p. 4.

Morris's final "Round-Up," in which he eschews "the meaningless sent[i]mentalism of most farewells" in favor of a "few closing words" on a topic he has previously addressed in the *Daily*

Texan: Americans' "sedate complacency" and their belief that success is measured by money rather than character (for example, see items 422 and 477). "I believe that the American genius, and particularly the Texas one, has gradually surrendered to a principle of acquisition.... I believe that we have built ourselves a coldly practical nation, and that in the severity of that practicality we have given over our national values to acceleration and to the material. We have developed a frigid disdain of thought and emotion, of all things intangible and irrelevant." Morris also believes that the University of Texas "has failed. It has traveled all too swiftly, I fear, toward beautiful buildings and sterling reputations. Its leaders, in submitting to those who relish the corporate purse, have too often and even without reluctance betrayed the corporation of ideas." In chapter 3, pages 193–94, of the "Texas" section of *North Toward Home*, Morris quotes from this column, admitting that he wrote it "with too many genuflections to Thomas Wolfe."

503 [Unsigned]. "There Will Be Similar Moments: A Word in Closing." *DT*, 20 May 1956, p. 4.

In an unsigned editorial (clearly written by Morris), the UT newspaper editor provides "one final word on the Daily Texan controversy before the defense rests its case. The year has been a clamorous one, amply supplied with its vicissitudes, but it has served to prove one point: free expression at this largest of Southern universities has undergone a trying chapter." Morris is encouraged that the university faculty recently "slapped back with a rare courage at those who take professorial rights lightly. In a measure, their action has compensated for the deep faculty silence on the Texan censorship case, which was but a manifestation of the same forces at work" (see item 497).

504 "Southerner in an Old World: Former Editor Explores One Isle Before Embarking for Another." *DT*, 24 October 1956, p. 2.

Morris visits Manhattan prior to his departure for England and Oxford University. "It is certainly common knowledge that everything happens here. In the tiny Southern city of my upbringing I can still clearly recall countless lazy summer afternoons when the sameness was almost never broken.... That explains why my fascination with the city was an awkward one. In the interval of two days Dwight Eisenhower, Adlai Stevenson, Harry Truman, and Tom Dewey came to town...."

Articles in the Texas Observer

The title *Texas Observer* is abbreviated in each citation as *TO*. See also items 945 to 949 and 958.

505 "Mississippian[s] Would Improve but Maintain Separate Schools." *TO*, 10 January 1955, p. 3.

To forestall integrating the state's school system, Mississippi voters have ratified a constitutional amendment approving "full equalization and adequate financing of Mississippi's segregated public schools." A special legislative session will convene this week to address the "segregation question," for the amendment also authorizes the "abolition of public schools as a possible 'last resort' measure to enforce a voluntary segregation program.... The voters in ratifying the amendment showed a willingness to preserve segregation, even in light of the cost of equalization."

506 "UT Faculty Rejects Proscription." *TO*, 16 May 1956, p. 8.

The University of Texas faculty "has repudiated a proposed regulation which would have prohibited professors from 'public advocacy of, or opposition to, candidates for governor, lieutenant governor, and legislature.'" The "suddenly outspoken faculty" instead has adopted a recommendation by Frederic Meyers, Associate Professor of Economics, which "maintains the present University political rule 'as it has been interpreted in practice,' which 'includes the right publicly to support candidates for any political office.'" An editorial note refers to Morris as the "crusading editor of The Daily Texan and a Rhodes Scholar from Texas this year." His coverage of the "proposed regulation" also appears in the campus newspaper (items 496 and 497).

507 "Letter from Yazoo City." *TO*, 10 October 1956, p. 3.

As Morris prepares to leave his hometown for Oxford University where he will study as a Rhodes scholar, he reflects on the *Daily Texan* "censorship episode" at the University of Texas. "Perhaps it was the most vociferous controversy in the history of university newspapers. After a summer here [in Yazoo City] I know we of the Texan sponsored our cause to an extreme, leaned too hard on the prerogatives of the college press, were too zealous and emphatic. Yet I am prouder now than ever of the principles we defended and nourished, even if it was with immoderation."

508 "Blakley's Campaign Turns on Union Leaders." *TO*, 27 June 1958, pp. 1, 5.

Reports on a Longview, Texas, rally supporting William Blakley, who is running for the United States Senate. "To the heart of East Texas came the Blakley Organization Tuesday, bringing along its select diet of well-barbequed constitutionalism.... Bill Blakley was there early, a tall, ruggedly handsome man with a smile that is warm, and winning, and unrehearsed. His wife, dark and serene and plump, was with him." An editorial note states that Morris has spent the last two years at New College, Oxford, as a Rhodes scholar. He "has joined the Observer staff for the summer, after which he will return to Oxford for his last year there."

509 "Precisely at 70." *TO*, 27 June 1958, p. 2.

A lyrical essay about the "sad, brutal, empty loneliness" of driving across the vast state of Texas. "Eight days before I had been in England, and here I was now driving alone in a '56 Plymouth with dual exhausts toward East Texas.... You don't have to worry about a damned thing. All you have to do is keep the speedometer precisely at 70, wheel-straddle the dead dogs, cats, buzzards, snakes, aim for the scaldering mirage that is heat rising up from the concrete a mile to the front of you."

510 "Daniel Gets Going." *TO*, 4 July 1958, pp. 1, 8.

Coverage of an Austin rally for Price Daniel, who begins his re-election campaign for governor. "The crowd, though sparse, numbering about 750, greeted Governor Daniel's official campaign opening with enthusiasm." Austin's Woodridge Park "provided the backdrop, and with a 55-station radio audience listening, Price took swipes at DOT [Democrats of Texas] and the federal government and reviewed his first-term record." The group Democrats of Texas comprised conservative Democrats who split with the national party. "Willie Morris, Associate Editor" appears on the *Texas Observer*'s masthead for the first time in this issue. See also item 543.

511 "Schools Need Teachers, Books." *TO*, 4 July 1958, pp. 1, 4.

Outlines the deficiencies of the public education system in Texas and the "important" efforts of the Committee of Twenty Four, which is working to improve the situation. "The Committee of Twenty Four was set up by the Legislature in 1957 to make a thorough study of Texas public schools. Four problem areas were named for specific recommendations: school program, teacher supply, school construction, and finance."

512 "Trees All Lanterned and Mossed." *TO*, 4 July 1958, p. 3.

Morris describes an "elegant" Houston wedding reception that he and his fiancée attended. "My black and white Plymouth with dual exhausts ... was a bit out of place among the Fleetwoods and the Jags, and the ragged sound of it was not quite meant for the setting: the shady drive lined with trees done up on moss, the undulating green lawn and the long, thin, ranch-style house that hugged close the ground behind. The swimming pool was not in view, but it was there somewhere, it had to be there somewhere."

513 "U. T.'s Lack: 'Broad Human Privacy.'" *TO*, 4 July 1958, p. 6.

The first of a two-part series of articles in which Morris presents "a rather diffuse comparison of the Universities of Oxford and Texas" (see also item 517). Morris left Oxford almost two years ago, "and sometimes that other University, the Texas one, seems of another realm, belonging with a set of experiences too alien, too removed, to be here with these. A university like Oxford, committed as it is to educating an intellectual elite sifted through one of the most rigid procedures ever, and a university like Texas, dedicated to the American's answer, education in the mass, stand theories, ways of life apart; the differences which separate them are almost defiant differences." Students are not compelled to attend classes at Oxford, and the university "is dedicated to the simple academic proposition of spare time, an almost unknown phenomenon in the do-and-do-often climate of a UT."

514 "Henry's Unorganized Organization." *TO*, 11 July 1958, p. 3.

A write-up of an Austin "$10-a-plate fund-raising dinner" for Texas Senator Henry Gonzalez, who is running for governor. "After ten minutes of his speech one sensed his genius with the spoken word, a facile genius given only a few politicians: Theodore Bilbo, Adlai Stevenson, perhaps Nye Bevan. He had spoken too long, he had repeated himself too much, but what mattered most to me was that he had spoken — and that he had spoken in Texas."

515 "A Symbol of Past on Texas Stump." *TO*, 11 July 1958, pp. 1, 5.

Morris follows the campaign trail of W. Lee

"Pappy" O'Daniel, who ran successfully for governor in 1938 and is now in the gubernatorial race again. "Doing West Texas, he is like a ghost riding the range. He looks old, he is old, he walks with an old man's shuffle, but there can be no denying that he yet weaves a magic spell.... Travelling through this lonely brooding country,... you see the legend alive again for a moment." Morris adapts material from this article for a profile of O'Daniel in chapter 7, pages 259–65, of the "Texas" section of *North Toward Home.*

516 "'What Is It?': On an Arrival." *TO*, 11 July 1958, p. 6.

Morris joins *Texas Observer* Editor Ronnie Dugger in the maternity wing of an Austin hospital as Dugger's wife goes into labor. "I am going to record this episode simply and briefly, without embellishment. Many years from now, when things may be going poorly for Celia Williams Dugger, when her men friends are drab and Republican, when the Sudanese are dropping H-Bombs on lower Manhattan, may she read this and note her strange beginnings, and take heart that she came to us as a woman of mystery."

517 "Pressures at U. T.: Students Free at Oxford." *TO*, 18 July 1958, p. 6.

The second of two articles that contrasts the University of Texas with Oxford University (see also item 513). Morris contends that the former institution often "has been caught in the vicious currents and crosscurrents of state politics." Because university administrators regard "legislative appropriations to be the most powerful of all considerations," they are unwilling "to combat political expediency with ideals." Students at Oxford University, however, "simply cannot comprehend" these concerns. "This lack of comprehension is embraced by many things: by that English tolerance of opposite ideas [and] by a popular respect for the man of ideas...." Oxford "is free, detached, not to be meddled with.... Student ideas are bandied about freely and with enthusiasm."

518 "And with Yarborough." *TO*, 25 July 1958, pp. 1, 6.

Morris spends a day in Houston with the campaigning Ralph Yarborough, who is running for re-election to the United States Senate. In a large shopping center, on top of a truck decorated with political banners and posters, a "hillbilly band ambled and rhythmed." As people gathered, Yarborough walked through the crowd shaking hands. "He took the cue when [violinist] Curley Fox started 'The Yellow Rose of Texas' and climbed up the steps onto the truck. He spoke for 15 minutes, ripped into his opponent with all the fire and fury of the political professional, then commended his own record with an opposite zeal. Finished, he waved and grinned to the accompaniment of 'The Eyes of Texas,' stepped off the truck to shake more hands, then left for another stop."

519 "A Long Hot Summer." *TO*, 25 July 1958, p. 2.

Morris satirizes the Texas governor's race with an imaginative report of a Latexo, Texas, campaign rally. "Silas Quinine, the Sam Wood-DOT [Democrats of Texas] candidate for Texas grand inquisitor, addressed a giant rally of the East Texas Pomegran[a]te Growers here last night in a speech watched closely through hidden cameras by big-city bosses in Detroit, Washington, Vladivostok, Beirut, and Leopoldville."

520 "A Roach, a Spider, and a Swim: One Fine Election Day." *TO*, 1 August 1958, p. 6.

Morris meticulously details his impressions of Election Day in Austin. "Then there was a breeze, and it was hot and prickly, like whiskers. A big fat woman furtively picked her nose in front of the HEB Food Store.... It was election morning and the People were going into Wooldridge School to make their Choices. I remembered our democracy and was glad."

521 "The Texas Poichase." *TO*, 1 August 1958, p. 3.

After hearing and reading statements that out-of-state "bosses" and "racketeers" purchased votes in the recent Texas elections, Morris concocts a fanciful interview with one of the mobsters. "We made a flying visit to Detroit Wednesday to see Ziggie Zoffazeck, the wiry out-of-state labor racketeer who controlled the Texas election last week."

522 "Integration in Boerne: Two Children in a One-Room School." *TO*, 8 August 1958, pp. 1, 6, 7.

Morris talks to black and white residents of Boerne, Texas, about a forthcoming referendum concerning the integration of the Boerne public schools. After he arrived in Boerne, a service station attendant directed him to the Kendall Inn, and from there he walked into town. "I had brought along a copy of the Boerne Star from the Kendall Inn and sat down on a bench in the park to look over it.... At the top of the seventh column was a story headlined in bold face, 'Let's Stay As We Are.'" See also item 524.

523 "Students Debate the Invasion." *TO*, 8 August 1958, p. 3.

Coverage of an "open debate on American intervention in the Middle East, sponsored by the University of Texas International Club." Soon after the discussion started, "tempers began to crackle. Arab students passionately tried to explain their resentment over the Leathernecks in Lebanon, and their American contemporaries out in the audience persisted in being slightly stupid and highly irrelevant.... The Arabs were fervid, articulate, indignant, and all things considered, remarkably patient."

524 "In a Refreshing Provincial Way." *TO*, 15 August 1958, p. 3.

States that a referendum that would permit the integration of public schools "was defeated in Boerne [Texas] by a rabid racist of an editor." Morris observes that the actions of the voters in this small town mirror those of countries and nationalities. "The good Anglo-Saxons of Boerne won their victory.... History in fact relates many victories, for didn't the Spanish butcher the Moors, and the Japanese mangle the Chinese,... and don't the Africans loathe the French and British, and vice versa and etcetera, mostly in the name of certain folks' genes? In the midst of this great complexity it should do our Anglo-Saxon hearts good to know that dusty little towns can nurture such massive instincts and be downright genetic too, in a refreshing provincial way." Republished in *Fifty Years of the "Texas Observer"* (item 920). See also item 522.

525 "A Thoroughgoing One-Issue Man." *TO*, 15 August 1958, pp. 1, 5.

Profiles Carter Wesley, editor and principal owner of the "militant" and "aggressive" *Houston Informer*, a "Negro weekly." Wesley "is optimistic now over the racial situation in the South. 'Legally,' he said, 'school desegregation is an accepted fact. Sure, it'll be a number of years before we have implementation of it, but Dallas and Houston are gonna lose their legal fight for sure.... The Negro in the South,' he said, 'just asks for equal opportunity. We wouldn't want you givin' us anymore than that.'" The essay is first in a series of character sketches featuring Texas newspaper editors. See also items 527, 529, and 531.

526 "An American Triumph." *TO*, 22 August 1958, p. 3.

Morris sarcastically congratulates the United States for successfully marketing its commercial television programs in Great Britain. "How heartwarming it is for us Americans to herald the triumph of all things American, no matter what. How encouraging to see our crime serials, our giveaway shows, our quiz games being exported, pandering to the same lazy passive tastes the world over."

527 "'A Function to Perform': Ray Bailey of the Luling Newsboy." *TO*, 22 August 1958, p. 8.

Profiles Ray Bailey, editor of the *Luling Newsboy*, a small-town newspaper in Luling, Texas, "that might typify Texas weekly journalism." Over cups of coffee "in a crowded cafe he chain-smoked and talked. 'You know,' he said, 'I could make more money doin' something else, but I look at it this way—here I think I'm performin' a function.' His function primarily is to help encourage the economic growth of Luling, to boost the more worthwhile community projects, to offer a source of information to home-town people about home-town things." The essay is second in a series of character sketches featuring Texas newspaper editors. See also items 525, 529, and 531.

528 "The Rain Fell Noiselessly." *TO*, 22 August 1958, p. 6.

Morris returns to his Mississippi hometown, Yazoo City, and visits his family and a close friend. He and his friend Bubba "talked in that fashion of friends so close that long separations can never embarrass, about the things boys who grew up together in small towns, one leaving and the other staying, talk about—and always about the people who died naturally or violently or by their own hand since the last trip home." Republished in *Shifting Interludes* (item 81).

529 "Both Barrels: Fullingim of Kountze News." *TO*, 29 August 1958, pp. 1, 4.

Profiles Archer Fullingim, editor and owner of the *Kountze News*, "one of Texas' most interesting" weekly newspapers. "There is Archer every week in his front-page column 'The Printer Fires Both Barrels,' telling yarns, chastizing the Republicans, and laughing out loud at the foibles of the good gentry of Kountze and their more worldly Texas neighbors." The essay is third in a series of character sketches featuring Texas newspaper editors. See also items 525, 527, and 531.

530 "A Routine Ritual on a Rainy Morning." *TO*, 29 August 1958, p. 6.

Morris and his fiancée drive to a county courthouse on a rainy morning in Houston to purchase a marriage license. "It was an ugly impassioned day, cold almost, and the skies were bleak and purple. When we parked outside the Courthouse it was raining so hard that my black and white Plymouth with dual exhausts, being the good proletarian car that it is, leaked water. Celia noticed my anger and said kind things, asking only for a Kountze News from the back seat to put over her head while we ran inside."

531 "An Editor the Sheriff Missed." *TO*, 19 September 1958, pp. 1, 6.

Profiles Ernest Joiner, who edits the *Ralls Banner* in Ralls, Texas, "and who gets quoted more than most newspapermen on the mass circulation dailies." Joiner "is a man of raw courage, a thorough non-conformist, and an idealist. Beneath the eccentricities of his weekly column, 'It Says Here,' a sensitive social conscience is at work, ridiculing political greed, jousting with religious dogma, lashing unkindness and inhumanity and pettiness and whatever else he thinks ills the human race, 2000 of whom have chanced to band together in this tiny community on the plains of West Texas." The essay is fourth in a series of character sketches featuring Texas newspaper editors. See also items 525, 527, and 529. As noted in the 27 June 1958 issue of the *Texas Observer* (item 508), Morris joined the staff while on summer vacation from Oxford University. After completing his series of newspaper editor interviews, he would not write again for the paper until the summer of 1960.

532 "Salvationists, Natural Childbirthists: It Won't Hurt So Bad." *TO*, 15 July 1960, p. 5.

Morris returns to the staff of the *Texas Observer* as associate editor. After watching the Democratic National Convention on television, he is resigned to the fact that Lyndon Johnson will not be the party's presidential candidate in the fall. "What really matters, way down here, is to explain to ourselves why a Texan can't get elected president these days, since we all seem to want one pretty badly." Although Morris did not attend the convention and saw it only on television, he believes that "it's not because the salavationists [sic] and natural childbirthists were pulling cords, that it might conceivably go a little deeper. It might be a Texan, a Southerner, can't be elected president of all the American people until that very day he becomes as progressive, as forward-seeing ... as the vast majority of average, decent Americans demand that he be."

533 "The Winds of Change ... And the Calculated Risk." *TO*, 15 July 1960, p. 4.

Morris opines that Senator John Kennedy made a "calculated gamble" in selecting Lyndon Johnson as his presidential running mate. Although Johnson may "keep most of the bristling and recalcitrant Southern states in line in November," he is "going to be a target of rhetoric for the Republicans this fall ... on oil, on labor, and on civil rights." Nevertheless, Johnson may in time "become a greater man than he is, a spokesman for all of America.... We need men sensitive to the great and overwhelming winds of change, to the downtrodden and the distressed all over the world."

534 "A Certain Vacuum in Our Land." *TO*, 22 July 1960, p. 5.

Dismisses Texas's metropolitan daily newspapers as "backward and narrow" and "lacking in the professional touch." A person can spend days "searching their sprawling grey interiors for the one occasional morsel of enlightenment and liberality."

535 "A Chapter in Technique: Franklin Spears and the Bexar Coalition." *TO*, 29 July 1960, pp. 1–2.

Profiles legislator Franklin Spears, a lawyer-politician who, at age twenty-eight, "has masterminded the most impressive campaign victory of the year in Texas. The only state House incumbent from San Antonio with liberal leanings," Spears began planning a "guarded political offensive" against members of a conservative Bexar County alliance six months before the May primary election. With support from "several dissatisfied groups" in San Antonio, "a coalition of four other young lawyers was assembled.... Before it was over, as Spears describes it, 'We had them on the defensive for the first time in their political lives.'"

536 "Houston Post, Texas Observer Push an Idea: A Virile Youth Force." *TO*, 29 July 1960, p. 4.

Satirizes the *Houston Post*'s idea of forming "a strong, well-organized American Youth Movement to counteract the subversive forces now gnawing away" on American girls and boys. Morris offers a number of "suggestions for the Post to work on," including: "Teach the kids how they can most courteously and without undue violation to the Fourth Commandment inform on recalcitrant and sneaky parents, as well as babysitters, friends, and double-dates caught reading subversive books or eating red popsickles" [sic].

537 "Constitutionalists in Search of a Hero." *TO*, 5 August 1960, p. 2.

Reports that members of the conservative Constitution Party met in Dallas to nominate their candidates for U.S. president and vice president. A pamphlet "listed the platform of the party. The foreign policy plank, listed seventh, advocated: 'That we immediately suspend all relations with Communist Russia and all Communist nations and satellites; withdraw the United States from the United Nations and its agencies immediately; ... discontinue all foreign aid to foreign nations....'" The party, which nominated General Douglas MacArthur in 1952, did not select any candidates at the convention, "but chose to await developments from conservative groups in other states."

538 "Johnson's 'Homecoming': Barbecue in Blanco." *TO*, 5 August 1960, pp. 1, 3.

Coverage of "Lyndon Johnson Day" in Blanco, Texas. "An organist played music while Johnson signed autographs, ate supper, shook hands with Sen. Ralph Yarborough, and talked with Percy Brigham, a banker from Blanco, sitting on his right.... Mayor Wayne Smith of Blanco remarked, 'I never seen so many people in my life. I didn't eat any supper I was so scared about what I was gonna say.' He called the Kennedy-Johnson ticket a 'kangaroo ticket, one with all its strength in the hind legs.'" Morris quotes from his reportage of the Johnson rally in chapter 6, pages 233–36, of the "Texas" section of *North Toward Home*.

539 "The Religious Issue: Methodist Upholds Jack's Stance." *TO*, 5 August 1960, pp. 1, 8.

Profiles Baxton Bryant, a Methodist minister who "has taken a lead in challenging the stand of a number of Texas Baptist leaders that Sen. John Kennedy's Catholicism is a bar to the presidency." Reverend Bryant believes that the "major issue in November is 'leadership, not religion.'"

540 "Who, After All, Is What?" *TO*, 5 August 1960, p. 5.

Charles Cullin, the editor of the *McLean News*, "has been tossing some pretty harsh adjectives" at H. M. Baggarly, editor of the *Tulia Herald*. "Prof. Cullin calls Baggarly a fool and a socialist. He wonders why the good people of Swisher County put up with him." Morris states that "we don't have anything against Prof. Cullin the person.... We merely object to self-righteousness of all kinds, especially in ourselves, which we seldom see until someone points it out to us."

541 "3 Nude Blondes Seen on Escalator." *TO*, 12 August 1960, p. 6.

Morris follows his eye-catching headline with news from a college friend who had "dropped by" to see him. The friend told him that in Austin "the only thing everyone is talking about ... this summer is sex. He said if the state's most popular Independent-Liberal newspaper doesn't start paying a little attention to this neglected area in Texas, then it will go the way of the old New York Sun, Grit, and the Weimar Republic." Morris facetiously adds that *Texas Observer* editor Ronnie Dugger is "out of town this weekend," but he, the associate editor, "humbly submits that we need more sex in this newspaper." See also item 545. The next issue of the paper contains Dugger's reply to Morris's proposal:

A Dugger, Ronnie. "2 Clothed Blondes on Escalator." *TO*, 19 August 1960, p. 6.

The editor of the *Texas Observer* explains that although "these days it's thought to be sophisticated to talk about sex, ... I feel bound to repudiate it in any and all of its forms and uses and preserve the Observer from its debilitating influence. Morris, a creative man, ought to know that one's best energies need to be reserved for the nobler life." We need to "make allowances" and excuse him for writing his article, however, "for he had just returned from four years abroad during which the English, the Parisians, and the Scandinavians were doing their best to infect him with alien ideologies."

542 "A Dismal Study — The Aged in Texas." *TO*, 26 August 1960, pp. 1–3.

Summarizes a "report on problems of Texas' old people," a study that provides facts on health, welfare, population trends, income, housing, and education. "The story it tells, in dispassionate, statistical tones, is in many ways a story of social failure.... The fact-finding report reveals that the plight of old people with no resources beyond the maximum $67.50 monthly old-age assistance is dire." See also item 543.

543 "Open Questions to a Governor." *TO*, 26 August 1960, p. 5.

A column directed to Governor Price Daniel, who during his "official campaign opening" two years ago (item 510) defended "our constitutional system of state-federal relations and local self-government." Morris lists some of the plights of "our old people" as outlined in a recent state report (item 542) and asks for Daniel's "leadership" to help solve the problems. "What are we to say about states' rights, Governor, when our own Texas investigators tell us at least 30 percent, and in some instances as many as 70 percent, of retired old couples in half our counties don't have the basic minimum income 'to maintain a decent standard of living'?"

544 Our Mississippi Correspondent. "The Frustrations of Bolting: Maneuverings in Mississippi." *TO*, 26 August 1960, p. 5.

Relates that Mississippi's "tall and gaunt segregationist governor," Ross Barnett, is "pushing an unpledged electoral slate bolt from the Democrats" this fall, while his "arch foe, ex–Gov. J. P. Coleman, will support the Kennedy-Johnson ticket." Although Barnett has few "party 'names'" supporting him, "his unbending segregationist drawing power may yet work its voodoo on Mississippi's still predominantly rural folks." Furthermore, "Kennedy's Catholicism may run into trouble" in the Northeast, "Mississippi's 'Bible Belt' of Protestantism." The election this November will decide "whether the bulk of the state's Democratic leaders can corral her inflammatory populace despite the presence of two combustibles—race and religion. Never before have both irritants been present." This unsigned article "From Our Mississippi Correspondent" is clearly by Morris.

545 "Prosecution Without Intimidation: Temptress Nabbed in Sidewalk Cafe." *TO*, 26 August 1960, p. 7.

On the heels of his tongue-in-cheek plea for more sex in the *Texas Observer* (item 541), Morris writes that "replies to the Observer's new Department S on Texus-Sexus continue to pour into this office. Seven lovely former Misses Cornstalk (1953–1957 inclusive) have been supplied us by the Jim Hogg County Corn Growers and Reapers Assn. to sort the mail, and the department is now firmly established in the storeroom next to the w.c., just back of us."

546 "Free Enterprise Wins, $51 to 82 Cents." *TO*, 2 September 1960, p. 5.

Contrasts America's "free private enterprise medicine" with "socialized medicine in England." Morris's ten-month-old son David was born in England and "cost us student parents 82 cents, and they never sent the bill." Last week Morris and his wife "took him to be circumcised in a local free private enterprise hospital.... The bill from the hospital alone was $51; like the socialists, they did not send it: they had my wife Celia, who was holding a screaming David in her arms just afterwards, sign a check for it then and there before she left the place." Republished as "$72 to 82¢" in the 2 March 1962 *Texas Observer* (item 677).

547 "Open Season on the Speakership: 'A Gentleman in Politics,' Spilman Is Conservative." *TO*, 2 September 1960, pp. 1, 3.

Profiles Wade Spilman, who is campaigning for Speaker of the Texas House. "Wade Spilman might be called a gentleman in politics. The 35-year-old McAllen lawyer, a leader of the conservatives in the Texas House, is gentle and deferential.... But Spilman is a man of strong views. Tall, slender, greying slightly at the temples, he is a soft-spoken advocate of a limited state government willing to deal adequately with what he calls its 'basic responsibilities.'"

548 "Journey to Recognition." *TO*, 9 September 1960, p. 6.

Inspired by his trip from Mississippi to Texas, Morris ponders his own mortality. "I left Mississippi in a grey and windy rainstorm. At Vicksburg, from the plane, the river was barely visible, rolling and winding beneath the darkening mists...." After the airplane landed in Dallas he took a "tiny two-motor Trans-Texas plane" to Austin, and from there he "drove through the streets of the city in the stifling September heat.... Later, in the cold waters of Deep Eddy, under the towering elms by the river, I saw myself for an instant as from a plane—under the elms by the river, in the city on the edge of the hills, in the middle of the vast rolling continent, caught there, in that mere moment, in the ebbs and flows of its own mortal destiny."

549 "On the Record: Only the Beginning." *TO*, 9 September 1960, p. 4.

Summarizes a few of the speeches, proposals, and recommendations made during this week's Conference on Aging in Austin. "All in all, the whole conference was an admirable project. But it is only the beginning."

550 "Two Views of a Campaign Tour: Sights, Sounds from a Truck." *TO*, 16 September 1960, p. 2.

Avers that the photographer's truck in front of the John Kennedy-Lyndon Johnson convertible "was the place to watch the unfolding drama of a presidential campaign.... Riding into a downtown, the two sat side by side, high up on the back seat. Johnson used his broad cowboy hat to wave to the crowds. Although Kennedy was given a black-and-white sombrero in San Antonio and a cowboy hat ... in Grand Prairie, he chose to remain bareheaded."

551 "The Baptist Issue." *TO*, 23 September 1960, p. 5.

Morris satirizes voters who have misgivings about Senator John Kennedy's Catholicism. "After giving the matter much thought, I have decided that I cannot vote for just any Southern Baptist for President this year.... I will admit that this is in part very emotional with me, although I have thought out my emotions. I come from a long line of Mississippi Methodists, and the Southern Baptist Church has always struck me as a very strange business. The doctrine of total immersion is shocking to an old Mississippi Methodist."

552 "Higher Education." *TO*, 23 September 1960, p. 7.

After quoting part of a news release that states the University of Texas begins the 1960-61 academic year with an emphasis on the "quality" of students "rather than quantity," Morris narrates how he and *Texas Observer* Ronnie Dugger were working in their office one afternoon "when we were roused by feminine giggles, screams, and shouts from across the street at the new Delta Zeta House.... We rushed outside, as our readers would of course expect us to do, and were greeted by a mad human stampede, composed of girls of all sizes, tall, small, and in between.... The girls rushing down the street from the campus had just made up their minds about which sorority to join."

553 "East Texas Sojourn: Allegiance and Dissent in a Baptist Town." *TO*, 30 September 1960, pp. 1, 6–7.

Morris talks to residents of Jacksonville, Texas—a small town in East Texas with a "pronounced Baptist character"—about the presidential election. One of the persons he meets is Barnes Broiles, newspaper editor of the "liberal Democratic" *Jacksonville Daily Progress*. "Back in the summer, Broiles says, 'You couldn't walk down the street without hearing about it'—the religious issue in the campaign. The talk has 'simmered down' since then, he believes. He thinks Sen. John Kennedy's statement before the Houston ministers September 12 has helped keep the situation 'under control.'"

554 Morris, Willie, and Ronnie Dugger. "'Kennedy Is Lying': Criswell's Attack." *TO*, 30 September 1960, pp. 1–2.

Morris and Dugger interview Rev. W. A. Criswell, pastor of the First Baptist Church of Dallas, the largest Baptist church in the world. "Is Sen. Kennedy's Catholicism the major issue in this campaign? 'It is,' Criswell said, 'and you'll not escape it. I don't care what Nixon, Kennedy, and most of all Lyndon Johnson say about it.'" Morris summarizes his and Dugger's interview in chapter 7, pages 253–55, of the "Texas" section of *North Toward Home*.

555 "Get Them Out of There: Hybrids Abound in Our School Tex[t]books." *TO*, 14 October 1960, p. 5.

Admiral J. Evetts Haley and his organization Texans for America "warned the state textbook committee the other day of some dire goings-on in our public schools." One member of the group "vigorously complained that some books promote class conflict," such as a volume that listed a biography of Negro baseball player Jackie Robinson among other "good books to enjoy." Another member of Texans for America asserted "that schools should emphasize ideas which tend to stress the strength, greatness, and nobility in American life.... 'The very young are not entitled to the impartial presentation of both sides of controversial questions which involve the traditional values of American civilization,' she declared." Despite the organization's protestations, the state textbook committee, "it is rumored, did not heed the Rear Admiral and put four or five of the irascible textbooks on their new list." See also item 694.

556 "Integration at U. T.: On-Campus Services Open; Housing, Sports Segregated." *TO*, 21 October 1960, pp. 1–3.

Four years after the University of Texas "opened its doors to Negro undergraduates," Morris talks to students (both white and black), faculty members, and administrators as he examines the integration "situation" at the institution. Frank Wright, director of the university YMCA, believes that although progress "'in integration'" has been steady since 1956, "'a great deal more needs to be accomplished.' ... Those in the University community who are anxious to press for equal rights for Negro students in all feasible areas continue to be concerned about housing segregation and the exclusion of Negroes from varsity teams. Negro students are also disillusioned by the attitudes of the majority of white students toward them. Those attitudes, many of the young Negroes feel, range from icy indifference to perfunctory courtesy."

557 "An Ex-Governor's Plaintive Cry: Shifting Contexts." *TO*, 28 October 1960, p. 4.

As former Governor Allan Shivers travels across the state campaigning against "that boy" [Senator John Kennedy], Morris admonishes him and other "conservative Republicans who style themselves Texas Democrats" for contending that the Democratic Party "has 'deserted' them and their kind." It strikes Morris, "as indeed it may have struck others, that Shivers' alleged individualism, principle, and courage have been somewhat over-played by our zealous gentlemen of the Republican press. For is this not a man who lacks the simple political fortitude to enjoin his deepest convictions and cast his lot with his true ideological kindred?"

558 "Teachers Told: To Go." *TO*, 28 October 1960, p. 2.

Reveals that "pressure was put on" the faculty of Allen Academy by its president, N. B. Allen, to buy tickets and attend a special lunch in honor of former Governor Allan Shivers. Allen Academy is a private preparatory school for boys with about forty faculty members. "A special faculty meeting was called last Friday. 'Mr. Allen told us we were going to have a distinguished guest and that 100 percent attendance was expected,' one of the teachers explained. 'He said that the school is not involved in politics, but that this is a private school and can do as it pleases.'"

559 "Experiment in Organization at College Station." *TO*, 4 November 1960, pp. 6–7.

Details the activities of the Citizens' Fellowship, an interracial, non-denominational group in College Station, Texas, that is vigorous "in pressing the Negroes' cases." For example, after a house burned down in one of the "Negro sections of town" due to the absence of fire hydrants in the area, the Citizens' Fellowship arranged for the city to install hydrants.

560 "In the Roosevelt Tradition." *TO*, 4 November 1960, p. 5.

Compares Senator John Kennedy's presidential campaign to the "reforming tradition" of former President Franklin D. Roosevelt. "Kennedy has emphatically, time and again, placed his domestic program in the Rooseveltian perspective." His various proposals, such as "medical care for the aged as a part of social security" and an "active 'moral leadership' in civil rights," are an "enlargement of New Deal humanitarianism in an even more complex and urbanized society."

561 "Texas Demos United, Jack Says in Wichita." *TO*, 4 November 1960, pp. 1–2.

Reports that five days before the presidential election, Senator John Kennedy "touched down at two Panhandle airports," Amarillo and Wichita Falls, "in a quick second visit to Texas." The Democratic candidate "stressed the endorsement by state officeholders of the party ticket and expressed incredulity that Texas, home of Democratic congressional leaders, would go Republican. He urged the election of a Democratic president to lead a Democratic congress."

562 "Johnson and the Election." *TO*, 11 November 1960, p. 5.

Argues that Senator Lyndon Johnson's place on the presidential election ballot "was a strength rather than a weakness to the Kennedy forces.... The South did not remain completely solid, just as it split in 1928, 1948, 1952, and 1956, but with Kennedy's strong stance on civil rights and his Catholicism as two towering obstacles, Johnson's candidacy was a crucial factor in preventing Nixon from making inroads elsewhere on the Southern front.... Nor have we been convinced that [Johnson] appreciably slowed down the ticket in key Northern states and in California." Morris quotes from the conclusion of his column in chapter 6, pages 237–38, of the "Texas" section of *North Toward Home*.

563 "The Press in Elections." *TO*, 11 November 1960, p. 4.

Observes that "big-city newspapers again supported the Republican presidential nominee in overwhelming numbers; this time, according to the New York Times, by about three or four to one." Morris believes that this happens "every four years" because "the big press is an appendage of big business, too suffused in the values of the big business community to even try to understand what the common, average American is thinking and feeling and wanting."

564 "A Tour in the Rain: Jack Visits LBJ Ranch." *TO*, 18 November 1960, 1–2.

President-elect John Kennedy tours Lyndon Johnson's ranch, accompanied by Morris and some fifty other newsmen. After an airplane carrying Kennedy touched down on a runway at the ranch, Mr. and Mrs. Johnson entered the plane. "In a few seconds they emerged again, bringing ... Kennedy with them. 'Shake hands,' the photographers shouted. Kennedy, looking lean and tan smiled and said to Johnson, 'I will if you'll take off that hat.' Then they made their way through the crowd. 'How're you doing?' Kennedy asked Johnson. 'Fine,' Johnson replied." Morris adapts material from this article for a passage on the Johnson ranch in chapter 6, pages 238–42, of the "Texas" section of *North Toward Home.*

565 "A Survey on Voting." *TO*, 25 November 1960, p. 4.

"How do Texas congressmen stand on the issue of federal power and responsibility? The widely respected *Congressional Quarterly* has just compiled an interesting study, based on 14 key votes in the Senate and 12 in the House during the 86th Congress...." The publication chose votes on major issues that "offered a clear choice between a larger and a smaller federal role," such as school aid and the minimum wage. Morris reports that Senators Lyndon Johnson and Ralph Yarborough "supported a larger federal role on 13 of the 14 test votes for a 93% rating."

566 "A Talk with Yarborough: Ralph on Education and Next Congress." *TO*, 25 November 1960, pp. 1–2.

U.S. Senator Ralph Yarborough (D-Tex.) "discussed the prospects of the new administration and his own views of the crisis in American education" during a two-hour interview with Morris. "Yarborough is fresh from a stint of hard campaigning for the Kennedy-Johnson ticket. He foresees a 'very active' administration and believes 'the caretaker phase of government is ended.' The early weeks of the new Congress should witness 'about a cross between the 100 Days and a normal rate of progression.'"

567 "Back in the Saddle Again: Blakley's Candidacy." *TO*, 2 December 1960, p. 4.

Regards William Blakley's second appointment to the United States Senate as "one of the disturbing commentaries on the tired cynicism of American one-party politics." Blakley was "roundly defeated" in 1958 during his campaign for the Senate, and in appointing him to fill the vacancy caused by Lyndon Johnson's resignation, Governor Price Daniel "must know he is participating in an indefensible perversion of the democratic process." Even with the support of both the Texas press and big business behind Blakley "against Ralph Yarborough, the people decisively and convincingly rejected him. Now he is being foisted upon them again...."

568 "Bolshevized Medicine Department: Too Late Now?" *TO*, 2 December 1960, p. 5.

A satirical article on the American Medical Association and its "consistent and creative opposition down through the years" to noteworthy medical and social programs such as health insurance, Red Cross blood banks, and now medical services for the elderly. "We heartily commend the American Medical Association and many of the Texas doctors who belong to the good brotherhood for their vigorous, forthright stand against bolshevized medicine. As we all know, the president-elect has again proposed placing medical care for so-called old people under the so-called social security program. This most pernicious scheme ... could very well be the death-knell of our American values of individualism, incentive and fair play."

569 "Consolidation or Separation?: Library Squabble." *TO*, 9 December 1960, pp. 1, 8.

"A controversy has developed on the six-member Texas library commission and in library circles over a proposal to re-organize the library system by consolidating the federally-financed rural program with the state library extension service." The consolidation would eliminate five staff positions, including the directorship of the rural library program.

570 "Outgoing, Incoming Editors Talk: Willie Morris." *TO*, 16 December 1960, p. 5.

Morris, the new editor of the *Texas Observer* (see item 1527), tells readers about himself and sets forth his ideas for the paper. "I was chased out of the state of Mississippi at an early age; my first confrontation with basic and honest criticism of a society, and its political adjunct, was in the pages of The Texas Observer. I am strongly committed, personally and ideologically, to the Observer tradition, which is itself in the tradition of American reform liberalism." Morris adds that he plans to publish articles on the church in Texas, the state's European ethnic communities, and "the pressing social issues in Texas still largely unmet: old age problems, [elee]mosynary institutions, welfare programs, education, and the rest."

571 "Observer Notebook." *TO*, 23 December 1960, p. 4.

A compilation of news items from around the state and comments on timely issues. "Archer Fulling[im], the colorful poet laureate of the Big Thicket, wrote in his column in the Kountze News this week: 'Does anybody in Kountze ever buy a good book outside of the paperbacks? How many people in Kountze ever read a novel by William Faulkner, who won the Nobel prize in literature? ... We have ceased to be the reading nation that we were in the 19th century and the early part of the 20th.'"

572 "'Operation Abolition' and the HUAC: Charges Swapped in Debate." *TO*, 23 December 1960, pp. 1, 6.

"A public debate on the House un–American Activities Committee and its film 'Operation Abolition,' which is now being shown by civic clubs, church groups, schools, and military installations in Texas, drew some hot exchanges before the Franklin Roosevelt Young Democrats at the University of Houston this week, symptomatic of the wider controversy it has provoked in the state." The movie charges that the San Francisco demonstrators who protested last spring against HUAC and its hearings on alleged communist and subversive activities were "communist-inspired." See also item 658.

573 "An Evangelical Mission: Anti-Communism Crusade Active in Texas." *TO*, 30 December 1960, pp. 1, 3.

Details the purpose and activities of the Houston-based Christian Anti-Communism Crusade. "Stressing 'a revival of pure religion' in the domestic and international struggle against communism, advocating a staunch moral basis in foreign relations, critical of 'pseudo-liberals,' 'pseudo-intellectuals,' and 'liberal theologians' who are often 'dupes' of the communists, the Christian Anti-Communism Crusade is bringing to civic forums and community platforms of Texas and the nation all the vigor of the sunrise evangelical revival."

574 "Focus on the 57th Legislature: Payroll Tax Cited; Governor Uncommitted." *TO*, 6 January 1961, pp. 1, 8.

The "central theme" of the new legislative session, which convenes next week, will be the "overriding issue of state finances, less settled than postponed in the fiery tax battles of the 56th legislature." Texas Governor Price Daniel's "advisory finance commission has emerged with a proposed 'payroll tax' to meet revenue needs, the governor replying that he would submit the recommendations of his unofficial advisory group but would remain uncommitted to any particular tax. See also item 575.

575 "Focus on the 57th Legislature: Some Responses, Appeals from State Agencies." *TO*, 6 January 1961, pp. 1–2.

Morris discloses that he asked the heads of "a number" of state government agencies to comment on Texas Governor Price Daniel's budget and "its possible impact on their administrative domains." The officials readily acknowledged the "present financial dilemma" and discussed the problems they had to face while contending with a "funds shortage." See also item 574.

576 "Historic Conflict: The Senate, the House, and the Session." *TO*, 6 January 1961, p. 5.

Despite the Texas Senate being "the bulwark of an entrenched and narrow-visioned conservatism," the "vitalized" House in the coming legislative session just may challenge its "hallowed immunity." A "hardy and experienced" group of liberals is returning to the House, which "as a whole will be more liberally disposed on taxation and economic legislation." Morris is hopeful that "the day of shallow justifications in our legislature is past, when niggardly appropriations for educating our children, for paroling our juveniles, for caring for our unfortunates, were rationalized on the crassest of grounds."

577 "Early Proposals on State Taxes: Eckhardt's Four-Part Pack." *TO*, 21 January 1961, pp. 1, 8.

While Texas Governor Price Daniel is seeking support in the House for his tax programs, "two major alternatives are being brought into shape: one by Rep. Bob Eckhardt, liberal from Houston, another by Rep. Maco Stewart, moderate-liberal from Galveston."

578 "Price's Choice: Payroll Levy, Deficit Plan." *TO*, 21 January 1961, pp. 1–2.

Governor Price Daniel proposed eliminating the state's sixty-three million dollar deficit "by a temporary three percent increase in the natural gas severance tax, a franchise tax aimed at the larger interstate corporations, an abandoned properties bill, and a change in general revenue financing of the rural roads program...." To raise over one hundred million dollars annually, he "offered the one percent payrolls earning tax brought forth by his advisory finance commission."

579 "Budget Board Slashes Agencies— But Less Than Usual." *TO*, 28 January 1961, pp. 1–2.

"The Legislative Budget Board's biennial budget, customarily as spare as a skeleton, has a little more meat on its ribs this year but still lags $20 million behind Gov. Price Daniel's 'hard economy' general revenue fund proposals." Although a number of state agencies "fared well," the board sharply cut proposed programs for public welfare, water projects, public health, and higher education.

580 "Senate Conservatives Rewarded: Ramsey's Choices." *TO*, 28 January 1961, pp. 1–2.

Lieutenant Governor Ben Ramsey has announced his appointments to state committees "in which the plums again were given the more solid Senate conservatives. As chairman of the two most important Senate panels, Ramsey chose two members of the conservative Senate 'team.'" He selected Wardlow Lane of Center, Texas, to head the state affairs committee and named Ray Roberts of McKinney to chair the finance committee.

581 "Lobby Makes Its Play — Against Texas Again: An Editorial." *TO*, 4 February 1961, pp. 1, 4.

Governor Price Daniel, as part of his tax plan to eliminate the state's deficit, has proposed "another tax increase on straight natural gas production — in other words, on the home-based independent Texas producer." Morris editorially denounces the "majors," the giant pipeline companies who are "the real source of the towering profits." These "absentee exploiters of our Texas resources" have avoided paying their fair share of taxes "by opposing any change in the present franchise tax, which favors the huge multi-state corporations by taxing the small and struggling and the entrenched and wealthy at the same rate."

582 "The Tax Committee: Sketches of Twenty-One." *TO*, 4 February 1961, p. 5.

Describes the "political allegiances and voting records" of the members of the state Revenue and Tax Committee. "By all odds the most important committee in the two houses this session, because of the pressing need for additional revenue and also because of the historic circumstances under which moderates and liberals have been summoned to control it, is the committee on revenue and taxation."

583 "Wright's Vigorous Bid: Defends 'Progressive Moderation' in Senate Race." *TO*, 4 February 1961, pp. 1, 3.

A "morning-long interview" with Congressman Jim Wright. In his current bid for the U.S. Senate, Wright "brings a sharp intelligence and a kind of sophisticated rural evangelism to the Texas hustings. The young Fort Worth congressman, elected to Congress in 1954 in a victory widely acclaimed by Texas liberals, has drifted toward the middle in the political spectrum in the last six years. He now describes himself as a 'progressive moderate.'"

584 "'Lot of Hell Ahead': Prisons Present Somber Warning." *TO*, 11 February 1961, pp. 1–2.

"O. B. Ellis, head of the Texas department of corrections, warned the House appropriations committee this week that if something isn't done to improve the salaries and working hours of guards in state prisons 'there's going to be a lot of hell ahead of us.'" The committee "heard Ellis' somber testimony that the department of corrections is $625,000 short to carry on for the rest of the biennium."

585 "Republican Tower Says He's Ahead." *TO*, 11 February 1961, pp. 1, 8.

A "lengthy interview" with John Tower, who six months ago "was an unknown government professor in an obscure West Texas college." He now "has an excellent chance to reach a second primary in the current campaign for the U. S. Senate. 'My conservatism,' John Tower says, 'is a matter of philosophical conviction.'"

586 "Abolish Inequities, Proponents Say: Franchise Tax Tussle — Pro and Con." *TO*, 18 February 1961, p. 3.

Businessmen "protested against a 'dangerous trend' in Texas tax policies, and got in a few plugs for a general sales tax in hearings this week before the House tax committee on Gov. Daniel's franchise tax aimed at the major interstate corporations." Representatives Franklin Spears and Joe Cannon defended the proposal, estimated to net ten million dollars annually, "on grounds that the present franchise levy discriminates against Texas companies doing most of their business in the state."

587 "Council Asks $$$: Total Request Refused in Budget." *TO*, 18 February 1961, pp. 2, 7.

Glenn Garrett, chairman of the Council on Migrant Labor, requested $10,335 from the House Appropriations Committee "to continue its operations for the year." The legislative budget board, however, "recommended cutting off the agency without any funds." Testified Garrett to the committee: "Surely $10,000 is not an exorbitant sum to devote to improving the well-being of over 100,000 Texas men, women, and children."

588 "A Curious Rapport: Tower's Chances." *TO*, 18 February 1961, p. 4.

Morris acknowledges that conservative U. S. Senate candidate John Tower and he have a "curious rapport." This mutual regard is not difficult to explain, as "there is a subtle respect for steadfast opinions honestly expressed." Nevertheless,

Tower's election to the Senate, "let there be no doubt, would be an unmitigated disaster for Texas and the nation.... This writer would like nothing better than to see him reach a runoff against some staunch maverick liberal — and get roundly trounced."

589 "Governor Warns of Special Session: Bankers Protest." *TO*, 18 February 1961, pp. 1, 8.

Governor Price Daniel has announced that he might call a special session of the legislature if it does not pass his abandoned properties law. His proposal "would put teeth in the present law by requiring those holding funds unclaimed for seven years or more to report them to the state treasurer." Bankers from all over the state warned that Daniel's plan would "violate the law of contracts, damage the relationship of banker to depositor, and do injury to the prestige of the banking community."

590 "Child Welfare Plea." *TO*, 25 February 1961, p. 1.

Department of Public Welfare officials have testified before the House Appropriations Committee asking "for more welfare workers to carry on essential services. John Winters, director of public welfare, told the committee the department's case load per fieldworker is the highest in the United States."

591 "Daniel Withdraws Payroll Proposal." *TO*, 25 February 1961, pp. 1–2.

The "big news" from the governor's office is that Governor Price Daniel has "abandoned his payroll-earnings tax, which he admitted had created little enthusiasm in either house, and pitched a campaign for a general broadening of selective sales taxes." He now proposes to "place new or increased taxes on beer, soft drinks, restaurant meals, cosmetics, car and boat parts, household appliances, liquor, and wine."

592 "One Committee: Come Down to Austin." *TO*, 25 February 1961, p. 4.

After observing "three weeks of important hearings" of the House Revenue and Tax Committee, Morris praises its hardworking members. "It is good to watch them at work, to understand what they represent in a state undergoing the most fundamental political changes. Those of our readers who haven't seen the legislature since those sordid days of the early '50's, when the large interests enjoyed a kind of final flowering, would do well to make a special trip to Austin someday soon just to watch."

593 "A Demolition Job: Conservative-Dominated Coalition, Three Dead Taxes." *TO*, 4 March 1961, pp. 1–2.

"In a mood ranging from bitter to bantering, a conservative-dominated majority stymied three of Gov. Price Daniel's deficit-retiring tax measures in the House this week. At the end of the torturous seven-hour session Wednesday, the escheats bill, the revised franchise tax on interstate corporations, and the gross receipts tax on utilities had been slapped down."

594 "Escheats Bill Fails: Old Foes and New 'Friends.'" *TO*, 4 March 1961, p. 2.

Reports that Governor Price Daniel's escheats bill was defeated in the legislature by a vote of 79–69. If passed, the measure would have required banks holding funds unclaimed for seven years to seek the "original depositors." If they could not be found, "the property would escheat to the state."

595 "Old Testament Retribution: Death Penalty Debated." *TO*, 4 March 1961, pp. 1, 8.

"The dynamics of Old Testament retribution, statistics on the social ineffectiveness of the death penalty, and warnings of increased state expense to keep condemned criminals alive who might deserve execution were debated in a dramatic hearing before the House criminal jurisprudence committee this week. After a five-hour session, the Bridges-Whitfield bill outlawing capital punishment was referred to a friendly subcommittee."

596 "Angry Atheist Hunt: Red Threat Also Cited in Hearing." *TO*, 11 March 1961, pp. 1, 3.

Warning of "rampant atheism in Texas education and creeping communism in schools and churches," Representatives W. T. Oliver, W. T. Dungan, and Joe Chapman have presented a bill before the House State Affairs Committee that would require "all public school and college teachers to take an oath acknowledging a 'Supreme Being.'" Witnesses opposing the measure, "all clergymen and theologians, argued that the bill is unconstitutional, injurious to good teaching, and in conflict with American traditions of individual conscience and religious liberty." See also items 606 and 614.

597 "'Saturation Limit' in State Juvenile Schools: 'Same Old Gang' — Or Parole System." *TO*, 11 March 1961, p. 2.

Representative Don Kennard and the Texas Youth Council have requested $668,000 from the legislature to fund a state juvenile parole system. "'We've reached the saturation limit,'" Dr. James Turman, executive director of the Youth Council, warned the House Appropriations Committee. "'We can't continue to build buildings to store people,' he said. 'Either we deal with these kids outside our schools or we must build more facilities each year to house them.'"

598 "A Day in Houston: Maury's Bid." *TO*, 18 March 1961, pp. 1–2, 7.

Morris spends a day in Houston on the campaign trail with senatorial candidate Maury Maverick Jr., who is running against Republican John Tower. "Campaigning on a solidly liberal platform in the current race for the U.S. Senate,... Maverick made the rounds of boat docks, Negro churches, and shopping centers in a one-day tour of Harris County. His theme, repeated before every group of voters: 'I'm a Franklin Roosevelt, Ralph Yarborough, John Kennedy Democrat. With John Kennedy, let us reach out for new frontiers, which is a reaching out for tomorrow.'"

599 "Judgments on House at Midway." *TO*, 18 March 1961, pp. 1, 8.

Analyzes "events so far" in the fifty-seventh Texas House of Representatives as it moved this week into the second half of the legislative session. "Two of Gov. Price Daniel's key deficit-retiring measures, the escheats bill and the revised franchise tax on interstate business, had been derailed, although proponents hope they might be revived later. Meanwhile, a wide range of taxes have been introduced and will probably be fought on the floor in the next several weeks."

600 "Remarks on Conservatism of Texas Students: The Time of Your Time." *TO*, 18 March 1961, p. 6.

Excerpts from a speech to students at Will Rice College, Rice University, in which Morris chides American — and particularly Texas—college students for their conservatism and conformity. He believes that "we young people are the most conforming generation in American history.... I think this conformity springs from the past eight years of a calm and unruffling national administration, which has set — after the pattern of most national administrations— a broad standard for the nation.... I would suggest, right here at Rice, an honest and probing appraisal of the college community in Texas, of the kind of people you are as college students, of what you want and where you are going and where America is going."

601 "Long, Hot Summer? Tax Fights Imminent." *TO*, 25 March 1961, pp. 1, 3.

As the Texas House of Representatives struggles with a "highly confusing tax situation," Morris predicts that the legislative body's "route" towards solving its revenue problems will be "warm and tortuous." The House is studying nine major tax programs, which embrace "every philosophy of taxation from a graduated personal income tax to a straight general sales tax without exemptions, with diverse selective sales taxes and levies on business and natural resources in between."

602 "Radical Mystique of an American Dictatorship: Houston, Austin Leaders Won't Disclose Strength." *TO*, 25 March 1961, pp. 6–7.

Discusses the membership and philosophy of the John Birch Society, an anti-communist organization that is particularly strong in Texas. "Membership in the John Birch Society is a curiously secret proposition. No one will disclose how many chapters or members there are in any given city. They will talk with you individually, once you learn they are members; but the bond of brotherhood is strong. If everyone 'knew of our activities, the enemy would work against us,' one West Texas member said." See also item 603.

603 "Radical Mystique of an American Dictatorship: The John Birch Society — Rooting Out 'Subversion.'" *TO*, 25 March 1961, pp. 6–7.

Relates that retired Boston candy manufacturer Robert Welch and a group of industrialists, with the goal of "rooting out communist subversion," formed the John Birch Society in 1958. "Two and a half years later this curious, American-made dictatorship of the far right, with its mystiques and its secrecies reminiscent of the Know Nothings and the KKK, its organizational techniques ironically akin to the embryonic stages of the very communism it seeks to destroy, has spread throughout the country." An unflattering profile of Welch and his organization. See also item 602.

604 "Rates Regulation Called Necessary." *TO*, 25 March 1961, pp. 1–2.

This week the House State Affairs Committee heard testimony concerning Representative Dan Struve's proposal to create a "telephone division in the Railroad Commission with power to fix rates and charges and [provide] reasonably adequate 'service and facilities impartially and without unjust discrimination.'" Proponents of the measure argued that "intrastate rates are disproportionally high because they are unregulated," while "telephone company officials countered that their companies are serving in the public interest and do not need to be regulated."

605 "House Coalition Wins Tax Battle." *TO*, 1 April 1961, pp. 1, 6.

After two days of debate, the Texas House of Representatives this week passed a forty-two million dollar tax bill. "A coalition of liberals, moderates, and [Governor Price] Daniel men were successful almost at every turn in sending to the Senate a diverse measure with amendments taxing air-conditioners and jukeboxes, changing certain bookkeeping methods to close loopholes and provide additional money for the embattled general revenue fund, establishing a new gift tax, raising license taxes on compact cars, [and] hitting inter-state corporations under a new franchise formula...."

606 "Supreme Oath Bill Endorsed by Panel." *TO*, 1 April 1961, pp. 1, 5.

"With several unsympathetic members absent, the House state affairs committee this week favorably reported the supreme being bill (item 596) to the House floor. The vote on the measure, which would require all public school and college teachers to take an oath acknowledging the existence of a supreme being, was 7–6."

607 "Conservatives to the Fore: Interpretation of a Sharply-Divided Senate Vote." *TO*, 8 April 1961, pp. 1–2.

With the U.S. Senate race of "six major candidates divided among two conservatives, two moderates, and two liberals, Goldwater Republican John Tower and Eisenhower-Kennedy Democrat William Blakley emerged with just about fifty percent of the slightly more than one million votes for places in the run-off." Both Tower and Blakley "ran as passionate foes of the Kennedy program, and for weeks the opposing camps jostled over the claim to 'true conservatism.'"

608 "Ralph Keeps Mum on Tower-Blakley." *TO*, 8 April 1961, pp. 1–2.

In an hour-long interview with Morris, Senator Ralph Yarborough "was cautious and diplomatic on the Senate campaign.... Asked whom he would support in the second primary of the Senate race, Yarborough said: 'There wasn't a party primary and there weren't any party conventions. It was purely a personal race. I think a statement now would be premature,' he said."

609 "Professor Hazed in Angry Hearing." *TO*, 15 April 1961, pp. 1, 6.

During a midnight hearing last week on a "controversial" bill, legislators directed "heated accusations" at Das Kelley Barnett, a professor of Christian Social Ethics at the Episcopal Seminary of the Southwest and a "major witness against the 'segregation bills' of 1957." The bill, heard by the House State Affairs Committee, "would provide a fine of $100–$500 for any person who refuses to leave the premises of a business when he is ordered to leave by the proprietor." Barnett was intensely questioned "on his background, his political beliefs,... and his views on civil disobedience and the sit-in movement." See also item 615.

610 "Speculation on Senate, Governor: Sales Tax Makes It." *TO*, 25 April 1961, pp. 1, 3.

Announces that the Texas House of Representatives passed a sales-tax bill that will "levy a two percent tax on all retail sales, with exemptions on food, medicine, farm machinery, and several other diverse items. [Charles] Wilson, who masterfully guided the bill through a host of amendments, estimated its yield at $127 million annually." If the Senate passes the bill, it will then go to the governor's office.

611 "Daniel's Firm Commitments: Political Honor." *TO*, 29 April 1961, p. 4.

Editorially reproves the members of the Texas House of Representatives for passing a general retail sales tax "at the expense of the average citizen of Texas [and] in naked defense of the wealthy interests which hire them." Morris hopes that Governor Price Daniel will "fight back" against the legislation, as he did against a similar measure in 1939 while a state Representative. Governor Daniel's "political prestige is now at stake. If he allows this tax to become law, it will not only be a mockery of the great public service he performed, along with his 55 other colleagues, in 1939. It will be a mockery also of his career as governor, and of his commitments to the people."

612 "Spy Adventure in Austin: An Intruder in Cell 772." *TO*, 6 May 1961, pp. 1–3.

In Morris's true story of a "cloak-and-dagger romp conducted in strictest secrecy," he describes clandestine meetings with "Young Mr. X," a member of an Austin cell (or chapter) of the John Birch Society. One day last week Young Mr. X told him that the society recently directed one of its most trusted members—the "Big Man"—to organize a highly selective group of University of Texas students to spy on their professors and ferret out any subversive activities. "The purpose of the project is to bring about a full-scale investigation of the University. The members, young patriots of resourcefulness and determination, had been working, quietly and efficiently, toward that goal." Morris, proceeding with caution, checked out his informant's allegations. Revised as "Cell 772, Or Life Among the Extremists" for *Commentary* (item 722). Morris expands on his *Texas Observer* "travails of a working journalist in the Age of John Birch" in chapter 8, pages 267–84, of the "Texas" section of *North Toward Home.*

613 "S-T Officials Mum on Funds: Sealy, Bracewell Won't Comment on Fees, Money Spent." *TO*, 13 May 1961, pp. 1–2.

The *Texas Observer* "learned from a reliable source this week that Tom Sealy, chairman of the Citizens for a Sales Tax organization, is receiving $25,000 for his services this session and Searcy Bracewell, former state senator and vice-chairman of the group, is receiving $20,000." Both Bracewell and Sealy refused to comment on the *Observer*'s information on the "grounds that the reporting of fees is not required by law and Citizens for a Sales Tax 'should not be singled out.'" See also item 624.

614 "Award Winners Revealed!" *TO*, 20 May 1961, p. 4.

A list of humorous awards compiled by *Texas Observer* staff members. "Texas Observer Ltd. this week announces its slate of Oscar-winners in the Texas House of Representatives." For example, Joe Chapman, W. T. Dungan, and W. T. Oliver, who sponsored a bill requiring teachers to take an oath recognizing the existence of a supreme being, each received "the Observer Prize for Being Supreme." Morris adds that "all three were adjudged equally supreme." See also item 596.

615 "Away from the Confederacy?: There Was Applause." *TO*, 27 May 1961, p. 5.

Editorially reports that after an "anti–sit-in" bill failed to pass in the Texas House of Representatives, the House members spontaneously applauded and cheered. "Some of the reporters sitting around the press table looked at one another and smiled. They knew it could not have happened five years ago. One-third of the Texas House of Representatives went on record against a thinly-disguised discrimination bill — and perhaps 15 others wanted to vote against it and did not...." During occasions like this, "we may assure ourselves that Texas is moving away from the Confederacy." See also item 609.

616 "Tax Impasse Seen: Conference Committee at Odds; Veto Threat." *TO*, 27 May 1961, pp. 1–2.

"House and Senate conferees were to meet over the weekend in one final effort to resolve their differences, but the likelihood of a compromise solution on a tax bill seemed all but futile. The regular session ends at midnight Monday."

617 "GOP's Triumph: New Political Era?" *TO*, 3 June 1961, pp. 1, 8.

John Tower's election to the U.S. Senate as the first Republican from Texas since Reconstruction "is an event of crucial significance. Tower's slim 10,000-vote margin over interim Sen. William Blakley serves notice to old-line Southern Democrats in both Texas and the deeper South that the traditional antipathy toward 'local' Republicans has become moribund and that Southern Republicans are becoming more aggressive and politically acute with each passing election."

618 "House Vetoes Tax in Anguished Finale: Turman's Vote Decides Struggle." *TO*, 3 June 1961, pp. 1–3.

On May 29, which will be remembered as "The Day the Speaker Killed the Sales Tax," Texas House conferees twice attempted to negotiate with their counterparts in the Senate to come up with a tax bill acceptable to the House before the legislative session ended at midnight. Both times the House members reported that the Senate would not change its mind. "Finally, in the dying minutes of the session, Speaker James Turman cast a deciding vote, creating a 72–72 tie and killing the Senate tax measure." See also item 627.

619 "Appropriations Examined: Disappointment Keen Over Tentative Slashing of Juvenile Parole." *TO*, 10 June 1961, pp. 1, 7.

"Continuing shortcomings in some areas, critical needs in others, an occasional expression of satisfaction — these were the reactions received by the Observer this week in querying a number of government agency heads on the $383 million appropriations bill passed by the Senate May 29."

620 "A Nibble at a Quibble." *TO*, 10 June 1961, p. 5.

Although the legislative session ended without the passage of a sales-tax bill, the measure will be raised again in a forthcoming special session. Morris editorially takes issue with "businessmen" who contend that the political negotiations over the bill failed due to a "quibble" over the proposed deductible amount that, when spent on certain items, would not be subject to sales tax. "We doubt rather seriously, for instance, that those thousands of Texas families with annual incomes of less than $2,500 or $3,000 consider the [Governor] Daniel-Senate struggle over the $10 exemption a quibble."

621 "Tormented Atmosphere of Houston." *TO*, 17 June 1961, p. 5.

Provides coverage of Houston's "proliferation of ultra-rightist organizations" such as the John Birch Society. This "renaissance of the radical right in the South's largest city" is not surprising, "since Houston geographically is a kind of metropolitan prop to the East Texas 'bible belt.'" Furthermore, "the city's extremist movements derive much of their native fervor from a mating of rigorous evangelical fundamentalism and 'pro-Americanism.'"

622 "Veteran Legislator Remembers the Days." *TO*, 17 June 1961, p. 1–2.

Interviews Charles Hughes, a ten-year member of the Texas House of Representatives. "Charlie Hughes is an old hand at the political game; his own career traces the end of one political era in Texas and the beginning of another. He has been in the House since 1951, when Allan Shivers was in full bloom, and he has noted the things that have changed." One summer evening two years ago he leaned back in his chair and said, "It's finally become acceptable for a man to be decent."

623 "Amarillo Solon Charges Pressure." *TO*, 1 July 1961, p. 1–2.

Texas House of Representatives member Ted Springer, who for sixteen years has worked as a printer for the *Amarillo Globe-Times* and the *Amarillo Daily News*, claims that newspaper publisher S. B. Whittenburg has fired him for voting against the sales tax bill. "Contacted in Amarillo, Whittenburg said he had established a new policy last March disallowing employees on his news media from seeking elective office." In a statement concerning the case, the newspapers declared that Springer's voting record "is not a point of issue."

624 "Observer Notebook: King Saud's Harem and Citizens for Sales Tax." *TO*, 1 July 1961, p. 4.

A compilation of news stories and comments on timely issues. "Citizen for a Sales Tax kingfish Tom Sealy was asked in Houston this week how much money his organization has received from various interests." He said that he could not recall exact figures but knew that he had received some contributions. "A very cynical associate of ours says the reason Gov. Daniel has gotten so ornery about this sales tax is that Tom Sealy is making twice as much money for his services this session as the governor is." See also item 613.

625 "Tormented Houston: On Sidelines, Cheering Them On." *TO*, 8 July 1961, p. 6.

Explains how the "loud and enthusiastic and spellbinding voices" of "first- and second-generation wealth" are influencing Houston's development. "Houston is a city of newcomers, and the newcomers are on the make: young men and women from East Texas who are turning the old swamps into vast new suburbias, a growing class of professionals and technicians and industrial managers all too ready to take the political nostrums of their superiors as their own."

626 "Floor Action Imminent: Governor Presses to Keep Coalition Together." *TO*, 15 July 1961, pp. 1–2.

"Governor Price Daniel was working overtime this week to keep a patchwork coalition of moderates and liberals behind his sales-tax–based compromise tax program. The results of his work will probably be seen Tuesday or Wednesday when H[ouse] B[ill] 20, sponsored by House tax committee chairman Charles Ballman of Borger, reaches the floor...."

627 "Compromise Squeezes By: $5 Deductible Advances to Third Reading." *TO*, 22 July 1961, pp. 1, 3.

"Speaker James Turman cast his second crucial tie-breaking vote of the 57th legislature on taxes Friday and by a 71–70 vote the House sent to third reading a compromise program of Austin Rep. Charles Sandahl staked mainly on a two percent sales tax on items over $5." See also item 618.

628 "The Wardlow Lane Stage: The Militant Fighter — How It Once Was." *TO*, 22 July 1961, p. 4.

Editorially chronicles the early political career of Wardlow Lane, president pro tempore of the Texas Senate. "Back in the 'forties, they say, he was the young man of deep compassion, a militant fighter and defender of those things more often than not deemed controversial." Now, unfortunately, he is "the hardened political practitioner who guts appropriations with accompanying belly-laughs [and] embraces grotesque tax bills and diverse vindictive schemes as a young man embraces his dreams of charity and renown."

629 "Anti-Aid Measure Gets 66, But Fails." *TO*, 29 July 1961, p. 2.

"A resolution which would have branded as 'irresponsible' the U.S. Department of Commerce's designation of 47 Texas counties as economically depressed areas drew 66–57 approval in the Texas House this week, but fell shy of a two-thirds majority needed to suspend the rules." Representative John Allen, who introduced the resolution, "charged that the designation of depressed area 'does a great deal of harm to the people of our area.'"

630 "Panel Recommends Lobby Legislation; Action Imminent." *TO*, 29 July 1961, pp. 1–2.

Next week the Texas House will discuss legislation that will require the reporting of all monies spent for lobbying. Representative Bob Mullen, "chairman of the subcommittee which worked over the measure, told the Observer the approach taken was 'to devise a bill that will get full disclosure of lobbying activities rather than punitive legislation which we probably have enough of already.'"

631 "Tax Showdown." *TO*, 29 July 1961, pp. 1–3.

This week the Senate Finance Committee completed its hearing on a House-passed tax bill and "referred the measure to the same subcommittee which threw back a straight sales tax in the regular session."

632 "TIPRO Declares War on Pipelines: Austin Speculates on the Gas Tax." *TO*, 29 July 1961, pp. 1–2.

The Texas Independent Producers and Royalty Owners Association has circulated a memorandum to its principal leaders throughout the state discussing its decision not to oppose a twenty-four million dollar natural gas tax. "In an unusually hard-hitting statement,... TIPRO President J. F. West wrote: 'It makes no sense for us to allow ourselves to be volunteered (by the pipelines) as a means of keeping taxes off pipelines.'"

633 "Eckhardt vs. Lane: Controversy Stirs on Pipeline Issue." *TO*, 5 August 1961, pp. 1–2.

"Sen. Wardlow Lane of Center and Representative Bob Eckhardt of Houston became involved this week in a sharp debate over the constitutionality of the tax on dedicated reserves of natural gas.... At stake is an estimated $18.5 million which the tax is expected to net."

634 "Long Day's Journey into Night: Fight to No Avail, Lane Bill Succeeds." *TO*, 5 August 1961, pp. 1–3.

Despite an eight-hour filibuster by one of its members, the Texas Senate approved a two percent general sales tax. "The vote on final passage for Sen. Wardlow Lane's $360 million tax package, which also includes an increase in the present one-factor corporate franchise tax and a gas pipeline tax which advocates contend was made unconstitutional [by the passage of an amendment], was 20–10."

635 "The Making of a Sales Tax: How It Happened; Price Goes for It, Wilson Key Figure." *TO*, 12 August 1961, pp. 1, 8.

Observes that "many diverse factors" contributed to the passage of the Senate's 354 million dollar tax bill in the House this week. "Mainly, however, it was the intervention of Gov. Price Daniel in favor of the bill and the decision of Speaker James Turman to take the lead in getting a favorable vote on any tax package with a chance of passing which broke the House deadlock." See also item 636.

636 "The Making of a Sales Tax: Pipeline Levy Truncated; Turman Oversees Passage." *TO*, 12 August 1961, pp. 1, 5.

Notes that on August 8, "a coalition of conservatives and moderates" in the Texas House, led by Speaker James Turman, "mustered 84 votes against 62 to join the Senate in enacting the state's first general sales tax.... Of the $354 million total, almost $320 million will be derived from the two percent sales tax. The rest will accrue from a greatly watered-down pipeline tax, an increase in the present corporation franchise tax, an increase in drivers' license fees, and minor bookkeeping amendments." See also item 635.

637 "Maury on Safari: Thoughts on LBJ." *TO*, 18 August 1961, p. 4.

"Our good friend," former member of the Texas House of Representatives Maury Maverick Jr., chats with Morris "over some good fifteen-cent beer" about Vice President Lyndon B. Johnson. "'He's really one of the most magnificent politicians in Washington today,' Maury said, 'whatever you think of him. And everyone in Washington tells me he's all for the Kennedy administration.'" Morris quotes from this article in chapter 6, pages 242–44, of the "Texas" section of *North Toward Home*: "Maverick had just returned from Washington, where he spent some time with Johnson, and I wrote a column quoting Maverick and praising the Vice-President. Subsequently, it was picked up by some of the big dailies, including the *Post-Dispatch*; Johnson himself was sure to see it."

638 "Mumbo-Jumbos of a Legislative 'Report': An Editorial." *TO*, 25 August 1961, p. 5.

Editorially condemns a "vindictive and unbalanced work" released by the Texas House "investigating committee" that purportedly examines "'racial agitation' in the state. After studying the somber mumbo-jumbos and the twisted conclusions of this rumbling work of prose, one can only reach the conclusion that the most vociferous communist 'dupes' in Texas are not the people given that quaint epithet in the report, but the six brave souls who had a hand in writing it."

639 "UT Student President: 'Mo' Holds His Ground." *TO*, 25 August 1961, pp. 1, 7.

"The University of Texas board of regents have found a tough adversary in Maurice 'Mo' Olian, 22-year-old president of the UT student body. When the regents decided this summer that racial integration on the main campus had gone far enough — branding student and faculty efforts for desegregation of housing and varsity athletics as the work of 'a vocal minority'— Olian minced no words. He called the regents' policy 'narrow-minded, backward, and hypocritical.'"

640 "Events in San Antonio." *TO*, 1 September 1961, p. 5.

Editorially criticizes the Fourth Army for agreeing to participate in a public program in San Antonio, inasmuch as right-wing "spellbinders and witchdoctors" will also be present. "The Fourth Army, as an official arm of our military establishment, is treading on dangerous ground in actively co-sponsoring a public affair which will feature some of the wildest 'revivalists of the far right' and Birch proselytizers in the land." See also items 641, 646, 648, 652, and 659.

641 "A Lively Controversy in SA: It Centers on Jaycee Seminar; Military in Politics?" *TO*, 1 September 1961, pp. 1–2.

A "lively controversy" has arisen in San Antonio after local civic groups and the San Antonio–based Fourth Army agreed to sponsor a "Let's Look at America" seminar on September 22 and 23. "Jaycee leaders say the program, designed to examine mostly internal communist subversion, is 'non-political' and 'non-controversial'; the Fourth Army, which is giving active organizational assistance, says it was invited to do so by the Jaycees and that the seminar is a civic function; critics say the whole affair is 'extreme right-wing' and the military has no business getting involved." See also items 640, 646, 648, 652, and 659.

642 "Observer Notebook." *TO*, 9 September 1961, pp. 1, 4.

A compilation of news stories and comments on timely issues. Senator Bill Proxmire from Wisconsin "tells in his latest newsletter why he opposed the appointment of Houstonian Lawrence O'Connor to the Federal Power Commission. 'I did this,' he writes, 'because there was a vast legal and economic case that had to be made to show the literal sitdown-strike against the consumer by the FPC.'"

643 "Cox of Breckenridge: Major Defection to GOP in Texas." *TO*, 15 September 1961, pp. 1–3.

Democrat Jack Cox, a "prominent conservative" from Breckenridge, Texas, has announced that the "Democrats are 'dedicated to a course which can lead only to the destruction of the basic political and civil rights guaranteed by our Constitution' and that he is enlisting as a 'buck private' in the GOP."

644 "Observer Notebook." *TO*, 15 September 1961, pp. 1, 4.

Morris asks several of his friends if they know where the South ends and the West begins. "A young man from Sweden was in town last week and wanted to know. He had been doing the South, talking to Freedom Riders on bail and in jail. By the time he reached CenTex, he wondered if he had imperceptively passed the barrier, silently and in the dark of night, or if the South were still upon him." Republished as "Where Does the South End?" in *Terrains of the Heart* (item 12).

645 "Eckhardt on Pipelines Tax: Did Lobby Err?" *TO*, 22 September 1961, p. 4.

Reports that in August, during the last few days of the Texas legislative session, lobbyists against a natural gas pipeline tax managed to secure the passage of an amendment that "apparently gutted the measure from $18 million to $3 million and let the pipelines off scot-free." Representative Bob Eckhardt, "who devoted most of his energies from the first day of the 57th legislature to a constitutional approach to pipeline taxation," now believes that despite the amendment the full tax is applicable "precisely as he originally intended."

646 "Sponsors: Jaycees, Army; Heated Exchange on Bexar Event." *TO*, 22 September 1961, pp. 1–2.

San Antonio's forthcoming "Americanism

Seminar," a program that has been "widely advertised in Bexar County," continues to generate controversy. The event's critics "resent the participation of the Fourth Army in what they consider a purely political project" and warn that the seminar is "actually providing a forum for right-wing extremists." Proponents claim that the speakers will be non-political and that the project is intended to show Americans how to oppose communist subversion. See also items 640, 641, 648, 652, and 659.

647 "Observer Notebook: Tower vs. Goldwater." *TO*, 29 September 1961, pp. 4–5.

A compilation of news stories and comments on timely issues, including a blunt appraisal of the John Birch Society. "The Texas Observer can bellow til doomsday, but it will be the conservatives themselves ... who must face, as ranking conservatives on the national level have long since faced, the unadorned truth that their own conservative cause in the long run is severely endangered by radical movements of the right."

648 Sherrill, Bob, N. P., and Willie Morris. "Jaycee-Army Seminar: Administration Appeases Soviets." *TO*, 29 September 1961, pp. 1, 3.

"Speakers at the Jaycee-Fourth Army 'Let's Look at America' seminar this week accused the Kennedy administration of appeasing Soviet Russia, urged immediate severance of diplomatic relations with the Soviet government, criticized American liberals as being soft on communism, and got in some harsh words on the United Nations." One of the program's leaders lambasted the seminar's critics, "arguing that no one is more qualified than the military on the communist menace." *Texas Observer* records cannot identify the co-author "N. P.," and Bob Sherrill does not recall the name. See also items 640, 641, 646, 652, and 659.

649 "Those One-Day Governors: An Austin Tradition Grows Bigger and Better." *TO*, 6 October 1961, pp. 1–2.

Describes Austin's annual "Governor for a Day" celebration. This "traditional ceremony" honors the president pro tempore of the Texas Senate, "the third man in line for the governorship and the acting chief executive when both the governor and the lieutenant governor are out of the state." Some people, "citing the receptions, banquets, and gifts, say that [the] quaint Texas custom ... actually amounts to payola in its more crass forms; others contend it provides an occasion to reward state senators for jobs well done."

650 Sherrill, Bob, and Willie Morris. "A Bitter San Antonio Feud: Gonzalez, Goode Fire from Political Opposites." *TO*, 13 October 1961, pp. 1, 3.

"In a city long noted for its unadorned political knocks, the Henry Gonzalez-John Goode congressional race is developing into an unusually bitter fight. Ideological lines have seldom been more tautly drawn in Texas." Because Goode is a "Goldwater-brand Republican" and Gonzalez a "warm admirer of Pres. Kennedy," this election "will furnish students of Texas politics with a kind of pristine partisan warfare seldom seen for a major office in a Texas constituency." Slightly revised as: "Bitter Texas Race Being Fought Along Ideological Lines." *Washington Post*, 29 October 1961, sec. A, p. 2.

651 "Poll Taxes Sought; Wright Quizzed." *TO*, 20 October 1961, p. 1.

Discloses that some two hundred liberal Democrats met in Austin this week, "but the only firm decision made on the state's forthcoming political wars was the organization of a sweeping poll tax drive."

652 "Another Rally: Long Hot Winter." *TO*, 27 October 1961, p. 4.

Morris satirizes the recent anti-communist rally held in San Antonio with his fictitious proceedings of the "Austin Americanism rally" at the city auditorium. "The crowd heard a report from S. V. 'Whitie' Finnletter. Subversives, he said, have infiltrated bookmobiles in Hays County with books upholding lasciviousness and other un-American doctrines. 'Better Dead than Bed,' he admonished the Youth for McKinley-Goldwater who crowded the balconies." See also items 640, 641, 646, 648, and 659.

653 "Intergration [sic] Dispute at UT: Negro Students Punished — Students, Teachers Protest." *TO*, 27 October 1961, pp. 1, 3.

"An undisclosed number of Negro students were placed on disciplinary probation last Saturday for defying 'properly constituted authority' when asked to leave a University dormitory during sit-in demonstrations two days before. They had been protesting University segregation policies in general, as well as regulations banning them from the lobbies of white dormitories." The disciplinary action provoked protests on the part of students "and generated a wave of hot anger in some faculty circles." In chapter 5, page 202, of the "Texas" section of *North Toward Home*, Morris refers to the title of his article and the "typographical error" that he and *Observer* staff members had missed: "For three hours we worked feverishly pasting the address labels by hand over the redundant 'r' in Intergration. The task was too much, and finally we gave up, turning over to our rickety address machine the job of placing the labels wherever it chose on the faulty front page."

654 [Unsigned]. "Observer Notebook." *TO*, 3 November 1961, pp. 4–5.

A compilation of news items from around the state and comments on timely issues. "In these times of high, evidently chronic unemployment, citizens may be grateful that Mr. Hunt, the Dallas billionaire, is doing his part for the national economy." A *Texas Observer* reader "has called to our attention" this classified advertisement in the October 19 *Wall Street Journal*: "GIFTED SPEAKER — To do advanced agent work in holding pro-freedom Life Line seminars in large cities. H. L. Hunt, 1704 Main St., Dallas 1, Texas." It is reasonable to assume that Morris wrote this unsigned article, as he wrote other "Observer Notebook" pieces. Furthermore, the work begins with: "The editor returned from four days...."

655 "Oscar Dancy of the Valley: A Gentle and Learned Judge." *TO*, 10 November 1961, pp. 1–2.

Profiles Oscar Dancy, dubbed "Mr. Democrat of South Texas," who has been the county judge of Cameron County, Texas, for thirty-nine years. During his time in office, "Dancy has used the position to help and encourage the Latins, to oversee construction of one of the finest road systems in the state, and to stress conservation of natural resources...."

656 "Slaughter in the Afternoon." *TO*, 10 November 1961, p. 6.

Describes an amateur bullfight in Reynosa, Mexico, a "stark caricature" of the "beautiful and noble" bullfights of Madrid. "This was a novillada, for young novice fighters.... We had heard how bad the bulls were in Mexico, but even Hemingway's outraged descriptions do them excess justice. They were miserable, scrawny creatures, more interested in leaping the barrera and galloping crazily in unfulfilled circles behind it than in coping with the frayed capes of the adolescent novilleros."

657 "Observer Notebook." *TO*, 17 November 1961, pp. 1, 4, 5.

A compilation of news items from around the state and comments on timely issues, including several paragraphs commending Texas Prison System Director O. B. Ellis. When Ellis testified before state appropriations committees, "He spoke with pride, justly so, of the improvements in the Texas prison system within the last decade. When he took over 13 years ago, the state's prisons bore close comparison with English gaols of the pre–Bentham era. His persistent pleas before conservative appropriations committees managed to keep the system a jump ahead of the crime boom...."

658 "A Public Apology: Whispers, Dissent in a Valley Town." *TO*, 17 November 1961, pp. 1, 3.

Relates that after a McAllen, Texas, woman questioned the accuracy of the House Un-American Activities Committee's film *Operation Abolition*, a local civil defense instructor referred to her as a communist in one of his open meetings. In addition, "to show all the things the McAllen lady gets into," the instructor told his audience that "she is 'membership chairman of the Hidalgo County Democratic Women's organization.'" When the woman and her husband threatened legal action, the instructor publicly apologized. See also item 572.

659 "Maverick on the Military: Off Constitutional Limits?" *TO*, 1 December 1961, p. 2.

In a speech to one hundred Democrats on November 26, attorney and former Texas legislator Maury Maverick Jr. "traced the background of the recent Americanism Seminar in Bexar County and warned that participation of the U.S. Fourth Army was symbolic of a 'horrifying danger' in America today." See also items 640, 641, 646, 648, and 652.

660 "Observer Notebook: Outrageous Juxtaposition." *TO*, 1 December 1961, p. 4.

A compilation of news items from around the state and comments on timely issues. "Jimmy Saxton, the great halfback for the Texas Longhorns, deserves all the honors he is getting. However, it must come as no mild shock to the members of that most vocal of minorities, the UT [University of Texas] board of regents, to note that Jimmy ... is the only white man in the all–American backfield."

661 "Texas Bankers vs. State: Daniel, Spears Lead Full-Scale Campaign for Escheat Legislation." *TO*, 1 December 1961, pp. 1–2.

Texas House of Representatives member Franklin Spears and Governor Price Daniel are "spearheading the most vigorous campaign yet waged to bring banks under a state escheat law, but the Texas banking community has largely snubbed them.... The countless attempts to put dentures in the state's abandoned property law offer a classic study in failure."

662 "Campus Controversy: A New Twist." *TO*, 8 December 1961, pp. 1, 6.

Sam Houston State Teachers College is embroiled in an "academic controversy with a slightly unusual twist." Conservative history teacher Glyn Turner asked that a number of books on the selected reading list of the John Birch Society be placed in the college library. After history department chairman John Payne denied his request, a group called "the ad hoc Friends Service Committee of the ACLU" denounced the decision as "an especially reprehensible example of book-banning."

663 "Observer Notebook." *TO*, 15 December 1961, p. 4.

A compilation of news stories and comments on timely issues. In the current issue of *Harper's Magazine*, Editor John Fischer quotes civil liberties lawyer Morris Ernst, who has established an award for exceptional teachers at the University of Texas. Ernst "felt convinced that 'this is the most underestimated campus in America ... that it is bubbling with more intellectual excitement than I have encountered at any Eastern college.'"

664 "Conservative Demos: Two-Party Warnings." *TO*, 22 December 1961, p. 2.

The recent increase of Texas Democrats joining the Republican Party has prompted two "conservative Democrats who wield influence in Democratic and governmental circles in the state" to publish "differing expressions of concern" in East Texas newspapers.

665 "A Texas Liberal's View: The Threats and Challenges of Communism." *TO*, 29 December 1961, pp. 1, 3–4.

Excerpts from a talk on "Communism: A Threat to the Liberal Position" that Morris gave on December 19 to a monthly community forum in El Paso. "I applaud a forum of this type. For some time I have been seriously concerned over the manner in which a certain hysterical mentality which manifests itself in times of stress in any free and complex society — and especially in ours, since ours is more complex and more openly democratic — has pre-empted the field of discussion on the subject of communism."

666 "Senator or Governor?: Ralph Mum on Texas Plans." *TO*, 5 January 1962, 1, p. 8.

Democratic Party leaders and others wonder if Senator Ralph Yarborough will challenge former Navy Secretary John Connally in the 1962 Texas gubernatorial race. Yarborough supporters throughout the state believe that the election of Connally "would be a major blow to the Yarborough organization. Connally's candidacy, they feel, constitutes an all-out effort on Vice-President Lyndon Johnson's part to expand drastically his influence on Texas politics."

667 "El Paso's Tom Lea: A Desert and Ranch Man." *TO*, 13 January 1962, pp. 1, 6.

Profiles Tom Lea, a painter and writer from El Paso. "As a boy, Lea began to sketch the designs he found on the pottery of the primitive Southwest.... In 1924, when he was 17, he left El Paso for the Art Institute of Chicago. He left, a brochure of a Lea exhibit at the Fort Worth Art Center last year describes him, 'with an inborn appetite for a knowledge of structures under the visible surfaces and textures of nature.'"

668 "A Breakthrough?: Latins and Votes." *TO*, 19 January 1962, pp. 1, 3.

Discusses the "increased political awareness" of Latin-Americans in Texas. "Rep. Jake Johnson of San Antonio, the tart-tongued liberal elected in the Bexar [County] coalition's sweep of 1960, says, 'These people are more enlightened now. They realize their leadership. The Latins are no longer a sleeping ethnic group.'" Latin-Americans are understanding what "sociologists have been telling minority groups for a long time: all power springs from the ballot, and the vote should come first."

669 "Don Yarborough: Young Aspirant Stresses Reform." *TO*, 26 January 1962, pp. 1, 8.

Profiles Democrat Don Yarborough, "the young lawyer who surprised a number of people this week by getting into the governor's race before Sen. Ralph Yarborough had formally announced he would not." Yarborough, who is not related to the senior senator from Texas, "makes it clear the tone of his campaign will be New Frontierish ('the people of Texas want to start moving again')."

670 Sherrill, Bob, and Willie Morris. "Intruders in the House." *TO*, 26 January 1962, pp. 1–2.

An interview with Kenneth Kohler and George Korkmas, the only Republican members of the Texas House of Representatives. They were both "chosen in 'sudden death' special elections to fill vacancies. Kohler got 45 percent of the vote, Korkmas only 28 percent, but they both testify to a growing GOP strength in their constituency and they both predict a considerably larger Republican delegation in the next House of Representatives."

671 "GOP's Leonard: 'One Movement.'" *TO*, 2 February 1962, pp. 1, 3.

Profiles Jim Leonard, the Executive Director of the Texas Republican Party. Leonard "observes with that curious mixture of melodrama and hard politics that characterizes the Texas GOP: '[Arnold] Toynbee says a movement requires enthusiasm, then a practical plan.... We feel that conservatism provides the enthusiasm; we have the practical plan. This explains why we're growing.'"

672 "The Daily Texan: Stifling a Free Student Newspaper at U.T." *TO*, 9 February 1962, p. 5.

Excerpts from an impassioned address on "the demise" of the University of Texas (UT) student newspaper that Morris recently presented before a meeting sponsored by the UT Student Union Speakers Committee. He decries the recent decision by the UT Board of Regents that the editor of the *Daily Texan* will no longer be elected by the student body but will be appointed by the university's Texas Student Publications Board. "I care not what the journalistic academics, or the administration, or least of all the present board of regents, tell us about this latest move to make the editorship appointive. The fact remains, and of this I am certain because I have experienced it as directly as a man can experience it, that the old and tested custom of electing Texan editors, of setting up a young man or a young woman in that job by direct popular mandate of the students themselves, has been the last great defense of the free tradition of the Daily Texan."

673 "General Launches Crusade." *TO*, 9 February 1962, pp. 1, 3.

General Edwin Walker begins his election campaign for the office of governor of Texas. "In a somewhat unusual press conference in the capitol last Saturday,... Walker made it clear that as Democratic candidate he is waging a fight against international communism, both abroad and at home. This also is his Texas program."

674 "Six Democrats: Sweeping Choice in Governor Race." *TO*, 9 February 1962, pp. 1–2.

Six Democrats, "ranging from the far fringes of the American right to New Frontier liberalism," are running for governor of Texas: Governor Price Daniel, Attorney General Will Wilson, Marshall Formby, former Secretary of the Navy John Connally, Don Yarborough, and former General Edwin A. Walker. The Republicans "will choose between Jack Cox, who tried for governor against Daniel in 1960 as a Democrat; wealthy oilman, cattleman, publisher Roy Whittenburg; and Harry Republican Diehl." See also items 689 and 715.

675 "Electoral Inequities Examined." *TO*, 16 February 1962, pp. 1, 3.

A study at the Institute of Public Affairs at the University of Texas discloses that "Texas cities and metropolitan areas remain seriously underrepresented in the state legislature, vitiating the ability of state government to find solutions to pressing urban problems."

676 "Visit Texas! Dazzling Suns, Falling Bricks." *TO*, 16 February 1962, p. 5.

Morris humorously suggests that the State of Texas can attract more tourists by publishing a "lively little brochure" that lists "the more indigenous facts about our Lone Star attractions." He highlights some of the details that the "propaganda piece," titled *Sunny Texas: Living Museum, Land of Fossils and Teddy Walker*, should include, such as: "See historic San Jacinto Monument, but beware falling bricks and if detect more than usual dropping plaster get hell out quick...."

677 "$72 to 82¢." *TO*, 2 March 1962, p. 5.

An essay originally published as "Free Enterprise Wins, $51 to 82 Cents" in the 2 September 1960 *Texas Observer* (item 546).

678 "Two Months to Go: Yarborough or Connally Fight for Run-Off?" *TO*, 2 March 1962, pp. 1–2.

With two months remaining until the Texas Democratic gubernatorial primary, the *Texas Observer* polled "the most widely-read newsmen in the state" concerning the probable outcome. "The general con[s]ensus—with exceptions and qualifications—was that Gov. Price Daniel was a certain bet for the run-off, with Don Yarborough and John Connally contending for the other second primary place."

679 "Where We Were Born: The Ground Is Bloody and Full of Guilt." *TO*, 2 March 1962, p. 5.

Morris, who studied for several years at Oxford University as a Rhodes scholar, recalls an evening he and three friends spent in Paris. "The nine of us lived a little like stray dogs during the long vacations away from school in England. We never bathed and we seldom shaved. We wandered to and from every capital in the NATO area." In September 1957, "Four of us were starting a new bottle of *rose* at a sidewalk affair on Blvd. San Michel. Flint of South Carolina (real name disguised), much the worse for wine and wear, looked around and said: 'Boys, the South is fully represented here tonight.' And so it was. There was McCall of Virginia and Steele of North Carolina and Morris of Mississippi...."

680 "Wheatley Clarion: 'Free Enterprise.'" *TO*, 9 March 1962, pp. 1, 3.

Profiles Keith Wheatley, who is running against "unbeaten veteran" Ben Ramsey for a position on the Texas Railroad Commission. "Clearly the underdog in a battle that will have the major financial sources against him, he calls himself 'a middle-class oil operator who knows what the struggle is to keep the "free" in free private enterprise....'"

681 "Institution Under Fire: Living Theology; Smith and the 'Y.'" *TO*, 23 March 1962, pp. 1–2.

The conservative *Dallas Morning News* has "launched a full-scale assault on the YM-YWCA at the University of Texas. 'University YM(?)A' was the title headline of reporter Jimmy Banks' front-page series, a label which went somewhat beyond implication to accuse, apparently, that old and occasionally controversial campus institution of being most heretically un–Christian."

682 "Broader Issues Raised: Hospital Fights to Survive." *TO*, 30 March 1962, pp. 1, 8.

The Texas Rehabilitation Center in Gonzalez, Texas, which offers rehabilitation services for the disabled, may close its doors due to a lack of funds. "The question of its continued existence raises broader issues, of course, for Texas and the whole society. In a state particularly noted for its extremely low expenditures in the welfare field..., can private charity, in partnership with state government, meet its responsibilities to severely handicapped people who need specialized help and can't afford it?"

683 Sherrill, Bob, and Willie Morris. "Crucial Consequences: Court's Decision May Affect Texas." *TO*, 30 March 1962, pp. 1, 3.

The Supreme Court has ruled in a "Tennessee apportionment case" that "lower federal courts may determine whether urban voters are being discriminated against unconstitutionally in legislative apportionment. The urban-rural issue has been a major conflict in most states, including Texas, where constitutional restrictions have severely limited representation" in the House and Senate from growing metropolitan areas.

684 "Tense and Vehement Clash on Textbooks." *TO*, 6 April 1962, pp. 1–3.

Reports that the Texas House Textbook Investigating Committee held its seventh hearing earlier this week in San Antonio, and as in previous hearings, the proceedings resembled a "tent revival or a political caucus." The many "booes [sic], catcalls, and handclapping," along with the accusations of subversion, "charged the atmosphere with enough electrical cross-currents to have kicked off a kind of ideological civil war in microcosm right there."

685 "Texas and Washington: The Crucial Showdown with John Connally." *TO*, 14 April 1962, p. 4.

Asserts that it would be "far-reaching and disastrous" for Texas if John Connally wins the election for governor. "John Connally's candidacy is not merely a threat to provincial reform, a bulwark in the path of the burgeoning liberal coalition in Texas.... The anointed candidate of that financial and industrial complex which has made the Texas myth and which has helped keep Texas far behind other modern urban states in minimum social responsibilities, he threatens an extension of the [Allan] Shivers era with a cool moderate veneer."

686 [Unsigned]. "A Smart Man Won't Get Bloody." *TO*, 21 April 1962, p. 3.

Chronicles the career and illegal "financial dealings" of swindler and one-time multimillionaire Billie Sol Estes of Pecos, Texas, an "architect of a thousand pyramid schemes" and "the original wheeler and dealer, the biggest wheeler and dealer there ever was." An unsigned article republished under Morris's name in *Fifty Years of the "Texas Observer"* (item 921). Revised with Morris's byline as "Estes Bolls 'Em Over" in the *Washington Post* (item 807). Part of the original article is republished in Morris's profile, "Billie Sol Estes," in the 27 December 1974 issue of the *Texas Observer* (item 708).

687 "Primary Turnout Pondered: Texas Republican Aggression on Large Scale." *TO*, 2 May 1962, p. 6.

The "sheer numbers of Republicans" who are running for state and congressional offices in Texas worry Democrats. The Republicans "are running candidates for every major statewide office. The governor's race between Jack Cox, the heavy favorite, and Roy Whittenburg is the second contested GOP gubernatorial primary in Texas history." Conservative Democrats "seriously fear that a heavy GOP vote will catch them in a vise between Republicans and liberal Democrats."

688 "Spotlight on Saturday's Primary: Senate Balance Wavers." *TO*, 2 May 1962, pp. 1, 7.

After the upcoming primary election, the balance of power in the Texas Senate, "for years one of the most unmistakably conservative upper houses in the country," might very well shift. "'Here we've been taking for granted all along that the Senate would stay conservative until some major miracle happened,' an Austin insider told the Observer. 'And now all of a sudden it could change overnight.'" See also item 689.

689 "Spotlight on Saturday's Primary: 3-Way Donnybrook in Governor's Race." *TO*, 2 May 1962, pp. 1, 5.

Six Democrats seek the Democratic nomination for governor in the primary election on May 5, which "has been widely described as the hottest race for governor in 16 years.... The battle for the two run-off berths is almost universally acknowledged to be between Gov. Price Daniel, former Navy Secretary John Connally, and Houston liberal Don Yarborough." See also items 674, 688, and 715.

690 "Observer Notebook: Thoughts on the Press." *TO*, 19 May 1962, p. 4.

A compilation of news items from around the state and comments on timely issues. Morris criticizes the Texas daily press for its "drab and relentless conservatism." After a reporter failed to print "what really happened" in his election coverage," Morris acknowledges that "we can understand all over again why talented young journalists who want a straightforward career in newspapering are tempted to leave Texas before they even start."

691 "Political Profile: Harris' Eckhardt." *TO*, 15 June 1962, pp. 1, 3.

Profiles Texas House of Representatives member Bob Eckhardt. "Many consider him the outstanding liberal in Texas public affairs today. Architect of the open beaches bill in 1959, one of Texas' two or three top authorities on the intricacies of oil and gas taxation, he is without doubt one of the most eloquent and persuasive politicians in the state."

692 "Margaret Carter: Egghead in Politics." *TO*, 7 July 1962, pp. 1–2.

Profiles the "liberal leader in Tarrant County," Margaret Carter. "Mrs. Carter, wife of Fort Worth lawyer Jack Carter, is unmistakably an intellectual in politics. She is well-educated, well-read, intensely ideological; her talk is laced with references to the responsibility of 'decent, civilized people,' to the consequences of 'unsophisticated' wealth in an atmosphere which fails to tolerate dissent, to the economic realties which undergird and shape politics."

693 "Key Is 'Support': Runner-Up Views Southern Politics." *TO*, 13 July 1962, pp. 1–2.

Democrat Don Yarborough, who is running for governor of Texas against John Connally, foresees "what he calls an 'imminent breakthrough' in Texas politics in terms of the broader South.... The South, he said, 'has been a millstone to the New Frontier' and to earlier reform efforts nationally. 'If we remain regressive in the South, remaining in the old unresponsive agrarian mold, then the South is going to continue to hold back the nation.'"

694 "Literary Review Answers Censors." *TO*, 24 August 1962, pp. 1–2.

The summer issue of the journal *Southwest Review* addresses "trends in censorship," particularly focusing on "the activities of the textbook investigating committee of the Texas House of Representatives." Nine well-known Texas literary figures "condemn Rep. W. T. Dungan's perambulating committee and J. Evetts Haley's Texans for America, the organization which provided the impetus to Texas' most recent censorship wars." See also item 555.

695 "Federal Amendment?: A Battered Issue Emerges." *TO*, 31 August 1962, p. 3.

Argues for the repeal of voters' poll taxes. "A permanent voter registration system is ... more conducive to voting than a yearly registration requirement.... Poll tax repeal, coupled with a liberal registration system, might revolutionize Texas politics, some Austin insiders feel."

696 "House Debate a Prelude?: Hot Exchange on Poll Tax." *TO*, 7 September 1962, p. 3.

The U.S. House has debated the anti-poll tax

constitutional amendment, and the members of the Texas legislature will likely address the measure "on two fronts" during the next session. "An attempt will be made to ratify the constitutional amendment approved by Congress, which would apply only to federal elections. Second, a serious showdown is almost certain ... on submitting to popular vote a state constitutional amendment repealing the poll tax in state and local elections."

697 "Somber Satirist: Mississippi's East." *TO*, 7 September 1962, pp. 1–2.

Profiles P. D. East of Petal, Mississippi, editor of the weekly *Petal Paper*. In East's autobiography, *The Magnolia Jungle*, "which was less the story of the somewhat eccentric boondocks humorist, which was his reputation, than of a man driven almost to the last edge of despair by his private sense of persecution and the institutionalized persecutions of a society, he said he had chosen to apply 'the feather rather than the elephant gun' to events in Mississippi." See also item 945.

698 "Angry Texas Labor to Reconsider Decision." *TO*, 21 September 1962, pp. 1, 3.

"Texas organized labor indicated this week it was moving even further in the direction of independence from the two major parties" when Hank Brown, president of the AFL-CIO (American Federation of Labor and the Congress of Industrial Organizations) announced that the group's political arm, COPE (Committee on Political Education), "would meet next month to reconsider its previous tentative recommendation of John Connally for governor." Brown said that some of the Democratic Party's "planks were worthy of labor's praise, but 'several planks are totally unacceptable to us.'"

699 "Brotherhood in El Paso: A Moderate-Conservative Tone." *TO*, 21 September 1962, pp. 1, 3.

Provides coverage of the Democratic state convention in El Paso. As one delegate pointed out, the convention this week "was less a convention than a coronation. Party brotherhood was the central theme, and despite shortlived rumblings from the far right and more threatening gestures from the liberal wing, gubernatorial nominee John Connally and his forces were in such close control that this Democratic state convention was the shortest and most emphatically the happiest in years." See also item 700.

700 "Brotherhood in El Paso: Circumspect Keynote." *TO*, 21 September 1962, pp. 1, 3.

The decision of gubernatorial nominee John Connally to deliver the keynote address at the Democratic state convention this week in El Paso "was illustrative of the central role he played" throughout the conference. "And the speech itself, noncommittal on specifics, critical of political extremes, and devoid of reference to either the Kennedy-Johnson administration or the national Democratic Party, set a dominant tone for the entire proceedings." See also item 699.

701 "Kennedy-Johnson Resolution Thwarted: Liberal Efforts Collapse." *TO*, 21 September 1962, p. 2.

Observes that the supporters of John Connally were in "complete control" of the Platform and Resolutions Committee during the Democratic state convention in El Paso this week. They "overwhelmingly approved the candidate's moderate-to-conservative platform virtually at the outset, then batted down both liberal and ultra-conservative moves without difficulty."

702 "Observer Notebook: The News' Dilemma." *TO*, 28 September 1962, p. 4.

A compilation of news items from around the state and comments on timely issues. Morris wonders which candidate for governor the *Dallas Morning News* will support, Democrat John Connally or Republican Jack Cox. "Its editorialists took a subtle backhanded poke at Cox last week by complaining that the Republicans made a 'bold bid' for the labor vote, despite the fact that they 'claim to be the real conservative party.' Does this portend an endorsement of Connally? Or is The News making an effort to keep us confused?"

703 "Political Summons in Bexar." *TO*, 5 October 1962, pp. 1, 8.

Members of the Political Association of Spanish-Speaking Organizations will meet in San Antonio on October 7 "to reconsider PASO's tentative endorsement of Democrat John Connally some weeks ago." Albert Pena, state chairman of the political action group, had pushed unsuccessfully at the Democratic state convention for "liberal planks in the Democratic platform committee."

704 "Ransom and the Regents: University of Texas; A Stunning Contrast." *TO*, 5 October 1962, p. 5.

Morris contrasts the "casual mediocrity" of the University of Texas in the 1950s, when he was a UT student, with the "intellectual vitality" of the university today. He also praises the leadership and "spirit of innovation and reform" of Chancellor Harry Ransom. Ransom's accomplishments "have had an unmistakable effect on the whole tone of the University. It is a campus which has become infused with a growing respect for intellectual controversy as the very substance of education, and where Ransom has insisted, despite the pressures, on the right of the teacher to be an individual." See also item 718.

705 "GOP Fields 17: Four Close Races for House Seats." *TO*, 12 October 1962, pp. 1–2.

"Texas' conservative-moderate dominated delegation to Congress will remain fairly much the same vote-wise after November, no matter how the Republicans fare in the general election." The Republicans are fielding seventeen nominees for congressional seats this year. "Their candidates are considered major threats in three races, two of them against staunchly conservative Democrats. GOP aspirants are waging vigorous fights in several other areas where general elections in the past have been little more than minor formalities."

706 "An Endorsement for Governor: Editorial." *TO*, 2 November 1962, p. 1.

"With considerable reluctance, but with the firm conviction that in these anguished moments in human affairs it is the more responsible and the less risky alternative, the Observer this week endorses John Connally for governor. It has been a most difficult decision," as the *Observer* has long been "Mr. Connally's most dedicated and persistent critic. But amidst the "gathering crises" in today's world, "this nation in the next days and months deeply needs as much moderation, restraint, and understanding of the world power structure as it can get, and in whatever locale, that compels us to support Connally over Cox."

Morris's name and his title "Editor and General Manager" appear on the *Texas Observer*'s masthead for the last time in the 9 November 1962 issue.

707 "Serious Thought and Writing by Concerned Young Men." *TO*, 11 December 1964, p. 3.

Morris, working for *Harper's Magazine* in New York City, remembers the grueling, but rewarding, hours that he and other "devoted" writers spent on the staff of the *Texas Observer*. What had been particularly important "was that provincial politics became the subject for serious thought and writing by young men concerned not just with reform at the state level, but with the broader reflection the Texas legislature and Texas politics and their terrible failures cast on social values in a democracy." Published in a ten-year anniversary issue of the *Texas Observer*. Revised as "The Other Texas: 20,000 Words a Week About the State As It Is" for the *New Republic* (item 724). Morris adapts his recollections for a passage on the *Texas Observer* in chapter 5, pages 198–202, of the "Texas" section of *North Toward Home*. See also item 1405.

708 "Billie Sol Estes." *TO*, 27 December 1974, pp. 50–51.

Describes the illegal "financial gymnastics" and "overt acts of fraud" (such as "financing with fictitious collateral") of Billie Sol Estes of Pecos, Texas. Morris republishes a section of his earlier unsigned profile (item 686) as he provides an update of the swindler's career. "Estes got an eight-year sentence in a state court proceeding, a 15-year sentence on federal convictions for mail fraud and conspiracy, and other lesser civil and criminal penalties."

709 "Billy Lee Brammer, 1929–78." *TO*, 3 March 1978, p. 20.

Morris reminisces about the first associate editor of the *Texas Observer* and the author of the 1961 novel *The Gay Place*. "That winter [December 1955], when I got a Rhodes scholarship, he told me whatever I did to stick to writing, to care for the language, not to be sidetracked by polemics. He told me that good writing endured beyond the momentary fashions, and to read, read, read. I honor him now for this."

Magazine and Journal Articles

710 "Mississippi Rebel on a Texas Campus." *Nation* 182 (24 March 1956), pp. 232–234.

University of Texas student editor Morris contributes his first article to a national publication by summarizing "the current controversy between my newspaper, the *Daily Texan*, and the University of Texas Board of Regents." Six weeks ago "the university regents, appointees of Governor Allan Shivers, announced they were tightening up on *Daily Texan* editorial policy. Obviously they had been highly disturbed by certain aspects of the *Texan's* categorical defense of student press freedom and its editorial comments on 'controversial' state and national issues." Republished in *Shifting Interludes* (item 80). Morris's article prompted a college newspaper editor to write the *Nation*:

A Meister, Dick. "A Cheer for Morris." *Nation* 182 (21 April 1956), p. 352.

Meister, editor of the Stanford University *Daily Stanford*, congratulates Morris on his article. "Mr. Morris certainly shows great perception of the problems involved in living in contemporary America, and his analysis of the college newspaper field hits the nail right on the head."

711 "Eisenhower." Oxford University *Isis*, no. 1292 (27 February 1957), p. 20.

Oxford University student Morris maintains that although President Eisenhower is a "popular" president, he is not a particularly effective one. "In his prouder moments, Ike speaks the idiom of international love and world peace in his own simple, Wilsonian fervour. In his least proud moments he is a fumbling, uninformed man, riding the portentous crest of party expediency and national prosperity, shunning controversy for the sake of its shunning." Republished in *Shifting Interludes* (item 64).

712 Morris, Will[ie], and Ed Yoder. "Down South We Fry Them on the Sidewalks." Oxford University *Isis*, no. 1298 (22 May 1957), p. 8.

Morris and Yoder, fellow students at Oxford University, argue that Adlai Stevenson's reputation as an "egghead" cost him votes during the 1956 presidential election and that his political future is now "very much in doubt." If the Democrats win in 1960, however, "Stevenson might conceivably be appointed secretary-of-state. The idea seems a good one: he has worked in the UN, knows international law, travelled widely, and has long been observant of the contemporary world." Republished in *Shifting Interludes* (item 65).

713 "A Texan at Oxford." *Texas Quarterly* 3 (Winter 1960), pp. 20–26.

Morris narrates his experiences at Oxford University, where he studied as a Rhodes scholar after graduating from the University of Texas. "I would prefer to avoid the gentle stereotype, even though it represents a very real part of Oxford. But being fresh out of the place and caring greatly for it, I still remember the strange, bewildering, and sometimes oppressive Oxford that confronts an American student just emerged from the provinces. The adjustment problem is often traumatic." Morris's essay appears in a "special issue" of the *Texas Quarterly* devoted to Britain. Republished as "The Other Oxford" in *Terrains of the Heart* (item 13).

714 "Houston's Superpatriots." *Harper's Magazine* 223 (October 1961), pp. 48–56.

Reports that "modern patrioteers" and "salvationists" are preaching "their diverse superpatriotic certitudes" to the residents of Houston, Texas. "In growing numbers, the citizens of that expansive country town are listening in rapt attention, believing — or fearing — that these compelling evangelists of the far right have found the definitive answer to the world's troubles."

715 "Texas Primary: A Democrat for Every Taste." *Nation* 194 (28 April 1962), pp. 372–74.

Examines the governor's race in Texas and profiles the leading Democratic candidates. "The Texas primary is May 5, and one political writer calls it 'the maddest scramble for the governor's office in sixteen years.' Six Democrats, ranging from the farthest reaches of the American Right to New Frontier liberalism, with a cluster of conservatives and moderates in between, are seeking the gubernatorial nomination." See also items 674 and 689.

716 "Texas Politics in Turmoil." *Harper's Magazine* 225 (September 1962), pp. 76–77, 82–87.

The "rapid industrialization and urbanization" of Texas are also changing politics and "power structures" in the state. The two large minority groups, Negroes and Latins, are becoming politically sophisticated, and "the long-dominant Democratic party is now a jungle of diverse groupings and weird coalitions, rent by a growing liberal-conservative cleavage."

717 "Texas." *Nation* 195 (27 October 1962), p. 257.

Reviews the upcoming gubernatorial and congressional elections in Texas. "This is Texas's first general election since Reconstruction in which a Republican nominee for governor is a serious mathematical threat. The race between Democrat John Connally, the former Navy Secretary and Lyndon Johnson protégé, and Goldwater Republican Jack Cox has overshadowed the Congressional elections in a state where November voting for Congress has seldom had much significance."

718 "Renaissance at the University of Texas." *Harper's Magazine* 226 (June 1963), pp. 76–79, 84–86.

The University of Texas has never enjoyed "steady blessings of influential public support," and over the years it has been "maimed by ruddy nabobs" on its governing Board of Regents. Today, however, the university is "one leap away from a certain greatness. Charged with intellectual vitality, full of energy and promise, it is a highly self-conscious place — a curious blend of the narrow and the cosmopolitan, trying, in an almost driven way, to discover its deepest possibilities." See also subsequent letter to the editor and Morris's reply: "Growing Pains at Texas U." *Harper's Magazine* 227 (September 1963), pp. 14, 16. See also item 704.

719 "Despair in Mississippi; Hope in Texas." *Dissent* 10 (Summer 1963), pp. 220–26.

An outraged Morris decries the racism in his native state. "I write about Mississippi with an almost total despair.... The tragedy of Mississippi is the tragedy of a society which not only does not allow dissent, but equates even silence with a kind of disloyalty. With a handful of exceptions, Mississippi is a monolith; its soul-force is its burning and raving and gnawing hatred." He is optimistic about Texas, although he admits that "there is a distressingly long way to go" in the state, given that many Texans last fall supported the rioters at the University of Mississippi who were protesting the admission of the school's first black student. "Yet in its basic aspects, Texas is another world from Mississippi. It is as pluralistic as Mississippi is monolithic; it is free, it stimulates dissent, things are happening." Republished in *Shifting Interludes* (item 82). See also item 1981.

720 "Memoirs of a Short-Wave Prophet." *New Yorker* 39 (30 November 1963), pp. 117–118, 120, 122–23, 126, 128, 130–32.

A teenage Morris uses a shortwave radio to pick up baseball play-by-play action several innings before his friends in Yazoo City hear a sports announcer broadcast the same "recreated" games over a local radio station. "The Old Scotchman [announcer Gordon McLendon] ... was not only several innings behind every game he described but was no doubt sitting in some air-conditioned studio in the hinterland, where he got the happenings of the game by news ticker.... Instead of being disappointed in the Scotchman, I was all the more pleased by his artistry, for he made pristine facts more actual than actuality. I must add, however, that this renewed appreciation did not obscure the realization that I had at my disposal a weapon of unimaginable dimensions." Morris began *North Toward Home* by writing these recollections of his youth, which his agent submitted to the *New Yorker*. A revised version appears in chapter 8 of the "Mississippi" section of his book; this segment of *North Toward Home* was subsequently republished as "The Phantom of Yazoo" in *Always Stand In Against the Curve* (item 33) and *After All, It's Only a Game* (item 51). The original *New Yorker* essay was republished in *Joy in Mudville* (item 887). Chapter 8 or excerpts from it also appeared in items 871, 876, 881, 886, and 919.

721 "Barely Winded at Eighty: Roger Baldwin." *New Republic* 150 (25 January 1964), pp. 8–10.

Profiles Roger Baldwin, founder of the American Civil Liberties Union. "He is 80 this week — January 21 — and he is the only man in America who has professionally covered the entire modern era of civil liberties. For three decades Baldwin *was* the ACLU, which he founded in 1920. Though technically 'retired' in 1950, he has remained active in its hierarchy, though he has devoted most of his activities to the International League, an organization accredited by the UN which aims to spread civil liberties around the world." Morris adapts material from this article for a passage on Baldwin in chapter 3, pages 350–55, of the "New York" section of *North Toward Home.*

722 "Cell 772, Or Life Among the Extremists." *Commentary* 38 (October 1964), pp. 31–39.

A revision of "Spy Adventure in Austin: An Intruder in Cell 772," published in the *Texas Observer* (item 612).

723 "Legislating in Texas." *Commentary* 38 (November 1964), pp. 40–46.

Morris chronicles his experiences and impressions of the Texas legislature, "a circus of ordinary follies." His "first exposure" to the state legislature was in 1960, when he assumed the editorship of the *Texas Observer*. "I was simply not prepared for it [the legislature]. It is difficult to convey exactly the way I reacted those first days there, but I remember it as a kind of physical sickness, the result of a continuing outrage, for which even writing was no outlet."

724 "The Other Texas: 20,000 Words a Week About the State As It Is." *New Republic* 151 (26 December 1964), pp. 6–7.

A revision of "Serious Thought and Writing by Concerned Young Men," published in the *Texas Observer* (item 707).

725 Foreword to "The South Today: 100 Years After Appomattox." A Special Supplement. *Harper's Magazine* 230 (April 1965), p. 126.

Morris marks the centennial of Robert E. Lee's surrender to Ulysses S. Grant at Appomattox Court House with a special supplement to *Harper's* that comprises essays, poems, and other observations on the American South of the 1960s. "The contributors—writers, historians, journalists—were encouraged to draw intimately upon the experiences of their own lives in describing the changes they have witnessed and the kind of future they foresee. Together, despite the inevitable contradictions, they have created a reliable composite portrait of present-day Southern society." Revised as the foreword to *The South Today* (see item 1). See also subsequent letters to the editor: "Reconstruction, 1965." *Harper's Magazine* 230 (June 1965), pp. 4, 6, 8.

726 "A Texas Education." *Commentary* 42 (August 1966), pp. 23–32.

Preliminary drafts of chapters 1, 2, and 3 of the "Texas" section of *North Toward Home.*

727 "A Provincial in New York: Living in the Big Cave." *Harper's Magazine* 234 (June 1967), pp. 43–51.

Excerpts from chapters 2 and 3 of the "New York" section of *North Toward Home.* The first of two parts to run in *Harper's Magazine* (see also item 728).

728 "The Bear on Madison Avenue: A Provincial in New York, Part II." *Harper's Magazine* 235 (July 1967), pp. 60–68.

Excerpts from chapters 3, 5, and 6 of the "New York" section of *North Toward Home.* The second of two parts to run in *Harper's Magazine* (see also items 727 and 1539). The publication of Morris's memoirs resulted in *Harper's* running two letters to the editor, with Morris replying to the second:

A "How to Become a New Yorker." *Harper's Magazine* 235 (August 1967), p. 4.

Two people comment on Morris's excerpts from the "New York" section of *North Toward Home.* The second reader, William North Jayme of New York City, wonders why Morris moved to Manhattan if he dislikes so much of the area. "Our island has never advertised itself as the ideal spot for a man with a wife and growing boy." Morris replies that "a certain irony escapes" Jayme. Morris reminds him that the title of his autobiography is *North Toward Home,* "which was prominently displayed" in the article. "This part of the narrative deals with one's introduction to the city, and I think it is a fairly common set of experiences. But even a place which is alien to the heart can become native to the mind—and hence, in a very basic way, home."

729 "The Yazoo Years." *Saturday Evening Post* 240 (7 October 1967), pp. 38–42, 44, 48–52.

Excerpts from chapters 1, 2, 3, 4, 6, 7, 8, 9, and 10 of the "Mississippi" section of *North Toward Home.* The *Saturday Evening Post* subsequently published four letters to the editor:

A "Growing Up in Yazoo." *Saturday Evening Post* 240 (18 November 1967), p. 4.

Readers respond to Morris's recollections. Writes John W. Boult: "In a poignant and moving narrative, Mr. Morris has stirred the fondest memories of those of us who passed through the magic delta and then departed." Says Robert E. Smith: "How sad that Willie Morris could not record some of the positive events which propelled him into the limelight at such an early age."

730 The editors. "June 6, 1968." *Harper's Magazine* 237 (July 1968), p. 16.

A brief notice of the death of Robert Kennedy. "Today, as this issue went to press, Senator Robert Kennedy died in Los Angeles. In the last four and one half years, Americans have witnessed the murder of three of our most resourceful and courageous leaders, men who stood before the international community as symbols of America's best and most enduring qualities." Although this article's byline reads "The editors," the *New York Times* of 8 June 1968 identifies Morris as the author (item 1566).

731 "Yazoo ... Notes on Survival." *Harper's Magazine* 240 (June 1970), pp. 43–50, 52–56, 61–64, 66–70.

Chapters 1–14 of Part 1 and excerpts from chapter 3 of Part 3 of *Yazoo: Integration in a Deep-Southern Town.* See also item 1576.

732 "The Last of the Southern Girls." *Ladies' Home Journal* 90 (March 1973), pp. 137–44, 149–50, 152–53.

Excerpts from chapters 1, 2, 4, 6, 7, 8, 9, and 10 of *The Last of the Southern Girls.*

733 "The Lending Library of Love." *Newsweek* 83 (11 March 1974), pp. 12–13.

Expresses dismay that there no longer seems to be any "ground rules to sexual love" and believes that "shuttling from one affair to the next" is bound to cause unhappiness. "In our country and our age, perhaps more than at any time in any advanced mass society, there has grown between lovers of my generation a fearful reluctance of any enduring mutual trust, an obsessive dwelling on the failings of the other, an urge to hurt and to tantalize — and all this buttressed and encouraged by strong and unprecedented social forces." An article for *Newsweek*'s "My Turn" column. Republished in *Terrains of the Heart* (item 19).

734 "Weep No More, My Lady." *Reader's Digest* 105 (October 1974), pp. 101–104.

Morris reminisces about his beloved maternal grandmother, Marion "Mamie" Harper Weaks, who had died earlier in the year at age ninety-seven. "When I was a boy, she and I took long walks around town in the gold summer dusk.... We must have been an unlikely pair on those long-ago journeys, she in her flowing dress and straw hat, I barefoot in a T-shirt and blue jeans, with a sailor's cap on my head, separated by our 60 years. Only when I grew older did I comprehend that it was the years between us that made us close; ours was a symbiosis forged by time." Republished in *Terrains of the Heart* (item 14) and *Shifting Interludes* (item 67).

735 "My Own Private Album: The Burden and Resonance of My Memory." *Southern Living* 10 (October 1975), pp. 72–75.

Excerpts from Morris's narrative in *A Southern Album.*

736 "The Sunbelt Comes Into Its Own." *Family Circle* 90 (February 1977), pp. 62, 66, 67.

Examines the rejuvenation and growth of the Sunbelt states. "Something exceptional is happening along the Sunbelt. It is there for the most jaded eye to see and does the heart good. The states of the Southern rim ... are undergoing a rebirth and revitalization that few would have dared predict a quarter of a century ago." See also item 1619.

737 "Yazoo City: South Toward Home." *Time* 110 (1 August 1977), pp. 13–14.

An account of President Jimmy Carter's visit to Yazoo City, Mississippi. "The Yazoo Motel was taken over en bloc by the White House, with the mystically regarded communications equipment quartered there. In Stubb's restaurant next door, Sheriff Homer Hood showed up in a suit and tie for the first time in recent memory, and at lunches there was an amalgam of reporters, cameramen, White House people, Secret Service and old country boys from the seed stores, feed stores and sawmills, who seemed to wish to preserve an integrity of disinterest but shamed themselves with sneaky over-the-shoulder glances at the outlanders." See also items 742 and 836.

738 "Christmas in Texas: Personal Stories of the Holiday in the Lone Star State." *Vision* 1 (December 1977), p. 13.

Morris and eight others contribute memories of Christmases spent in Texas. "One Christmas afternoon in Austin about 17 years ago, in a temperature of something like 80 degrees, a group of us sneaked into Texas Memorial Stadium, empty and ghostly still, and played a rousing hour or so of touch football, sweating profusely all the while. What would Irving Berlin have thought of that?" *Vision* is a publication of the Public Communications Foundation for North Texas.

739 "A Friendship: Remembering James Jones." *Atlantic Monthly* 241 (June 1978), pp. 47–50, 52–53, 58–64.

Excerpts from chapters 1, 2, 11, 12, 13, 14, 15, 16, 17, and 18 of *James Jones: A Friendship.*

740 "Pete, 'The Mayor of Bridgehampton.'" *Reader's Digest* 113 (December 1978), pp. 114–17.

A revision of "The Day I Followed the Mayor Around Town," published in *Shifting Interludes* (item 87). Republished as "The Mayor of Bridgehampton" in *Animals Can Be Almost Human* (item 869).

741 "'From Here to Eternity.'" *TV Guide* 27 (3 February 1979), pp. 14–17.

Morris summarizes the various achievements of his friend James Jones shortly before NBC airs the movie *From Here to Eternity*. "In August 1942, he shipped out to Guadalcanal, where he was involved as an infantryman in some of the bloodiest fighting of the war. He was awarded the Bronze Star and the Purple Heart and was among the first large waves of wounded sent home to the States." Jones's novel about "life in the peacetime Army," *From Here to Eternity*, "took four years of diligent work" and is a "rich, complex tale of violence, adversity, valor, passion and the search for belonging."

742 "The Day the President Left Yazoo." *Jackson: The Mississippi Magazine* 2 (March 1979), pp. 24–27.

In July 1977 President Jimmy Carter came to Yazoo City "for one of his town meetings" (see item 737). Morris recalls that on the day President Carter left Yazoo, he (Morris) and some young friends paid an evening visit to the town cemetery that was unexpectedly cut short by a local policeman. "At last, near midnight, we got to the [cemetery] entrance. As we drove through, all around us were the spooky graves of my childhood, the familiar names on the tarnished stone, the magnolias which seemed to hover like specters there, and in the inky darkness the rows of dead so etched on my memory." Republished in *Terrains of the Heart* (item 18). See also item 836.

743 "A Sense of Place and the Americanization of Mississippi." *Southern Quarterly* 17 (Spring/Summer 1979), pp. 3–13.

Morris discusses recent changes in his native state, such as the "massive integration" of its public schools. Mississippi is now "catching up to the older social ideals and values of the more pristine America," but he admits that "we have a long, long way to go." Although the state's "rapid development" in the twentieth century has its advantages, he believes that the "communal heritage of our native land is threatened by that relentless urge to mobility and homogeneity which I fear is the hallmark of the greater society." Consequently, Morris wonders if the state can "retain those qualities of the spirit that have made it unique" in the face of this "Americanization." Morris delivered these remarks in October 1978 during a two-day symposium on "Sense of Place" at the University of Southern Mississippi in Hattiesburg. The conference's papers were published in this special issue of the *Southern Quarterly*, titled *Sense of Place: Mississippi*, and in a book of the same title (item 870). Morris's keynote address was excerpted as "The Americanization of Mississippi" in *Terrains of the Heart* (item 28). See also item 1625.

744 "About the Author: William Styron." *Book-of-the-Month Club News*, Midsummer 1979, pp. 3, 5–6.

Morris profiles his friend William Styron upon the Random House publication of Styron's "extraordinary novel" *Sophie's Choice*. "From these many years of knowing Bill in numerous moods and moments, from the antiseptic lounges of Los Angeles and the oyster bars of the French Quarter to the watering spas of Manhattan and the faculty suites of Ivy League universities, I believe I grew to recognize in him the sources of his genius as one of America's foremost novelists. Writing fiction is a hard and draining calling, and at the core of his talent, both protectively and toward the fruition of high creativity, lay always an abiding humane intelligence...."

745 "The Education of an Editor: Burroughs Mitchell's Gift." *Horizon* 22 (December 1979), pp. 56–57.

A tribute to editor Burroughs Mitchell, who died in the summer of 1979 at age sixty-five. Burroughs worked for Maxwell Perkins at Scribner's and edited the works of such authors as Marjorie Kinnan Rawlings, C. P. Snow, Thomas Berger, and James Jones. "'Mitch,' as many of us who knew and loved him called him, was an old-fashioned editor who felt in his soul the abiding language—old-fashioned too because he felt an editor should not be a public figure, nor intrude on the private commitment and sensibility of the writer. He appreciated the courage and tenacity of fine writing, and he knew how tenuous, and often maddening, is the urge toward its creation."

746 "The Ghosts of Ole Miss." *Inside Sports* 2 (31 May 1980), pp. 99–107.

Morris explains why he made a "final homecoming" to Mississippi and reflects on his love for his native state, particularly Ole Miss, the university in Oxford. The University of Mississippi "is a place of authentic ghosts. Few other American campuses for me—W & L [Washington and Lee] perhaps, or VMI [Virginia Military Institute] in a different way because of the Battle of New Market, or U. Va. [University of Virginia]—envelop death and suffering and blood, and the fire and sword, as Ole Miss does." A revised essay was published in *Terrains of the Heart* (item 29), while another revision appeared as "Ghosts of Ole Miss" in the *Ole Miss Alumni Review* (item 751). See also items 1637 and 1700.

747 "Good Friends: Dogs, Sons and Others." *Parade*, 7 September 1980, pp. 6, 8–9.

Morris values and extols friendship, for it is a "rare blessing" and an "emotion of esteem and affection." When he sees an "honored friend again after years of separation, it is like reassuming the words of an old conversation which had been halted momentarily by time. Surely as one gets older, friendship becomes more precious to us, for it affirms the contours of our existence. It is a reservoir of shared experience, of having lived through many things in our brief and mutual moment on earth." Republished in *Terrains of the Heart* (item 20). The essay from Morris's book was excerpted in *Mosaic I* (item 882).

748 "Faulkner's Ghost Stories." *American Bookseller* 4 (October 1980), pp. 40–41.

A brief account of William Faulkner's annual "Hallowe'en ritual" of telling ghost stories to Faulkner family children and their friends as well as a promotional piece for a newly published collection of the tales. "With all the lights turned off in his big, antebellum home," which he called Rowan Oak, "and two big jack-o'-lanterns flickering on either side of his front steps, Mr. Bill gathered the children around him for a ghostly tale." Faulkner's niece, Dean Faulkner Wells, "has recounted her uncle's ghost stories" in *The Ghosts of Rowan Oak.* She describes him and his home "with a rare eye and with the Faulkner care and genius for words, and with the emotion of love." Revised as "The Stable" for *Terrains of the Heart* (item 27). See also items 749 and 927.

749 Untitled. In "The Werewolf: William Faulkner." *Paris Review* 23 (Spring 1981), pp. 200–201.

Excerpts from Morris's introduction to *The Ghosts of Rowan Oak: William Faulkner's Ghost Stories for Children* (item 927), followed by the collection's "The Werewolf." See also item 748.

750 "Coming on Back." *Life* 4 (June 1981), pp. 108–110, 113–114, 116, 120, 123.

After living in the East for "nearly 20 years," Morris returns to his native Mississippi. In "Coming on Back" he reflects on his southern roots and the "enduring past" of his homeland, and as the state "catch[es] up to the social ideals and values of the older America," he confidently looks forward to its future. "If it is true that a writer's world is shaped by the experience of childhood and adolescence, then returning at long last to the scenes of those experiences, remembering them anew and living among their changing heartbeats, gives him ... the primary pulses and shocks he cannot afford to lose." Republished in *Shifting Interludes* (item 88) and excerpted in *Life* magazine (item 770). Revised for *Terrains of the Heart* (item 9), with this revision excerpted in *A Place Called Mississippi* (item 900).

751 "Ghosts of Ole Miss." *Ole Miss Alumni Review* 30 (September 1981), pp.10–13.

A revision of "The Ghosts of Ole Miss," published in *Inside Sports* (item 746).

752 "A Love That Transcends Sadness." *Parade*, 13 September 1981, pp. 18, 20.

Morris feels at ease "wandering among the stones" in cemeteries and admits that "I am no stranger to graveyards. With rare exceptions, ever since my childhood, they have suffused me not with foreboding but with a sense of belonging and, as I grow older, with a curious, ineffable tenderness. My dog Pete and I go out into the cemeteries, not only to escape the telephone, and those living beings who place more demands on us than the dead ever would, but to feel a continuity with the flow of the generations." Condensed as "I Am No Stranger to Graveyards" in *Reader's Digest* (item 756). Original version republished in *Shifting Interludes* (item 89) and *Remembering Willie* (items 914 and 2081).

753 "John Birch Society Beans." In "The Famous Writers' Cooking School." *Playboy* 28 (October 1981), p. 188.

A recipe originally published in Dean Faulkner Wells's *The Great American Writers' Cookbook* (item 872).

754 "The Search for Billy Goat Hill." *Ole Miss Magazine* 1 (October 1981), pp. 12–14.

Twenty-five years after graduating from the University of Texas, Morris returns to Austin. He soon becomes lost and "inutterably disarranged" while searching for familiar landmarks on a campus that has more than tripled in size since the spring of 1956. "Was this the university where I had spent the most ebullient years of my existence, or had I been tricked, set bodily in the middle of UCLA, or Ohio State, or the University of Illinois at Champa[ign]–Urbana?" Slightly revised for *Always Stand In Against the Curve* (item 38). Morris served as the faculty advisor to the *Ole Miss Magazine*, a student-edited publication sponsored by the University of Mississippi Department of Journalism. The magazine premiered with this issue. See also items 755 and 1445.

755 "Pete and Frances." *Ole Miss Magazine* 1 (December 1981), p. 6.

The second issue of *Ole Miss Magazine* (see also item 754) includes a brief article chronicling the friendship between Frances Mitchell, Morris's "neighbor across the way on Faculty Row," and Pete, "my big black Labrador retriever who came down with me when I moved here from New York." Revised as the introduction to *Pete and Me: Twenty Poems* (item 929). Subsequent issues of the short-lived *Ole Miss Magazine* bear the dates spring 1982 and 30 September 1982.

756 "I Am No Stranger to Graveyards." *Reader's Digest* 120 (January 1982), pp. 171–72, 174.

A condensation of "A Love That Transcends Sadness," published in *Parade* (item 752).

757 "The Saga of Willie and Pete." *Parade*, 14 March 1982, pp. 14–15.

Morris describes his remarkable canine companion Pete and the intense bond they share. "What is the mysterious chemistry that links a human being and a dog? I only know that the friendship between me and this dog, like the few truly fine things in life, is God-given, buttressed by shared experience and fidelity and a fragility of the heart. I grew up—from childhood through adolescence and to maturity—with honored dogs. Pete, the dog of my middle age, is the best of them, for he has endless kindness, imagination and good cheer."

758 "Our Finest Hour." *Families* 2 (April 1982), pp. 102–12.

Excerpts from chapters 1, 8, and 9 of *Good Old Boy*.

759 "Willie Morris—Misty, Water-Colored Memory of My First College Football Game." Special Football Section. *Southern Living* 17 (September 1982), pp. 10s, 13s–14s, 16s.

A revised excerpt from chapter 16 of *The Courting of Marcus Dupree*. Morris reminisces about "the first college football game I ever saw," to which he traveled with his father in the autumn of 1941. "It was, indeed, the first genuine journey of my life. My father had promised me for weeks. I was lying in my front yard one night that fall, in the grass wet with dew, my head resting on a football as I looked up at the sky, when my father came out of the house and said, simply: 'I'm going to take you to Memphis to see Ole Miss play.'" See also item 891.

760 "At Ole Miss: Echoes of a Civil War's Last Battle." *Time* 120 (4 October 1982), pp. 8, 11.

Morris examines changes at the University of Mississippi in the twenty years since rioters protested the admission of James Meredith, the school's first black student. "Many blacks complain that they do not feel they are a significant part of campus life. I was privy to this emotion in a small class I taught last semester. I had encouraged the young whites and blacks to be candid about the realities of their relationships here. What ensued was sudden and torrential." Republished in *Shifting Interludes* (item 90). See also item 1932.

761 "My Friend Marcus Dupree." *Parade*, 30 October 1983, pp. 10, 12.

A profile of a "swift and powerful" young black football player and the subject of Morris's book, *The Courting of Marcus Dupree*. "I first got to know Marcus when he was 17 years old, a senior in the high school at Philadelphia, Miss., in Neshoba County. That was more than two years ago, and even then he was a legendary figure in his native state and in much of Dixie. He came from a poor black family; he lived with his mother, who was a schoolteacher, his crippled brother, Reggie, and his grandparents." Republished in *Shifting Interludes* (item 70).

762 "A Conversation with Willie Morris: Football Has 'Helped Moderate Southern Racism.'" *U.S. News & World Report* 95 (28 November 1983), p. 78.

Morris states that even though "the Deep South still has immense problems," the region "has changed enormously in the past two decades." For example, integration of the public schools in the South has come about "more harmoniously than elsewhere," and high-school sports, particularly football, have been a contributing factor. "Football is an expression of what the South is, a place in which parts of the terrain have been ignored and forgotten by the rest of America." Some small southern towns are isolated, "and football helps to combat the loneliness.... And because football is so visible, that makes the integration of athletics in the region all the more important." A "conversation" with Morris soon after the publication of *The Courting of Marcus Dupree*.

763 "What It Takes for a Son to Understand a Father." *Parade*, 26 August 1984, pp. 16, 18–19.

Morris, the father of a twenty-four-year-old son, David Rae, believes that the father-son relationship is "one of the most fundamental of human relationships, deep in the blood and primitive in its intensity, baffling in its emotions and ambivalences, in the pain and joy on both sides." He looks back at his own long-dead father, admitting that "it has taken me a long time to get to know [him]. But much in life comes full circle sooner or later, and I discover myself dreaming about him these days—his loping gait in the woods with a shotgun over his shoulder, his quiet drawl, the way he chuckled deep in his throat." Republished in *Shifting Interludes* (item 71).

764 "The Women and Dogs in My Life." *Playboy* 32 (January 1985), pp. 128–30, 250, 252, 254.

Morris remembers the dogs and women he has loved over the years and "unabashedly" confesses that he is a "woman-and-dog man." He adds that "women and dogs have been — inseparably —

at the core of my existence" and that he comprehends "perhaps more than any other American male those ineffable qualities that fine women and fine dogs share," such as love, independence, courage, loyalty, intelligence, kindness, and friendship.

765 "Percy Took Me by the Hand." *Southern Exposure* (Durham, N.C.) 13 (March-June 1985), pp. 32–33.

Excerpts from chapter 4 of the "Mississippi" section of *North Toward Home.* "Several times every summer I went the 42 miles to Jackson, to the brick house on North Jefferson, to stay with my grandmother Mamie, my grandfather Percy, and my two great-aunts. In Jackson I did not have to go to church unless I was foolish enough to volunteer; I could remain a heathen for days on end."

766 "Ed Yoder As Essayist." *American Oxonian* 72 (Spring 1985), pp. 98–100.

An excerpt from the introduction to *The Night of the Old South Ball, and Other Essays and Fables* (item 932).

767 "'Now That I Am Fifty.'" *Parade*, 21 April 1985, pp. 16–17.

Morris, who shares his thoughts about turning fifty, contends that "time and remembrance matter. Memory is a release from the narrowness of circumstance; it gives one a sense that there is something beyond the miserable details of everyday life." Furthermore, "No matter what one feels or dreams or fears in one's loneliest being, others among us have felt or dreamed or feared these things too. There is a community of the heart, and friendship is the closest community of all." Republished in *Shifting Interludes* (item 91).

768 "Were We the Best?" *Parade*, 18 August 1985, pp. 16–17.

Rhodes scholar Morris talks with fellow members of Oxford University's class of 1956 as they assess what the scholarships to study at Oxford meant to them. "What all of us finally found at Oxford was a continuity with the best historical, literary and intellectual tradition of the Western world. 'What I think Oxford imparts is an attitude, a certain style of mind,' says Ed Yoder, a Washington-based columnist who won a Pulitzer in 1979. We left with broader outlooks on life, higher standards, tolerance for differing views and a respect for ideas."

769 "Southern Hospitality? Try the 10 Sets on at Shine Morgan's with His Son Ed Switchin' the Channels." *TV Guide* 34 (5 July 1986), pp. 36–40.

A lighthearted article about small-town life in the South. Ed Morgan, the owner of a furniture and appliance store in Oxford, Mississippi, keeps eight or ten television sets on all the time and runs the business—"more accurately, the *institution*"—as a "daytime hostelry." The establishment is "host to a steady stream of people coming in to see what Ed Morgan might be watching on TV. These curious interlopers will include a vivid cross section of the vicinity: bankers, druggists, soybean farmers, tire salesmen, football coaches, law-school deans, history professors, Federal judges, legal secretaries, a perambulating bum or two and certified public accountants."

770 "Arts & Letters: Voices from Life." *Life* 9 (Fall 1986), p. 201.

Life magazine's special fifty-year anniversary issue includes excerpts from the concluding three paragraphs of "Coming on Back," published in the June 1981 issue (item 750). "Driving up Highway 7 past the little lost hard-scrabble towns and the rough exteriors of an isolated America that has been forgotten, I sight the water towers of Ole Miss and the town silhouetted on the horizon...."

771 "The South and Welcome to It: Does It Still Exist?" *Southern Magazine* (Little Rock, Ark.) 1 (October 1986), pp. 39–40, 43, 45, 47.

After a friend wonders "if the South as we once knew it still exists," Morris wrestles with the question and lists "a few of the qualities that, in my own, most personal view, still make the South different, or at the least are more characteristic of the South than of other regions." His bulleted paragraphs feature: "A heightened sense of community, of mutuality," "Manners," "Ritual," "A stronger feeling of morality," "Whites and blacks trying to live together within a common history," and "Continuity." Republished in *Shifting Interludes* (item 85). Republished as "Is There a South Anymore?" for the web page *The Southerner* (item 1998). "The South and Welcome to It" comprises five articles, the first of which is Morris's. The others include: "The Southern Mind," "The Southern Heart," "The Southern Body," and "The Southern Soul." See also item 1678.

772 "A Return to Christmases Gone." *Mississippi* 5 (November/December 1986), pp. 38–43.

Part I is a revision of "Christmases Gone" from *Terrains of the Heart* (item 15). In Part II,

Morris remembers Christmas day in 1985 when he drove to Yazoo City from Oxford to place roses on his parents' graves, the spot behind his boyhood home where his dog lay buried, the parking lot where his grandparents' home once stood, and other old familiar places. "And here, on Grand Avenue, is the house—*my* house. I park surreptitiously across the street to take a look. I do not even know who lives in it now. But I know every inch of this house; my sweetest dreams and bleakest nightmares are filled with it. It exists in my deepest blood." Illustrated with photographs by Morris's son, David Rae Morris. Republished in *Homecomings* (item 46). See also item 839.

773 "The Capote Chronicles: A Drunk, A Drug Addict, A Genius—And a Man Alone." *Southern Magazine* (Little Rock, Ark.) 2 (May 1988), pp. 26, 28–29.

Morris reminisces about his close friend, writer Truman Capote. "I liked Truman, and, for whatever reason, he liked me. I don't know if this mutual affection was because we were both small town Southerners in a place where there were few of us to be found. It may well be so; the small town South never left Truman, though it always seemed subtly at war with his cosmopolitan instincts." Revised as "Capote Remembered" for *Homecomings* (item 44).

774 "Texas-Oklahoma: Like the Clash of Armies." Special Football Section. *Southern Living* 23 (September 1988), pp. 10s, 14s, 16s, 19s.

Discusses the "storied rivalry" between the football teams of the University of Texas and the University of Oklahoma. "Over the years no American intercollegiate football rivalry has quite matched Texas–OU in its histrionic sweep. It is more than a mere event; it represents American society at its ultimate modern edge—violent, flamboyant, unpredictable, and withal somewhat self-righteous."

775 "Faulkner's Mississippi." *National Geographic* 175 (March 1989), pp. 313–39.

A paean to William Faulkner's hometown of Oxford, Mississippi, the inspiration for the author's fictional Yoknapatawpha County. With photographs by William Albert Allard. "William Faulkner's imaginative, intuitive cosmos—Yoknapatawpha County—was one of the most convincing ever conceived by a writer. His own 'little postage stamp of native soil,' as he called it, was a spiritual kingdom that he transmuted into a microcosm not only of the South but also of the human race." Revised as *Faulkner's Mississippi*. Excerpted in *From the Field* (item 902). See also items 1693, 1694, 1697, and 1704.

776 "Southern Comfort." *Memories* 2 (October/November 1989), pp. 21–22.

Morris compares the South of his boyhood with the new South of today. "The South is still the least nomadic, the most ingrown and settled, of the American terrains, and much remains of its older values. I pray that it will never wholly lose its ornery rebelliousness against the norms of blandness and faddishness, and that there yet remains a certain warmth and ease and kindness and grace that have been its finest and most indwelling hallmarks."

777 "Here Lies My Heart." *Esquire* 113 (June 1990), pp. 168–70, 172, 174–75.

Morris pensively remembers his ex-wife, Celia Buchan Morris. "Yet the further I grew from those painful moments, the more the bitterness faded; one is left with a kind of mellowing sadness, and recollections of the beginnings of love when one was young, the heightened promise and trust. I also comprehend now that in many ways I grew and developed into the adult I am today, for better or worse, because of her, and of her values." Republished in *Shifting Interludes* (item 93), *Magazine Article Writing* (item 889), and *Here Lies My Heart* (item 909). Revised as chapter 11, "Fame, Family, Failure," of *New York Days*. See also item 1972.

778 "In the Spirit of the Game." *Southern Living* 25 (November 1990), pp. 90–93.

An essay originally published as "The South" in *Game Day USA* (item 883). Republished in *Shifting Interludes* (item 74) and *A Century of Heroes* (item 892).

779 "Deja-Vu's of the Old Bold." *Southron* (March 1991), pp. 5–7.

Morris recalls the Jackson, Mississippi, of his "childhood years" for a local publication. "The Chamber of Commerce, in its buoyant solicitudes, chooses to present the Jackson of the waning years of the century as the Bold New City. I prefer to call it The Old Bold, for my clandestine aspect of it, in truth, exists in another time, when it was nothing if not a somnolent state capital town, drowsy in those wartime summers, and indwellingly rooted."

780 "America: The Art of the Country." *American Photo* 2 (May-June 1991), pp. 55, 62–65.

An introductory essay to a "special section"

of photographs taken around the country. "As I thumb the photographs chosen for this issue of *American Photo*, I am taken with how each, in its own way, seeks to come to terms with the feel of America, its varying and unexpected textures, its icons and ideals and idiosyncracies, its copious western horizons and small towns and large cities, its unattended silhouettes and eclectic paraphernalia. I am impressed that these are some of the things I too look for in my haphazard peregrinations on the American road, and how I too feel the subtle arcane shadings and nearly imperceptible blendings of South into West, Midwest into East, and how the land so profoundly shapes the people who dwell upon it...."

781 "In a Shifting Interlude." *American Way* 24 (15 September 1991), pp. 62–70, 140, 145–146, 148, 150, 152, 157–58.

Morris—along with his wife, JoAnne—revisits Oxford, England, where he studied as a Rhodes scholar after graduating from the University of Texas in 1956. "I have not been back in more than thirty years. The old, brave, magnificent town is suffused for me with youth and death, and forever imbued in my memory with an uncommon maze of emotions, some felicitous, others premonitory. Quite frankly, I am a little afraid of the incontrovertible burden of its past, and of memory itself, to go back again. There are old, buried fears of it. Is my return certain to be strange and magic and sad?" Republished in *Shifting Interludes* (item 86).

782 "Asphalt." *Oxford American* 2 (1992), pp 7–13.

A revision of "The Blood Blister," published in *After All, It's Only a Game* (item 50).

783 "Last of the Great Desultory Southern Drivers." *Car and Driver* 38 (July 1992), pp. 173.

Rhapsodizes about the pleasures in the early 1950s of "driving over long Southern distances.... I loved to see some unfamiliar stretch of road unfold before me in the darkness and the sleepy little towns of the Southland slip by me and the splattering of the insects on the windshield. I would look at the darkened houses along empty streets and wonder who lived in them and what kind of people they might be."

784 "The John Foster Dulles." *Car and Driver* 38 (November 1992), p. 184.

Morris relates that in 1957, while he was at Oxford University, he and some friends "were plotting" an excursion for their forthcoming spring break and purchased a 1927 Buick town car they named "John Foster Dulles" after the U.S. "peregrinating Secretary of State of that era." While driving through the "tiny village of Surrey we began looking for a pub. As we turned sharply at an innocent corner there came a sound I had never before or since heard in an automobile, a succession of esoteric bumping scrapes, metronomic in their intensity, soon followed by a strange hissing sensation, and then an horrific sort of blast." Republished in *Shifting Interludes* (item 94).

785 "New York Days." *New York* 26 (23 August 1993), pp. 36–42.

Excerpts from chapters 9, 14, and 15 of *New York Days.*

786 "New York Days." *American Way* 26 (15 December 1993), pp. 68, 70, 80, 82, 84, 86.

Excerpts from chapter 7 of *New York Days.*

787 "Watch Out or You'll Get a Note from a Witch (And See a Cat Drive My Car)." *New Choices for Retirement Living* 34 (April 1994), pp. 66–69.

An inveterate prankster as a boy, Morris now sees no "particularly good reason for growing up" and details some of the jokes he has played on children of his acquaintance. "What in heaven, the reader may justly inquire, do the kids involved in such deviltry *think* of it? They appreciate unmitigated nonsense and invariably come back for more—and occasionally seek their own retribution for my accumulated crimes against them...."

788 "Justice, Justice at Last." *New Choices for Retirement Living* 34 (June 1994), pp. 42–46.

Recounts the proceedings of the third murder trial and the conviction of white supremacist Byron De La Beckwith, who in 1963 shot and killed civil rights leader Medgar Evers. The trial and the investigative work that led to it "constitute one of the most unusual episodes of criminal prosecution in American history. After the passage of 31 years, people finally came forward to tell the truth. A cowardly assassin who shot a man in the back and openly boasted about it finally got what he deserved." The importance of this story "lies not merely in the fact that justice was finally served; the outcome of this case establishes beyond doubt that prejudices can be examined and reversed, that people and places *can* learn from their mistakes." See also item 801.

789 "The Water in Which You Swim." *American Heritage* 45 (July/August 1994), pp. 70–77.

Morris interviews "prolific writer" William Ferris, the co-editor of the *Encyclopedia of Southern Culture* and the director of the Center for the Study of Southern Culture at the University of Mississippi in Oxford. "I returned from the East to my native Mississippi in 1980, only a year or so after Ferris himself had done so, and our friendship goes back to those early days at Oxford. The father of a young daughter, Bill is a tall, agile fellow, a figure of fine company whose moods, depending on the milieu, swing easily from serious to whimsical to mischievous. He is noted for a certain sartorial casualness, having reputedly worn a suit and tie only four times since coming home."

790 "The Wild One." *Esquire* 122 (August 1994), pp. 68–69.

Under the collective title "Women We Love," Morris and other writers "pen mash notes to their favorites." Morris's choice is "the first naked woman in America," Betty Page. "Her body was of the Fifties, *my* Fifties, full and opulent as the replenishing epoch itself, not the taut, slender, athletic silhouette of the Nineties models nor of today's high-ballasted strippers with the silicone aspect."

791 "My Friend Forrest Gump." *Oxford American*, March/April 1995, pp. 42–44, 46–48.

Recollections about author Winston Groom, with whom Morris worked at the *Washington Star* newspaper in 1976. "I was the first person to read the manuscript of his novel *Forrest Gump*, which he sent me in Oxford in about 1986 while I was writer-in-residence at Ole Miss, and which I liked enormously, but that is a story that requires a little background." Republished in *Shifting Interludes* (item 75).

792 "Skip and Me and Our Crush on Rivers Applewhite." *At Random* 4 (Summer 1995), pp. 34–37.

Excerpts from chapter 5 of *My Dog Skip* in Random House's trade magazine. "Often in the languid nights Skip and I would climb up to this private place [a tree house] and absorb the sounds of nature all around and look up at the moon. I would whisper to him about things of growing up. One of those subjects was Rivers Applewhite." See also item 1433.

793 "The Man in the Back Row Has a Question." *Paris Review* 37 (Fall 1995), pp. 86–107.

A special issue on humor includes authors' responses to a questionnaire on topics such as the importance of "humor in a literary work," the existence of concepts that are "universally funny," and writers who have "succeeded admirably at humor." Morris's replies are on pages 92, 94, 98, and 101. On the latter subject Morris selects Ralph Ellison (*Invisible Man*), William Styron (*Sophie's Choice*), William Faulkner ("Spotted Horses"), Saul Bellow (*Herzog*), Mark Twain (*Roughing It*), and Walker Percy. "Once at a dinner party down here in Mississippi I read the hilarious early section of Walker Percy's *The Moviegoer* about William Holden strolling through the French Quarter to Gene Hackman and other Hollywood people. 'Percy knows what he's talking about,' Hackman said."

794 "Tennessee Sightings." *Mississippi Quarterly: The Journal of Southern Culture* 48 (Fall 1995), p. 577.

Morris recalls some of the occasions he's seen playwright Tennessee Williams. "I saw him for the first time when I was seventeen years old. It was the spring of '52 and my fellow members of the graduating class of Yazoo City, Mississippi, high school and I were staying in the Monteleone in New Orleans.... By chance he and I were the only passengers on the elevator one afternoon. My floor came first. 'Good luck, Mr. Williams,' I said as I got off. 'Good luck to you, young man,' he replied."

795 "Miss Eudora." *Southern Living* 30 (October 1995), pp. 104–108.

A tribute to author and native Mississippian Eudora Welty. "As a writer and person, her example has meant much to me. When I first read her short story 'The Worn Path' in the eighth grade, it made me feel I wanted to be a writer. Once I told her this. 'I'm glad,' she said. I honor her adventurous independence, her bravery, her humor, her spirit."

796 "The Big Kick." *Oxford American*, December 1995/January 1996, pp. 30–31.

Morris calls to mind the drama and "incredible intensity" of a 1986 University of Mississippi–Louisiana State University football game that he saw with his son, David Rae, on the young man's twenty-seventh birthday. "In the course of human events, as all mystics comprehend, there can be a magic defying all logic, a magic that will seize a moment, and this, of course, is the material of poets. This is how I wish to remember that ball game. It was not played for any National Championship, but it dwells vividly in the sinews of my memory."

797 "As the Years Go By, Do We Grow ... Crankier—Or More Tolerant?" *New Choices: Living Even Better After 50* 36 (April 1996), pp. 34–36.

As Morris recounts some of his "transgressions" and "past guilts of my lifetime," he narrates a few anecdotes to show that he has "grown more tolerant with time" and "more forgiving of others' transgressions toward *me*." He adds that he has "grown more tolerant because I see now I do not have all the time in the world. My feelings of humility deepen the more frequently I look around a room, or a dinner table, and acknowledge that I am the oldest person present." Republished in *Shifting Interludes* (item 95) and *Are You Old Enough to Read This Book?* (item 899).

798 "Going Home with Mark Twain." *American Heritage* 47 (October 1996), pp. 64–74, 76.

A condensation of Morris's introduction to *Life on the Mississippi* (item 940).

799 "Super Bowl Sunday in the Cybersouth." *Reckon: The Magazine of Southern Culture* 1 (Winter 1996), pp. 84–85.

Morris provides a tongue-in-cheek description of his "best Super Bowl viewing experience." He and his friends met beside the grave of a friend who had recently died. "On one table was our battery-operated 68-inch TV. On other tables were battery-operated word processor computers equipped for e-mail, two battery-operated fax machines, and four cellular telephones. The computers were hooked up to ESPNnet/Prodigy and other sports information nexuses."

800 "Barry Moser's Bible." *Oxford American*, no. 19 (1997), pp. 31–33.

Morris describes the latest project of his friend, artist Barry Moser, with whom he collaborated on *A Prayer for the Opening of the Little League Season*. Moser is illustrating the Bible "with a dexterity and adroitness that the great masters might envy," and his talent "has resulted in a colossal publishing project. In the fall of 1999, Penny Royal Caxton Press of North Hatfield [Massachusetts] will publish a limited edition of 400 Bibles that will feature approximately 250 Moser illustrations (he's so far completed eighty-three of them). Each book will cost $10,000."

801 "Back to Mississippi." *George* 2 (January 1997), pp. 68–71, 88–90.

Morris chronicles the Hollywood filming of a motion picture about the slaying of Mississippi civil rights leader Medgar Evers and reflects on the "virulent" racist past of his native state. The story of the 1994 third and final trial of Byron De La Beckwith, who shot and killed Evers in 1963, "touched deeply upon every significant facet of my Mississippi upbringing, my roots in the South, my wanderings as an editor and writer, the things I considered important as an American. The making of the film embraced for me two extremes of the American dream: racism, which alone prevented Medgar Evers and other blacks of the era from succeeding, and Hollywood, whose chimera can anoint anyone with success." See also items 788, 1441, 1772, 1813, and 1977.

802 "Words for Evans Harrington." *Oxford Town*, no. 225 (4–10 December 1997), p. 7.

Morris remembers his "dear friend and mentor" Evans Harrington, former chairman of the University of Mississippi's English Department, who died on December first. "I loved Evans very much. When I finally returned to live in my native Mississippi after many years in the East, I was full of odd hesitations. Evans befriended me and gave me invaluable guidelines—both intellectual and emotional."

803 "Mississippi Queen." *Vanity Fair*, no. 465 (May 1999), pp. 180–83, 198–201.

Morris's recollections of fellow Mississippian and author Eudora Welty, whom he first met in a Jackson grocery store when he was "eight or nine" years old. "One afternoon during World War II, on one of my many sojourns into Jackson from my home in Yazoo City, I accompanied my great-aunt Maggie, who was wearing a flowing black dress, to fetch a head of lettuce, or a muskmelon perhaps. Eudora was at the vegetable counter when my great-aunt introduced us. I remember her as tall and slender, her eyes luminous blue. As we were leaving, my great-aunt whispered, 'She writes those stories *her own self.*'" Republished in *Shifting Interludes* (item 77). See also item 1811.

804 "Grow to Be a Thinker ... A Thought for Freshmen." *American Oxonian* 89 (Winter 2002), pp. 10–11.

An article originally published as "A Thought for Freshmen: Grow to Be a Thinker..." in the University of Texas *Summer Texan* (item 346).

805 "An Unexpected, Unimagined Thing." *American Oxonian* 89 (Winter 2002), pp. 7–9.

An article originally published as Morris's "Round-Up" column in the *Daily Texan* (item 405).

Newspaper Articles

806 "Far-Away Student Writes Recollections of Home Town." *Yazoo City Herald*, 5 May 1955, p. 4.

An article originally published as Morris's "Round-Up" column in the *Daily Texan* (item 280). See also item 1473.

807 "Estes Bolls 'Em Over." *Washington Post*, 29 April 1962, sec. E, pp. 1–2.

A revision of "A Smart Man Won't Get Bloody," published in the *Texas Observer* (item 686).

808 "A Word in Defense of Texas." *New York Times Magazine*, 5 April 1964, pp. 23, 107–108.

Examines and attempts to dispel various stereotypes and myths about Texas, "a favorite object of enmity among Easterners.... In part this animosity is understandable; we have all lived through a national trauma [John F. Kennedy's assassination]. But in part, also, it is symptomatic of the endemic fear and suspicion which those Easterners who have never ventured far beyond the Hudson River feel about the American hinterland as a whole. For many, the United States begins just north of Cape Cod and ends somewhere in the vicinity of Hoboken. The rest is vast and miasmal, to be taken seriously only for its larger barbarisms."

809 "Southern Comforter." *New York Times*, 10 August 1973, p. 31.

Expresses pride that a fellow southerner, Senator Samuel "Sam" J. Ervin Jr., is the head of the Watergate committee. Morris relates that after a New Englander told him he "feared there would be a whitewash" of the Watergate scandal because "there were too many Southerners" on the investigating committee, "I suggested that he might be proven wrong. I told him that I had been on the opposite end of many fights with the old Southern conservatives, but that after all it was their people who had largely founded this nation, the laws and ethos of it, that they would be at their best on the profound constitutional issues now before the country...." Republished in *Shifting Interludes* (item 66). Morris's op-ed piece prompted a letter to the editor:

A Rabinove, Samuel. "'Southern White Comforter.'" *New York Times*, 24 August 1973, p. 32.

Contends that Senator Ervin's record on "civil rights for black citizens" is "sadly wanting," though it is outstanding in other areas. "Beyond his fervent praise for 'Senator Sam,' Willie Morris delivered a paean to Southern aristocratic tradition, roots, civility and erudition."

810 "Bridgehampton: The Sounds and the Silences." *New York Times*, 1 March 1974, p. 29.

Morris details why he is drawn to Bridgehampton, New York, which features "the most beautiful terrain in America.... It is a land that enlists loneliness, and also love. It reminds me a little of the Mississippi Delta, without the Delta blood and guilt — no violence to this land, and it demands little. The village itself remains part of the land that encompasses it." An op-ed piece republished in *Shifting Interludes* (item 83).

811 "'I Am a Southerner.'" *(Memphis) Commercial Appeal*, "Mid-South" section, 7 December 1975, pp. 36–39, 42.

Excerpts from Morris's narrative in *A Southern Album*. These passages also appeared in the *Houston Post* of 23 November 1975.

812 "Another CIA Story Still Lurks in a Shopping Bag." *Washington Star*, 25 January 1976, sec. C, pp. 1, 6.

In September 1965 Morris, then a "very junior editor" at *Harper's Magazine*, was sent to Washington, D.C., to help former Central Intelligence Agency Director Allen Dulles write a "defense" of the agency's involvement with the disastrous 1961 Bay of Pigs invasion. The "rebuttal," however, was never written, for the mind of the "old gray eminence" often wandered. Morris recalls: "I had come to realize he was old and weary, that something had been lost to him forever from those days of derring-do and adventure with Nazis and Italians that could never now be retrieved...." Republished as "Memoir of a Legendary Spy" in *Newsday* (item 813) and as "8" of "Vignettes of Washington" in *Terrains of the Heart* (item 16-H). Morris also relates this story in chapter 2, pages 34–36, of *New York Days*.

813 "Memoir of a Legendary Spy." *Newsday*, 27 January 1976, p. 35.

An essay originally published as "Another CIA Story Still Lurks in a Shopping Bag" in the *Washington Star* (item 812).

814 "'The Past Is Never Dead,' And Violence Goes On." *Washington Star*, 27 January 1976, sec. B, pp. 1–2.

After an elderly woman in Washington, D.C., is killed during a mugging, Morris observes that "the talk here today is of violence." He believes that the "central thread that runs through us as a people is the relationship between the white man and the black man in America" and adds that in large cities, residents are "paying the terrible price of slavery." Republished as "6" of "Vignettes of Washington" in *Terrains of the Heart* (item 16-F).

815 "Everyone Came to Town, But Power Stayed Home." *Washington Star*, 29 January 1976, sec. C, pp. 1, 5.

On the third anniversary of Lyndon Johnson's death, Morris chats with Horace Busby, one of the President's former aides. "'My relationship was not that of someone who comes and joins the White House staff,' Busby was saying to me. 'My relationship all along was with the man.' And he speaks of the illusion of power at the center. 'This isn't a system of power.... Johnson, Truman, Kennedy, all addressed themselves to the perception that it wasn't an office of power but of persuasion. You don't order people, you don't command them — you persuade them to do it themselves.'"

816 "A Down-Home Pilgrim's Progress." *Washington Star*, 1 February 1976, sec. C, pp. 1, 5.

Morris is living in Alexandria, Virginia, and because he views Washington, D.C., as an "inextricable maze," he takes a taxicab "to meet an appointment in the District." But the cab driver is also unfamiliar with Washington's streets, and they are soon lost, "foundering in horrendous traffic." Republished as "3" of "Vignettes of Washington" in *Terrains of the Heart* (item 16-C).

817 "Only the Strong Go Back to the Hustings." *Washington Star*, 3 February 1976, sec. C, pp. 1, 6.

An interview with Joyce Burland, a leading Democrat in Suffolk County, New York, and the daughter of Clark Gifford, who served as legal counsel to President Harry Truman. "Rarely do we hear of someone who grew up in Washington, inured to its rhythms, molded in the textures of a prominent Washington family, who chooses to go far out into the provinces for a life in provincial politics, bringing to that difficult and often prosaic calling the memories of a political childhood here. 'I grew up with the unpredictability of politics,' Joyce Burland says, 'with its tragedies and its surprises. I remember how people would come and go.'"

818 "What About the Girl Who Stays Here?" *Washington Star*, 5 February 1976, sec. C, pp. 1, 3.

Morris presumes that young women come to Washington "out of the same impulses of ambition" as those who travel to New York City. Fiction in America, however, tends to dramatize only those "who are drawn to Manhattan." Recently he had dinner with a twenty-six-year-old southern woman, "a friend of mutual friends," and asked her "to tell something of herself, and of her life here. It is just a Washington story, no more, no less, a vignette about the sexual revolution, and I wanted to put it down." Republished as "1" of "Vignettes of Washington" in *Terrains of the Heart* (item 16-A).

819 "The Saga of Wilbur Mills ... 'As a Man, Not Merely as Colossus.'" *Washington Star*, 8 February 1976, sec. A, pp. 1, 7.

Morris spends an afternoon with U.S. Representative Wilbur Mills (D-Ark.), the once powerful chairman of the Ways and Means Committee who resigned his chairmanship after several highly publicized incidents linked him with burlesque dancer Fanne Fox. "We sit in an air of calm through the afternoon, interrupted by the telephone only two or three times. He talks to me of what Congress was like when he first knew it, and of the South, and of the Democrats.... 'The secret of the South was to elect a young person and try him out one or two terms, and if he was any good to leave him there until he got seniority. The South has always been more aware of this than the rest of the nation.'"

820 "Girl from Silver Spring with Songs of Lament." *Washington Star*, 10 February 1976, sec. D, pp. 1, 3.

Profiles Martha Sandefer, a singer in the lounge of a "brand-new Holiday Inn" in Alexandria, Virginia. "I started coming in there occasionally, after long days with various eminent souls in the District. Martha's songs, her lyrics of loss and lament, of old loves betrayed or forgotten, were something I looked forward to after I came in off the icy, deserted streets, and I began talking with her a little during her breaks." Republished as "9" of "Vignettes of Washington" in *Terrains of the Heart* (item 16-I).

821 "It Took More Than Good Men to Win the War." *Washington Star*, 12 February 1976, sec. C, pp. 1, 4.

Morris tells stories about his "old buddy" James Dickey, the poet and novelist who has "dipped into Washington" from his home in South Carolina. "Big Jim, or sometimes just Jimbo to those of us who know he's a good man to ride the river with, was the Poet-in-Residence at the Library of Congress 10 years ago. 'I had a splendid office with the best view of the Capitol in the city. It's appropriate that the poet's office should have the finest view, don't you think?'" Republished in *Shifting Interludes* (item 68).

822 "'It's the Last Gentleman Thing in This Town.'" *Washington Star*, 15 February 1976, sec. C, pp. 1, 5.

Interviews Leon Hinkle, "as we shall call him," about his experiences as a bookie in the Washington, D.C. area. "His clients here are doctors, lawyers, businessmen, 'a little bit of everybody.' But no politicians. 'The pols go through a second person, such as a friendly bartender. They're being careful. I don't know of any pols who place their own bets.'" Morris met Hinkle through a mutual friend, one "Joe Bob Duggett." A character by the same name is featured in the first chapter of the author's *Good Old Boy*. Republished as "5" of "Vignettes of Washington" in *Terrains of the Heart* (item 16-E).

823 "Prelude to Setting Off in a Camper to History." *Washington Star*, 17 February 1976, sec. C, pp.1–2.

Morris, writer James Jones, and their teenage sons visit the Jefferson Memorial, "the most beautiful edifice in Washington" and a monument that "perfectly catches the spirit of the man" and his era. "The four of us are about to take a red pickup truck with a camper in the back down to Chancellorsville, Spotsylvania, and the Wilderness to listen to the rustlings of the ghosts of 18-year-old boys, and then on to Harpers Ferry and Antietam...." Republished in *Shifting Interludes* (item 84) and *Willie Morris: An Exhaustive Annotated Bibliography and a Biography.*

824 "Honeymoon and Stars at Harpers Ferry." *Washington Star*, 19 February 1976, sec. C, pp. 1, 3.

As Morris, writer James Jones, and their sons tour Civil War battlefields, they spot the same honeymoon couple at various sites. In Harpers Ferry, West Virginia, Morris and his companions watch as the young groom hands a map to another tourist, "a singer of masculine eminence." The celebrity "thanked him warmly," waved good-bye, and walked down the street. "The boy went back to his bride, and he too was smiling.... In his casual brush with greatness, in this village of blood and lost causes, of pillage and rapine, perhaps he felt he had performed well before her." Slightly revised and republished as "7" of "Vignettes of Washington" in *Terrains of the Heart* (item 16-G). In the revision, Morris names Glen Campbell as the singer. Original version republished in *Willie Morris: An Exhaustive Annotated Bibliography and a Biography.*

825 "The Fields of War Become a Cold Companion." *Washington Star*, 22 February 1976, sec. H, pp. 1, 4.

Morris, his friend and neighbor James Jones, and their teenage sons are visiting Civil War battlefields. "Doing those battlefields between the Rapidan and the Rappahannock, my friend had been haunted, as any superior writer of fiction might be, by the knowledge that these armies in the spring of 1864 were fighting on the same terrain of battles of a year before, so that the boys who had survived that year and come back again to Virginia saw the old scenes of devastation, the skeletons of men and horses, the burnt-out woodlands, the makeshift graves." Morris adapts material from this article for a summary of the battlefield tour in chapter 15 of *James Jones: A Friendship*. Article republished in *Willie Morris: An Exhaustive Annotated Bibliography and a Biography.*

826 "God's Pulpit Can Be Even a Hamburger Stand." *Washington Star*, 24 February 1976, sec. C, pp. 1, 4.

Profiles Ben Walton, an uneducated fifty-three-year-old "man of God" who makes $2.45 an hour cooking hamburgers and serving them through the window of a diner near Washington called the Little Tavern. "Now he feels he is working for God and that his pulpit is the serving window" at the restaurant. "'This is truly spoken,' he says. 'The only thing people are studyin' around here today is how to cut other people's throats. I work at the Little Tavern, but I also work for everyone in the universe. I lie down in bed all day and read my Bible. I may not even sleep three hours, but I'm back behind that counter every night refreshed. People don't respect God enough.'"

827 "Universal Truths on the Porn Film Scene." *Washington Star*, 26 February 1976, sec. C, pp. 1, 3.

Morris goes to see *Behind the Green Door*, a "dirty movie" starring Marilyn Chambers. "At 4:30 in the afternoon there were a large number of well-tailored men with briefcases sitting by themselves who could have dropped in from a meeting on farm parity or the cost index en route to their wives in Reston.... There were six or eight couples scattered here and there, and sometimes a few males sitting together, but mostly it was silent men enveloped in their solitary hallucinations."

828 "'I've Found My La Belle Aurore.'" *Washington Star*, 29 February 1976, sec. C, pp. 1–2.

Praises Dominique's restaurant, "a joyous little place," and interviews its "generous and buoyant owner," Dominique D'Ermo. "One of the cliches about Washington is that people go to restaurants to be seen,... but my friend Dominique says that the same people who go to Rive Gauche or the Sans Souci to look and be looked at come to his place just to enjoy themselves." Republished as "11" of "Vignettes of Washington" in *Terrains of the Heart* (item 16-K) and as the foreword to *Dominique's* (item 933).

829 "The Native Who Loves to Come Home Again." *Washington Star*, 2 March 1976, sec. C, pp. 1, 3.

Morris talks to Shaun Sheehan, a native Washingtonian. After serving in Vietnam, Sheehan returned to Washington, "because he knew he couldn't go anywhere else, and he speaks of the vitality it has, the people who come from other places and live among the children like himself who grow up here. 'A Colonel would live next door to us and then move away, and for awhile we'd get Christmas cards from him.... A congressman or senator living in the same block. This is something kids growing up here notice. They absorb it into their experience. They wouldn't get it in other cities.'"

830 "Washington Loneliness Has a Special Quality." *Washington Star*, 4 March 1976, sec. C, pp. 1–2.

Senses that "there is a special quality to loneliness" in Washington, D.C., "having to do with Washington's own notion of its commonality. Loneliness most of the time springs from disappointment. One develops a love affair with Washington, especially when you're young, having to do with new latitudes and possibilities, but just as with love the realities of it, not even to mention what it stands for, will sometimes let you down."

831 "The Real Meaning of Washington." *Washington Star*, 7 March 1976, sec. C, pp. 1, 7.

Morris attends a showing of *The American Adventure*, a "multi-media show" that "explores quite effectively and realistically not merely the genesis of this compromise city built out of its swamps but the way Washington itself has encompassed the sorrows and triumphs of the imperfect experiment." Although Americans during this Bicentennial year have heard "a lot of trite words" about "tolerance" and the courage of this country's founders, Morris believes that the "real meaning of Washington as our fortuitous political focus goes deeply into the wellsprings of our history." Republished as "4" of "Vignettes of Washington" in *Terrains of the Heart* (item 16-D).

832 "A Happy Story That Promises a Happy Ending." *Washington Star*, 9 March 1976, sec. D, pp. 1–2.

Relates the story of Kensington Moore, "as we shall call him," an "attractive and intelligent black kid of 15" from an all-black neighborhood. Moore studied hard to make good grades, and he now attends an exclusive private school in the District of Columbia on a full scholarship. "What does all this say about Kensington, and about the city where he has placed his roots? That it is an atypical little tale. That a counsellor in a black public school was sensitive to the promise of an 11-year-old child.... That there have been gambles for the child, beyond his knowing perhaps and ours, and challenges to his soul to come."

833 "When Your House Is 8 Feet Wide, You Get Visited." *Washington Star*, 11 March 1976, sec. C, pp. 1, 3.

Morris, who lives in "the most curious house you ever saw," a building only eight feet wide, is constantly bothered by tourists and gawkers. His house is listed in "one of the Bicentennial guides to the walking tour of Old Alexandria [Virginia]. The tourists, reading their guidebooks, are instructed to turn right off Royal [Street], and the book says: 'Take a close look at 4 — Prince. How wide do you think this house is?'" Republished as "2" of "Vignettes of Washington" in *Terrains of the Heart* (item 16-B).

834 "A Long Visit with a Country Lawyer." *Washington Star*, 14 March 1976, sec. E, pp. 1, 5.

Morris travels to Morganton, North Carolina, to chat with Senator Samuel "Sam" J. Ervin Jr., the former Senate head of the Watergate investigating committee. "It wasn't just the things we talked about through that long day, I suppose, although we talked about God, war, Shakespeare, Tennyson, Churchill, Kipling, Lincoln, Tom

Wolfe,... Jefferson, greased-eels who lie in public, the United States of America and poker-playing Protestants, to an extent that I can only touch the surfaces of it here, as it was the substance and texture of him, the gestures of a brilliant and happy and very funny man, the playfulness and then the intensity on some of the old verities, and the pleasure of two men of different ages so spontaneously getting along...." Republished as "10" of "Vignettes of Washington" in *Terrains of the Heart* (item 16-J).

835 "Of Northern Fears, Southern Realities and Jimmy Carter." *New York Times*, 8 July 1976, p. 31.

Wonders why northerners have a "lingering antipathy" and "disaffection" toward Jimmy Carter. Morris believes that the "fears that abound" about the presidential candidate from the Deep South "are misguided, certainly, responsive as they are to the regional clichés and the negative images, and damnably naïve about a lot of things, including the realities of national politics." He adds that "intelligent Southerners have made a more conscientious effort to understand the non–Southern regions of this country, the disparities in them, the dispositions and impulses of their history, than their Northern counterparts have made to understand the South." An op-ed piece republished in *Shifting Interludes* (item 69). See also subsequent letter to the editor: Beizer, James. "Questions About Carter." *New York Times*, 21 July 1976, p. 32.

836 "Dear Mr. President: Let Me Talk of Yazoo...." *Washington Star*, 17 July 1977, sec. A, p. 14.

Morris writes an "open letter" about his hometown to President Jimmy Carter, who is scheduled to visit Yazoo City in a few days. "Just for the record, you are the second sitting president to visit Yazoo. Teddy Roosevelt came bear hunting on the western fringes of the county in 1902. He was lavishly entertained despite the fact that no one could find a soul who had voted for him." Republished as "Dear Mr. President: Let Me Tell You About Yazoo City" in the *Yazoo Daily Herald* (item 837). See also items 737 and 742.

837 "Dear Mr. President: Let Me Tell You About Yazoo City," *Yazoo Daily Herald*, 21 July 1977, sec. A, pp. 1, 7.

An article originally published as "Dear Mr. President: Let Me Talk of Yazoo..." in the *Washington Star* (item 836).

838 "Bill Bradley: A Sense of Where America Is." *Philadelphia Inquirer*, "Today" section, 22 October 1978, pp. 12–13, 34, 36.

Morris profiles his friend Bill Bradley, who is running as a Democrat from New Jersey for the U.S. Senate. "There is little to say about the public Bill Bradley that is not well-known — the son of a small-town banker, the legend at Princeton, the Rhodes Scholar, the professional basketball player who made teamplay his hallmark.... What is less known, perhaps, about Bradley is his generous private personality, his wonderful decency, his insatiable curiosity and his profound feeling for the promise and complexity of America."

839 "Christmases Gone in Mississippi." *Newsday*, "LI" section, 24 December 1978, p. 8.

Morris nostalgically looks back at Christmases spent with his family in Yazoo City, Mississippi. "For me those mornings of Christmas were warm with the familiar ritual. We would wake up at dawn in our house in Yazoo — my mother, my father, my dog Old Skip, and I — and open the presents. My mother would play two or three carols on the baby-grand — then we would have the sparsest of breakfasts to keep room for the feast to come." Revised as "Christmases Gone" for *Terrains of the Heart* (item 15). Further revised as "A Return to Christmases Gone" for *Mississippi* (item 772), which was republished in *Homecomings* (item 46). The *Homecomings* essay was republished as "Christmases Gone Revisited" in *Christmas Stories from Mississippi* (item 917).

840 "Willie Morris Talks to the East End's 'Toots Shor.'" *Newsday*, "LI" section, 1 July 1979, pp. 13–14, 34–35.

Morris interviews Long Island's Billy DePetris, an "athlete approaching middle age with grace" and owner of a restaurant in Bridgehampton, New York.

841 "Different Terrains of the Heart: Willie Morris; Ole Miss vs. Long Island." *Bridgehampton (New York) Sun*, 11 June 1980, pp. 1, 7.

Proclaims his affection for Mississippi and Long Island, "the two places I love above all others. The same emotions are engendered for a place as for a woman: belonging, serenity, fulfillment, remembrance, torment, fed by buried anguish that is sexual, almost, in its intensity. So it is for me, with my Mississippi and my Long Island." Republished as "Different Terrains" in *Terrains of the Heart* (item 23).

842 "A Man for All Seasons." University of Mississippi *Daily Mississippian*, 26 February 1981, pp. 1, 9.

Upon the opening of the University of Mississippi baseball season, Morris profiles baseball coach Jake Gibbs for the campus newspaper. "This is Jake's tenth season at Ole Miss, and we should pause now to consider whom we have here. He may be the best college baseball coach in America, and he certainly is the best college coach who chews tobacco with dignity. He was the last Ole Miss athlete who was all–American in two sports, football and baseball." Republished in *Terrains of the Heart* (item 26).

843 "Bringing Football Back to Its Glory in Mississippi." *New York Times*, 28 August 1983, sec. 5, p. 2.

An optimistic Morris believes that the University of Mississippi football team will improve now that Billy "Dog" Brewer, who played for Ole Miss in the late 1950s, has returned as head football coach. "To our tortured and beautiful locale, as my friends are saying: 'The Dog's come home.' And indeed he has— Billy (Dog) Brewer. He has inherited the once-mighty Ole Miss Rebels football team, a decade of losing, in a university that rightly or wrongly has a dubious national reputation on race." Republished as "The Dog Comes Home" in *A Century of Heroes* (item 890) and as the foreword to *The Dog Comes Home* (item 930).

844 "The 'Marcus Legend' Began Early, and Spread Quickly." *Clarion-Ledger/Jackson Daily News*, 16 October 1983, sec. A, pp. 16–17.

Excerpts from chapter 3 of *The Courting of Marcus Dupree*. Part 1 of a three-part series (see also items 846 and 847).

845 "Halftime: Scenes from a High School Football Game." *Atlanta Journal and Constitution*, "Atlanta Weekly" section, 23 October 1983, pp. 10–11, 13.

Excerpts from chapters 5 and 10 of *The Courting of Marcus Dupree*. See also item 54.

846 "Process of Elimination a Factor in Dupree's Decision." *Clarion-Ledger/Jackson Daily News*, 23 October 1983, sec. A, p. 15.

Excerpts from chapters 19, 22, and 25 of *The Courting of Marcus Dupree*. Part 2 of a three-part series (see also items 844 and 847).

847 "There's Sadness in the Splendor of a Beautiful Cheerleader." *Clarion-Ledger/Jackson Daily News*, 6 November 1983, sec. A, p. 15.

An excerpt from chapter 10 of *The Courting of Marcus Dupree*. Part 3 of a three-part series (see also items 844 and 846). The series of excerpts was scheduled to conclude "next Sunday," but the fourth part was not published. See also item 54.

848 "Irwin Shaw's Quiet Craft: Friendship & the Bridge of Writing." *Washington Post*, 18 May 1984, sec. B, pp. 1–2.

Reflections on Irwin Shaw, "a worldly and profoundly sensitive American writer," who died on 16 May 1984. "These words are shaped by affection; Irwin Shaw ... was my friend. He was one of the most generous and kind-spirited men I ever knew. One doubts if any writer had more admiring friends. His fun and mischief were contagious; his laughter was memorable, but he was a sad man too, and did not take cruelty lightly."

849 "Rebs Too Tall for 'Shorty.'" *Jackson (Miss.) Daily News*, 21 November 1986, sec. D, pp. 1, 7.

The fifth of a five-part series "in which prominent Mississippians recall their most memorable Ole Miss–Mississippi State football games. Today's flashback recalls the [University of Mississippi] Rebels' 33–14 victory in 1947." Writes Morris: "I was thirteen and it was a golden, luminous November's afternoon, my first Ole Miss–State game in person. My emotions were ambivalent. I was a Yazoo City boy. As Yazoo was half delta and half hills, it was also half Ole Miss and half State, and remains so to this day: a most schizophrenic locale. I loved both teams." Revised as "North Toward Starkville" for the *Clarion-Ledger* (item 850).

850 "North Toward Starkville." *Clarion-Ledger*, 23 November 1991, sec. C, p. 2.

A revision of "Rebs Too Tall for 'Shorty,'" published in the *Jackson (Miss.) Daily News* (item 849). Revised for *After All, It's Only a Game* (item 53).

851 "Remembering Hitler, and How the Luftwaffe Spared Yazoo." *Clarion-Ledger*, 10 March 1993, sec. D, p. 1.

Despite Morris's intense dislike for Adolf Hitler, which reaches "back to my childhood in Yazoo City in World War II," he remains fascinated "with the sorry bugger, who in my lights became the ranking swine in all of history's long and ineluctable sweep." Morris admits that "I am a sucker for any television documentary" on the German dictator and lists facts about him that he learned from a program "featuring the newly released Soviet film footage pertaining to Hitler's last days in his fetid Berlin bunker." Morris recollects meeting a former newspaper correspondent, "an elderly gentleman in bucolic tweeds," who told him that he once had tea with Hitler. "And what was he like—what was Hitler really like? 'Well, actually,' the old man replied, 'I found him rather charming.'"

852 "Here's a Prayer for Little Leaguers Here, Everywhere." *Clarion-Ledger*, 17 April 1993, sec. C, p. 1.

Today Morris will throw out the first pitch at the opening day ceremony of a youth baseball league in Jackson, Mississippi. He will also read a baseball prayer he wrote that is "being published as a signed and numbered limited edition" print. Part of it reads: "Bless, Dear God, the little infielders from the bad bounces and assuage the wounded lips when the blood mixes with the infield soil; grant them the deft shovel dips and 6–4–3 double plays." The prayer is revised as *A Prayer for the Opening of the Little League Season*.

853 "If You Liked the '60s, You'll Love the '90s." *Los Angeles Times*, 5 September 1993, sec. M, pp. 3, 6.

An "adaptation" (that is, a revision) of an excerpt from chapter 16, the last chapter, of *New York Days*. The passages prompted a reader to write a letter to the editor:

A Powers, Michael. "The '60s, the '80s." *Los Angeles Times*, 20 September 1993, sec. B, p. 6.

"As Willie Morris gushes on about the lost '60s, maybe he should recall that while the '60s was a 'time of immense pristine hope and idealism,' it was also the period when America lost a great deal of its moral bearings...."

854 "A Provincial on the Upper West Side." *New York Times Book Review*, 5 September 1993, p. 15.

A three-paragraph excerpt from chapter 4 of *New York Days* that accompanies a front-page book review (item 1206).

855 "Heady Days, Hedy Nights: Starstruck Memories of Manhattan in the '60s." *Washington Post*, 12 September 1993, sec. C, pp. 1, 3.

An excerpt from chapter 8 of *New York Days*.

856 "Remembering Dennis Potter, 1935–1994: The Moviegoer." *Village Voice*, 21 June 1994, pp. 32–33.

Morris looks back on his friendship with writer and filmmaker Dennis Potter, whom he first met in 1956 when they were both students at Oxford University. Morris soon discovered during their initial conversation that Potter was "zealously inquisitive with a fine sense of absurdities, brilliant, gregarious, as curious about America in all its whim and detail as any foreigner I would ever know. In the medieval dining hall that evening he asked me the precise odor of a skunk, the physiognomy of armadillos, and whether rattlesnakes could bite through shoes."

857 "The Air Down There." *New York Times*, 22 October 1994, p. 23.

Profiles Steve (Air II) McNair—the quarterback for Alcorn State University of Lorman, Mississippi, and a leading candidate for football's Heisman Trophy—and describes the "bucolic, undulating terrain" surrounding Lorman. "To have a true sense of Alcorn and, I suppose, its quarterback, you have to absorb and understand something of the seductive, nearly spooky earth that encompasses it for miles around." An op-ed piece republished as "Air II Makes Sports History in an Area Fertile with Memories" in the *Clarion-Ledger* (item 858).

858 "Air II Makes Sports History in an Area Fertile with Memories." *Clarion-Ledger*, 25 October 1994, sec. A, p. 11.

An article originally published as "The Air Down There" in the *New York Times* (item 857).

859 "Versatilities of the Heart." *Olympic Atlanta* 2 (24 March 1996), p. 39.

A few months before the commencement of the 1996 Atlanta, Georgia, Olympic Games, the *Atlanta Journal / The Atlanta Constitution* devotes its special Olympics magazine to "96 people who are shaping the region in a variety of fields." In a brief commentary on the selected persons, Morris contends that "above all, this roster demonstrates anew how diverse the Southern species is—that far from being the monolith many persist in viewing it, it embraces a remarkable range of individual distinctions, contrasts and varieties." Furthermore, although "all of these people are Southerners," a major consideration for Morris is "how much like other distinguished Americans this group seems to be. The issues they deal with are not just regional but matter to all Americans who care for our beloved, complex society."

860 "20 Years Later, The King Reigns." *USA Today*, 13 August 1997, sec. A, p. 13.

A tribute to Elvis Presley twenty years after his death on 16 August 1977. "Much of the mystique lies in the fact that Elvis was both model and icon of American beauty and sex and excess, of everything about America, from narcissism to self-destruction to fame to Vegas to pills to deep-fried banana sandwiches. People still need Elvis, I think, because he represents the highest pinnacle and the deepest pit, the glamorous and the dangerous, the man who seemingly had everything but was in the heart of him as vulnerable as anyone else."

861 "Money, Logistics Dictated Filming Site." *Yazoo Herald*, 27 May 1998, sec. A, p. 4.

"Guest columnist" Morris explains why the movie version of his book *My Dog Skip* is being filmed principally in Canton, Mississippi, rather than his hometown. "The director and producer liked Yazoo City but eventually chose Canton for reasons having to do almost entirely with logistics and money. 'My Dog Skip' is being filmed on a limited budget, and the movie company had to make the most of the money they had."

862 "The Relationship Between Mississippi and Her Residents." *Madison County (Miss.) Journal*, 30 December 1999, http://onlinemadison.com/19991230/willie.html (accessed 7 October 2000; page now discontinued).

As Mississippi nears that "auspicious landmark — the year 2000," Morris offers his perspectives on the state's past and future. "At the new century, it is the juxtapositions of Mississippi, emotional and in remembrance, and the tensions of its paradoxes that still drive us crazy. Faulkner understood how deeply we care for it despite what it was and is— the gulf between its manners and its morals, the apposition of its kindness and violence." In 1999, the Associated Press invited Morris and other prominent citizens of Mississippi to comment on the state and the new century. Morris died while the series was being prepared. In an email to Jack Bales dated 10 May 2002, the publisher of the Ridgeland, Mississippi, *Madison County Journal* stated that the newspaper "did not print the story by Willie Morris— it only appeared on our website.... All we had in the print edition that week was a web-only promotion."

Contributions to Books

Includes Morris's original and republished works in books written or edited by others. The exceptions, however, are his introductions and forewords, which are cited in the following section (items 922–944).

863 "The Daily Texan." In *The Cactus*, 1956 [yearbook of the University of Texas], edited by James Van Richards. Austin: Texas Student Publications, University of Texas, 1956, p. 158.

Morris sums up his year as *Daily Texan* editor, noting that "in many respects it was a crossroads year. The Texan stuck to its guns that it was the campus newspaper's duty to concern itself with 'all issues, no matter how controversial.' Through its additional news coverage and editorial policy, it endeavored to maintain accurate news, intellectually stimulating editorial page matter, and freedom of comment."

864 "Shrimp de Jonghe." In *Bayou Cuisine: Its Tradition and Transition*, edited by Mrs. Arthur Clark Jr. Indianola, Miss.: St. Stephen's Episcopal Church, 1970, pp. 289, 297.

Morris contributes a recipe for Shrimp de Jonghe to a church cookbook that is a "pot pourri [sic] of Delta cookery, art, and history — reflecting cultural influences traditionally and transitionally." See also: Hoge, Tom. "Shrimp de Jonghe from Willie Morris." *Houston Post*, 26 September 1974, sec. AA, p. 14.

865 "Yazoo City." In *As Up They Grew: Autobiographical Essays*, compiled by Herbert R. Coursen Jr. Glenview, Ill.: Scott, Foresman and Co., 1970, pp. 259–65.

An excerpt from chapter 1 of the "Mississippi" section of *North Toward Home* is included in an anthology designed to help students "learn how to write about their experiences." In the passage, Morris looks back on his boyhood in his hometown, Yazoo City, Mississippi.

866 "The Awakening." In *Love, Capitalism, Violence, and Other Topics: A College Reader*, edited by Jan Pinkerton. Boston: Allyn and Bacon, 1971, pp. 394–96, 422–23.

A college anthology "focusing on contemporary issues" includes the first few pages of chapter 1 of the "Texas" section of *North Toward Home*. In the selection, Morris has just arrived at the University of Texas after a long bus ride from Yazoo City. "But for so many of us who converged on Austin, Texas, in the early 1950s, from places like Karnes City or Big Spring or Abilene or Rockdale or Yazoo City, the awakening we were to experience, or to have jolted into us,... was the acceptance of ideas themselves as something worth living by."

867 "Notes from an Anonymous Parent to the Class of '77." In *Reflections*, 1977 [yearbook of the Baldwin School of New York], edited by David Rae Morris. N.p., 1977, p. 3.

Morris anonymously contributes a brief essay to a high school yearbook edited by his son. The Baldwin School "is a good old school, small enough to bring out the individual in each of you, and your years here have encouraged in you an openness, a fine informality, and a sense of belonging in the world's greatest city which you will value as time goes by."

868 "From *North Toward Home*." In *An Anthology of Mississippi Writers*, edited by Noel E. Polk and James R. Scafidel. Jackson: University Press of Mississippi, 1979, pp. 439–50.

An anthology of selections from "the best and most representative writers of nearly a century and a half of Mississippi's literary culture" includes chapter 2 of the "Mississippi" section of *North Toward Home*. "Willie Morris" on page 438 is a one-paragraph biographical sketch. See also item 1895.

869 "The Mayor of Bridgehampton." In *Animals Can Be Almost Human*, edited by Alma E. Guinness. Pleasantville, N.Y.: Reader's Digest Association, 1979, pp. 215–17.

An anthology of animal stories includes an article originally published as "Pete, 'The Mayor of Bridgehampton'" in *Reader's Digest* (item 740).

870 "A Sense of Place and the Americanization of Mississippi." In *Sense of Place: Mississippi*, edited by Peggy W. Prenshaw and Jesse O. McKee. Jackson: University Press of Mississippi, 1979, pp. 3–13.

Morris's remarks during a two-day symposium on "Sense of Place" were simultaneously published in this volume and a special issue of the *Southern Quarterly*. See item 743 for a summary of his keynote address.

871 "From *North Toward Home*." In *Baseball Diamonds: Tales, Traces, Visions, and Voodoo from a Native American Rite*, edited by Kevin Kerrane and Richard Grossinger. Anchor Books ed. Garden City, N.Y.: Anchor Press, 1980, pp. 88–101.

This "anthology of contemporary baseball writing" includes chapter 8 of the "Mississippi" section of *North Toward Home*. The book is a revision of *Baseball, I Gave You All the Best Years of My Life*, published in 1977. See also item 720.

872 "John Birch Society Beans." In *The Great American Writers' Cookbook*, edited by Dean Faulkner Wells. Oxford, Miss.: Yoknapatawpha Press, 1981, pp. 165–67.

Wells's cookbook is comprised of recipes sent her by "writers of novels, short stories, history, commentary, plays, poetry, reportage, columns, and criticism." Morris's John Birch Society Beans "are so named because of the intense internal reaction they produce. I learned how to prepare them from a border-rat Texan I once knew years ago, and I have been refining them ever since." Republished as part of "The Famous Writers' Cooking School" in *Playboy* (item 753). See also item 873.

873 "Mamie's Fried Chicken." In *The Great American Writers' Cookbook*, pp. 87–88 (see item 872).

A writers' cookbook includes a recipe for fried chicken handed down to Morris by his maternal grandmother. "My grandmother Mamie cooked me this fried chicken after our baseball games when I was a boy in Mississippi. After I grew up, she told me her recipe, which I have used many times."

874 Untitled. In *Ole Miss*, 1983 [yearbook of the University of Mississippi], edited by John Hall. University: University of Mississippi, 1983, p. 4.

Morris loves the University of Mississippi, but he also believes that its problems "remain to be solved" and need to be addressed. "Now, in 1983, Ole Miss is a subtle blend of everything the Deep South was and is—the Rebel flags, the Kappa Alphas in Old South, the beautiful sorority girls who will marry at age twenty-one in their Delta weddings. It is the best and the worst of an older South which has survived into the new age. Many of the white students live the most sheltered of lives. Their proximity with the young blacks of Ole Miss seems both mystifying and exhilarating." A one-page essay.

875 "From *Good Old Boy*." In *Mississippi Writers: Reflections of Childhood and Youth*, edited by Dorothy Abbott. Vol. 1: Fiction. Center for the Study of Southern Culture Series. Jackson: University Press of Mississippi, 1985, pp. 433–39.

Each selection in this anthology devoted to Mississippi authors of the twentieth century "expresses the theme of Mississippi childhood and youth or its relevance to the life of the writer." Morris is represented by chapter 2 of *Good Old*

Boy, which is republished in Abbott's *Mississippi Writers: An Anthology* (item 884).

876 From *North Toward Home*." In *Mississippi Writers: Reflections of Childhood and Youth*, edited by Dorothy Abbott. Vol. 2: Nonfiction. Center for the Study of Southern Culture Series. Jackson: University Press of Mississippi, 1986, pp. 461–78.

An anthology of works written during the twentieth century by Mississippi authors. "The selections here are mainly prose narratives or autobiographical essays in which both the well-known and the unheralded reflect upon the Mississippi they experienced during their formative years." One of the passages is an excerpt from chapter 8 and the complete chapter 10 of the "Mississippi" section of *North Toward Home*, republished in Abbott's *Mississippi Writers: An Anthology* (item 885). See also items 720 and 877.

877 "From *The Courting of Marcus Dupree*. In *Mississippi Writers: Reflections of Childhood and Youth*. Vol. 2, pp. 479–83 (see item 876).

An anthology includes chapter 1 of *The Courting of Marcus Dupree*.

878 "Willie Morris." In *A Celebration of Teachers*, by the National Council of Teachers of English. New ed. Urbana, Ill.: National Council of Teachers of English, 1986, pp. 35–36.

The National Council of Teachers of English celebrates its Diamond Jubilee with a collection of "thank-you notes" from fifty-three "famous former students who are entranced with words" to some of the teachers who influenced them and "who cared a lot about language." Morris is among the writers who responded to the solicitation; his testimonial honoring Omie Parker, his high school English teacher, is based on a passage from chapter 9 of the "Mississippi" section of *North Toward Home* (pages 134–35). "Among many of the students Mrs. Parker was a scorned woman. They bad-talked her behind her back and said that she worked people ... hard out of plain cruelty. I myself sometimes joined in this talk, because it was fashionable. I fully appreciated her only when I went far away to college and made straight A's in English." The Educational Resources Information Center (ERIC) republished *A Celebration of Teachers* as *A Celebration of Teachers for the Diamond Jubilee of the National Council of Teachers of English*, new ed., 1986. ERIC, ED 269756. See also item 1640.

879 "The American Classroom." In *American Classroom: The Photographs of Catherine Wagner*, by Anne Wilkes Tucker. Houston: Museum of Fine Arts; New York: Aperture, 1988, pp. 7–11.

An exhibition of Wagner's photographs of American school classrooms was held at Houston's Museum of Fine Arts from 10 September to 27 November 1988. In an essay accompanying the exhibition catalog, Morris relives a few of "my own experiences" with schools, classrooms, and teachers. "Grade school classrooms have always had a certain smell, palpable yet indefinable, an old layered scent of chalk, ancient wooden desks, dust, talcum, a faint encompassing residue of youth and mortality and time. Here in grade four the red-nosed Miss Abbott, etched not with especial affection in *North Toward Home*, claimed St. Louis the capital of Missouri and performed hymns on a plastic Woolworth's flute and read us the Scriptures half the livelong day and forbade Coca-Colas because of their high alcoholic content...."

880 "The Deep South." In *Discover America!: A Scenic Tour of the Fifty States*. Washington, D.C.: National Geographic Society, 1989, pp. 118–28.

Photographs and essays focusing on nine regions of the United States reflect "the diversity of our many views of America." According to Morris, "There are places that exist as a song in the heart — only certain places one truly loves, any of us. For me the Deep South has been abrupt departures and bittersweet returns."

881 "The Phantom of Yazoo." In *Elements of Literature: Third Course*, edited by Robert Woodruff Anderson and others. Austin: Holt, Rinehart and Winston, 1989, pp. 452–61.

A secondary school reader includes an excerpt from chapter 8 of the "Mississippi" section of *North Toward Home* in the unit "The Elements of Nonfiction: Biography and Autobiography." The selection is not as long as the book excerpt of the same title published in *Always Stand In Against the Curve* (item 33) and *After All, It's Only a Game* (item 51). See also item 720.

882 "Good Friends ... Dogs, Sons and Others." In *Mosaic I: A Reading Skills Book*, edited by Brenda Wegmann and Miki Prijic Knezevic. 2d ed. New York: McGraw-Hill Publishing Co., 1990, pp. 224–27.

Mosaic I, a reader for "in-college or college-bound nonnative English students," includes an excerpt from Morris's essay in *Terrains of the Heart* (item 20), which originally appeared in *Parade* (item 747).

883 "The South." In *Game Day USA: NCAA College Football*, produced by Rich Clarkson. Rochester, N.Y.: Professional Photography Division of Eastman Kodak Co; Charlottesville, Va.: Thomasson-Grant, 1990, pp. 67–73.

Photographers and writers capture the spectacle of National Collegiate Athletic Association college football in four regions of the country. In "The South," Morris recounts the agonizing University of Mississippi–Vanderbilt game of 28 October 1989, in which Ole Miss cornerback Roy Lee "Chucky" Mullins was paralyzed after he tackled an opposing player. "Within hours of Chucky Mullins' injury a trust fund had been started for him. LSU [Louisiana State University] collected donations at its Purple-Gold basketball game in Baton Rouge. The University of Delaware shut down a football practice an hour early for a prayer session. Calls from coaches—and the White House—came from all over America." Republished in *Popular Culture: An Introductory Text* (item 888) and as "In the Spirit of the Game" in *Southern Living* (item 778). The *Southern Living* essay was republished in *Shifting Interludes* (item 74) and *A Century of Heroes* (item 892). See also items 937 and 1700.

884 "From *Good Old Boy*." In *Mississippi Writers: An Anthology*, edited by Dorothy Abbott. Center for the Study of Southern Culture Series. Jackson: University Press of Mississippi, 1991, pp. 146–53.

The numerous twentieth-century Mississippi writers featured in this anthology "have published creative or interpretive literature—fiction, poetry, drama, literary essays—that has received critical attention." The selected passage from *Good Old Boy* is an excerpt that Abbott first reprinted in her *Mississippi Writers: Reflections of Childhood and Youth* (item 875). See also item 885.

885 "From *North Toward Home*." In *Mississippi Writers: An Anthology*, pp. 332–50 (see item 884).

The passages from *North Toward Home* reprinted in this anthology are excerpts Abbott first reprinted in her *Mississippi Writers: Reflections of Childhood and Youth* (item 876).

886 "From *Northward* [sic] *Toward Home*." In *The Yankees Reader*, edited by Miro Weinberger and Dan Riley. Boston: Houghton Mifflin Co., 1991, pp. 219–28.

An anthology of essays celebrating the New York Yankees baseball team includes an excerpt from chapter 8 of the "Mississippi" section of *North Toward Home*. See also item 720.

887 "Memoirs of a Short-Wave Prophet." In *Joy in Mudville: The Big Book of Baseball Humor*, edited by Dick Schaap and Mort Gerberg. New York: Doubleday, 1992, pp. 81–92.

An essay originally published in the *New Yorker* (item 720) and subsequently in *North Toward Home* is reprinted in an anthology of stories, essays, cartoons, and other works of baseball humor.

888 "The South." In *Popular Culture: An Introductory Text*, edited by Jack Nachbar and Kevin Lause. Bowling Green, Ohio: Bowling Green State University Popular Press, 1992, pp. 392–97.

A volume that "presents methods and examples for studying the entire breadth" of popular culture includes an essay originally published in *Game Day USA* (item 883).

889 "Here Lies My Heart." In *Magazine Article Writing*, by Betsy P. Graham, 2d ed. Fort Worth: Harcourt Brace Jovanovich College Publishers, 1993, pp. 179–86.

An essay originally published in *Esquire* (item 777) and subsequently in *New York Days* is reprinted in a book of "step-by-step instructions for writing a magazine article."

890 "The Dog Comes Home." In *A Century of Heroes*, edited by Larry Wells. Atlanta: Longstreet Press, 1993, pp. 107–114.

A collection of sports-related essays celebrating one hundred years of football at the University of Mississippi contains an article originally published as "Bringing Football Back to Its Glory in Mississippi" in the *New York Times* (item 843). See also items 891, 892, and 930.

891 "Heroes in the Rain." In *A Century of Heroes*, pp. 45–51 (see item 890).

An excerpt from chapter 16 of *The Courting of Marcus Dupree*. See also items 759 and 892.

892 "In the Spirit of the Game." In *A Century of Heroes*, pp. 117–25 (see item 890).

An article republished from *Southern Living* (item 778). See also items 883 and 891.

893 "Memoir." In *Grisham: An Exhibition*, by Thomas M. Verich and the Department of Archives and Special Collections, University of Mississippi. University: University of Mississippi Libraries, 1994, pp. 6–7.

An exhibition of the works of "mega-selling author and fellow Lafayette Countian, John Grisham," was held at the University of Mississippi's John Davis Williams Library from 10 April to 10 August 1994. In a brief piece written especially for the exhibition catalog, Morris recalls that he first met Grisham in 1988 in Oxford, Mississippi, when the fledgling author was beginning his first book and that he "advised him" on several literary matters. "I liked John and could tell he was serious about wanting to write. He told me he had recently compiled a list from trade journals of dozens of literary agents around the country and sent letters and samples of his writing to these people. Most had not given him the courtesy of a reply."

894 "Farewell." In *Leaving New York: Writers Look Back*, edited by Kathleen Norris. Saint Paul, Minn.: Hungry Mind Press, 1995, pp. 60–87.

An anthology of essays, stories, poems, and other works that describe writers' experiences in New York City contains chapter 15 of *New York Days*.

895 "Always Stand In Against the Curve." In *A Modern Southern Reader: Major Stories, Drama, Poetry, Essays, Interviews and Reminiscences from the Twentieth Century South*, edited by Ben Forkner and Patrick Samway. Rev. ed. Atlanta: Peachtree Publishers, 1996, pp. 598–605.

An anthology of "the best of modern Southern writing" includes an essay originally published as the title piece in *Always Stand In Against the Curve* (item 34).

896 "Blessed That We Were." In *Picturing the South: 1860 to the Present; Photographers and Writers*, edited by Ellen Dugan. Atlanta: High Museum of Art; San Francisco: Chronicle Books, 1996, pp. 90–92.

An exhibition of more than 160 photographs taken since the Civil War era was held at Atlanta's High Museum of Art from 15 June to 14 September 1996. In one of seven essays accompanying the 223-page exhibition catalog, Morris observes that the "photographs share an ineluctable thread: people gathered in clusters in towns and stores, by creeks and levees, the very façades of buildings with their signs and posters inviting the native human species: *community*. All these evoke the words of my friend Eudora Welty, two of whose photographs grace this exhibition, about the South's profound sense of place, not simply in the historical or philosophical way, 'but in the worlds of sight and sound and smell, in its earth and water and sky and in its seasons, and in its sense of generations and continuity.'"

897 "The Blood Blister." In *Full Court: A Literary Anthology of Basketball*, edited by Dennis Trudell. New York: Breakaway Books, 1996, pp. 123–36.

An anthology of basketball stories and poems "with a literary focus" includes a story originally published in *After All, It's Only a Game* (item 50).

898 "A Prayer Before the Feast." In *Centennial Olympic Games: Official Souvenir Program, July 19–August 4, 1996*. New York: Sports Illustrated, 1996, pp. 26–28.

In the introductory essay to the souvenir program for Atlanta's Centennial Olympic Games, Morris declares that the festivities represent the "quintessential coming out party for the modern-day American South." He adds that the Olympic Games "have always provided a way of viewing in microcosm the history of world politics and human rights—and the inherent tension between the two.... Ironies have forever abounded. Three years after the doves of peace were released at the 1936 Berlin Games, mankind would be enveloped in nearly terminal destruction." See also items 1445 and 1757.

898a "Willie Morris." In *The Writer's Desk*, by Jill Krementz. New York: Random House, 1996, pp. 40–41.

Noted photographer Jill Krementz captures fifty-six writers at work, including Morris. Each black-and-white photo is accompanied by the subject's remarks on the writing process or personal work habits. "I'm an afternoon writer," Morris says. "I draw sustenance from my strange nocturnal dreams. My workroom is on the second floor of an old Mississippi house. I work on an enormous oak table that I had especially built."

899 "As the Years Go By, Do We Grow ... Crankier or More Tolerant?" In *Are You Old Enough to Read This Book?: Reflections on Midlife*, edited by Deborah H. DeFord. Pleasantville, N.Y.: Reader's Digest Association, 1997, pp. 36–38.

A collection of essays, interviews, and quizzes that examines the positive sides of middle age includes an article originally published in *New Choices* (item 797). See also item 1969.

900 "From 'Coming on Back.'" In *A Place Called Mississippi: Collected Narratives*, edited by

Marion Barnwell. Jackson: University Press of Mississippi, 1997, pp. 432–38.

An anthology of "narratives by explorers, travelers, historians, social observers, artists, writers, and musicians all writing about Mississippi" includes excerpts from *Terrains of the Heart*'s "Coming on Back" (item 9), a revision of an essay published in *Life* magazine (item 750).

901 "From *North Toward Home.*" In *The Oxford Book of the American South: Testimony, Memory, and Fiction*, edited by Edward L. Ayers and Bradley C. Mittendorf. New York: Oxford University Press, 1997, pp. 487–91.

An excerpt from chapter 5 and the complete chapter 10 of the "Mississippi" section of *North Toward Home* are included in an anthology of fiction, memoirs, diaries, essays, and other works of "writing by Southerners about the South."

902 "Who Did He Think He Was?" In *From the Field: A Collection of Writings from "National Geographic,"* edited by Charles McCarry. Washington, D.C.: National Geographic Society, 1997, pp. 220–22.

Excerpts from "Faulkner's Mississippi" that originally appeared in *National Geographic* (item 775) are reprinted in an anthology of material published over the magazine's 109-year history.

903 "Other Voices, Other Tastes." In *Backroad Buffets & Country Cafes: A Southern Guide to Meat-and-Threes & Down-Home Dining*, by Don O'Briant. Winston Salem, N.C.: John F. Blair, 1998, p. 141.

A guide to "mom-and-pop restaurants" in the South includes Morris's (and his wife's) recommendation for Doe's Eat Place. "I have many favorite restaurants in the great and sovereign state of Mississippi, but I'll single out Doe's Eat Place in Greenville because it's the establishment JoAnne and I drive the farthest to from Jackson just to have dinner." Morris is mentioned on pages 145 and 149–50.

904 "The Place, the People, and the Vision." In *Making Things Grow: The Story of Mississippi Chemical Corporation*, by Jo G. Prichard. Yazoo City, Miss.: Mississippi Chemical Corporation, 1998, pp. 13–17.

Making Things Grow commemorates the fiftieth anniversary (1948–1998) of Mississippi Chemical Corporation, a nitrogen fertilizer plant based in Yazoo City, Mississippi. In four chronologically arranged essays (items 904 to 907), Morris intertwines historical facts about Mississippi and the United States with significant events in the company's history. His first essay covers the years 1948 to 1956. "The formative years of Mississippi Chemical were bellwethers of important and critical milestones in American and Mississippi history. In 1947, only a few months before MCC's incorporation, at Delta State Teachers College in Cleveland, Mississippi, only eighty miles from Yazoo City in the middle Delta, Under Secretary of State Dean Acheson, substituting for the ailing Secretary George Marshall, first disclosed to a public audience the concept of the Marshall Plan." See also item 1803.

905 "Expanding Horizons." In *Making Things Grow*, pp. 67–71 (see item 904).

Morris's second essay describes events from 1956 to 1973. "In Mississippi in the early 1960s industrial employment at last equaled agricultural, largely because of the monumental decrease in farm workers since World War II. To nurture industrial development in the state, [company President] Owen Cooper, with the support of Mississippi Chemical's shareholders, founded the state's original venture capital enterprise, First Mississippi Corporation." See also items 906 and 907.

906 "Rising to the Challenges." In *Making Things Grow*, pp. 135–39 (see item 904).

Morris focuses on the two decades from 1973 to 1993 in his third essay. "The optimism of the early 1960s in America began to descend into frustration and a lessening of confidence and trust in the decade of the 1970s following Vietnam, Watergate, Iran, and the exigencies in Southern school integration. The period 1973 to 1993 was characterized by a sharpening impact of far-reaching world events on MCC, on both its success and its failures." See also items 905 and 907.

907 "The World Beyond." In *Making Things Grow*, pp. 199–203 (see item 904).

Morris's fourth essay deals with the years 1993 to 1998. "It is 1998, and the world has taken more than a few turns.... Inevitably shaped by the modern television culture, by the electronics and communications and computer revolutions, the young are not nearly so sequestered in Yazoo as in my day.... And how can one calculate the difference Mississippi Chemical Corporation's presence has made on the town, its international connections bringing the distant horizons right to its door? My Yazoo City was the Gateway to the Delta, and now it's a gateway to the world. And this is good." See also items 905 and 906.

908 "Willie Morris: From *North Toward Home.*" In *Southern Selves: From Mark Twain and Eudora Welty to Maya Angelou and Kate Gibbons; A Collection of Autobiographical Writing*, edited by James H. Watkins. New York: Vintage Books, 1998, pp. 189–202.

The "rich autobiographical tradition" of the South is highlighted in this collection of works by southern autobiographers and memoirists. Includes chapter 6 of the "Mississippi" section of *North Toward Home.*

909 "Here Lies My Heart." In *Here Lies My Heart: Essays on Why We Marry, Why We Don't, and What We Find There*, edited by Deborah Chasman and Catherine Jhee. Boston: Beacon Press, 1999, pp. 165–77.

An anthology of twenty essays that examine the multifaceted aspects of marriage contains Morris's article on his ex-wife, originally published in *Esquire* (item 777).

910 "Paradise Road." In *Eudora Welty: Writers' Reflections upon First Reading Welty*, edited by Pearl Amelia McHaney. Athens, Ga.: Hill Street Press, 1999, pp. 71–72.

Morris's tribute to Welty is one of twenty-two "discerning reports of first encounters with and recollections of Eudora" collected to celebrate her ninetieth birthday. "My connections with Eudora go back considerably. I was born in a house two blocks from hers in the Belhaven neighborhood of Jackson. I was christened in the church of her childhood, the Galloway Memorial Methodist Church.... She knew my mother, my grandparents, and my eccentric spinster great-aunts Maggie and Susie Harper."

911 "The Distinguished Adversary." In *The Crimson Tide: An Illustrated History of Football at the University of Alabama*, by Winston Groom. Tuscaloosa: University of Alabama Press, 2000, pp. 168–69.

In this chronicle of University of Alabama football, Morris, a "fervid" University of Mississippi fan, recounts "two beguiling pilgrimages" he and his wife made to Birmingham, Alabama. "During them, it was my pleasure to honor our distinguished and long-standing adversary, the Crimson Tide, for one of the most noble football traditions in American history, an achievement accompanied over the years by considerable grace and dignity, not to mention tenacity and resilience."

912 "A Faded Photograph." In *Biography and Autobiography*. Prentice Hall Literature Library. Upper Saddle River, N.J.: Prentice Hall, 2000, pp. 28–33.

A collection of biographical and autobiographical essays and book excerpts (compiled for juvenile readers) includes chapter 1 of *My Dog Skip*.

913 "From *Good Old Boy: A Delta Boyhood.*" In *Where the Red Fern Grows, and Related Readings*, by Wilson Rawls. The Glencoe Literature Library. New York: Glencoe/McGraw-Hill, 2000, pp. 194–99.

Rawls's semi-autobiographical novel of a boy and his dogs is followed by "related readings," one of which is chapter 4 of *Good Old Boy*. An editorial statement informs readers that in the book excerpt, "Mississippi writer Willie Morris recalls his boyhood and the special friendship he had with his dog, Old Skip."

914 "A Love That Transcends Sadness." In *Remembering Willie.* Jackson: University Press of Mississippi, 2000, pp. 113–17.

An essay originally published in *Parade* (item 752). See also item 2081.

915 "Willie Morris." In *Three Minutes or Less: Life Lessons from America's Greatest Writers*, by the PEN/Faulkner Foundation. New York: Bloomsbury, 2000, pp. 289–91.

The PEN/Faulkner Foundation hosts a gala every fall at the Folger Shakespeare Library in Washington, D.C., during which well-known writers speak for three minutes each on a preselected topic. This anthology comprises more than 150 of these authors' short essays. On 27 October 1997, Morris and eleven others spoke on "Confessions." Among "several brief and esoteric confessionals," Morris admits "to being the last remaining white Democrat in the state of Mississippi. No, I'm a little wrong. There are three of us remaining white Democrats there, one in Itta Bena, I'm told, the other in downtown Alligator. There may be a fourth in Belzoni, but she is inaccessible." See also item 916.

916 "Willie Morris." In *Three Minutes or Less: Life Lessons from America's Greatest Writers*, pp. 322–24 (see item 915).

On 28 September 1998 at the PEN/Faulkner celebration, Morris and eleven other authors delivered prepared remarks on the subject "Reunion." Morris's memoir *My Dog Skip* was made into a motion picture over the summer, and Morris describes the filming as "a reunion of profound emotion and remembrance." One day he was watching "a scene from a distance and was drawn to several figures sitting together in rickety baseball bleachers. There were Kevin Bacon, playing my father; Diane Lane, playing my mother; the little actress playing Skip's and my girlfriend, Rivers Applewhite; and yes, the Jack Russell terrier named Enzo playing my dog, Skip, himself. And I divined the supple whisperings of my vainglorious heart: you've come back to me, all of you."

917 "Christmases Gone Revisited." In *Christmas Stories from Mississippi*, edited by Judy H. Tucker and Charline R. McCord. Jackson: University Press of Mississippi, 2001, pp. 197–203.

A memoir republished from *Homecomings* ("A Return to Christmases Gone," item 46). See also item 839.

918 "North Toward Home." In *Voices in Our Blood: America's Best on the Civil Rights Movement*, edited by Jon Meacham. New York: Random House, 2001, pp. 32–41.

Chapter 6 of the "Mississippi" section of *North Toward Home* is republished in a collection of the "strongest story-telling about the world in which the [civil rights] movement took shape and played itself out." Recounts in the book's introduction Morris's 1957 meeting of Mississippi native Richard Wright in Paris (an anecdote from the opening chapter of *North Toward Home*). See also item 2063.

919 "Willie Morris: From *North Toward Home*." In *Baseball: A Literary Anthology*, edited by Nicholas Dawidoff. New York: Library of America, 2002, pp. 374–85.

An excerpt from chapter 8 of the "Mississippi" section of *North Toward Home* appears in an anthology of "excellent writing about baseball in any form," such as fiction, song lyrics, newspaper columns and reportage, essays, poetry, oral histories, and sections of biographies and memoirs. See also item 720.

920 "In a Refreshing Provincial Way." In *Fifty Years of the "Texas Observer,"* edited by Char Miller. San Antonio: Trinity University Press, 2004, pp. 91–93.

A compilation of ninety-one pieces from the *Texas Observer* marks the fiftieth anniversary (1954–2004) of the muckraking "journal of free voices." Morris's essay originally appeared in the 15 August 1958 issue (item 524). See also item 921.

921 "A Smart Man Won't Get Bloody." In *Fifty Years of the "Texas Observer,"* pp. 36–38 (see item 920).

An essay originally published in the 21 April 1962 issue of the *Texas Observer* (item 686).

Introductions and Forewords

Includes Morris's introductions and forewords to other writers' books.

922 Foreword to *...And Other Dirty Stories*, by Larry L. King. New York: World Publishing Co., 1968, pp. v–vii. [Ellipses are part of title.]

Morris praises the essays of his *Harper's* colleague, some of which are reprinted in this collection. King's "writing has been characterized by a deep and abiding commitment to America and to authentic American values— almost to an older and vanished America whose expressed ideals of democratic justice and humanity touched somehow the unsophisticated young men in its provinces and shaped them into maturity: a belief that poverty could be overcome and that one would be the better for having experienced it; a belligerent regard for the underdog, for the wayward tramp, for the homeless lost brother; an allegiance to free expression and a hope that in the clash of strong voices some truth might prevail; and an almost mystical country boy's faith that this nation was the last great hope of the world."

923 Introduction to *You Can't Eat Magnolias*, edited by H. Brandt Ayers and Thomas H. Naylor. New York: McGraw-Hill Book Co., 1972, pp. ix–xiii.

Observes that the "unifying theme which undergirds" this collection of twenty-two essays on the problems and changes in the modern American South "is that out of a meaningful working partnership between whites and blacks the South stands an exceptionally good chance of solving its old egregious faults and its more contemporary ones, while both preserving the best in its own unique heritage and offering more than a few crucial lessons to other Americans." The authors of the essays are white and black "writers and editors and politicians and teachers and scholars, who believe passionately in the South and who intend to remain there advancing its most enduring interests."

924 Introduction to *Yazoo: Its Legends and Legacies*, by Harriet DeCell and JoAnne Prichard. N.p.: Yazoo Delta Press, 1976, pp. xi–xii.

Morris contributes his impressions and memories of his hometown to a well-documented history of Yazoo County, Mississippi, "a place which has touched all of us who have known, at one time or another, its ineluctable pull.... I among many was nourished in these legacies of Yazoo's past, and as I grew older they taught me, as they did others, something tangible in what it was to be both a Southerner and an American." Republished as "Legacies" in *Terrains of the Heart* (item 22). Morris reviewed the volume for the *(Memphis) Commercial Appeal* (item 955). DeCell, Morris's high school algebra teacher, spoke at his funeral (see item 2088). Morris married Prichard in 1990 (see item 1703).

925 Introductory note to *Whistle*, by James Jones. New York: Delacorte Press, 1978, pp. xv–xvii.

Morris states that at the time of Jones's death on 9 May 1977, the novelist had completed nearly thirty-one of the thirty-four chapters of *Whistle*. Jones had also "plotted in considerable, and indeed almost finished detail his remaining material" and had asked Morris, his friend and neighbor in Bridgehampton, New York, to finish the book. As Morris explains, "In tape recordings and conversations with me over several months prior to his death, he left no doubt of his intentions for the concluding three chapters." Morris's ending of *Whistle*, "reconstructed from [Jones's] own thoughts and language," appears on pages 447 to 457.

926 Introduction to *A Cook's Tour of Mississippi*, by Susan Puckett and Angela Meyers. Jackson, Miss.: *Clarion-Ledger / Jackson Daily News*, 1980, pp. 13–19.

A cookbook of Mississippi recipes evokes for Morris "many memories of the food of my childhood, and the fine rituals of cooking as it then existed. I remember my grandmother's stories of the Sunday suppers in the 1880s at the family house in Raymond when the preacher came, and since she was the youngest of the seventeen children, she sat at the farthest end of the table. 'By the time the fried chicken got down to me, all that was left were the necks and the wings,' she would tell me, pausing to add, 'But they were still mighty good.'" Excerpted as "A Cook's Tour" in *Terrains of the Heart* (item 25).

927 Introduction to *The Ghosts of Rowan Oak: William Faulkner's Ghost Stories for Children*, recounted by Dean Faulkner Wells. Oxford, Miss: Yoknapatawpha Press, 1980, pp. 7–10.

William Faulkner was a "story teller by profession," writes Morris, and Dean Faulkner Wells, his niece, "has put down here Mr. Bill's ghost stories as he told them to her," her cousins, and other children who played at his home in Oxford, Mississippi, which he called Rowan Oak. In these tales, Wells "has recaptured the sorcery of her uncle's story-telling, and the mood and texture of those vanished moments when he told them. After having recounted them for years to her own children, she has saved them for a new generation of young readers." Excerpted as an introduction to Faulkner's "The Werewolf" in the *Paris Review* (item 749). See also item 748.

928 Foreword to *Mississippi Heroes*, edited by Dean Faulkner Wells and Hunter Cole. Jackson: University Press of Mississippi, 1980, pp. xi–xiii.

Biographical essays of ten deceased "figures who influenced the course of Mississippi history, beginning with the Territorial period and continuing up to the recent past." Morris explains that the Mississippians profiled are not "'heroes' in the old-fashioned sense." Wells's and Cole's "criteria of valor were more subtle. They have selected individuals who have contributed to the state's distinctive culture, people from different backgrounds and sections of the state, figures nurtured by Mississippi who in turn nurtured their state and whose influence is still felt — people who have made us what we are as Mississippians."

929 Introduction to *Pete and Me: Twenty Poems*, by Frances Mitchell. University, Miss.: Pete's Press, 1981, n. pag.

A revision of "Pete and Frances," published in *Ole Miss Magazine* (item 755). Morris's "friend and neighbor," Frances Mitchell, often takes his dog Pete for walks around the University of Mississippi; she "has written a collection of poems about their countless strolls. These whimsical little poems describe their evanescent journeys through the changes of the seasons on the lovely terrain of this campus...." See also item 1894.

930 Foreword to *The Dog Comes Home: Ole Miss Football in 1983*, by Don Whitten. Oxford, Miss.: Yoknapatawpha Press, 1984, pp. vi–ix.

An account of Billy "Dog" Brewer's "brilliant rookie season" as head football coach at the University of Mississippi includes as its foreword a piece originally published as "Bringing Football Back to Its Glory in Mississippi" in the *New York Times* (item 843). See also item 890.

931 Introduction to "Coffee" section of *Taste of the South*, compiled by the Symphony League of Jackson, Mississippi. Jackson: Symphony League of Jackson, 1984, p. 37.

The introductions to the various sections of this cookbook are by "acclaimed Mississippians," including Morris. "As with a few other writers I know, I am a nocturnal figure, a prowler of the shadows by nature, a sleeper into the late mornings. Only coffee awakens me from my most prolific and complex dreams."

932 Introduction to *The Night of the Old South Ball, and Other Essays and Fables*, by Edwin M. Yoder Jr. Oxford, Miss.: Yoknapatawpha Press, 1984, pp. xii–xvi.

In his introduction to a volume of essays and other short pieces, Morris reminisces about the author, "my old friend," whose work he first read "in the fall of '55, when we were twenty-one. He was the editor of *The Daily Tar Heel* at the University of North Carolina, I of *The Daily Texan* at the University of Texas. I began to notice his brilliant, incisive pieces, the best in college journalism of that era.... In *The Night of the Old South Ball* Yoder takes his superlative talents among the ebb and flow of the human events of his lifetime." Excerpted as "Ed Yoder As Essayist" in the *American Oxonian* (item 766).

933 Foreword to *Dominique's*, by Dominique D'Ermo. New York: E. P. Dutton, 1987, pp. xi–xvi.

A cookbook from Dominique's restaurant includes as its foreword an essay originally published as "'I've Found My La Belle Aurore'" in the *Washington Star* (item 828).

934 Introduction to *The Great College Coaches' Cookbook*, edited by Ron Borne. Gulfport, Miss.: Stanley-Clark Publishing Co., 1988, n. pag.

A cookbook that "contains the favorite recipes of some of America's most famous college coaches." Morris believes that "there is an ineluctable relationship between coaching and cooking. From my experience not every coach is a skilled chef, but those who choose to be are ingenious zealots in a kitchen."

935 Introduction to *Life After Mississippi*, by James A. Autry. Oxford, Miss: Yoknapatawpha Press, 1989, n. pag.

Morris avers that in this compilation of "distinguished verse," his friend and Mississippi native Autry "shares with us the power of his faith in mankind, his sense of community in the face of adversity. He takes us back and forth between the past and present, between the youth that we remember and the future we face together." In addition, Autry's poems "reflect the lessons life teaches."

936 Foreword to *Stories from Home*, by Jerry Clower. Jackson: University Press of Mississippi, 1992, pp. xiii–xvii.

A collection of tales by humorist and entertainer Jerry Clower, whose "hard-earned artistry" Morris admires. "In his work and in his example he has been a civilizing influence in the South and the nation on those things that matter deeply. Even at his most uproarious his humor has been characterized by a commitment to an older and more elusive America whose expressed ideals of democratic justice and humility touched somehow the unsophisticated young men and women in its provinces and shaped them into maturity...."

937 Foreword to *A Dixie Farewell: The Life and Death of Chucky Mullins*, by Larry Woody. Nashville: Eggman Publishing, 1993, n. pag.

Morris notes that he and his wife, JoAnne, were present at the October 1989 University of Mississippi–Vanderbilt football game when Ole Miss cornerback Roy Lee "Chucky" Mullins was paralyzed after he tackled Vanderbilt fullback Brad Gaines. "I would never forget that moment, nor would many others. What follows is a complex and many-faceted story about race relations in the modern-day Deep South, about indelible friendships between the young black orphan Chucky ... and his college coach Billy Brewer, between Chucky and his white teammate Trea Sutherland, between Chucky and his black contemporaries." But to Morris "the quintessential tale here" is about Mullins, from an "impoverished small-town upbringing," and Gaines, the "product of a privileged white background in Nashville." See also items 883 and 1700.

938 Foreword to *Another Coat of Paint: An Artist's View of Jackson, Mississippi*, by Wyatt Waters. Brandon, Miss.: Quail Ridge Press, 1995, n. pag.

Morris reminisces about his youth and the "old enduring landmarks" of the city of his birth. "Among my favorite scenes in this book are the ones set along East Capitol from North State to Mill Street, certain stretches of which have changed hardly at all from my boyhood time. At the crest, of course, is the old Capitol itself. How

I loved it then!—its splendid sheen of the past, its majestic colonnades, its big round top, its hushed and tender greenswards. My great-great uncle served as governor here, and my great-grandfather as state legislator from Raymond, and before the arrival of air-conditioning, it seemed forever cool and damp and impervious."

939 Introduction to *For Us, the Living*, by Myrlie B. Evers with William Peters. Jackson: Banner Books / University Press of Mississippi, 1996, pp. ix–xviii.

Morris considers Myrlie Evers's recollections about her husband, "the most prominent and visible advocate in the state for equal justice for blacks" until his assassination in 1963, to be "one of the finest of our American memoirs." Morris describes Medgar Evers's struggles as field secretary for the Mississippi NAACP in the 1950s and early 1960s, his brutal murder at the hands of a white racist, and the 1994 conviction of his killer. First published in 1967, *For Us, the Living* "deeply affected" Morris when he read it while editing *Harper's Magazine* in New York City, and he recalls "the power of its writing, its poignance and passion and candor and beauty.... Why should this book be read three decades after its original publication? Its importance lies in its human dimensions, its everlasting themes: courage, sacrifice, grief, loyalty, and love, Old Testament in their intensity."

940 Introduction to *Life on the Mississippi*, by Mark Twain. The Oxford Mark Twain. New York: Oxford University Press, 1996, pp. xxxi–lii.

Morris compares his small-town boyhood in Yazoo City with that of young Sam Clemens in Hannibal. "His Hannibal, Missouri, and my Yazoo City, Mississippi, are symbiotic for me, evanescently linked in detail and sensation and remembrance; the two most vivid towns of my youth were my own and his—his fictional Hannibal, which in breath and substance if not in exact geography was as Southern a place as my own. Reading him as a boy on rainy days in the muted old library in Yazoo City, I felt palpably in my heart, Why, that town's like this one now." Condensed as "Going Home with Mark Twain" in *American Heritage* (item 798). The Oxford Mark Twain series "consists of twenty-nine volumes of facsimiles of the first American editions of Mark Twain's works."

941 Introduction to *A Pictorial History of Yazoo County*, by the *Yazoo Herald*. [Lincoln Center, Mass.]: Heritage House Publishing, 1996, p. 1.

The photographs in this county history remind Morris of his "complex and indwelling heritage." He adds that the *Yazoo Herald* newspaper "has performed a service in bringing together these photographs, ranging from woodcutters in Phoenix in the 1890s to the steamboats loaded with cotton at the foot of Main Street to the legendary trolley on Grand Avenue to the catastrophic flood of '27. Old family photographs from the notable Quekemeyers and others are among the most fascinating of all." Morris is featured on page 97 of the volume.

942 Foreword to *The Provincials: A Personal History of Jews in the South*, by Eli N. Evans. Rev. ed. New York: Free Press Paperbacks, 1997, pp. xi–xii.

Morris recalls that when he was editor of *Harper's Magazine* "a quarter of a century ago," he had a conversation with Evans about the Jewish experience that "eventually led Eli to a magazine and a book contract." That book was *The Provincials*, published in 1973. Morris adds in his foreword to the volume's revised edition that had his friend "chosen to write a straightforward history of Jews in the South, his book would have, of course, been in itself an enormous contribution. But in wisely concluding to intertwine this significant historical background with his own personal reminiscences, he endowed his narrative with a rueful human texture which elevated it to literature."

943 Foreword to *The Daily Texan: The First 100 Years*, by Tara Copp and Robert L. Rogers. Austin: Eakin Press, 1999, p. vii.

Morris looks back on the year he served as editor of the University of Texas's campus newspaper. "The world has taken a couple of turns since my University years, but I would take nothing for my experience on *The Daily Texan*.... I remember as yesterday the fun and camaraderie in the old journalism building of that 1950s era, and also the bone-wearying work, the late-night deadlines, the arduous responsibility we all felt when we stood up to the Board of Regents on censorship." See also item 1942.

944 "My Two Oxfords." Foreword to *They Write Among Us: New Stories and Essays from the Best of Oxford Writers*, edited by Jim Dees. Oxford, Miss.: Jefferson Press, 2003, pp. 15–27.

An anthology of fiction, verse, and nonfiction by Oxford, Mississippi, authors features as its foreword an essay originally published in *Homecomings* (item 45). Dees credits Morris with turning the small university town into a thriving literary community.

Book Reviews

945 "P. D. East: Life and Times of a Southern Editor." *Texas Observer*, 26 August 1960, p. 6.

Reviews *The Magnolia Jungle* (Simon and Schuster), a "brutally honest" autobiography by newspaperman P. D. East, editor of the *Petal Paper* in Petal, Mississippi. "Out of the deepening anguish of Mississippi, home of the world's greatest living novelist, the best college football team in the land, two consecutive Miss Americas, and the timid expatriate who writes this response, comes a remarkable document of the times." See also item 697.

946 "Sophisticated and Lively: A Full-Fledged UT Murder Mystery." *Texas Observer*, 22 September 1961, p. 6.

Reviews *Close His Eyes* (Harper & Brothers), by Olivia Dwight, the pseudonym for the wife of a University of Texas English professor. Dwight "has given us a full-fledged murder mystery, and the events and landmarks, not to mention some of the people, are unerring enough to place it in the geographic center of the Forty Acres."

947 "Respectable and Rich: Saving Long Island Polo." *Texas Observer*, 19 January 1962, p. 7.

Reviews *The Revolt of the Conservatives: A History of the American Liberty League* (Houghton Mifflin) by George Wolfskill. Wolfskill, a professor of history at Arlington State University in Texas, "has given us a greatly needed and thoroughly documented, if not graciously written or aptly organized, study of the American Liberty League of the 'thirties."

948 "Turn of the Tide: Texas and the Delicate Vote Balance of '60." *Texas Observer*, 23 February 1962, p. 6.

Reviews *Texas in the 1960 Presidential Election* (Institute of Public Affairs, University of Texas) by Professor O. Douglas Weeks, whose "analysis of the Texas vote is sound and comprehensive." His "calculations on the religious issue in the voting largely follow the Observer analysis."

949 "The KKK in Texas: An Adventure in Moral Authoritarianism." *Texas Observer*, 14 September 1962, pp. 1, 4.

Reviews *Crusade for Conformity: The Ku Klux Klan in Texas, 1920–1930* (Texas Gulf Coast Historical Association) by Charles C. Alexander. Historian Alexander's study covers the Klan's "first tentative organizations in 1920, through the years of violence and the conscious turn toward politics from 1921 to 1924, to the Klan's disastrous political rout in the elections of 1924.... For students of Texas politics, it is a welcomed contribution."

950 "The Devil Theory." *Nation* 198 (13 January 1964), pp. 56–58.

Reviews *When the Word Is Given: A Report on Elijah Muhammad, Malcolm X, and the Black Muslim World* (World Publishing) by Louis E. Lomax. Although Lomax, an active member of civil rights organizations, does not agree with the militancy of the Black Muslims, "he writes with a deep understanding of the causes of their alienation." His book "is good journalism, written during the period of Birmingham and the March on Washington to relate the Muslims to the main stream of the Negro revolt."

951 "What Makes Dallas Different?" *New Republic* 150 (20 June 1964), pp. 20–22.

Reviews *Dallas, Public and Private: Aspects of an American City* (Grossman) by Warren Leslie and *The Decision-Makers: The Power Structure of Dallas* (Southern Methodist University Press), by Carol Estes Thometz. At the time of President John F. Kennedy's assassination, there was no other metropolitan area the size of Dallas (outside of the Deep South) "where intolerance and the closed mind were so inclusive, and where violence could be so manifestly political.... Any study of this most disturbed and disaffected of American cities must confront the hardest question of all: how was Dallas different? Neither of these books, unfortunately, is adequate to the task; Mrs. Thometz' is too much the graduate school thesis, Mr. Leslie's is too tentative, ambivalent, and facile."

952 "Norman Mailer's *The Armies of the Night*." *Literary Guild*, July 1968, p. 15.

Reviews *The Armies of the Night* (Literary Guild edition) by Norman Mailer, excerpts of which Morris published in the March 1968 issue of *Harper's Magazine* under the title "The Steps of the Pentagon." Mailer's "physical descriptions of Washington as a place and his evocations of Washington as an idea are probably the best ever written by an American writer, certainly since Henry Adams. His mediations into the American past and into what we have summoned from ourselves as a people and a civilization are as true and as touching as any I have read in years."

953 "Old Hopes and Present Realities." *New York Times Book Review*, 6 July 1969, p.6.

Reviews *America in Crisis* (Holt, Rinehart, and Winston), with text by Mitchel Levitas and photographs by Magnum Photos; edited by Charles Harbutt and Lee Jones. "The theme underlying this impressive and often moving book is that terrible emotional conflict between America's old hopes and present realities.... Mitchel Levitas has contributed an appropriately restrained text—on the ideals we have made for ourselves, on our poverty,... on Vietnam, on the politics of 1968 and on the quality of our environment and of our national life. In format and design the editors have allowed these magnificent photographs to speak for themselves, and the message they bring us is the social history of a decade."

954 "Capote's Muse Is Heard." *New Republic* 169 (3 November 1973), pp. 21–22.

Reviews *The Dogs Bark: Public People and Private Places* (Random House) by Truman Capote, a collection of nonfiction works. "All the pieces in [Capote's] latest volume have appeared at one time or another over the last three decades. They have touched me, reminding me of the things I most cherish and fear and need to remember, things having to do with the nature of the calling."

955 "A History of the Yazoo Homefolk." *(Memphis) Commercial Appeal*, 16 January 1977, sec. G, p. 6.

Reviews *Yazoo: Its Legends and Legacies* (Yazoo Delta Press) by Harriet DeCell and JoAnne Prichard. The result of DeCell's and Prichard's "imaginative instinct[s], reportorial fortitude, and administrative tenacity" is a "handsome, well-designed exploration into our history, filled with maps, newspaper reproductions, photographs, and a considerable amount of clean, incisive prose." See also item 924.

956 "Books About the South." *Southern Living* 21 (July 1986), p. 118.

Reviews *Rommel and the Rebel* (Doubleday) by Larry Wells. A breezy essay about Yoknapatawpha Press and Wells, its publisher, as well as a review of his book. "Now Larry, who has patiently and benignly edited and published books of others, is soon coming out with his own first novel, *Rommel and the Rebel.*" He "has weaved a rich, whimsical narrative—funny, bright, assiduously researched, gracefully written."

957 "Terkel's America." *Chicago Tribune Books*, 11 September 1988, pp. 1, 23.

Reviews *The Great Divide: Second Thoughts on the American Dream* (Pantheon) by Studs Terkel, which is the writer's "most ambitious" book yet. "A subtle calculus of epiphanies in a period that has been marked by a kind of retrenchment of the American spirit, 'The Great Divide' is in some measure a departure for the author. 'Division Street: America,' 'Working,' 'The Good War' et al. dealt with the manner in which diverse Americans remembered their past. 'The Great Divide' concentrates, deeply and panoramically, on the present."

958 "The Epistolary Soldier." *Texas Observer*, 18 May 1990, pp. 18–19.

Reviews *To Reach Eternity: The Letters of James Jones* (Random House), edited by George Hendrick. Morris weaves quotations from Jones's letters throughout a biographical essay about his friend. "In reading these letters, selected and edited by George Hendrick of the University of Illinois with resourceful, descriptive, biographical bridges, I acknowledge anew how serious and impassioned Jim was about being a writer, that it was his whole life...." Republished in *Shifting Interludes* (item 73).

959 "Wonderful Wanderlust: Charles Kuralt Remembers His Years on the Road." *Chicago Tribune Books*, 4 November 1990, pp. 7–8.

Reviews *A Life on the Road* (Putnam), a "candid and affecting autobiography" by Charles Kuralt. From the traveling Kuralt does for his CBS *On the Road* pieces, "He likely knows more about the isolated byways and unknown recesses and surreptitious yearnings of America than any living person." His "prose is clean, flexible and incisive, its context his own generous humanity. He himself is the best testimony to the quiet civilization that lies beneath our many layers."

960 "Delta Blues." *New York Times Book Review*, 11 February 1996, pp. 9–10.

Reviews *Mississippi: An American Journey* (Knopf), a "fine and brave" memoir by Anthony Walton that is "enmeshed in history; in its unfolding, it becomes a compassionate meditation on this country and the South, their past, present and future."

Letters to the Editor

961 "From Willie to Bo, Others." *Yazoo City Herald*, 19 October 1967, sec. 1, p. 1.
See item 1543-A.

962 "Southern Liberalism." *Commentary* 60 (September 1975), pp. 4, 6, 8.
Morris protests Michael Novak's perception of him and other southern liberals in Novak's article "Tom Wicker's Attica" (*Commentary*, May 1975). "I haven't written a letter to the editor pertaining to my own work in about fifteen years. But the suggestion in Michael Novak's article that I have paid deference to the Yankee liberal-chic on questions of race in America is not only patently dissembling and absurd — misrepresenting the very substance of my books and everything I have stood for over the years— it imputes a dishonesty before the conventional Northern fashions which I consider a personal affront."

963 "The Battle Over 'New York Days.'" *New York Times Book Review*, 19 December 1993, p. 31.
See item 1206-C.

964 "Native Son Takes Issue with Writer's Comments on Marker." *Yazoo Herald*, 11 April 1998, p. 4.
See item 1789-B.

PART III
Published Writings About Willie Morris

CONTENTS

Book Reviews

- *The South Today: 100 Years After Appomattox.* Edited by Willie Morris. New York: Harper & Row, 1965 (item 1).

965 "Non-Fiction." *Virginia Kirkus' Service* 33 (1 June 1965), p. 559.

Briefly discusses the book's essays, which are all written by "men of some distinction." Contends that "the most fascinating contributions here lie in the aspect of homecoming, as of Louis Lomax to Valdosta, Georgia; or of William Styron's seeking of the setting of Nat Turner's rebellion in Virginia. Indeed, it is the sense of attachment rather than alienation prevalent in so much that has appeared recently which gives this book its particular quality."

966 Carter, John M. Review. *Library Journal* 90 (August 1965), p. 3302.

Summarizes the eleven "excellent essays by that many experts on the South and its problems," but asserts that "Willie Morris' introduction is elementary, as if aimed primarily at those who know nothing of the South."

967 O'Connor, John J. Review. *America* 113 (13 November 1965), pp. 598–600.

A review essay of I. A. Newby's *Jim Crow's Defense* and *The South Today.* "Willie Morris' collection of essays—by Southerners, and about the South—also underscores the fact that the white man in Dixie never really knew the Negro and is now confronted with a moral imperative to quiet traditional bombast so that he may stop and think." The two books imply that when Negroes win their rights, "the end of much of our racial bigotry will be in sight."

968 Review. *Choice* 2 (February 1966), p. 882.

These "beautifully written impressions of the South" are written by "sensitive, skilled authors who know the region well.... While each essay stands by itself, one recurrent theme is that the South now stands at the threshold of a new era as it begins to accept the changes that will admit Negroes into the mainstream of life."

- *North Toward Home.* Boston: Houghton Mifflin Co., 1967 (item 2).

969 "Non-Fiction." *Kirkus Service* 35 (1 September 1967), pp. 1108–109.

North Toward Home provides "a feeling for people and places and principles, a sense of roots and regionalism transferred and transmuted—the experience of an individual and a generation."

970 Cayton, Robert F. Review. *Library Journal* 92 (15 September 1967), p. 3034.

Recommends this "beautiful account of a young man maturing" and praises the author as a "compassionate observer of life, with a reporter's desire for honesty." Morris's *North Toward Home* is an "intellectual autobiography in which he determinedly steers clear of reporting, other than superficially, any emotional involvements."

971 Review. *Publishers' Weekly* 192 (2 October 1967), p. 54.

Speculates that few memoirs are "of this fine quality, humor, perception, and frank and even unfavorable self-analysis," though the book's segment on Morris's early years in Mississippi is "the better part, evocative, pictorial, intensely real. The sections on Texas politics and on New York literary life are essentially journalism, thoughtful, competent journalism but not the work of art, disciplined memory and emotional synthesis which the Mississippi part of the book is."

972 Hayes, Harold. "Yahoo from Yazoo Makes Good." *Washington Post Book World*, 15 October 1967, pp. 3, 18.

Hayes, the editor of *Esquire*, admires the book's "lyrical" first part covering Morris's Mississippi youth and applauds "the author's strong voice, reacting decisively and with enthusiasm to the new people and places he encounters." He criticizes, however, the volume's "structural weaknesses," such as "extraneous vignettes of good friends and professional associates, short asides on encounters with great men..., and other journalistic excursions into the irrelevant."

973 Greene, A. C. "The Printed Page." *Dallas Times Herald*, 22 October 1967, sec. E, p. 11.

Extols this "beautiful, wise and important book" and declares that Morris's journey from Mississippi to Texas to New York "is not a process of sophistication or a mere climb to success. It is a reckoning with himself. And either through artistry or sheer power of revelation inherent in such a spiritual discovery, Willie Morris does more to make this clear to Texas readers than anything I have ever read."

974 Haygood, William C. "From Yazoo to Manhattan's 'Cave': An American Journey Is Retraced." *Milwaukee Journal*, 22 October 1967, sec. 5, p. 4.

Avers that Morris's "account of his transformation from raw provincial to active liberal ... seems curiously abrupt and inconclusive." Of the book's three parts, "The section on Mississippi is not up to the others, either in substance or in style. The Texas section is the most informative and entertaining, the New York section easily the most brilliant...." Favorably mentions the author's "sure feel for history and his balanced perspective." See also item 1546.

975 Jones, Madison. "Journey from Yazoo." *New York Times Book Review*, 22 October 1967, p. 5.

"Of the book's three sections the most vivid and coherent is the one that treats the author's growing up in Mississippi," argues Jones, a well-respected southern novelist, in this discerning appraisal. He affirms that because this part and the two on Morris's years in Texas and New York "succeed each other as fragments, ordered according to the principle of chronology instead of by a compelling central thing," the book "has no really solid center and ... fails to achieve any meaningful unity." However, Jones concludes that *North Toward Home* "clearly has its virtues. There are the many vivid sketches of persons and places, moments when the spirit of things is caught with affecting precision.... And there is also the pleasure of encountering a prose that is extraordinarily clean, flexible and incisive."

976 Sanders, Leonard. "Morris' Book Bell-Ringer." *Fort Worth Star-Telegram*, 22 October 1967, sec. G, p. 6.

States that although it may seem "audacious" for a thirty-two-year-old to write his autobiography, "Morris has the uncanny ability of placing his memoirs in a timeless framework. In effect, his book is the story of a large segment of a generation," focusing on the author's "continual sense of wonder at the differences among people of different origins."

977 Fremont-Smith, Eliot. "A Sense of Self in Two Fine Books." *New York Times*, 23 October 1967, p. 43.

Reviews the "engaging, revealing and beautifully told" *North Toward Home* and Frank Conroy's *Stop-Time*. Summarizes Morris's career, pointing out that "the contrasts in Mr. Morris's life — between then and now, between his small-town, Deep-South upbringing and his current eminence in the New York literary swirl — give the book its focus and its tension.... A recurrent theme in this book is how crassly provincial is the typical Northern intellectual's attitude toward the South and Southerners."

978 Review. *Christian Century* 84 (25 October 1967), p. 1382.

A brief notice of publication. "*Harper's* new young editor-in-chief offers an 'up-from-slavery' reminiscence of his ascent from typical southern small-townery to New York city."

979 Ochs, Martin. "It's a Long Way from Yazoo City." *Chattanooga Times*, 26 October 1967, p. 6.

Salutes Morris for writing "a good autobiography at an age when many men are just attaining senior membership in the country club." Reasons that while the author now feels at home in New York, "The past clings to him with every old buddy from Yazoo who comes to town.... His widening gulf with boyhood comrades in the racial agony cannot shut out the sympathy and love for the town he knew, unhurried in its isolation and personal, so personal in its relationships."

980 O'Connor, John J. "From a Southerner's Point of View." *Wall Street Journal*, 2 November 1967, p. 18.

Recognizes *North Toward Home* to be a "sensitive and affecting portrait" of a southern expatriate; that is, "a man of liberal tendencies who rejects certain of the values he has inherited — particularly in the areas of race and social structure — while gradually discovering and accepting that his past is firmly locked inside of himself." Also maintains in this critical essay that even though Morris has not led a particularly notable life, his autobiography "is a fascinating and poignant documentation of a man honestly searching for a small, unassuming area of personal meaning in the madnesses of our modern existence...."

981 S., R. A. "From Yazoo to the Cave." *Newsweek* 70 (6 November 1967), pp. 96–98.

Opines that Morris's career and "effortless swoop" to the editor's office of *Harper's Magazine* is marked by a certain degree of "charming temerity." Because his "elemental reserve saves him from the intrinsic egotism in the act of telling one's own story,... what we do get is an acute observer's well-wrought account of what he has seen on his circuitous travels 'north toward home.'"

982 "North by South." *Time* 90 (10 November 1967), pp. 61–62.

Descriptive, rather than evaluative, reviews of *North Toward Home* and Vermont Royster's *A Pride of Prejudices.* Southern authors and editors bring to their writing "a closeness to the soil, an abiding sense of tradition, a refreshing wonderment at the city's delights along with a certain wariness."

983 Schweder, William H. Review. *Best Sellers* 27 (15 November 1967), p. 325.

"It may seem strange that a man of 32 should write his autobiography at that age, but so much has been changing so swiftly since 1935 and Morris has been engaged in so much of the action of these hectic years that his report is worthy of print. Morris has, besides, two talents: enthusiasm and a feeling for the concrete and personal." The second characteristic prevents him from "regarding abstractions and ideas as if they were real events. His enthusiasm ... enables him to see good in many things, has helped him to keep an open mind and to be able to call himself today a Liberal Democrat." *North Toward Home* "will please Morris' friends, but not his enemies. For the reader who is neutral there is much to keep him interested in the education of Willie Morris, especially in his early years."

984 Beaufort, John. "Southerner's Odyssey: On to 'The Big Cave.'" *Christian Science Monitor,* 16 November 1967, p. 15.

"'North Toward Home' can perhaps best be read as history — essentially personal but set perceptively in the context of larger events and their implications.... It is the relating of the personal elements to the larger context (regional, social, political, psychological, etc.) that gives 'North Toward Home' its force." Beauford adds that the book "displays a falling off" when Morris recounts his years in New York, because the author has not found the metropolis to be as "wonderful" as cities in Mississippi and Texas. "Mr. Morris has left the South. All the way home he is not — yet."

985 Carroll, J. Speed. "Bright Boy from Yazoo." *New Republic* 157 (18 November 1967), pp. 32–34.

This lengthy positive, yet critical, review points out that Morris does not merely wish to narrate his life's story, but "explain in large part what was happening in America in the forties, fifties, and sixties. It is this ambitious attempt to relate recent personal experience to history that gives *North Toward Home* its character and attraction.... The Yazoo section is the most satisfying, probably because, having passed from his original love through a stage in which he rather hated Mississippi, he can now see it clearly.... Willie has some harsh words for the East's facile intellectualism, feeling it is voguish and superficial, less honest somehow than the intellectualism of the provinces which is so much more difficult to come by."

986 Hickey, Dave. "North Toward Home." *Texas Observer,* 24 November 1967, pp. 7–8.

One of the most critical of *North Toward Home* reviews, appearing in a publication that Morris once edited. Although the memoir is a "pleasant and intelligent book," Hickey wonders if the scholars and academicians who have praised it would regard Morris's "confessions" so highly if he was not "our kind" of southerner and "if his liberal credentials were not so elegantly in order." Hickey suggests that the book needs "some tightening of the syntax" and that it would be a much better work if it were one-third shorter. He also considers it to be "more of a travel book than an autobiography. Family, friends, and colleagues, unbetrayed, function as figures in a landscape of surfaces which completely dominate them...."

987 Schrag, Peter. "Homecoming." *Reporter: The Magazine of Facts and Ideas* 37 (30 November 1967), pp. 44, 46–48.

Summarizes Morris's career and notes that *North Toward Home* should probably be subtitled "The Education of Willie Morris," whose author "is part Henry Adams, part Huck Finn, and part pioneer with a compass that jammed while it was pointing north instead of west." Morris "can write about his country because he knows whence he came, and why. He is also a very funny man who has produced a magnificent book. Autobiography it surely is, peopled with the great and small of Texas politics and New York publishing, and full of anecdotal color...." In addition, Schrag writes in his detailed evaluation that the author came home to New York "not because that's where the heart is" but because "that's where the action is, and because its very distance gives the Americanism of Texas and Mississippi its meaning."

988 Hassenger, Robert. "Willie Morris Tells It Eloquently in an Autobiography in Mid-Passage." *National Observer,* 4 December 1967, p. 23.

Particularly singles out the New York portion of *North Toward Home* in this complimentary review. Morris uses his struggles in New York City "to weave together some of the most perceptive social commentary this side of Norman Mailer (and with considerably more compassion than Mr. Mailer)." Whether he is "discussing the cold abrasiveness of the urban metropolis" or "the ancient and mysterious stigma shared by Negroes and Southern whites," Morris "is at once eloquent and intuitive, tragic and hilarious."

989 Corbett, Edward P. J. "Book Reviews." *America* 117 (9 December 1967), p. 720.

Morris's *North Toward Home* is "one of the best books of the year in any category.... What is especially remarkable is that this man could so early in life have achieved the maturity that enables him to render and assess his experiences with so much discrimination and balance. And his consummate skill with words makes us ask once again what there is about the atmosphere of the South that has caused it to produce so many first-rate writers in this century. *Harper's* is indeed in good hands."

990 Friedenberg, Edgar Z. "Boy's Life." *New York Review of Books* 9 (21 December 1967), pp. 3–4.

In this noteworthy review essay of *North Toward Home* and Frank Conroy's *Stop-Time*, Friedenberg acknowledges that "Morris is a superb raconteur: colorful, amusing, with a wry but sympathetic eye for the quaint detail...." He contends, however, that "*North Toward Home* is so preoccupied with status and power as to seem rather old-fashioned; growing up in a small Southern town has given Morris not only an eye and an ear for the nuances of social class, but an archaic faith that society has enough structure to permit one to care which are the important people." Friedenberg also comments that although Morris's "style is genial and warm" and his attitudes are "consistently generous and liberal," the book is still impersonal, with significant portions of his life "omitted or dealt with summarily." For instance, Morris includes little of his experiences abroad as a Rhodes scholar at Oxford University. Although he writes about his son, the reader has "no sense of the Morris domestic scene." The author may simply be modest, "but an autobiographer must start with the assumption that the core of what he has to offer is his own special perception of and involvement with reality. If he does not, his work becomes a sort of travelogue; which is what *North Toward Home* is—though a discerning one whose narrator has a real grasp of the terrain through which he guides his reader."

991 Weales, Gerald. "Making It Home." *Kenyon Review* 30, no. 2 (1968), pp. 282–88.

A review essay of *North Toward Home* and Norman Podhoretz's *Making It*. Weales realizes that for Morris, "home" in New York City "is not a place but an accumulation," which involves not a severing of his ties to Mississippi and Texas, "but a carrying of those places." Weales prefers the "remarkably revealing" section covering Morris's Texas years over the chapters on Mississippi and New York because the latter two "contain much of the material of conventional reminiscence." Although the author "is at his best in portraits of people,... strangely enough, the one portrait that is absent is that of Willie Morris. He is present in the early chapters,... but once he leaves Yazoo we glimpse him only occasionally and never come to understand what makes him work."

992 Bode, Elroy. "A Long Way from Yazoo City." *Southwest Review* 53 (Winter 1968), pp. 95–98.

A former University of Texas student from the early 1950s provides a flowery summary of his classmate's "book of education: one person's spiraling out from innocence to a greater knowledge of the world beyond." Comparing this "work to honor" to a Horatio Alger success story, Bode exclaims that Morris "not only has plenty to say but says it all in a style that is impressively clear and engaging. Writing with great honesty, perceptiveness, intelligence, and humor, he has produced a remarkable work."

993 Epstein, Joseph. "Most Likely to Succeed." *Commentary* 45 (January 1968), pp. 74–77.

Commends Morris for his "Northern values and Southern manners" as well as for "that rarer literary gift, a voice of his own." This latter characteristic refers not only to the author's "unique style," but it also signifies that he "has succeeded in stripping away all artificiality from his prose, that he has mastered the various techniques of writing, and that he understands himself well enough to be able to surmount the usual barriers between writer and reader.... But what finally makes Willie Morris so winning a writer is ... his civility; his regard, that is to say, for individual people with their 'flaws and weaknesses and absurdities.'" A serious and thought-provoking assessment of Morris's book.

994 Jones, Elliott. "Books: Reviews and Interviews." *Delta Review* 5 (January 1968), 18–19.

Each of the book's three parts works "its sadness and humor on the shaping of Willie Morris," a writer who "can tell a good country story and make sweeping perceptions and still sound humble."

995 Kapp, Isa. "Man from Yazoo City." *New Leader* 51 (1 January 1968), pp. 19–20.

A "delight" of Morris's "absorbing" autobiography is his "constant and pleasurable relation to his environment." This "old Southern magic" of conveying a "mesmerizing" sense of place is particularly noticeable in the book's first part. Although his remembrances of his youth are not as "provocative" as his New York narrative, "they are more tranquil and much better written." An "arresting aspect" of this Mississippi part is the "flat, objective tone in which Morris sets down his community's derisive and taunting behavior toward its Negroes." This may at first seem strange, but his literary and journalistic craftsmanship "prevents him from imposing the liberal hindsight of the future on the responses of his childhood." Morris's "colorful reporting" of early 1960s Texas politics gives his book "its main distinction." Although he detests the rudeness of New Yorkers, Kapp wonders if Morris will eventually notice the "layers of warmth and temperamental community behind the irritable facade of the New York intelligentsia."

996 Barkham, John. "On 'North Toward Home': Saturday Review Praises Morris' Book." *Yazoo City Herald*, 4 January 1968, sec. 1, p. 5.

Declares that Morris is a "rare breed of cat" because he absorbed the "manners and mores" of Mississippi while growing up, yet felt enough of a sense of restlessness and discontent "to break out of his comfortable cocoon." *North Toward Home* "is an honest and unsparing memoir of a boy growing up in the gentility and bigotry of Yazoo City, Miss., of grappling with a wider world at the University of Texas, where he worked on the campus newspaper, of encountering a still wider world as a Rhodes Scholar at Oxford, and of assimilating it all while remaining essentially the simple Southern boy he had always been." In a note preceding this review, the editor of Morris's hometown newspaper states: "After reading scores of critical reviews of North Toward Home we wrote for permission to reprint the following as the one that comes closest to our own surmising — were we able to write authoritatively on the subject." Barkham's review was distributed to newspapers around the country by the Saturday Review Syndicate.

997 Hicks, Granville. "How to Succeed at an Early Age." *Saturday Review* 51 (13 January 1968), pp. 77–78, 81.

A noted literary critic and editor reviews *North Toward Home* and Norman Podhoretz's *Making It*, each of which "is primarily a contribution to the intellectual history of the United States in the Fifties and Sixties." He perceives Morris to be a "master" at "telling a story and telling it in a lively and charming fashion" and is pleased that before coming to *Harper's* in New York City, the author first lived in other areas of the country. "He is no sentimental apologist for Mississippi and Texas; he knows their evils and he has fought against them; but they are part of what he has become."

998 Review. *Booklist* 64 (1 February 1968), p. 621.

Views the Mississippi part of the three book sections as "freshest and frequently entertaining," while "least attractive" is Morris's portrayal of New York City, "which is in many respects dehumanized, bombastic, and pseudo intellectual." *North Toward Home* is "a very interesting if sometimes unclear portrayal of a reactionary Southerner turned liberal."

999 Lardner, Susan. "Willie Morris (b. 1934-) and Frank Conroy (b. 1936-)." *New Yorker* 43 (3 February 1968), pp. 106, 109–111.

A critical, probing review essay of *North Toward Home* and *Stop-Time* by Frank Conroy. Asserts that Morris "is at his best" while writing about his years in Texas, as he furnishes "a vivid picture of the territory" and its state politicians. On the other hand, his "main fault is a tendency to be distracted from facts, details, characters, anecdotes, by issues and themes, and so he is better in Mississippi and Texas than he is in New York, where he gets immoderately entangled in analyzing his ambivalence toward the place. Apart from that, there are rough spots in 'North Toward Home' that an editor ought to have ironed out," such as "unnecessary repetition and mistimed explanations."

1000 "Lives & Letters." *Virginia Quarterly Review* 44 (Spring 1968), p. lxii.

The memoir "is the story of an eminently civilized man, told with grace, humor, and abundant reserve.... From any perspective, it provides one of the finest literary contributions of the year."

1001 Eaton, Clement. Review. *Journal of Southern History* 34 (May 1968), pp. 333–34.

Eaton, in his review of *North Toward Home* and Joseph L. Morrison's *W. J. Cash: Southern Prophet*, recommends Morris's autobiography as "a valuable source for the study of the political, social, and intellectual life of Mississippi, Texas, and New York during the period.... His liberalism and social criticism are admirable, but one keeps wondering if there is not another side to be presented — a kinder point of view toward the South to be written by an intelligent and understanding conservative."

1002 Chase, Edward T. "Three Autobiographies." *Dissent* 15 (May-June 1968), pp. 272–75.

Chase raises significant issues in his thoughtful review essay of *Making It* by Norman Podhoretz, *North Toward Home*, and *Stop-Time* by Frank Conroy. He argues that although Morris "has a great feel for the colorful in people and events, and a remarkable gift as a raconteur,... he never raises any [questions] as interesting as Podhoretz's or Conroy's. This is partly so because his book is a chronicle, a memoir of considerable poignancy and unfailing intelligence, but not an analytical account of making it nor an evocation of one's innermost emotional life. One is entertained, but not gripped. The main reason, though, is that Morris confronts political and social problems that are of such heroically unsubtle dimensions— the incredible caricatures of Southern and Northern racists, colorful Texas Neanderthal politicians— that the reader's response is confined to amusement or horror."

1003 Moynahan, Julian. "Whiz Kid from Yazoo." *Observer (London)*, 7 July 1968, p. 27.

Believes that Austin, the "political hub" of Texas, was a "great place" for Morris to learn "political realities in a hard school." Moynahan "found Mr. Morris much more interesting and imaginative on Yazoo and Texas than on the New York literary world about which he editorialises in his final chapters. Is it because one of his strong points is humour and there isn't a laugh in a carload either in the *New York Review* crowd which rebuffed him or the middle-brow WASP crowd at *Harper's* which took him to its bosom? Maybe it's because he has his New York career still to make and isn't giving any secrets away."

1004 Rosenthal, T. G. "Grub Street and Fakin' It." *New Statesman* 76 (6 September 1968), p. 293.

Reviews James Hepburn's *The Author's Empty Purse and the Rise of the Literary Agent*, *North Toward Home*, and John Clellon Holmes's *Nothing More to Declare*. Morris's memoir "reads with much more honesty than usual." His "analysis of Texan politics is devastating and his version of LBJ's campaigning style judicious and acute.... *North Toward Home* is notable for the warmth and tolerance of its descriptions of outrageous events and characters. Only when he turns his unjaundiced eye on the New York literary scene does Morris become sharp and critical."

1005 "From Mississippi to Manhattan." *Times Literary Supplement*, 12 September 1968, p. 985.

An erudite summary and critical appraisal. Deems the title of Morris's *North Toward Home* to be "a boast and challenge to everything his heart holds dear: his book as finely poised as a scholastic dispute, moving through its triadic structure from Mississippi to New York. It is this dialectic between heart and reason — with Texas as its ambiguous pivot — that makes this autobiography so fascinating. However casual and amusing, it is a report from a battlefront."

1006 Reynolds, Stanley. "American Times and Lives." *(Manchester, Eng.) Guardian Weekly*, 12 September 1968, p. 14.

Reviews the British edition of *North Toward Home*, John Clellon Holmes's *Nothing More to Declare*, and John Kobler's *Henry Luce: His Time, Life, and Fortune*. Morris's "writing has the easy flow of the Southern drawl." He "writes with a feel for the land and the people of the South that reminds one of Mark Twain. In fact, this is the best picture of a Southern boyhood since Mark Twain, a portrait at once timeless in its characters and scenery and timely in the insight it gives into segregation and the South of the newspaper headlines." Morris is "cutting" while describing Texas politics or the small-minded intellectuals of New York City, "but when he deals with the people of the South he seems to rise above his white liberal stance and writes with a combination of pity and distaste that is at times Olympian. He could become a big writer."

1007 Sanders, Scott. "North Toward Home." *Cambridge Review* 90 (22 November 1968), pp. 164–65.

Critically and favorably evaluates the British edition of "this humouress and intensely human" memoir. "With the rhythms and eloquence of those Southern writers he so much admires— Faulkener [sic], Robert Penn Warren, William Styron, Thomas Wolfe, Ralph Ellison — with the lively rhetoric of a revivalist or stump-politic[i]an, with a novelist's sharp sense of person and place, Willie Morris has recreated a fascinating life, caught at midpassage."

1008 Osborn, George. Review. *Journal of Mississippi History* 31 (August 1969), pp. 254–56.

Descriptive summaries of *North Toward Home* and Ira B. Harkey Jr.'s *The Smell of Burning Crosses: An Autobiography of a Mississippi Newspaperman.* "Perhaps only a person who has lived in a small Mississippi town can fully appreciate how poignantly [Morris] has caught the flavor of time and place.... His observations on the political climate of Texas during the Kennedy-Johnson years fill more than a hundred of the most interesting pages of the book."

1009 "Biography and Autobiography." *Publishers' Weekly* 198 (27 July 1970), p. 76.

A one-paragraph review of the paperback edition. "Most of all, it's a book about the American South today.... It is a very good book."

1010 Hays, William Scott. "Book Reviews." *Journal of Mississippi History* 45 (November 1983), pp. 314–15.

A "new assessment" of *North Toward Home* after its republication in 1982 by Oxford, Mississippi's Yoknapatawpha Press. "What is often neglected in reviews of *North Toward Home,* oddly enough, is Morris's fundamentally dark vision which he never really overcomes. Each of the three sections concludes with an escape motif that culminates, with the finest touch of unity, in the book's final sentences.... For all its other achievements, and there are many, *North Toward Home* principally articulates the lonely search for truth against the hypocrisy that prevailed in all sectors of America during the time of Morris's experience."

- *Yazoo: Integration in a Deep-Southern Town.* New York: Harper's Magazine Press, 1971 (item 3).

1011 "Non-Fiction." *Kirkus Reviews* 39 (15 March 1971), p. 344.

As the reviewer notes, the U.S. Supreme Court ruled in Alexander v. Holmes (1969) that Mississippi had to integrate its public schools. Morris, "a haunted son of that 'bedeviled and mystifying and exasperating region,'" returned to his hometown "to record the historic moment." Although many feared that white students would enroll in "private segregationist academies" rather than attend classes with black students, 80 percent remained in public schools. "This is a tribute, occasionally misty-eyed, to the decent people of the New South as well as a subdued eyewitness account of a quiet revolution."

1012 Review. *Publishers' Weekly* 199 (29 March 1971), pp. 47–48.

Observes in this brief review that "two striking observations" are apparent after reading *Yazoo.* "One is the almost universally expressed conviction that the kids, left alone, have no trouble integrating. The more significant conclusion is that the South ... is really the vanguard of a cultural revolution." Affirms that the book "is one of the more eloquent and convincing descriptions of evolving race relations in the South."

1013 "This Week." *Christian Century* 88 (5 May 1971), p. 570.

Brief notice of publication. Morris "tells the story of integration in a Mississippi city in a you-can't-go-home-again mood, but with a spirit that offers some hope."

1014 Sheppard, R. Z. "Boy's Home Town Makes Good." *Time* 97 (10 May 1971), p. 93.

Discusses Morris's return to Yazoo City to report on how the town complied with the October 1969 Supreme Court order that Mississippi's school districts desegregate their schools. Opines that "the mood of the '60s, with its racial violence and political assassinations, mutes Morris' blend of journalism and autobiography. It puts graceful reins on his prose, which sometimes seems about to run wild like Thomas Wolfe's or feed royally on itself like Norman Mailer's." However, "It is Morris' tone of voice ... that gives *Yazoo* a nuance and emotional impact far more revealing than any amount of facts or figurings."

1015 Wolff, Geoffrey. "You Can Go Home Again." *Newsweek* 77 (10 May 1971), pp. 110, 112.

Applauds Yazoo City for responding "gracefully" after a federal court orders the town to integrate its public schools by 7 January 1970. "Morris took six trips to Yazoo to measure the effects of a social revolution imposed upon his townspeople by law...." In *Yazoo* he "faces down the contraries at war within him, comes to terms with the present and future of the place whose past he abandoned, and rids himself of romantic, unlocated dread to come to terms with the workaday facts of school desegregation in the town where he was raised."

1016 Taylor, Robert. "A Sense of Hope for the South." *Boston Globe,* 14 May 1971, p. 34.

The "tension between private and public lends 'Yazoo' a remarkable depth. The ex-wife who hated Mississippi with a passion, as something elementally evil. The all-white private school which held its classes in churches.... From the materials of myth and current event Morris constructs a South so much a part of his flesh and bone that, in the end, it does partake of the universal.... From his book arises a sense of the shared burden as well as the curse of slavery, of so[m]ething lived, and strangely enough in an age of voguish pessimism, a sense of hope."

1017 Powell, Lew. "Yazoo." *(Greenville, Miss.) Delta Democrat-Times*, 16 May 1971, sec. 1, p. 5.

A laudatory review written in conjunction with Powell's interview with Morris following a successful book-signing session in Greenville (item 1591). "Many fine reporters have written about school desegregation in Mississippi, but none has done it with the skill and passion of Willie Morris. His peculiar brand of advocacy reporting — an advocacy of decency and hope — adds a dimension to Yazoo that is simply unattainable in conventional journalism."

1018 Wakefield, Dan. "A Time of Pain and Anger, Gentleness and Decency in Mississippi." *New York Times Book Review*, 16 May 1971, pp. 42–43.

In a lengthy, cogent essay, Wakefield, a respected journalist, explores integration in Mississippi as well as reviews Morris's book. The volume "succeeds, I think, because it is not only the story of Yazoo and Mississippi and the black-white battle in this society, but also because it is the story of Willie Morris, and the hopes and anguish of his own personal history, which are intertwined with those of the place from which he came, and the place where he arrived. Those who want 'just the facts' and statistics of a social phenomenon may regard Willie Morris's own personal reflections as irrelevant, but I believe that it is these very elements that make the book live, that enrich the outside events he is writing about." See also items 1023 and 1036.

1019 Lehmann-Haupt, Christopher. "The Irony of Southerners." *New York Times*, 24 May 1971, p. 29.

Reviews *Confessions of a White Racist* by Larry L. King (who worked on *Harper's Magazine* with Morris) and *Yazoo*. During visits to Yazoo City, Lehmann-Haupt points out, Morris discovered that blacks and whites were "getting along" in the newly desegregated schools, despite some fears and uncertainties. "What he concluded was that while the integration order had come as a shock, there were a thousand signs that it was working.... It is a cheering book that Mr. Morris has written. And an emotionally rich one too, filled with nostalgia and pride and affection and mixed feelings...."

1020 Weeks, Edward. Review. *Atlantic* 227 (June 1971), pp. 101–102.

Congratulates Morris for writing "a very human document, with its flashes of courage, bigotry, mean taunts, and hopeful compromise." Includes observations from "the more liberal leaders of the community [who recognized] that change was inevitable and might be for the better."

1021 Cayton, Robert. Review. *Library Journal* 96 (1 June 1971), p. 1958.

A one-paragraph review of a "forceful book," a volume that is written with "appealing sensitivity" and "with a superb understanding of contemporary Mississippi and the South." Morris believes, states Cayton, that "integration, as it is happening in Yazoo, is important because it represents people enriching their human integrity."

1022 Holmes, William F. Review. *Saturday Review* 54 (5 June 1971), pp. 31–33.

A lengthy, significant essay detailing the transition from segregation to integration in the Deep South and how Morris "realized the magnitude of what was taking place" in his hometown. Avers that Morris's book is "an extremely well-written account" of how Yazoo City handled the court-ordered integration of its public schools and that "Morris has a sense of perspective about the state that is essential. He realizes the importance of what is happening in Yazoo, and he presents the change with its full historical significance." Because Morris grew up in the town and knows its residents, "He instills into his narrative a degree of compassion and understanding rarely seen in modern journalism." On the other hand, this same "personal involvement" is partly responsible for an "inevitable" weakness, for "Yazoo is written almost totally from the point of view of the whites, focusing upon their fears, hopes, and adjustments in confronting school integration. Morris is not sufficiently sensitive to the problems of blacks."

1023 Review. *New York Times Book Review*, 6 June 1971, p. 38.

The "touching, very personal" *Yazoo* is included in "A Selection of Recent Titles," a list of books "reviewed since the Christmas Issue of Dec. 6, 1970." See also items 1018 and 1036.

1024 Wisch, Steve. "'Yazoo' Tells Southern Crisis." University of Texas *Daily Texan*, 10 June 1971, p. 13.

Considers Morris's *Yazoo* to be "a unique paradigm of human understanding. He communicates a below-the-surface understanding between southern whites and southern blacks, one that just falls short of the two races reaching out for each other to resolve a human predicament."

1025 Herman, Tom. "Of Integration, Yazoo-Style." *Wall Street Journal*, 1 July 1971, p. 10.

Commends Morris for relating personal anecdotes that show how students and adults have reacted to the integration of the Yazoo City schools. Although the author reports incidents that reveal "the darker aspects of the Yazoo experience," he "plays down these unfortunate facts, leaving himself open to the charge that he wrote his book too heavily from the point of view of a white man and did not account fully for the feelings of blacks." This criticism implies "that if Mr. Morris' emotional and highly personal approach is the strength of the book, it also is its weakness."

1026 Carter, Hodding, III. "There's a Snopes in Each of Us, But Will He Win Out?" *Washington Post Book World*, 4 July 1971, p. 3.

The editor of the *Delta Democrat-Times* of Greenville, Mississippi, and member of a leading southern political family reviews *Yazoo* and Larry L. King's *Confessions of a White Racist*, "two brilliantly realized personal statements." He provides quotations from several paragraphs of Morris's book while contending that the volume "is a rare combination of superb reporting and lyric, loving insights forged from a shared past."

1027 McPherson, William. "Rediscovery ... Reconciliation." *Washington Post*, 6 July 1971, sec. B, pp. 1, 4.

McPherson, the book editor of the *Washington Post*, sums up Morris's "sanguine" conclusions concerning integration in the South as he quotes liberally from *Yazoo*, "a good and thoughtful and deeply sensitive book" that is "part reportage, part rediscovery of self and country, part reconciliation.... If Morris's 'true human revolution' does finally come to pass, he believes that it will be the young people of the South who may finally bring it about." These youths, Morris writes, "are as American as they are Southern, but it is this common bond in the South — the rhythms and tempos, the ways of speaking and of remembering, the place and the land their people knew and out of which they suffered together — that makes them, young blacks and whites, more alike than dissimilar; and it is this, before it is all over, that will be their salvation."

1028 Goodman, Walter. "The Search for America." *Commentary* 52 (August 1971), pp. 87–90.

Goodman examines *Yazoo* and four other books that "bring America back to the folks at home" in his review essay. *Yazoo* "shows what can be accomplished by a writer of intelligence and sensibility involved with a subject of manageable proportions." Morris, who has lived in Texas and Europe, wonders why he is still drawn to the South. Goodman replies that others besides Mississippians "need to come to terms" with their early lives. "Still, the South seems to have its special power, particularly for the literary imagination, and in a series of quiet conversations and reflections, Morris works his way into the contradictions of the home town which he fled but cannot escape." His book is "heartening because it reminds us, without the hint of preachment, that some injustices, even those which excite the most violent passions, can be alleviated, and that it is within the capacity of ordinary men to play a part in that process."

1029 Friedenberg, Edgar Z. "Southern Discomfort." *New York Review of Books*, 2 September 1971, pp. 7–8.

Southerner Friedenberg opines in his lengthy, absorbing review essay of Larry L. King's *Confessions of a White Racist* and *Yazoo* that the problem with books about the American South is that writers "so easily select from it themes and issues that reveal their own concerns more clearly than they do its essence." Although Yazoo is about the "moral predicament of the South," Morris focuses on "situations so trivial and commonplace" that his eloquence "seems forced and even empty" and his anecdotes "as static as snapshots in an album." The volume, however, has its strong features. "The liveliest, most convincing, and most moving parts of the book are those that show how much conflict in the South already resembles conflict in the rest of America: the ease with which black and white students begin to know one another and the petty determination with which their elders block their efforts to come together, not so much out of prejudice as out of political fear."

1030 Cosgrave, Mary Silva. Review. *Horn Book Magazine* 47 (October 1971), pp. 506–507.

A one-paragraph descriptive summation of *Yazoo*. Between January and November of 1970, Morris visited his native state "to observe the effects" of the Supreme Court's ruling ordering Mississippi "to integrate thirty school districts immediately." By the end of the year, "He was proud to report that Mississippi had quietly achieved school integration and, at the same time, he, himself, had come to terms with his 'old warring impulses ... to be both Southern and American.'"

1031 "Notable Nominations." *American Libraries* 2 (October 1971), p. 1010.

The American Library Association has selected *Yazoo* and seven other titles as "Notable Books of 1971." Morris's "lucid, sensitive account aptly portrays a southerner's profound love for his native land, and his conviction that what is happening in Yazoo will provide a pattern for peaceful black-white relations in other troubled communities."

1032 Review. *Booklist* 68 (1 October 1971), p. 122.

Refers to *Yazoo* in this short review as a "balanced report" of Morris's visits to his hometown. See also brief review in 15 October 1971 *Booklist*, page 191.

1033 Review. *Choice* 8 (November 1971), p. 1253.

Regards *Yazoo* as "even more significant" than the author's *North Toward Home*. "Yazoo tells us much about the human condition, boyhood memories on a collision course with adult realities, court orders and human ploys to block them, dedicated black and white youth changing the racial scene, an excellent balance of personal recollection and objective reporting...."

1034 Kellogg, Jean. "Sound the Warning." *Christian Century* 88 (17 November 1971), pp. 1362, 1364.

Believes that Morris "has produced an evocative, courageous, and yet tragic portrayal of his native town's 'progress' toward integration." While commenting on the "tone of sadness that underlies Morris' warm and vital picture of the town of Yazoo," the reviewer wonders if "the protests" and "the bloodshed" that led to integration were pointless if students of both races "are moving into new and more subtle forms of isolation."

1035 Marsh, Pamela. "1971— Always the Unexpected." *Christian Science Monitor*, 26 November 1971, sec. B, p. 3.

Book editor Marsh includes *Yazoo* in her list of notable books published in 1971. "What characterizes them all is the quality of saying what we least expect."

1036 Review. *New York Times Book Review*," 5 December 1971, p. 88.

Morris's "report on integration in his old hometown" is included in "1971: A Selection of Noteworthy Titles," a list that "has been selected from titles reviewed during the past year." See also items 1018 and 1023.

1037 "Paperbacks." *Publishers Weekly* 201 (15 May 1972), p 55.

Praises *Yazoo* as an "important book" and "a brilliant perspective on a modern small town" in the South. Deems Morris in this one-paragraph review to be "a good writer, and remarkably objective and astute in his ability to see his home town clearly, as it was and as it is now, and as it seems to be going."

1038 "Varia." *Best Sellers* 32 (15 August 1972), p. 244.

A notice of the paperback publication. "Willie Morris sought for a crystallization of some of America's problems and came up with a book about his home town, 'Yazoo.'"

- *Good Old Boy: A Delta Boyhood*. New York: Harper & Row, 1971 (item 4)

1039 "Older Non-Fiction." *Kirkus Reviews* 39 (1 November 1971), p. 1167.

"Unmistakably firsthand but demonstrating perhaps the shifting sights of memory, these recollections of a Mississippi boyhood contain many of the episodes and much of the wording of the first part of *North Toward Home* (1967), but without the probing complexity of Morris' adult book.... All told this version is less revealing but more of a story, with Spit, Bubba, Muttonhead and the others reappearing like fictional characters...." It is difficult "to separate the facts from fiction here," but "Morris' 'rich, slow' Southern atmosphere makes for an affecting encounter."

1040 "'Good Old Boy' a New Book About Willie Morris' Boyhood." *Yazoo City Herald*, 11 November 1971, sec. B, p. 6.

A reviewer for Morris's hometown newspaper writes that "although the face of America has changed greatly in the past quarter century, 'Good Old Boy' richly portrays the excitement and warmth of boyhood life in a small town. In this fascinating reminiscence, Willie Morris reminds young readers that something of value from the past does and should remain, compelling allegiance and love."

1041 Review. *Publishers' Weekly* 200 (22 November 1971), p. 41.

"Willie Morris's running commentary on childhood remembrances," writes the author of this short review, "is an affectionate, nostalgic story, full of humorous incidents (some fact, some fiction) and an appealing atmosphere."

1042 Review. *Time* 98 (27 December 1971), p. 61.

A brief review. *Good Old Boy* "is drenched in crawdads, squirrel dumplings, Delta woodlands, and Peck's-bad-boy jokes. But Morris eases out of realism into fantasy and back with no strain, and it's nice to think that somebody more contemporary than Huck Finn could remember it all that way."

1043 Anson, Brooke. Review. *Library Journal* 97 (15 January 1972), p. 290.

Although the author of this succinct review admits that the book contains charming anecdotes and "many fine descriptions of growing up" in a small southern town, "the lack of a well-defined plot and the setting in the near past will likely limit the book's appeal to a small but highly appreciative audience."

1044 H[aviland], V[irginia]. "Autobiography." *Horn Book Magazine* 48 (February 1972), p. 60.

A nationally known authority on children's literature endorses *Good Old Boy*. Morris furnishes "an account for his son of what it was like to grow 'up in the deep South.' There is a classic American quality about the reminiscences of a boy who, 'let alone to grow' in the 1940's, had roamed about the Delta forest with a gang of boys, dogs, and one delightful girl in a red Model-A Ford; who played tricks and suffered schoolroom trials; and who was addicted to baseball.... The author vividly recalls a range of highly individual town characters of varying age and status; the feel of the hot, rich Delta land; the intimacies of a boy's delights and sorrows; 'the softest, most bittersweet sadness' of a summer's being almost gone; and the remarkable dog Skip that 'walked the woods with a natural sense of the impossible.'"

1045 Review. *Booklist* 68 (1 February 1972), p. 466.

Parts of this "rich personal reminiscence of a boyhood in Yazoo City" originally were published "in different form" in *North Toward Home.* "Here, writing straightforwardly rather than introspectively as in the other book," author Willie Morris focuses principally "on his friends" and "the adventures they shared." A one-paragraph, short review.

1046 Smith, Jennifer Farley. "Books for the Children of Light." *Christian Science Monitor*, 24 February 1972, p. 7.

The newspaper's children's book editor declares that *Good Old Boy* "is a fine example of just how exciting an adventure tale can be when it's well-written as well as filled with action." Occasionally narrating "in the carefree accents of a boy" or as a "master ghost-story teller," Morris ingenuously "rambles up to the book's central episode: an encounter with seven giant tattooed C[h]octaw Indians in—yessirree—a haunted house that will make your hair stand on end."

1047 Stahel, Thomas H. Review. *America* 126 (25 March 1972), pp. 324–25.

This "delightful boyhood reminiscence" is a "shortened and somewhat simplified" adaptation of the first section of *North Toward Home,* written in a tone that is "more straight-forward, good-spirited and casual than the earlier version. Here the emphasis is on sports, dogs (especially Ol' Skip, the football-playing fox terrier), practical jokes, school days and clever country ruses.... Good reading, especially for boys, but also for anyone who appreciates reminiscences vividly remembered and lovingly recounted."

1048 Sutherland, Zena. Review. *Saturday Review* 55 (22 April 1972), p. 86.

A concise review. These "loosely connected series of anecdotes ... bring the torpor of a small Southern town and the indefatigable business of its younger residents vividly to life."

1049 Review. *Observer (London)*, 17 March 1974, p. 37.

A review of the British edition. Morris wrote this "potty little memoir" for his son, so the boy would know what his father experienced growing up in Yazoo City, Mississippi, "back in the days when Pop was knee-high to a bottle of

Coke." The reader just has "to sit back and let Dad get on with the job of imprinting his own sentimental Southern jingoism on the urbanised infant."

1050 "Born to Sorrow." *TLS, The Times Literary Supplement*, 29 March 1974, p. 326.

Points out the "lack of coherence" in *Good Old Boy* and dismisses the book as a "pleasant, ambling read, and a loving evocation of one small American town, but nothing more."

1051 Walker, Martin. "Angled Views." *(Manchester, Eng.) Guardian*, 30 March 1974, p. 22.

A purported review essay of *Good Old Boy* and Loren Eiseley's *The Night Country*, though little is said of the former book. Walker provides his interpretation of a "Good Ole Boy," summarizes Morris's life, and succinctly labels the author's volume as "tales of childhood daring-do, of closeness to the earth, of youthful comradeship, a kind of Enid Blyton for grown-ups."

1052 Wordsworth, Christopher. Review. *New Statesman* 87 (24 May 1974), p. 738.

A brief notice of publication. "Willie Morris recalls his Mississippi home town, escapades in swamps and squirrel-woods, blacks and whites in harmony."

1053 L[ogue], J[ohn] D. "Books About the South." *Southern Living* 16 (February 1981), p. 8.

"Willie Morris' own book of his boyhood, *Good Old Boy*, is happily reprinted.... No one, not even 'Mr. Bill' [William Faulkner], was better at capturing the sounds and textures and lazy days and lost moments of youth than Mr. Morris."

1054 Review. *Kliatt Young Adult Paperback Book Guide* 17 (Winter 1983), p. 44.

Good Old Boy is "a celebration of childhood, written by one of America's most gifted storytellers."

- *The Last of the Southern Girls*. New York: Alfred A. Knopf, 1973 (item 5).

1055 Review. *Publishers Weekly* 203 (12 March 1973), p. 62.

"Despite some good moments, this novel is a distinct disappointment, coming from a writer of Morris's ('North Toward Home') proven sensitivity and perception.... Morris, from whom you'd expect considerably better, has come up with yet another novel about Washington pols and their ladies."

1056 Hills, Rust. "Fiction." *Esquire* 79 (May 1973), pp. 66, 68.

A short, disparaging review. "This seems to be a *roman à clef* about a girl who rises to great heights in Washington society — plans the President's parties, and so on — then falls mightily." The "book makes you wish the bad 'moneymen' had let Morris go on doing whatever he thought he was doing as editor of *Harper's*...."

1057 B[arthelme], S[teve]. "Southern Girls, Last of." *Texas Observer*, 11 May 1973, p. 15.

A reviewer for the publication Morris once edited concludes that although the author has "written books and edited magazines with a considerable amount of skill and daring," his first novel is "not very good." Although Morris is fascinated with Washington, D.C., the setting of his novel, "he fails to transfer his feeling. Instead, he *explains* it, and the explanation is not enough to make you care." Barthelme also objects to Morris's use of language, calling it "petty lyricism," and adds that the "weaknesses of contemporary journalism overwhelm" the book. "An atmosphere of pseudo-significance and portentousness combine with the abuse of language to produce a book which reads as if it were written by a computer.... It's a graveyard of 60's pop sociology."

1058 Avant, John Alfred. Review. *Library Journal* 98 (15 May 1973), p. 1601.

Lauds *The Last of the Southern Girls* as an "extraordinarily beguiling first novel" and an "awfully good read," distinguished by a title character possessing "charm and brilliance" with "overtones of both Zelda and Scarlett." Concedes that "there are a couple of long, lethargic sequences, but this book delivers a lot: childhood scenes that evoke the feeling of *To Kill a Mockingbird*; a unique sense of place that no other Washington novel has suggested; in the last pages, the heroine's strong vision of grass roots America." See also item 1080.

1059 Yardley, Jonathan. "Yen for Power." *New Republic* 168 (19 May 1973), pp. 28–29.

A prominent literary critic — and an obvious admirer of Morris's work — contributes a mixed review of the author's first novel. Although this "witty, intelligent and engaging book about Washington" is "great fun" as a roman à clef, "it has its drawbacks: Morris has difficulty weaving expository material into his story, and in a few passages his descriptive prose lapses—surprisingly, and most uncharacteristically for a writer of his skill and taste—into mush." Other paragraphs from the book suggest that Morris's biggest problem as a novelist is that "he tends to march out his themes with ruffles and flourishes.... He too often uses expository rather than fictive methods; he is didactic where he ought to let his themes flow subtly and naturally from the story itself. The result is that the novel moves in fits and starts, its flow broken from time to time by extended passages of exposition." That said, Yardley does urge readers to peruse chapter 3, an account of the protagonist's childhood in De Soto Point, Arkansas, to see what the author "can do at his best," as "we have few writers more capable than Morris of making childhood believable."

1060 Coppel, Alfred. "The Thin Fictional Veil of 'Southern Girls.'" *San Francisco Sunday Examiner & Chronicle*, 20 May 1973, "This World" section, pp. 38, 42.

Describes the extensive media coverage given "a pair of His and Hers books," *The Last of the Southern Girls* and *Laughing All the Way* by Washington socialite Barbara Howar, explaining that "Howar has written a personal biography and that Morris has immortalized Howar" as the heroine of his "droning bore" of a book. Coppel chides Morris for the "fawning awe" his title character "engenders in her creator" and recommends that he "refrain from writing novels about beloved friends at least until time and distance allow some perspective."

1061 Mano, D. Keith. Review. *New York Times Book Review*, 20 May 1973, p. 7.

A lukewarm endorsement of a "workmanlike" novel. "There's nothing wrong with 'The Last of the Southern Girls.' It doesn't offend; it doesn't astonish. It doesn't bore; it doesn't enthrall. It is serviceably written with a kind of tepid elegance." Mano is "not much persuaded" by the author's "descriptions" of the novel's settings—De Soto Point, Arkansas, and Washington, D.C.—but he recognizes that "Morris writes fine dialogue; it's his best asset. When a character is described as glib and clever, that character talks glib and clever." See also item 1078.

1062 Hoffman, Marjorie. "Morris' 'Southern Girls' Shows Misplaced Talent." *Austin American*, 25 May 1973, p. 4.

Traces Morris's career and summarizes *The Last of the Southern Girls*, drawing a parallel between it and Barbara Howar's "simultaneous book," *Laughing All the Way*. Hoffman laments that his book "seesaws from interesting fiction to badly (and sometimes needlessly) disguised fact." She also hopes that he "has not abandoned what he does best: autobiographical non-fiction," for even though his novel is "at times lively reading," it demonstrates that fiction "is not his forte." See also Hoffman's interview with Morris (item 1607).

1063 Review. *New Yorker* 49 (2 June 1973), p. 123.

Hypothesizes that Morris is "too complex a writer" to write a novel about a "charming, ambitious Southern woman's ups and downs among the Washington notables." The reviewer compares *The Last of the Southern Girls* to the author's "beautiful autobiography," *North Toward Home*, and regrets that although the descriptive passages of the heroine's childhood are "superb" and the Washington, D.C., setting is "believably evoked," the "writing is mostly slick and ... disappointingly shallow."

1064 Porterfield, Christopher. "Such Good Friends." *Time* 101 (4 June 1973), pp. 92, 95.

A review of Barbara Howar's memoir *Laughing All the Way* and *The Last of the Southern Girls*, the latter a work of fiction written by Howar's "constant companion" and "transparently based" on her life. Morris's novel is a "disappointment," and admirers of his writing "may not know what to make of it, unless they shrug it off as the indulgence of every man's right to do something silly to impress his girl friend." Although a few sections "hint at the book that he might have written," the volume "most resembles a political novel in the way its narrative keeps jerking to a halt like a campaign train, while Morris hops off to deliver a high-flown speech."

1065 McMurtry, Larry. "Wringing the Belle." *Washington Post Book World*, 17 June 1973, p. 3.

A lengthy review essay of *The Last of the Southern Girls* and Barbara Howar's *Laughing All the Way*. Bookstore owner and novelist McMurtry—who years later would earn accolades with *The Last Picture Show*, *Terms of Endearment*, *Lonesome Dove*, and other works—considers Morris to be "one of the two or three finest editors of his time." With *The Last of the Southern Girls*, however, he now "seems to have fallen victim to total editorial paralysis. What can the noble house of Knopf have been thinking of, to so passively allow him to foist this canard on his own reputation?" Morris, McMurtry allows, "writes a beautiful prose sentence," is "highly informed," and is "keenly sensitive to place." As the author clearly wanted to write a novel about love, "he might have written a wonderful long memoir on what it's like to be in love in this particular capital, in our particular day and age.... Instead he has served up some gracefully written but lukewarm Balzac, about a remarkably insipid girl from the provinces who comes to Washington and loses her illusions."

1066 Perry, James M. "Can a Belle Make It Big in Washington? Morris Muses ..." *National Observer*, 30 June 1973, p. 23.

Roundly criticizes this "surprisingly, spectacularly bad book. The basic problem is that Morris, who has written some first-rate nonfiction, knows nothing—*nothing*—about writing a novel. Thus the flaws in this book include an inability to structure a plot, develop a character, or carry a dialog. Other than that, he doesn't know very much about Washington or how it works."

1067 Sanborn, Sara. "Scarlett Lives—in Washington." *Nation* 217 (2 July 1973), pp. 23–25.

In this detailed, critical study of Morris's novel, Sanborn praises Morris's "Southern language and habits of mind," qualities that are especially noticeable in the chapter devoted to the childhood of his main character, Carol Hollywell. While discussing the novel's plot, Sanborn ponders Hollywell's "inability to go home again," and wonders if "perhaps we are to assume that Carol has been corrupted by ambition and the craving for power. That is what the book jacket would have us believe. Unfortunately, there is little warrant in the novel for such a pretentious interpretation." Concerning the novel's structure and tone, the reviewer sees "Morris letting himself off too lightly. Carol Hollywell's character and her personal worlds in Washington and Arkansas are fully evoked," but more substantial issues, such as the significance of her career and women's liberation, "are only invoked."

1068 Fuller, Edmund. "Gadding About Washington with a Southern Lady." *Wall Street Journal*, 5 July 1973, p. 6.

Barbara Howar's memoir receives most of the attention in this joint review of *Laughing All the Way* and *The Last of the Southern Girls*. Fuller considers Morris, the "former boy-wonder editor" of *Harper's Magazine*, as "one of the last of the Southern boys, and a highly talented one, whose possible powers as a novelist are clearly visible in the best parts of this uneven, essentially slight book.... His novel remains an unfinished story but he writes with skill, often with penetration. There are fine sequences, notably a passage on Carol's childhood and her friend Buddy Carr, 'a good old boy.'"

1069 Review. *Booklist* 69 (15 July 1973), pp. 1049–50.

A short review, asserting that readers of *North Toward Home* who regard Morris "as able and sensitive will be disappointed to find his first novel is a soap opera, somewhat redeemed by a writing style several cuts above the plot line."

1070 Coyne, John R., Jr. "Barbara/Carol." *National Review* 25 (20 July 1973), pp. 797–98.

Coyne notes in his review of Barbara Howar's *Laughing All the Way* and Morris's *The Last of the Southern Girls* that Carol Honeywell [sic], the heroine in Morris's novel, is based on Washington, D.C., hostess Barbara Howar. Most of *The Last of the Southern Girls* "reads like a dramatization of *Laughing All the Way*, and like Mrs. Howar's own book it fails to answer one central question—what makes Barbara/Carol run?" Coyne believes that Morris intended to "add substance" to his protagonist by focusing on her southern roots and childhood as a way of explaining why she behaves the way she does. "But she is not Zelda, Morris is not Faulkner, and despite magnolias and moonlight on the Mississippi and good ole boys and monuments to the Confederate dead, Barbara/Carol would probably have behaved the same way had she been born in Sioux Falls or Bend, Oregon." Although in some places "Morris writes beautifully," too often he seems to be "rewriting chunks of *North Toward Home* and *Yazoo* without deepening the perceptions of the Southern experience that illuminated those books."

1071 Egerton, John. "Out of the South." *Progressive* 37 (September 1973), pp. 54–55, 58.

A review essay of Tom Wicker's *Facing the Lions* and Morris's novel. After capsulizing *The Last of the Southern Girls*, Egerton concludes that "as a fantasy, a fairy tale with a not-so-happily-ever-after ending, it is amusing and clever. There is an especially fine chapter about Carol's Arkansas childhood.... But most of the rest is dinners and cocktail parties and charming repartee, apropos of nothing."

1072 "Notes on Current Books." *Virginia Quarterly Review* 49 (Autumn 1973), p. cxxxvi.

A one-paragraph review of a "thinly disguised roman à clef." The volume ends "at an arbitrary point that leaves the reader with no sense of resolution. Mr. Morris' book is at best ineffective and ephemeral."

1073 Review. *Choice* 10 (October 1973), p. 1196.

North Toward Home and *Yazoo* "were splendid achievements, but readers felt that Morris was somewhat confined by the genre of nonfiction. With this first novel, Morris displays a newfound freedom and has fulfilled the promise anticipated by his early readers." He "has vividly created a picture of the intoxicating, addicting life of politics...."

1074 Magid, Nora L. "Willie & Barbara & Barbara & Willie." *Commonweal* 99 (26 October 1973), pp. 89–92.

A commentary on Morris's novel and Barbara Howar's *Laughing All the Way*. To support her statement that *The Last of the Southern Girls* "was rumored to be a fictionalized version" of Howar's memoir, Magid compares two similar passages from the books. "The point is not just that Willie Morris has translated the incident and softened it, but that he has done so to no purpose.... Clichés abound. The southern deb, the brittle New York prodigy who understands the 'trap in being golden.'"

1075 "Novels in Brief." *Observer (London)*, 3 March 1974, p. 37.

Avers that the British edition of *The Last of the Southern Girls* is "shrewd and enjoyable for all its lush and reverential tone."

1076 "Bulldozered." *TLS, The Times Literary Supplement*, 8 March 1974, p. 229.

Examines "the rise and fall" of central figure Carol Hollywell. "Though his descriptions of the South are masterful, Willie Morris has set himself a difficult task. His is not simply the problem of deriving wit and effective dialogue from a society unable to 'understand the consequences of words'; it is that of bestowing reality on a woman and a world deliberately identified with the fictional."

1077 Review. *Observer (London)*, 17 March 1974, p. 37.

"It is unfortunate for Morris that events have somewhat devalued the kind of story that chooses to concentrate, amid all the affairs of capital and Capitol, on 'one vital and beautiful woman who conquered it all' (we are more likely these days to look out for the several slimy and ferocious men who might undermine it all), but it is hard to imagine a good old boy like Mr Morris changing anything much in the light of hard news."

1078 Review. *New York Times Book Review*, 14 April 1974, p. 23.

"Larded with much gossipy detail," Morris's novel "set tongues wagging from Georgetown to McLean" after its original publication. This single-paragraph review of the paperback edition quotes from the original *New York Times* critical piece (item 1061).

1079 McLellan, Joseph. "Paperbacks." *Washington Post Book World*, 2 June 1974, p. 4.

A brief notice reporting that the novel is "based on the plausible premise that Washington is 'starved for a beautiful, irreverent woman.'"

1080 Rogers, Michael. "Classic Returns: Fiction." *Library Journal* 120 (15 May 1995), p. 100.

Quotes from *Library Journal*'s original review (item 1058) in a short evaluation of the Louisiana State University Press paperback edition. "Though a bit like a soap opera, the novel is nevertheless 'an awfully good read.'"

- *A Southern Album: Recollections of Some People and Places and Times Gone By.* Edited by Irwin Glusker, narrative by Willie Morris. Birmingham, Ala: Oxmoor House, 1975 (item 6).

1081 Review. *Publishers Weekly* 208 (25 August 1975), pp. 287–88.

"Immediately the non–Southern reader will be impressed by the blend of regional pride, grace, candor and sense of human community that emanates like an aura from photos and text.... Willie Morris's memory-laden introductory memoir of his Mississippi boyhood illuminates the entire book most beautifully."

1082 Staggs, Sammy. Review. *Library Journal* 100 (15 November 1975), p. 2160.

Applauds both the photographs and the selections from southern writers in this coffee-table book. "Like many of the excerpts, the introduction by Willie Morris is lyrical and nostalgic, evoking a genuine love of the legendary South."

1083 Hoagland, Edward. "Down Memory Lane." *New York Times Book Review*, 7 December 1975, pp. 4, 86.

Hoagland's review essay of four "picture

books" includes his scathing observations on "an appalling piece of balderdash called *A Southern Album*.... Willie Morris's unfortunate prose contribution here is derivative drivel.... The whole zombie narrative ... is so mercifully brief that it might be more accurate to describe him as lending his name to this book rather than contributing to it. The rest of the prose comes in dabs alongside the pictures and was chosen by a specially selected panel of eleven Ph.D.'s and two M.A.'s and is therefore predictable.... The pictures are okay — as pictures in such books generally are. They are at least *complete*, whereas the word snippets quoted are a jigsaw puzzle."

1084 Dunlap, Benjamin. Review. *New Republic* 173 (13 December 1975), pp. 27–28.

As Dunlap reflects on southern authors and their writings, he asks: "But how did Willie Morris and Irwin Glusker, who have done such splendid work, get mixed up with this hardcover super issue of *Southern Living*?... The best Southern novelists no longer write about the South as a peculiar people; and the rest of America, with its own experience of defeat and guilt, has become more like the South as the South has become more like it.... Morris writes persuasively of those moments that 'elicit some deep interior tension and seem to mirror all the longings and intuitions of one's existence'; but none of the recent pictures record such moments, perhaps because — whatever the eleg[ia]c eloquence of Morris' introduction — the publishers had something blander in mind." A correction to Dunlap's text is noted in: "Correction." *New Republic* 173 (20 December 1975), p. 31.

1085 "Notes on Current Books." *Virginia Quarterly Review* 52 (Spring 1976), p. 60.

In a brief paragraph, the reviewer excoriates the book's photographs as "strikingly bland" and "poorly reproduced," the quoted passages from southern authors as "appropriately saccharine remarks," and Morris's narrative — which "sets a new standard for nostalgic trivialities" — as a "pretentiously disjointed rhapsody on The Meaning of The South That Was."

1086 Thatcher, Gary. "Deep South Paid Honor in Album." *Christian Science Monitor*, 14 June 1976, p. 30.

Congratulates Glusker and Morris for perfectly describing "the ambivalence many Southerners feel as industrialization and urbanization change their region. On the one hand, they applaud the near-elimination of many forms of racism and inequality that existed for so long, yet mourn much vanished charm and grace. Mr. Glusker has captured both emotions, sometimes in one picture and its accompanying text.... The introduction by Willie Morris is perceptive and stirring, as he ponders whether his is the last generation to 'have known, and lived, the old warring impulses to be both Southern and American.'"

- *James Jones: A Friendship*. Garden City, N.Y.: Doubleday & Co., 1978 (item 7).

1087 "Non-Fiction." *Kirkus Reviews* 46 (1 September 1978), p. 994.

Morris's memoir is "a lament for a dead friend and a eulogy for his works. For the most part, Morris is clear-eyed about Jones' victories and failures.... The only flaw in this labor of love is that the quotes from Jones' works are so much more vigorous and hard-edged than the book we're reading."

1088 Review. *Publishers Weekly* 214 (4 September 1978), p. 108.

Morris's "affectionate tribute" to his friend, writer James Jones, is a "moving document." The "penultimate scenes in this book are stunners: Jones, moribund, unhooking the monitoring machines in the hospital intensive care unit and talking urgently to Morris about the last, unfinished chapters of 'Whistle'; reciting aloud Yeats's 'Lake Isle of Innisfree' as he lay on his deathbed...."

1089 Babyak, Blythe. Review. *Washington Monthly* 10 (October 1978), p. 63.

Summarizes the literary career of "a super life, a funny, raucous, loving, vivid man." Although Morris writes about his friend "with beauty and sensitivity, the book never quite lets us reach Jones, touch him, know him." Babyak opines that "two problems" with *James Jones* account for this flaw. First, Morris should have waited several years before beginning it, so that "memories of the man dying no longer shrouded memories of the man." For example, the anecdotes Morris recounts sound as if he interviewed people just days after Jones's funeral "when they were still paralyzed with grief." Second, Morris "makes himself too large a part" of his memoir. He seems to have difficulties "coming to terms with his own reputation and work. He spends far too many pages 'correcting' reviews he considers unfair to Jones and generally flailing against the critics in an artlessly immediate way." Near the end of *James Jones*, Morris complains about a negative review of one of his own books. "In all his justification for Jones then, part of Morris' game is justifying himself."

1090 Kelly, Richard J. Review. *Library Journal* 103 (15 October 1978), p. 2114.

"This is a refreshing tribute to a man who, it appears, was as impressive a human being as he was a writer." Morris describes his friendship with Jones "movingly and evocatively," and his "skillfully rendered" recollections add up to "an engaging portrait; anecdotal and affectionate, witty and wise." A brief review.

1091 Krim. "Versions of Jones." *Nation* 227 (28 October 1978), pp. 447–48.

An insightful, plainspoken appraisal by a man who knew Jones. Because of Morris's obvious "hero-worship" of the fifteen-year-older writer, his memoir is regrettably a "starry-eyed performance" and "litany of love and admiration." But Morris is not solely responsible for making his book "too sweet a package"; Krim also blames Jones, though in the "best sense" of the accusation. "By this I mean that J.J. was a commanding presence among the male writers of his generation because ... he wrote about the most central masculine experience of his time, The Army and The War." His appeal "went far beyond the writing and gave Jones among men of all sorts something of the charisma of a heavyweight boxing champion." Unfortunately, "The complex element of buddyship among American men is something that Morris hardly tries to analyze in the book, but it was basic to all of Jones's writing."

1092 Fremont-Smith, Eliot. "Short Circuits." *Village Voice*, 30 October 1978, p. 113.

This "act of affectionate tribute" is a "lovingly anecdotal remembrance" that "presents Jones as all good things—loyal, bright, wise, funny, forgiving, manly,... shrewd, gentle, frank, caring, and brave." Fremont-Smith concludes in his one-paragraph write-up that "Morris, very sincere, controls the catch in his throat just enough to elicit ours, and to render suspicion of disbelief as evidence of callousness or worse."

1093 Isaacson, Rose Levine. "Morris' Moving Testimony to Friend Jones." *Clarion-Ledger / Jackson Daily News*, 5 November 1978, sec. G, p. 7.

A pedestrian review that pays homage to a local author. "What a beautiful testimony to a friend and to a friendship.... The book also gives us an insight into Willie Morris. He writes beautifully and movingly."

1094 Thomas, William. "An Illumination of a Friend." *(Memphis) Commercial Appeal*, 5 November 1978, sec. G, p. 6.

This book is not a scholarly, critical biography of Jones but is rather about "a writer's concern for his life's work." It is Morris's "sad-funny tribute to a fellow writer," and although he "praises Jones to unnecessary extremes," this is forgivable, "because Morris is writing about friendship here as much as art and craftsmanship." Thomas mentions that Jones, before his death, and Morris lived in the same neighborhood in the village of Bridgehampton, New York, and that both men "shared a number of interests, not the least of which was Memphis.... So the book is about places and writing and being a writer. But, finally, it is about friendship—and it is on this level that Morris gives it his best shot."

1095 Brashler, William. "Willie and Jim: An Illuminating Memoir." *Chicago Tribune Book World*, 12 November 1978, p. 4.

James Jones "is full of anecdotes and gossip, of the good and wild times of the hundreds of writers and characters ... who knew Jones and liked him. But Morris is the guiding hand and the inquisitive eye throughout the book. With him we ... watch as Jones imitates for his kids the way the cartoon character Deputy Dawg walked, plays poker, drinks at Bobby Van's tavern, or simply look over Jones' shoulder as he reads poetry. At the core of every scene, however, is a look at the writer's mind and temperament." Morris disparages critics of Jones's books, "and at times he simply tries too hard to defend Jones' novels from the arrows." Nevertheless, "this thin but rich book is everything Morris claims for it: 'Not a work of scholarship or literary criticism, but an illumination of a friend.'"

1096 Lehmann-Haupt, Christopher. "Books of the Times." *New York Times*, 15 November 1978, sec. C, p. 27.

A writer who knew James Jones questions Morris's "critical objectivity" for extolling his friend's books "in the framework of his personal devotion to the man" and for "closing his eyes to Jones's shortcomings as a writer." Lehmann-Haupt acknowledges, however, that Jones "comes off as an appealing person in these pages," and Morris "reveals the deep feelings behind his affection—his identification with Jones's middle-American, small-town outlook on things" and his "admiration for what he saw as Jones's constancy, straightforwardness and 'bedrock integrity.'" *James Jones*, therefore, "is as much an autobiography as it is a portrait of another, and, as self-exploration, it stands as a fitting embellishment" to Morris's *North Toward Home*.

1097 Review. *Booklist* 75 (15 November 1978), p. 521.

Morris writes "from the heart" and "from the depth" of his friendship with James Jones "in a memoir that is valuable not only for its illumination of a distinguished and deadly earnest novelist, but as a record of the international community of American writing during the 1950s, '60s, and '70s."

1098 West, Woody. "Willie Morris on James Jones: 'Illuminations' of a Friendship." *Washington Star*, 19 November 1978, sec. D, p. 10.

James Jones: A Friendship "is biographical but not a biography; it is about writing, but it is not a work of literary criticism. Morris calls it 'an illumination of a friend' and that is nicely descriptive." He "makes a passionate case" that James Jones is among the "first rank" of American writers. That theme is a dominant one, "but as paramount, and especially moving, is that 'illumination' of the friendship between the two writers."

1099 Barbato, Joseph. "Decency and Integrity." *New Leader* 61 (20 November 1978), pp. 17–18.

Morris's volume of remembrances and anecdotes is a testimony to his friend, and the author "wisely makes no claims for objectivity." At the same time, however, the book "is a fine and keenly felt memoir that takes pains to record the integrity of Jones' life and art when the people who remember him are still present."

1100 Ross, Mitchell. Review. *New Republic* 179 (25 November 1978), pp. 37–38.

"The messages of this book are that James Jones was great as a writer and as a man, and that Willie Morris is his prophet. The result is a fairly dull gospel.... Morris is on his knees here from the first page to the last; when he is not worshiping the master, he is sending off smoke signals to the 'critical establishment' he feels has done Jones wrong. All of this is very boring, the more so because Morris writes like a copy boy being given his first crack at the Sunday features section." Nevertheless, persons interested in Jones's life "will find this memoir serviceable until a full biography comes along."

1101 Middleton, Harry. "The Life and Times of an American Novelist." *(Baltimore) Sun*, 26 November 1978, sec. D, p. 5.

This book "is not a biography or a critical study, though it has elements of both, but a fond remembrance of a friend and an affectionate celebration of James Jones's rich life and the substantial achievement of his writing." Morris "writes of Jones's life the way he must, never separating the man from his writing." With the assistance of Jones's family and friends, he "traces the Jones odyssey with insight and care." Although Jones had the reputation of being a "hard-drinking, hard-living, perpetual soldier," in reality he was "more complex and more interesting than that. He was, as Morris and Jones's other friends tell us, a compassionate, sophisticated, thoughtful, generous and gentle man, determined to be kind and caring in spite of life's cruelty, meanness and injustice."

1102 Dunne, Peter F. "Loving Tribute." *(Springfield, Ill.) State Journal-Register*, 10 December 1978, p. 42.

Morris's book "is a tribute to a friend, to a man who marched to a different drummer.... Comments from peers add to the picture of fond remembrance of one of America's favorite writers."

1103 Manning, Margaret. "A Loving Kind of Truth." *Boston Globe*, 11 December 1978, p. 28.

Although Morris, in this "quick biography" of James Jones, surrounds his reminiscences with an "aura of mushy adoration," he is "so clearly sincere, so warmly admiring, so loving, that what he has to say about Jones becomes the kind of truth about human relationships we ought to have a lot more of."

1104 Christy, Jim. "James Jones Was Old-Fashioned, They Said. But Old-Fashioned in All the Best Ways." *Globe and Mail* (Toronto), 16 December 1978, sec. 3, p. 37.

Both a sympathetic biographical essay and book review. Literary critics, notes Christy, said that James Jones was old-fashioned, "but he was old-fashioned in all the very best ways. He was honest, compassionate, funny, emotional and damned human. Morris must be very much the same way and this moving story of their friendship possesses all of those old virtues.... Aside from being a wonderful memoir, A Friendship makes one want to go out and reread all of those big dramatic war books, books about human dignity and books of a kind we are not about to ever see again."

1105 Flaherty, Joe. "Pleasant Memories." *New York Times Book Review*, 17 December 1978, p. 14.

Because James Jones was a "mythic figure" to not only his readers but also World War II veterans, Morris has set for himself a "tough task" in writing about the novelist. Much of what Flaherty calls Morris's "private vision" succeeds, "and perhaps most of it would have if Mr. Morris had called his book a 'memoir' instead of a 'friendship.' His daring title suggests he is about to explore male friendship," but this subject is one that Morris "seems reluctant to explore.... Instead, he spends the first half of his book rehashing Jones's Paris years, when he wasn't present, so we get filtered-down tales. To Mr. Morris's credit, he's honest here, in that his writing makes it clear he would have loved to be in attendance during those gaudy days."

1106 Kirsch, Robert. "Memoir of an Author As a Friend." *Los Angeles Times*, 26 January 1979, sec. 4, p. 4.

James Jones "is an admiring memoir, idealizes the Jones I knew, though the book tells some fine truths about him and his work that must be said. Morris shows the kindness and gentleness beneath the Popeye exterior, the natural gift of storytelling which was Jones' central force, the courage and decency of the man."

1107 Wilson, Robert. "Brief Notices." *Washington Post Book World*, 11 February 1979, p. 5.

Morris "heaps on his high opinion of Jones' work," but his loyalty and praise—while "hard on the reader of this book"—are understandable. "Success, which came to James Jones at age 30 with the publication of *From Here to Eternity*, seems to have tamed him. His life was not the spectacle it might have been; instead, he lived privately and was dedicated to his family and friends, and to his work." The two men met when Jones returned to the United States from France in 1973 and began work on *Whistle*, his last novel. "Morris' loosely biographical book is at its best when it describes these last years, when the two men became close friends."

1108 Bianco, David. Review. *Best Sellers* 38 (March 1979), p. 393.

"Willie Morris's book is not simply, or even primarily, an account of the friendship between these two writers. Rather, the book is a portrait of James Jones as writer, lover, husband, drinking companion, and general *homme du monde*. A number of people whose lives were touched by James Jones ... furnished Willi[e] Morris with their personal recollections. These accounts range from general statements of character to tales of wild and unusual exploits, and they are quoted in half-page excerpts. Combined with the writer's sensitive understanding of his subject, they furnish a balanced yet many-sided picture of James Jones."

1109 Brown, Chris M. "Father and Friend As Close Subjects." *Christian Science Monitor*, 30 March 1979, p. 18.

Reviews Morris's memoir and Ralph Schoenstein's *Citizen Paul: A Story of Father and Son.* "'James Jones' is an eloquent, intensely moving and perfectly painted portrait of a rare and precious friend.... Incredibly rich, warm and honest, this account could only come from a writer's deepest thoughts, feelings and affections." Morris "vividly portrays Jones's deep sensitivity and warmth" and "imports to the reader every ounce of his own devotion to James Jones's towering spirit. And as the book nears its conclusion, a sense of personal loss may rise in the throat of even the most cynical reader."

1110 "Paperbacks: New and Noteworthy." *New York Times Book Review*, 4 November 1979, p. 53.

This brief notice upon the paperback publication of *James Jones* reports that half of the book is "well-told yet second-hand tales" of Jones's life through his post–World War II years in France while half is "an affectionate memoir of Willie Morris's fraternal relationship with him ... during the last 10 years of his life."

1111 "A Selection of the Best Books of 1979." *New York Times Book Review*, 25 November 1979, p. 15.

This brief notice recommends *James Jones* as "a sweetly affectionate memoir."

1112 Noble, Donald R. Review. *Southern Humanities Review* 15 (Summer 1981), pp. 272–75.

A review essay of works about Henry Miller, James Jones, Alfred Hitchcock, and Joe Orton. Morris knew Jones for just the last decade of the older man's life, "but the quality of their friendship, the affection these men had for one another, warms every page." Morris does not attempt to present a full biography (though he does cover the "major phases" of his friend's career), but instead focuses on "what it was like to know Jones, to talk with him, drink and eat with him, be his friend. The result is a sincere and warm book."

- *Terrains of the Heart and Other Essays on Home*. Oxford, Miss.: Yoknapatawpha Press, 1981 (item 8).

1113 Hoffman, Barbara. Review. *Best Sellers* 41 (November 1981), p. 312.

"Willie Morris, in returning to Mississippi and collecting these essays on his native soil and all significant terrains and people in between, has given us all reason to pause and consider our roots. So much in this collection spoke to me, because its regionality was rooted in warm and universal portraits of humans wherever the author found them.... Throughout the book Morris enriches the past; he does not juggle/distort it with sentimentality or revisionism." He "has come home and his heart is in the right place."

1114 Bayles, Martha. "Nonfiction." *New York Times Book Review*, 1 November 1981, p. 16.

The essays on the author's "other homes" (those outside his native state) "have some strength," but "he tends to see only the commonplace: the impersonality of commuter trains, loose morals on Capitol Hill," and "black crime as a legacy of racism." Bayles regrets that Morris's writings about race relations in Mississippi and the changes that homogenization have brought to the Old South do not appear in this collection. "Perhaps because it is organized around the theme of 'home,' the book describes his comings and goings—meetings with friends, football games—in a self-absorbed manner far less complex and passionate than the vision of his home state conveyed by his earlier works. A bit too long on rhetoric and short on perception, it draws an imperfect map of this heart's true terrain."

1115 Petrakis, Harry Mark. "Going Home Again with Willie Morris: A Nostalgic Journey." *Chicago Tribune Book World*, 1 November 1981, p. 3.

Discusses and quotes from some of Morris's essays in an introspective review that is complimentary without being effusive. The author "reveals his love of a place where individuals, relationships, the link with generations gone not only matter but buttress the everyday life.... Whether writing of talking to the great former Sen. Sam Ervin, or his visit with his 10-year-old son to see his dying grandmother, or in the loving memoir of his friend, the novelist James Jones, Morris recaptures vividly and movingly a sense of soil and time, the shades of darkness and light, and the pleasures of growing up in an aura of stories.... Willie Morris makes us understand his people and his land. For the first time in my life I feel an urgency to see that lovely, haunted, and lore-riddled region for myself."

1116 Atchity, Kenneth John. "Mississippi to Manhattan and Return." *Los Angeles Times*, 13 November 1981, sec. 5, p. 26.

To support his contention that "these essays make hard claim on the reader's heart," Atchity complements his various appraisals with passages from the author's writings. For example, the structure of an essay "allows nostalgia where stricter forms demand analysis: 'I like the way they sell chicken and pit-barbecue and fried catfish in the little stores next to the service stations.'"

1117 H[ooper], W[illiam] B[radley]. Review. *Booklist* 78 (15 November 1981), pp. 422–23.

A brief review. Although Morris has lived in a variety of cities in the United States and abroad, "It is his native Mississippi ... that remains Home, its peculiarities forming an atmosphere eminently sustaining. Wit and compassion mark the essays, which should really be read aloud, for his illuminating thoughts are couched in a lilting style that is intoxicating."

1118 L[ogue], J[ohn] D. "Books About the South." *Southern Living* 16 (December 1981), p. 120.

Logue considers Willie Morris to be "in a class by himself" among American essay writers, adding that *Terrains of the Heart* is "vintage Morris." Throughout the book "always there is the aspect of home: from his youth in Yazoo to the death of his mother, the 'burden and resonance of time' weighs powerfully on his mind." A quotation from the essay "The Ghosts of Ole Miss" (item 29) encompasses more than half of the review.

1119 Jones, John G. Review. *Journal of Mississippi History* 44 (February 1982), pp. 91–93.

A scholar of southern literature provides a sagacious analysis not only of the essays in *Terrains of the Heart* but also of the "intensely personal nonfiction style of Willie Morris." Jones argues that "with a strong sense of the past, formed around a complex and abiding bond with his native state, Morris writes of the verities, naming them, illustrating by what peculiar process his—to use one of his favorite words—'peregrinations'—brought him unto these mystical terrains. His ability as a raconteur of the southern school, and his fascination for the nature of 'old time dying' make his work always enjoyable to the reader. *Terrains of the Heart* is no exception." Jones thoroughly examines the essays representative of the author's assorted "homes" and perceives that the ones published in the *Washington Star* during Morris's tenure as writer-in-residence in 1976 offer "an escape from the kind of suffocating regionalism that differentiates the good essayist from the artist." Other non–Mississippi localities, "and the people and events experienced along the way, are evoked with characteristic mirth and pathos." Of the Mississippi essays, Jones avers that Morris "knows when he writes that Mississippi 'is a blend of the relentless and the abiding,' that regardless of the extreme manifestations of the relentless, causing many of the aberrations which have come to define Mississippi for the nation in modern times, at least here there is something that abides, that endures across the sweep of time."

1120 Clifford, Craig Edward. Review. *Texas Observer*, 7 May 1982, pp. 25–26.

Believes that Morris's book of essays "is a testament to the power of native soil and communal memory, or at least to Southern soil and memory." With this sense of remembrance, "The writer does not live in the past, in the painless escape of nostalgia; he suffers through the truth of himself and his people and his place. The spectrum of guilt and pain, joy and exhilaration, failure and meanness, serenity and humor, which Willie Morris dredges up out of his vagabond past and the mud of Mississippi is a spectrum of human *possibility*, not simply a report on what has been." Clifford found while reading the essays that although "death is pervasive," humor is as well. "The enduring insight of these essays and stories is that life is neither tragic, nor comic, but both."

1121 Cook, Thomas. "The Guilt of the Land." *Atlanta* 22 (June 1982), pp. 54, 56.

Contends that the book's theme of home "is a bit misleading," for *Terrains of the Heart* is "simply a selection of Morris essays on various subjects. Still, in those essays which actually seem to be about home, the South emerges as the real subject." Cook remarks that Morris "does not, by and large, romanticize or sentimentalize the South.... In general, he writes with a sorrowful understanding of the Southern past, and he has learned to honor the rural virtues without overly exalting them."

1122 L., W. E. Review. *Kliatt Young Adult Paperback Book Guide* 17 (Winter 1983), p. 32.

The reviewer is pleased that these essays about Morris's "time in the South, his growing up and his family, the mix of pain and exhil[a]ration that he feels when he dreams of, looks back upon, and even sometimes returns to the region, have been collected together in *Terrains of the Heart*."

- *The Courting of Marcus Dupree*. Garden City, N.Y.: Doubleday & Co., 1983 (item 30)

1123 "Non-Fiction." *Kirkus Reviews* 51 (15 August 1983), p. 944.

Marcus Dupree is an outstanding black football player in a high school in Philadelphia, Mississippi, a small town with a racist past, though it is now integrated. Morris visits Philadelphia to write about Dupree and his 1981–82 football season, but the author's "relevant/irrelevant digressions" often overpower his main story. "He indulges in autobiographical effusions— on his own high-school days, his lifelong interest in sports, his love for dog Pete (whose death will later provide a maudlin fadeout), [and] his feelings of symbolic kinship with Marcus...." Although "a more disciplined reporter might have made a small, powerful book out of the personal/football/sociological interplay here, Morris' sprawling treatment — at its very best in the interview-evocations of daily life in today's Philadelphia — is only fitfully involving, only obliquely provocative."

1124 Review. *Booklist* 80 (1 September 1983), p. 6.

A one-paragraph review. Morris relates the story of superb high-school football player Marcus Dupree "from poverty to high-school stardom to fame as a University of Oklahoma [running] back who in his freshman year, last season, very nearly won college football's Heisman trophy. But, more important, Morris conveys the grace and strength of this singular athlete as well as Marcus Dupree's place in the South of the 1980s and in high-stakes American sport."

1125 Review. *Publishers Weekly* 224 (16 September 1983), p. 110.

Recognizes that *The Courting of Marcus Dupree* is concerned not only with the recruitment of an outstanding black football player, but it is also "about the South and especially about the new, integrated South.... Although Morris's account of Dupree's "courtin'" by football coaches is "overlong," the author, "good ol' boy and sophisticate simultaneously, has used his considerable talents to produce a work as absorbing as it is important."

1126 Branston, John. "Tales of Dupree, Oxford and Philadelphia." *(Memphis) Commercial Appeal*, 16 October 1983, sec. G, p. 3.

Although Morris includes some "startlingly touching scenes" of Dupree's friendships with his coach and teammates in *The Courting of Marcus Dupree*, the book "lacks the freshness" of some of the author's earlier works. While researching his story, Morris met many sportswriters, and he "quotes generously from practically every one of them." The volume, however, is "not particularly enlightening on the subject of college football recruiting." Furthermore, he touches upon the vague rumors people hear about illegal gifts and payoffs, but the tales are "never really explored in detail."

1127 Lehmann-Haupt, Christopher. "Books of the Times." *New York Times*, 17 October 1983, sec. C, p. 18.

Lehmann-Haupt maintains in this stinging review that Morris reads too much into the sociological importance of Philadelphia, Mississippi. Marcus Dupree was born in Philadelphia in 1964, the same year that three civil rights workers— Michael Schwerner, Andrew Goodman, and James Earl Chaney— were murdered nearby. Seventeen years later, Dupree, a black member of the town's first high school senior class in which blacks and whites have gone through all twelve grades together, is a star football player and "pride of Philadelphia." Among his many devoted admirers is the son of one of the white men implicated in the killings. Lehmann-Haupt wonders why "Dupree's apotheosis" carries such "profound significance" for the author. The volume itself lacks definition, though perhaps if Morris had spent more time with Dupree and "got acquainted with the hero as well as the mob of characters that was collecting around him, a drama would ensure, with the happy consequence that 'The Courting of Marcus Dupree' would shape itself." Morris's book, however, never develops. "Lacking any other points to make, he succumbs to reminiscing about the soil, his own upbringing and all the good old boys he got to know in the progress of his assignment."

1128 Gold, Don. "Of Football, the South and a Search for Truth." *(Chicago) Sunday Sun-Times*, 23 October 1983, p. 27.

The managing editor of *Playboy* congratulates Morris for his "noble account" about "football, college recruiting, race, Southern politics and one man's quest for sane judgments." As the author wandered through Marcus Dupree's hometown of Philadelphia, Mississippi, he was determined to move "into the shadowed past, to revive the bad times of the '60s, to recapitulate the murders, the attitudes, the clamor of those times— and to assess the present. People talked to Morris and he was up to the tasks of listening attentively, reporting accurately and writing astutely.... In observing Dupree, his teachers and coaches, the survivors of the tainted past and those who never knew it, Morris could confront both American dreams and American nightmares. He emerged, as the book vividly points out, changed in ways he could not have anticipated."

1129 Yardley, Jonathan. "Marcus Dupree and the Other Philadelphia Story." *Washington Post Book World*, 23 October 1983, pp. 3, 8.

Yardley finds little to applaud in his biting review of Morris's book, though he agrees with him on one point: in the twenty years since three civil rights workers were murdered on the outskirts of Philadelphia, Mississippi, the town in particular and the South in general have changed from localities of "racial estrangement to racial accommodation." The residents of Philadelphia have embraced the young black football player Marcus Dupree, whose life, according to Morris, is a metaphor for the "new" South. Yardley acknowledges that "there are signs and portents in this marvelously ironic juxtaposition," but the author "attempts to carry the tale to extremes it cannot sustain, freighting Marcus Dupree with a significance he in no way possesses." Morris wildly searches for a "unifying theme," at various times writing about his own life, race relations, southern history and culture, college sports recruiting, and life in Philadelphia, all of which "add up to precious little." Yardley particularly faults him for falling under Dupree's spell. "In his own account he is as breathless and goggle-eyed about Dupree's college prospects as any cheerleader or booster-club member." Morris's consequent lack of objectivity prevents him from analyzing the significant issues he raises in his book, such as college recruiting practices and the pressures faced by teenage athletes.

1130 Boozer, William. "Marcus Dupree: The Symbol of a New South." *Detroit News*, 26 October 1983, sec. B, pp. 1, 3.

Morris, affirms Boozer, "is one of a talented

fraternity of writers who have made a profession of being Southerners and who keep proving that the pen is mightier than the sword." *The Courting of Marcus Dupree* contains not one but three books. The first chronicles the story of high school football phenomenon Marcus Dupree "and the recruiting wars that preceded his selection of [the University of] Oklahoma." The second shows how Dupree's home, Neshoba County, has progressed in terms of race relations since the "dark days of 1964, when Michael Schwerner, James Earl Chaney and Andrew Goodman were murdered and buried in an earthen dam." The third is Morris's own story, a sequel of sorts to his "classic" *North Toward Home*. Boozer, the editor of the *Faulkner Newsletter*, summarizes Marcus Dupree's remarkable accomplishments but suggests that "more important than being a football hero, he is a symbol of a new day that has supplanted the one that saw that memorial to Schwerner and Chaney and Goodman planted in front of Mount Nebo Baptist Church down the street from his house."

1131 DeLapo, Josephine A. "Social Science." *Library Journal* 108 (1 November 1983), p. 2095.

A brief review of a volume that is part story of a talented black athlete, part "retrospective" on the brutal murders of three young civil rights workers in 1964, and part memoir. Morris has combined these three elements "into an exceptional book," one that is "not for everyone, certainly not for the average fan looking for a simple football story, this is for a special audience."

1132 Rapoport, Ron. "For Marcus Dupree a Sad State of Affairs No More." *(Chicago) Sun-Times*, 2 November 1983, p. 119.

A book review as well as a Morris interview and news story, which reports that college freshman Marcus Dupree suddenly quit the University of Oklahoma and enrolled in the University of Southern Mississippi. Morris finds the situation "kind of touching.... He's come home. Mississippi is a strange and bewitched state. It exerts a strong pull on its native sons." Although Morris regards Dupree as a symbol of the integrated, changing South, Rapoport writes that "there are times when Dupree the young man almost seems to vanish from the book in deference to Dupree the symbol. And there are times when we wish we could hear more from his mother, his teachers and his uncle, who played a key role in Dupree's choice to go to, and probably to leave, Oklahoma."

1133 Lambert, Pam. "Dixie-Style Football Follies." *Wall Street Journal*, 8 November 1983, p. 32.

If the "recruiting carnival" of a record-breaking black athlete from an integrated town with a "bloodstained past"were combined with "a bit of old-fashioned gridiron drama," a writer would have enough ingredients to write "a page-turner with substance." Regrettably, in *The Courting of Marcus Dupree*, Morris "fumbles badly." As the author drives through his native state, he is "sidetracked by so many detours that he loses sight of where he's going." The book is padded with irrelevant information such as "his chest-puffing accounts of rubbing elbows with the glitterati of Manhattan, his three-page ode to the cheerleaders and baton twirlers of Mississippi and the slobberingly sentimental treatment of his dog, Pete." Morris's overwriting is particularly evident when he "attempts to mesh the dramatic events of the summer of '64 with the story of Marcus's senior year." In addition, he "sadly fails in his task when it comes to Marcus, who remains blurry, like a photograph in a faded newspaper clipping."

1134 Wilkinson, Jack. "Dupree's Tale: A Man, Town and the South." *Atlanta Journal / The Atlanta Constitution*, 13 November 1983, sec. H, p. 8.

Emphasizes that this "beautifully crafted story" is not just a book about a talented black high school football player. It is also an account of "violent" Philadelphia, Mississippi, where in 1964 — the year Marcus Dupree was born — the Ku Klux Klan murdered three civil rights workers. "Morris and many others view Dupree as a symbol of the progress that blacks and Philadelphia have made in the course of Marcus Dupree's lifetime." The author's book is "a longing, loving, lyrical look at the South, at the Mississippi homeland Morris finally returned to after too many years in Manhattan...."

1135 Crews, Harry. "A Pet Peeve: Morris Fumbles Recruiting Story." *Chicago Tribune Book World*, 20 November 1983, p. 35.

Novelist and autobiographer Harry Crews states that Morris's account of the murders of three civil rights workers in 1964 is a "powerful" one, and the author plays this incident off Marcus Dupree's boyhood and football career. "In those dark days of the '60s when civil rights workers were murdered, Dupree could have done very few, if any, of the things that were possible for him to do in 1980." Crews recognizes that *The Courting of Marcus Dupree* is not a biography, nor a football book, but instead centers on "the changes that have come about in the South" since Dupree was born in 1964. The book also focuses on the changes in Willie Morris, a native Mississippian. The author's musings tend to be overlong; he contributes a genealogy, which "goes on for quite a long while, and it is a little difficult to see what it contributes to the story." His "running commentary" about his dog, Pete, "goes on for a long, long time and tells us more than we really want to know about the dog." Furthermore, his narrative about the death and burial of Pete is "representative of a sentimentality that crops up again and again."

1136 Wall, Chris. "True Story Too Good To Be True." *Los Angeles Times Book Review*, 20 November 1983, p. 17.

Reports that Marcus Dupree has left the University of Oklahoma and moved back home to Mississippi, but "this latest development does not reflect badly on Morris' book.... Morris is a Mississippi boy himself, writing about the changes he sees in the South he knew and left for the Big City." *The Courting of Marcus Dupree* is "a provocative look at race relations in a part of the country that once provided some of our sorriest social history. It is also an intelligent, firsthand view of the pressures that big-time college football place upon a 17-year-old recruit."

1137 "Picks & Pans." *People Weekly* 20 (21 November 1983), p. 20.

"Morris' aim was to go beyond a mere sports story and to say something profound about the changed relations of whites and blacks in the South today. But the book is poorly organized and too long (452 pages). The story, moreover, is too specific; Dupree is black, but seems too special to qualify as a symbolic character."

1138 Stratton, W. K. "A Tale of Old Patterns and New Heroes." *Texas Observer*, 25 November 1983, pp. 20–21.

An admiring review that ranks, "in the genre of sports writing," *The Courting of Marcus Dupree* with *The Boys of Summer* by Roger Kahn. Stratton recounts how Ku Klux Klan members murdered three civil rights workers outside Philadelphia and buried their bodies beneath an earthen dam. "That a child born to a poor, black family in that town during that dark summer would become, just seventeen years later, a statewide hero is a remarkable story. And Morris successfully conveys its significance." Stratton also describes the fierce recruiting of Dupree, adding that the author's "reporting on the sordid practices used by college recruiters make *The Courting of Marcus Dupree* the best account I've read of athletic recruiting." Because it is essentially about the South, the book gives Morris "the opportunity to concern himself with those things about which he writes best: small-town cemeteries, old men sitting on benches outside courthouses, willowy Southern girls, football stadiums, dogs, old friends, whiskey, the lay of the land.... He has the ability to make us feel that we're in the somnolent Mississippi towns with him. And that's no small part of the appeal of this book."

1139 Adams, Phoebe-Lou. Review. *Atlantic* 252 (December 1983), p. 116.

The Courting of Marcus Dupree "includes, naturally, such matters as football recruiting methods (alarming) and coaches' salaries (outrageous). It does not include the reasons for Dupree's decision to go to [the University of] Oklahoma, and this omission exemplifies the slight vagueness in Mr. Morris's attempt to describe the modern South. He is an intelligent observer, a fine reporter, and a southerner, but one is left with the suspicion that in Philadelphia he encountered an invisible and impenetrable wall."

1140 Bradley, David. "Race and the Halfback." *New York Times Book Review*, 18 December 1983, pp. 11, 18.

A contemplative, balanced review of a "well-conceived and well-crafted book that has topical impact" and a "document of significance and undeniable truth." Although some might wonder why Willie Morris would be interested in writing about a high school athlete, the reviewer discerns that Morris "sees Mr. Dupree as a symbol that reaches beyond college football." Bradley traces the facts of the shocking Neshoba County, Mississippi, murders of 1964 (called "the Troubles" by community residents), and clarifies why Morris connects them to Dupree, who was born a month earlier in the same area. "As Mr. Morris subtly shows, Mr. Dupree's date of birth exempted him from the terrors of a South twisted by the aftermath of slavery ... and provided an environment in which white men would pursue him with sleek executive jets instead of patrol cars and pick-ups.... This is the irony that molds the structure of the book. Chapters go back and forth between accounts of Mr. Dupree's senior season, the history of Mississippi and the Troubles and anecdotal, often hilarious accounts of the world of college football." There are, however, "a lot of things wrong with 'The Courting of Marcus Dupree.' Mr. Morris is given to sentimentality. He also drops names.... One wishes occasionally he had spent less time talking to the townspeople, more to Mr. Dupree."

1141 Sigal, Clancy. Review. *Nation* 237 (24 December 1983), p. 670.

The Courting of Marcus Dupree "is overwritten and occasionally impossibly rhetorical. Southern writers hardly ever use one word when ten will do. But the core of Morris's book is a moving meditation on the South's present fix: the old patterns persist, with new accommodations."

1142 McPherson, James Alan. "Southern Exiles." *Esquire* 101 (January 1984), pp. 91–92.

A review essay of three books on the South (*The Courting of Marcus Dupree*, *Womenfolks* by Shirley Abbott, and *Southern Honor* by Bertram Wyatt-Brown), volumes which "attempt to explain the cultural factors that, in addition to racial antagonism, went into the making of a way of life." On one level, Morris's book records his attempt "to redefine his present self against the background in which he grew up. On another level the book is about the progress being made in the experiment called social integration. But on its most significant level it is about the moral reintegration of Philadelphia, Mississippi, and the attempts made by *average* people there to reclaim the sense of moral integrity, or honor, lost in 1964 with the murders of civil rights workers Michael Schwerner, Andrew Goodman, and James Earl Chaney."

1143 Review. *Playboy* 31 (January 1984), p. 30.

Morris's book is not merely an inside look at a high school football star and the "desperate and often sleazy business" of college recruiting. It is "about being black in Mississippi and about being white there, about the land and the people and their history." The story is told "with such a sure narrative voice that it is bound to take a place among the best books written about the modern South."

1144 Seyler, Harry E. Review. *Best Sellers* 43 (January 1984), pp. 373–74.

Behind the book's "somber" subjects of race relations in Mississippi and the "wooing" of Marcus Dupree, the reader is aware of the "rueful spell of the South, and Mississippi. Nostalgia and love have brought the narrator home to the poor, beautiful, vexed land from which he had come. He witnesses the increasing integration of the whites, blacks, and Choctaws who live in Neshoba County."

1145 Snider, Norman. "Football As a Species of Religion." *Globe and Mail* (Toronto), 11 February 1984, sec. E, p. 19.

Asserts that *The Courting of Marcus Dupree* has "large faults as well as large virtues," yet it is an "oddly compulsive book and Morris a writer whose charms are more than equal to his lacks." Unfortunately, the volume is "literary in the worst sense. Not only does the shadow of Faulkner hang heavy over every page but also those of Thomas Wolfe, William Styron, Walker Percy and just about every other Southerner who ever put pen to paper. So, instead of getting a fresh look at the New South" of shopping malls and fast-food restaurants, "we get a repetition of the insights of all these writers." Morris is not a particularly good sports writer. Nevertheless, "his account of the shadowy world of the college recruiters, much more than his rehash of civil rights history..., is the best part of his somewhat unfocused book." Although Morris is "garrulous, digressive, sentimental, snobbish and overblown," he still "makes for an agreeable, suspenders-snapping companion."

1146 Review. *Choice* 21 (March 1984), p. 1016.

"This is a highly personalized journalistic account of the pressure-cooker world of big-time college recruiting.... But this is far more than an inside look at sports, for Morris is really concerned with understanding the character and values of the residents of southern hamlet towns. Morris juxtaposes the placid Philadelphia [Mississippi] of today with itself in 196[4] when it was the scene of the murder of three civil rights workers."

1147 Lardner, Susan. "Good Old Dichotomous Boy." *New Yorker* 60 (5 March 1984), pp. 136–39.

Lardner provides a detailed summary of Dupree's life and observes that Morris was "dutiful in his legwork" while researching *The Courting of Marcus Dupree*. In the end, however, "He doesn't come to know Dupree any better than the nomadic recruiters do, or the citizens of Philadelphia [Mississippi], who were kept guessing until the last minute which school he would choose to attend. Morris labors to see something of himself in Dupree, but the effort fails, and he is driven to rumination and rhetorical questions." Lardner is extremely critical of how Morris expresses these reflections and other passages in his work, for "although he is capable of composing an unadorned factual statement," he favors a "more inflated, roseate prose, a grander diction: words like 'archetype,' 'indwelling,' 'inchoate,' and 'suffused';

phrases like 'an apprehensive chord,' 'the omniscient hope,' and 'the insatiable injunctions of television.'" A thoughtful analysis of an "autobiographical extension" of *North Toward Home.*

1148 Hood-Adams, Rebecca. "Almost Persuaded." *Delta Scene* 11 (Spring 1984), pp. 28–30.

A candid review by a southerner and one of "Willie Morris' fans" who bluntly declares in her penultimate paragraph: "I expect more from one of the most gifted writers in America today." She grants that he "has a great gift" for describing small-town life in the South, and he "excels as he reveals the fabric of life in Neshoba County and the machinations to get Dupree's coveted signature on the dotted line." Morris, however, is "looking for The Big Symbol and frankly, for me, that's where *The Courting of Marcus Dupree* strains credibility. In Morris' view, Dupree represents the redemption of Philadelphia for its sins of racism in the sixties." Hood-Adams concedes that the author's narration of the civil rights murders "is riveting, but Morris' forced connection to Dupree wears thin." Moreover, not only does he have a tendency to descend into "pompous, ponderous writing," but occasionally he also "goes badly off course. There's a whole cloying chapter on Morris' dog Pete, a fine animal to be sure. But when Morris starts putting Pete's supposed thoughts in quotes, I gagged on the cuteness."

1149 Jones, John G. Review. *Journal of Mississippi History* 46 (May 1984), pp. 142–46.

Jones, who is well familiar with Morris's work, contributes this lengthy and trenchant review. He notes that when both white and black sports fans cheer the athletic exploits of black Marcus Dupree, Morris infers that this represents a "substantive change in the social fabric of Mississippi." This view is a "fallacy," however, as fans have cheered for outstanding sports players, regardless of color, for decades. But because Morris "relates his own story with Dupree's life as a backdrop," the athlete perhaps gives the author's "thesis the touch of reality it requires." Dupree's indifference to the civil rights movement—"the very topic which motivates Morris"—is the "best testament to the fact that, at least for the 225-pound tailback with lightning speed, and maybe others, racial prejudice in Mississippi is no longer a pervasive condition." Jones adds that Morris's "prodigious gifts" include "a particular ability to render a time and a place. Perhaps, of all Mississippi writers except Eudora Welty, Morris is in closest touch with that which informs the writer's heart: memory."

1150 Robinson, George. "High School Star." *Progressive* 48 (June 1984), pp. 42–44.

A serious, deliberate essay. Robinson muses that while the two principle themes of the book are race relations in the South and Marcus Dupree's "extraordinary" high school senior year, the volume is also a "chronicle" of Willie Morris himself, "a son of Mississippi, coming home at last. The bittersweet but immensely satisfying realization that his home state has finally joined the Union pervades the entire book." The reviewer points out that nearly two decades after the 1964 racial murders of Philadelphia, Mississippi, the community has "embraced"the black Dupree, who seems to be "a reflection of some deeper sense of the cohesion that has come slowly to the town in the aftermath of the turbulence of the civil rights movement." Although *The Courting of Marcus Dupree* is an "illuminating addition to the literature of integration," with Morris particularly adept at comparing past and present Philadelphia, the volume is marred by "structural flaws." The author "digresses often, commenting on everything from the comparative psychologies of cheerleaders and baton twirlers to a biography of his dog Pete and reminiscences of literary lunches in New York bistros." Also, "the one figure who remains disturbingly vague in this mixture of history, athletics, sociology, autobiography, and anecdote is Dupree himself."

1151 Brown, Beth. Review. *Journal of Black Studies* 17 (June 1987), pp. 511–513.

"Morris's journalistic treatment of the Dupree story succeeds because of the interweaving of episodes from the early twentieth century and the history of Dupree's career." The author interviewed many of the residents of the young football star's hometown, Philadelphia, Mississippi, and "although Marcus Dupree seldom emerges from the pages to take a stand for himself, he is viewed from all sides." Morris's research "culminated in a tremendous piece of reporting, historical analysis, and biography in an exciting, although cumbersome, combination."

1152 Norton, Margaret W. Review. *English Journal* 82 (November 1993), pp. 83–84.

Reviews the 1992 paperback edition. "This modern classic, describing high-school life a generation ago in a small town, includes the moral dilemma of college-football recruitment and a perceptive flashback to events of the Civil Rights Movement.... The story of the town, its history, and its people unfolds along with the exciting tales of sport and recruitment. Interspersed are facets of Mississippi life and references to Southern writers, inspiring teachers, and the local establishment. Race and both real and potential exploitation are explored in exemplary prose."

• *Always Stand In Against the Curve and Other Sports Stories.* Oxford, Miss.: Yoknapatawpha Press, 1983 (item 31).

1153 "At the Library." *Yazoo Herald*, 30 November 1983, sec. B, pp. 1, 4.

"Yoknapatawpha Press has just brought out a perfectly delightful set of essays by Willie Morris that describe[s] sports from Yazoo City to Long Island.... 'Always Stand In Against the Curve' is bound to be an immediate favorite for Yazooans, those who love sports and those who love a well told story."

1154 Weatherly, Jack. "Morris Revisits Playing Fields of His Youth." *(Little Rock) Arkansas Gazette*, 18 December 1983, sec. C, p. 6.

An in-depth examination of the collection's sports pieces by someone obviously familiar with the author's life and works. While researching *The Courting of Marcus Dupree*, Willie Morris followed the high school athlete Dupree around Mississippi. These travels "awoke in Morris memories of his days on the playing fields of the Delta. As much as anything, the six autobiographical essays and one short story in *Always Stand In Against the Curve* are about losing, and a sense of loss. Morris dissects adolescent strivings and yearnings on and off those fields, when just about everything is divided into two categories: Losing and winning. And, looking back from his perspective of three decades, he feels a nostalgia for his youth."

1155 Wells, Robert W. "Youth and Truth in Yazoo City." *Milwaukee Journal*, 25 December 1983, "Entertainment" section, p. 13.

The "seven segments of youthful autobiography" in this book are "mostly about Morris' heady triumphs and abysmal tragedies as a high school athlete in Yazoo City, Miss." Wells especially likes "The Fumble" (item 32), but all of the stories "bring back what it was like to be 17 in small-town Mississippi. More important, they revive memories of what it was like to be an adolescent anywhere."

1156 Cawthon, Raad. "Morris' Latest Recalls the Athletic Fields of Everyone's Childhood." *Clarion-Ledger / Jackson Daily News*, 15 January 1984, sec. F, p. 6.

Discusses the various "sports memoirs" in Morris's "superbly done volume," *Always Stand In Against the Curve*. "And through the gracefulness of his art and the pointed meanderings of his prodigious memory we can all once again grace the playing fields of a lost time.... In this series of seven short memoirs the full range of emotion that sport provokes—fear, anger, pain, humor, wistfulness, jubilation—is given to us through Morris' eyes. And they are perceptive eyes that can distinguish, even from the distance of a quarter-century, the subtle palp[i]tations of a young man's heart."

1157 Freeman, Don. "A Tender Look at Dixie." *San Diego Union*, 22 January 1984, sec. E, pp. 1, 7.

"A slender volume, full of riches, this new collection of stories is vintage Willie Morris, which is to say that its essence is as unswervingly Southern as the name of the publishing house and its locale—Yoknapatawpha Press in Oxford, Miss." Freeman avows that "Morris has given us a memory book which includes a classic of unfulfilled dreams, entitled 'The Fumble,' and six autobiographical essays.... If the book's title is evocative metaphor, it is also a summing-up of how Willie Morris would indeed always stand in against the curve as he went to bat facing life's bitter bruises and its golden times. Both are remembered with equal grace in this exquisitely written search for the past."

1158 Point, Michael. "Communicates Athletic Experience: Morris in Championship Form." *Houston Post*, 5 February 1984, sec. F, p. 13.

Praises Morris—who is "not so much a sportswriter as a writer who loves sports"—for explaining "to those who do not understand the almost primal pull of sports" that "the pull is on the heart, not the head." In this collection of autobiographical essays, Morris traces the "various high and low spots" of his own sports career and "steps forward as a modern-day champion at communicating the athletic experience." He is "the perfect guide for those seeking to either attain or regain the particular spirit of wonder that infuses the mystique into the world of sports." Of the seven memoirs, the longest one, "The Fumble" (item 32), is a "certifiable minor masterpiece" and "Morris's finest effort in the volume."

1159 O[tt], B[ill]. Review. *Booklist* 80 (15 March 1984), pp. 1022–23.

"Willie Morris' love of sports and of his native Mississippi is very evident in these autobiographical essays. The high and low points of Morris' career as a high-school athlete form the basis of most of the tales, which Morris tells in a straightforward, heartfelt manner.... He remembers sports fondly and writes about them with care and precision." Revised for an annotated bibliography of recently published sports books: Estes, Sally. "Growing Up Jock." *Booklist* 90 (1 November 1993), p. 535.

1160 Ott, Bill. "Quick-Bibs: New and Recent Books on a Timely Topic." *American Libraries* 15 (April 1984), p. 203.

Brief reviews of Morris's book and other recently published works on baseball. "These sports-related essays by the former *Harper's* editor concern his youthful ballplaying days."

1161 Rosta, Paul. "Title Page." *Los Angeles Times Book Review*, 20 May 1984, p. 12.

"Charm and mischief mark the best stories, as when Morris tells of driving his college mascot, the University of Texas' longhorn steer, all the way to a football game at Notre Dame. In his weightier efforts, Morris grapples with change and tends to overwrite." However, "all the pieces are deeply felt."

- *Good Old Boy and the Witch of Yazoo.* Oxford, Miss.: Yoknapatawpha Press, 1989 (item 39).

1162 Hood, Orley. "Willie's Back in 'Good Old Boy and the Witch of Yazoo.'" *Clarion-Ledger*, 1 October 1989, sec. F, p. 3.

"The Yazoo gang returns with high adventure in the sequel to Morris' *Good Old Boy.*" The plot "goes like this: The boys are bored. Nobody in Yazoo is getting a kick out of seeing Skip drive Bubba's car down the street. So, naturally, mischief fills the gap."

1163 Naughton, Jim. "The Awkward Age." *Washington Post Book World*, 5 November 1989, p. 21.

Although Morris "keeps matters moving at a brisk, enjoyable pace," *Good Old Boy and the Witch of Yazoo* is "marred by indications that he has not taken much care with this work. Bubba, Billy and Henjie, Willie's three best pals, are sketched so cursorily that they become almost indistinguishable. The plot hinges on several implausible turns.... The result is a naive but often diverting book that is not so much about youth as the idealization of the past."

1164 Sweeney, Joyce. "'Good Old Boy' Steals Characters, But Tale Is New." *Atlanta Journal / The Atlanta Constitution*, 19 November 1989, sec. L, p. 9.

Sweeney chides the author for borrowing characters from Mark Twain's *Huckleberry Finn* ("the only thing Willie doesn't do is build a raft"), as Morris is an excellent writer and "too good to rely on crutches." His story is "original, meaningful, funny and moving. He writes in a way that both children and adults can appreciate, without insulting the intelligence of either. He makes scores of points without hammering them home. He shows small-town prejudice and hysteria in their most laughable light.... Mr. Morris understands the 13-year-old mind" and "captures with effortless grace the smell of a Southern spring evening and the joys of playing catch against a cloudless October sky."

1165 Van Strum, Carol. "Adventures for Ages 12 and Up." *USA Today*, 24 November 1989, sec. D, p. 4.

A brief review. Yazoo, Mississippi, once again "comes to life" in this sequel to *Good Old Boy.* "Willie and his elderly neighbor, targets of a town witch hunt, keep their heads and humor amid mass hysteria and violence."

1166 Sparks, Jon W. "Gift Wrap Morris's Mississippi Mischief." *(Memphis) Commercial Appeal*, 10 December 1989, sec. G, p. 4.

Willie Morris, the "bright trickster of these pages, lives the everyboy fantasy in search of adventure." His book is a "smartly blended mix of Mississippi culture, small-town sensibilities, lurking evil, trust and betrayal, and the impulsiveness of youth.... It's an entertaining story told by a master."

1167 Bolle, Sonja. "Fiction in Brief." *Los Angeles Times Book Review*, 1 April 1990, p. 6.

"Willie Morris' sly psychology, uproarious dialogue and lyrical descriptions of Mississippi life make 'The Witch of Yazoo' a book to read aloud, preferably to one's children."

- *Homecomings.* With the art of William Dunlap. Author and Artist Series. Jackson: University Press of Mississippi, 1989 (item 40).

1168 Lucas, Sherry. "Essays and Art." *Clarion-Ledger*, 16 November 1989, sec. D, pp. 1–2.

Two native Mississippians, author Willie Morris and artist William Dunlap, collaborate on a book for the University Press of Mississippi's Author and Artist Series. "Morris' words and Dunlap's art bond memory, experience and emotions of home into parallel, complementary statements in *Homecomings*." Morris's six essays relate "his personal journeys" while Dunlap's "vivid, 'charged' landscapes, recreated on color plates within *Homecomings*, echo the homing instincts and the historical layers in landscapes and memory." Morris said that he was pleased with the collaboration. "Bill's work enhances the themes I'm trying to get into about place, the past and belonging."

1169 Hood, Orley. "'Homecomings' Stares into Our State's Soul." *Clarion-Ledger*, 19 November 1989, sec. F, p. 3.

The pairing of Willie Morris and William Dunlap on *Homecomings* "is a marriage of Mississippi souls, bodies that left Mississippi and hearts that could never break the bond of home. The graceful volume includes six of Morris' essays, subjects ranging from his grandfather to the infield fly rule as explained by a drop-dead gorgeous Ole Miss darling, from Truman Capote to the Oxfords, Mississippi's and England's. Dunlap's sketches and paintings bring home back home,... not illustrating the stories but illuminating the *feeling* that 'home' engenders...."

1170 Luft, Kerry. "Eloquent Essays on Matters of Heart." *Chicago Tribune*, 25 December 1989, sec. 5, p. 3.

Opines that *Homecomings* is about "things close to the heart." The collaboration of Morris and Dunlap "seems to be especially fortunate, for both men produce works that expand and improve with each viewing, or reading. Morris aptly describes Dunlap's art as 'visual poems.' For a reader, though, it is Morris' own work that is worth the price of the book." Luft discusses three essays she particularly likes: "Anybody's Children," a narrative of a 1987 murder trial; "Capote Remembered," a memoir of the author's friend, Truman Capote; and her favorite, "A Return to Christmases Gone," a remembrance of Morris's youth.

1171 "Hardcovers in Brief." *Washington Post Book World*, 7 January 1990, p. 13.

A one-paragraph notice. Morris has contributed six essays to *Homecomings*, while "William Dunlap has provided surreal landscapes and still li[f]es."

1172 Sparks, Jon W. "Morris Pays Rich Homage to South." *(Memphis) Commercial Appeal*, 7 January 1990, sec. G, p. 4.

Homecomings is a "rich combination of words and art" and a "handsomely produced" volume. "It is a profound affection for his native Mississippi that drives Morris, and these six essays are charming love letters to and about his passion." William Dunlap's "multi-media work does not illustrate the essays but stands on its own as Dunlap's view of his South." Sparks contends in his summary of the pieces in Morris's book (which "have little in common outside the Southern theme") that "the strongest character sketch is his portrait of his friend, Truman Capote."

1173 Caldwell, Gail. "Willie Morris' Southern Fire Is Still Burning." *Boston Globe*, 10 January 1990, p. 69.

Extols Morris's writing in an insightful review. William Dunlap's art "is somewhat commanding, and makes a handsome edifice for Morris' prose; the opening dialogue between the two men casts a telling glance at the internal and external landscapes that form the creative sensibility." The six essays "range from the poignant to the peripheral to the searingly acute.... There are two stunners: a haunting account of a 1987 murder trial in Oxford, and a reminiscence of Morris' fellow Southerner and old friend, Truman Capote." After scrutinizing each of Morris's works, Caldwell concludes that "there's damn fine life left in this man's prose."

1174 Lannon, Linnea. "Recommended." *Detroit News and Free Press*, 21 January 1990, sec. J, p. 9.

A brief review. Morris's essays "sparkle." He "writes of disparate events ... with skill and grace."

1175 Pearson, Michael. "'Homecomings' Opens Door to Willie Morris's Past." *Atlanta Journal/The Atlanta Constitution*, 11 February 1990, sec. N, p. 9.

"The artwork of William Dunlap is fascinating, but the book draws its life from Mr. Morris's words." Although the introductory dialogue between the two men "seems strained" and is "by far the weakest part" of the book, the essays "are all interesting. Some are brilliant. Mr. Morris is a romantic, and most often he recalls the past in dreamy colors, but these essays show all facets of his personality — his playfulness, his sentimentality, his honesty, his anger." Pearson especially admires "Anybody's Children," which recounts an Oxford, Mississippi, murder trial. After reviewing some of the other works, he asks: "Is there another essayist writing today who can describe the South with such honesty and affection?" Also published as "The South by a Specialist in Going Home" in the 4 March 1990 issue of the *(Norfolk) Virginian-Pilot and The Ledger-Star.*

1176 B., M. W. "Books About the South." *Southern Living* 25 (August 1990), p. 59.

As explained in the "opening dialog" between author and artist, the heart of *Homecomings* is how a person's past, his experiences, and his memory of those experiences relates to both the people and the landscape around him. "The book, then, is the telling of the familiar made more meaningful when related as a remembrance. Morris relates six wonderful experiences that will hit home. Even if you don't know the people and places by name, you'll certainly recognize them within the framework of your own life...." Dunlap's "inspiring" art is an "ideal accompaniment to these essays as it triggers the imagination to enjoy the intimacy that lurks beyond the surface of your existence."

- *Faulkner's Mississippi.* Photographs by William Eggleston. Birmingham, Ala: Oxmoor House, 1990 (item 47).

1177 Review. *Library Journal* 115 (15 September 1990), p. 51.

A brief notice of publication that labels Morris's narrative as a "meditation on Faulkner's fictional world" and Eggleston's photographs as "forthright images of Deep South landscapes."

1178 Holditch, W. Kenneth. "Sentimental Journey." *(New Orleans) Times-Picayune*, 25 November 1990, sec. E, pp. 6–7.

Holditch, Research Professor of English at the University of New Orleans and a southern literature scholar, recalls that William Faulkner had "intense and ambivalent feelings" about Mississippi; this "love-hate relationship" is the crux of Morris's "perceptive and beautifully written" *Faulkner's Mississippi.* "Morris writes with understanding of this complex man.... This is a serious biographical and literary analysis, but Morris is also adept at writing in a humorous, sometimes gently satirical tone...." His childhood in Yazoo City, his years in New York, his studies in Oxford, "and his own status as an author equip him with a unique viewpoint and insights into this great American novelist." Although some of the volume's photographs are "near perfect," Holditch has "always felt that Eggleston's work is overrated, for he has a tendency to draw attention to subjects by use of garish color and by a gimmicky way of shooting pictures; for example, twisting the camera to warp the image." Many photos are "simply inappropriate to the text.... The end result is a distinct and disruptive contrast between the perceptive, realistic, but often almost idyllic text of Morris and the disturbing subjects and their presentation in the pictures; between author's genuine sentiment and photographer's almost unrelenting cynicism."

1179 Goldsmith, Sarah Sue. "Faulkner's Mississippi Comes Alive." *(Baton Rouge) Sunday Advocate*, 9 December 1990, "Magazine" section, p. 16.

Writer Willie Morris and photographer William Eggleston "joined forces to create a gorgeous coffee-table book." Morris's text "sketches a verbal picture of Faulkner's frustrations and animosities, his peculiarities and pleasures," while the Mississippi scenes of Eggleston's photographs "reflect the settings of Faulkner's Yoknapatawpha stories." Readers "old enough to remember a Mississippi (or Louisiana, for that matter) of several decades ago will find the book a nostalgic look at the past."

1180 Koeppel, Fredric. "Faulkner Territory Made Timeless in Morris Prose, Eggleston Photos." *(Memphis) Commercial Appeal*, 9 December 1990, sec. G, p. 4.

Faulkner's Mississippi benefits from an "evocative text" by Morris and "even more evocative images by Memphis photographer William Eggleston.... Morris, who tends to lapse into highly metaphorical biblical–Faulknerian prose himself in many writings, mainly restrains himself and produces a moving yet fairly impressionistic biographical study of Oxford's Nobel Prize–winning novelist." The author has talked to Faulkner's "remaining family members" and is "best at capturing the spirit of Oxford and Faulkner's presence there." Eggleston's color photographs "evoke in uncanny fashion the spirit—calm, grandiose, lurid—of the mansions, hamlets and towns Faulkner's characters inhabited."

1181 Jackson, Ken. "Faulkner Book Monumental." *Tulsa World*, 23 December 1990, sec. D, p. 6.

Morris "offers a new, invaluable and inherent perception, an insight, into the complication that was Faulkner the man.... The lyricism of Morris, coupled to his down-home writing style and his honesty and writing economy, make the book a near-must for Faulkner lovers, of whom I am obviously one."

1182 Harrist, Ron. "Faulkner, South Come Alive As Morris Tackles a Legend." *Washington Times*, 26 December 1990, sec. E, p. 2.

Both a book review and an interview with the author. Morris's "'good old boy' love for the South" and his interest in William Faulkner have led to this "moving tribute" to the late novelist. "'He was a fellow Mississippian and a fellow writer, and I wanted to present him as a human being, not as an icon,' said Morris.... 'I tried to assess in the most human way the way Faulkner's native Mississippi and the South shaped him as a man and as an artist and also the way that he shaped Mississippi and the South.'" Possibly "the most noteworthy section" of the book, according to Harrist, is the part covering Faulkner's views on civil rights. "Morris describes Faulkner's stand in trying to be a moderating force in a time of hysteria and passion in a way that helps the reader understand the man and the times." This Associated Press review appeared in other newspapers, including the *Houston Post* of 30 December 1990 and the *Richmond (Va.) Times-Dispatch* of 10 February 1991.

1183 Pearson, Michael. "A Paean to Faulkner, a Portrait of His State." *(Norfolk) Virginian-Pilot and The Ledger Star*, 3 February 1991, sec. C, p. 2.

"This book is a paean to Faulkner's genius and a lovingly photographed portrayal of the state of Mississippi." The eye of photographer William Eggleston is "uncanny," and he "brings Mississippi to life" with his "lyrical collection of color photographs." Willie Morris "intertwines Faulkner's story with Mississippi's, and he manages to tell it by doing some fine reporting."

1184 Shulevitz, Judith. "The Real Yoknapatawpha." *New York Times Book Review*, 17 March 1991, p. 22.

The author explores "not only Faulkner's life and geography but also the colors and gossip of his own childhood." Photographer William Eggleston frames "fragments of Faulkner's cherished landscape in a bright, crisp noonday light that makes them appear, to a reader of Faulkner, both uncannily familiar and wonderfully strange."

1185 Lindgren, Carl E. "Library." *PSA Journal* 57 (July 1991), p. 9.

Lindgren, writing in the official publication of the Photographic Society of America, argues that Morris's book "reveals the textures of Faulkner's Mississippi—cultural, linguistic, and social—making an exceptional commentary on southern life. Morris accomplishes the task of seizing and capturing the imagination of the reader. This image is heightened by the stark, often haunting photographs of Eggleston which combines the reality of Mississippi's landscape with an almost spiritual journey through Faulkner's mystical Yoknapatawpha County."

1186 Smith, Galen. "Faulkner's Mississippi Explored." *Park City (Ky.) Daily News*, 21 July 1991.

Morris "sincerely did his homework" while preparing for this book, and he "writes with a journalistic flair." He "brings together a community of people who knew and loved Faulkner" and "interviews many Oxford residents who curiously knew, watched and viewed Faulkner on [o]ccasions."

1187 Lyday, Lance. "Faulkner Criticism: Will It Ever End? *South Carolina Review* 25 (Fall 1992), p. 183–92.

Faulkner's Mississippi and eight other Faulkner works are analyzed in a "highly selective survey of some of the more interesting books" related to the author that have been published in the last few years. This "handsome" coffee-table volume, an "expansion" of Morris's March 1989 *National Geographic* essay (item 775), "is light-years better than the average book of this type, even though parts of it appear to be aimed at an audience that likes to read biographical anecdotes about famous people but has no intention of reading Faulkner's novels. It is good that not all writing about Faulkner is aimed at specialists and scholars, and even better that someone as talented as Morris can communicate about Faulkner with the lay reader."

- *After All, It's Only a Game.* With art by Lynn Green Root. Jackson: University Press of Mississippi, 1992 (item 49).

1188 Hood, Orley. "Morris Gives Games Perspective." *Clarion-Ledger*, 30 October 1992, sec. E, p. 1.

For Morris, sports are people, and the "games provide neat backgrounds for the follies and foibles and farces that balance the human experience with the avalanche of tragedy inherent in the human condition." Morris's purpose in "this quiet and lovely collection" of fiction and nonfiction sports stories "is to put the games themselves in their rightful place, to set them down in context, in place and in time, gently allowing human frailty and small-town naivete and the pure joy of being alive to spin webs of mystery and fascination." *After All, It's Only a Game* also includes Lynn Green Root's "breathtakingly bold illustrations."

1189 Salter, Sid. "Willie Morris Jostles Awake Memories of Small-Town Sports." *Clarion-Ledger*, 7 March 1993, sec. G, p. 3.

The editor of Mississippi's *Scott County Times* reminisces about his past glories as a high-school athlete and gives his admittedly biased opinion about "my old friend's latest offering." *After All, It's Only a Game* is a "loving, whimsical and moving tribute to the dreams of small boys in small towns playing kids' games in the cauldron of adult expectations. It's the best book I've seen about high-school sports, and it is as compelling and comfortable to me as the old red-and-black wool letterman's jacket hanging in my closet." Willie Morris "reminds us that in this age of million-dollar salaries, strike seasons and arbitration, the only real glory that remains in the world of sports is the game played on that obscure high-school field, in a dim, small gymnasium or on a crude baseball diamond hewn from a cow pasture."

1190 Gietschier, Steve. Review. *Sporting News* 215 (22 March 1993), p. 46.

Commends this collection of stories by "one of America's most distinguished Southern writers" as a "gem." The short pieces "evoke the simplicity and confusion of youth" and "recapture the halcyon days before television." They are made even more appealing by the "captivating illustrations by Lynn Green Root, a bold and colorful painter."

1191 Liss, Barbara. "In Willie Morris' Lyrical Fiction/Memoir, The Game Is the Way Home." *Houston Chronicle*, 4 April 1993, "Zest" section, p. 21.

Morris's book "is a mix of memoir and fiction (with Morris, it's hard to make the distinction). And it's a fine opportunity for anyone who hasn't met this intelligent, sensitive writer. Nobody has written more lyrical, lucid prose than Morris about sports as a rite of passage for boys—and girls, too, who cheered and twirled their teenage hearts out—in a more innocent place and time, the small Southern towns of the 1940s and '50s." Liss regrets that just two of the six essays are new: "The Blood Blister" and "North Toward Starkville."

1192 Gamache, Ray. Review. *Aethlon: The Journal of Sport Literature* 10 (Spring 1993), pp. 143–44.

A ringing endorsement of *After All, It's Only a Game*. "In this slim volume is one man's love of sport, eloquently remembered and given life as it must have happened in the back roads and locker rooms of his experience. Morris is able to breathe the Mississippi air, its people, and their love of sport into his work. By focussing on the simple, everyday aspects of sport, he touches a chord that rings true with clarity." After Gamache offers his interpretations of the essays, he observes that "in this age of up-to-the-minute, wall-to-wall sports broadcasting, Morris' *After All, It's Only a Game* reminds us that sport is best appreciated in our own memories, etched forever in our consciousness.... Lynn Green Root's ten art pieces are a dazzling display of color which captures the swirling emotions and atmosphere of Morris' Mississippi."

- *New York Days*. Boston: Little, Brown and Co., 1993 (item 56).

1193 Hooper, Brad. Review. *Booklist* 89 (July 1993), p. 1915.

This "delectable sequel" to Morris's "delicious memoir" *North Toward Home* is an "extended essay on time and place, an especially beautiful piece of writing in which Morris attempts to answer the question we all shy away from with regard to roads we've taken: 'What did it all mean?' ... Journalistic memoirs abound, but few are as full of heart and as gracefully expressed as this one."

1194 "Non-Fiction." *Kirkus Reviews* 61 (1 July 1993), pp. 842–43.

As editor of *Harper's Magazine*, Morris was "the toast of the intellectual town" until he was forced to resign in 1971. Morris relies "too much on nearly year-by-year recapitulations of what his magazine published.... Portraiture here is at a minimum; mostly there are names and more names. That all of these are names culturally significant to the era gives the book its interest—but finally even they can't quite help it see much beyond its own bumped and bruised nose."

1195 Review. *Publishers Weekly* 240 (19 July 1993), p. 242.

"Morris writes, sometimes eloquently, sometimes with a little too much rhetorical rodomontade, about the magic of New York City and the distinguished writers with whom he worked" at *Harper's*. He "recaptures splendidly the heady sense that he and his magazine were helping to shape the culture of the times by focusing opposition to the Vietnam war and by taking the complicated beat of the contemporary American pulse."

1196 Williams, Wilda. "Social Sciences." *Library Journal* 118 (August 1993), p. 114.

A "vivid sequel" to the author's "classic memoir" *North Toward Home*. "There's plenty of name dropping and ego here, but Morris also ruminates on the personal costs of a celebrity-filled 'glamorous' life (the dissolution of his marriage). Morris obviously loves words; his prose is at times over-ripe and portentous in its lyricism but never dull." A starred review.

1197 Peede, Jon Parrish, with Steve Mullen. "Willie Morris: The Return of the Good Ole Boy." *(Oxford, Miss.) SouthVine*, 18 August—1 September 1993, pp. 6–7.

Not only a review but also an examination of Morris's career and an interview with the author prior to his August 26 visit to sign copies of *New York Days* (see item 1718). In this "long-awaited sequel to his classic memoir, *North Toward Home*," he reflects on the events leading up to his resignation from *Harper's* and on the failure of his marriage. "'I think that I needed the perspective of a quarter of a century to comprehend those events in my own personal life,' Morris said from his Jackson home. 'New York is a city that, if one's not careful, it can devour you.'" His book "does more than just document life in the fast-paced publishing world of the late sixties and early seventies; it explores the collective psyche of the country during the most turbulent period in its post–Civil War history." A cover story published in the small university town where Morris once lived and taught classes.

1198 Matthias, Heady-Dale. "Morris Writes Love Letter to New York in 'New York Days.'" *Clarion-Ledger*, 25 August 1993, sec. D, pp. 1–2.

Describes Morris's years in New York City, adding that he is "best when telling tales" about the writers who worked for him. His account of his "sense of estrangement from New York" after he resigned from *Harper's* "is also his best writing, perhaps his best writing ever.... If there are any faults with this book, they are few. However, the first third of the book, despite the seeming excitement of meeting New York's rich and famous in one salon soiree after another, is slow and encyclopedic. But by the seventh chapter, Morris finds his shimmering voice, and the rest is (literary) history."

1199 Samway, Patrick H. Review. *America* 169 (28 August—4 September 1993), p. 19.

A brief descriptive synopsis among other reviews in a "Fall Book Roundup." Morris's memoir "recounts the exhilarating and devastating New York years of the youngest-ever editor-in-chief of Harper's."

1200 King, Florence. "'Days' Rush by in a Blur of Words That Run You Over." *Washington Times*, 29 August 1993, sec. B, pp. 8, 6.

King, author of *Southern Ladies and Gentlemen*, finds "some" of *New York Days* to be "vivid" but dislikes most of the rest of it. "Unfortunately, Mr. Morris confuses evocative with exhaustive. His imitation of Thomas Wolfe's frantic purple prose starts on Page 1 with hosannas to New York.... Despite Mr. Morris' vaunted liberalism, the book frequently lapses into a testosteroniad reminiscent of novels belonging to the all-the-fine-young-men genre. After tossing off a cavalier tribute to 'the secretaries, God bless them one and all!' he proudly describes how he and staffers David Halberstam and Larry L. King turned the staid Harper's offices into an Ole Miss frat house...."

1201 O'Connell, Peter. "Heady Days in New York." *Natchez (Miss.) Democrat*, 29 August 1993.

Both a review and an interview with Morris. "Much of 'New York Days' concerns the friendships Morris [as editor of *Harper's*] formed with writers and other celebrities in the nation's 'cultural capital.' Morris shares his wonder at the famous and infamous with whom he mingled as a peer." After he resigned from the magazine, he had definite ideas on what he wanted to do next. "I'm a writer. I consciously decided when I left publishing that I was going to devote my life to my writing. It's very hard to be both an editor and a writer, too."

1202 Cryer, Dan. "Tales of the Big Apple from a 'Callow Imposter.'" *Newsday*, 30 August 1993, sec. 2, p. 40.

New York Days is a "spirited apologia, a treasuretrove of anecdotes and a more limited evocation of an era when unprecedented excitements and lunacies were appealing daily. It is also a bittersweet paean to the city of New York, which for this small-town southerner was 'sometimes ally, sometimes antagonist, but never for a moment neutral.'" The book is "strongest when focused on the magazine, when the author's personal journey intersects with the zeitgeist. Morris is indelible as the outsider as insider, 'half Yazoo boy, half cosmopolitan man.'" His "portraits" of the *Harper's* editors and administrators "are especially vivid." Even if *New York Days* "only occasionally rises to the charged eloquence" of his earlier memoir, *North Toward Home*, the book "still must be considered essential testimony documenting the life and times of literary New York in the late '60s."

1203 Kakutani, Michiko. "On Being Young, Hot and Literary in the 60's." *New York Times*, 31 August 1993, sec. C, p. 15

Morris's "chatty, anecdotal volume" is "not only filled with descriptions of his encounters with the powerful and famous,... but it is also animated by a sense of wonderment at the social and cultural pleasures afforded by the city." Unfortunately, *New York Days* is padded with descriptions of some of the articles he published in *Harper's*, and although Morris "rehashes, at rather wearying length," major news stories of the 1960s, he "doesn't have anything particularly new to say about any of these events, and his accounts of them feel both familiar and perfunctory, as though they had simply been added to the book to lend the narrative historical resonance and weight." Indeed, the "liveliest" sections of *New York Days* focus not on the "big, momentous events" of the decade, but on the "smaller, pettier ones" that occurred in the *Harper's* offices. Morris "nimbly conjures up the hectic, adrenaline-driven atmosphere" that he and his staff relished, "communicating to the reader what it must have been like to be young and gifted and ambitious in New York" at that time. The numerous anecdotes surrounding the famous people the author knew "might make another young person from the provinces want to come to New York, but they don't have much to do with the story Mr. Morris sets out to tell about 'the city itself in the 60's' and they ultimately distract the reader from the merits of this otherwise evocative book."

1204 Hills, Rust. "The Second Life of Willie Morris." *Esquire* 120 (September 1993), p. 52.

Harper's in the period Morris edited it "was a truly remarkable magazine. His accounts of the creation of various articles in that turbulent decade are fascinating...." Now back home in his native Mississippi, he "has summoned up the glory days of his past with what seems to be total recall. ('I'm blessed, or cursed, with an incredible memory,' he says.) Despite the presence of the celebrated, the tone is as down-to-earth American as its author."

1205 Donaldson, Scott. "A Memoir of 'Harper's' Heyday." *USA Today*, 3 September 1993, sec. D, p. 4.

Suggests that Morris was forced to resign from *Harper's* because of his "conflict of personality" with magazine owner John Cowles Jr., not because the publication lost money. "The end was implicit in the beginning when the young editor, who was constitutionally disinclined to kowtow to authority, fashioned his vision of what *Harper's* should become: a magazine determined 'to assume the big dare, to move out to the edge, to make people mad.'" Although Morris was "editing *Harper's* for himself," and in the process perhaps made himself more prominent than the magazine itself, "it would be wrong to criticize or in any way diminish the accomplishment of *Harper's*, 1967–1971. Down with the exhausted establishment, down with empty conventional mores, Morris and his contributors proclaimed, and they did so in some of the finest and most personally revealing writing ever to appear between magazine covers."

1206 Hardwick, Elizabeth. "'I Had Had My Pinnacle.'" *New York Times Book Review*, 5 September 1993, pp. 1, 13–15.

A respected novelist and a New York publishing insider not only reviews Morris's memoir, but she also provides her detailed, lengthy perspective on his years at *Harper's*. Morris "has cast his story in the streets of the city with a fluent affection and an acute rendering of the turmoil of the years: the assassinations, the civil rights movement and the Vietnam War.... The book gives credibility to his aims and achievements. It is a mixture of pride and heartache." Although other biographies and autobiographies are centered around American magazines, "no other comes to mind as having such a measure of chagrin as 'New York Days.' A certain naïveté made Willie Morris care too greatly and too painfully about the alliance with Harper's. A fragility of temperament, beneath the sunny sociability, inhabits the book and brings, or can bring, the reader to much sympathy for this composition of nostalgia and hurting regret in Mr. Morris's total recall of the lost days and nights." See also items 854, 1223, and

1723. After the appearance of Hardwick's review, three significant letters were published in the *New York Times Book Review*:

A Blair, William S. "'New York Days.'" *New York Times Book Review*, 10 October 1993, p. 35.

Blair, the publisher of *Harper's* "for most of the time described" in *New York Days*, writes that "Miss Hardwick accepts certain statements at face value," such as Morris's circulation figures of the magazine. Blair also points out the author's "inaccuracies" and concludes: "It is sad to see that this disdain for fact in favor of fantasy, which was the root cause of his problems at Harper's, continues to this day."

B Lapham, Lewis. "Advertisements for Themselves: A Letter from Lewis Lapham." *New York Times Book Review*, 24 October 1993, pp. 3, 39.

A writer who worked with Willie Morris at *Harper's Magazine* and who is presently editor-in-chief contributes a lengthy rebuttal to both Elizabeth Hardwick's review and Morris's interpretation of events in *New York Days*. "My own memory of the time and place so flatly contradicts his portrait in nostalgic pastel (in the specific instances as well as the general propositions) that on reading his book and its attendant publicity, I assumed that one of us was looking at the reverse images seen in a mirror. What Mr. Morris presents as a golden age I remember as an age of tinsel; his cast of fearless prophets I remember as a crowd of self-important pharisees; ... and well before I had reached the end of 'New York Days' I thought that it captured, all too perfectly, the spirit of an age that debased the currency of its idealism with the coinage of celebrity." See also item 1732.

C Morris, Willie. "The Battle Over 'New York Days.'" *New York Times Book Review*, 19 December 1993, p. 31.

Morris responds to Lewis Lapham's "inchoate quarrels and roily resentments" against *New York Days*. "There are only six references to Mr. Lapham in 'New York Days,' and they are niggardly. I never once considered him a stalwart personage in this chronicle. To tell the truth, I came damnably close to not mentioning him at all.... He has introduced the misinformation that 'New York Days' holds him responsible for the narrator's editorial departure from Harper's, and this mightily intrigues me, since I neither wrote nor even remotely implied any such thing." (This letter to the editor is also documented as item 963.)

1207 Swindle, Michael. "Literary N.Y.C. in the '60s." *Los Angeles Times Book Review*, 5 September 1993, pp. 4, 9.

A descriptive summation of *New York Days* as well as an evaluative review. Morris's account of his days in New York City "doesn't move in a strictly linear way. Like memory itself, the narrative indulges tangents here and there, or circles back to embellish certain episodes, before plunging onward in a prose style at times approaching the Biblical.... This book drops names—of the rich and famous, the powerful, the talented and interesting, and the merely weird—the way names were meant to be dropped: with concomitant stories that are enlightening, revelatory, touching, and uproariously funny." After the appearance of Swindle's review, the following letter was published in the *Los Angeles Times Book Review*:

A Margiloff, Irwin B. "The Editor's Duty." *Los Angles Times Book Review*, 3 October 1993, p. 15.

A letter to the editor written in response to Michael Swindle's review. Margiloff, a long-time reader of *Harper's*, believes that Morris's decision to devote an entire issue "to Norman Mailer was simply irresponsible and self-indulgent.... Vietnam was certainly an important topic but by no means the only one worth reading about that month. So the editor breached his duty to the readers. That is why he was fired."

1208 Yardley, Jonathan. "Young Man in a Hurry." *Washington Post Book World*, 5 September 1993, p. 3

A critical, fair-minded appraisal of an "alternately charming and vexing memoir." Yardley regrets that "Morris, the unconventional editor, has written a conventional editor's memoir," one that is "avuncular, nostalgic and paternalistic." Although each author is free to write his or her own biography, "it remains that Morris has not written in *New York Days* the book for which he is almost uniquely suited: the story of the youth from the provinces who is seduced by the city and in the end finds his glittering candle prematurely snuffed. Did all of the blame for his decline lie with those bloodless souls in the corporate counting houses whom he so bitterly portrays, or might Morris himself have played a major part in his story's unhappy outcome? ... However loutish he may have found those counting-house cretins, might they not have labored under burdens and responsibilities he was too single-minded and inexperienced to understand?" Rather than address these and other questions, Morris is instead "content to rehash old stories from the '60s, to recall high times among the evanescently eminent, and to cosset himself in illusions of persecution."

1209 Skube, Michael. "Morris's Memoir a Story of Loves Lost." *Atlanta Journal / The Atlanta Constitution*, 12 September 1993, sec. N, p. 8.

Skube does not review the book as much as he sympathetically sums up the author's "brilliant but brief" editorial years in New York. "'New York Days' is a love story, full of remorse and remembrance, and not a little recrimination.... The years produced enough scar tissue to go around. For Morris, the New York days were a time in the life of the nation that saw the perversion of promise, the corruption of purest ideals. But all that is past. Harper's, under Lewis Lapham — the Judas Iscariot of this tale — is in rigor mortis. Willie Morris, happily remarried, writing with confidence, has found redemption."

1210 Smith, Wendy. "Those Halcyon Days at Harper's Magazine," *Chicago Sun-Times*, 12 September 1993, "Arts & Show" section, pp. 12–13.

"Like most of America in the late '60s, *New York Days* is disorganized, given to hyperbole, inclined to chronicle events in a self-serving fashion, yet ultimately exciting and moving due to its passionate conviction that this was an important moment in our nation's history." During Morris's editorship, *Harper's* published notable and controversial articles about some of these events, so he "can be forgiven a little hyperbole.... Still, it does get to be annoying after a while when every Harper's writer — indeed, practically everyone Morris meets— is described as 'talented,' 'a consummate stylist,' 'a genius of the language,' even 'inspiring.' His portraits read more like press releases than perceptive personal sketches...." As he did in *North Toward Home*, Morris "tells his personal story in tandem with a history of the times" and he "sensitively evokes the pain, anger and fear prompted by the violence and polarization of American politics in an age tormented by the intractable, murderous problem of Vietnam."

1211 Elson, John. "Willie Boy Was Here." *Time* 142 (13 September 1993), p. 76.

A derisive review in which Elson accuses Morris of reading too much Thomas Wolfe. "Symptoms of the disease are truly terrible: a bloviation of the prose, with clichés clanging at irregular intervals; a golly-gee nostalgia for the glitz of Manhattan when one was young, yearning and oh-so-talented; and, for a few, an incurable lust to strew names like sunflower seeds." Elson acknowledges that *Harper's Magazine* "scored some exceptional coups" with a few of its articles. "But it also ran too many indulgently edited articles that dribbled on until reeled the mind."

1212 McDonald, Duncan. "His Own Driven Man: Willie Morris Recalls His Days As the Volatile Editor of Harper's Magazine." *Chicago Tribune Books*, 19 September 1993, p. 3.

Although Morris "brought a special vitality to Harper's that matched the tension and foment of the late '60s," he "still seems not to fully understand the seizures and arrests that were taking place in the magazine industry of the '70s, and that still haunt the trade today. For this and other reasons, I prefer Willie Morris as the writer, not the editor. He marches his verbs, nouns and adjectives in a glorious precision that sometimes hints of rebellion and of delicious anarchy. How I wish he would have given more of his soul and less of his spleen in 'New York Days'; there is simply too much anger and pining for the hobnobbing days to give the non-insider a clear vision of the importance of Harper's during the Vietnam era."

1213 O'Connell, Shaun. "Falling from Gotham's Heights and Telling About It." *Boston Globe*, 19 September 1993, p. 93.

Although Willie Morris's *New York Days* is "a compelling record of this articulate and reflective man's transforming love affair" with New York City, it is also "uneven, occasionally oblique and at times overwrought." For example, "Too often Morris recounts the outsized characters and the tumultuous events of his day — JFK, LBJ, Vietnam, Martin Luther King Jr., RFK, the Chicago riots— in a summary fashion, with little critical engagement." He instead quotes liberally from articles on the 1960s that appeared in *Harper's* "as though he were editor, rather than author, of his book. Though it is personal, his memoir is guarded, leaving mysterious gaps— particularly on his life at Harper's.... At times, Morris' prose, ever grandiloquent in the high Southern manner, overreaches itself as he tries to grasp the ineffable wonder of the city — 'a seething zenith from which to perceive the frustrations and the possibilities of the national scene.'"

1214 Pope, John. "Tales of the City." *(New Orleans) Times-Picayune*, 19 September 1993, sec. E, pp. 7–8.

In *New York Days*, Morris "mixes rhapsodic accounts about the Manhattan and the people he met with bitter tales of craven corporate behavior. It is, for the most part, exhilarating." His "narrative power" is "first-rate" while he is focused on *Harper's*, such as how Norman Mailer came to write about the anti-war demonstration in Washington, D.C., "The Steps of the Pentagon." Also, he is "on firm ground" with his descriptions of the "magic" of Manhattan and the "fascinating individuals" he encountered. "These are marvelous stories, but, unfortunately, Morris doesn't know when to stop; as a result — especially in a long chapter on Elaine's— he veers from scene-setting to name-dropping. And his attempts to define the Great Themes of the 1960s come off as windy pop sociology." In spite of these weaknesses and several factual errors, *New York Days* "is well worth the ride. Morris was lucky enough to be at an important spot during a turbulent time,... and he was skillful enough to interpret what happened." See also item 1724.

1215 Menand, Louis. "Willie's Version." *New Yorker* 69 (20 September 1993), pp. 121–26.

Both a review of *New York Days* and an analysis of American literary journalism in the 1960s. "The memoirs of literary people are traditionally so unreliable that to call them 'self-serving' is nearly a redundancy. Just as long as nobody mistakes them for history. Morris's *Harper's*, though, *is* history, and when he leaves off reminiscing about the lunches at the Century and the parties at George Plimpton's he does manage to give us some idea of what being an editor was like back in the days when journalism was New." After quoting a paragraph from *New York Days*, Menand declares this type of writing to be "corny. There is a lot of corniness in sixties literary journalism, and the reason for it sounds a little corny, too. It's that those writers still cared about America. It's not that they loved it, or sought to honor it; it's that they found it endlessly and intoxicatingly interesting."

1216 Manning, Robert. "Heating Up *Harper's*." *Columbia Journalism Review* 32 (September/October 1993), pp. 58–59, 61–62.

Manning, editor of the *Atlantic Monthly* during Morris's editorship and a "friendly but highly competitive" rival of him, provides an insider's view of magazine publishing when he summarizes the "painfully familiar" financial problems that Morris had to face. Manning argues that although Morris's practice of putting "a team of several writers on modest retainer" produced some fine articles, it also created problems: not only was it expensive, but he "in effect deeded a disproportionate part of the magazine's pages to the same voices issue after issue, and the heavy drain on his limited money for articles obliged him to use their material whether they were on or off their feed." And while Madison Avenue decreed *Harper's* to be a "hot" magazine, it was not popular enough to justify an increase in advertising rates, "nor did the people out there west of the Hudson respond with a flow of subscription checks." Manning disagrees with some of Morris's assertions, such as his claim that *Harper's* "was the first major established institution in America" to protest the Vietnam War. "But nobody I know, and certainly not I, cares to quarrel with that bright, friendly, admirable, 'complicated old southern boy' or 'Mississippi bullhead,' as Willie Morris describes himself, nor deny him any of the praise due him for the achievements he records in *New York Days*, all with good humor, engaging candor, and appropriate pride."

1217 Logue, John. "Books About the South." *Southern Living* 28 (October 1993), p. 78.

Contends that this "sequel to the classic memoir, *North Toward Home*," is "greater" than the first book. "The joy of editing one of America's oldest magazines, *Harper's*, is rampant in the narrative of Morris's *New York Days*, and the pain of losing that magazine — and all that had gone into it — bleeds on every page. Currents of the book run deep through the human heart."

1218 Leonard, John. "Tossing the Salad Days." *Nation* 257 (25 October 1993), pp. 463–64, 466.

A review essay of *New York Days* and Paul Krassner's *Confessions of a Raving, Unconfined Nut*. "Willie, whose sweet tooth for the elegiac is notorious," has "some nice passages" on Manhattan, marriage, and his years as a Rhodes scholar in Oxford. "Most of the reviews of Willie's book, like most of the book itself, were devoted to his days at *Harper's*. So be it. The only revenge a writer's got on the bean counters and backstabbers who buy and sell him like a yo-yo or a porkbelly future is to give us a book that pins them through their buggy little eyes down to a page of style, impales then on a consummate disdain." Even if Morris and his friends drank and ate too much and too often, "Any magazine that in five years managed to publish [Norman] Mailer on the armies of the night, [David] Halberstam on the best and the brightest, Irving Howe on the New York intellectuals, and Seymour Hersh on the My Lai massacre was doing wonderfully, thank you, no matter what they thought in Minneapolis."

1219 Brookhiser, Richard. "Metropolitan Diary." *Commentary* 96 (November 1993), pp. 56–58.

After quoting a paragraph from *New York Days*, Brookhiser, a senior editor of *National Review*, deadpans: "As these sentences indicate, the incandescent days are not the only windy things in Morris's book. But he does manage to capture the thrill of being at what feels like the center of the world. *New York Days* is less effective when it tries to capture the spirit of the 60's. Morris's account of the times is bland and summary, like riffling through the minutes of old editorial story conferences, not least because the stories which those conferences produced have fixed the period so vividly, and so rigidly, in our minds." His "most interesting take on the 60's derives from his awareness of the role that white Southerners played in articulating its discontents." *New York Days* "is not a flashy book.... But the flashes existed, and Morris takes pardonable pride in having helped generate some of them."

1220 Wolcott, James. "Remaking It." *New Republic* 209 (15 November 1993), pp. 31–32, 34–36.

Wolcott reviews *Kafka Was the Rage* by Anatole Broyard and *New York Days* by "starry-eyed" Willie Morris. "Time and memory have not shrunk his sense of wonder. He goes through the entire book agape and agog, the Thomas Wolfe of the three-martini lunch." Wolcott briefly discusses some of the best-known writers of the sixties and avers that although Morris had a "bird's-eye view of the decade," he "has nothing original or revisionist to say," for *New York Days* is simply "reheated punditry, smothered with quotation." The reviewer maintains that "the sole selling point of a book like this has to be its gossip. As Morris waxes Proustian about his days at Oxford ... or plays pop sociologist..., you find yourself muttering: yeah, yeah, get to the good stuff. The negative surprise of the book, aside from its gaseous prose, is how little good stuff there is." Nevertheless, "none of this diminishes what Morris accomplished at *Harper's*." His publication of such controversial articles as Norman Mailer's "The Prisoner of Sex" and Seymour Hersh's piece on the My Lai massacre "displayed a nerve, an instinct and a capacity for encouragement rare among editors. Each issue was proof that writers will settle for less money, if less money means more freedom and space."

1221 Copetas, A. Craig. "Like a Boll Weevil to a Cotton Bud." *London Review of Books* 15 (18 November 1993), pp. 26–27.

Remembers the "dynamism" of the sixties and states that under Morris, *Harper's* was "one hell of a magazine," as it "reported the events and articulated the cravings that defined the generation." Copetas recounts various passages and incidents from *New York Days*, especially the events leading to Morris's resignation from *Harper's*.

1222 Hart, Jeffrey. "Books in Brief." *National Review* 45 (29 November 1993), pp. 72, 76.

"In the shadow of the North Carolina windbag [Thomas Wolfe], Mr. Morris serves up a prose stuffed to the bursting point with multiple adjectives, an inflated prose full of paste gems and exaggerated nostalgia." Although he believes he recruited first-rate authors for *Harper's*, "Most of his admired writers are less writers than celebrities.... One cannot begrudge Mr. Morris the fact that he had a ball as editor, but his book is an embarrassment."

1223 Review. *New York Times Book Review*, 5 December 1993, p. 52.

New York Days—"Mr. Morris's memoir of his star-crossed romance with Harper's Magazine"—is included in a list of "notable books" of 1993. The volumes have been "selected from books reviewed since the Christmas Books issue of December 1992." See also item 1206.

1224 Gaillard, Frye. "A Time to Remember." *Progressive* 58 (February 1994), pp. 42–43.

Despite such flaws in Morris's book as his overwriting and "star-gazing" (for example, his "breathless accounts" of cocktail parties with the rich and famous), *New York Days* is a "gripping memoir — brilliant in places— by one of the finest editors of our time." Morris frequently quotes from authors whose articles he published in *Harper's*, "revealing a pride in his own work as editor, but displaying also the key to his success. Then as now, he loved good writing and admired good writers. And all in all, he was the kind of editor most of them prayed for.... Morris recounts his memories of *Harper's*, the bitter and the sweet, but he does a great deal more than that. He gives us a passionate account of the 1960s, with all their pain and confusion and hope, a subject grand enough for his words."

1225 "New & Noteworthy Paperbacks." *New York Times Book Review*, 18 December 1994, p. 36.

A brief review of the new edition of *New York Days*. After Morris became editor of *Harper's Magazine*, he brought in "fresh talent and an irreverent slant — a move that ultimately caused conflict with the venerable publication's corporate owners."

1226 Review. *New York Times Book Review*, 11 June 1995, p. 60.

New York Days is among "a noteworthy collection" of paperbacks.

- *My Dog Skip*. New York: Random House, 1995 (item 57).

1227 Hooper, Brad. "Adult Nonfiction." *Booklist* 91 (15 March 1995), p. 1282.

Reviews *A Dog's Life* by Peter Mayle and *My Dog Skip*. "Morris remembers back to the boy-and-his-dog days in his small hometown in the Deep South, where Skip was involved in all of his pranks and escapades. Poignancy rather than humor is the pervading tone of this ode to a steadfast presence."

1228 Skube, Michael. "The Adult Pastime Called Childhood." *Atlanta Journal / The Atlanta Constitution*, 26 March 1995, sec. M, p. 8.

A review of Morris's *A Prayer for the Opening of the Little League Season* and *My Dog Skip*. The latter volume "is at least as much an adult's book as a child's. It is an elegy to the loyalty of a smaller creature and the inevitability of one day telling it goodbye." See also item 1253.

1229 McCaig, Donald. "A Boy's Best Friend." *Washington Post*, 27 March 1995, sec. D, p. 2.

During his youth in a small Mississippi Delta town, Morris's companion was a fox terrier named Skip. *My Dog Skip* is his "tribute to the dog, the place and the time.... Readers will enjoy this marvelous, modest memoir, but after they have closed the book and come blinking into the bright sunlight of everydayness, they may say to themselves: 'Play football? Go to the store for his own bologna? Read a boy's mind? A dog can't do that!' But in a romantic Delta town in the '40s, with Willie Morris as a pal, a dog named Skip could, and did, live up to his potential." A favorable review also published in the *Chicago Sun-Times* of 13 April 1995.

1230 Hood, Orley. "Willie Morris' Dog-Gone Book Is Purely Heartfelt." *Clarion-Ledger*, 30 March 1995, sec. D, p. 1.

A heartfelt reminiscence about the author and his love of dogs as well as a book review. After Morris's dog Pete died, "The phone lines between New York and Oxford were burning hot with condolence calls from Willie's writer pals.... This skin deep brother love Willie holds for all things canine bursts forth" in *My Dog Skip*.

1231 Zythum, Lester V. "Willie Morris Signs April 4." *Oxford (Miss.) Eagle*, 30 March 1995.

Savors the "cleanly written, enchanting prose" of this "irresistibly sweet, poignant story about a boy and his dog. Although young Willie Morris grew up in the rural South during World War II, his carefree adventures speak eloquently of the universality of childhood experiences. You do not need to be of the place or the generation to cherish these heartwarming reminiscences, you just need to be a bit of a kid at heart."

1232 Williams, Wilda. Review. *Library Journal* 120 (1 April 1995), pp. 117, 119.

A "sweetly sentimental if slight memoir" in which the author "recalls growing up with Skip in the small, sleepy town of Yazoo, Mississippi.... For anyone who has ever loved a dog, Morris's loving tribute will be a delightful read."

1233 Arson, Susan. "This Dog Will Hunt." *(New Orleans) Times-Picayune*, 2 April 1995, sec. E, p. 6.

A "slim, sweet memoir of a boy and his dog.... Young adults will enjoy this book for its evocation of childhood in a bygone era, when a boy could send his dog down to the grocery store for some bologna, or trick a friend into walking across a cemetery in the dark. Older readers will feel its bittersweet charm, too, thinking of a sweeter, perhaps more innocent time, but remembering as well the reality of World War II, such a grand imaginary adventure for a young boy."

1234 Teachout, Terry. "Willie Morris' I-Had-a-Dog-Once Memoir." *(Baltimore) Sun*, 2 April 1995, sec. F, p. 5.

The plot of *My Dog Skip* is "embarrassingly obvious," and Morris misses no opportunity to tug at the reader's heartstrings. "The really irritating thing is that there is a slender, affecting tale trapped somewhere inside this gassy, overblown book. Though Morris works the small-town pedal a bit too hard, he has a marvelous eye for detail. What is missing from 'My Dog Skip,' and from everything else its author ever wrote, is a sense of selectivity. Presumably as a result of premature exposure to Thomas Wolfe, Morris writes in a boozily pseudo poetic style in which every other sentence contains at least one adjective too many...."

1235 McCall, Bruce. "Good Dog! Bad Dog!" *New York Times Book Review*, 9 April 1995, p. 11.

McCall reviews *My Dog Skip* and Peter Mayle's *A Dog's Life*, two "canine recollections." Morris has written "a memoir of his beloved boyhood friend, companion and fellow prankster, Skip, set in the small-town South of 40 to 50 years ago. This allows Mr. Morris to expand on the theme of dog love less cutely and more honestly than Mr. Mayle, and to work in a lot more atmosphere. It's a richer experience all around, and a richer wallow still for the dog-struck.... Skip seems every bit as unique and memorable as Mr. Morris thinks he is, and I'd take him home in a shot."

1236 Wilkie, Curtis. "Willie Morris Writes of His Love for Skip." *Boston Globe*, 10 April 1995, p. 3.

"More than a generation after William Faulkner expounded on the glories of the mule, another Mississippi writer, Willie Morris, has emerged as a literary champion of dogs." *My Dog Skip* is a "funny, sentimental book, a march back into time to the innocent cadence of an old Booth Tarkington novel."

1237 Hartman, Diane. "Story of Skip a Trip to Past." *Denver Post*, 16 April 1995, sec. E, p. 10.

Describes a few of Skip's adventures with young Willie Morris. "This paean to the dog part of a boy and his dog will have readers fondly remembering their own adventures, dog at side."

1238 Wilson, Craig. "Willie Morris' Pet Project Evokes Mississippi Memories." *USA Today*, 20 April 1995, sec. D, p. 4.

A combination book review and interview with Morris. "You can't beat the age-old story of a boy and his dog. And no one knows that better today than Willie Morris.... Although Skip is the dog that runs through Morris' charming memoir, the real tale lies in the daily truths of a small Southern town during World War II. Why is it, Morris is asked, that Southern small towns always seem more romantic places than all the rest? 'I like to say Mississippi is America's Ireland. A society of small towns, where the old tradition of storytelling is still alive. I grew up before TV, the great silencer of conversation.... We all had to fall back on ourselves for our entertainment then. If the fire truck went by, we all followed it.'"

1239 Merriman, Ann Lloyd. "Between the Bookends." *Richmond (Va.) Times-Dispatch*, 23 April 1995, sec. F, p. 5.

My Dog Skip is "a delightful little memoir by Willie Morris.... Skip was his boyhood companion, linked forever to the long-ago days of his youth when youngsters played and roamed and discovered, and all was right with the world."

1240 Warren, Tim. "Dog's Life Isn't Morris' Best." *Houston Chronicle*, 23 April 1995, "Zest" section, p. 23.

Warren is an admirer of Morris's work but finds *My Dog Skip* "to be a narrow, not very deep piece of writing. It's Morris Lite. For although there are indeed many affectionate reminiscences about what seems to have been a remarkable dog, and there are times when the author gives us the graceful, moving writing of which he is capable," his latest book is a "lesser effort. Ultimately, how much can you write about a dog that could do all kinds of tricks and that you loved very much?" The story "seems forced, and way too long. That's a shame, for in a time when the memoir has flourished, Morris has become perhaps the pre-eminent American memoirist."

1241 Adams, Phoebe-Lou. "Brief Reviews." *Atlantic Monthly* 275 (May 1995), p. 125.

A one-paragraph review. Although a dog grows old as its owner grows up, the owner's later reminiscences about their youthful escapades together "will affectionately and extensively include his dog."

1242 McCampbell, Marlene. "Picks & Pans: Pages." *People Weekly* 43 (29 May 1995), p. 28.

"Morris evokes the 'spooked-up and romantic' atmosphere of life in a small Delta town where swimming holes beckon on languid afternoons and the air is fragrant with honeysuckle.... This book is both a loving tribute to his companion and a lyrical remembrance of vanished innocence."

1243 Lyons, Gene. Review. *Entertainment Weekly*, no. 277 (2 June 1995), pp. 52–53.

An "unpretentious saga" of a boy and his dog and an "unabashedly sentimental ode to a bygone world." Morris's dog Skip appears to have been a "remarkable" dog, "even if readers are apt to suspect the author of telling what Huck Finn called a 'stretcher' now and again." Review grade: B.

1244 Vosburgh, Mark. "Reflections on Childhood's Dog Days." *Chicago Tribune*, 12 June 1995, sec. 5, p. 4.

Morris "weaves childhood memories of an ordinary fox terrier into an extraordinary tribute to dogs and their boys." He "lets his doggie anecdotes meander in and out of plausibility and back and forth in time. This, Morris tells potential critics, is as it should be. 'My memories of Skip move in and out and around in time anyway, from my grade school years through junior high and high school and beyond, which is likely as it should be because if the existence of all creatures is a continuum, there is still plenty of room to weave and backtrack and drift and glide." Review originally published in the *Orlando Sentinel* of 4 June 1995.

1245 Carlton, Michael. "Books About the South." *Southern Living* 30 (October 1995), p. 110.

A brief review. "If you've ever had a dog, or if your child has one now, make this a family must-read. The book, simple *and* simply wonderful, teaches much about love and loyalty, about growing up and innocence — even about death."

1246 McCaig, Donald. "Dogography." *Dog World* 80 (October 1995), pp. 64–65.

"The best dog stories are never content to be as simple as they seem, and 'My Dog Skip' is a fine dog story. Sure, it's Skip's biography, but it is also a sweet-natured account of growing up in a more courteous America of ballparks, fishing holes, courthouse squares, nightly radio broadcasts about the war and the weekly Kiddie Matinee at the Dixie Theater." Although Morris is "best known" for *New York Days*, his "brilliant recollections" of his years as editor of *Harper's Magazine*, "I wonder if he won't come to be remembered for this modest, honorable, marvelous memoir of a boy and his dog."

1247 "Nonfiction Reprints." *Publishers Weekly* 243 (1 January 1996), p. 69.

A brief review of the paperback edition.

1248 Reynolds, Susan Salter. "In Brief." *Los Angeles Times Book Review*, 4 February 1996, p. 10.

"There used to be fine places to raise children who would grow up ... in a cushion of community and security and loyalty to an environment. This book, Willie Morris' tribute to his childhood dog, Skip, is such a memoir: Mark Twain, Nehi sodas, baseball, until you think he must be kidding, this can't be real, this is Norman Rockwell and Jimmy Stewart. But damn if you don't dread the day when this dog dies, which you know must happen.... Because when this dog dies, all that will be over, childhood will be over, that kind of friendship will never happen again."

1249 Schnedler, Jack. "Willie Morris Lets His Dog Wag This Tale." *(Little Rock) Arkansas Democrat-Gazette*, 10 March 1996, sec. J, p. 7.

A review of the paperback edition, which is reported to be "selling briskly in Central Arkansas." While Skip is the book's main character, "Morris has crafted much more than a warm and fuzzy memoir of a boy and his pooch. 'My Dog Skip' is a fresh mining of a lode worked over the years by the author of 'North Toward Home'—what it was like growing up in a Mississippi delta town of 10,000 a half-century ago, when the South was still a very distinct and separate corner of America." Although Morris's "stream of recollection" occasionally takes "a soppy turn," he generally "underpins keenly remembered anecdotal detail with perceptions as frisky as Skip the puppy must have been."

1250 Eighner, Lars. "A Dog and His Boy." *Texas Observer*, 31 May 1996, p. 18.

Eighner wishes that *My Dog Skip* "were a little less charming, and the picture of this life of boy and dog a little less pretty and seductive." Morris fails to include among his "idyllic scenes of boyhood" any indication that there was "an ugly reality beneath his nostalgia." He recollects "with amusement that Skip did not deign to eat anything except bologna (which Skip would fetch himself from the shopkeeper, paying with money carried in a backpack). The humor of Skip's refined palate is lost if one recalls that this was a time that many Americans stood in long lines for thin soup, but neither the boy Morris nor the author Morris seem to know of the Depression."

- *A Prayer for the Opening of the Little League Season.* Illustrated by Barry Moser. San Diego: Harcourt Brace & Co., 1995 (item 58).

1251 Review. *Horn Book Guide* 6 (January-June 1995), p. 378.

"The language will delight sophisticated, knowledgeable followers of the game but has little general child appeal. Young ball players of both genders are portrayed in this book written *about* children — not *for* them."

1252 Plaut, David. "These Books Cover All the Bases." *USA Today Baseball Weekly* 4 (1 March 1995), p. 13.

A brief review. "Words of wisdom and compassion for all participants of Little League and youth baseball to consider as they prepare for their first game on the schedule."

1253 Skube, Michael. "The Adult Pastime Called Childhood." *Atlanta Journal / The Atlanta Constitution*, 26 March 1995, sec. M, p. 8.

Reviews *My Dog Skip* and *A Prayer for the Opening of the Little League Season.* Morris's Little League prayer is a "tongue-in-cheek appeal to the Great Scorekeeper. Position by position, Morris asks that the Almighty intercede to help the little players on close calls and tough plays. The book is as fun and fanciful as 'Casey at the Bat,' and yet when I read this, I thought of every child I've ever seen standing on a baseball field in a uniform three sizes too large, looking lost...." See also item 1228.

1254 "New and Recommended." *Chicago Sun-Times*, 2 April 1995, "Showcase" section, p. 19.

A brief review. Morris and "distinguished artist" Barry Moser have collaborated on a "charming ... children's book that will tug the heartstrings of adult fans." Includes a few lines from their baseball prayer.

1255 Lind, Angus. "Let It Be a League of Their Own." *(New Orleans) Times-Picayune*, 16 April 1995, sec. E, p. 6.

A Prayer for the Opening of the Little League Season is "somewhat schmaltzy but well-crafted" and is "excellently illustrated in Norman Rockwell style by prize-winning illustrator Barry Moser.... Morris's prayerful prose reflects his Southern upbringing and the small-town values of life in his hometown of Yazoo City, Miss."

1256 Review. *Library Talk* 8 (May 1995), p. 15.

A brief review. "The 'prayer' notes the tribulations of the different positions ... but asks for comfort for all playing children, their wrathful fathers and faithful mothers, and their umpires."

1257 "The Books on Baseball." *St. Petersburg (Fla.) Times*, 15 May 1995, sec. D, p. 5.

"Willie Morris offers a prayer for youthful catchers and pitchers, little infielders, eager outfielders and all those who have yet to get a hit." Quotes several lines from the prayer.

1258 Hurlburt, Tom S. "Nonfiction." *School Library Journal* 41 (June 1995), p. 104.

"While the picture-book format will make this title visually attractive to a young audience, the text includes such words as ordinance, inexorable, and assuage, which will require adult interpretation. Morris's skillful prose melds neatly with Moser's fine paintings, creating an end product that will delight all who participate in, or follow the game of baseball."

1259 Gibson, Nancy. "New Baseball Books Make Their Pitch." *Columbus Dispatch*, 8 June 1995, p. 24.

A short review. Author Morris and artist Moser "get downright reverent in their collaboration" on this "humorless reminder of the joys and pitfalls of juvenile baseball."

1260 Goedhart, Bernie. "Between the Covers at the Old Ball Game." *Gazette* (Montreal), 23 June 1995, sec. G, p. 2.

Goedhart suspects that "nostalgic adults" will enjoy *A Prayer for the Opening of the Little League Season* more than adolescent ball players. "'Save the young pitchers from all erratic affliction as the line drives whip past their heads' is not a phrase likely to roll off the tongue of any young reader.... The illustrations, in fact, are the best thing about this book — and probably the reason it's marketed as juvenile literature."

1261 "Picture Book Reprints." *Publishers Weekly* 246 (26 April 1999), p. 85.

A brief notice upon the publication of the paperback edition. "Lofty language couches a wry appeal to the 'Great Umpire in the Heavens' for a happy baseball season."

1262 Fenly, Leigh. "Just for Kids." *San Diego Union-Tribune*, 23 April 2000, "Books" section, p. 5.

Reviews the paperback edition. "The tone is optimistic, the language reverent but funny. By the last page, Morris has explained the reasons why baseball creates the kind of memories that last."

- *The Ghosts of Medgar Evers: A Tale of Race, Murder, Mississippi, and Hollywood.* New York: Random House, 1998 (item 59).

1263 "Non-Fiction." *Kirkus Reviews* 65 (15 December 1997), p. 1819.

"A certain modesty of scope, a specificity of observation, and an adherence to the ingrained understanding of a native are what make this 'the-making-of' story a surprisingly successful book about the legacy of the civil rights movement." Willie Morris provides a "good-natured chronicle" of the making of Rob Reiner's motion picture, *Ghosts of Mississippi*, which recounts Byron De La Beckwith's 1994 conviction for killing Medgar Evers some thirty years previously. "It's a curious mixture of a serious civil rights history and a whimsical peek into the Hollywood fiction factory. But these elements are held together because the movie was based on such fresh facts that it became a small part of the history itself." Although Morris reveals little about his own experiences growing up in Mississippi, he does expound on the state's "deep, distinctive past and uses his childhood recollections to otherwise great effect in observing the movie's dramatization of that past."

1264 Smothers, Bonnie. Review. *Booklist* 94 (1 and 15 January 1998), p. 742.

Morris ponders "the ghosts of racial healing and progress" in this "multilayered study" of the film *Ghosts of Mississippi*. The movie, directed by Rob Reiner, "is about Mississippi assistant D.A. Bobby DeLaughter (Alec Baldwin) reopening the case against Byron [D]e [L]a Beckwith (James Woods) for the murder of civil rights activist Medgar Evers and, with the aid of the widow Evers (Whoppi Goldberg) bringing the murderer to justice." Morris's work "reads like a series of long magazine articles," each of which focuses on various aspects of the making of the motion picture and its critical and popular reception.

1265 "Forecasts." *Publishers Weekly* 245 (5 January 1998), pp. 52–53.

Rob Reiner's 1997 motion picture *Ghosts of Mississippi*, about the murder of civil rights leader Medgar Evers and the thirty-year-long pursuit of the assassin, was a "commercial flop" and generally considered to be "earnest but uninspired." Nevertheless, Morris's "account of the making of the film might have been an interesting investigation into the politics of race and popular culture." Instead, the book, though "well-meaning," is an "overly detailed, credulous account of the minutiae of Hollywood filmmaking." Movie buffs will already be familiar with many of the technical details that the author finds so intriguing. "Most disappointingly, Morris, who knew or shared acquaintances with many of the real figures in the case, speaks of the thorny problem of race mostly in grandiloquent platitudes."

1266 Morgenstern, Joe. "Black and White in Color." *Wall Street Journal*, 2 February 1998, sec. A, p. 20.

A perceptive and thought-provoking review. Morris covered the third murder trial (the all-white juries in the previous two trials deadlocked) of white supremacist Byron De La Beckwith, accused of shooting civil rights activist Medgar Evers some thirty years earlier. The author persuaded a producer friend of his that the trial and the story behind it could make a major motion picture, and *The Ghosts of Medgar Evers* is his "often eloquent but sometimes exasperating account of how 'Ghosts of Mississippi' came to be made and yet failed to make the grade." Although the book is an "impressive evocation of the period," Morris is "curiously indiscriminate" as he relates film production details. "Mr. Morris covers a lot of ground, and doesn't he ramble as he invokes not just the ghost of Medgar Evers but Faulkner, Emily Dickinson, Elvis Presley, long-dead black slaves and tenant farmers, longer-dead Indians and, not incidentally, ghosts of his own movie-going past." Morgenstern disagrees with some of Morris's reasons behind the movie's failure at the box office, such as his "dubious conclusion that 'more than ever, perhaps, we are unable to think clearly and rationally about racial matters.'" Instead, Morgenstern lays part of the blame on the motion picture itself: "Working from a pedestrian screenplay, the director crafted a slow-paced, earnest film that young (and not-so-young) audiences inevitably perceived as old-fashioned. What I perceived was a plain old failure of imagination."

1267 Ewing, Jim. "Actual History, Making of Movie Combined in Book." *Clarion-Ledger*, 4 February 1998, sec. E, p. 3.

In *The Ghosts of Medgar Evers*, Morris combines an historical account of Evers's 1963 murder with an insider's view of the making of a film based on the tragedy and its aftermath. "The book is a tale of dichotomies, of odd juxtapositions that only a native Mississippian can fathom and explain. How Morris intertwines the two is a product of his genius, as a writer, a journalist, a Mississippian."

1268 Shribman, David M. "Mississippi Goes Hollywood." *Globe and Mail* (Toronto), 7 February 1998, sec. D, p. 16.

The Ghosts of Medgar Evers "is a combination history primer, program note and gazetteer to that elusive and alluvial swath of God's earth called Mississippi." In it Morris "examines two distinctly American cultures, Mississippi and Hollywood, finding in them both an innate sense of drama and an even deeper sense of insecurity. Hollywood, he finds, is 'enigmatic, almost demented,' and my only quibble might be with the word 'almost.' The same might be said, of course, of Mississippi."

1269 Bernstein, Richard. "Recalling a Racial Killing and the Movie About It." *New York Times*, 11 February 1998, sec. B, p. 12.

Bernstein is disappointed that Morris focuses on the making of the movie based on the killing of Medgar Evers and the murderer's trial rather than on the actual historical event. "His book includes a few luminous pages of boyhood memoir and some powerful reflections on Southern racism, but mostly it is a detailed, almost starstruck account of the making of the movie 'Ghosts of Mississippi.' And it is an explanation for that movie's commercial failure, which Mr. Morris sees as a reflection of the contemporary American feeling about race." Although the author's insights are "certainly valuable," the book "has a meandering quality, and its arguments offer little that is especially deep."

1270 Adam, Anthony J. "Arts & Humanities." *Library Journal* 123 (15 February 1998), p. 144.

Morris's *The Ghosts of Medgar Evers* "ranks among the best of the on-the-spot-coverage film books of recent years. He blends perceptive regional awareness with a sharp wit and eye.... Moreover, Morris's fluid prose reminds us that Southern writing is very much alive."

1271 Ealy, Charles. "Morris Fritters Away His Script with Trivia." *Dallas Morning News*, 15 February 1998, sec. J, p. 9.

Ealy is surprised that Willie Morris examines Byron De La Beckwith's third murder trial "not from his own worldly perspective but in the context of a Hollywood movie" as *Ghosts of Mississippi* was neither successful at the box office nor well reviewed by critics. Furthermore, "The author fails to deliver a complex and fully reasoned portrait of race and its interaction with Hollywood. Instead, he lets the tale devolve into meandering musings, needless name-dropping and off-point anecdotes, without ever exploring in depth the central question of Hollywood's treatment of the civil rights movement."

1272 Liss, Barbara. "In Hollywood We Trust: Reverent Take Undermines Tale of Evers Film." *Houston Chronicle*, 15 February 1998, "Zest" section, p. 29.

Although *Ghosts of Mississippi* is a "triumphant story of evil brought to justice," the motion picture is "somber and magisterial. Morris recounts the historic events and the filming of them in tones even more hushed and reverential than the movie's." The author is "characteristically insightful and poetic when he concentrates on the Delta and its people. But when he turns his attention to the filmmakers, he surrenders his clear eye. The problem is that he's dazzled by 'the industry'; he takes these guys too seriously, not recognizing how much self-promotion is going on."

1273 Anderson, John. "Mississippi Meets Hollywood." *Newsday*, 22 February 1998, sec. B, p. 10.

In *The Ghosts of Medgar Evers*, "Morris delivers a keening lament for the blood-soaked soil of Mississippi, some humorous if naive observations about how movies are made and an apologia for an unquestionably well-intentioned film whose failure should have been as predictable to its makers as Medgar's murder was to him.... But what the author misses in marrying the stories of Medgar Evers, the murder case and the movie is that they were mutually exclusive to begin with. Evers' life wasn't about his own murder. Neither was it about a murder case. And the movie business isn't about noble purposes. It's about stars, drama and happy endings."

1274 Campbell, Julia. "Picks & Pans: Pages." *People Weekly* 49 (23 February 1998), p. 40.

The film *Ghosts of Mississippi* "wasn't a blockbuster, and Morris's somewhat cluttered account helps explain why. But most affecting is the author's sensitive rendering of the vivid human landscape of his Mississippi Delta homeland, a place still very much haunted by the ghost of Medgar Evers."

1275 Duke, Dan. "Mississippi Meets Hollywood in Morris' Irony-Filled Chronicle." *(Norfolk) Virginian-Pilot*, 9 March 1998, sec. E, p. 5.

In the first section of his book, Morris narrates the story of assassin Byron De La Beckwith, who in 1964 "escaped justice through two mistrials" for shooting civil rights leader Medgar Evers but was finally convicted thirty years later. The book's second part details the filming of *Ghosts of Mississippi*, a motion picture that "chronicles the struggle to bring Beckwith to justice. Only Morris could have written 'The Ghosts of Medgar Evers.'... He is the guide, the voice of his state, the interpreter, but never the apologist.... The interplay between Mississippi and Hollywood, and between the past and present, fills Morris' book with irony, incongruity and humor."

1276 Carr, Jay. "Following 'Ghosts' to Hollywood." *Boston Globe*, 13 March 1998, sec. F, p. 9.

Morris's "richly textured, compassionate memoir" is a "rueful reminder that it takes more than good intentions to make a successful movie." After *Ghosts of Mississippi* finished production, Medgar Evers's wife, Myrlie Evers, did not wholeheartedly praise it, "partly, she said, because she thought her family would be at the film's center, not the white district attorney who prosecuted the case at some personal cost." In addition, the movie "was attacked for putting a white man at the center of a story about the death of a black hero.... Gentlemanly to the end, Morris decries in civilized fashion the political correctness he feels stood in the way of the film getting a fair shake." Although he is "amusing in his innocent-abroad contrasting of Mississippi and Hollywood, his evocation of Mississippi is what leaves the most indelible impression. That, and his reminder of the abiding struggle attached to blacks and whites trying to live there together."

1277 Hinckley, David. "Pale 'Ghosts.'" *(New York) Daily News*, 15 March 1998, "Sunday Extra" section, p. 26.

Despite the many decades Morris has spent "ruminating on the troubled soul of his native state," even he "cannot find sturdy or enduring truth" in the making of the motion picture *Ghosts of Mississippi*. Nevertheless, Morris has written a book about it, though the volume's "richness grows exponentially when Morris drives past the movie and on his own confronts the movie's subject, the 1963 murder of civil rights leader Medgar Evers." In the process he travels back to the beloved Delta of his boyhood, "where he was surrounded by the seeds and fruit of the mistrust and hatred that made Evers' death inevitable. While Morris limits these trips to snapshots, they are nonetheless so much more vivid and emotionally arresting than anything from the movie." Because the film was a commercial disaster, Morris was left with these "passing snapshots of a real story and extensive videotape of a footnote. He weaves them together with charm, grace and style. But backstage anecdotes about celebrities ... do not provide the infrastructure for the book Morris presumably had hoped to write."

1278 Rosengarten, Theodore. "A Death in Mississippi." *New York Times Book Review*, 15 March 1998, p. 32.

A lengthy, evenhanded review. Rosengarten summarizes the lives of white supremacist Byron De La Beckwith and civil rights activist Medgar Evers, whom Beckwith shot and killed in June 1963. The title character of Morris's *The Ghosts of Medgar Evers* "is indeed a ghost, more shadow than substance," for the hero of the book is Bobby DeLaughter, the white attorney who managed to convict Beckwith in 1994 after two previous trials thirty years earlier ended in hung juries. He is also the hero of *Ghosts of Mississippi*, a major motion picture based on the murder case and third trial. Morris's story "tells what happened when Hollywood came to Mississippi" to make that movie. The reviewer believes that had the production not "flopped at the box office," *The Ghosts of Medgar Evers* "would have been a different book. Morris might not have felt compelled to write nearly 300 pages in defense of the film. He might have developed some of the fertile themes that get smothered in a futile legal brief." Rosengarten praises the author as "a living icon of Mississippi's phenomenal literary tradition. At his best when he is making an allegory of his life and using the external world as a stage for his inner drama, Morris seems to abandon his craft by the end of the book. The last 25 pages consist of critical reviews and fan letters laid out like a scrapbook. We can overlook the occasional passages of purple prose that flirt with the 'implacable' Faulkner vocabulary,... but it is more difficult to pardon Morris for taking us down the road of sour grapes." See also items 1283 and 1285.

1279 Chappell, David L. "Through the Looking Glass." *(Raleigh, N.C.) News & Observer*, 22 March 1998, sec. G, p. 4.

Willie Morris, "a master story-teller from Mississippi with a distinguished record in journalism, has written an engaging book" about the history behind the movie *Ghosts of Mississippi*. He "describes with admirable thoroughness and insight" the "storm of controversy" over the motion picture, and he "makes clear how truth and fiction, past and present, have gotten all tangled up in our hyper-mediated society."

1280 Nordan, Lewis. "Triumphant Tribute: Good Intentions of 'Ghosts of Mississippi' Moviemakers Make a Better Book Than Film." *Pittsburgh Post-Gazette*, 22 March 1998, sec. G, p. 8.

Although the movie *Ghosts of Mississippi* was

"apparently a labor of love by its makers" who worked hard to ensure historical accuracy, it lost money and "was far from an unqualified success." *The Ghosts of Medgar Evers* is "a chronicle of the hazards, pitfalls and surprises involved in making 'a meaningful, dramatic, nondocumentary movie based on authentic and recent history.' But the book ends up being far, far more than such a description is able to convey." Nordan finds the story of the murder and trial "riveting," for "Morris writes with such brilliance and elegance of the facts themselves." Nordan admits, however, that "there are places in the book where less would have been more. Do I really care what the full menu for the movie set was on any given day, for example?" Nordan, a creative writing professor at the University of Pittsburgh and native Mississippian, sprinkles anecdotes about Evers and Byron De La Beckwith throughout his review.

1281 Core, George. "Murder, Movemaking in Mississippi." *Washington Times*, 5 April 1998, sec. B, p. 7.

In this "engaging book," Morris not only revisits the vicious murder of the famed civil rights worker, but he returns to "many of the subjects that have attracted him over his long career as a writer — Mississippi, William Faulkner, racism and integration, North and South. The best parts of this memoir involve these subjects that Mr. Morris has explored from various angles for over 30 years. The author is not so skillful in dealing with Hollywood." He could have explored Evers's death and the three trials of his murderer "in greater detail than he allows himself here. Instead he has given precedence to the movie about the series of events involving Evers' death, its background and the third trial and conviction — after a delay of 30 years— of a wretched little man." Core, editor of the *Sewanee Review* since 1973, writes that Morris is a "considerable stylist despite sometimes overwriting as though he had swallowed the collected works of William Faulkner or, more often, lapsing into the bad habits of journalism, as when he writes of 'the unmitigatingly tragic, memory-obsessed Mississippi earth' and 'the fashionable boulevards of popular tinsel dreamland.'"

1282 Jenkins, McKay. "On Death and on Film in Mississippi." *(Newark, N. J.) Star-Ledger*, 14 May 1998, p. 6.

While there are flaws in the "curious and fascinating" *Ghosts of Medgar Evers*, "such as frequently empty behind-the-scenes glimpses at the way the film [*Ghosts of Mississippi*] was put together, the book also contains some poignant details: James Woods, playing De La Beckwith, learning to mimic the creepy facial tics of his character; Beckwith's little grandson, Byron VIII, referring to some in the courtroom as 'sorry Jews'; Evers's daughter Reena, cast as a jury member, weeping as Alec Baldwin, playing prosecutor Bobby DeLaughter, gives his closing argument. As a lens through which to take another look at a state and a history that continue to intrigue this country, Morris's book offers a worthy read."

1283 Review. *The New York Times Book Review*, 31 May 1998, p. 26.

The Ghosts of Medgar Evers appears in a briefly annotated listing titled "Vacation Reading." The selected books were chosen from volumes "reviewed since the Holiday Books issue of December 1997" and are "meant to suggest some of the high points in this year's fiction, poetry, nonfiction, mysteries and science fiction." See also items 1278 and 1285.

1284 Fraiser, Jim. "Morris Again Shows Masterful Way with Words." *Yazoo Herald*, 25 July 1998, p. 4.

A sympathetic review of Morris's "uniquely lyrical and poignant" book that appeared in his hometown newspaper. "It is Morris' way with words that sets this and all of his books apart from the pack.... Even when Morris gets hung up delineating the minutiae of moviemaking,... he quickly returns to his singular talent for poetic observation with such comparisons as 'the unmitigatingly tragic memory-obsessed Mississippi earth on the one hand, the fashionable boulevards of popular tinsel dreamland on the other.'" Fraiser does fault Morris, however, for "his bias, in favor of friends and against political enemies, within the context of a non-fiction story," as it "lessens his effectiveness." For instance, his "praise" of a local newspaper columnist and his "unremitting vilification of Republican Gov. Kirk Fordice, regardless of how justified in a limited context, detract the reader from the heart of his otherwise noteworthy story of race and redemption in Mississippi."

1285 Review. *New York Times Book Review*, 6 December 1998, p. 80.

The Ghosts of Medgar Evers is among the *New York Times Book Review*'s "Notable Books of 1998." The volumes in the briefly annotated bibliography were "selected from books reviewed since the Holiday Books issue of December 1997." The list is "meant to suggest some of the high points in this year's fiction, poetry, nonfiction, children's books, mysteries and science fiction." See also items 1278 and 1283.

- *My Cat Spit McGee*. New York: Random House, 1999 (item 60).

1286 Hooper, Brad. Review. *Booklist* 95 (August 1999), p. 1983.

Morris "follows his 1995 boy-and-his-dog memoir, *My Dog Skip*, with an equally moving account of the cat he owned in adulthood, who traveled under the name Spit McGee.... Like the previous book about his dog, this one is particularly poignant without being maudlin. You've read pet books before but never one as meaningfully or even beautifully written as this one and its predecessor."

1287 "Nonfiction." *Kirkus Reviews* 67 (15 September 1999), pp. 1482–83.

Willie Morris, "an inveterate dog lover," is dismayed when his fiancée tells him she wants a cat. Her son gives her an abandoned kitten, who bears a son, the central character of the author's book. "Through a series of linked cat tales, Morris tries to get a grip on why he became a menial to this cat and in the course of his attempt draws a deeply affectionate picture of the evolution of their friendship." The book is a "tender, melodious tribute," and the stories in it "flash with humor."

1288 Williams, Wilda. "Science & Technology." *Library Journal* 124 (1 October 1999), p. 125.

A "slim, sentimental memoir" that is "made poignant by Morris's death.... Despite the flowery, overwrought prose, cat lovers and even dog owners who think they hate cats will enjoy this."

1289 "Forecasts." *Publishers Weekly* 246 (11 October 1999), p. 64.

"Morris named his cat Spit McGee after a mischievous, resourceful boy" in his children's book *Good Old Boy*. "A quirky iconoclast, Spit will win the hearts of both cat lovers and those who are cat-neutral, in this enjoyable sequel" to the author's *My Dog Skip*. "With self-deprecating humor and Southern charm, he charts his metamorphosis from ailurophobe to 'valet, butler, and menial' of Spit...."

1290 Steelman, Ben. "Final Novel Is Plea for Tolerance (Even for Cats)." *(Wilmington, N.C.) Sunday Star-News*, 31 October 1999, sec. D, p. 4.

Although a few of Morris's fans of *My Dog Skip* confronted him and "angrily" asked how he could possibly have a cat, "His salute to the estimable Spit McGee is mostly a jovial, light plea for interspecies tolerance. There's nothing deep here, but the book makes a graceful exit for a considerable literary talent."

1291 Stephenson, Anne. "New & Notable." *(Phoenix) Arizona Republic*, 31 October 1999, sec. E, p. 12.

Although Morris was "a confirmed dog man most of his life," in his later years he loved cats, particularly one he named Spit McGee. "Do you have to love cats to love this book? We'll be honest with you — it helps. A little Spit McGee goes a long way." After quoting a few lines from the book, Stephenson opines that Morris's dogs Skip and Pete "are probably spinning in their graves." This review was also published in the *Milwaukee Journal Sentinel* of 7 November 1999.

1292 Butler, Wanda. "Books About the South." *Southern Living* 34 (November 1999), p. 124.

"The reader is treated to a warm, humorous, and sometimes reluctant personal look at a good ol' Southern boy who grew up with a substantial feline phobia. But then, after falling in love with his future wife, referred to often as 'Cat Woman,' Morris begins a tortured conversion to catdom."

1293 Reynolds, Susan Salter. "Discoveries." *Los Angeles Times Book Review*, 7 November 1999, p. 15.

"I admit that you have to be willing to throw yourself into a Norman Rockwell-Mayberry frame of mind to really appreciate Willie Morris. The world he describes in 'My Cat Spit McGee' is about as far from where I'm sitting in downtown L.A. as Jupiter.... Morris puts the brakes on daily life, and I have to say it is soothing."

1294 Yardley, Jonathan. "Small Tale: Learning to Love Cats." *Washington Post*, 17 November 1999, sec. C, p. 2.

Speculates that Morris's *My Cat Spit McGee* is probably "the last of his intensely personal works," though "all of Morris's work was intensely personal, as he was, throughout his three-plus decades as editor and writer, wholly in the grip of autobiography." The book is a "sequel of sorts" to *My Dog Skip*, and "like its predecessor, it teeters at the edge of the maudlin — a pitfall into which Southern writers with a gift for lush prose are wont to tumble — but it is also, like its predecessor, funny and endearing. It is the testament of a man who grew up hating cats and learned to love them, and as such is sure to touch a responsive chord in other people — their numbers surely are legion — who have had similar experiences."

1295 Winecoff, Charles. "Nonfiction." *Entertainment Weekly*, no. 514 (26 November 1999), p. 86.

A brief review of a "remarkably engaging sequel" to *My Dog Skip*, in which "Morris poignantly captures the deep, elusive kinship between man and kitty." Review grade: A-.

1296 Green, Ranny. "Meet Spunky Spit McGee, Who Converts Passionate Dog Man into a Feline Fan." *Seattle Times*, 5 December 1999, sec. H, p. 8.

My Cat Spit McGee is an "engaging new sequel" to *My Dog Skip*. Green recounts several episodes in which the author saves his cat's life. "With Morris and Spit, you cross many other emotional intersections on this free-spirited ride, where the author delightfully channels energy into charisma. A trusting faith, infused with spirit and confidence, surfaces time and again between the pair."

1297 O'Brien, Joan. "If You Can't Roller Skate in a Buffalo Herd, Try 'Dancing with Cats.'" *Salt Lake Tribune*, 9 January 2000, sec. D, p. 8.

Reviews eight books on animals and pets, the first being *My Cat Spit McGee*. Morris "writes elegantly of his newfound affection for cats. He dwells lovingly on cats' eccentricities, their resourcefulness, and how they are shaped by their jungle origin."

1298 C[raig], D[avid] C[obb]. "Book of the Week." *People Weekly* 53 (24 January 2000), p. 45.

An "astonishing love story" and "surely one of the most engaging cat books ever written. With lithe artistry and heaps of humorous Dixie detail, Morris chronicles his conversion from die-hard 'dog man' ... to a blubbering middle-aged mass of affection seduced by a newborn kitten with one blue eye and one yellow eye."

1299 Fierman, Daniel. Review. *Entertainment Weekly*, no. 576 (5 January 2001), p. 65.

A notice of the paperback publication. Chronic dog lover Morris "realizes there's room in his life for one eccentric cat with mismatched eyes."

1300 Howard, Jennifer. "New in Paperback." *Washington Post Book World*, 7 January 2001, p. 10.

A brief review of the Vintage paperback edition. Morris "discovers, after a lifetime of cat-hating, the joys of feline companionship."

1301 Flaherty, Dolores, and Roger Flaherty. "Ailurophobe Turns into Ailurophile." *Chicago Sun-Times*, 21 January 2001, sec. D, p. 14.

A review of the paperback edition. Traces Morris's "conversion from cat hater, or ailurophobe, to cat lover, or ailurophile." His "tribute to Spit, though less substantial than his earlier volume honoring Skip, is nonetheless a charming book, filled with the down-home humor and warmth that characterized much of his writing."

• *My Mississippi*. Photographs by David Rae Morris. Jackson: University Press of Mississippi, 2000 (item 61).

1302 Hooper, Brad. Review. *Booklist* 97 (1 September 2000), p. 5.

Despite the many years Willie Morris lived away from Mississippi, "it was a place that always remained in his heart." This posthumously published book, "written in his characteristically limpid, lyrical prose, offers a heartfelt appreciation of his home state." The volume "is not a defensive recitation of Mississippi's virtues nor is it a whitewash of its less-than-attractive features." Morris speaks of the physical beauty of the region, "then, with both pride and understanding, he brings into sharp focus Mississippi's peculiar tensions and ambivalence and also its passions." His son, a professional photographer, contributes photographs that "informally capture ordinary moments in the lives of Mississippians.... Together, the text and the photographs showcase Mississippians doing what they do best — being themselves completely without artifice."

1303 Arana, Marie. "Photography." *Washington Post Book World*, 10 September 2000, p. 10.

Arana, editor of *Book World*, includes *My Mississippi* in her "Fall Forecast" of "titles that stand out in the great stampede of upcoming publication" and which "I await with great anticipation."

1304 Lucas, Sherry. "'My Mississippi.'" *Clarion-Ledger*, 10 November 2000, sec. E, pp. 1–2.

A lengthy commentary that includes remarks by Morris's widow, JoAnne Prichard Morris; his son, David Rae Morris; and his publisher, Seetha Srinivasan. "The father's four-part essay explores the land, its people, the paradox and promise of the state and the creative spirit. The son's full-color photographic narrative, 'Look Away,' provides a striking complement. Portions of each echo with the state's proud accomplishments, its shameful shortcomings, its treasured eccentricities and teasing ironies. Brightening each is a sure, sometimes sly storyteller's hand."

1305 Smith, Andrew Brodie. "Social Sciences." *Library Journal* 125 (15 November 2000), p. 87.

Morris's *My Mississippi* is a "tribute to his home state, which he feels has been much maligned and misunderstood. In a four-part essay, the author addresses one of Mississippi's central paradoxes: the state finds itself at the bottom of all rankings in terms of social, educational, and human services but near the top at producing people of creativity and imagination." In this "balanced portrait," he applauds the state's numerous contributions in the arts and technology, while denouncing its storied history of racism. The photo essay by Morris's son, David Rae Morris, "does not so much illustrate as complement the text."

1306 O'Briant, Don. "Morrises' Mississippi: Collaboration Showcases Dad's Son's Love for State." *Atlanta Journal-Constitution*, 3 December 2000, sec. M, p. 2.

Published in collaboration with Morris's photographer son, David Rae Morris, *My Mississippi* is a "tribute to the people and places that the author of 'North Toward Home' knew so well. Through words and photographs, the book expresses how the state has changed and gives a glimpse of what Mississippi is like as it enters the 21st century." In Willie Morris's introduction he "describes the 'snarled confluence of the past and present.'" David Rae Morris writes of his photographs that "I have tried to strike a careful balance between the history and tragedy of Mississippi and the beauty and magic of the land and the people."

1307 Kemp, John R. "Mississippi Yearning: A World According to Willie and Son David Rae Morris." *(New Orleans) Times-Picayune*, 10 December 2000, sec. D, p. 6.

A lengthy, perceptive commentary on the narrative and photographs of *My Mississippi*. Kemp states that in spite of Willie Morris's "long love affair" with his native state, the author does not fail to recognize Mississippi's flaws, such as its legendary racism. "Willie's engagingly written, impressively researched 103-page text gives readers a thorough, passionate view of Mississippi today. He explores the land and people, and the dark ironies and tragic contradictions that have plagued the state for generations. David Rae's 96 superb color photographs give a sensitive glimpse of ordinary Mississippians going about their lives. Each part tells a story of human connection to place and history." While the elder Morris's introduction "speaks to the intellect," his son's photographs "demand emotional response" and "stare you in the face."

1308 Smith, Tammy M. "Morris and Son Send Love Letter to 'My Mississippi.'" *(Biloxi, Miss.) Sun Herald*, 16 December 2000, sec. B, p. 1.

Willie Morris's essays look "at the land itself, a sense of place, the paradox of our way of life here, the creative spirit of Mississippians and what makes residents of the Magnolia State so unique." David Rae Morris's color photographs "evoke images of the Mississippi that Mississippians know and cherish," such as "the decorative pageantry of the Confederate Pageant at the springtime Natchez Pilgrimage."

1309 Lampton, Lucius. "*My Mississippi*: A Must-Have Morris Meditation." *Magnolia (Miss.) Gazette*, 28 December 2000, sec. A, pp. 1, 4.

An eight-by-ten-inch photograph of Willie and Davie Rae Morris dominates the entire front page of this issue of Pike County's *Magnolia Gazette.* Willie Morris surveys "every aspect of Mississippi imaginable: its contrasting regions, paradoxical history, diverse peoples, creative spirits, fluctuating economy, and promising future." His son's "varied photographs celebrate Mississippi's ordinary scenes in an extraordinary way. The everyday subject matter may disappoint some, but the artist accomplishes his goal by providing a glimpse of the real Mississippi at the end of the twentieth century." In his review, *Gazette* editor Lampton singles out references in the book — both textual and pictorial — to Pike County. He also records several errors that "slipped through" during the editing process, which Morris, had he lived to polish his text, "would have caught." An adaptation of this review appeared as: "The Physician's Bookshelf." *Journal of the Mississippi State Medical Association* 42 (March 2001), pp. 72, 74, 76.

1310 Buchholz, Brad. "Mississippi Yearning." *Austin American-Statesman*, 7 January 2001, sec. K, p. 6.

A probing, analytical review of a volume that is "more scholarly, less lyrical" than Morris's other books. Although *My Mississippi* "is not his best" work, it is nevertheless "rewarding and insightful — though mostly for what it reveals about Morris, not Mississippi. Beyond that, there's a compelling generational drama at play within the pages, as father and son use different narrative techniques to 'portray' modern Mississippi in the context of race and economics, family and faith, art and landscape.... Traveling together, working independently, father and son frequently convey similar messages through different media. Yet there are times when one storyteller accentuates a vision that the other relegates to background."

- *Taps: A Novel.* Boston: Houghton Mifflin Co., 2001 (item 62).

1311 "Fiction." *Kirkus Reviews* 69 (15 February 2001), p. 209.

This "lush, lazy tale of growing up in Mississippi during the Korean War" centers on sixteen-year-old trumpet player Swayze Barksdale of Fisk's Landing, who plays "Taps" at the military funerals of local youths killed overseas. "Each ceremony calls up a world of memory, and the dead men's stories are laced through a larger storyline" involving Swayze and his friends. As more servicemen return home in coffins to be buried, "the boy's understanding of the world broadens." Like some of Morris's other works, *Taps* "contains many fondly elegiac passages and dozens of charming descriptions of small-town life, but it lacks a substantiating depth that might have truly conveyed Swayze's metamorphosis. Instead, it reads very much like the recapitulations of a mature adult amused to find there was a time when he didn't know so much."

1312 Hooper, Brad. "Adult Fiction." *Booklist* 97 (15 February 2001), pp. 1084–85.

Refers to the author's books as "gritty but poignant," with the posthumously published *Taps* being a "summary statement of Morris' fondness for the Mississippi where he came of age, and as such, the novel reads like a memoir of childhood and youth.... Plotlines are kept to a minimum; this is a novel of characters rather than story, and what delicious, real, and beautifully conceived characters they are."

1313 Arana, Marie. Review. *Washington Post Book World*, 25 February 2001, p. 4.

Taps is included in *Book World*'s "Spring Preview," an annotated listing of "titles we are meant to fall in love with."

1314 "Fiction." *Publishers Weekly* 248 (26 February 2001), p. 55.

Declares that Morris's now-dead literary voice "resonated with a particular Southern grace and eloquence. This posthumous novel, by turns poignant, funny, heartwarming and suspenseful, is worthy of comparison" to the author's "classic" *North Toward Home*. "Illuminating the rich interior lives of the inhabitants of a Southern backwater, this tale of young love, intrigue, jealousy, treachery and violence is a deeply affecting swan song by one of America's most beloved writers.... It plays a fitting 'Taps' for a literary genius cut down in his prime." A starred review.

1315 Klise, James. "Day Is Done, Gone the Sun: Willie Morris' Last Novel Plays 'Slow and Proud.'" *Chicago Sun-Times*, 1 April 2001, sec. D, p. 10.

This "autobiographical novel" is set in Fisk's Landing, the "fictional stand-in" for Morris's hometown, Yazoo City, Mississippi. The author "paints a complex, warts-and-all portrait of a town he loved during a very specific time in our history." His prose is "lyrical and lush in the Southern tradition. And how could it not be, when Morris is describing his feelings for people so close to his heart?"

1316 Paddock, Polly. "A Graceful Parting Gift from Willie Morris." *Milwaukee Journal Sentinel*, 4 April 2001, sec. E, p. 2.

A Knight Ridder syndicated review. *Taps* takes place during the Korean War in the small Mississippi Delta town of Fisk's Landing, which is "clearly modeled after Morris' hometown of Yazoo City." The novel's sixteen-year-old main character, Swayze Barksdale, plays trumpet in his high school band, and when the first local soldier is killed early in the conflict and returned for burial, a World War II veteran enlists him to play "Taps" at his funeral. As the graveside services multiply, the young man begins to learn "more than he ever imagined — about the fragility of life, the heart's capacity for both wonder and suffering, and what it means to be a man. 'The sense one makes of the past often derives from small, evanescent moments, seldom the grand designs,' Swayze muses, looking back from the vantage point of middle age. 'Taps' is filled with such small moments — some hilarious, some heartbreaking, some simply the ordinary stuff of daily life. Morris' writing is as graceful and evocative as ever, summoning up a time, a place and a mind set with breathtaking assurance."

1317 Conrads, David. "Portrayal of Small-Town Life Travels Familiar Ground." *Christian Science Monitor*, 5 April 2001, p. 21.

Pans *Taps* as a "tepid, coming-of-age story" burdened with a "singular lack of drama" and "two-dimensional characters." Morris's works of nonfiction "are consistently thought-provoking and readable. Yet, somehow, these skills are largely absent in Morris's fiction, which may explain why he wrote only a few novels in his productive career. Set in the small Mississippi Delta town of Fisk's Landing in the 1950s, 'Taps' covers a year in the life of 16-year-old Swayze Barksdale, the only son of a widowed mother. The story meanders through a long series of incidents in Swayze's life and the life of the town, few of them of any real consequence."

1318 Bell, Bill. "And So, Goodbye, My Bittersweet Youth: A Late Author's Moving Requiem for His Past." *(New York) Daily News*, 8 April 2001, p. 20.

Taps is a "song of the South, rich with grace notes and total, nostalgic recall of the small moments that add up to something large and defining." After teenager Swayze Barksdale is called upon to play "Taps" on his trumpet for hometown soldiers killed in Korea, "The funerals become the measure of the boy's maturing and introduce a marvelously varied cast of characters, starting with his mother, who teaches tap-dancing. They also include his moody high-school buddy, his first love, the town bully, a profane coach, a racist landowner, a half-dozen veterans and the town undertaker...." *Taps* is not "simply a series of character studies." It is "also the stories of a half-dozen overlapping families unable to tame their passions and natures.... This is a coming-of-age story lyrically and lushly described, with moments of knee-slapping humor, perceptive insight and painful stabs to a young man's heart."

1319 Pearson, Michael. "'Taps' Provides Fitting Epitaph for a Soulful Southern Voice." *Atlanta Journal-Constitution*, 8 April 2001, sec. C, p. 3.

Taps is Morris's "best book, a story written with genuine passion and soulful understanding. It is an old-fashioned Dickensian sort of novel, but with a Southern accent, filled with main characters one is compelled to love and hate and minor characters one is unable to forget." The story, narrated by central figure Swayze Barksdale and "written as a funny and poignant backward glance at young love, depicts an evolving understanding of all the heartbreaking beauty and sadness and unearned terror the world can offer." The characters in *Taps* "are truly and memorably drawn," and although "at times Morris' style may seem ornate or antique to some, ... it is the sound of wind rustling through magnolia leaves, plaintive and lovely." Pearson's review also appeared as: "Fiction." *BookPage: America's Book Review*, April 2001, p. 4.

1320 Sayers, Valerie. "Southern Requiem." *Washington Post Book World*, 8 April 2001, p. 15.

In Morris's *Taps*, "as in so much of his writing, he attempts to capture a slow-moving, formal, gracious, brutal, funny, guilt-inducing culture with prose that might be described with all the same adjectives." The novel's sixteen-year-old narrator, Swayze Barksdale, plays "Taps" at the funerals of local servicemen killed in Korea. "The deaths he now marks on his trumpet connect him to a wider world, and a wider sense of the ways men are expected to comport themselves in love and war and small-town America. The plot of *Taps* takes its time unfolding, but Morris's evocation of time and place are worth the slow buildup of tensions." Although the novel contains "lyrical passages," the author's "excessive impulses" also appear, particularly in the overwritten descriptions of the "intensifying intimacy" between Swayze and Georgia, his girlfriend. However, "The prose is less orotund in describing the second-hand effects of war on Swayze and his neighbors." Morris's novel "does not break literary ground, but it is engaging and its hero is often endearing."

1321 Patterson, J. C. "Morris' Novel Unexpected Privilege." *Clarion-Ledger*, 15 April 2001, sec. G, p. 4.

Quotations from an interview with JoAnne Prichard Morris, the author's widow, are interspersed throughout this review. Morris's "lush and literary farewell novel" is "much more than a coming of age tale. 'It brings together the land and its effects on people and races,' said Prichard Morris.... Told with warmth, respect and a keen eye for his surroundings, Willie Morris' 'baby' will echo for generations to come."

1322 Minzesheimer, Bob. "'Taps' Plays Lyrical Farewell to Morris: Novel Hits Flourishes of Greatness." *USA Today*, 19 April 2001, sec D, p. 4.

Taps is "not a great novel, but there are flashes of greatness." The book is "about growing up lonely, about finding and losing love, about learning about 'flawed people and all their dark inheritance.' It's at its best describing the supporting characters and a sense of time and place: the pre-civil-rights South when blacks and whites 'were consumed by the unrelenting land....' The writing is leisurely, a series of long, flowing, ornate sentences.... Morris loved words, and some of them sent me to my dictionary: 'meretricious' and 'peregrinating' and 'suzerainty.' A bigger problem is that the novel didn't start clicking for 100 pages, a long warm-up for a sense of impending doom and a sharp, violent end."

1323 Brown, Scott. "Fiction." *Entertainment Weekly*, no. 592 (20 April 2001), p. 66.

A one-paragraph review. *Taps* is about Willie Morris and his "coming to grips with the twin burdens of memory and mortality, which together seem to have awakened in him more operatic verbosity than insight." The "sex scenes" involving the central character "resemble something akin to a chat-room encounter between Danielle Steele and Faulkner." Review grade: C+.

1324 Carter, Ron. "Willie Morris' Last: Glow Tints Tale of Young Love." *Richmond (Va.) Times-Dispatch*, 22 April 2001, sec. F, p. 4.

The military funerals at which the novel's protagonist, Swayze Barksdale, plays "Taps" on his trumpet "anchor a sequence of vividly realized scenes that at first seem random but that coalesce into a story of young love and heartbreak, of long-standing feuds and the violence they beget, and of a somewhat improbable bond between two couples—Swayze and his longtime sweetheart, and Luke Cartwright, a World War II veteran, and his lover, the unhappily married Amanda Godbold." Although Morris occasionally engages in "rhetorical excess," *Taps* has a "sad beauty" that "readers jaded by the dissonance and complexity of contemporary life will find appealing."

1325 Core, George. "Last Book Written by the Southern Author Who Gave Us 'My Dog Skip.'" *Washington Times*, 22 April 2001, sec. B, pp. 8, 7.

Although Willie Morris "always wrote exceptionally well," he occasionally overwrote. In *Taps*, however, "from beginning to end, the prose is near-perfect, as is the tone, clear as the heart-wrenching tune for which the novel is named.... The author not only presents the story of a boy's coming of age through the measured and moving memories of Swayze, but he shows the reader the impact of the war on a small town in the Mississippi Delta, Fisk's Landing (which is modeled on Yazoo City, Miss.) as it loses a disproportionate number of soldiers from its National Guard unit." Core, editor of the *Sewanee Review*, contends that while the characters "may at first glance seem flat and predictable" and appear stereotypical (for example, the strict but softhearted coach, the heartless plantation owner, the stern but compassionate librarian), "many take on a surprising complexity and humanity. In 'Taps,' the author has painted an enduring portrait of small-town Southern life—or life in any small American community—in the early 1950s."

1326 Eder, Richard. "Southern Elegy." *New York Times Book Review*, 22 April 2001, p. 23.

The most notable features of *Taps* are the "backgrounds," such as the "long summer evenings with children playing out late." Morris "essays a great sweep of a book, taking in the processes of history, the specifics of a region and a community and the ache of adolescence.... The past is more real than anything that follows. Funerals are its talismans and 'Taps' is at its strongest when it describes them." Eder believes that the "most successful" of the book's characters is the town's undertaker. "Otherwise, though, Morris's writing fails to match his ambition. The principal figures are set down in large explanatory details that struggle unsuccessfully to take shape as portraits.... Morris's passion to convey the South's character and its past is evident and at times moving, but for much of the time, 'Taps' is a lush plod."

1327 Kuhlken, Ken. "'Taps' for a Great Writer: Willie Morris' Gemlike Last Work Is Powered by His Love for Life's Beauty." *San Diego Union-Tribune*, 22 April 2001, "Books" section, p. 8.

The narrator and protagonist of *Taps*, Swayze Barksdale, "attempts to reach manhood alive and un-maimed by the forces that threaten him: the near-mad hysteria of his widowed mother, a tap-dance instructor; a culture plagued by racism and defined by class privilege; the Korean War he might soon be called to fight, from which hardly anybody seems to return whole; and most treacherous of all, the perils of young love." The core of Morris's novel "lies in the narrator's exploration of beauty. Swayze sees beauty in the earth with its woodland hills, ponds and rivers, in the courage and resilience of men, and in women's tender strength." Morris, who died in August 1999, packs a "lifetime of wisdom" into *Taps*, and his "passion for life and a fervor to expose its depths are clear on every page."

1328 Levins, Harry. "Morris Goes Out with a Bang in 'Taps.'" *St. Louis Post-Dispatch*, 22 April 2001, sec. F, p. 8.

Taps is "a coming-of-age story set in Morris' Mississippi Delta in the Korean War years. And surely, it's the novel Morris would have wanted to go out on. It is, by turn, funny, sentimental, overwritten, warm, overwrought and insightful. The word 'bittersweet' seems to fit best.... When Morris was good — oh Lord, he was really good. His plot gets less and less humorous and more and more dark as 'Taps' moves toward a sad and violent climax that you can smell coming from a long way off. Even so, his final chapter ... is just wonderful. It's philosophical, and poignant, and it makes you wonder whether Morris smelled his own death coming, even as he wrote."

1329 Martin, Philip. "Posthumous Novel Plays Elegant *Taps* for a Writing Life." *(Little Rock) Arkansas Democrat-Gazette*, 22 April 2001, sec. H, p. 4.

Taps is "obviously a product of great worry and care." Morris "was always a memoirist, and *Taps* seems like yet another chapter in his own story...." The book's "descriptive passages are sweetly evocative without ever tipping over into the kind of maudlin overkill to which Morris was occasionally susceptible.... But the chief pleasure of *Taps*— as with any of Morris' work — is his beautiful, melancholy way with language, a kind of minor-key wistfulness that sings and sighs and elicits ineffable sad yet sweet feelings."

1330 Swindle, Michael. "Southern Voices— Morris Makes the Old New Again." *(Memphis) Commercial Appeal*, 22 April 2001, sec. G, p. 1.

Taps takes place during the Korean War, and "the story is recounted by 16-year-old Swayze Barksdale, who lives in the small Delta town of Fisk's Landing, fictional stand-ins for Morris and Yazoo City, respectively." A trumpet player in his high school band, he is asked to play "Taps" at the graveside services of hometown servicemen killed in Korea. "While the military funerals are the central event in Swayze's coming of age story, Morris, as one would expect, paints a full and vivid and moving picture of what it was like to be 16 in the Delta in the 1950s, when 'the resolution of all the world's ennui did indeed lie in 'riding around,' main street to country club, boulevard to cemetery, flatland to hills, then all over again, the rubric and imprimatur of the generation.... This is pure quadruple-distilled Willie Morris, speaking through his fictional alter-ego. For if Morris did one thing, he remembered. And in his past, he found treasure beyond knowing." *Taps* is a "quite magical thing."

1331 Buchholz, Brad. "The Last Goodbye: Forever Melancholy, the Late Willie Morris Plays the Saddest and Most Elegant Notes in His Farewell Novel, 'Taps.'" *Austin American-Statesman*, 24 April 2001, sec. E, p. 1.

Buchholz incorporates insights from Morris's widow, JoAnne Prichard Morris, into his extensive assessment of *Taps*. The prose of the novel "is breathtaking and beautiful, making us wonder what might have been had its author pursued fiction all along. Morris takes great care to let us feel 'rain as shy as tears' and the 'fusty twilights.' We come to know the muggy, buggy beauty of a Mississippi summer.... Most of all: There is sorrow. A delicate sorrow. There is more sorrow within these pages than in anything else Willie Morris ever wrote." Buchholz observes that Morris first wrote about many of his novel's images and characters' experiences in *North Toward Home* and that "'Taps' rivals 'North Toward Home' in its lyricism and poignance." According to JoAnne Prichard Morris, "In some ways, I think Willie revealed more of himself in fiction — even though he made a lifelong career out of writing very personal nonfiction."

1332 Kellman, Steven G. "Trumpeter Swan Song." *Texas Observer*, 27 April 2001, pp. 20–21.

An insightful review, written by an academician well versed in the author's writings and career. "*Taps* is a fitting valediction to a man whose work deserves to echo. Its title refers not only to the tattoo that teenage Swayze, whose widowed mother happens to teach tap dancing, plays in memoriam to his fallen townsmen. It also recalls the lesson that an adolescent learns about the place of death in human life." Morris "writes in gorgeously redolent sentences that seem to grow directly out of the lush Delta landscape they evoke. Sometimes, as when he describes the ecstasy of first sex ('the glowing, pillowy rapture of joy'), Morris's prose is colored purple, but it never lacks the same awe over the power and pathos of words that Swayze, listening to the funereal weeping as to 'the murmur of mourning doves at dusk, or the breathless flow of water in a summer's stream,' brings to the music he releases from his trumpet."

1333 Mitchell, H. Gregory. "Coming of Age in the South: Lessons of Life Begin with Death." *(Fredericksburg, Va.) Free Lance-Star*, 29 April 2001, sec. F, p. 6.

Taps is a "powerful, compelling novel" and "classic Willie Morris, full of both the mischief for which he is so widely known and his ambivalent reverence for the South. It is a moving and unforgettable coming-of-age story set in the Mississippi Delta country of Morris' youth. More, it is an examination of the American South — warts and all — and its profound, enduring effect upon all who live here."

1334 Nugent, Phil. "Last Call: Willie Morris' Posthumously Published 'Taps' Recalls One Writer's Shaky Beginnings." *(New Orleans) Times-Picayune*, 6 May 2001, sec. D, pp. 6–7.

Taps is "part fool's errand, part labor of love. The love isn't undeserved; 'Taps' isn't terrible," but "it doesn't feel very necessary" and "it never flirts with greatness." The novel is set in Fisk's Landing, a small Mississippi Delta town, in 1951. Swayze, the sixteen-year-old narrator of the story, is "caught between childhood emotions and adolescent experience." Local youths are going off to fight in Korea, and when some of them return home in coffins, he is "pressed into service," playing "Taps" on his trumpet at their funerals. "It's easy to believe that Morris began writing this book before he really found his voice; the strongest passages feel like pure, uncut memory, but they're pressed into a clumsy fictional framework. Morris is at his most relaxed describing the women in Swayze's life. These creatures— the brazen young Georgia and the sweeter yet more distant, tragedy-tinged Amanda — are bewildering to him, yet he pays them rapt attention, enjoying the show and hoping to get a clue."

1335 Fuson, Ken. "'Taps' Has Finality, But Color It Celebratory." *Seattle Times*, 21 May 2001, sec. D, p. 5.

Like young Willie himself, teenager Swayze Barksdale is called upon to play "Taps" at the funerals of local soldiers killed in Korea. "Swayze, his trumpet-playing partner, Arch, and his girlfriend, Georgia, are coming of age in a town that remains mired in the losses and longings of the past and the morbidity of the present. Swayze's feelings for Georgia — he knew her forever, loved her, hurt her, left her and eventually made his peace with her — mirrors Morris' conflicted feelings for the South." Fans of the author's work "will recognize his familiar themes, shared with good humor, about love, growing up and the South's peculiar ability to exhibit mercy and cruelty simultaneously." Morris spent many years, off and on, working on *Taps*. "He once said he put everything he knew into it, and his obvious ambition to create something grand and lasting occasionally overwhelms the narrative." Although *Taps* is not the literary masterpiece he hoped it would be, "There's joy to be cherished in watching a master take his best shot."

1336 Park, Mary Jane. "A Last Bugle Call." *St. Petersburg Times*, 27 May 2001, sec. D, p. 5.

"Morris' mastery of the language is vast enough to send even the erudite to their dictionaries, his word pictures so clear that you may recapture your own longings, your own rapturous days, your own sweet, sad mysteries.... Fisk's Landing in the 1950s is the setting for friendship, romance, suspense and violence in a rich, moving narrative on which Morris worked for years." The "spinner of golden stories" died in August 1999, and *Taps* is "a sorrowful reminder of just how extraordinary a writer he was."

1337 McLeese, Don. "Review & Opinion." *Book: The Magazine for the Reading Life*, no. 16 (May/June 2001), p. 73.

Taps is "a fitting elegy for Morris. The author, a renowned memoirist, has written a novel that, like so much of his writing, is a tribute to the author's Mississippi homeland.... Morris's new novel brings his career full circle, and the plot mainly provides pegs on which the author can hang his descriptive raptures and down-home philosophies."

1338 Whitehead, Julie L. "Southern Scrapbook." *Mississippi Magazine* 19 (May/June 2001), pp. 10, 13.

Morris's novel is "often both hilarious and profound. Set in fictitious Fisk's Landing during the Korean conflict, *Taps* is a book about Mississippi and how it shapes those growing up in its small towns." The author's "characters are all very human," and with the exception of the few villains in the book, the reader will empathize with them. "'Willie had great empathy and sympathy for all people,' JoAnne Prichard Morris said. 'He truly saw good in everybody.'"

1339 Young, Dianne. "Books About the South." *Southern Living* 36 (June 2001), p. 46.

"No one has ever been better than this author at writing from the heart. In *Taps*, the late Willie Morris takes a scene from his own Mississippi Delta boyhood and spins around it an engaging and thoughtful novel set in the fictional town of Fisk's Landing.... As always, Willie Morris's language rings with poetry and meaning...."

1340 Gibson, Sharan. "Morris' Posthumous Novel Flawed but Welcome." *Houston Chronicle*, 3 June 2001, "Zest" section, p. 18.

Morris worked on *Taps* throughout his long literary career, but it "lacks the cohesiveness of his more polished books. The story works itself out in slow, leisurely stretches and ends abruptly with the death and funeral of a rather key character." The "real beauty of this story in which people 'play seven-card stud with God' is the flatland itself with its violent extremes, its tumultuous elements and its selective memory. It is a land whose 'Negroes' attend 'High School Number Two' and study hand-me-down textbooks from the white school.... It is a landscape of unpainted establishments covered with chewing-tobacco and soft-drink advertisements...." *Taps* is "a sad book, sad because we must acknowledge the loss of a mid-century innocence...."

1341 Price, Naomi Kaufman. "Fiction." *(Portland) Oregonian*, 3 June 2001, sec. F, p. 8.

The narrative of *Taps* "doesn't so much move forward as meander.... The characters are real enough, in their way, but it is almost as if they are too close to Morris, who indeed blew taps at Korean War funerals. He creates too much emotional distance between them and the reader, and they become too much like caricatures: Georgia, who is Swayze's slightly rebellious girlfriend; the goof-off Arch, who has little use for small-town conventions; Luke, the moral and immoral hero...." Although *Taps* should have been edited "into a cleaner read," the book "is, unarguably, Willie Morris, and we're poorer without him."

1342 Woolley, Bryan. "Safe in Sleep: Willie Morris' Last Novel a Solemn Tale of Life, Death." *Dallas Morning News*, 10 June 2001, sec. C, p. 8.

Morris "always refers to Jackson as 'the capital city" and Vicksburg, recognizable to any reader who has been there, as 'our big river town.' This unnecessary and useless device always rings false, especially in dialogue. So does Mr. Morris' clunky attempt to tell of soldiers' experiences in Korea through their letters home. But these are tiny flaws in a novel that's simultaneously warm and terrifying, sentimental and tough, funny and heartbreaking."

1343 "Editors' Choice 2001." *Booklist* 98 (1 & 15 January 2002), p. 762.

The Adult Books editors of *Booklist* included *Taps* among their "Top of the List" books for 2001, the titles that are "representative of the year's outstanding books for public-library collections." *Taps*, by the "gritty, feisty, and eloquent" Morris, "reads like a summary statement of his fondness for his native state."

1344 Core, George. "Comedy with a Southern Accent." *Virginia Quarterly Review* 78 (Winter 2002), pp. 178–88.

A review essay of *Taps* and three other novels that all take place in southern towns. *Taps* includes some of Willie Morris's "finest prose and shows few, if any, signs of the habit of overwriting in which he occasionally indulged himself." Morris is "more nearly a memoirist, a keeper of memory, than a novelist; and *Taps* is beautifully recounted as a sustained act of memory in the lyrical and elegiac mode that Morris enacts through the character and voice of Swayze Barksdale." Morris does, however "know his business" as a writer of fiction. "His use of the playing of Taps as the controlling image of the action is but one artfully deployed technique. And Morris ... uses the veterans of the world wars as choral figures to comment upon the Korean War as it grinds on and takes its grisly toll on the small town of Fisk's Landing (Yazoo City)."

1345 C[ore], G[eorge]. "Current Books in Review." *Sewanee Review* 110 (Summer 2002), p. lxviii.

"At his best Morris writes beautifully, and in this novel he does not indulge in his worst vice—overwriting."

- *Shifting Interludes: Selected Essays.* Edited by Jack Bales. Jackson: University Press of Mississippi, 2002 (item 63).

1346 Hood, Orley. "'Interludes' Offers More Wonders from Willie." *Clarion-Ledger*, 3 November 2002, sec. F, p. 1.

A warm reminiscence of Morris as well as a review of a "sweet volume" of "Willie's greatest hits." In this book of essays "there is the serious—Willie's monumental argument against censorship of the *Daily Texan*—and the hilarious—the tale from his Rhodes Scholar days of trying to drive a car named 'John Foster Dulles' from Oxford to Paris—and the sublime—his ode to his dead grandmother, Mamie. Bales ... played bartender with *Shifting Interludes*, mixing many ingredients from Willie's remarkable life into a cocktail of charm and humor and occasional outrage, balancing the spring of youth with the autumn of age, giving even novices a firm foundation into the distinctive Morris idiom."

1347 Stauffer, Todd. "Meeting Willie." *Jackson Free Press: The City's News and Culture Magazine*, 1 (21 November 2002), p. 21.

Morris's *Shifting Interludes* includes magazine essays and newspaper articles that "round out a picture of this man. Here you can read Morris as the early Daily Texan firebrand, the young adult prognosticator in New York, the middle-aged, intense observer and 'exiled' artist, and the slightly-more-middle-aged narrative historian, back home for good.... After reading 'Shifting Interludes' I feel, in a small way, that I've finally met Willie Morris. The relevance and power of Morris' essays—on politics and Christian fundamentalism, race and culture, baseball and death—remind me that we call him a great writer because he has something resonant and different and universal to say the moment you pick up and start reading."

1348 Hammett, Chad. "Shifting into Reverse." *Texas Books in Review* 22 (Fall/Winter 2002), p. 9.

A mixed review. Hammett recounts how he "first encountered Willie Morris' writing" on a trip to New York City. He was contemplating visiting the author during his return trip to Texas when he heard on his car radio that Morris had died. Since then, Hammett's relationship with the writer's works "has been somewhat personal," which is why he "regretfully" has to declare that readers already familiar with Morris's books and articles need only to browse through *Shifting Interludes*. "Though editor Jack Bales deserves credit for tracking down the heretofore unpublished (or unpublished in book form) Morris essays and, though he at times strikes gold with his discoveries, much of the material in *Shifting Interludes* has been expanded upon and previously published in some form.... The essays that do manage to stand out in *Shifting Interludes* are the ones that show us the Willie Morris we didn't know: a Willie Morris, who, in 'Mitch and the Infield Fly Rule,' lusts heartily after a southern belle Ole Miss coed and uses her intelligence to stand gender roles on their ears.... But these essays come too few and far between. For the most part, the book reads like a medley or a 'Greatest Hits' collection of a favorite musician."

1349 Lampton, Lucius. "Shifting Interludes: More Essays from Willie Morris." *Magnolia (Miss.) Gazette*, 2 January 2003, sec. A, p. 2.

Praises Morris's "ambitious prose" and recalls that the author "loved forceful language and the beauty of the written word. *Shifting Interludes* is full of that great talent which long ago spilled its heart to us, comforting Mississippians like a warm morning cup of coffee." The essays in this "varied anthology" are all "worthy of Morris, and reveal much not only about his thinking, but also about his development as a writer." Lampton's "one and only complaint" is that Bales should have included each essay's "date and source of original publication either at its beginning or end" instead of listing all the works on one page. "But, don't let this complaint slow you down. The dust jacket photo of Morris is worth having the book, and Morris's essays are Mississippi songs to sing you to sleep."

1350 Park, Mary Jane. "Traveling with Boomer 'Girls' Through Past and Present." *St. Petersburg Times*, 26 January 2003, sec. D, p. 5.

A brief notice of publication. "This anthology includes work from Willie Morris' 40-year career as writer and editor...."

1351 Spikes, Michael B. Review. *Arkansas Review: A Journal of Delta Studies* 34 (April 2003), pp. 49–50.

Spikes not only reviews this "important new collection" of Willie Morris's writings, but he also provides his own interpretation of the author's works. Spikes affirms that "Morris is a personal essayist" and that he "infuses his prose with the sort of heartfelt emotion, verbal panache, and attention to place and the personal details of people's lives that is reminiscent of the autobiographical fiction of a fellow Southerner of an earlier generation, Thomas Wolfe, a writer Morris admires and cites several times." After the reviewer quotes from "Here Lies My Heart," an essay that particularly "captures the artistry and sensitivity pervading the collection as a whole," he concludes that the volume is "vintage Morris. These are the sorts of intense, poignant, deeply personal insights that the reader is treated to throughout *Shifting Interludes*."

Biographical and Critical Entries from Reference Works

1352 "Morris, Willie." In *Current Biography Yearbook, 1976*, edited by Charles Moritz. New York: H. W. Wilson Co., 1977, pp. 271–74.

A lengthy biographical and critical essay published in a well-known library reference set. Raised in the Deep South, Morris "brings to his work the complex sensibility of a man who has fought his way through the prejudices on which he was reared, and whose liberalism is informed by a long historical memory." In his writing, he has been "intolerant of any form of parochialism and, like all enlightened Southerners, has used his regionalism as a vantage point from which to survey the larger issues affecting American society." Includes bibliographic references.

1353 Hobson, Fred. "Willie Morris (1934–)." In *Southern Writers: A Biographical Dictionary*, edited by Robert Bain, Joseph M. Flora, and Louis D. Rubin Jr. Baton Rouge: Louisiana State University Press, 1979, p. 322.

A brief biographical sketch. "As editor-in-chief of *Harper's* from 1967 to 1971, [Morris] particularly cultivated southern writers of promise and published sensitive treatments of southern life during a period of crisis and change." His book *North Toward Home* "is in the broad tradition of southern self-examination, yet is a far more personal and autobiographical account than most works in this tradition." Includes primary bibliography.

1354 "Morris, Willie." In *The World Almanac Book of Who*, edited by Hana Umlauf Lane. New York: World Almanac Publications; Englewood Cliffs, N. J.: Prentice-Hall, 1980, p. 53.

A brief paragraph about the "U.S. editor, novelist, nonfiction writer."

1355 Bobbitt, Joan. "Willie Morris." In *Dictionary of Literary Biography Yearbook, 1980*, edited by Karen L. Rood, Jean W. Ross, and Richard Ziegfeld. Detroit: Gale Research Co., 1981, pp. 270–76.

An excellent illustrated overview of Morris's life and works, providing in-depth commentary on *North Toward Home*, *Yazoo*, *Good Old Boy*, *The Last of the Southern Girls*, and *James Jones*. Includes primary and secondary bibliographies. "Willie Morris, journalist, essayist, novelist, is a writer whose life and work are inseparable. Not only is most of Morris's writing about himself, but it is also about how his experience reflects a larger regional and national experience."

1356 Richardson, Thomas J. "Morris, Willie: 1934– ." In *Lives of Mississippi Authors, 1817–1967*, edited by James B. Lloyd. Jackson: University Press of Mississippi, 1981, pp. 344–46.

A perceptive essay that discusses Morris's works in context with his life and Mississippi heritage. His relationship to his hometown, Yazoo City, "and to the rest of Mississippi and the South, is deep and complex, perhaps as ambivalent as the town's location. Throughout his career, Morris has been attracted to Yazoo's sense of place, its values of community, neighborliness, and friendship, and, like Mark Twain, much of his best writing gains significance and meaning through the power of memory — a memory which draws upon the attractiveness of the small town he knew as a boy." Although his "critical sophistication and spiritual distancing from Yazoo City" are easily noticed in his writings, "He continues to treasure the values of the old community—friendship, caring, a general sense of decency, kindness, [and] personal integrity...."

1357 Paneth, Donald. "Morris, Willie (1934–)." In *The Encyclopedia of American Journalism*. New York: Facts on File Publications, 1983, p. 304.

A one-paragraph sketch emphasizing Morris's editorial careers with the *Texas Observer* and *Harper's Magazine*. "On each occasion, he produced a probing, provocative periodical."

1358 "Morris, Willie 1934– ." In *Contemporary Authors: A Bio-Bibliographical Guide to Current Writers in Fiction, General Nonfiction, Poetry, Journalism, Drama, Motion Pictures, Television, and Other Fields*, edited by Linda Metzger. New Revision Series, vol. 13. Detroit: Gale Research Co., 1984, pp. 378–79.

Primary and secondary bibliographies accompany an extensive vita of Morris's life and literary career. The "Sidelights" analytical essay includes quotations from published criticism. "In all of his books, Willie Morris writes of the American South, presenting its people, traditions, and problems through his own experiences."

1359 "Morris, Willie." In *World Authors, 1975–1980*, edited by Vineta Colby. New York: H. W. Wilson Co., 1985, pp. 535–37.

A biographical/critical essay with bibliographies listing works both by and about the "American journalist, memoirist, and novelist."

1360 Taft, William H. "Morris, Willie (1934–)." In *Encyclopedia of Twentieth-Century Journalists*. New York: Garland Publishing, 1986, pp. 239–40.

A brief essay that focuses on Morris's editorship of the *Daily Texan* at the University of Texas and of *Harper's Magazine*. It contains a few errors: Morris left the University of Mississippi in 1991, not 1981, and his books do not include *The Ghosts of Ole Miss and Other Essays*.

1361 Moss, William. "Morris, Willie." In *Encyclopedia of Southern Culture*, edited by Charles Reagan Wilson and William Ferris. Chapel Hill: University of North Carolina Press, 1989, p. 967.

A biographical sketch with brief bibliography. "Willie Morris, Mississippi-born journalist, editor, essayist, and novelist, continues the long-standing tradition of the southern man of letters as explainer of the South to the rest of the nation, to itself, and to himself. Seeing the South as 'the nation writ large,' he has probed the complexities of the region and of the country."

1362 Ward, Martha E., Dorothy A. Marquardt, Nancy Dolan, and Dawn Eaton. "Morris, Willie 1934– ." In *Authors of Books for Young People*. 3d ed. Metuchen, N.J.: Scarecrow Press, 1990, p. 511.

A short paragraph of biography. "For young people [Morris] wrote *Good Old Boy*."

1363 "Morris, Willie." In *The Writers Directory, 1992–1994*. 10th ed. Chicago: St. James Press, 1991, p. 698.

A concise vita of Morris, author of "novels/short stories" and "social commentary."

1364 Amende, Coral. "Morris, Willie (1934–)." In *Legends in Their Own Time*. New York: Prentice Hall General Reference, 1994, p. 170.

A very brief entry in a biographical dictionary covering some ten thousand well-known living and deceased people. Morris's occupation is listed as "Am. editor/novelist/nonfiction writer."

1365 Raper, Julius Rowan. "Willie Morris (1934–)." In *Contemporary Poets, Dramatists, Essayists, and Novelists of the South: A Bio-Bibliographical Sourcebook*, edited by Robert Bain and Joseph M. Flora. Westport, Conn.: Greenwood Press, 1994, pp. 377–87.

A superb scholarly essay, divided into sections titled Biography, Major Themes, Survey of Criticism, and Bibliography (organized into Works by Willie Morris, Interviews with Willie Morris, and Studies of Willie Morris). Raper affirms that Morris's "major contribution has been to make available to contemporary American journalism the considerable resources of the Southern 'literature of memory'—themes and techniques developed by early Modernist novelists Thomas Wolfe and William Faulkner and later Modernist novelists Ralph Ellison and William Styron.... With Faulkner and especially with Ellison, Morris shares the soul-wrenching conviction that both the South and America must find a way to reconcile racial diversity with brotherhood. Like these masters, Morris knows that the best Southern writing dramatizes the individual heart in conflict with itself, a struggle often centered on the conflict between the challenge of change and the demands of memory—between the present and the past."

1366 Shirley, Aleda, Susan M. Glisson, and Ann J. Abadie. "Willie Morris (1934–)." In *Mississippi Writers Directory and Literary Guide*. University, Miss.: The Center for the Study of Southern Culture, University of Mississippi, 1995, pp. 32–33.

A short entry, with photograph, in an "alphabetized list of writers who live in Mississippi now. We have included an address where the writer can be contacted, his or her publications, and major awards."

1367 "Willie Morris, 1934– ." In *American Decades, 1960–1969*, edited by Richard Layman. Detroit: Gale Research, 1995, pp. 366–67.

Morris appears with other "Headline Makers" in the "Media" section of a volume devoted to "this decade of promise and protest." Although the article outlines the author's entire career, it principally covers his years with *Harper's Magazine*. Includes a brief list of sources. An excerpt from *North Toward Home*, titled "Magazine Life," appears on page 353.

1368 Applegate, Edd. "Willie Morris (1934–)." In *Literary Journalism: A Biographical Dictionary of Writers and Editors*. Westport, Conn.: Greenwood Press, 1996, pp. 183–87.

An essay on "journalist, editor, and novelist Willie Morris" with commentary on his books. Includes listings of primary and secondary works.

1369 "Morris, Willie." In *Who's Who in America, 1999*. 53d ed. Vol. 2. New Providence, N.J.: Marquis Who's Who, 1998, p. 3157.

A brief vita of this "author, editor."

1370 Bales, Jack. "Morris, Willie." In *Encyclopedia of American Literature*, edited by Steven R. Serafin. New York: Continuum Publishing Co., 1999, pp. 784–85.

A summary of Morris's career and bibliography of critical sources.

1371 Bear, Perry. "Morris, Willie." In *Contemporary Southern Writers*, edited by Roger Matuz. Detroit: St. James Press, 1999, pp. 270–72.

A vita, a listing of Morris's works organized by genre, and a critical essay. "Willie Morris draws upon personal experience to evoke local color and to connect significant events in his native Mississippi with larger issues in contemporary America. Whether recalling boyhood mischief-making..., or examining race relations from his experiences with desegregation and violence, or exploring more general topics, Morris' observations are infused with his Southern sensibility and, therefore, celebrate the region's culture and history."

1371a Hamilton, Stacey. "Morris, Willie." In *American National Biography, Supplement 1*, edited by Paul Betz and Mark C. Carnes. New York: Oxford University Press, 2002, pp. 432–34.

A biographical and critical article covering the life and major literary works of a "master storyteller and essayist." Morris "wrote eloquently about the complex struggle that most southerners face: how to celebrate their heritage without forgetting the sins and horrors of the past. He spoke of a 'certain burden of memory and a burden of history' that most 'sensitive southerners' feel. Having spent much of his life trying to distance himself from the world of his southern upbringing, he found himself ultimately drawn back to the place."

1372 Perkins, George, and Barbara Perkins. "Morris, Willie (1934–1999)." In *HarperCollins Reader's Encyclopedia of American Literature*, edited by George Perkins, Barbara Perkins, and Phillip Leininger. 2d ed. New York: HarperResource, 2002, p. 701.

A paragraph of biography and commentary on "novelist, essayist" Morris. "The South was his perennial subject. In his autobiography, *North Toward Home* (1967), Morris uses his own life history to cast light on the history of his native region as it was impacted by the social and political changes of the post–World War II period."

1373 "Willie Morris (1934–1999)." In *The Chronology of American Literature: America's Literary Achievements from the Colonial Era to Modern Times*, edited by Daniel S. Burt. Boston: Houghton Mifflin Co., 2004, p. 569.

A year-by-year record of America's literary history selects *North Toward Home* for its "Modernism and Postmodernism, 1950–1999" section. "Morris's autobiography is an ambitious attempt to link his personal history with American experience from the 1940s through the 1960s."

Magazine and Journal Articles

1374 "Youth for *Harper's*." *Time* 89 (19 May 1967), p. 56.

John Fischer has resigned as editor-in-chief of *Harper's Magazine* so he can "indulge his preference" for writing. Willie Morris, who "has long breathed the breezes of freewheeling dissent," will replace him as editor. Joining the thirty-two-year-old Morris will be David Halberstam, age thirty-three; Larry L. King, thirty-eight; and Robert Kotlowitz, forty-two. "'These additions,' said Fischer, 'will give *Harper's* the best-balanced — and youngest — editorial staff in its 117 years.'"

1375 "A Spur for Harper's." *Newsweek* 69 (22 May 1967), pp. 68, 71.

Recounts Morris's "scathing attacks" as editor of the University of Texas's *Daily Texan* and how he "dug his spurs into graft-hungry politicians" while writing for the *Texas Observer*. Adds that "last week, in a move that will keep the spurs to the status quo, the 32-year-old native of Yazoo City, Miss.," was appointed editor-in-chief of *Harper's Magazine*. "But while Harper's once catered to the tastes of genteel literati, in recent years it has become decidedly middle-brow. Already, Morris has hired Pulitzer Prize–winner David Halberstam, late of The New York Times, to make a three-month trip to Vietnam for a progress report, and Larry L. King, a Texan with a Mencken touch, to take up residence in Washington."

1376 Fischer, John. "The Editor's Easy Chair: Announcing Some Changes." *Harper's Magazine* 235 (July 1967), pp. 24, 26–27.

Fischer, who has been editor-in-chief of *Harper's Magazine* for fourteen years, informs his readers that he is going to resign his position so he can return to writing, his "addictive habit." Morris, presently executive editor, will become editor-in-chief on July 1. "From the day he joined the staff in 1963 he was a confident and resourceful editor, ready to carry his full share of responsibility." Fischer summarizes the careers of Morris and those of Robert Kotlowitz, David Halberstam, and Larry L. King, three other newly hired staff members. He also outlines the "audience and purpose" of the magazine.

1377 Smith, Roger H. "Authors & Editors: Willie Morris." *Publishers' Weekly* 192 (9 October 1967), pp. 21–22.

An interview with Morris upon the publication of *North Toward Home*, "one of the most talked-about nonfiction books" of the year. "'For a long time, I worked on this material in fictional form,' Mr. Morris told *PW* in an interview the other day. 'Then I decided: Why not tell it like it really was?'" Although Morris did not answer when asked if Mississippi is now "a better or a worse place than it was" during his youth, he did remark that "more recently, there has been recognition that racial sickness is a national thing; it belongs to us all. The South, at its best, could lead the country out of this social madness." Morris's "basic concerns these days" center around *Harper's Magazine*, which he has edited since July 1. Republished in *The Author Speaks: Selected "PW" Interviews, 1967–1976*, by *Publishers Weekly* editors and contributors. New York: R. R. Bowker, 1977, pp. 314–15. Republished in *Conversations with Willie Morris* (item 1946).

1378 DeCell, Harriet C. "Where Is Home for Willie Morris?" *Delta Review* 5 (October 1968), pp. 54–55, 61.

A teacher at Yazoo City High School relates how "conversation crisscrossed the town" when Morris, accompanied by a few of his colleagues from *Harper's*, came back to his hometown as a speaker for National Library Week. "'He's bringing somebody named William Styron, who's writing a book about a slave uprising.' ... 'Good grief, why?'"

1379 Whittington, Mary Jayne Garrard. "Willie Morris." *Delta Review* 5 (October 1968), pp. 53–54, 60.

Morris is interviewed about *Harper's Magazine*, writing, and his memoir. When asked why he chose *North Toward Home* as a title, since he clearly "deplores" New York City, he replies: "Certainly I don't feel alienated from the South, far from it; the feelings are very complicated, but the older I am the more it means to me, the closer the ties.... The title was chosen in a way for its irony." Some "purists" point out the book's "inaccuracies" and consequently do not think it should be called an autobiography. "Of this dispute on semantics the author says, 'It's true the Mississippi section of the book is more an evocation of a time, a place, and its people; reflections on a composite picture of what it was like at home, the good and bad that's always a part of a person, or a place.'" Republished in *Conversations with Willie Morris* (item 1948).

1380 Mitchell, Paul. "*North Toward Home*: The Quest for an Intellectual Home." *Notes on Mississippi Writers* 2 (1970), pp. 105–109.

Mitchell perceives Morris's travels from Mississippi to Texas to New York in *North Toward Home* to be the author's "search for a challenging, compatible intellectual climate.... Willie Morris' emphasis on various modes of travel — bus, old car, train, and airplane — also points toward the quest motif which serves as the artistic center of and gives meaningful unity to *North Toward Home*." In the "Mississippi" section of the book, Morris delineates "the intellectual and social pall of his hometown" and begins his "quest for an intellectually lively home" by enrolling in the University of Texas. "Texas," the book's second part, is both the memoir's "physical and spiritual center" as Morris wanders "physically and intellectually in this section in search of his full identity." He reaches "the final stage of his quest" in the third part of *North Toward Home*, "New York," when he joins the staff of *Harper's Magazine*. "The intellectual quester had outgrown his previous surroundings of total intellectual dearth in Mississippi and newly jubilant intellectual discovery in Texas to assume his detached position in New York City as the social and literary critic who created *North Toward Home*."

1381 "South Toward Home." *Time* 95 (1 June 1970), p. 77.

A profile of Morris upon the publication of "Yazoo ... Notes on Survival" in the 120th anniversary issue of *Harper's Magazine* (item 731). The 22-page article that describes how his hometown of Yazoo City, Mississippi, responded to court-ordered integration is "thoughtful, deeply personal and brutally honest." As editor of *Harper's*, "Morris acts more as a filter than an originator of ideas, but his greatest strength is in understanding, in [David] Halberstam's words, 'writers' prerogatives, what they feel, what they are, what is important to them.' Often what is most important to them is to be given the freedom to write in the length and style they want to."

1382 Shalleck, Jamie. "Remaking It Since McLuhan." *Print* 24 (July/August 1970), pp. 30–35.

Shalleck interviews Ralph Graves, the managing editor of *Life* magazine, and Morris, the editor-in-chief of *Harper's*, as she compares the two periodicals and examines their editorial policies. Morris "answered each question tentatively, pausing as long as a minute to think.... 'Editing a magazine is like politics, a hit-or-miss affair.

Hindsight is always clearest. But a magazine does have to have a vision and stand for something, for better or worse. It is, of course, a reflection of its editor — what he feels in his heart and guts. I am obsessed with the fact that Harper's must embody the best in the American experience. This is my only working principle.'" Shalleck is the editor of And/Or Press.

1383 Nobile, Philip. "Willie Morris and Harper's." *National Catholic Reporter* 7 (22 January 1971), p. 14.

An interview with and a profile of Morris, emphasizing his editorship of *Harper's*. Some of the controversial articles in the magazine, avers Nobile, are "mighty dumb but parts are marvelously restorative." As editor, "Morris has performed exceedingly well," particularly for publishing Norman Mailer's excellent pieces. "Also under Morris' tutelage, a talented corps of contributing editors have leavened Harper's content with a constant stream of lively intelligent prose. The magazine has peaked. It is in top form." Some people, however, "devoutly" despise Morris and *Harper's*, perhaps for "the seeming ingenuousness. You can take Willie Morris out of Yazoo but not the reverse."

1384 "The Coup at Harper's." *Newsweek* 77 (15 March 1971), p. 64.

Reports that Morris, "in a move that caught the entire communications industry by surprise, bitterly submitted his resignation as Harper's editor in chief." Although he certainly helped "revitalize a literary magazine that had grown stodgy, predictable and tediously middle-brow" by bringing in new writers, his success failed to increase either circulation figures or advertising revenue. Morris declared that "it boiled down to the money men against the literary men. And, as always, the money men won." However, according to publisher William S. Blair, *Harper's* "money man," finances were only part of the problem, as he disagreed with Morris over his editorial policies as well.

1385 "Hang-Up at *Harper's*." *Time* 97 (15 March 1971), p. 41.

Discloses that a "showdown" between *Harper's* editor Morris and publisher William S. Blair led to Morris's resignation last week, which was "quickly accepted." At a business meeting two weeks ago, Morris read a 21-page memo by Blair, "most of it critical of the magazine's editorial performance. Blair's attack was based largely on economics, but some of the discussion went farther. 'Who are you editing this magazine for?' asked someone sharply. 'A bunch of hippies?'"

1386 "Morris Quits at Harper's; Cites 'Severe Disagreements.'" *Publishers' Weekly* 199 (15 March 1971), p. 51.

Willie Morris, editor-in-chief of *Harper's Magazine*, "resigned suddenly March 4 in what he described as a dispute with management over editorial direction." In a public statement, "He cited 'severe disagreements with the business management.'" Morris also mentioned Norman Mailer's controversial article, "The Prisoner of Sex," published in the March issue, as figuring in the dispute, saying that it "has deepely [sic] disturbed the magazine's owners." *Harper's* publisher William Blair "expressed surprise at the move and denied Mr. Morris's claims."

1387 Kitman, Marvin. "On Selling Out." *Antioch Review* 31 (Spring 1971), pp. 79–96.

Morris and assorted "members of the literary and other establishments" respond to the question: "Why did you (or did you not) sell out?" Morris answers: "I have sold out, not once but many times. People in Mississippi believe I sold out to Texas radicals. The Texas radicals argue I sold out to Lyndon [Johnson].... The hate mail I have received more or less steadily since the age of 19 might suggest to the scholar and sociologist Professor Kitman that I have sold out more often and more bodily to more pernicious influences, counter-currents, revolutions, and urban contaminations than any American since Andrew Johnson."

1388 "After the Fall." *Newsweek* 77 (22 March 1971), p. 69.

Relates that following Morris's resignation from *Harper's* as editor-in-chief, the publication's "remaining editors" met with its business managers to discuss the future of the magazine. The two groups, however, "had very different ideas about the direction in which Harper's should go." At a meeting between *Harper's* board chairman John Cowles Jr. and the editors, Cowles read from a prepared statement. He said that although the magazine was an "artistic success," it was "a circulation disappointment" and that it "cannot live only on favorable press notices and dinner-party conversation." After Cowles told them that *Harper's* publisher William Blair, "whom several of the editors regard as the man who undermined Willie Morris's position during the past two years," would choose the new editor-in-chief, Morris's former colleagues resigned and "stormed out of the room."

1389 "The Walkout Continues." *Time* 97 (22 March 1971), p. 51.

Reports that after Morris resigned from *Harper's Magazine,* six of the contributing editors decided to quit as well "after a frequently bitter and fruitless confrontation with *Harper's* Chairman John Cowles Jr." At the beginning of the meeting, Cowles read a statement that addressed the owners' "dissatisfaction" with the periodical. "While the magazine was losing money over the past few years, he said, *Harper's* nevertheless 'dramatically increased' Morris' editorial and promotional budgets, hoping to gain in newsstand sales and subscription renewal rates. Neither hope was fulfilled." The editors had hoped that Cowles would permit them to "keep *Harper's* as it is" and allow them to "play a major role in the choice of a new editor," but they were "frustrated on both counts."

1390 Little, Stuart. "What Happened at 'Harper's.'" *Saturday Review* 54 (10 April 1971), pp. 43–47, 56.

A comprehensive article on the events leading to Morris's and his colleagues' resignations from *Harper's Magazine.* The dispute between Morris and "management" was not "so simple" as Norman Mailer's profanity in his piece on the women's liberation movement in the March 1971 issue, nor was it related to the occasional book-length articles or the salaries paid the various contributors to *Harper's.* "Rather, the trouble sprang from a serious philosophical difference over how to edit an intellectual magazine in today's publishing market — and from a disputed evaluation of the magazine's editorial achievement under Morris. It was the way management seemed to belittle the Morris years, which to many people in publishing produced the 'hottest' magazine in America, that most angered the wounded Morris men — a sense of being misunderstood, misvalued, underappreciated, and undercut." After Little's article appeared, author Norman Mailer wrote a letter to *Saturday Review*:

A Mailer, Norman. "Norman Mailer's Side on 'Harper's.'" *Saturday Review* 54 (12 June 1971), p. 56.

Corrects four errors in a "combination of inaccuracy and unattributed reporting" in Stuart Little's article.

1391 Curtis, Charlotte. "An Adventure in 'The Big Cave.'" *More* 1 (June 1971), pp. 11–13.

Curtis's irreverent essay on what she calls the "Great Harper's Flap" appears in the inaugural issue of the journalism review *More.* "According to the now almost mythologized script, Willie Morris and his talented staff resigned during that fateful week in March because the bright young editor had created the 'hottest' publication in America only to be harassed and ultimately knifed by publisher William S. Blair." The real story, however, reads "more than somewhat different. More accurately, it is an unhappy tale of an almost willful failure to communicate and often astonishing inexperience — of a confused publisher who had never published a national magazine, of a headstrong editor who had never edited one, and, not least, of a well-meaning owner, John Cowles, Jr., who had never owned one." Republished in *Stop the Presses, I Want to Get Off!: Inside Stories of the News Business from the Pages of "More,"* edited by Richard Pollak. New York: Random House, 1975, pp. 243–58.

1392 M[ount], D[ouglas] N. "Authors & Editors: Willie Morris." *Publishers' Weekly* 199 (14 June 1971), pp. 15–16.

A profile of and an interview with Morris. "He does not care to talk about what happened at *Harper's* ('Enough's already been written about that'), or about his future, and when talking to him one often has the impression of a lot of energy with no place to go." He is living on Long Island at work on a novel, "and he says that he has no desire at this time to edit another magazine."

1393 "Filling the Morris Chair." *Newsweek* 77 (28 June 1971), p. 61.

Robert Shnayerson, a former *Time* magazine senior editor, replaces Morris as editor-in-chief of *Harper's.* "While Shnayerson is genuinely impressed by the flashes of brilliance that Harper's displayed under Morris, he is bluntly critical of the way the monthly has been run. 'It became a writer's magazine,' he says matter-of-factly, 'and I often had the feeling that a lot of non-writers never quite got around to reading it. I want a different mixture — one that will hold the present subscribers, attract new readers and still smuggle a little reason into American life.'"

1394 "New Head at *Harper's.*" *Time* 97 (28 June 1971), p. 46.

Harper's chairman John Cowles Jr. and publisher William Blair have selected *Time* senior editor Robert B. Shnayerson to succeed Willie Morris as editor-in-chief. "The future? There will be a shift in the editorial mix: rather than encourage writers to strut their stuff unhindered by editorial pencils, as they tended to do under Morris, Shnayerson will edit more tightly."

1395 Kadushin, Charles. "Who Are the Elite Intellectuals?" *Public Interest*, no. 29 (Fall 1972), pp. 109–125.

Morris is included among "The 70 Most Prestigious Contemporary American Intellectuals (1970)," the results of a study that "attempts to identify and describe the top American intellectuals objectively, with statistics, and to give some indication of their stand on social and political issues." See also item 1603.

1396 "Willie Morris: *The Last of the Southern Girls*." *Library Journal* 98 (1 February 1973), pp. 441–42.

Morris's remarks on how he began *The Last of the Southern Girls* are a part of "First Novelists," edited by Irene Stokvis Land, in which twenty-three new writers of fiction "discuss their first published novels." Morris recalls that after he left *Harper's Magazine* in 1971, "I came here to the tip of Long Island, to a little town by the ocean, feeling very sorrowful. I had given up what I had always wanted professionally. As an act of will, and out of loneliness, I was determined to learn fiction. It was slow and bruising. It drew on another part of the brain. It was the most demanding and at the same time most gratifying, almost *sensually* gratifying, work I had ever done."

1397 Fallows, James. "'Making It' Revisited: Nader, Podhoretz, and Morris." *Washington Monthly* 5 (July/August 1973), pp. 57–64.

Fallows, an editor of *Washington Monthly*, argues that consumer advocate Ralph Nader, *Commentary* editor Norman Podhoretz, Morris, and others who long for celebrity status often place more significance on "making it" (public acclaim) than "doing it" (working at one's profession). For instance, in May 1973 Fallows attended a *Washington Post* luncheon in which Morris and three other writers were asked to discuss their recently published works. But instead of talking about his first novel, *The Last of the Southern Girls*, Morris compared himself to the "Southern Greats": authors William Faulkner, Thomas Wolfe, and William Styron. "The value he appeared to emphasize was no longer his work but his reputation; he seemed more intent on being called a 'great writer' than in writing great literature.... In comparison with his earlier writing, Morris' goal seemed to have changed, from expressing a message to projecting himself, from 'doing it' to 'making it.'"

1398 Moore, Robert H. "The Last Months at *Harper's*: Willie Morris in Conversation." *Mississippi Review* 3, no. 3 (1974), pp. 121–30.

"This exchange occurred while Willie Morris was editor in chief of *Harper's Magazine*, but was withheld from publication in the context of Morris' differences with his publisher which culminated in his resignation in March 1971." Moore's correspondence, now among the Willie Morris papers in the University of Mississippi's Department of Archives and Special Collections, J. D. Williams Library, shows that Moore talked with the author during the summer of 1970 soon after *Harper's* published his "Yazoo ... Notes on Survival" (item 731). Moore's questions produced lively discussions on William Faulkner, *North Toward Home*, the autobiography as a literary form, and Morris's *Harper's* article on school integration. Republished in *Conversations with Willie Morris* (item 1950).

1399 Haden-Guest, Anthony. "Out Here in the Hamptons: Snapshots of the Literary Life." *New York* 8 (1 September 1975), pp. 43–47.

Haden-Guest wonders if the writers who live in New York's Hamptons discuss projects with or seek encouragement from one another. He talks to Morris and some of the other writers to see if a writers' community creates a "Literary Life." Opinions vary and "one just can't generalize." Morris says of James Jones: "'Jim and I are close. We'd be close even if we were truckdrivers.' Pause. 'Sometimes I think we should be truckdrivers.'"

1400 Eastland, Terry. "South Toward Home." *National Review* 28 (28 May 1976), pp. 563–64.

An editorial writer for North Carolina's *Greensboro Daily News* covers Morris's address to the Historical Book Club in Greensboro. Morris admits that he very much likes the South, but when asked why he doesn't return to his native land, he evades the question. "A teasing answer: no answer. In *North Toward Home*, how had Morris put it? There was that terrible burden he felt whenever he returned to places south, and only when departing did he feel any relief." But now Morris seemed "light-hearted and witty; now he was recollecting delightfully and enjoying the pleasure of his audience. And so you mused: maybe the burden has finally been unpacked. But then why does the man *still* keep house up north, up on Long Island?"

1401 Kahn, R. T. "James Jones: A Talk Before the End." *Book Views* 2 (June 1978), pp. 6–7.

Kahn records a conversation between James Jones and Morris in the spring of 1977, just three months before Jones's death. When Jones asks Morris if he, as a writer, has problems with discipline, Morris replies: "I think all writers have a severe problem with discipline. The discipline itself, I think, is almost a symbol for controlling the moods and the emotions and the feelings that a writer has about being a human being, about living. I don't think it's a cliché that writing is a terribly lonely thing, because it means that your best hours of the day you're spending pretty much alone; not just physically alone, not just detached from your fellow creatures, but also alone in the most intense, emotional way."

1402 Bobb, F. Scott. "The Editors of *The Daily Texan*." *Alcalde* 65 (July/August 1978), pp. 28–32.

Willie Morris and other former editors of the *Daily Texan* reminisce about their experiences working on the campus newspaper. In 1956, Morris "increasingly found himself fighting for 'freedom of expression for *The Daily Texan*, in the absolute Jeffersonian sense,' as he says, 'against those forces which would stifle it then as presumably now, or shape it to their own ends.' The fight over censorship of the *Texan*, he says, 'may have been the most basic in the history of college journalism.'" *Alcalde* is the University of Texas alumni magazine.

1403 Cummings, Mary. "*Hampton Life* Interviews Willie Morris." *Hampton Life* 4 (October 1978), pp. 10–11.

Morris shares his views on Bridgehampton, the South, and his writing during an interview with a resident of the Hamptons on Long Island, New York. "I don't like it [writing] when I'm doing it. I like it when it's finished. I can't think of any writers who do really like it. But after a while you have no choice. It's such an expression of your self. Like so many writers I know, I feel I have no choice." Republished in *Conversations with Willie Morris* (item 1955).

1404 O'Grady, Tom. "The Writer's Power: An Interview with William Styron, James Dickey and Willie Morris." *Hampden-Sydney Poetry Review* (Winter 1979), n. pag.

A five-page interview with Styron, Dickey, and Morris at Hampden-Sydney College in Virginia, where in the spring of 1978 the three friends met "for a day of readings and lectures." Magazine editor Tom O'Grady asked if writers had any "political power," and Morris responded: "Writing has its own power, as Mr. Faulkner from my native state of Mississippi always said, the power to survive and endure. I think that is really where the power of great fiction or great poetry resides—in the fact that great writing lasts." Another of O'Grady's questions focused on the effect of writing "on the individual life." Morris told of James Jones's courage in trying to finish his book *Whistle* while dying. "The writers whom I have known, some of the greatest writers in America and of our generation, are people of immense courage because they fight hard to keep the act of the imagination going."

1405 Duffy, Susan. "Paper Tiger." *Texas Monthly* 9 (April 1981), pp. 108, 111–12.

Reports that *Texas Observer* founder and publisher Ronnie Dugger is back in Austin "to resume the helm" of the biweekly. He began the publication in 1954, and "despite the efforts of dedicated writers and interim editors like Larry Goodwyn, Willie Morris, Bill Brammer, and Robert Sherrill, the pace Dugger set for himself was punishing.... As Morris wrote in the tenth anniversary issue: 'For two men each to write some twenty thousand words of presumably literate journalism a week under deadline, read all the copy and galley proofs, hobnob with politicians, and keep up a correspondence means staying up all night two or three nights in succession.'" See also item 707.

1406 Griffith, Thomas. "Cutting Down to Size." *Time* 121 (17 January 1983), p. 45.

Protests *Washington Post* reporter James Conaway's "recent treatment of Willie Morris" (item 1655). After quoting several of Conaway's derogatory comments from his article about the author, Griffith concludes: "It was as if Morris had let the reporter down, this reporter who gives the impression of having come to ingratiate and had stayed to harpoon. The real question is why a paper like the Washington *Post* should publish across two pages, seven full columns in all, a long and wounding hatchet job."

1407 Axthelm, Pete. "The Trophies of Marcus Dupree." *Newsweek* 102 (31 October 1983), p. 93.

Axthelm refers to Morris as he recounts the turbulent athletic career of erstwhile football star Marcus Dupree. Nineteen years after three civil rights workers were murdered in Dupree's hometown, Philadelphia, Mississippi, "Dupree himself had emerged as a symbol of how far Philadelphia had come. He was the star of an integrated team, hero of blacks and whites alike, even the subject of a book, 'The Courting of Marcus Dupree,' by celebrated Mississippi writer Willie Morris."

1408 Watson, Bret. "Having Headed South Toward Home, Willie Morris Brings a New Book North." *Avenue* 8 (December-January 1984), pp. 136–40, 142, 144, 146, 148.

A significant, extensive biographical essay and commentary based on interviews with Morris and his friends. "Morris' editing as much as his writing won him the respect and devotion of many writers" during his editorship of *Harper's Magazine*. His "personal charm had much to do with his success as well. Recalls Bill Moyers, who first met Morris during their student days at the University of Texas: 'When I left *Newsday* on Long Island, I didn't know what I'd do next. Willie said: "Why don't you go out into the country and just listen, and I'll give you the whole magazine." I wrote "Listening to America," which he turned into a little book that became a best-seller. That's one of the things you like about Willie: he has good ideas for you and he feels a sense of mission in finding a way for you to do what you can do.'"

1409 Barra, Allen. "In Search of Marcus Dupree." *Inside Sports* 7 (May 1985), pp. 35–44.

Traces the controversial football career of star athlete Marcus Dupree. Morris, "the world's foremost Dupree scholar," spent two years "observing Marcus and his pursuit by the nation's football powers. The remarkable book that resulted, 'The Court[ing] of Marcus Dupree,' was almost without precedent in American literature.... Aside from bloodless tomes such as James Michener's 'Sports in America,' serious attempts to probe the psychological and sociological meaning of sports in American culture scarcely exist."

1410 Perry, Richard L. "The Front Porch As Stage and Symbol in the Deep South." *Journal of American Culture* 8 (Summer 1985), pp. 13–18.

A passage from chapter 1 of the "Mississippi" section of *North Toward Home* is included in a study of the southern front porch as a symbol of "social identity." In his memoir, "Willie Morris tells of lying near death as an infant" with his parents unable to locate either their family doctor or any white doctor in town. They finally called the local negro doctor, who immediately came and saved the baby's life. Years later, Morris asked his grandmother if the doctor had come in the front door or back door. "'I declare,' she said, pausing to remember.... 'I believe he came around back.'"

1411 Jenks, Tom. "How Writers Live Today." *Esquire* 104 (August 1985), pp. 123, 125–27.

Writers' "expressions of today's life are rightly to be found in their work." Morris and forty other authors "tell the way of their own lives." Morris is asked about the "promise and curse" of New York. "It would be easy to berate the tough intellectual life of New York City. I won't do it. As a writer, I've been abused by New York—who hasn't?—but it gave me much in my comprehension of my country and civilization. New York was a promise when I arrived, a curse when I left."

1412 Johnson, Don. "Willie Morris, Marcus DuPree [sic], and the New South." *Arete: The Journal of Sport Literature* 3 (Fall 1985), pp. 129–35.

Although Morris states in *The Courting of Marcus Dupree* that his book is "a tale about the South," Johnson argues that the volume is more about "Morris's ideal vision of the South" presented from the perspective of a "Southern-born intellectual." Johnson writes that early on in his book, Morris implies that Dupree is a "heroic figure, not merely a sports phenomenon," and because of the young man's ability to unite both blacks and whites, he is "also a redeemer, someone 'sent' to atone for Philadelphia's transgressions." Residents of the town wondered if the community would benefit from Dupree's success. A black minister in Philadelphia remarked to Morris that Mississippi football recruiters should have told Dupree that he could not play football forever and that "he had a responsibility to his people here, that he could do so much for them." Johnson believes that what the minister "had in mind was a genuinely heroic enterprise, one in which the victor ... brought home gifts to his people." Dupree's career suggests that this will not likely happen; moreover, "money is anathema to the heroic venture. But money, as the minister saw, may be at the heart of the new South, and Marcus Du[p]ree, in eschewing the ideal and heroic for financial security might, ironically, be the South's new man. If such is the case, then *The Courting of Marcus Du[p]ree* is not so much a book about the South but a book about what the South was, or what Morris wished it to be."

1413 Lennon, J. Michael. "Glimpses: James Jones, 1921–1977." *Paris Review* 29 (Summer 1987), pp. 205–36.

Interviews with some of writer James Jones's family members and friends "excerpted and arranged from those conducted for 'James Jones: Reveille to Taps,' a ninety-minute television documentary, which was broadcast on PBS in 1985 and 1986." Says Morris: "There was never any doubt in my mind that [Jones] considered the war works to be the supreme part of his creative life. World War II was such an all-consuming event, perhaps the most momentous event in the history of the human race. Millions upon millions of men and women were caught up in it, many destroyed by it, consumed by it, and this small-town boy from Robinson, Illinois, has given us this stunning corpus of work, perhaps the most significant and distinguished corpus of work there is on that catastrophic set of years."

1414 Andrews, William L. "In Search of a Common Identity: The Self and the South in Four Mississippi Autobiographies." *Southern Review*, n.s., 24 (Winter 1988), pp. 47–64.

Compares four autobiographies that "emanate from a common geocultural region," the Mississippi Delta: William Alexander Percy's *Lanterns on the Levee* (1941), Richard Wright's *Black Boy* (1945), Morris's *North Toward Home* (1967), and Anne Moody's *Coming of Age in Mississippi* (1968). Morris and Percy write from their perspectives as white members of economically well-to-do families, while Wright and Moody "record the bitter socialization of the children of those near the bottom class of the South's subordinate caste." But aside from these differences, "One can also see some commonness of purpose between these two generations of autobiographers," for the authors share "experiences, perspectives, and literary motives." However, "Our investigation of the communal identifications of these autobiographers needs to go deeper than the question of who's different from (or similar to) whom? We need to ask ourselves, foremost, what difference does difference make in the narrations of these writers and to a search for 'a common identity' among black and white autobiographers of the modern South?" Andrews explores these questions by examining caste, class differences, place, and the authors' quests for selfhood.

1415 Borne, Ron. "Great Mississippi Dogs I Have Known: Great Dog #1." *Mississippi Magazine* 6 (May/June 1988), p. 91.

Profiles Morris's dog Pete in a "new series on Mississippi's most remarkable dogs, living and dead." Pete, a black Labrador, "was already a famous three-year-old when he and his keeper, Willie Morris, first met in Bridgehampton, New York, in 1974. Pete would wander those streets, meet various business owners and public servants, receive their friendly pats, and then settle under an elm tree at the Shell station to watch the day go by. He handled these tasks with great dignity, became the semiofficial mayor of that Yankee community, and answered to the title of 'Your Honor.'"

1416 "Conversations About Literature." *Humanities* 9 (September/October 1988), pp. 4–9.

A 29 June 1988 interview in Oxford, Mississippi, with Cleanth Brooks, Gray Professor Emeritus of Rhetoric at Yale University, and Morris, writer-in-residence at the University of Mississippi. The two men "held a wide-ranging conversation lasting more than two hours" about "writing and writers in America."

1417 "Good Old Boy." *Disney Channel Magazine* (9 October–20 November 1988), pp. 24–26.

A promotional article on the movie *Good Old Boy*, which premieres on television's The Disney Channel on November 11. "*Good Old Boy* recreates the childhood world of author Willie Morris, who grew up in Yazoo City, Mississippi, where the film is set. It was an outdoor world of Burma Shave signs and dusty dirt roads, sprawling cotton fields and overgrown marshes, secluded water holes and small town stadiums. As a boy Morris swam, fished, and dreamed of one day becoming a big league ball player."

1418 Cobb, James C. "Southern Writers and the Challenge of Regional Convergence: A Comparative Perspective." *Georgia Historical Quarterly* 73 (Spring 1989), pp. 1–25.

Examines southern literature within the context of the relationship — particularly the "interregional tensions" — between the North and the South. "In 1967, Willie Morris published *North Toward Home*, a transitional work that bridged the gap between the 'shame and guilt' era and the post-civil rights period." The memoir "owed much of its incisiveness and clarity of detail concerning life in his native Mississippi to the striking 'unsouthernness' of a New York so intimidating and foreign that Morris called it 'The Big Cave.'"

1419 King, Larry L. "Writers Si, Editors No!" *Roundup Quarterly*, n.s., 3 (Fall 1990), 6–10.

A discussion of the "adversarial" relationship between writers and editors in the publication of the Western Writers of America. Although King thinks of "Writers and Editors in terms of Us versus Them," he mentions a few "excellent editors" with whom he has worked. "I don't mean to rank editors like college football teams, but my Number One All-Time editor was Willie Morris at *Harper's* magazine. Willie had a knack for putting the right writer with the right subject. He spent a lot of time with his writers, listening to them ramble and talk, and when a writer's eyes began to glow and his narrative drive shifted into high gear and he refused to be interrupted, Willie said, 'Write me a piece about that.'"

1420 Plimpton, George. "The Art of Fiction CXIX: Maya Angelou." *Paris Review* 32 (Fall 1990), pp. 144–67.

A formal interview with Maya Angelou. After Plimpton asks her if she has ever "been back" to her hometown of Stamps, Arkansas, she recalls that in "about 1970," she, Morris, and Bill Moyers "were at some affair.... The suggestion came up: 'Why don't we all go back South.' Willie Morris was from Yazoo, Mississippi. Bill Moyers is from Marshall, Texas, which is just a hop, skip, and a jump — about as far as you can throw a chitterling — from Stamps, my hometown." Although the three of them did not return to the South together, "after a while" Angelou drove to Stamps with broadcast journalist Moyers, who "was doing a series on 'creativity.'"

1421 Hobson, Fred. "Surveyors and Boundaries: Southern Literature and Southern Literary Scholarship After Mid-Century." *Southern Review* 27 (October 1991), pp. 739–55.

As Hobson traces changes in the nature of contemporary southern writing and southern literary scholarship, he points out that "as late as the 1960s" the works of many white southern writers were characterized by the traditional "pride-shame" feelings toward the South. This "love-hate relationship" is particularly evident in "nonfiction works of contrition and confession" such as Morris's *North Toward Home* and Larry L. King's *Confessions of a White Racist.* "These books ... were very much in the tradition of George W. Cable, W. J. Cash, and Lillian Smith, a tradition which required that the writer probe deeply and painfully his relationship to his homeland. But something seemed to be missing in these latter-day confessionals. They are interesting and eloquent — *North Toward Home* has become, deservedly, something of a southern classic — but one wonders if their authors really *meant* it as deeply as Cable and Cash and Smith had, if they were risking all in their truth-telling as their predecessors had." Hobson presents the same argument on pages 5–6 of his *The Southern Writer in the Postmodern World.* Athens: University of Georgia Press, 1991.

1422 Moore, Gary. "William Faulkner's Oxford." *Memphis* 17 (April 1992), pp. 34–47, 64–65.

William Faulkner, who died in Oxford, Mississippi, thirty years ago, fostered a "literary legacy" that the residents still maintain. This "portrait of literary Oxford" includes vignettes of Morris and other figures identified with the small university town. "If ever a man was made for Oxford in the 1980s it was the literary lion who took refuge during the yuppie decade and made Faulkner's old haunts and characters into living myths that turned right around on barstools and spoke back to you, the man they still revere around Square Books in whispers and chuckles though now he has dried out and married anew and moved to Jackson: Willie Morris."

1423 Devereaux, Elizabeth. "Willie Morris's New York Memoir." *Publishers Weekly* 240 (7 June 1993), p. 18.

An interview with Morris shortly before the publication of *New York Days.* In his book, which he calls a "sequel" to his first memoir, *North Toward Home*, he recalls the sixties "with an unusual clarity, conjuring up conversations as if they'd just taken place. 'For some reason, I have the memory of a herd of elephants,' he says. He hadn't kept a journal, but he had notes, as well as all the back issues of the magazine. 'They were like a cherished diary for me. Every article, every story, evoked specific memories of happenings, events.'"

1424 Hills, Rust. "The Second Life of Willie Morris." *Esquire* 120 (September 1993), p. 52.

A brief profile of Morris upon the publication of *New York Days.* In his second autobiography, he provides "fascinating" accounts of the people he met and the articles he published in *Harper's.* "Morris has summoned up the glory days of his past with what seems to be total recall. ('I'm blessed, or cursed, with an incredible memory,' he says.) Despite the presence of the celebrated, the tone is as down-to-earth American as its author."

1425 Parshall, Gerald. "The Yarn Spinner from Yazoo." *U.S. News & World Report* 115 (13 September 1993), pp. 75–76.

A lively interview with and an anecdotal portrait of Morris upon the publication of *New York Days*, the "worthy sequel" to the author's *North Toward Home.* "Morris is the throbbing personification of the Southern tradition of back-porch storytelling. As he talks, you can almost hear the night bugs hitting the screen and the rockers squeaking.... He is happiest when telling true stories in which he himself is a character, and so much the better. The prism of his well-nourished ego magnifies his vision of the world in wondrous ways."

1426 Shnayerson, Michael. "He'll Always Have Elaine's." *Vanity Fair* 56 (October 1993), pp. 130, 132, 134, 138, 140, 144, 146.

A lengthy, in-depth profile of Morris based on interviews with the author and many of his friends. Shnayerson writes of Morris's "ascension" to the editorial offices of *Harper's* and provides a penetrating look at the "controversial evening" when he and most of his colleagues resigned from the magazine following a dispute with the publication's owner. "And so began a far more complex journey — a coming to terms after the fall — that sent Morris first into self-imposed exile in the Hamptons, then to Oxford, Mississippi, and only recently to Jackson, where the circle has completed itself with the writing, at last, of *New York Days*, just published by Little, Brown." Shnayerson is the son of Robert Shnayerson, who replaced Morris as editor of *Harper's*. In the December issue, *Vanity Fair* published two responses to "He'll Always Have Elaine's" as well as its author's reply to them under the title "Men of Letters":

A Lapham, Lewis H. Letter to the editor. *Vanity Fair* 56 (December 1993), pp. 40, 46.

Quarrels with Shnayerson about his "account of Willie Morris's sudden exit from the New York literary stage. Shnayerson doesn't know how or why Morris destroyed his career or defeated his own best hopes, and so he elects me to the office of villain...."

B Marzorati, Gerald. Letter to the editor. *Vanity Fair* 56 (December 1993), p. 46.

To counter Shnayerson's "hagiography of Willie Morris" and Morris's personal "grudge against Lewis Lapham," a former deputy editor of *Harper's* lists a few of the latter's accomplishments.

C Shnayerson, Michael. Letter to the editor. *Vanity Fair* 56 (December 1993), p. 46.

The author of "He'll Always Have Elaine's" replies to Lapham's and Marzorati's letters, insisting that his article "contains not one word of criticism or spite from me about Lapham."

1427 Manly, Lorne. "In a New York Minute." *Folio: The Magazine for Magazine Management* 22 (1 October 1993), p. 26.

Avers that Morris's "tales of his tenure" as editor of *Harper's* are entertaining because the "dirt" surrounding the resignations of him and his staff "is dished flavorfully." A one-paragraph piece about *New York Days*.

1428 "Absolut Morris" [advertisement]. *Southern Accents* 17 (January/February 1994), pp. 22–23.

Morris holding court at Elaine's restaurant in New York City is the focal point of an advertisement that promotes both Absolut Vodka and the author's *New York Days*.

1429 Sansing, David G. "The Other Mississippi." *Xavier Review* 14 (Fall 1994), pp. 19–28.

Sansing, professor of history at the University of Mississippi, believes that "for every trait or characteristic that is typical of Mississippi, there is a corresponding opposite trait that is equally typical. That corresponding opposite is the other Mississippi." For instance, "Mississippi's ready resort to violence and its hostility to outsiders is legendary, but so too is its gentility, its hospitality, and its hint of yesterday." Regrettably, most people perceive only the stereotypical characteristics that make "good press" in the newspapers and on television. Sansing quotes from Morris's *Yazoo* and notes that he — "one of our most famous expatriates" — and other prominent writers are allied with the state's other, lesser-known side. Morris occasionally refers to his friend Sansing in his own works, such as the following passage from chapter 1, page 8 of *The Ghosts of Medgar Evers*: "There has always been what historian David Sansing cites as 'the *other* Mississippi,' the Mississippi not of illiteracy but of literary tradition, not of ignominy but of nobility, not of nihilism and injustice but of charity and humanity."

1430 Swindle, Michael. "The Last of the Southern Boys: Willie Morris at 60." *Double Dealer Redux* 2 (Winter 1995), pp. 28–30.

The publication of the Pirate's Alley Faulkner Society provides a detailed account of Morris's "North (Jackson) Toward Home Birthday Bash," held in Jackson, Mississippi, on 29 November 1994, his sixtieth birthday. "David Halberstam, calling Willie 'America's best magazine editor,' presented him with a silver Tiffany's box from his former colleagues at *Harper's*." See also item 1741.

1431 Chappell, Charles. "Lawrence Wells of Oxford: An Interview." *Mississippi Quarterly: The Journal of Southern Culture* 48 (Spring 1995), pp. 319–36.

Wells, author of *Rommel and the Rebel* (1986) and *Let the Band Play Dixie* (1987), is co-owner with his wife, Dean, of Yoknapatawpha Press, which published some of Morris's works when the author lived in Oxford. "When Willie came to teach at Ole Miss, something happened that was remarkable. In 1980 he was teaching — one of his courses was sort of an appreciation of modern writers, you might say — he taught eight or ten novels. And for Willie to teach fiction, to teach novels was an amazing thing. His appreciation, his instincts, and his astute observations — he had people *running* to that class...." Wells also comments on the "great encouragement" Morris gave him and other aspiring writers.

1432 King, Richard H. "Reflections on Southern Intellectuals." *Southern Cultures* 1 (Spring 1995), pp. 335–46.

Examines some of the issues facing southern intellectuals and offers "some suggestions about their past and present roles in the life of the region." King asserts that there has been a decline of "public intellectuals," that is, persons who debate and speak out on matters of general concern. "Perhaps the last southerners who made up something approaching a coherent cadre of public intellectuals were the writers Willie Morris gathered, as companions or contributors, at *Harper's* in the mid-to-late 1960s. In his brief tenure at *Harper's* Morris transformed one of gray ghosts of American magazine journalism into a lively publication devoted, it often seemed, to whatever happened to be on the minds of selected southern intellectuals."

1433 Burt, Elsa. "Willie Morris's Dog Days." *At Random* 4 (Summer 1995), p. 37.

An interview with Morris in the house organ of Random House, which accompanies excerpts from the recently published *My Dog Skip* (item 792). "In revisiting his past, Morris got caught up in the way of life of the 1940s and 50s, the years before television, which he calls 'the great silencer of conversation.' *My Dog Skip*, he admits, is 'about the only book I've ever written that I enjoyed doing.'"

1434 Holland, Richard. "Archives of Southwestern Writers: Larry L. King at Harper's." *Southwestern American Literature* 21 (Spring 1996), pp. 61–72.

Maintains that the sixties was an "unusually rich period in American journalism and essay writing" and that the success Morris had as editor of *Harper's Magazine* in publishing such excellent works was its "high point." Texan Larry L. King — an "ebullient letter writer" as well as a "great storyteller with an eye for the telling detail" — was one of Morris's staff writers, and in 1992 he gave over 15,000 pieces of correspondence to the Southwestern Writers Collection at Southwest Texas State University (now Texas State University–San Marcos). Holland reprints a few of King's *Harper's*-era letters to "reveal something of the character of this remarkable archive."

1435 Ott, Bill. "Literary New York." *Booklist* 92 (1 & 15 June 1996), p. 1776.

One-paragraph excerpts from *New York Days* and four other books that are representative of "literary New York." Morris wrote in *New York Days* that "I came to the city, and it changed my life." These words "have been paraphrased by a thousand other literary types who have done time on the island of Manhattan both before and after Morris."

1436 Crowther, Hal. "The Hounds of Heaven." *Oxford American* (June/July 1996), pp. 18–19.

Alludes to Morris's affection for dogs in an essay expounding on the animals' virtues. "They still appreciate dogs in Mississippi. In two recent Mississippi memoirs — *On Fire* by Larry Brown and *My Dog Skip* by Willie Morris — the death of a favorite dog is the most painful thing the author remembers. There's no false stoicism, either, no tough-guys-don't-cry stuff to insulate the reader from the pain."

1437 King, Larry L. "To Buster, with Love." *Washingtonian* 31 (July 1996), pp. 48–51, 89–91.

A man who at one time "harbored a deep fear of and something bordering on hatred for dogs" is now the proud owner of the "Top Individual Dog in the World." King, who worked with Morris on *Harper's Magazine*, humorously recalls how astonished he was some ten years ago when his long-time friend, sounding "distraught and zombie-like," telephoned to tell him that his dog, Pete, had just died. "And [Morris] began to weep. 'Well, hell, Willie,' I said. And then, inanely, 'Say, how's the Ole Miss football team looking?' Willie choked out, 'I can't talk now,' and hung up; I sat wondering how much he'd been drinking because I simply couldn't *identify*."

1438 "Willie Morris Papers Available at the University Library." *Southern Register* (Summer 1997), p. 19.

The newsletter of The Center for the Study

of Southern Culture at the University of Mississippi publicizes the university's acquisition of "the personal papers of Mississippi man-of-letters Willie Morris." The papers will be housed in the Library's Department of Archives and Special Collections and include 17,000 letters, postcards, clippings, photographs, and "notes from political figures, relatives, school children, critics, and admirers." See also item 1765.

1439 Bales, Jack. "Willie Morris: An American Writer Who Comes from the South." *Firsts: The Book Collector's Magazine* 8 (January 1998), pp. 46–55.

A sympathetic portrait of Morris and his literary career. Includes a first edition "Checklist with Approximate Values." Morris is "particularly well known for the books and articles in which he compares his experiences and his long and complex Southern heritage to America's own history. 'I am an American writer who happens to have come from the South,' he emphasized in the spring of 1997. 'I've tried to put the South into the larger American perspective.'"

1440 Dees, Jim. "Willie Morris, Mississippi's Writer in Residence: A Yazoo Way of Knowledge." *Oxford Town*, no. 234 (5–11 February 1998), p. 8.

A warm tribute to Morris shortly after the publication of *The Ghosts of Medgar Evers*. "The topics to which he has turned his ear and eye (and heart) take on added hues when seen through the prism of his Southern sensibility: racism, childhood magic, sports, death, writing, memory and history, and of course, dogs. Morris's work is driven by his presence in the storytelling.... In fact, re-reading various pieces that make up his books reveals that it is his empathy, coupled with his consummate skill and craftsmanship, that gives his distinguished canon its life." A photograph of Morris "cheering an Ole Miss touchdown" dominates the cover of this issue of *Oxford Town*, which is published by the *Oxford (Miss.) Eagle*.

1441 D[ees], J[im]. "Willie's Ghosts." *Oxford Town*, no. 234 (5–11 February 1998), p. 9.

An interview with Morris upon the publication of *The Ghosts of Medgar Evers*. Morris tells Dees that "the genesis of the book" came from John F. Kennedy Jr., who telephoned and asked him to write an article on Senator Jesse Helms for *George* magazine. "I told him I couldn't do it because I was involved with this movie, *Ghosts of Mississippi*. I also told him that on the night before Medgar was assassinated, his father was on the radio and TV giving the most emphatic speech ever given by an American president on civil rights." Kennedy then asked him to write a piece on the making of the motion picture (item 801). "So I did. And then the more I got involved with the movie, I said, this has to be a book."

1442 Decter, Midge. "Southern Comforts." *Commentary* 106 (July 1998), pp. 26–33.

Decter, formerly Morris's executive editor at *Harper's*, recalls her association with him and the other "men of the Left" on the magazine. She remembers that in the 1960s, they and other "Southern Boys" declared that black people in the North had a far more difficult life than southern blacks. "In the South, it was argued, blacks had always lived cheek-by-jowl with white folks, while in Northern cities they had been forced to remain isolated in ghettos, as poor as ever but faceless into the bargain." This "falsehood" about racism in the North relieved the blacks of that region from assuming "responsibility for the improvement of their own social and economic condition." This in turn led to failures in the struggles for civil rights. Morris's idea "that the North is more racist than the South is not only untrue, it has proved a very rickety political and cultural crutch for all too many black leaders and perhaps an even more rickety one for my former good buddies."

1443 Summer, Bob. "Remembrances of Willie." *Publishers Weekly* 246 (16 August 1999), p. 30.

Announces two weeks after Morris's death the forthcoming publication of books both by and about this "highly regarded" author. These include *My Mississippi*, *My Cat Spit McGee*, and *Conversations with Willie Morris*, a volume in the University Press of Mississippi's "extensive author interview series" (item 1945).

1444 "Black Mississippi Man Receives Cornea Donated by Late White Author Willie Morris." *Jet* 96 (20 September 1999), p. 22.

After Morris's death in August, his family donated his two corneas. A recipient of one of the cornea transplants, Ozie Longino of Monticello, Mississippi, said "I was speechless" upon hearing who the donor was and added that "I'm planning on taking real good care of everything." Dr. Connie S. McCaa, the surgeon who performed the operation, stated, "It was a great gift for Morris to give to someone — the gift of sight." See also items 1818 and 1832.

1445 Hamblin, Robert W. "'The Shadow Beneath the Act': Willie Morris and the Metaphor of Sports." *Aethlon: The Journal of Sport Literature* 17 (Fall 1999), pp. 29–37.

Observes that Morris, "one of the most significant contemporary Southern authors," is not only well known as a memoirist, editor, novelist, cultural historian, and essayist but also as a sportswriter. Because he is an author "concerned with broader social and cultural issues, Morris's interest in sport is scarcely ever for the mere sake of sport itself—in sports as sports. As he notes in the preface to his collection of sports narratives, *Always Stand In Against the Curve*, 'As a writer I have often viewed sports as a metaphor for much that transpired in the greater society, for the shadow beneath the act—a reflection of the American hyperboles.'" Hamblin examines several of these "'hyperboles'" in Morris's book *The Courting of Marcus Dupree* and his essays "The Search for Billy Goat Hill" (item 754) and "A Prayer Before the Feast" (item 898).

1446 Q[uinn], J[udy]. "More Morris." *Publishers Weekly* 246 (1 November 1999), p. 29.

Announces that the University Press of Mississippi will be publishing "an 'instant' hardcover edition" of the late Willie Morris's *North Toward Home* on November 29, his sixty-fifth birthday anniversary. Other Morris-related books that the firm will be releasing soon include *Remembering Willie*, a collection of eulogies and memorial tributes (item 2081); *Conversations with Willie Morris*, a volume of interviews (item 1945); and Morris's *My Mississippi*, which he "delivered shortly before his death." Random House, the author's trade publisher, will be bringing out his new book *My Cat Spit McGee* in December and a Vintage paperback edition of *North Toward Home* next year. See also item 1820.

1447 "Talking with Writers." *Publishers Weekly* 247 (3 April 2000), p. 76.

Reports that writers Charles Bukowski and Willie Morris are featured in two forthcoming books of interviews. Morris, who died in August 1999, "had a knack for taking a person's story and elucidating the larger themes behind it." The twenty-five "interviews and profiles of the prolific Southerner" in Jack Bales's *Conversations with Willie Morris* (item 1945) are "thoughtful pieces [that] provide insight into Morris's personality, influences and beliefs."

1448 Swoboda, Ron. "Negative's Re-Enforcement: A Son's Photos, His Father's Words." *New Orleans Magazine* 34 (1 May 2000), pp. 30–31.

An interview with David Rae Morris, whose photographs will accompany his father's text in their book *My Mississippi*, scheduled for publication in September. Morris's "images take you to Confederate Day celebrations and Martin Luther King Day parades; they show you the faces of Mississippi today.... 'In order to do any kind of study of Mississippi today, you had to confront the past, and to confront the past you had to take a fairly strong stance against racism. And so there are moments in my pictures where I get in your face,' Morris says."

1449 Lapham, Lewis H. "Hazards of New Fortune: *Harper's Magazine*, Then and Now." *Harper's Magazine* 300 (June 2000), pp. 57–72.

The editor of *Harper's* commemorates its 150th birthday with a history of the magazine. In his summary of the Willie Morris era, the time in which he joined the staff, Lapham acknowledges that Morris's editorial "strategy matched the go-go expectations of the Age of Aquarius, and for two or three years it seemed to hold out the promise of astonishing success." But whereas the liberal magazine was "much talked about" in New York City, "elsewhere in the country the reviews were not so kind," with both readers and advertisers soon losing interest in it. Many subscribers believed that "intellectuals were indebted to society and therefore obliged to apply their knowledge to its service.... Morris enlisted a company of writers who regarded the society's principal institutions (schools as well as government) as their natural enemies, which was a brave and noble pose and maybe even true, but not one that sold a lot of copies in Detroit." A year-end accounting of the magazine in 1970 showed a loss of $700,000 and a paid circulation below 300,000. For tax reasons, owner and midwestern newspaper magnate John Cowles Jr. restructured *Harper's* as a department of his *Minneapolis Star and Tribune*. "Blaming Cowles for the unwelcome news, Morris abruptly resigned in March 1971, and for the next thirteen years the magazine drifted through a period of financial and editorial instability."

1450 Wells, Lawrence. "The Days of Wine and Letters." *Southwest Airlines Magazine* 30 (October 2000), pp. 66–69, 143, 146–47.

Wells and several other of Morris's long-time friends remember "the old days" of the 1970s when writers, artists, and their families and friends congregated at the Hamptons on the east end of Long Island and at Bobby Van's in Bridgehampton. Owner Bobby Van says that after Morris wrote an op-ed piece on the restaurant in March 1974 for the *New York Times* (item 810), "The next day it was pandemonium. People were pushing to get inside the place. We had to lock the doors during regular hours. People were wild to get in, and it wasn't for the bluefish."

1451 Walsdorf, Jack. "Something About Books." *Against the Grain* 12 (November 2000), p. 84.

Walsdorf, who was responsible for the publication of Morris's *My Two Oxfords*, writes both an affectionate tribute to his friend and a review of Jack Bales's *Conversations with Willie Morris* (item 1945). "Along with Willie's life long passion for writing came his belief in the written word. As he said, 'The written word, when well done, is one of the few endeavors of the human race that lasts and matters. If you write something good, it's going to last; it's that simple.'"

1452 Thorn, J. Dale. "The Writer Willie Morris and His Legacy for Race Relations in Mississippi." *McNeese Review* 39 (2001), pp. 1–9.

Quotes from Morris's works and secondary sources to show his lifelong commitment to civil rights and racial equality. "Ultimately, he graced us with his writings of Mississippi's transformation and the lyrical literature of his homecoming. It was Willie's special gift to his readers that, although he looked on racism as Mississippi's 'everlasting albatross,' there was so much about his home state that he loved, that he made us love it as well, not because of its past but despite its past. Like no other Mississippian of his time, Willie grasped the tremendous complexity of Mississippi and race."

1453 Rosen, Judith. "Fond Farewell: 'Taps' for Willie Morris." *Publishers Weekly* 248 (2 April 2001), p. 19.

Interviews with Morris's widow and several of his friends are featured in a promotion piece for his last book, *Taps*. Although the author is best known for his nonfiction, "The novel *Taps* is one of his most autobiographical works. The central image of a 16-year-old boy playing taps at the funerals of the Korean War dead in Yazoo City, Miss., is something that Morris did. 'He actually had the experience and it was so powerful on him as a child,' said his widow, JoAnne Prichard Morris. 'It brought together and established his point of view on the land, death, and the presence of death in life.'"

1454 King, Larry L. "The Book on Willie Morris." *Texas Monthly* 29 (May 2001), pp. 138–39, 170–72, 196, 198–200.

A straightforward appraisal of Willie Morris's life. Larry L. King was one of Morris's chief contributing writers at *Harper's*, and the two stayed in touch after they—and most of the staff—resigned in March 1971. King interviewed many of Morris's friends for this fascinating, provocative article, which the Texas Institute of Letters praised in March 2002 as the "Best Work of Magazine Journalism" of 2001. "Everybody thought they knew [Morris]. Few truly did. Willie Weaks Morris was a man of many parts. Some did not mesh with the others. The private Willie Morris—the brooder, the loner, the man who could lose himself in sleep because wakefulness was too painful, the man who called his telephone an instrument of torture and hid it in the refrigerator to muffle its rings, the man who at bottom was as stubborn as any mule William Faulkner ever owned, the man who became known, in plain ugly language, as the town drunk—well, that contentious and complex fellow is a Willie Morris his adoring public never met."

1455 Long, Robert Lee. "A Good Old Boy Goes Home." *Mississippi Magazine* 19 (May/June 2001), pp. 79–84.

These interviews with Morris "shortly before he died" and with other Mississippians explain the "sense of longing" that residents have for their native state. "The late Willie Morris, the state's beloved writer, wrote about 'home,' and leaving, loving, and longing for its warm, comforting embrace more than any other Mississippi writer. For a time, Morris lived in New York City, or the 'Big Cave' as he called it, and later, on the eastern end of Long Island. Like Morris did, most homesick exiles long to come home, at one time or another."

1456 West, Jennifer. "From the Editor." *Mississippi Magazine* 19 (May/June 2001), pp. 6–7.

Recalls how "flabbergasted" she was when she read Morris's vivid descriptions of her native state in *North Toward Home*. "How could this famous writer know so well something that I knew so well? I guess my surprise stemmed from my reading so many books about places and people who seemed so far away and so different from me...." As she read his other books, "I felt a deep sense of kinship and connectedness with a man whom I had never met."

1457 Bales, Jack. "'A Bright Sparkle'—Willie Morris at the University of Texas." *American Oxonian* 89 (Winter 2002), pp. 5–6.

Introduces the reprinting of two of Morris's essays from the *Daily Texan* (items 405 and 346) by recounting his journalistic career at the University of Texas. Although a few of his newspaper columns "are tinged with a certain amount of self-righteousness, readers should bear in mind that this small-town youth at a huge state university was, to quote one longtime acquaintance, simply 'exploding with ideas.'" The *American Oxonian* is the magazine of the Association of American Rhodes Scholars. Morris attended Oxford University from 1956 to 1960.

1458 "Remembering Willie Morris Festival." *Mississippi Magazine* 20 (May 2002), p. 12.

"The second festival honoring Mississippi writer Willie Morris will take place May 24–26 in his hometown of Yazoo City." Last year's celebration "drew visitors from all over Mississippi and more than a dozen other states."

1459 Spong, John. "L. on Wheels." *Texas Monthly* 33 (January 2005), pp. 104–107, 170–73.

A lengthy interview with and entertaining profile of Larry L. King, "the crotchety West Texan who wrote some of the greatest magazine stories of all time" and Morris's former colleague at *Harper's*. Says King: "Willie Morris really did make my career. He gave me a place to write and insisted that I find my own voice.... He'd sit and drink with a writer and start 'em to talking about something, and then when their eyes started glowing, he'd say, 'Why don't you write about that for me.' He could tell when you really cared and were bound to write a good piece. He was just brilliant that way."

1460 Murphy, Kate. "Mississippi: A Literary Tour Through the State Evokes the Voices of Percy, Welty, Williams, and More." *Business Week*, no. 3922 (28 February 2005, p. 101.

A "literary tour" of Mississippi highlights the homes of a few of "the state's sons and daughters [who] went on to become renowned authors," including Walker Percy (Greenville), Eudora Welty (Jackson), Tennessee Williams (Clarksdale), William Faulkner (Oxford), and Morris (Yazoo City). "Touring the state, you can see their homes and papers as well as experience the quirky Southern charm that inspired their work.... Author Willie Morris grew up less than an hour's drive northwest of Jackson, in Yazoo City (yazoo.org). Morris warmly portrayed his boyhood in this sleepy riverside town in *North Toward Home* and *My Dog Skip*."

Newspaper Articles

1461 "Phi Eta Sigma Elects Officers: Morris to Head Men's Honorary." *Daily Texan*, 21 April 1953, p. 3.

Morris is elected president of Phi Eta Sigma for the 1953-54 academic year. The national honorary scholastic fraternity is open to male freshmen.

1462 [Chambers, Anne]. "'30' on Last 'Notes' Marks End for This Texan Editor." *Daily Texan*, 17 May 1953, p. 4.

In her final column, the outgoing editor of the *Daily Texan* recalls when she first met Morris, her soon-to-be colleague. "During a rainy registration day last September,... [a] young freshman peeked his sunshiny face around the corner of the office and introduced himself. Dear Willie (Yazoo City) Morris, who was too sleepy on his all-night–awake stand to notice that the chimes don't ring at night, has been a bright sparkle in our sometimes over-cynical staff crowd."

1463 Forsvall, Murray. "Sports Staff Small but Highly Capable." *Daily Texan*, 20 September 1953, p. 3.

The *Daily Texan* sports editor introduces Morris and the other members of the "highly capable and ambitious" sports staff to the newspaper's readers. "We can't forget Willie Morris. He was intramural co-ordinator last year. Willie, with his flair for the spectacular, has that certain ability to get the story that no one else can get. A very handy man."

1464 "On Humanizing." *Daily Texan*, 23 September 1953, p. 3.

A brief editorial recognizing Morris's new column, "The Round-Up" (see item 177). "On the front page today, we begin a new feature — a weekly column in which the writer will attempt to humanize this great big University by reporting the humorous, trivial and human incidents which make a school as big as this one livable. Wish him luck; it's an ambitious undertaking."

1465 "Seven Texan Awards Announced for Month." *Daily Texan*, 3 November 1954, p. 3.

Morris is among the winners of September's *Daily Texan* awards. His article "Bevo Is Sensation on Midwest Jaunt," published in the September 24 issue (item 234), won the best feature story award. "Judges said that interest in the topic was high and that Morris seemed to get the most out of his material.... The September 22 front page which Willie Morris day edited and Will White night edited won the award for best page one."

1466 "Morris, Watkins File for Editor of Texan." *Daily Texan*, 21 April 1955, p. 1.

Morris, a candidate for editor of the *Daily Texan*, lists his qualifications for the position and announces his election platform. Some of his principles include: "Fair, hard-hitting editorials; free-thinking, tolerant, virile, liberal Texan; conscious desire to prevent an inert, indifferent University populace; sincere effort to make Texan respected, if not agreed with; elimination of cliques on staff; more staff spirit and unity; complete editorial independence; daily columns by editor, managing editor...." A similar article appears as item 1470.

1467 Burgen, Carl. "UT Voters Put Farabee, Morris, Siegel, Holder, Richards In; Yell Leader Run-Off." *Daily Texan*, Election Extra, 27 April 1955, p. 1.

"Ray Farabee and Willie Morris glided to landslide victories Wednesday for the offices of President of Students' Association and Editor of the Daily Texan."

1468 Goulden, J. C. "Candidates Want Desegregated UT." *Daily Texan*, 27 April 1955, p. 1.

Candidates running for student offices address a "Stump Speaking crowd" and present their views on the controversial issue of desegregating the university. "First to catch a question on the subject was Willie Morris, Mississippi-born candidate for Texan editor, whose views have been rhetorically pondered during the campaign.... He answered: "'There's an inner turmoil in the United States; there's an inner turmoil in me. The Supreme Court decision was inevitable, but I don't think any universal rule can be applied to the entire nation when the time for integration comes,' Morris said. 'I don't think Ole Miss is ready for integration. I think The University of Texas is.'"

1469 Hall, Jerry, and J. C. Goulden. "Voting Machines Color Scene." *Daily Texan*, Election Extra, 27 April 1955, p. 1.

Notes that as Morris campaigned for editor of the *Daily Texan*, shaking the hands of passersby, he "tried to read 'The Grapes of Wrath' between handshakes. He finally gave up trying to study amidst all the turmoil and became a full-time smiler."

1470 "Texan Editor." *Daily Texan*, 27 April 1955, p. 4.

Morris, a candidate for the position of *Daily Texan* editor, announces his election platform and lists his qualifications. He has worked on the *Daily Texan* for three years and has a 2.73 grade average. "He was originator and author of 'The Round-Up,' a weekly front-page column in the Texan. Morris is currently sports editor; he has served as exchange editor, intramurals co-ordinator, day editor, and night sports editor.... On the Texan this year he has won monthly awards for best feature story, best news story, best front page, and best departmental page." A similar article appears as item 1466.

1471 Goulden, J. C. "It's Farabee, Morris in Record Vote: Siegel, Holder, Richards Win." *Daily Texan*, 28 April 1955, p. 1.

"A record-breaking vote gave Ray Farabee and Willie Morris overwhelming victories for president of the Students' Association and Daily Texan editor Wednesday. A total of 5,505 students cast votes, breaking by 1,020 the previous record of 4,485 set in 1954." Morris, who ran for editor against Edgar Watkins, "racked up a substantial 1,443 majority over" his opponent. The official tally was 3,357 votes for Morris to 1,914 for Watkins.

1472 "Outstanding Students, Belles Named for 1955." *Daily Texan*, 5 May 1955, p. 1.

Morris is one of twenty-four persons named as "outstanding students" at the University of Texas. They were selected by a committee comprised of the Dean of Men, Dean of Women, the Assistant Dean of Student Life in charge of campus organizations, and several student officers.

1473 Yerger, Louise M. "'Willie' Reaches High Rung in His Ladder of Success." *Yazoo City Herald*, 5 May 1955, p. 4.

Morris's hometown paper profiles him shortly after he is elected editor of the *Daily Texan*. "The only son of Mr. and Mrs. H. R. Morris, 'Willie' was the rare individual in high school—a combination honorman in his class, letterman in athletics and 'a regular guy' as well.... Anyone who knew him never doubted that he wouldn't achieve his ambitions." Morris's reminiscences of Yazoo City that he wrote for the *Daily Texan* earlier in the year (item 280) are reprinted alongside this biographical article (item 806).

1474 "Texan Presents Annual Awards: Keys Are Received by 92 Journalists." *Daily Texan*, 17 May 1955, p. 6.

The *Daily Texan* annual awards—gold keys,

silver keys, bronze keys, and certificates—are presented at the *Texan* picnic. Morris is among eleven journalists who receives a gold key.

1475 "Willie's Got 'Em on the Record and He Hopes to Keep 'Em There." *Texas Observer*, 20 June 1955, p. 3

Discloses that after Texas journalists "scolded" students at the University of Southern California for protesting the selection of Texas Governor Allan Shivers as USC's commencement speaker, University of Texas students reminded the reporters and Governor Shivers that Eleanor Roosevelt was not allowed to speak at UT in 1953. The paper quotes Morris: "Certainly Governor Shivers should have been allowed to speak in California. At the same time, however, Eleanor Roosevelt should have been allowed to speak here in 1953. Shivers and the newspapermen said open-mindedness should have prevailed. We will remember their stand."

1476 "Students Have Own Government." *Daily Texan*, 12 August 1955, sec. 1, p. 5.

Brief profiles of Morris and other officers of the UT Students' Association. "Willie Morris, Daily Texan editor: senior journalism–English major from Yazoo City, Miss., Silver Spurs, past president of Phi Eta Sigma, Delta Tau Delta." Silver Spurs is a men's service organization, Phi Eta Sigma is a national honor society for male freshmen, and Delta Tau Delta is a social fraternity.

1477 "Friars Select Four New Members." *Daily Texan*, 6 November 1955. p. 1.

Friars, a UT men's honorary organization, chooses Morris and three other students for membership. "The Friars are selected for outstanding scholarship, leadership, good character, and unselfishness." Morris's biographical profile states that his "2.7 [grade] average has satisfied requirements for Phi Beta Kappa. A member of Delta Tau Delta, he served on the Inter-Fraternity Council. He is a past secretary of Silver Spurs and was selected an Outstanding Student by the Cactus last year.... He was a member of the University freshman baseball team and has played intramural football, basketball, softball, and track."

1478 "Morris Selected Rhodes Scholar in Region Finals." *Daily Texan*, 11 December 1955, p. 1.

Reports that *Daily Texan* editor "William W. Morris" was one of four southern college students awarded a Rhodes scholarship during the regional competition in New Orleans December 9. "Morris, one of 32 students throughout the United States chosen for the scholarships, will study at Oxford University in England for two years.... [He] was advanced to the regional finals last Wednesday when he was chosen in the state finals in Houston." This issue of the *Daily Texan* includes Morris's article about New Orleans, "City of 1,000 Secrets..." (item 411).

1479 "Morris to Enter Oxford Next Fall." *Daily Texan*, 4 January 1956, p. 6.

In the fall, Morris and thirty-one other Rhodes scholarship winners will begin their classes at England's Oxford University. "Winners represent 30 states and 23 colleges and universities. They will begin a program of at least two years of study.... Scholarship winners are selected on the basis of leadership, character, intellect, and interest in sports."

1480 Harvill, Doyle, and Vaden Smith. "'Banned' Editorials Accepted After Five-Hour TSP Meeting." *Daily Texan*, 7 February 1956, p. 1.

Announces that yesterday evening the Texas Student Publications (TSP) Board approved for publication in the *Daily Texan* "editorial matter" submitted by Editor Morris and the paper's managing editor. This material had been rejected that morning by Harrell Lee, TSP's editorial director, and Dr. DeWitt C. Reddick, chairman of the Editorial Advisory Committee and acting director of the UT School of Journalism. At a February 4 meeting of the Student-Regent Liaison Committee, the newspaper's editorial policy was questioned "for not presenting opinions of the 'majority of the student body,' and not presenting both sides of every story." One of the three items rejected, for instance, was a guest editorial from the *New York Times* critical of the Fulbright-Harris natural gas bill pending in Congress. Morris called a meeting of the TSP Board to appeal Lee's and Reddick's decision. "In reference to [Lee and Reddick] Morris said, 'I think that in your analysis of the editorials, you are enforcing, in the strictest sense, the policies laid down in the TSP Handbook which, if enforced, would take away all rights of the editor.' Editorial Director Lee said, 'It is my opinion, the Regents don't feel the Texan is being edited with the zeal which would bring favorable feelings toward the University.'" Morris defends the principle of freedom of the press in the same issue of the newspaper (item 438).

1481 "Students Lead on TSP by 6–5." *Daily Texan*, 7 February 1956, p. 3.

Clarifies who sits on the Texas Student Publications Board, which directs campus publications and which supports Morris's right to publish his editorials (see item 1480). "Texas Student Publications, Inc., is an independent corporation responsible only to the Board of Regents of the University. The corporation is governed by a board with a six–five student majority." Its student members include the editor of the *Cactus* (yearbook), the editor of the *Ranger* (humor magazine), the editor of the *Daily Texan* (newspaper), the president of the Students' Association, and two student representatives. Faculty members on the board include three professors of journalism, a professor of English, and a professor of architecture. See also item 1494.

1482 "The Firing Line: Students Respond to Texan Censorship. *Daily Texan*, 8 February 1956, p. 4.

This issue's "Firing Line" (the title of the letters-to-the-editor section of the *Daily Texan*) contains letters supporting and criticizing Morris's editorial stand on freedom of the press. For example, Eugene Smith writes: "Several times last semester I found occasion to disagree with many of your editorial comments. I have, at times, even felt that you did not represent true student opinion; but only the most narrow-minded would, should, or could condemn your right to express yourself as the duly-elected editor of the official 'student publication.'" Roger Turner has a different opinion: "As [Morris] says, maybe the free press is endangered. But don't you think it's about time? It's trying to stir us up, putting ideas into the minds of innocent youths, making them think sometimes for themselves.... Our youth must be saved from themselves, and the great men of our state must not be embarrassed."

1483 "Regents' Statement: Statement of the Board of Regents of The University of Texas." *Daily Texan*, 8 February 1956, p. 1.

The UT Board of Regents declares that it "is much concerned with the editorial matter" that has appeared in this year's *Daily Texan*. The editorials "have the impact of being considered as implying attitudes and positions of the University. No such editorials, therefore, may violate the statutory prohibition against using appropriated funds of the University to influence the outcome of any election or the passage or defeat of any legislative measure.... Editorial preoccupation with state and national political controversy is also manifestly a distortion of the basic function of The Daily Texan." Because "it is clear" that the *Daily Texan*'s editorial pages "have violated the foregoing policies many times,... the [UT] President is requested to take steps immediately to have the Board of Directors of Texas Student Publications take firm and positive action to assure future compliance with these policies." The President is also asked to begin a "restudy and clarification" of the policies outlined in the Texas Student Publications *Handbook*. See also item 441.

1484 Smith, Vaden, and Doyle Harvill. "Regent Message Requests Self-Survey by TSP Board." *Daily Texan*, 8 February 1956, p. 1.

Reports that Morris and other members of the Texas Student Publications (TSP) Board met yesterday with the President's Student Advisory Cabinet to examine the editorial policies of the *Daily Texan* and to discuss a statement from the UT Board of Regents (item 1483). The Regents contend that the *Daily Texan* violated the rules prescribed by the Texas Student Publications *Handbook*, and they asked the TSP Board to review those rules and report on its findings. "In a protest at the Regents' Intervention Editor Willie Morris said he would still continue to fight the limitation laid down in the message." UT President Dr. Logan Wilson stressed that the *Daily Texan* is viewed as the university's newspaper "and that, as the Regents stipulated in their request, 'Editorial preoccupation with state and national political controversy is a distortion of the basic function of The Daily Texan.' ... Morris said, 'If put into effect, it (the Regents' statement) would take away the Texan's right to editorialize on controversial issues, and would absolve the Texan's status as a student newspaper.'"

1485 "A Student-Regent Crisis." *Texas Observer*, 8 February 1956, p. 1.

Because Morris has published articles in the *Daily Texan* critical of Governor Allan Shivers's administration, the University of Texas Regents has declared that the newspaper "should not be 'preoccupied' with state and national political issues" (see item 1483). In spite of the Regents' resolution, the students on the school's publications board "voted to override the university's editorial director and acting journalism dean and approve editorials written by Willie Morris, the student editor."

1486 "Assembly to Get Review of Texan Policy Problem: Dr. Reddick, Morris Invited to Thursday Student Meeting." *Daily Texan*, 9 February 1956, p. 1.

Students' Association President Roland Dahlin has invited Morris and Dr. DeWitt Reddick, acting director of the UT School of Journalism and vice chairman of Texas Student Publications, to a meeting of the Student Assembly today. "Dahlin said he hopes the Assembly discussion of the Texan problem will result in a positive expression of what assemblymen expect from their student newspaper."

1487 "Dobie Blasts Regents." *Daily Texan*, 9 February 1956, p. 1.

Discloses that J. Frank Dobie, renowned Texas writer and folklorist, sent a letter to the *Daily Texan* that is "highly critical of the Regents' statement of Texan editorial policy. 'They (the Regents) don't want any controversial ideas aired around the University,' Mr. Dobie wrote, 'unless those ideas coincide with their own. Yet they are fearful enough of democracy not to order the University newspaper run entirely by their own flunkies.'" The *Daily Texan* was not allowed to publish Dobie's letter in its entirety, but the *Texas Observer* ran it under the title "Dobie Unexpurgated" (item 1504). Morris writes in chapter 3, page 190, of the "Texas" section of *North Toward Home*: "The Board of Regents, Dobie's letter said, 'are as much concerned with free intellectual enterprise as a razorback sow would be with Keats' "Ode on a Grecian Urn"'—a well-known statement now despite the fact that this phrase, and many another colorful one, were deleted after I had gone home to sleep and the paper was going to press."

1488 "The Firing Line: More Response on Texan Censorship." *Daily Texan*, 9 February 1956, p. 4.

Seven letters to the editor in support of Morris and the *Daily Texan*, including one signed by 145 UT students. Writes Pete Gunter: "You have the students behind you; we appreciate your position and the right of free speech which you defend.... Keep up the good work, Willie. A lot besides censorship can be improved because of your stand."

1489 Smith, Vaden. "Dahlin Calls Friday Meeting of TSP Board for Analysis." *Daily Texan*, 9 February 1956, p. 1.

Roland Dahlin, chairman of the Texas Student Publications Board and president of the Students' Association, has announced that the Board will analyze the *Daily Texan*'s editorial policy, "which has received national interest." Dave Garroway of the National Broadcasting Company in New York "mentioned the controversy over a national television broadcast" and both United Press International and Associated Press have covered the story. Editor Willie Morris will appear on a local television program tomorrow. "Morris said he regretted there has not yet been enough space in the Texan to publish all the letters addressed to the Firing Line, the readers' column."

1490 "Student GOP Backs Editor." *Daily Texan*, 9 February 1956, p. 1.

The UT Young Republicans club has passed a resolution "commending The Daily Texan and its editor for their stand against press censorship. Vote on the resolution was 40–0." The formal statement, which was approved on February 8, noted that the paper "should be free to exercise these rights (free press) at its discretion."

1491 "Young 'Demos' Backing Texan." *Daily Texan*, 9 February 1956, p. 1.

The *Daily Texan* has received a "unanimous vote of confidence" in a resolution passed by the UT Young Democrats club on February 7. "The resolution cited the Texan and Editor Willie Morris for 'the courageous stand for free discussion of current governmental questions.' The vote was 40 to 0."

1492 "Gas Issue Stirs Texas U. Dispute." *New York Times*, 10 February 1956, p. 3.

"Editors of the student newspaper and the administration of the University of Texas are feuding again." The "faculty supervisors" of the *Daily Texan* refused to allow the newspaper to reprint a *New York Times* editorial that was "critical" of the Fulbright-Harris gas bill, which the U.S. Senate passed this week. "It was rejected by the faculty editorial director on the grounds that material on the other side of the issue had not been presented in balance."

1493 Lindsey, Byron. "Student Assembly Supports Free Editorial Policy 25 to 1: Principles, Not Issues Dr. Reddick's Concern." *Daily Texan*, 10 February 1956, p. 1.

The UT Student Assembly has "passed a resolution supporting a free editorial policy for The Daily Texan by a vote of 25 to 1." Prior to the vote, the group heard interpretations of the Board of Regents' statement on *Daily Texan* policies by Editor Willie Morris and Dr. DeWitt Reddick, vice-chairman of the Texas Student Publications Board and acting director of the UT School of Journalism. Reddick defended the UT Regents when he said that "'they have the right and the duty' to draw attention to something at the University that they find wrong." Morris's remarks followed Reddick's. "'This is a state university where freedom of expression and thought abound,' Morris said. 'If we falter here and surrender a principle, we will have violated the principles of a hundred newspapers and a hundred universities.'"

1494 Lindsey, Byron. "Texan Reports on TSP Board: Directors' Records Show Qualifications." *Daily Texan*, 10 February 1956, p. 4.

The Texas Student Publications Board, which manages the various publications of the university, includes the president of the Students' Association, two students from the Student Assembly, five faculty members, and the editors of the *Daily Texan* (newspaper), the *Cactus* (yearbook), and the *Ranger* (humor magazine). Lindsey summarizes the "record" of each person on the board, observing that all eleven voting members have "a knowledge of academic and professional principles." He writes that Morris was "elected editor of The Daily Texan last spring by the student body in a 2–1 vote." See also item 1481.

1495 Jones, Bil. "UT Editor Gets Mild Reprimand." *Austin American*, 11 February 1956, pp. 1–2.

Reports that the five faculty and six student members of the Texas Student Publications Board of Directors "suggested" during a meeting yesterday that Morris, editor of the *Daily Texan*, "tone down his editorials of his running battle" with the University of Texas Board of Regents.

1496 "Daily Tar Heel Co-Editors Backing Morris' Position." *Daily Texan*, 12 February 1956, p. 1.

Louis Kraar and Ed Yoder, co-editors of the *Daily Tar Heel*, the student newspaper at the University of North Carolina at Chapel Hill, have sent a telegram to the *Daily Texan* "strongly backing Texan Editor Willie Morris' stand in defense of college press freedom.... 'We join the editor of The Daily Texan, Willie Morris, in his unswerving defense of college press freedom,' Kraar and Yoder said in the wire."

1497 "The Firing Line: More Response on Texan Censorship." *Daily Texan*, 12 February 1956, p. 5.

Assorted letters to the editor on the "Texan censorship" issue. Although most of the writers defend Morris, John A. Clary does not. "No, Mr. Morris, we do not have and cannot have freedom of the press or complete freedom of anything. For every freedom that is extended, there accompanies a corresponding responsibility. I hope that you are not trying to kid yourself into believing that any newspaper can print whatever the editors wish; if so you are even more naive than I thought."

1498 Harvill, Doyle. "Suggestions for Interim Given to Morris Friday." *Daily Texan*, 12 February 1956, p. 1.

The Texas Student Publications Board has given *Daily Texan* Editor Willie Morris some "suggestions" relating to the campus newspaper's "editorial policies." The board recommended on February 10 that he "avoid 'facetiousness' in his editorials," reduce the amount of space devoted to the *Texan* dispute, and "use good judgment in commenting on controversial issues." After Morris heard the "suggestions," he replied, "If I submit to any restrictions, we will be fighting censorship with censorship, but I realize the wisdom of the board and in a broad sense the suggestions are good. I accept the suggestions, but I will not under any circumstances accept any restrictions."

1499 H[aston], N[ancy]. "Regental Censorship: Texan Issue Heads Week." *Daily Texan*, 12 February 1956, p. 4.

Morris's stand against the UT Board of Regents dominates a "campus cavalcade" of news stories. "Some students disagreed with The Texan's and Morris' stand. But the majority of the student populace joined the line-backers.... One thing is good. This explosively potent situation has caused students and those closely associated with the University to wake up from a somewhat passive indifference. It has caused them to think."

1500 "This Week's Guest Editorial: The Star-Telegram." *Daily Texan*, 12 February 1956, p. 4.

A reprinting of an editorial from the *Fort Worth Star-Telegram*. The piece suggests that both the UT Regents' opinions about Morris's editorial philosophy and Morris's attitude about the Regents "are as natural as the progress of the seasons. We are inclined to think that the Regents may be unduly concerned about the influence the views of the Texan editor might have over thinking of the state's citizens—including those young citizens at the University. Regent C. W. Voyles of Austin has said the Regents do not want to make a big issue of the matter—which certainly seems wise."

1501 Burgen, Carl. "Campus Commentary: Texan Staff Backs Editor in Policies." *Daily Texan*, 14 February 1956, p. 4.

The managing editor of the *Daily Texan* announces that the newspaper staff presented a report to the Texas Student Publications Board that "outlined the staff's recommendation on what policies the Texan should follow and expressed unqualified support of the present editor, Willie Morris."

1502 "The Firing Line: More Response on Texan Censorship." *Daily Texan*, 14 February 1956, p. 4.

Letters to the editor both for and against Morris. Writes Gene A. Templeton: "To the Regents of The University of Texas I would ask a question: Who are you, supposedly the protectors of our way of education and our traditions, to say what we should read in our newspaper? Another question, please: Why should The Texan, a student newspaper, be suppressed and kept from printing student opinion on state and national matters." From William S. Bussey: "Well, Willie, you have my sympathy and condolences, because you have made headlines and in a way that puts you forth as a young fool in the eyes of anyone outside the confines of the Forty Acres.... I do hope you get out of the situation without having to eat 'humble pie.' If so, I hope you learn a lesson from this experience.... An editor or newspaperman never criticizes the publisher or owners of his paper — that is, if he wants to retain his job."

1503 Harvill, Doyle. "TSP Board Lists Controversial Issues." *Daily Texan*, 14 February 1956, p. 1.

Daily Texan Editor Morris and Dr. DeWitt Reddick, acting director of the UT School of Journalism, addressed the Texas Student Publications (TSP) Board on February 13 concerning the "editorial policy" of the newspaper. "In answer to criticism that there was not a balanced editorial policy, Morris said that he had tried to contact several of the people on the opposite side several times for comment, but was unable to get statements...." Reddick said that freedom of the press rests not with the editor, but with the TSP Board, "and through the Board the editor gets his responsibility."

1504 Dobie, J. Frank. "Dobie Unexpurgated." *Texas Observer*, 15 February 1956, p. 3.

A reprinting of the letter J. Frank Dobie sent to the *Daily Texan* (see item 1487). The sentences that a UT faculty-appointed newspaper supervisor chose to remove are highlighted in italics.

1505 [Dugger, Ronnie]. "Regents Should Resign." *Texas Observer*, 15 February 1956, p. 2.

Editorial denouncing the "inquisitorial arrogance" of the University of Texas's Board of Regents for "muzzling" Willie Morris and the *Daily Texan* newspaper. "The nine Regents, by their censorship of student expression, have publicly demonstrated their opposition to the highest principle of higher education: free inquiry, free discussion. The next governor should demand that their resignations be on his desk the morning he arrives there so that Texas may once again have a free university."

1506 D[ugger], R[onnie]. "Report of the Regents' Ire Over 'Politics.'" *Texas Observer*, 15 February 1956, pp. 1, 4.

A lengthy, incisive article detailing how Morris's editorials in the *Daily Texan* on Governor Allan Shivers, segregation, higher taxes, and the natural gas bill have incited a "clampdown" on the campus newspaper at the University of Texas. Both Morris and members of the University's Board of Regents expressed their strong opinions at a meeting of the Texas Student Publications Board on February 13. Regent Leroy Jeffers, an attorney from Houston "who is an expert in labor relations for management, said ... that the issue is not freedom of the press but compliance with state law, a rider on the university's appropriations bill that state funds shall not be used for 'influencing the outcome of any election, or the passage or defeat of any legislative matter.'" Morris accused the Regents of attempting to censor the newspaper and spoke out "adamantly against the exercise of policy-making over the Texan by the Regents or the publications board. 'The editor should form his own decisions,' he said. 'He is responsible to the students who elected him.'"

1507 "From Dallas News: Lynn Landrum Says Rider Does Apply." *Daily Texan*, 19 February 1956, p. 5.

A reprinting of a *Dallas News* piece by the "salty old" columnist Lynn Landrum, who "has struck a hard blow for the advocates of fettered higher education." Landrum calls Morris's editorials "propaganda" and believes that no one "has the right to divert taxes or tax uses to his own propaganda politics." Landrum reasons: "An economist has the right to discuss economics in an economics class. He is hired to do that. But when he begins to campaign in his class for clear-cut political purpose for one party or another, out he goes and out he ought to go. Tax-endowed partisanship is an invasion of the rights of tax-bearing citizens."

1508 "Texas U. Editor Pushes Crusade." *New York Times*, 19 February 1956, p. 60.

Daily Texan editor Morris "is pressing his challenge to the administration" of the University of Texas. Editorials from the *New York Times* and the *Christian Science Monitor* that he submitted for reprinting in the campus newspaper were recently rejected by the university's faculty editorial director, Harrell E. Lee, and the acting director of UT's School of Journalism, DeWitt C. Reddick. Both editorials concerned a natural gas bill that was then pending in Congress. "The regents of the university cited a provision of a state appropriations law forbidding the use of state funds to influence the outcome of any election or the passage or defeat of any legislative measure. They declared that the editorials from other newspapers, if printed in The Texan, would violate the law."

1509 D[ugger], R[onnie]. "Willie and the College Yell." *Texas Observer*, 22 February 1956, p. 6.

A profile of Morris and a passionate tribute to his "current stand" against the University of Texas's Board of Regents. "Now, twenty-one, six feet tall, full cheeked, boyish, he is defending the student newspaper he edits against the massed opposition of the University of Texas Regents and its constituted agents.... This doesn't fit the stereotype of tight-lipped American youth paralyzed into conformity, but then there aren't many like Willie. When the Regents declared two weeks ago that The Daily Texan, the student paper, would thereafter be prohibited from editor[i]alizing on state policies, one of them, rancher-oilman Claude Voyles, explained to a newspaperman: 'We're just trying to hold Willie to a college yell.'"

1510 "Student Editorials 'Questionable.'" *Texas Observer*, 22 February 1956, p. 1.

Reports that the student-faculty publications board of the University of Texas declared on February 20 that "it had found 'some errors of fact and some instances of questionable editorial presentation' in The Daily Texan, the student newspaper, under fire from the university Board of Regents. Student Editor Willie Morris, the only dissenter to the finding, called it 'direct appeasement' of the Regents and 'admitting to guilt.'" On February 22, however, the board stated that the editor has the right to "express his opinions on state policies if he has laid a factual basis for them."

1511 "TSP Drafts Interim Report for Regents." *Daily Texan*, 23 February 1956, p. 1.

The Texas Student Publications Board has presented an "interim progress report" to the UT Board of Regents. In the document the board stated that the *Daily Texan* would emphasize campus news, but that due to students' "increasing interest in state and national affairs," the paper should be free to discuss subjects in these areas. "Editor Morris, in commenting on the progress of the board so far, said, 'We have approved certain broad principles which affirm the Texan's obligations to comment on state and national issues.'"

1512 "Texas U. Reports Accord on Paper." *New York Times*, 25 February 1956, p. 19.

A student-faculty publications board at the University of Texas has decided how the *Daily Texan* should handle "sensitive political news." The board agreed this week that the newspaper, edited by Morris, "should lay a factual background on which to base editorial comment. The policy revision, in which Mr. Morris is participating, provides that the paper will not make statements about state officials or political or legislative matters that include errors of fact."

1513 "Lee Withholds Texan Editorial." *Daily Texan*, 26 February 1956, p. 1.

Discloses that Harrell E. Lee, editorial director of Texas Student Publications, yesterday withheld an editorial scheduled for publication in today's *Daily Texan* "on the grounds that it was 'unduly partisan' and not in line with 'wise editorial management.'" The piece quoted part of a position statement in the *Amarillo (Tex.) News* that the newspaper would not support Governor Allan Shivers's bid for a fourth term in office. "A blank space appears on the editorial page where the editorial was to have run.... 'Censorship of this editorial is plainly but another manifestation of a great fear,' [Editor Willie] Morris said. 'The situation which brought it about is nothing less than tragic.'"

1514 "Guest Writer: Collegiate Censorship." *Daily Texan*, 28 February 1956, p. 4.

A reprinting of an editorial from the *Cornell Daily Sun*, "one of our more respected collegiate colleagues," which summarizes the controversy surrounding the *Daily Texan* and upholds Morris's right of freedom of the press. "The college newspaper, like any other, has the responsibility, editorially, of providing a platform for independent criticism of and comment upon any matter which is of importance to students and faculty as members of the academic community and as an intelligent portion of the citizenry of the United States."

1515 "TSP Director Lee Withholds Editorial." *Daily Texan*, 28 February 1956, p. 1.

Dr. DeWitt Reddick, acting director of the UT School of Journalism, and Harrell Lee, editorial director of Texas Student Publications, have withheld from publication in today's *Daily Texan* "an editorial concerning the political consequences of the natural gas bill." Lee "called the editorial 'unduly partisan comment on a political issue' and also 'in conflict with wise editorial management.'" A blank space headed by the phrase "This Editorial Withheld" appears on the editorial page where the piece would have been published.

1516 "Gas Editorial Ban Ordered at Texas U." *New York Times*, 29 February 1956, p. 16.

The *Daily Texan* "was ordered to withhold from today's publication an editorial on political consequences of the veto of the natural gas bill.... Today's development was the latest in a growing controversy between Willie Morris, student editor, and the Board of Regents over editorial views." In protest of the decision, part of the editorial page in the campus newspaper "was left blank."

1517 "Regents Told Texan Free." *Texas Observer*, 29 February 1956, p. 6.

The University of Texas student-faculty publications board has written the Board of Regents that as long as the *Daily Texan* "gives the factual basis on an issue, the editor has a right to express his opinion on it editorially." Nevertheless, editor Morris was not permitted to excerpt an editorial from the *Amarillo (Tex.) News*, and he "published instead a blank space in his editorial column and the announcement, 'This Editorial Censored.'"

1518 "A Rebuttal: Case Against Autonomy." *Daily Texan*, 20 March 1956, p. 4.

A reprinting of an article from the *Tar Heel*, the student newspaper at the University of North Carolina. Although *Daily Texan* editor Willie Morris "argues that a college paper must be open to all views for both educational and ethical reasons," the publishers of the paper, the members of the UT Board of Regents, feel that "they—like any publisher—can prevent an editor from publishing a given editorial." Admittedly, "Any student freedom exists at the pleasure of a university's administration. But that freedom is too valuable an educational force to be taken away merely because it causes controversy. If Texas journalism students are going to be taught in the classroom about the free press, they must enjoy that same free press."

1519 "The Firing Line: Editor Falls in Mud, Rants Incessantly, Blathers Inanely." *Daily Texan*, 25 March 1956, p. 6.

Several readers express their dissatisfaction with Morris's editorials. James H. Keahey, for instance, lists a "few observations" about the editor's writing: Keahey writes: "Thesaurus-thumbing is not to be confused with style. The function of journalism is communication of ideas, not semantic pyrotechnics or spurious erudition."

1520 "The Week in Texas." *Texas Observer*, 28 March 1956, p. 8.

Reports that Morris editorialized in the *Daily Texan* that the Texas Student Publications Board is threatening the right of a free press (item 479). "He singled out a proposed rule under consideration that criticism of state officials and legislators will be published 'only when it seems, in extreme situations, to be in the best interests of the University.'"

1521 Harvill, Doyle. "Editorial Policies Set; Regents Will Consider." *Daily Texan*, 29 March 1956, p. 1.

The Texas Student Publications Board has completed, passed, and released the editorial policies that will guide the *Daily Texan*. The chairman of the board will give the documents to UT President Logan Wilson, who will in turn present them to the Regents. After much discussion, the board stipulated that the campus newspaper should not favor one politician over another during a state or national election. "In reference to editor Willie Morris' criticisms of state and national officials, the committee making recommendations to the board stated that 'violent or personal criticism of legislators or other state officials may influence legislation affecting the University and the student body,' and that criticism in this area will be tolerant, reasoned, and well-founded in factual situations. To this proposal Editor Morris and several members of the board took issue as to what is tolerant and reasoned criticism.... In consideration of 'significant' controversy treated within the Texan, the policy report stipulated that provision shall be made for the publishing of a diversity of opinion should such comment be available. Editor Morris pointed out to the board that in all cases a diversity of opinion is not available." Ernest Sharpe, Professor of Journalism, replied that it is the newspaper's responsibility "to go in search of the opposing view."

1522 "A Minute of..." *Texas Observer*, 11 April 1956, p. 2.

Editorial opining that the UT *Daily Texan* "is just about dead." For over fifty years "student editors said what they thought when they thought it the way they thought it. No more. A faculty member will take over nightly supervision of all news stories and editorials next September, as soon as the fiery young editor, Willie Morris, is safely in Oxford, England, on his Rhodes Scholarship."

1523 "Student Editor Pessimistic: Says Texan Being Killed by a 'Subtle Paralysis.'" *Texas Observer*, 11 April 1956, p. 6.

The Board of Regents at the University of Texas "met last weekend and delayed action on the new editorial policies set up by the Board of Publications. These policies permit the editor [of the *Daily Texan*] "the privilege and the responsibility of developing an editorial program ... and of expressing his own views." The newspaper may not endorse candidates or discuss "personalities" in an election, but it may analyze the "issues." The Board also voted favorably on a "reorganization plan." Beginning in September, a faculty member working as "night supervisor" over the staff "will, in effect, supervise everything that goes in the paper." *Daily Texan* editor Morris believes that because of these restrictions, the newspaper's "editorial independence is being killed."

1524 Dugger, Ronnie. "The Firing Line: A Student Voice." *Daily Texan*, 20 May 1956, p. 4.

The editor of the *Texas Observer* congratulates Morris as he finishes his term as *Daily Texan* editor. "You have refused to be embarrassed in the act of confessing that you believe in high principles.... As you go on I hope you will come to prefer failing at your own work to succeeding at somebody else's. Good luck." A letter to the editor.

1525 "William Morris Graduates with Highest Honors." *Yazoo City Herald*, 7 June 1956, p. 3.

"William Morris received his Bachelor of Arts degree from the University of Texas at the 73rd annual commencement exercises Saturday, June 3, graduating Magna cum Laude."

1526 "Hot Flashes." *Texas Observer*, 10 October 1956, p. 2.

Recalls that after an "impertinent" Morris editorialized in the *Daily Texan* against state sacred cows, the University of Texas Regents threatened him "with total censorship and emasculated the newspaper by giving it a full-time censor."

1527 "Morris Is to Edit Continuing Observer." *Texas Observer*, 16 December 1960, pp. 1, 5.

Announces that the *Texas Observer* "is continuing publication with former Rhodes Scholar Willie Morris the editor and general manager." Includes a few paragraphs of biography and a statement by Morris "about the change in the Observer editorship" (see item 570).

1528 "Observer Changes to a Fortnightly." *Texas Observer*, 9 November 1962, p. 1.

Texas Observer editor Willie Morris "has decided to resign and move to California." Ronnie Dugger, former editor of the weekly publication, "will return to the editorship, and the Observer itself will become a fortnightly."

1529 "Dialogue: A Writer on Morris' Observer." *Texas Observer*, 16 November 1962, p. 7.

Readers of the *Texas Observer* comment on the periodical in general and Morris's editorship in particular. Writes Roger Shattuck: "What has kept the paper ticking under Willie's direction is his search for sturdy style in himself and in his contributors. By keeping his attention constantly on the writing, he could keep the issues and the personalities in perspective. In Texas they loom so large they would overwhelm a mere journalist who thought only in terms of news."

1530 Sutherland, Tom. "Adios to W. M." *Texas Observer*, 16 November 1962, p. 1.

As Morris prepares to leave the *Texas Observer*, one of its contributing editors writes a poignant — but not maudlin — tribute to his friend and colleague. "As editor, Willie Morris gave the Observer an individualistic, judicious direction, outstanding, without a doubt, in intelligence and perspective and brilliant in exposition of his point of view." Sutherland occasionally sees Morris in "vignettes" of his memory, "as when in an ancient cantina he surprised the international company assembled there, by borrowing, with courtesy, the professional trumpeter's horn and blowing a long blast of pure Dixieland bugle notes until the night was full and the mesquite shook on both sides of the border."

1531 D[ugger], R[onnie]. "Observations." *Texas Observer*, 13 December 1962, pp. 14–15.

In the second section of this three-part article, Dugger remembers Morris's last few hours in Texas. "Willie's gone. He left the other night. He wanted to have a few beers at the tavern and then leave directly from there in the station wagon he was driving to an auction in Los Angeles.... At the tavern, two others and he and I talked for longer than we though[t] we would, two hours? It was the kind of talk without which he, and before him I, could have gone mad in the isolation of the Observer, the loneliness and exhaustion."

1532 Weedman, Joyce Jane. "Harper's Employs Ex-Editor of Texan." University of Texas *Summer Texan*, 4 June 1963, p. 1.

Morris, a "youthful legend" at the University of Texas, has been named an assistant editor of *Harper's Magazine*. "Morris was graduated from the University in 1956 after a memorable battle with the administration over articles written for the Texan."

1533 "Texan Ex-Editor to Speak Here." *Daily Texan*, 12 October 1965, p. 1.

Former *Daily Texan* editor Morris will return to campus on October 13 "to speak on 'The University of Texas in the 1950's.' ... He will speak in connection with the Program in Criticism of the College of Arts and Sciences."

1534 Maddigan, Jack. "'I'm Proud': Ex-Texan Editor Recalls His Days on Controversy." *Austin American*, 14 October 1965, sec. A, p. 7.

Relates that Morris, during a speech yesterday at the University of Texas, said that "those days in 1956 were the proudest of my life, and they always will be." While he was editor of the *Daily Texan*, he became embroiled in a "controversy over whether student editors have the right to discuss sensitive state and national issues in their publications." Morris noted that the mid–1950s on campus were "stolid and unimaginative times." The "general mood of complacency and 'smugness,' Morris said, made the desire of The Daily Texan to speak on important issues seem out of place." See also: Shelton, Sharon. "1950's: Morris Says Administration Stifled Ideals It Spawned." *Daily Texan*, 14 October 1965, pp. 1, 3.

1535 King, Larry L. "The Ole Country Boys." *Texas Observer*, 24 June 1966, pp. 10–12.

A humorous account of a weekend at Morris's country home in Putnam County, New York. Besides King and his wife, the guests included "Famous Arthurs" William Styron, Robert Penn Warren, and C. Vann Woodward. "I might have calmed myself before the Famous Arthurs appeared had not Willie kept asking me if I'd go over the names of the guests, and the books they'd written, just one more time. Nothing personal, he just wanted to be sure I had it down pat."

1536 Raymont, Henry. "Harper's Shifting Its Top Personnel." *New York Times*, 12 May 1967, p. 44.

Reports both the resignation of *Harper's* editor-in-chief John Fischer and the appointment of Morris, the magazine's thirty-two-year-old executive editor, as his successor. Morris's first editorial decision will be to announce today the appointment of writers David Halberstam and Larry L. King as contributing editors. "In an interview last night, Mr. Morris expressed the hope 'that the magazine will have a stronger appeal to younger readers— young in age, young at heart.'"

1537 "Yazoo Native Is Harper's Editor." *Clarion-Ledger*, 24 May 1967, p. 12.

"New York City's youngest editor, William Weaks Morris of Yazoo City," has been appointed editor-in-chief of *Harper's Magazine*. "Mr. Morris was in Yazoo City the middle of April where he spoke in observance of National Library Week."

1538 "Harper's Is Placed in Willie's Hands." *Texas Observer*, 26 May 1967, p. 11.

"Two contributing editors of the Texas Observer have moved into key positions with *Harper's* magazine, the influential, 117-year-old monthly journal of national affairs. Willie Morris has, at 32, become editor-in-chief of the publication and has named Larry L. King, 38, as one of his contributing editors." Morris graduated from the University of Texas in Austin "and is well-remembered on the campus for his fight against censorship of the Daily Texan while serving as that paper's editor."

1539 "His Terrible Swift Sword." *Richmond (Va.) News Leader*, 6 July 1967, p. 12.

An editorial commentary on Morris's "The Bear on Madison Avenue," a section of *North Toward Home* serialized in *Harper's Magazine* (item 728) that contains "panoramic vignettes of his life in Gotham." Two "vignettes" featuring Morris's angry confrontations with racists are recounted, with the editorial writer concluding, "We trust that all this purges and redeems the Mississippi blood of Editor Morris in the eyes of his *Harper's* clientele."

1540 "Excerpt to Appear from Morris' Book." *Yazoo City Herald*, 28 September 1967, sec. 1, p. 2.

Announces that the *Saturday Evening Post* will publish part of Morris's autobiography *North Toward Home*. "Entitled, 'The Yazoo Years,' the selection deals with the author's impressions as a child of his surroundings." See item 729.

1541 Mott, Norman, Jr. "Random Thoughts." *Yazoo City Herald*, 5 October 1967, sec. 1, p. 1.

In a page-one article, the editor and publisher of Morris's hometown newspaper supports the author for writing candidly in "The Yazoo Years" (item 729) and providing excerpts from his forthcoming memoir *North Toward Home*. "Nothing in recent years has caused such a local stir as Willie Morris' article in the Saturday Evening Post entitled, 'The Yazoo Years.' We liked his story and thought it fascinating.... Some of what Willie wrote offended many Yazooans who are chauvinistic to the degree they wish nothing but flattering accounts would be published concerning their hometown." Although this view is "admirable" and one that Morris "understands," he "wrote his impressions as he honestly recalled them from his childhood and adolescence."

1542 Kenny, Herbert A. "2 Southern Writers Display Different Brands of Courage." *Boston Globe*, 11 October 1967, p. 12.

Brief profiles of two southern authors: William Bradford Huie (*The Klansman*) and Willie Morris (*North Toward Home*), with "the two of them a vivid contrast in determinations and attitudes." Huie is a "fighter" and a "man who has elected to take the side of the Negro in Alabama and put his life on the line." Morris is a "self-admitted exile, repelled by the brutality of the South," whose book title "reveals his estrangement." In *North Toward Home* he "may have done a courageous thing" by choosing "to challenge, ridicule and denounce the super-parochialism of New York City."

1543 Collins, Clifton (Bo), Jr. "'Bo' Collins to Willie." *Yazoo City Herald*, 12 October 1967, sec. 1, p. 1.

One of Morris's childhood acquaintances rebukes the author for using "ridicule and exaggerations" while describing him in the *Saturday Evening Post* excerpts from *North Toward Home* (item 729). Morris has "deeply hurt my parents, and brought undue hurt and embarrassment to the school, church and friends. I'm proud to be a Yazooan, and I'm proud of my Graball heritage." In chapter 1, pages 21–22 of the "Mississippi" section of *North Toward Home*, Morris writes that the "'redneck' boys" are from the Graball Hill area of Yazoo City. "I particularly liked one of these boys, the gentlest one from Graball. His name was Bo. He was the slowest reader in the class, and he wore the same clothes every day." Morris's response to the letter appeared in the newspaper a week later:

A Morris, Willie. "From Willie to Bo, Others." *Yazoo City Herald*, 19 October 1967, sec. 1, p. 1.

Morris replies to Collins's "touching and generous letter" in the *Herald*. "The little boy named 'Bo' ... was not you, not by any means. It was a composite portrait of many little boys I was fortunate enough to grow up with and whom I loved. I did not have you in mind when I wrote it, and it is not a specific reference to you." Morris adds that Collins should be proud of his Graball Hill heritage, "which represents one of many great heritages in Mississippi, in the South, and in America." (This letter to the editor is also documented as item 961.)

1544 Quinn, Bert. "Letter to the Editor." *Yazoo City Herald*, 12 October 1967, sec. 1, p. 2.

Does not appreciate Morris's depiction of Yazoo City in "The Yazoo Years" (item 729). Perhaps the essay "is a literary one, coming from the editor of Harper's, but I could not see where it was flattering to the home town.... Doubtless Mr. Morris wrote of things as he saw them during his years of growing up, but my recollections of an earlier era were a bit brighter than he painted."

1545 Nordell, Roderick. "Harper's Turns to New Audience." *Christian Science Monitor*, 17 October 1967, p. 7.

An interview with Morris, who as the editor of *Harper's* is attempting "to reach a younger audience with a long familiar product." The magazine "is seeking a freshened 'attitude of mind,' pertaining to 'engagement,' 'involvement,' and 'the use of the language.' Mr. Morris said he was convinced intellectual content and entertainment could be combined. He is trying to release writers' talents through giving them 'as much elbow room as possible.' In this way, he said, 'If you get the right writers, the results can be good.'"

1546 Cross, Leslie. "Willie Morris, All-American." *Milwaukee Journal*, 22 October 1967, sec. 5, p. 4.

An interview with Morris upon the publication of *North Toward Home*. He "started the book as fiction, then decided it would be better to tell his experiences as they happened. 'I tried to use the techniques of fiction, though,' he explained. 'I wanted the book to be a work of imagination as well as fact, with a steady narrative flow.'" Republished in *Conversations with Willie Morris* (item 1947). See also item 974.

1547 Yarbro, Louise Joseph. "'Willie, You're a Dilly.'" *Yazoo City Herald*, 26 October 1967, sec. 3, p. 4.

A long, rambling letter to the editor concerning Morris's "The Yazoo Years" (item 729). "I am sure your book is a great achievement and you should be proud to be its author; I wish only you had not used such elaborate words for it is rather boring to fumble through the dictionary as if it were a telephone directory."

1548 Exum, Kinchen. "Chattanoogan on Willie." *Yazoo City Herald*, 2 November 1967, sec. 1, p. 6.

A letter to the editor in which a native of Yazoo City finds "no offense" in Morris's "The Yazoo Years" (item 729). "Politics might give rancor to some; most politics do, at one time or another. His sensitivity to racial conditions might alienate others, but we have been aware of these changing racial relationships" for many years. "Leave Willie Morris alone — and hope that he will write more." Exum is an associate editor of the *Chattanooga News-Free Press*.

1549 A Herald Reader. "'Red Neck' Likes It." *Yazoo City Herald*, 2 November 1967, sec. 1, p. 7.

A reader of the *Yazoo City Herald* "enjoyed" Morris's "The Yazoo Years" (item 729) "very much" and believes that city residents "should take pride that one of our town, that a lot of us knew, has made good in the literary world." A letter to the editor.

1550 Gary, Nelson. "Post Article Appalls." *Yazoo City Herald*, 9 November 1967, sec. 1, p. 6.

A former resident of Yazoo City writes the town newspaper to say he "was appalled" at Morris's article in the *Saturday Evening Post* (item 729). "The impression given of Yazoo by Mr. Morris hasn't been the same impression I've given of my old home town."

1551 Grittner, Carolyn Powell. "Willie Meant No Harm." *Yazoo City Herald*, 9 November 1967, sec. 1, p. 6.

Grittner writes in her letter to the editor that it was "a pleasure" to read Morris's "The Yazoo Years" (item 729), and she "was very surprised" at the many letters in the newspaper that criticized it. "I got the distinct impression from reading the article that Mr. Morris loved Yazoo and really cherished the memories of his boyhood and his friends."

1552 Frederick, J. J. "Willie's Book Is Finest!" *Yazoo City Herald*, 16 November 1967, sec. 2, p. 8.

A Jackson, Mississippi, resident writes the editor of the *Herald* that Morris "writes with deep feeling and integrity" in *North Toward Home* and she considers the book to be "one of the finest I have read this year."

1553 Kelly, Carol. "Willie's Honesty Admired." *Yazoo City Herald*, 16 November 1967, sec. 1, p. 5.

Morris has "filled" his article on "how life was" in Yazoo City during his youth (item 729), "with warmth, humor and the sincerity that only one who looks deep within himself can know. He has offered Yazoo City a precious gift — if only Yazoo City will accept it." A letter to the editor.

1554 O[lds], G[reg]. "Willie Morris in Texas." *Texas Observer*, 24 November 1967, pp. 8–9.

After reading *North Toward Home*, a staff member on the *Daily Texan* during Morris's editorship reminisces about "this remarkable young man" and his years in Texas. "There are many well-told tales of Texas public life in this book, a number of which will be familiar to Texans but which are brought vividly alive by Willie's engaging style." Olds "had no voice in the decisions that led to the *Texan* making its memorable stand against the board of regents' censorship. Nonetheless I am proud that, along with every other staff member, from the managing editor to the last freshman copy reader, we were all prepared to resign should someone on high have removed Willie from the editorship."

1555 Powell, Gene Harlan. "Willie's Book Honest." *Yazoo City Herald*, 7 December 1967, sec. 1, p. 2.

Powell, a Jackson, Mississippi, folklorist and frequent contributor to the *Herald*, recommends Morris's memoir in a letter to the editor. "I think anyone who reads 'North Toward Home' will come out of it with a little better understanding, a keener eye, and a better knowledge of our generation." See also item 1557.

1556 "Yazoo in Limelight." *Yazoo City Herald*, 14 December 1967, sec. 1, p. 2.

An editorial acknowledging the "national publicity" Yazoo City has been receiving since the publication of *North Toward Home*, such as the *Saturday Evening Post* excerpts (item 729), the book's numerous reviews, and Morris's December 13 appearance on NBC's *Today* show. While discussing his autobiography on television, "Mr. Morris was especially effective in telling everyone how proud he was of being a Mississippian and what an immense value he placed on his heritage. His interview undoubtedly helped others, particularly Yankees, to understand the correct perspective of the context of his book."

1557 Powell, Gene H. "'Write, Willie, Write!'" *Yazoo City Herald*, 21 December 1967, sec. 1, p. 16.

An open letter to Morris praising *North Toward Home*. "I am proud to see your book is on an uphill ride; and I hope it is doing well in other parts of the nation. And I am proud enough of what you have done for Yazoo City, the old hometown, that, at times, I feel like gathering up about a dozen staunch, high-volume Willie Morris supporters, and climbing to the Dome of the Old Capitol, and shouting, 'Write, Willie, Write.'" See also item 1555.

1558 "North Carolina's Sacred Cow." *Chapel Hill (N.C.) Weekly*, 28 January 1968, p. 2.

Points out the similarities between Texas's oil and gas industry — one of Morris's "favorite targets" when he edited the *Texas Observer* — and North Carolina's tobacco industry.

1559 Dann, Joanne. "Harper's Editor Labels Suburbia 'Boring As Hell.'" *(Mount Kisco, N.Y.) Patent Trader*, 3 February 1968, p. 1.

Morris, who once commuted to New York City from Putnam County, New York, disparages suburban life in an interview. "Mr. Morris, who describes upper Westchester from the commuter run as 'little bedroom towns with Indian names, the names as pathetic as the names one saw on the little lower-class houses in the working districts in England, and artificial, so unlike the raw towns with Indian names I had once known in the Mississippi delta,' lived in a suburb 30 miles south of San Francisco for awhile. 'I missed a real feeling of community there in the broad sense. In New York, I get that feeling almost despite the city. Here I'm involved with the most exciting writers in the country — though the backbiting of the intellectual community is somethin' to behold.'"

1560 Raymont, Henry. "Harper's and Atlantic Put Out 'Vietnam' Issues." *New York Times*, 19 February 1968, p. 14.

Both *Harper's Magazine* and the *Atlantic Monthly* are devoting most of their March issues to "single articles" on the Vietnam War. *Harper's* will publish Norman Mailer's 90,000-word article "The Steps of the Pentagon," which covers "his experiences during the Washington peace demonstration last October." In an interview, Morris said "he had initially asked Mr. Mailer to write a 20,000-word piece for Harper's February issue. But the article 'just kept growing and growing into what I think became Norman's best work ever, so we decided to run it all in March,' he added cheerfully."

1561 "Morris Joins Ranks of Letters Institute." *Daily Texan*, 17 March 1968, p. 1.

"Willie Morris, a former student at the University, was among the six new members elected to the Texas Institute of Letters, Joe Frantz, Institute president, said Thursday. Morris is a former editor of The Daily Texan and the Texas Observer."

1562 "Harper's Editor Cites U.S. Role." *Dallas Times Herald*, 24 March 1968.

Morris has won the Texas Institute of Letters' Carr P. Collins Award for *North Toward Home*, "the best nonfiction book of the year by a Texan." At the awards banquet, Morris said that "I strongly believe our country truly needs a national magazine, young and courageous enough to carry the language to its limits to reflect the great tensions, complexities and even madnesses of the day; to help give the country some feel of itself and what it is becoming." See also: "Willie's Book Wins $1000 Texas Award." *Yazoo City Herald*, 28 March 1968, sec. 1, p. 2.

1563 Holt, David Earl. "New Book News." *Austin American-Statesman*, 12 May 1968, sec. T, p. 24.

Reports that on May 9 in the University of Texas's Hogg Auditorium, Norman Podhoretz, editor of *Commentary* magazine, and Morris addressed a near-capacity audience on "Interpretations of Contemporary American Thought." Morris "said that he started 'North Toward Home' as fiction, then threw away that part (he wanted to describe what it was like in America's three 'most violent societies'); recalled the latest report from Yazoo City was that the book had split the town in half (those not mentioned comprised the maddest half!); and spoke of his own devotion to human causes and dedication to 'civility.'" He thought that the *Texas Observer* "provided a platform for dissenters," and he characterized his editorship as "cleansing." See also: Davis, Linda. "Morris, Podhoretz: Editors View Social Trends." *Daily Texan*, 10 May 1968, p. 1.

1564 "Ford Chooses Panel to Award TV Grants." *New York Times*, 15 May 1968, p. 95.

"The Ford Foundation yesterday named the panel of judges who will select recipients of its grants for cultural and public affairs programs." One of the panel members is "Willie Morris, editor in chief of Harper's Magazine."

1565 "Willie Gets Degree." *Yazoo City Herald*, 30 May 1968, sec. 3, p. 5.

Announces that Willie Morris, "the youngest editor of the 117 year old Harper's magazine," will receive an honorary doctor of literature degree from Gettysburg College during its annual commencement ceremony on June 2.

1566 Raymont, Henry. "Magazines Rushing to Change Material After the Assassination." *New York Times*, 8 June 1968, p. 22.

Following the assassination of Senator Robert F. Kennedy, some magazine publishers are either "eliminating material now regarded in poor taste" or "adding commentaries on the tragic event." *Harper's Magazine* "held up its July issue for two days to insert an editorial note by Willie Morris written the morning of the Senator's death" (item 730). Morris said that the August issue would include an "expanded version" of a speech Arthur M. Schlesinger gave at City University's doctoral commencement ceremonies on June 5. "In the speech Professor Schlesinger called on all Americans to 'uncover the roots of hatred and violence.'" See also item 1567.

1567 Raymont, Henry. "Max Ascoli Leaves Harper's in Rift Over Schlesinger Article." *New York Times*, 14 June 1968, p. 44.

Dr. Max Ascoli, an editorial board member of *Harper's Magazine*, has resigned "in protest over the magazine's plans to publish an article in its August issue by Prof. Arthur Schlesinger Jr. on the conflict between traditional liberals and the theorists of the New Left." Ascoli, who "had been working on a similar article for the same issue," said he was "shocked" when he read in the *New York Times* that Morris had asked Schlesinger to contribute the piece (item 1566). The decision, he observed, "can be justified only by an incurable youthfulness."

1568 Raymont, Henry. "Harper's Magazine Will Shift Executives Today." *New York Times*, 26 August 1968, p. 36.

Harper's Magazine, Inc. is planning to restructure the publication "into a more aggressive topical magazine." Among several personnel changes, Morris "will continue as editor in chief, a post he has held since May, 1967, and become executive vice president."

1569 Wilson, Dana. "Willie Morris Views Texas." *Daily Texan*, 27 September 1968, pp. 1–2.

In an address at Southwestern University in Georgetown, Texas, Morris talked about Texas "as seen through the eyes of a university student, a liberal Texas editor, and the editor of one of America's most relevant magazines." While discussing promising young writers and intellectuals of the state such as Bill Brammer, Ronnie Dugger, and Larry McMurtry, "He spoke of there being 'real potential here,' and attributed it in great part to a certain dedication to human causes and a 'sense of place' in our depersonalized world shared by these writers."

1570 Raymont, Henry. "A New Weekly Newspaper Makes Debut Here." *New York Times*, 14 November 1968, p. 40.

Morris is on the advisory committee of the *Manhattan Tribune*, a new weekly tabloid newspaper "conceived as an interracial enterprise."

1571 Whitcraft, Carol. "Harper's Editor Willie Morris Due 'Roundup' Honors." *Austin American*, 16 November 1968, p. 33.

A summary and brief appraisal of *North Toward Home*, one of eleven books that will receive honors at the twentieth annual Texas Writers Roundup on November 23. The Roundup is an "annual benefit program" sponsored by the Austin Professional Chapter of Theta Sigma Phi, a national society for women in journalism, to provide scholarships for women in American colleges and universities.

1572 Raymont, Henry. "Harper's Editor Hails Polk Prize for Mailer." *New York Times*, 28 March 1969, p. 57.

While presenting the George Polk Memorial Lecture at the Polk annual awards luncheon program, Morris advised writers and editors "to use 'the full richness and inventiveness and daring of the American idiom,' in the portrayal of current events, but not to exploit bold language solely to create a sense of shock." Morris praised Norman Mailer, who won the 1969 George Polk Memorial Award for magazine reporting, as "the finest writer working in America today." The awards are named for a CBS correspondent killed in Greece in 1948.

1573 Cohen, Richard. "*Harper's* Willie Morris." *Women's Wear Daily: The Retailer's Daily Newspaper*, 19 August 1969, pp. 38–39.

Morris discusses his plans for *Harper's Magazine* in one of his earliest interviews for a national publication. "*Harper's* has not only survived — it's 116 years old, America's oldest magazine — but it has retained its influence. The primary reason it's been able to do that is because it has always changed with the times. I want *Harper's* to continue to reflect the American experience. As a magazine it must show the outrages, the faults, the failures of American society. For if America doesn't make it, the whole human race isn't going to make it. We want to be a liberal magazine with uncommitted liberal writers who know a lot about this country, who can capture something of the feeling of the country right now." Republished in *Conversations with Willie Morris* (item 1949).

1574 Burton, Marda. "Willie Morris Shows His Heart Stays in Yazoo." *Yazoo City Herald*, 23 April 1970, sec. A, p. 8.

After meeting with Morris and some of his friends in New York City, a free-lance writer from Laurel, Mississippi, offers her impressions of the writer "as a person and as the editor of Harper's magazine." Although Morris titled his book *North Toward Home*, "His heart is a far piece from the concrete jungle; it's right down on the Yazoo. Sure, New York is where it's happening in the literary world and is where he has to be, but he is admittedly 'obsessed by the South.'" His position as editor of *Harper's* "is an awesome responsibility and he is dedicated to making the magazine a living thing, a humane and civilized voice of our society." See also item 1597.

1575 Rebuffoni, Dean. "Willie Morris: From Yazoo City to New York 'Literary.'" *St. Louis Globe-Democrat*, 29 April 1970, sec. C, p. 1.

An interview with Morris prior to his address at Washington University in St. Louis. "And Willie Morris tells you that being editor-in-chief of Harper's isn't so much Horatio Alger as it is being a young man in a young man's business, which he says the magazine business is. He claims he got there because he's a Southerner, saying this with a big grin and a Yazoo City 'hee-haw.'" During his presentation in the university chapel, "He tells his audience that America 'seems profoundly at war with itself,' that he has great faith in the South, that the Southern white and the Southern black have more in common than they do with people in the North and that he believes all American magazines are better than they have ever been."

1576 "Yazooans Complimented...." *Yazoo City Herald*, 28 May 1970, sec. A, p. 1.

A page-one editorial announcing the publication of Morris's cover story in the June issue of *Harper's Magazine* on how citizens of Yazoo City reacted to the Supreme Court–ordered integration of their public schools (item 731). "Our way of life is being forced to change to accommodate the very real and unrelenting pressures which are affecting all similarly situated communities." Morris's lengthy article "pertains to the editor's observations and evaluations of how his hometown met its biggest challenge and did so in a manner that not only brought national acclaim for its citizens but also exemplified what can be done when leaders rise to their responsibility.... Our purpose here is to say that Willie Morris' article is bas[ic]ally a factual account of how our community went through the historical crisis."

1577 Mitchell, Henry. "Harper's Editor Resigns." *Washington Post*, 5 March 1971, sec. B, pp. 1, 8.

Morris has resigned from *Harper's* "over what some of his friends called the long-range development of the 121-year-old magazine. Morris was named editor in 1967 to bring a sense of the surging American scene to the stately journal." Some of his friends "said that for more than a month he had seemed to 'lose heart.' The usual reason given for this was that Morris was spending more money" on the magazine than its publishers "thought was justified."

1578 Whitman, Alden. "Morris Resigns in Harper's Dispute." *New York Times*, 5 March 1971, pp. 37, 71.

Thirty-six-year-old Morris has "resigned unexpectedly" as editor of *Harper's Magazine*, a position he had held for the past four years. "Mr. Morris, in a statement last night, said he had quit in a dispute between 'the money men and the literary men.' He added that '[The] Prisoner of Sex,' an article by Norman Mailer in the current issue dealing with the women's liberation movement, had also 'deeply disturbed' the magazine's owners." Morris stated that "I deeply loved the magazine" and the day he submitted his resignation was "the saddest day of my life." A detailed account.

1579 Frazier, George. "The Lit'ry Life." *Boston Globe*, 6 March 1971, sec. 1, p. 6.

Laments Morris's resignation from *Harper's*, which "was announced abruptly and shockingly and very, very sadly." Morris "is one of the few authentically great editors. In four years, he converted a moribund, stuffy, utterly humorless Harper's into one of the very best magazines ever published in America." He managed to acquire a staff of writers "who not only write like dreams but have insatiable investigative zeal."

1580 Mitchell, Henry. "Willie Morris' Options." *Washington Post*, 6 March 1971, sec. E, p. 5.

Discloses that prior to Morris's March 4 resignation as editor of *Harper's*, he attended a meeting with magazine owner John Cowles Jr. and publisher William S. Blair to review possible solutions for solving the publication's budget problems. Yesterday Morris discussed with his staff the various scenarios, which included: stop publishing the magazine, "retrench" and pare circulation, trim the budget by half, and fire the principal staff writers. "Since none of the choices was acceptable to Morris, he resigned."

1581 "Editors Will Meet with Harper's Head." *New York Times*, 7 March 1971, sec. 1, p. 29.

John Cowles Jr., chairman of Harper's Magazine Company, will meet with the magazine's staff writers in two days to talk about the future of the publication following Morris's resignation last week as editor-in-chief. "Mr. Morris, who called his departure 'a protest against the calculated destruction of Harper's,' charged that the magazine's 'money men' had won a dispute with its 'literary men' and that the management intended to change the publication 'to a more specialized journal.'" Morris also contended that the magazine's publishers wanted to reduce the editorial budget and "get rid of" the magazine's contributing editors.

1582 "Mailer Through with Harper's." *Washington Post*, 8 March 1971, sec. B, p. 2.

Author Norman Mailer declares he will not write for *Harper's Magazine* now that Morris is no longer editor. Mailer, who said he was "shocked" when he heard that Morris had resigned, insisted, "At the bottom of it all is a profound disagreement about what direction Harper's is going in." He said "he suspected there was 'a strong connection' between Morris' resignation and publication in Harper's this month of 'The Prisoner of Sex,' a long Mailer essay dealing with women's liberation."

1583 "3 Pulitzer Winners Make Harper's Plea." *New York Times*, 10 March 1971, p. 40.

Pulitzer Prize winners Arthur Miller (playwright), William Styron (novelist), and Arthur M. Schlesinger Jr. (historian) "are among a number of prominent writers who have signed an appeal to John Cowles Jr., chairman of the board of Harper's, asking that he rehire Willie Morris as editor-in-chief." Others who signed the telegram that emphasized how Morris "had been instrumental in making the monthly an important and exciting publication" include James Jones, John Kenneth Galbraith, Gay Talese, and Tom Wicker.

1584 Schumach, Murray. "6 Harper Editors Resign After Talk with Cowles." *New York Times*, 11 March 1971, p. 43.

Harper's managing editor Robert Kotlowitz; contributing editors David Halberstam, Larry L. King, John Corry, and Marshall Frady; and poetry editor John Hollander have resigned after meeting with *Harper's* board chairman John Cowles Jr. They offered to stay if Kotlowitz was appointed editor, but Cowles replied that *Harper's* publisher William S. Blair would select the successor to Morris, who quit his position as editor-in-chief last week. "At the opening of the meeting on Tuesday night, Mr. Cowles read a statement in which he stressed declines in the magazine's advertising and circulation."

1585 "An Interim Editor Named at Harper's." *New York Times*, 16 March 1971, p. 35.

Harper's publisher William S. Blair has announced that John Fischer, editor-in-chief of the magazine from 1953 to 1967, will return as its interim editor. "The magazine lost its editor in chief, Willie Morris, two weeks ago when he resigned in a dispute with John Cowles Jr., the principal proprietor of Harper's." Blair said that he was "a long way" from selecting a permanent editor.

1586 "Harper's to Select a New Editor Soon." *New York Times*, 19 March 1971, p. 36.

"A new editor in chief for Harper's Magazine to succeed Willie Morris will be chosen in six to eight weeks, William S. Blair, the periodical's publisher, said yesterday." Blair added that although he was seen as the villain in the clash between Morris and *Harper's* owner John Cowles Jr., he was merely attempting to strengthen the magazine's shaky financial condition.

1587 "Notes on People." *New York Times*, 6 May 1971, p. 48.

"Willie Morris, out of a job since he resigned as editor of Harper's magazine in a bitter dispute with its publishers last March, has been offered a visiting professorship at Duke University 'for a week, a month, a year, as long as I like,' he said." While considering the offer, he will "travel about plugging his new book," *Yazoo: Integration in a Deep-Southern Town.*

1588 "Willie Morris Coming to Delta East-West." *Yazoo City Herald*, 6 May 1971, sec. A, p. 12.

Announces that Morris will be in Yazoo City on May 11 at the Delta East-West store on Main Street for a "book party" in honor of his latest book, *Yazoo.* The volume "chronicles the experiences of his hometown during the historic court ordered integration of the public school system."

1589 "Noted Yazooan Is Visitor." *Yazoo City Herald*, 13 May 1971, sec. A, p. 1.

A photograph of Willie Morris, Marion Morris (his mother), and Mr. and Mrs. Wyeth Ramsay that was taken after the author's book-signing party at the Delta East-West store in Yazoo City (see item 1588). "Mrs. Ramsay reports her store sold out of the initial order of 100 copies of 'Yazoo,' Mr. Morris' new book and she has re-ordered."

1590 Cotton, Gordon. "Yazoo Author: Back Home Again." *Vicksburg (Miss.) Evening Post*, 14 May 1971, p. 5.

An interview with Morris after he returns to his hometown to sign copies of his recently published *Yazoo: Integration in a Deep-Southern Town.* "'Yazoo was one of the first 30 school districts to integrate under the Alexander [v. Holmes] Decision,' Morris said, 'and since I grew up here I decided to see what would happen.... The book is reportorial in its core and it is also highly objective,' he stated. 'In a sense it's also autobiographical, but it also has a journalistic base to it. I've been a great believer in this sort of personal, autobiolgraphical [sic] writing.'"

1591 Powell, Lew. "On Being the Famous Writer Willie Morris." *(Greenville, Miss.) Delta Democrat-Times*, 16 May 1971, sec. 1, p. 5.

In a question-and-answer session during a stop on his book tour for *Yazoo*, Morris discusses the strengths and flaws of *North Toward Home*, his years at *Harper's*, his literary career plans, and the difficulties he faces while writing fiction. "I've been living in New York City for eight years and ran this magazine which I think was a truly great one — the best magazine of our day — but now that that's really behind, all I want to do is to do my work. That's what I've always wanted to do — to tell stories and everything — and the most gratifying thing in the world to me is my own writing. It's not much fun to do it, but it's immensely gratifying, and I do want to spend the rest of my life at it — and I'm going to." Republished in *Conversations with Willie Morris* (item 1951). See also item 1017.

1592 Kass, Carole. "Writer Says South Will Pioneer Racial Harmony." *Richmond (Va.) Times-Dispatch*, 19 May 1971, sec. B, p. 6.

During an interview, Morris talks about his book *Yazoo*, race relations, and his editorship of *Harper's Magazine.* He believes that "the 'harmonious living together of the races' will be pioneered by the South," for as he shows in *Yazoo*, the residents of his hometown, Yazoo City, peacefully integrated their public schools. He remarks to a reporter that "one of the crazy ironies is that while adults are stirring up antagonism, the kids are handling the situation well." Morris "describes Harper's as 'encouraging and defending our best writers and journalists against the distractions and philistinisms of modern America.'" After resigning as editor in March, "He looks back on his magazine experience as failure ... 'I'll never go back to a magazine,' he said yesterday, firmly, regretfully and reflectively. 'It didn't work.'"

1593 The Mule Rider. "Remember the Mule." *Yazoo City Herald*, 20 May 1971, sec. C, p. 11.

An anonymous writer from Benton, Mississippi, defends Morris in a disjointed letter to the editor. The reason for the defense is not given, although it probably relates to Morris's book *Yazoo.* "I have said before and will say again that Willie has written of the South objectively and from the heart. I predict that someday Willie will be the man who will project the real image of the south for the world to see."

1594 Hayes, Marcia. "Harper's Limps Along Without Morris." *Boston Globe*, 23 May 1971, sec. 1, p. 38.

Recounts the controversial dispute between Morris and the management of *Harper's* and muses about the Mississippian's possible successor as editor-in-chief. The magazine "is taking its time replacing the talented staff that walked out in a huff over policy last March." *Harper's* president and chief executive William S. Blair said that he has "a good list of prospects," but "he would not say who was on the list to replace Willie Morris." Editors in New York and Boston who were polled on the subject mentioned Bill Moyers (former *Newsday* publisher), Otto Freidrich (former editor of the *Saturday Evening Post*), and Jim Thomson (Harvard University professor). All three are believed "to have turned down the job, largely because of fierce editorial loyalty to Morris."

1595 Raymont, Henry. "Shnayerson, Time Editor, To Get Top Job at Harper's." *New York Times*, 16 June 1971, p. 35.

"Robert Shnayerson, a senior editor of Time magazine, has been selected as the new editor in chief of Harper's magazine, succeeding Willie Morris, who resigned last March in a dispute with the magazine's management."

1596 "Mrs. Morris Reports on Visiting Willie." *Yazoo City Herald*, 8 July 1971, sec. A, p. 7.

At the request of the *Yazoo City Herald*, Marion Morris contributes an "interesting account" of her trip to Wainscott, New York, to visit her son, Willie. "One of the most interesting evenings was the one spent with the Dick Cavetts at their home at Montauk on the tip of Long Island, 18 miles from Wainscott. Willie is a friend of Dick Cavett and of his wife, Carrie Nye, and has appeared as a guest on the Cavett show several times." Morris recalls the visit with Cavett and Nye in chapter 13, pages 289–92 of *New York Days*.

1597 "Willie Morris on TV Monday, Channel 29." *Yazoo City Herald*, 4 November 1971, sec. A, p. 12.

A brief article notes that Marda Burton's interview with Morris will be televised on November 8 during a fifteen-minute segment of "Southern Perspective," a production of the Southeastern Television Network. "In the interview Morris talks informally about himself as he writes of his life inside and outside Mississippi, stressing the importance of his roots in the South to his work. In a level-headed, self-assured manner, he talks frankly and clearly about the South, his future and the literary establishment." Burton's April 1970 profile of Morris in the *Yazoo City Herald* (item 1574) "won a national award for feature writing." See also item 1600.

1598 Dugger, Ronnie. "Fallow Fields." *Texas Observer*, 5 November 1971, pp. 21, 23.

Discusses and evaluates the books and literary careers of Texas writers John Graves, Elroy Bode, Larry McMurtry, Bill Brammer, Shirley Ann Grau, Morris, and several others. "Willie Morris is now working on his book. I do not know what book, and would not ask, because when a man as grave, passionate and fine as Willie says he is working on his book, that is all you need to know." Dugger believes that Morris "has his best work ahead of him."

1599 [Mott, Norman, Jr.] "Random Thoughts." *Yazoo City Herald*, 11 November 1971, sec. A, p. 12.

The newspaper's editor brags that "this week Yazooans can have two causes for vicarious pride," as two local authors have published their books. One of the volumes is *Good Old Boy* by Morris, "a collection of his adventures as a boy growing up in Yazoo in the 1930's and 40's."

1600 Burton, Marda. "Willie Morris on ETV: TV Interview Is Recapped." *Yazoo City Herald*, 23 December 1971, sec. B, p. 6.

Burton, who earlier this year interviewed Morris for Mississippi Educational Television (see item 1597), brings readers of the author's hometown newspaper up to date on his plans and gives her opinion of his book *Yazoo: Integration in a Deep-Southern Town*. Now that Morris has resigned from *Harper's*, "He intends to 'just write,' something he's [sic] always plenty of time to do and something many people think he should have been doing all along." Although his recently published *Yazoo* is an "absorbing and affecting document which deserves all its kudos," Burton regrets that "our spokesman" did "not warn of complacency over the peaceful integration of our schools, which in itself has little impact upon the economic situation."

1601 Johnson, Ellen. "Family, Music, Antiques—Marion's Loves." *Yazoo City Herald*, 9 March 1972, sec. B, pp. 3–4.

A profile of Morris's mother, Marion Morris. When Johnson asked Mrs. Morris "how it felt to be the mother of a famous son, she replied, 'Well, no different! He's just the same old boy. He wrote of his youth and his friends in "Good Old Boy," but it should have been "Bad Old Boy."' She hastened to explain that he 'wasn't really bad—just mischievous and full of pranks as boys are.'"

1602 Murray, Jake. "Willie Morris, Once of Yazoo." *East Hampton (N.Y.) Star*, 15 June 1972, sec. 2, p. 5.

Reports that Morris is now living in the Hamptons on Long Island at work on a novel. "Willie chose the East End in which to live and work instead of Martha's Vineyard where many of his friends go because of our potato fields that run across the outwash plain to the dunes.... In a world afraid to use such phrases anymore, Willie Morris is a sweet man. A very private person. Which may be one reason he dislikes teaching and lecturing; so much so, in fact, that he turned down an offer from Duke to do a lecture series that would have paid him almost what Harper's did as managing editor. He simply prefers life by himself here on the East End."

1603 Leonard, John. "The Top 70 Intellectuals." *New York Times Book Review*, 29 October 1972, p. 63.

Humorous comments on *Public Interest*'s list of prestigious intellectuals (item 1395). Morris's name appears in the last of the four rating categories. "You could cut the gloom with an alpenstock last week down at The Lukewarm Cavity, a watering spa.... The intellectual ratings had come out, and quite a few Lukewarmers were afraid that their credibility was about to get cancelled. They hadn't made the Top 70."

1604 Holland, Beth. "Willie Morris Source of Inspiration Likened to Japanese S[h]intoism." *Yazoo City Herald*, 18 February 1973, sec. 1, p. 2.

Examines Morris's reflections on his ancestors in *North Toward Home*, *Yazoo*, and *Good Old Boy* and argues that "the way in which Morris regards his ancestors parallels the beliefs of the S[h]into religion. This religion is a loosely organized religious cult of Japan which emphasizes loyalty to the throne and gratitude to ancestors." An editor's note indicates that Holland, a student, wrote this essay for a class assignment.

1605 MacPherson, Myra. "Belle, Books and Scandal." *Washington Post*, 13 May 1973, sec. K, pp. 1–2, 3.

Detailed profiles of and interviews with Morris, author of the novel *The Last of the Southern Girls*, and Washington, D.C., socialite Barbara Howar, who wrote the memoir *Laughing All the Way*. Morris and Howar "are friends and lovers, who have simultaneously but coincidentally, they insist, hit the market with books on similar themes: Washington and the trappings of power." Critics and readers believe that Morris modeled the heroine of his novel on Howar. Morris calls his book a "serious work of fiction" and says during an interview that "it's very, very bad timing.... It just so happens that a woman, whom I love deeply, has come out with a book about herself that coincides with my first novel."

1606 Casey, Phil. "Lunch with the Authors." *Washington Post*, 18 May 1973, sec. B, p. 3.

Relates that Morris, his friend Barbara Howar, John Kenneth Galbraith, and Chalmers Roberts were special guests at yesterday's *Washington Post* Book and Author Luncheon, attended by about 1,200 people. Morris's novel *The Last of the Southern Girls* has received both mixed reviews and notoriety, as "some people believe [Howar] is his book's heroine." Morris, however, "has confidence in his work. He does serious work and believes it will endure, he said, and he's not going to be done in by the temporary fads and fashions of today's critics."

1607 Hoffman, Marjorie. "Willie Morris Comes Home Again." *Austin American*, 25 May 1973, p. 4.

Morris, a former student at the University of Texas, returns to Austin to sign copies of his new book *The Last of the Southern Girls*. "'There were some difficulties (in switching to fiction writing),' he said. 'But then I'm a natural born liar,' he added with amusement. 'I tend to dwell in my dreams and memories a lot and I call on my impressions of things. Fiction draws on a different part of your brain.'" Notwithstanding "what reviewers tend to think of the book, Morris believes it's a durable one, 'a strong, sturdy work that is going to last.'" Republished in *Conversations with Willie Morris* (item 1952). See also Hoffman's book review (item 1062). See also "Willie Morris Here Thursday." *Austin American*, 23 May 1973, p. 43.

1608 Jacobs, Jody. "Cause Celebre with a Southern Drawl." *Los Angeles Times*, 11 June 1973, sec. 4, p. 1.

Interview with Morris upon the publication of *The Last of the Southern Girls*, a novel whose southern heroine "finds a measure of fame and quite a bit of notoriety" in Washington, D.C. Morris explains that although many books feature young men and women who travel to New York to achieve success, prior to his novel, nothing had been written "about young people from the South who go to Washington." However, "Some people are saying that the book really grew out of Morris' 'friendship' with ... Barbara Howar who was a confidante and fashion-social adviser to the Johnson women when they were in the White House." Morris "claims he doesn't read reviews and so what's been written about the book doesn't 'disturb me.'"

1609 Buckley, Tom. "80 Notables Gather in the Hamptons for a 'Rebel' Party Without Cause." *New York Times*, 29 July 1974, p. 27.

Reports that Morris, who lives in the village of Bridgehampton on Long Island, hosted eighty friends at a restaurant dinner party last night. "The invitation described the gathering as an old-time rowdy Southern party, a reflection of Mr. Morris's origins in Yazoo City, Miss., and said it would celebrate 'all of our living impulses.'"

1610 Hendricks, David. "Two Authors Read Own Works: Morris, Styron Discuss Loneliness in Writing." *Daily Texan*, 17 October 1974, p. 1.

During a program last night at the University of Texas, Morris read from *North Toward Home* and William Styron read "from an unfinished novel he is writing." At a reception afterwards, both men also discussed the loneliness of the writing profession. "Although 'it does not matter where a serious writer lives,' Morris added at the reception, 'the only thing we [writers] have is the past, the memory and dealing with it.'"

1611 Goodwyn, Larry. "Dugger's Observer." *Texas Observer*, 27 December 1974, pp. 3–5, 7–8.

Notes that on 6 November 1974, the Southern Historical Association sponsored a forum on "Recent Texas Writing: Larry McMurtry and *The Texas Observer* Group." Goodwyn, a professor of history at Duke University and a *Texas Observer* editor in the 1950s, traces the publication's impact on Texas politics and culture — and also on the lives of some of its writers. "The form of the *Observer's* literary response to the world of democratic corruption varied in interesting ways.... Willie Morris never ceased to be offended by the gracelessness of it all. Few of the plunderers seemed to him to possess a redeeming style and none seemed to have more than fleeting intuition about the human costs involved in 'the game.' Willie attempted to extract humor from the more grotesque examples of corporate regime in Austin, but the laughter often was hollow and, at such times, the underlying despair in Willie became visible."

1612 "Witch Is Coming Back, Says Willie." *Yazoo City Herald*, 30 March 1975, p. 1.

After a fourth-grade class at a local school read *Good Old Boy*, the students "decided to share their feelings with author Morris." Each one wrote him a letter, commenting on the book. His reply to the class, in which he added personal notes to some of the students, is published here. "You asked me a few questions. The most requested one is: was Spit McGee a real person? Well, yes indeed he was. In fact, he is still living out in the swamps. He lives with about 75 stray dogs. He never comes into town."

1613 Morris, David. "James Jones Talks About 'Whistle.'" *East Hampton (N.Y.) Star*, 17 July 1975, sec. 2, p. 12.

Although Morris is not mentioned in this interview (conducted by his fifteen-year-old son), it is cited because Morris completed *Whistle* after Jones's death in 1977. "Asked what he was going to do when he finished 'Whistle,' the novelist laughed and said 'I'm gonna sit on the porch.' He paused and added, 'And then I'm gonna write more books.'" A photograph of Jones taken by David Morris accompanies the interview. From page 197 of *James Jones*: "One summer [David] worked as a cub reporter on the East Hampton *Star* and did a piece on Jim about the work he was doing on *Whistle*."

1614 Morris, Dave. "Coach Morris Undone." *East Hampton (N.Y.) Star*, 24 July 1975, sec. 1, p. 9.

Coverage of a benefit softball game between the Golden Nematodes, managed by Morris, and the Spindrift Players. "When Spindrift took a 6–3 lead in the fifth inning, the Nematodes' coach, Willie Morris, decided to make several changes." He replaced the pitcher and the players at first, second, and third bases. "With this strong infield combination, the Nematodes dropped two more runs on Alan Birtwhistle's triple to left field." Dave Morris is Morris's son. See also: "Benefit Softball Sunday." *East Hampton (N.Y.) Star*, 17 July 1975, sec. 1, p. 12, which includes a photograph of Morris, "manager of the Golden Nematodes," along with Kaylie Jones, one of his players. Jones is the daughter of novelist James Jones.

1615 Morris, Dave. "Artist-Writers' Game on Saturday." *East Hampton (N.Y.) Star*, 21 August 1975, sec. 1, p. 14.

Morris's son reports that the twenty-first annual softball game "between the artists and the writers is coming up Saturday.... On deck for the writers will be such masters of the bat as Senator Eugene McCarthy, Willie Morris, Tom Paxton, and James Jones." See also: Morris, Dave. "Writers Wreak Revenge on Artists." *East Hampton (N.Y.) Star*, 28 August 1975, sec. 2, p. 5.

1616 O'Briant, Don. "A Southern Album: A New Book Attacks the Social Issues Through a Nostalgic Tour of the South. *Atlanta Constitution*, 18 October 1975, sec. B, p. 2.

An interview with Morris, Irwin Glusker (editor of *A Southern Album*), and John Logue (editor-in-chief of Oxmoor House) upon the publication of Glusker's and Morris's book. As Logue singles out a photograph in the book of a family on the front porch of a dilapidated farmhouse, he says: "What I think is great about the pictures, and the whole book, is that it shows poor people, but not the despair of so many pictures. There's hope in the faces of these people. They're a proud people. Many people can't understand that you can be poor and proud, too."

1617 "Willie Morris Begins As Star Guest Writer." *Washington Star*, 25 January 1976, sec. A, p. 2.

Morris begins writing a regular column today as the *Washington Star*'s fourth writer-in-residence. "Morris will be writing Tuesdays, Thursdays and Sundays in The Star's Portfolio section until March." Morris's columns include items 812, 814–834, and 836. See also items 16, 1618, and 1975.

1618 Delaney, William. "Willie Morris: Fiction Still Alive in U.S." *Washington Star*, 19 March 1976, sec. A, p. 1; sec. F, p. 12.

Morris has finished his term as writer-in-residence for the *Washington Star*. During an interview with *Star* staff writer William Delaney, he talks about American literature, writing, and his own career. Writing is "just something you have to dedicate your whole life to. And I think one of the things—I haven't completely thought this out—but just being down here for two months writing these pieces three times a week on all sorts of people and things in the Washington area, it's given me more of a sense of my own work and of the absolute necessity of privacy, in the deepest human sense, that I've never had before." Republished in *Authors in the News*, edited by Barbara Nykoruk. Vol. 2. Detroit: Gale Research, 1976, pp. 204–205. Republished in *Conversations with Willie Morris* (item 1953). See also item 1617.

1619 "South Toward Home." *Texas Observer*, 11 February 1977, p. 17.

Opines that Morris should "head South toward home, at least for a refresher course," because in a *Family Circle* article on "the glories of the South" (item 736), he writes that San Antonio is on the Trinity River.

1620 Whitman, Alden. "James Jones Hailed by Friends at a Memorial Service on L. I." *New York Times*, 16 May 1977, p. 33.

Morris, Irwin Shaw, and William Styron eulogize fellow writer James Jones during a Long Island memorial service. "Mr. Jones 'couldn't stand fraud or phoniness or cruelty,' Mr. Morris said of a writer best known for his books on war. 'One of the ironies about this most unusual man is that he knew so much about human cruelty in all its manifestations—but as a person was so ... deeply tender and caring.'"

1621 Healy, Robert. "Carter at Home Again." *Boston Sunday Globe*, 24 July 1977, sec. A, p. 7.

Compares Morris to President Jimmy Carter in a story covering Carter's speech in Yazoo City, Mississippi. Morris's book *Yazoo* "told the story of the southerner returning home and how he learned to appreciate the southern things he disclaimed when he had left for New York. There was a lot of Morris in President Carter's town meeting in Yazoo City, Miss., last Thursday night."

1622 Klemesrud, Judy. "Party Hails Publication of Jones's Last Novel." *New York Times*, 23 February 1978, sec. C, p. 15.

Morris and some 270 friends of the late James Jones attend a dinner party to celebrate the posthumous publication of the novelist's *Whistle*. Jones died last May before he finished the book, and by working with tapes and Jones's notes, Morris then completed the last three and one-half chapters of it. "'He was one of the most beloved authors that's ever been around,' Willie Morris said. 'He inspired close friendships because of his utter honesty, and because he wasn't into the competitive game. He was a man of rare generosity to his friends.'" See also Wadler, Joyce. "Famous Friends Throw an Old-Fashioned Wake." *Washington Post*, 24 February 1978, sec. D, pp. 1, 4.

1623 Dickerson, James. "Willie Morris Comes Home Again to the Delta." *Greenwood (Miss.) Commonwealth*, 4 April 1978, p. 2.

A descriptive summary of Morris's two-day participation in Greenwood's annual arts festival. "Morris, who said he tries to write five or six hours every afternoon, described writing as an 'universal, private calling.'" He added that "on my first novel I learned something that's almost impossible to put into words. I learned about the discipline of fiction. I learned a lot about dialogue and I learned how very, very tough the writing of fiction is.... I'm just a writer, always will be. I'll stick to fiction. That's what my life is." Republished in *Conversations with Willie Morris* (item 1954).

1624 Flynn, Pat. "Who's Buried in the Witch's Grave." *Yazoo Daily Herald*, 2 July 1978, sec. B, p. 1.

An excellent summation of the local legend surrounding the Witch of Yazoo of Yazoo City, Mississippi. Some longtime residents of the town who are knowledgeable about the area's history and its folklore "think the witch existed only in the fertile mind of the author Willie Morris, who thrilled children [in his book *Good Old Boy*] with his description of the mean old woman who lived down by the river and cast spells on hapless fishermen who wandered too near her domicile." When the witch died, "so Morris' story goes," citizens of Yazoo buried her in the local cemetery and placed a heavy iron chain around the site "to keep her from fulfilling her threat to come from the grave and burn the town." Yazoo actually was destroyed by fire in 1904, and Morris wrote that after the flames were out, townspeople went to the cemetery and discovered that the chain had been broken in two. For years, various legends have surrounded the tomb "with its corroded chain, one link mysteriously missing." No one knows who actually is buried there, because the Glenwood Cemetery records "went up in smoke with the rest of the town" in the 1904 fire. See also: Gerrard, Ben. "Did the Witch Cause the 1904 Fire?" *Visions* (1983), p. 7 [Yazoo City High School student magazine].

1625 Baumann, Melissa. "Willie Morris: 'I Will Forever Consider This My Home.'" *Clarion-Ledger / Jackson Daily News*, 8 October 1978, sec. G, pp. 1–2.

An interview with Morris as he visits his native state to participate in a conference at the University of Southern Mississippi in Hattiesburg on "Sense of Place" (see item 743). "'Growing up there [in Yazoo City], there was always the feeling of time standing still,' Morris said, his gaze still fixed outside the window. 'And one of the things I remember,' he said, 'we were always playing tricks over there in Yazoo. It had to do with a sense of fancy. There wasn't too much going on over there in the summer — this is before the TV and the big expressways — and we had to do something in a place where the intellect wasn't much accepted.'" Republished in *Conversations with Willie Morris* (item 1956).

1626 Thomas, Phil. "Willie Morris Pays Tribute to His Friend James Jones." *(New Orleans) Times-Picayune*, 17 December 1978, sec. 3, p. 10.

An interview with Morris upon the publication of *James Jones*. He "says he has no doubt Jones' work will be remembered. 'I think just on the basis of this war fiction "From Here to Eternity," "The Thin Red Line," and "Whistle" that posterity is going to regard these books with enormous respect. I don't think it is too farfetched to say that many years from now people are going to be reading Jones' fiction of World War II to see what it really was like for human beings during those years.'"

1627 "Native Yazooan Slated to Lecture." *Yazoo Daily Herald*, 5 September 1979, sec. B, p. 1.

Announces that Morris will be teaching courses in the American novel and creative writing at the University of Mississippi during the spring 1980 semester. The University of Mississippi Foundation, through the Department of English, is sponsoring the Willie Morris Visiting Lectureship. "'Our students should benefit greatly from having the opportunity to study with such a distinguished writer,' said Ole Miss Chancellor Porter L. Fortune Jr."

1628 Podhoretz, Norman. "How the North Was Won." *New York Times Magazine*, 30 September 1979, pp. 20, 50, 53, 55–64.

The erudite editor of *Commentary* magazine examines the influence of Morris, Truman Capote, Gore Vidal, and other southern writers and intellectuals who in the 1960s moved to New York into journalistic and literary "positions of power." Podhoretz contends that these "transplanted white Southerners" believed that racism was as widespread in the North as it was in the South. They therefore "could present themselves — and the South as a whole — as specialists, experts, in the spiritual contention with racism." Similarly Morris, in his book *Yazoo*, "could say that the South was showing the rest of the nation the way to racial integration and harmony. In this, alas, he was wrong. The South was undoubtedly showing the rest of the nation the way to something, but it was not a greater harmony, racial or any other kind." Through the efforts of these mostly white, prominent literary and political figures, "The

South pioneered in the rise of a new liberalism characterized by a resurgent hostility toward business, a hypocritical repudiation of ambition and other 'middle-class' values, and a simplistic notion of the relation between the races."

1629 Williamson, Randy. "Willie Morris: Author Joins UM Staff." University of Mississippi *Daily Mississippian*, 16 October 1979, p. 3.

Morris is slated to join the University of Mississippi's English Department "for one semester to teach courses in creative writing and the American novel." Morris will teach just one section of each class, so interested students will probably have to apply for admission to the courses by submitting samples of their writing. The first article in a three-part series "concerning the Willie Morris Guest Lectureship at Ole Miss." See also items 1630 and 1631.

1630 Williamson, Randy. "Morris Says State Is Unique." University of Mississippi *Daily Mississippian*, 17 October 1979, p. 3.

Morris addresses "a group of people" at the public library in Clarksdale, Mississippi. "Mississippi's distinctiveness is a result of an awareness of community and a profound feeling of community origins, Morris said." The author will be a visiting instructor in English at the University of Mississippi during the spring semester. The second article in a three-part series. See also items 1629 and 1631.

1631 Williamson, Randy. "Morris Coming Home." University of Mississippi *Daily Mississippian*, 18 October 1979, p. 3.

Morris is looking forward to his forthcoming position as instructor and writer-in-residence in the University of Mississippi's English Department. "'It's for me a kind of reaffirmation of the heart to come down here and see all over again just how wonderful and open the people down here are,' he said." His two classes will include "a writing workshop and a course in the American novel." The third article in a three-part series. See also items 1629 and 1630.

1632 Davidson, Chandler. "Of That Time, Of This Place." *Texas Observer*, 28 December 1979, pp. 60–63.

A former associate editor of the *Texas Observer* remembers its various writers "with fondness and fascination" in the publication's twenty-five-year anniversary issue. Willie Morris "was an angry young man" at the *Observer*, but not merely because his "political sensibilities" were offended. "It was his aesthetic sensibilities as well. It was not only that the public good was being violated, the public till plundered by the oil moguls, the race-baiters, the corn-pone con artists who worked for the Establishment. It was that they had no style.... The Yahoos of the Texas ruling class were more effectively exposed, in all of their pompous banality, by Willie's finely-wrought satire in the *Observer* than at any time before or since — at least until another itinerant satirist named Molly Ivins came on the scene almost a decade later."

1633 Bennett, Elizabeth. "The Daily Texan: A Look at the Workings of a Campus Paper and Its Editors." *Houston Post*, 13 January 1980, sec. BB, pp. 1, 4.

Twenty-five years after Morris walked into the editor's office of the student newspaper at the University of Texas, former editors of the *Daily Texan* and school administrators reminisce about working on "one of the half-dozen best college publications in America." DeWitt Reddick, professor of journalism emeritus at the university and a teacher who spent some fifty years working with students on the *Daily Texan*, recalls Willie Morris: "I kind of felt like he always wrote and felt from the heart, but his experience on The Texan taught him to write from the head. To Willie, facts weren't very important. Once he wrote an editorial — a short editorial — where there were seven errors of fact. When I pointed it out to him he said, 'Oh, it's the idea that counts.'"

1634 Thomas, William. "Willie Morris, Home Again." *(Memphis) Commercial Appeal*, "Mid-South" section, 2 March 1980, pp. 6, 8–10.

A lively interview with Morris, who has returned to his native state to teach classes at Oxford's University of Mississippi. "I wanted to come home. It's no more complicated or simple than that. I'm at a kind of juncture in my life, and I felt it was time. Besides, my nerve ends come alive when I cross the Mississippi line. I'm not exaggerating. It's got to have something to do with that whole business of the burden of memory — the memory that serves one's imagination as a writer." Republished in *Conversations with Willie Morris* (item 1957). See also item 2068.

1635 "Now, Willie." *Yazoo Daily Herald*, 18 April 1980, p. 1.

A photograph of Morris in Yazoo City's Ricks Library, where last night he spoke "as a part of National Library Week festivities." See also: "Morris to Speak." *Yazoo Daily Herald*, 16 April 1980, sec. A, p. 1.

1636 Rose, Willard P. "Willie Morris Finds You Can Go Home Again." *Chicago Tribune*, 19 April 1980, sec. 1, p. 15.

This portrait piece states that Morris is "having the time of this [sic] life" back in Mississippi. "Some have speculated that Morris' decision to finally go home is tied directly to the deaths two years ago of his mother and his best friend, novelist James Jones.... 'I think he needs that sense of place so important to Southerners now more than ever,' said one of Morris' old Mississippi friends. 'He went away so young that he was deprived of a lot of the old ties to his home. Those ties are important to a Southerner.'" Syndicated by Knight-Ridder Newspapers, this article also appeared as: "Willie *Did* Go Home." *Houston Post*, 4 May 1980, sec. AA, pp. 1, 12.

1637 Ewing, Jim. "'Ghosts of Ole Miss' Live On — Morris." *Jackson (Miss.) Daily News*, 21 April 1980, sec. A, p. 5.

Reports that Morris spoke at the Yazoo City, Mississippi, public library on April 17 in honor of National Library Week, and the following day he "shared his experiences" with local high school students. During his first session, he read from his article, "The Ghosts of Ole Miss," which is scheduled to be published next month in *Inside Sports* (see item 746).

1638 "Harper's: Hail and Farewell." *Washington Star*, 19 June 1980, sec. A, p. 18.

"The demise of *Harper's* magazine is certainly regrettable," begins this editorial, though it adds that the news is "hardly surprising. The magazine had a long and distinguished history, but it hadn't contributed much to that history in recent years— the energetic efforts of its final editor, Lewis H. Lapham, notwithstanding.... In the late '60s, under the imaginative and unpredictable editorship of Willie Morris, it enjoyed a brief revival; but that ended when Mr. Morris quit in a dispute with his publisher, taking with him many of the writers and editors who had given the magazine a distinctive character."

1639 King, Larry L. "Lamenting the Best and Brightest of Magazines." *Dallas Times Herald*, 6 July 1980, sec, K, p. 1.

Harper's is expected to cease publication soon. King — who wrote twenty-six articles for it under Morris's editorship — remembers this "golden era" and offers insights as to why the magazine "became a victim of changing times and tastes." Those years at *Harper's*, writes King, "were the most exciting of my writing life. Willie turned me loose to carve on LBJ, Nixon, Rockefeller, Joe Pool, Congress in the aggregate.... My generation at Harper's became a band of brothers. There was a camaraderie such as I had not experienced before, or since." Unfortunately, people now "read specialized magazines— about motor boats and sex and sports— or they read such trash as People and worse if they can find it." See also items 1888, 1903, and 1943.

1640 "Former School Teacher Reminisces About Willie." *Yazoo Herald*, 8 November 1980, sec. B, p. 1.

Morris has dedicated a new edition of his book *Good Old Boy* to Omie Parker, one of his favorite high school teachers. Parker, who was a faculty adviser to the student newspaper staff, looks back on her long-time friendship with the writer. "'Willie was editor of the school newspaper, The Flashlight, for more years than he should have been, really,' Mrs. Parker said recently during some reminiscing time. 'But he had a creative mind.' ... Mrs. Parker said she always felt that Willie would be famous someday. 'He had all the earmarks. He had ambition,' she said." See also item 878.

1641 "Authors Discuss Worth of Children's Literature." *Yazoo Herald*, 10 December 1980, sec. B, p. 1.

Photographs of Morris, author Dean Faulkner Wells, and others as they participate in a symposium at the Yazoo City, Mississippi, public library.

1642 Yoder, Edwin M., Jr. "Rambles in Faulkner Country with Willie Morris." *Washington Star*, 12 February 1981, sec. A, p. 12.

Yoder, whose "friendship with Willie Morris is now a quarter century old," recalls the recent "brilliant midwinter day" when he joined the author and his dog in Oxford, Mississippi, as they "set out in Willie's old Plymouth to prowl the Faulkner country." Morris "knows every gulley and crossroads store of the steep, red-clay hills and hollows of rural Lafayette County where Faulkner found his Snopeses and McCaslins." Republished in *American Oxonian* 68 (Fall 1981), pp. 169–71.

1643 Bird, David. "Discovering the Hamptons in Winter." *New York Times*, 20 February 1981, sec. C, pp. 1, 22.

A travel article on the pleasures of visiting Long Island's Hamptons during the winter. In a section titled "Eating and Drinking," Bird notes that Morris's favorite restaurant in Bridgehampton is Bobby Van's. "Although Mr. Morris is spending this winter in Mississippi, 'He calls back all the time,' Mr. Van said the other day. 'I guess there are no good bars down there.'"

1644 "Dickey Visits." *Oxford (Miss.) Eagle*, 5 March 1981.

A photograph of several students chatting with the novelist and poet James Dickey, who "recently spoke at The University of Mississippi as part of the Willie Morris Visiting Lectureship." Morris, writer-in-residence at the university, has also invited authors Winston Groom, John Knowles, and William Styron to speak at Ole Miss and meet with students.

1645 Mullener, Elizabeth. "Like Other Mississippi Exiles, Writer Willie Morris Comes Home." *(New Orleans) Times-Picayune*, 15 March 1981, sec. 3, p. 10.

Morris relates several *Harper's*-era anecdotes, and although he admits that he misses "a few specific people" from his years in New York, he is delighted to be home again in Mississippi. "Oxford, Miss., is a far cry from the glamorous Manhattan literary scene. But Morris seems to be adjusting just fine. 'I missed it at first,' he says. 'I missed the perquisites of power.... But in Mississippi, there is for me a kind of oneness with myself as a writer that I could never feel up there. It wasn't that I was out of place so much. But I wasn't in my own culture.'" Republished in *Conversations with Willie Morris* (item 1959).

1646 "Knowles to Speak at UM Tomorrow." *Oxford (Miss.) Eagle*, 16 March 1981.

Announces that John Knowles, author of the novel *A Separate Peace*, will speak on March 17 "as part of the Willie Morris Visiting Lectureship at The University of Mississippi." Earlier in the semester the program brought writer Rose Styron and novelist and poet James Dickey to the university. Other Lectureship-sponsored authors scheduled to speak at Ole Miss this spring include Winston Groom, Larry L. King, and William Styron. See also "Knowles to Lecture on 'Craft of Fiction.'" *(Memphis) Commercial Appeal*, 13 March 1981.

1647 "William Styron to Speak at UM." *Oxford (Miss.) Eagle*, 2 April 1981.

The Willie Morris Visiting Lectureship at the University of Mississippi is bringing author William Styron to campus on April 9. Styron won the Pulitzer Prize for his 1968 novel *The Confessions of Nat Turner*, and his most recent novel, *Sophie's Choice*, received widespread critical praise. "The lectureship is sponsored by contributions to The University of Mississippi Foundation."

1648 [Photograph]. *Oxford (Miss.) Eagle*, 15 April 1981.

A photograph of Willie Morris, formerly editor of *Harper's Magazine*, who "recently spoke at The University of Mississippi as part of Journalism Week." The program was held for Mississippi high school and junior college students.

1649 Harrist, Ron. "Willie Morris 'Never Really Left' Yazoo City." *(Baton Rouge) Morning Advocate*, 21 October 1981, sec. C, p. 3.

An anecdotal interview with Morris. Although the author has traveled all around the country and abroad since his youth in Yazoo City, his "heart and his thoughts have never strayed far from his Mississippi roots. 'I've never really left this place emotionally,' says Morris.... 'Everything is compounded by the fact that I am a writer, and writers by the very nature of our strange calling deal in memory. I've always found myself coming back to Mississippi in my thoughts.'" Syndicated by the Associated Press, this article also appeared as: "Mississippi Revisited: Author Has Found Memories." *Clarion-Ledger / Jackson Daily News*, 18 October 1981.

1650 "South Toward Home." *Washington Post Book World*, 29 November 1981, p. 15.

A light piece about Morris's move from New York City to Oxford, Mississippi. "Writers have been known to transfer their affections from one hangout to another; in the case of Willie Morris (*North Toward Home*, *Yazoo*) it's been a matter of a 1,200-mile removal. The Warehouse, in Oxford, Mississippi, may not be Elaine's (the New York restaurant where big-name literati watch each other munching fried zucchini), but it's where Morris, now teaching contemporary lit at the University of Mississippi, takes friends ... who've come down there to talk to his classes."

1651 Mitchell, Frances. "'Pete the Magnificent.'" *Oxford (Miss.) Eagle*, 2 July 1982, p. 3.

A lengthy, animated profile of Morris's black Labrador, contributed by a woman who regularly walks him around the University of Mississippi campus. "That's the way it goes during our campus ambulations. People stop us, asking questions and wanting to pet the famous dog; and some have Labs of their own. At times students will hang half out of car windows, when noticing us. 'Hi Pete!' they yell." See also item 1894.

1652 Cawthon, Raad. "Willie Morris Turns South Toward Home." *Clarion-Ledger / Jackson Daily News*, 15 August 1982, sec. E, pp. 1, 15.

Muses that Morris, "once the golden boy of Mississippi letters" who "had it all" before he abruptly left *Harper's Magazine* in New York, is content in his native state teaching at the University of Mississippi, writing, and "developing friendships with the locals." The residents of the small university town recognize the author "and speak of him in affectionate terms, like a rowdy but lovable younger brother." Observes Morris: "There is something deep in the people of Mississippi, the ones who were born here, that cannot be denied or chased away. It can be buried for a while or sometimes ignored, but never successfully. Sooner or later you have to come home."

1653 Blades, John. "Small Publisher Becomes Expert in Printing Mistakes." *Chicago Tribune*, 10 November 1982, sec. 4, pp. 1, 5.

An interview with Dean and Larry Wells, owners of Yoknapatawpha Press in Oxford, Mississippi, as well as a straightforward account of the hard work and tenacity that small publishers need to succeed. The firm is named for William Faulkner's fictional county. "After Faulkner, the writer with whom Yoknapatawpha Press is most closely identified is Willie Morris, three of whose books the Wellses have published, with more to come."

1654 Blades, John. "Touring Faulkner's Stomping Grounds with Author Willie Morris." *Chicago Tribune*, 21 November 1982, sec. 11, pp. 3–4.

Morris provides a tour of Oxford, Mississippi, the home of author William Faulkner. "As much as any one person, it was William Faulkner who drew Morris to Oxford.... Says Morris: 'In personal terms, I wouldn't want to make too much of it, but Faulkner's presence is definitely here and I can feel it.' ... To his everlasting regret, Morris never met Faulkner, but, he says, 'I have no doubt that Mr. Bill and I would have been friends.'"

1655 Conaway, James. "Willie Morris in the Land of Faulkner." *Washington Post*, 28 December 1982, sec. C, pp. 1, 3.

A malicious, lengthy portrait of Morris, who is living in Oxford, Mississippi, and teaching at Ole Miss. The article's conclusion indicates that while Conaway was trying to talk to him, Morris brushed him off. Whatever occurred, the result of the interview is a petty diatribe—complete with a caricature of a bloated Morris—that paints the author as a "broad of beam" individual who wears "a pair of wrinkled trousers torn in the seat." While he "sips his bourbon," his dog Pete, "a black Lab with the canine equivalent of a beer belly, sleeps noisily on the rug." Conaway dismisses one of Morris's books as "a disappointment to his admirers," while he quotes from a negative review of another. The article's mean-spiritedness prompted *Time* magazine to publish an entire column criticizing Conaway's "long and wounding hatchet job" (item 1406).

1656 Freeland, Lee. "Pete Was a Good Ol' Dog." University of Mississippi *Daily Mississippian*, 2 February 1983, p. 1.

A tribute to Pete, Morris's black Labrador, who died on February 1 in the author's yard of his campus house. "Morris said, 'I'll never have another dog. I'll get a wife before I'll get another dog.' ... Morris and a small group of friends gathered in a late afternoon rain Tuesday and Dean Fa[u]lkner Wells, niece of the late William Fa[u]lkner, read from the 1928 Episcopal Prayer Book in the memorial service at a cemetery." See also item 1666.

1657 "Willie Morris to Be Speaker at Dinner Honoring Journalist." *Clarion-Ledger*, 9 October 1983, sec. B, p. 2.

"Mississippi writer Willie Morris will be featured speaker at a Dec. 9 Pike County Arts Council dinner honoring the late Charles B. Gordon, journalist and historian." Gordon, a "veteran reporter and columnist" for several Mississippi newspapers, died in November 1982.

1658 Biffle, Kent. "Willie Morris Writes the Saga of Marcus Dupree." *Dallas Morning News*, 13 November 1983, sec. G, p. 6.

During a promotional tour for *The Courting of Marcus Dupree*, Morris chats with a reporter about the college recruitment of student athletes as well as about the young hero of his latest book. Biffle gushes that the work "needs promotion about as much as the Dallas Cowboys need promotion" and that when Morris began following Dupree's career, the author had no idea he "would become the most famous teenager in the United States this side of Brooke Shields." Morris realizes that reforms are needed in college sports; recruiters exploit student athletes and most scholarship winners do not graduate from college. "Researching his book, Morris met college recruiters as tough as $2 steaks, coaches and agents who would attempt almost any tactic to win the prized

Dupree — while stiff-arming aside the other recruiters."

1659 McNeely, Dave. "The Courting of Willie Morris: Mississippi Roots, Teaching Job Lure Writer South Toward Home." *Austin American-Statesman*, "Onward" section, 15 November 1983, pp. 8–9.

An interview with and biographical sketch of Morris as he stops in Austin while promoting *The Courting of Marcus Dupree*. Morris tells a reporter that the book is more than just a narrative about a talented football player. "'I use football as sort of a motif, a thread that runs through the story, and Marcus himself. But it gave me the chance to be personal, and to describe a lot of the sights and sounds and smells of the South today, and how the South has changed — and not changed.' ... That Willie is also back in Mississippi, and likes it, and apparently plans to stay there in William Faulkner's hometown of Oxford, is testimony to changes in both the man and the state." Also published as "Willie Morris Comes Home to the Land of Faulkner." *Atlanta Journal / The Atlanta Constitution*, 20 November 1983, sec. A, p. 2.

1660 Reeves, Garland. "Mississippi Writer, Athlete Have Deep Ties." *Clarion-Ledger*, 15 November 1983, sec. B, p. 3.

Suggests that there is a "kinship" between Morris and football player Marcus Dupree, the central character of Morris's book *The Courting of Marcus Dupree*. Although the two are "seemingly different," there exist "root-deep ties between the two. They are fellow Mississippians. Both — perhaps dazzled by fame and glamour — left home to seek their fortunes, only to find that Mississippi is where they wanted to be. And they came home again."

1661 Bandler, Michael J. "The Good Old Boy's Taste in Books." *Chicago Tribune Book World*, 20 November 1983, pp. 35–36.

In a formal question-and-answer session with the book columnist of *American Way* magazine, Morris discusses, among other subjects, "the evolution of his reading taste." After Bandler asks him if any books gave him "perspectives on the North" during his youth, he replies that in the public schools he was principally reading the "English classics," but "then I started going to the library and dipping into books.... I went off on a sort of Thomas Wolfe tear.... I started living my life out of the pages of Thomas Wolfe — those wonderful sequences of going off to the East, and to New York City. Wolfe's feelings of the small-town provincial Southern boy in New York affected me deeply.'" Republished in *Conversations with Willie Morris* (item 1961).

1662 "At the Library." *Yazoo Herald*, 30 November 1983, sec. B, pp. 1, 4.

Relates "with some consternation" that Morris's *Good Old Boy* is "universally classified on the United States–wide Union Catalog under biography. The cataloguer obviously believed that, in truth, ten foot high Indians do exist in our environs. So there, in non-fiction, sits the tallest tale you've heard."

1663 Watson, Robbie N. "Minutia: 'The Fumble' Not Such a Big Deal." *Yazoo Herald*, 30 November 1983, sec. B, pp. 1, 4.

The "Lifestyle" editor of Morris's hometown newspaper reminisces about his own Mississippi football career after reading "The Fumble" in the author's *Always Stand In Against the Curve* (item 32). "That's just great Willie, just great — fretting about a fumble that cost Yazoo City High School a win some 30-odd years ago. I only wish I had been big enough to get in a game."

1664 Cass, Julia. "Willie Morris Stays Home: Author Finds Write Stuff in Mississippi." *Chicago Tribune*, 2 January 1984, sec. 5, pp. 1–2.

A reporter for Knight-Ridder Newspapers interviews Morris and several of his friends in Oxford, Mississippi, and discovers that what the author likes about Oxford is "its small-townness— seeing the same people every day.... He likes it that people know not to bother him until after noon and also know where they can find him at night." Publisher Larry Wells, who brought out the author's *Terrains of the Heart*, insists that Morris "stirred things up and made us better." Morris says that "everything comes together for me here, and a writer has to be selfish. You have to be in a place where you can work." This syndicated article also appeared as: "Old Love in the New South: Writer Willie Morris Relishes His Return to a Better Mississippi." *Kansas City Star*, 8 January 1984, sec. F, pp. 1, 7.

1665 Weidie, Wayne W. "Mississippi Holds 'Grip' on Natives." *Belzoni (Miss.) Banner*, 11 January 1984, p. 8.

Regrets that Morris's books are not read by more Mississippians, as "Willie understands the 'grip' that Mississippi holds on its natives and even some people who are not natives." Recommends the "totally delightful" *Always Stand In Against the Curve*, "a collection of sports stories that should appeal to anyone who has ever kicked, thrown or dribbled a ball." Also published as an op-ed piece: "Mississippi Author, Willie Morris, Lauded." *(Hernando, Miss.) DeSoto Times*, 12 January 1984, p. 4.

1666 Harrist, Ron. "Remembering Pete, the 'Deputy Mayor.'" *Washington Post*, 13 February 1984, sec. C, p. 12.

Morris remembers his dog Pete, who died almost a year ago. "'I lost a brother that day,' said Morris, whose love for the black dog is woven into his literary works.... 'I think it was old age. He just went out in my front yard and died,' Morris said in an interview. 'We buried him on a beautiful hill here in Oxford, and there's not a single day that goes by that I don't think about him.'" This article, written by an Associated Press reporter, also appeared in the *Los Angeles Times* of 16 February 1984. See also item 1656.

1667 Lammons, George. "Willie Morris' Agent Says TV Wants Marcus Dupree Story." *Jackson (Miss.) Daily News*, 1 March 1984, sec. A, pp. 1, 12.

"Author Willie Morris and his agent say they are negotiating with a major television network on turning Morris' book, 'The Courting of Marcus Dupree,' into a made-for-TV movie." Lammons, however, could find no television executives interested in the project.

1668 Williams, Toni. "Workshop Benefits Young Writers, Teachers." *Clarion-Ledger*, 19 April 1984, sec. B, p. 4.

Morris is scheduled to be one of the speakers at the statewide Writer's Workshop on April 21. This annual program encourages high school students "to express themselves through their writing."

1669 Groom, Winston. "Requiem for an Old English Sheep Dog." *Washington Post Book World*, 15 July 1984, pp. 7–8.

Groom (who years later would achieve fame as the author of *Forrest Gump*) reviews four books about pets and their owners. His own dog, Fenwick, recently died, and he writes that "I phoned Willie Morris, who is the writer in residence at the University of Mississippi, and who, more than anyone else I know, has a way of helping you through times like these.... Willie shared my sadness, but mostly he talked about the memories.... They were, of course, painful, those memories, but cathartic too, and Willie, raised in the tradition of old southern bereavement knew they were a needed tonic."

1670 Kotz, Mary Lynn. "Willie Morris Is Home Again at Ole Miss." *St. Petersburg (Fla.) Times*, 22 July 1984, sec. D, p. 8.

Morris has eased into a comfortable lifestyle in Oxford, Mississippi, and has become a close friend and literary mentor to the students in his classes at the university. "'I agreed to come for one semester as writer in residence at Ole Miss,' says Morris. 'I had no idea that I'd be here for four years. But I fell in love with Oxford.' ... There is no question but what he is loved here, as sincerely and as deeply as 20-year-old college students first discovering literature are capable of loving.... Willie knows their pain and their joys, because they confide in him, and he shares his with them." Republished in *Conversations with Willie Morris* (item 1962). A variation of this article appeared as "Morris in Mississippi." *Texas Observer*, 13 July 1984, pp. 20–21.

1671 Myers, Leslie R. "Morris Stop Pledges Evening of Reflection." *Clarion-Ledger*, 23 October 1984, sec. C, p. 1.

On October 25, Morris "will share his reflections on the South in a lecture/reading" at Millsaps College. "The literary-evening's theme is likely to embody such Morris-trademark topics as being Southern, what makes Southerners different and why traveling Southerners (eventually) long to return home."

1672 Myers, Leslie R. "Evening with Willie Entertains His Fans." *Clarion-Ledger*, 26 October 1984, sec. C, p. 1.

Morris "shared his long saws and short punch lines with a captive audience" during a lecture/reading at Millsaps College on October 25. His remarks, which were "spiced with humor," were also "rich with references to other Southern writers," such as Eudora Welty and William Faulkner. He also read excerpts from some of his works, especially his "classic" *North Toward Home* and the recently published *The Courting of Marcus Dupree.*

1673 Salter, Sid. "Willie Morris Passes a Milestone." *Scott County (Miss.) Times*, 2 December 1984, sec. F, p. 3.

Newspaper editor Salter salutes his friend Morris, who celebrated his fiftieth birthday on November 29 in Oxford, Mississippi. "There were some impressive names on the guest list from Up

East, yet most of the revelers were just common Mississippi folk.... Of the many gifts Willie Morris possesses, perhaps the greatest is his appreciation of ordinary people, those unaffected by the trappings of the literati."

1674 Lewis, Bill. "Mississippi's Willie Morris Concedes Bit of Trouble in 'North Toward Home.'" *(Little Rock) Arkansas Gazette*, 8 December 1984, sec. B, p. 1.

Morris, in Little Rock signing copies of his books, recalls that half of the residents of his hometown liked *North Toward Home* "or at least didn't mind it, and the other half were miffed, mainly because they weren't mentioned." In his second book about Yazoo City, Mississippi, *Yazoo*, he discusses the town's and schools' integration. "If Mississippi can be said historically to have been the state most likely to hold out against desegregation longest, then the community with that distinction might easily have been Yazoo City, where racial lines were indelible and where the rigid pre–1954 social order most nearly approached feudalism. For all of that, Yazoo City had its aristocrats, many of whom, in the final counting, proved to be far more pragmatic than anyone would have suspected. Desegregation there, Morris said, has been accepted and seems to be working well...."

1675 Harrist, Ron. "Willie Morris Turns 50." *Victoria (Tex.) Advocate*, 9 December 1984.

An Associated Press reporter catches up with Morris as the author turns fifty years old. Morris spent part of his birthday "taking a drive in his weathered car. 'I was doing some reflecting, something one does when one grows older,' he said. 'It's not the grandiose things that over the years matter so much, it's the elemental ones like family and friendships—a sense of community reality.'" He stays in touch with friends in New York, and novelist Philip Roth and playwright Arthur Miller once asked him if he would be interested in editing another magazine. "'I told them I enjoyed running Harper's, but that was not for me,' he said. 'It's a young man's calling. As far as the future, I'll always be writing.'"

1676 "Willie Morris Featured on 'Postscripts.'" *Clarion-Ledger*, 29 January 1985, sec. D, p. 3.

Morris "talks about teaching and writing on the next edition of *Postscripts* at 7:30 tonight on Mississippi ETV.... *Postscripts* is a new eight-part series of interviews with Mississippi writers."

1677 McKenzie, Danny. "Willie, Words and Wisdom." *Jackson (Miss.) Daily News*, 4 March 1985, sec. D, p. 1.

A sports writer admires Morris's sports knowledge and his rapport with athletic coaches and directors. "When you're in Oxpatch, Ace, you pay attention to one Willie Morris, the Magnolia State's poet laureate—who also happens to know a thing or two about sports."

1678 Claffey, Charles E. "Does the 'Southern Writer' Really Exist." *Boston Globe*, 9 December 1986, pp. 71, 72.

James Dickey, Shelby Foote, Morris, Walker Percy, Eudora Welty and other writers from the South ponder the definition of the term "southern writer" and wonder "whether there exists such a being." In the inaugural issue of *Southern Magazine* (item 771), Morris "posed the larger question of whether the South itself still exists. He concluded that it does: 'Perhaps in the end it is the old, inherent, devil-may-care instinct of the South that remains in the most abundance and will sustain the South in its uncertain future.'" The first article in a two part-series (see also item 1679).

1679 Claffey, Charles E. "In the Heart of the Literary South, A Tradition Lives On." *Boston Globe*, 10 December 1986, pp. 93, 96.

Authors Morris, Barry Hannah, and Larry Wells discuss William Faulkner and Oxford, Mississippi, a "small university community that has become the capital of literary Mississippi and perhaps of the literary South." Wells "says of Morris that 'Willie has gotten all the love here the people knew they should have given Faulkner in his lifetime.'" Morris "said that '25 years ago I would have been intimidated living in Oxford, given the intimidating presence of Faulkner. As I aged, instead of being intimidated I have drawn sustenance from the place he wrote about so powerfully.'" The second article in a two-part series (see also item 1678).

1680 Drake, Rebecca B., comp. "Willie Morris Reminisces His Raymond Ancestry." *Hinds County (Miss.) Gazette*, "Special Supplement," 8 May 1987, pp. 9–10.

Excerpts from *North Toward Home* provide biographical material on Major George W. Harper and several other ancestors of Morris's. Morris, the great-grandson of Harper, who founded the *Hinds County Gazette*, will speak on May 9 at the dedication of new grave markers in the Confederate section of the Raymond, Mississippi, city cemetery. Related articles in this issue of the newspaper include "Renowned Author and Great-Grandson of *Gazette's* Founder Speaks at Dedication Ceremony" (page 5) and "George W. Harper" (page 8). See also item 1996.

1681 Uthoff, Christine. "Markers Placed on Confederate Gravesites." *Clarion-Ledger*, 10 May 1987, sec. B, pp. 1, 3.

Morris, his son, David, and more than two hundred other persons gather in the Cemetery for Confederate Dead in Raymond, Mississippi, during the "dedication of new gravemarkers for 109 of the dead soldiers who have now been identified as being buried in the cemetery." Both Morrises spoke during the ceremony, and the two also "erected a stone honoring Civil War Major George W. Harper — Willie Morris' great-grandfather — in the family burial plot." Besides fighting in the Civil War, "Harper founded the Hinds County Gazette, the county's weekly newspaper, and served in the Mississippi Legislature before his death in 1894."

1682 Johnson, Hayes. "Yankees 1st to Buy Film Rights to Morris' Book." *Clarion-Ledger*, 3 September 1987, sec. A, pp. 1, 12.

Multimedia Entertainment, a New York production company, has purchased the motion picture rights to Morris's *Good Old Boy*; filming will take place in Natchez, Mississippi. "*Good Old Boy*, set in the 1940s, is about growing up in the rural South. 'The book is an adventure story, primarily,' said Morris, who wrote the book in 1971 when he lived in Long Island, N.Y.... 'It's the only book I ever wrote that I truly enjoyed writing.'" See also: Associated Press. "Morris' 'Good Old Boy' to Be Filmed in Natchez." *(Baton Rouge) Morning Advocate*, 4 September 1987, sec. B, p. 12.

1683 "Southern Writers Are Unique In Sense of Past, Morris Says." *(Little Rock) Arkansas Gazette*, 16 September 1987, sec. B, p. 2.

In a speech at the University of Arkansas at Monticello, Morris tells students that "southern writers are different because they have a sense of community, a sense of the past and of the flow of generations.... Morris said that school desegregation was the predominant change in the South in the last 20 years." He added that "if there is such a thing as the 'new' South, he hoped the beneficiaries of it would be 'a new generation of blacks and whites, growing up together,' and doing it better than the previous generations."

1684 Polman, Dick. "A Son of the South: Author Willie Morris Speaks Out from the Land He Chronicled in the '60s on Life There in the '80s." *Philadelphia Inquirer*, 9 March 1988, sec. D, pp. 1, 4.

Morris, who has sequestered himself in McComb, Mississippi, to write a novel, talks with several friends and journalist Polman about urban sprawl, politics, and race relations in Mississippi. "Just the other night at the cafe, not long before the Super Tuesday presidential primaries, he was greatly bemused by the changes that homogenization has wrought on the ways and mores of the Old South. 'Seems like there's Republicans everywhere now,' he said." Polman captures the private — even brooding — side of Morris in his lengthy article. Syndicated by Knight-Ridder Newspapers, it also appeared as: "Willie Morris Wrestles Demons: The Past, Writer's Block." *Houston Chronicle*, 21 March 1988, sec. 5, p. 3; "Burned-Out Writer Tries to Ignite Muse in South." *Chicago Tribune*, 31 March 1988, sec. F, p. 13. Republished in *Conversations with Willie Morris* (item 1963).

1685 Hale, Leon. "Author of 'North Toward Home' Has Settled in South." *Houston Chronicle*, 24 May 1988, sec. 2, p. 1.

A Texan fails to engage Morris in conversation about the author's leaving New York to return to his native state. "I tried a time or two to draw a comment about that but it didn't work. A sore point, maybe." The author apparently "is in Mississippi to stay. 'I served my time in New York. I'm not going back. I went up there not long ago to a dinner for a friend, and I came back the same night.'"

1686 Myers, Leslie R. "'Good Old Boy' Begins Filming in Natchez." *Clarion-Ledger*, 6 June 1988, sec. D, pp. 1, 4.

Good Old Boy, the full-length movie based on Morris's 1971 book of the same name, "will begin filming today in Natchez. The production by Multimedia Entertainment of New York is being made for The Disney Channel.... The movie script retains Morris' Yazoo City setting, although the scenery will reflect picturesque Natchez instead of the hilly city on the edge of the Delta flatlands." Filming will wrap up on July 7. See also sidebar article: Myers, Leslie R. "Co-Starring Role Must Go to a Dog." *Clarion-Ledger*, 6 June 1988, sec. D, pp. 1, 4.

1687 Myers, Leslie R. "Mia's Mom and Tarzan's Jane." *Clarion-Ledger / Jackson Daily News*, 10 July 1988, sec. E, pp. 1, 2.

Profiles actress Maureen O'Sullivan, who plays Morris's "eccentric and endearing" Aunt Sue in the movie *Good Old Boy*. "'I feel it's like Huck Finn of the '40s,' O'Sullivan, 77, said. 'That's why

I decided to do it. It's lovely for a change and I hope people will see it and enjoy its basic values of life. I've only read the screenplay, which I love enormously,' she said of the adaptation by Paul Cooper." The movie is based on Morris's autobiographical "childhood adventure story."

1688 Myers, Leslie R. "Disney Gets Dream Dog." *Clarion-Ledger*, 28 July 1988, sec. F, pp. 1, 6.

An Airedale named Moose, who once played Little Orphan Annie's dog Sandy in the Broadway musical *Annie*, has been selected to portray Morris's boyhood dog Skip in the movie *Good Old Boy*. "For Morris, seeing Moose on the set was a dream come true. 'Moose and I got along real well,' Morris, 53, said. 'He barks with a Southern accent.'" The production is the "movie version" of Morris's autobiographical *Good Old Boy*.

1689 Edwards, Jeff. "'Good Old Boy' Debuts on Disney Channel." *Jackson (Miss.) Daily News*, 10 November 1988, sec. B, pp. 1, 7.

Good Old Boy, a film based on Morris's book of the same name, is scheduled to premiere on Friday, November 11, on The Disney Channel. Morris "claims the movie is 'splendid, very true to the spirit of my book and my experiences growing up in Yazoo City.'"

1690 Myers, Leslie R. "Morris Celebrates Movie, Reissued Book in Oxford." *Clarion-Ledger*, 11 November 1988, sec. D, p. 1.

This evening Morris and two hundred friends will gather at The Hoka, a theater/cafe in Oxford, to celebrate the world premiere of *Good Old Boy*, the movie adaptation of his "adventure story." The film, which "mixes the fantasy and reality of Morris' childhood," will be shown in the theater at six o'clock and simultaneously on cable television's The Disney Channel. The book *Good Old Boy* is being reissued by Yoknapatawpha Press of Oxford. See also the *Clarion-Ledger*'s review of the film: Lucas, Sherry. "'Good Old Boy': The Movie." *Clarion-Ledger*, 11 November 1988, sec. D, pp. 1, 3.

1691 Rejebian, Michael. "Oxford Guests Attend Debut of Morris Movie." *Clarion-Ledger*, 12 November 1988, sec. A, p. 1.

Reports that Morris and more than one hundred other guests attended a formal party last night at The Hoka, an Oxford theater and cafe, where they watched the premiere of the two-hour motion picture *Good Old Boy* on cable television. The author, whose 1971 autobiographical work inspired the movie, "told the crowd that the film stuck to the spirit of the book. 'It brought back to me, in a bizarre rush, the past,' said Morris, who viewed a videotape of the movie earlier this week."

1692 Blackadar, Bruce. "Good Old Boy Is a First-Class Family Film." *Toronto Star*, 8 January 1989, sec. C, p. 2.

Recommends the movie *Good Old Boy*, which will be televised this evening on the Family Channel. Adapted from Morris's book, the film is "about how the young Willie grows up in the heart of bayou country, in Yazoo City, Miss., during World War II — and generally it's a fine, sensitive, amusing and ultimately cheering production."

1693 Trueheart, Charles. "A Visit to Yoknapatawpha." *Washington Post*, 21 February 1989, sec. C, p. 7.

"Name-brand writing in National Geographic is not frequent, but the March issue offers a lovely exception in 'Faulkner's Mississippi,' by Willie Morris. The novelist and former Harper's editor, a Mississippian, recalls the life and work of the ornery Nobelist while paying tribute to the 'little postage-stamp of native soil' William Faulkner called Yoknapatawpha County" (item 775).

1694 Thomas, William. "Faulkner Land Deftly Treated by Morris." *(Memphis) Commercial Appeal*, 16 March 1989, sec. B, p. 1.

Extols Morris's "Faulkner's Mississippi," a "superb biographical sketch of the literary genius and his mindscape" published in the March *National Geographic* (item 775). "Willie Morris has always written about Mississippi with a burning passion. But his prose has seldom been better than in this month's National Geographic cover story, where, an editor says, 'you can hear Willie's heart beating.'"

1695 Cawthon, Raad. "A Torn-Up Dreamer: Marcus Dupree Carried a Football Like Few Ever Have, But an Injured Knee Has Made Him a Memory at Age 24." *Atlanta Journal / The Atlanta Constitution*, 30 April 1989, sec. C, pp. 1, 20.

Reviews the disappointing athletic career of Marcus Dupree, the one-time star football player and the subject of Morris's book *The Courting of Marcus Dupree*. "Even as 'The Courting of Marcus Dupree' was being released, the magical career was soiled. Dupree dropped out of college and went pro. Then, before anyone could catch their breath, he was out of football, living again in his mother's house in Philadelphia [Mississippi]."

1696 Hood, Orley. "President Bush Makes a Hit with Willie Morris at the White House." *Clarion-Ledger / Jackson Daily News*, 30 April 1989, sec. E, pp. 1–2.

Tells of Morris's friendship with President George Bush and their mutual interest in baseball. "'Bush and I started writing letters about baseball back when he was vice president,' Morris said the other day. Willie was in town a few days ago for the Jackson premiere of the Disney-produced TV movie made from his book *Good Ol' Boy*, two days before he dined with President Bush at a state dinner for the king and queen of Jordan."

1697 Greenberg, Paul. "Some Southern Exposure: Taking It Easy and Faulkner." *Tulsa World*, 9 May 1989, sec. A, p. 6.

A syndicated editorial that acclaims the South, William Faulkner, and Morris's "Faulkner's Mississippi" (item 775). "The next best thing to reading Faulkner may be to read about him, a theory borne out by Willie Morris' fine piece on 'Faulkner's Mississippi' in the March issue of the National Geographic. He quotes a line from Faulkner that swings open a door. It explains why my first, unthinking reflex to anything Southern, and maybe my last as well, is still a smile: 'Memory believes before knowing remembers. Believes longer than recollects, longer than knowing even wonders.' Memory is a kind of autonomous faith." Greenberg adds that "Morris recites the best Faulkner stories, which tend to get even better with repetition."

1698 Miller, Robin. "Morris Saw Book Potential in Cult Scare." *(McComb, Miss.) Enterprise-Journal*, 13 October 1989, p. 7.

A detailed report on the small-town "satanic scare" that inspired Morris to write *Good Old Boy and the Witch of Yazoo*. While the author was in Pike County, Mississippi, working on his novel *Taps*, he began hearing tales about "satanic cult activity" in the area. New stories cropped up daily, and before they were revealed as a hoax, worried parents kept their children home from school as "Pike County was swept by hysteria." Morris followed local newspaper articles about the rumors, and he "immediately saw fictional possibilities in the situation — the scare was the perfect setting for a sequel to his classic children's novel, 'Good Old Boy.'" See also items 1816 and 2078.

1699 "Willie Morris to Sub for Plimpton at Ole Miss Faulkner Conference." *Clarion-Ledger / Jackson Daily News*, 28 July 1990, sec. B, p. 2.

Announces that author/editor George Plimpton will not speak at the University of Mississippi's Faulkner and Yoknapatawpha Conference on July 30. "In Plimpton's place, Ole Miss Writer-in-Residence Willie Morris will read from his forthcoming book *Faulkner's Mississippi*."

1700 Glauber, Bill. "All for One, One for All." *Los Angeles Times*, 18 August 1990, sec. C, pp. 1, 16.

Chronicles the "story of a Rebel heart and a Southern miracle." On 28 October 1989, University of Mississippi football player Chucky Mullins was paralyzed after tackling a Vanderbilt University receiver. Since that day, a "grass-roots campaign" that began at the university in Oxford, Mississippi, but which "swept the South" has collected hundreds of thousands of dollars for him. "A simple, elegant courthouse square anchors Oxford, but the campus of Ole Miss dominates the town. Author Willie Morris, a writer-in-residence at the school, wrote: 'Almost no other American campus envelops death and suffering and blood, and the fire and sword, as Ole Miss does.'" (This passage is from "The Ghosts of Ole Miss," item 746.) Morris wrote the foreword to *A Dixie Farewell: The Life and Death of Chucky Mullins* (item 937) and covered the fateful Ole Miss–Vanderbilt game in his essay "The South," first published in *Game Day USA* (item 883).

1701 "Nashville Hosts Book Festival Oct. 12–14." *(Memphis) Commercial Appeal*, 26 August 1990, sec. G, p. 4.

Morris and more than one hundred other "well-known writers will discuss their works at the second annual Southern Festival of Books in Nashville, Oct. 12–14.... Topics for panel discussions will include the Civil War, Southern poetry, Dr. Martin Luther King Jr., Elvis Presley, Southern expatriates and Vietnam."

1702 Rogers, Joe. "Notable Nuptials." *Clarion-Ledger*, 14 September 1990, sec. E, pp. 1, 4.

Announces that JoAnne Prichard, senior editor at the University Press of Mississippi, and Morris will marry today "in a private, family ceremony." The two first met in 1967 when Morris—then editing *Harper's Magazine* in New York City — "came home to Yazoo City on a tour after publication of his *North Toward Home*. He gave a reading at Yazoo City High School, where Prichard taught. They became friends." He wrote the introduction to a history of Yazoo City that Prichard and a colleague wrote (item 924), but "the two really got together" last year when Prichard edited Morris's and William Dunlap's *Homecomings*. She went to Oxford, Mississippi, to interview the two men, and "then I just found I was going back to Oxford more and more."

1703 "Morris and Prichard Wed in Private Ceremony." *Yazoo Herald*, 15 September 1990, p. 1.

"They're calling it a marriage made in literary heaven. Two of Yazoo City's favorite literary folks tied the knot yesterday in Oxford.... Willie Morris, 55, and [JoAnne] Prichard, 46, were married by Supreme Court Judge James Robertson, a mutual friend."

1704 "Just Call Those Faulkner Eyes." *Clarion-Ledger*, 25 October 1990, sec. E, p. 2.

Morris is planning to sign copies of his new book, *Faulkner's Mississippi*, tomorrow at Lemuria bookstore in Jackson. Based on the author's lengthy article in *National Geographic* (item 775), the volume "is an expanded examination of mythic Mississippi as seen through Faulknerian eyes. It features the impressionistic photographs of William Eggleston ... and illustrates the fictional and real events mapping Yoknapatawpha County."

1705 Myers, Leslie R. "Disney's Planning to Rerun Morris' 'Good Old Boy.'" *Clarion-Ledger*, 18 September 1991, sec. D, p. 1.

The Disney Channel intends to broadcast "encores" of the movie *Good Old Boy*, which is based on Morris's book, during the last week of September. "The writer's fondness for his only brush with Hollywood endures. So does the movie. 'They did a very good job of it. I think Disney captured the spirit of the book,' Morris said this week. 'The communication I get from kids who've watched it is, they love it. I think it's a movie they'll be watching for a long, long time.'"

1706 Lucas, Sherry. "Yazooans Hold Out Hope You'd Rather Witch Than Switch." *Clarion-Ledger*, 8 October 1991, sec. D, p. 1.

A tourism plan in Yazoo City, Mississippi, Morris's hometown, is stirring up controversy. According to a "fertile folk legend" and Morris's book *Good Old Boy*, on 24 May 1904, the witch of Yazoo City broke a heavy chain around her grave and burned much of the town. Several weeks ago a local tourism committee, Discover Yazoo, decided to capitalize on the story by starting a contest for a witch logo. When the contest began, "A few sensitive citizens didn't like the idea of having a witch logo flying around their town. Thought it was inappropriate at least and a beacon for Satan worshipers at worst." Morris "urged Yazooans to poll their children on the subject. 'It's the kids who really matter. Unlike people who get older and use witches to mask their own internal fears, kids enjoy being frightened — it's part of being kids.'" See also item 1707.

1707 "Ellzey Draws Winning Witch." *Yazoo Herald*, 30 November 1991, sec. A, p. 1.

John Ellzey, a librarian at the Yazoo City public library, has submitted the winning drawing in the Discover Yazoo tourism committee's logo contest, but his drawing of the town's controversial Witch of Yazoo will be used only on material related to the witch legend. "Controversy developed" in Yazoo City last month when the tourism committee announced its contest (see item 1706). "Church leaders and parishioners reacted with charges that the contest fostered and encouraged endorsements of the occult.... When asked about his reaction to the controversy, [Ellzey] said, 'I've never even taken the legend seriously. We have people coming (into Ricks Memorial Library) almost daily inquiring about the witch. It's nothing more than a very interesting legend.'"

1708 Myers, Leslie R. "'New York' Preview Proves Willie Morris in Peak Writing Form." *Clarion-Ledger*, 5 April 1992, sec. F, p. 1.

The Arts columnist for the *Clarion-Ledger* listens as Morris reads from the manuscript of his work-in-progress, *New York Days*, which focuses on the years he edited *Harper's Magazine*. "Now, at 57, Willie is 'consciously trying to root myself in that era ... the tumultuous 1960s. I'm trying to catch the mood of that very important decade in America from the vantage point of our cultural metropolis ... when I was young and everything was so full of promise.'"

1709 [Photograph]. *Clarion-Ledger*, 29 October 1992, sec. A, p. 1.

A photograph of Morris handing presidential candidate Bill Clinton "a limited edition, signed copy of his new book *My Two Oxfords*." Both men were Rhodes scholars at England's Oxford University. Clinton gave a speech in Jackson on October 28 during a campaign stop.

1710 Myers, Leslie R. "Mississippi Writers Gather for Mutual Admiration Society." *Clarion-Ledger*, 20 December 1992, sec. F, p. 1.

Relates that last weekend Morris played host "to some of America's best writers—all Mississippians—who met for Mississippi Homecoming in Jackson. They came from across America for the fifth Mississippi Writer's Day at the Old Capitol Museum. For the better part of 36 waking hours, their revelry didn't stop as friendships were begun or renewed." Besides Morris, the authors included Richard Ford, Barry Hannah, Rebecca Hill, Beverly Lowry, James Whitehead, and Beth Henley.

1711 Booth, William. "South by Northeast: A Not-Too-Southern Son Makes Good." *Washington Post*, 20 January 1993, sec. F, p. 4.

"Southern scholars, writers, cooks, politicians and artists" ponder the "southernness" of Bill Clinton. "'Of course Bill is a southerner,' says Willie Morris, the former editor of Harper's magazine and the author of 'North Toward Home,' one of the South's great coming-of-age memoirs, about his early life in Yazoo City, Miss." Southerners, according to John Floyd, editor of *Southern Living* magazine, are "very emotional," and "Morris remembers a Clinton hug. The year was 1980, and Morris was in Greenville, Miss., dining at the original Doe's Eat Place. Morris had not seen Clinton since 1968.... Clinton marched up to the table and threw his arms around Morris like a long-lost brother."

1712 Campbell, Sarah C. "Citizens of Yazoo City Among Nation's Movers and Shakers." *Clarion-Ledger*, 30 January 1993, sec. A, p. 13.

Mike Espy, the U.S. Secretary of Agriculture, and Haley Barbour, the national chairman of the Republican Party, join Morris and humorist Jerry Clower as well-known Americans who grew up in Yazoo City, Mississippi. "'This just doesn't happen. History was made here,' said Mayor Hugh McGraw."

1713 Kaufman, Elaine, and Charles Kipps. "Names, Names, Names: Elaine Looks Back." *New York Times*, 25 April 1993, sec. 9, p. 9.

On the thirtieth birthday of Elaine's restaurant in New York, owner Elaine Kaufman remembers some of the well-known people who have frequented her establishment over the years. "The first customers were the writers.... The editors followed the writers. Willie Morris, who was at Harper's then, liked to do contracts on a napkin."

1714 Thomas, William. "Willie Morris Odyssey, Part Two, Tells of Dizzy Days at Literary Peak." *(Memphis) Commercial Appeal*, 30 May 1993, sec. A, pp. 1, 6.

Morris talks about his new book, which will be published this fall. "Although his stormy break with Harper's is at the core of his forthcoming memoir, *New York Days*, it is not the whole story. 'Readers are going to find out what happened at Harper's,' Morris said in an interview at his home in Jackson. 'But the book is much more far-ranging. It's also about New York in the '60s, an intense and turbulent time, and it's about how sweeping events enveloped the city, the nation and my personal life.'"

1715 Skube, Michael. "Southern-Born Morris Finds Grail Back Home." *Atlanta Journal / The Atlanta Constitution*, 6 June 1993, sec. N, p. 9.

Recounts Morris's "triumphal return" to the South. After he resigned from *Harper's Magazine* in 1971—"four years after having written a book quite unlike any other in modern American letters"—he moved to Long Island where "he was a man at loose ends." By 1980, however, he had returned to his native state to teach at the University of Mississippi. While in Oxford, "he helped revitalize literary and intellectual life" and "he became a presence again." This September, some twenty-five years since the appearance of *North Toward Home*, Little, Brown and Company will publish Morris's second memoir, *New York Days*. "He is, his friends say, a man at peace with himself and as happy as it is possible for a man of conscience to be in a world that knows more injustice than justice."

1716 Myers, Leslie R. "Grisham's Success Challenges Oxford Literary Tradition." *Clarion-Ledger*, 8 August 1993, sec. F, p. 1.

Best-selling author John Grisham and his family have little privacy in Oxford, Mississippi, and have purchased a second home in Charlottesville, Virginia. Morris, who moved to Jackson when he married JoAnne Prichard, also felt the "pressures of popularity" in the university town. "'I love Oxford,' Morris said.... 'But I lost my privacy there. I lost it in a big way. Toward the end ... people were knocking on my door at all hours of the day and night for me to sign books or to give advice. Two times people crawled in the window,' Morris mused."

1717 Myers, Leslie R. "Fans Can't Read 'New York Days' Yet, But Willie Will." *Clarion-Ledger*, 15 August 1993, sec. F, p. 1.

Announces that on August 17, Morris will read from two sections of his forthcoming memoir, *New York Days*, at Lemuria bookstore in Jackson. This sequel to *North Toward Home* will be published "within a week," though Morris "absolutely will not sign books until Aug. 25, when Lemuria will hold a second party to launch his national book tour."

1718 "Willie Morris: Oxford Days." *(Oxford, Miss.) SouthVine*, 18 August—1 September 1993, p. 7.

Prior to Morris's return to Oxford to sign copies of *New York Days* (see item 1197), "SouthVine interviewed several of his friends from that period of his life." These include David Sansing (historian), Donna Tartt (novelist), Richard Howorth (owner of Square Books), and Evans Harrington (writer and professor of literature). Harrington said in part: "But Willie was more than a literary influence in Oxford. Coming to us as a celebrated Rhodes Scholar, author, and editor, he radiated wit, sentiment, humor, sadness, a love of high-jinks, and social concern. His evaluation of our people and customs were clear-eyed and articulate, yet tempered with tact and generosity.... Perhaps the most valuable influence Willie brought to us was his human warmth and decency."

1719 Myers, Leslie R. "New York Dazed." *Clarion-Ledger*, 25 August 1993, sec. D, pp. 1–2.

Reflections from Morris, William Styron, and Lauren Bacall highlight this capsule summary of Morris's literary years in New York, which the author has chronicled in the just-published *New York Days*. "A quarter century after surviving the city, the writer who grew up in Yazoo City recalls Manhattan — that Oz of wishers and wanderers— where, for four, brief, splendent years, he was the man at the controls. At age 32, he was the youngest-ever editor-in-chief of *Harper's* magazine.... 'I certainly did find myself. I certainly did find my past,' Morris said of the tangential rewards of writing these second memoirs, a sequel to *North Toward Home*. 'I found out what those years genuinely meant to me, how profoundly gratifying ... how innovating they were.'"

1720 Harris, Chico. "North Toward Oxford." *Oxford (Miss.) Eagle*, 26 August 1993.

A formal question-and-answer session with Morris upon the publication of *New York Days*. When asked if the United States will ever experience again "a chapter" like that described in his book, Morris replies: "No, I don't think so. There was something about the sixties, the deepening tragedy of Vietnam and the racial and class and generational divisi[ve]ness [which] gave a kinetic energy to those years that will probably never happen again. Some see the sixties in an unfavorable light as a time of coming apart. I disagree with that. In some ways, many things came together."

1721 Sheffield, Christopher. "State Author Offers Second Autobiography." *(Tupelo) Northeast Mississippi Daily Journal*, 26 August 1993, sec. B, p. 1.

Morris is scheduled to sign copies of *New York Days* today in Oxford and tomorrow in Tupelo. "Already teachers [in Tupelo] have planned to bring students to see Morris, whose third book, 'Good Old Boy' and its sequel, 'Good Old Boy and the Witch of Yazoo' have almost amassed a cult following by teens enthralled by the story of Morris' adolescent days in his Delta hometown. 'A lot of the kids can really relate to it,' said Brenda Key, a teacher at Tupelo's Middle School."

1722 Camphor, Sandra. "'New York Days' Is a Retrospective for Morris." *(Greenville, Miss.) Delta Democrat-Times*, 5 September 1993.

An interview with Morris during a stop in Greenville to promote *New York Days*. Morris set high goals for *Harper's*, but he clashed with the "money men" who controlled the magazine, and he resigned as editor in 1971. "In retrospect, Morris said, 'It's not realistic for a magazine to have lofty aspirations, but we were young and full of hope. We were trying to shape our country in a better way. A magazine should be judged by how much it tries, how big a dare it takes,' he concluded. Morris believes the problems he encountered at 'Harper's' reflected the 'tone of the times— it was part and parcel of the 1960s struggle,' he explained."

1723 Harshaw, Tobin. "The Secretaries, the Glamour, the Power." *New York Times Book Review*, 5 September 1993, p. 14.

A telephone interview with Morris that accompanies a front-page review of *New York Days* (item 1206). "Mr. Morris hasn't picked up a new issue of Harper's since he resigned in 1971. 'Sometimes I even avert my gaze when I see one on the newsstand,' he admitted. He doesn't miss the day-to-day hassles of running a magazine, which he called a 'young man's game.' But he admitted he misses its perquisites, 'the secretaries, the sense of glamour and a certain kind of power.'"

1724 Larson, Susan. "Home Free: Harper's Editor Recalls His 'New York' Days." *(New Orleans) Times-Picayune*, 19 September 1993, sec. D, pp. 1, 5.

A lengthy and upbeat interview with Morris shortly after the publication of *New York Days*, "a romantic chronicle of one man's sojourn at the heart of one of the most exciting periods in American writing and journalism." Reading back issues of *Harper's Magazine* while writing the book "was like reviewing 'a cherished diary,' Morris said. 'Every issue elicited memories.... And it made me feel proud. It brought back an immense rush of feelings—the energy of those days and the turbulence of the '60s themselves.... Everything seemed to be falling apart, but at the same time a lot of things seemed to be coming together.'" See also item 1214.

1725 Warren, Tim. "Willie Morris' Return to His Legendary, Literary Past." *(Baltimore) Sun*, 22 September 1993, sec. C, pp. 1, 8.

Assesses Morris's accomplishments during his years at *Harper's* as he, his magazine colleagues, and numerous friends gather in New York to celebrate the publication of *New York Days*. "As editor of *Harper's*, this former Rhodes Scholar from Yazoo City, Miss., published nearly every contemporary American writer of note, from Norman Mailer to Bernard Malamud to William Styron to John Updike." Guests at the book party embrace many of "New York's literary old guard," including David Halberstam, Larry L. King, Norman Mailer, George Plimpton, Mike Wallace, Arthur Schlesinger Jr., and William Styron. "'Willie is just a gifted, extraordinary, intuitive editor,' says Mr. Styron when asked how his friend of nearly three decades could draw such a crowd. 'He's got a great combination of honesty, intelligence and a touch of genius.'"

1726 Kakutani, Michiko. "Two Writers Revisit the City of Promise." *New York Times*, 24 September 1993, sec. C, pp. 1, 32.

Explores New York City as depicted in two recently published memoirs: Willie Morris's *New York Days* and Dan Wakefield's *New York in the Fifties*. "Some of the same friends and colleagues turn up in both books—William Styron, Norman Podhoretz and the ubiquitous Norman Mailer—but Mr. Morris's New York of the 60's tends to be a racier, more glamorous place, more public in its gestures, less introspective in its passions."

1727 Myers, Leslie R. "'New York Days,' Morris Find Friends Wherever They Go." *Clarion-Ledger*, 26 September 1993, sec. F, p. 1.

Comments on the many famous persons attending the parties held in honor of Morris and his memoir *New York Days*. "Nearly a dozen Pulitzer Prize winners and a sea of top journalists—as well as eastern actors, artists, every ilk of writer and Mississippians from all walks of life—crowded Little, Brown & Co. confabs held in New York and near Washington, D.C., in the past two weeks.... 'They were wonderful, renewing old friendships,' Morris, 58, said of the parties that drew 250 friends to Elaine's and 350 to the Warrenton, Va., farm of writers Nick and Mary Lynn Kotz. 'It was totally exhausting—but fun,' said Morris...."

1728 Spanberg, Erik. "Willie Morris' *New York Days*." *(Baton Rouge) Sunday Advocate*, 26 September 1993, "Magazine" section, pp. 3–4.

Morris discusses his years with *Harper's* and his literary career during a personal interview. "Wearing a pullover shirt stained by one of his three beloved cats, a pair of White Sox gym shorts and Nikes, Morris looks more like a Little League baseball coach than a man of letters.... 'The 1960s were probably the most turbulent era in American history since the Civil War,' Morris says. 'There was a lot going on, and I was right in the middle of it. I also traveled a lot in those years to college campuses, so I had a sense of what college students and the rest of America were thinking about. Everything in those days was touched by the war—you couldn't escape it; it was everywhere.'"

1729 Lanham, Fritz. "Southern Days, Northern Memories: Willie Morris Recalls Those Remarkable, Heady 'New York Days.'" *Houston Chronicle*, 3 October 1993, "Zest" section, p. 16.

Morris remembers his exhilarating years as an editor in New York City during a promotional tour for *New York Days*. "There was, Morris says, something special about that period in American history and journalism, a remarkable intersection of talent and time. 'I think there are good magazine writers any time,' he says. 'But there was something in the nature of the times, the temper of the 1960s, that drove a lot of our best writers to writing for magazines. I'm not just talking about the best journalists but novelists. It was a time of great kinetic energy.'"

1730 Smith, Wendy. "Willie Morris: When North Was Home." *Newsday*, 3 October 1993, "Fanfare" section, pp. 34–35.

Morris talks about *New York Days* and future writing projects during a New York City interview. Says Morris: "'I sent about 45 letters to my friends and colleagues of that time, from

David Halberstam to Billy Moyers, asking them to jog my memory by furnishing their own reflections, and their responses were invaluable to me. When I had a draft, I sent portions of the manuscript that pertained to other people to make sure they were accurate.'" Morris "hopes to get back to fiction now with a novel set during the Korean War years. 'I've been working on it off and on for several years; it's one of those things that obsesses you and gives you such problems, because you want it to be just right.'"

1731 "Morris Explains Origins of Southern Fiction." *Oxford (Miss.) Eagle*, 15 October 1993.

At a book-signing in Fairhope, Alabama, Morris provides a "down-home explanation for why Southerners seem drawn to fiction: lies and liquor. 'In the first place, they are natural-born liars and they don't hurry around like a lot of other people,' said Morris. 'They like to entertain and there's also, indubitably, something in the quality of the sour mash bourbon.'"

1732 Reidy, Chris. "Lit Snit." *Boston Sunday Globe*, 14 November 1993, p. 75.

Reports that several authors are engaged in public literary feuds and laments that the disputes are "meaner and less witty" than the ones that transpired back in the "days before the literati were *glitterati*." In the "controversial book" *New York Days*, "Morris attempts to settle a 20-year-old grudge. According to Morris, Lapham abetted his ouster as the editor of Harper's Magazine in 1971. At the time, Lapham was a staffer. Five years later, he was given Morris' old job, which he holds now." Incensed by *New York Days*, Lapham "massively aired his pique" by writing the *New York Times Book Review* (item 1206-B).

1733 McKenzie, Danny. "Morris Resting Up Before He Tackles Trilogy's Third Leg." *Clarion-Ledger*, 3 December 1993, sec. B, p. 1.

While on a promotional tour for *New York Days*, his sequel to *North Toward Home*, Morris has been planning his next memoir. "'I've given it a great deal of thought, and I'm gonna round out the trilogy,' Morris said during a recent interview at his north Jackson home." The book, which he'll probably call *South Toward Home*, "will deal with the changes he found in his homeland. 'Oh, it will have to,' he said. 'It will be about things in Mississippi and in the South that have changed and things that haven't, and about myself and how I've changed in some ways and haven't in others.'"

1734 "Morris to Receive Statewide Award." *Yazoo Herald*, 29 January 1994, pp. 1, 10.

Announces that on February 10 in the Old Capitol Museum in Jackson, Morris will receive a Governor's Award for Excellence in the Arts. The Governor and the Mississippi Arts Commission sponsor the annual awards "to honor significant contributions to the state's artistic and cultural life." Morris will receive the Artist's Achievement Award, and in announcing the prize, the Arts Commission said: "Morris is a mentor and inspiration to many artists and writers who has helped bring Southern literature to gr[e]ater prominence throughout the world. His writing gives poetic expression to the memory of people, places, and terrains of the heart."

1735 McKenzie, Danny. "Governor's Awards an Annual Reminder Why State Is Special." *Clarion-Ledger*, 11 February 1994, sec. B, p. 1.

A "handful" of artists selected by the Mississippi Arts Commission have received the annual Governor's Award for Excellence in the Arts. Morris was honored with the Artist's Achievement Award. Artist William Dunlap, master of ceremonies, "introduced Morris as 'the catalyst for the renaissance of creative writing in Mississippi' and called the Yazoo City native 'the heart, soul and conscience of Mississippi.' The emotional Morris said, 'All of what Mississippi was and is compelled me to my writing. It is especially gratifying to be recognized by one's own people.'"

1736 Reynolds, Christopher. "Southern Sanctuary." *Los Angeles Times*, 20 March 1994, sec. L, pp. 1, 12–13.

Morris is mentioned in a travel article on Oxford, Mississippi. This detailed piece is the first in a series of articles on "unscientifically selected" small American towns. "[John] Grisham is the biggest name, but he's only one among many successful writers around.... Author Willie Morris, born south of here in Yazoo City and celebrated in New York as the editor of Harper's magazine in the late 1960s, resided in Oxford a while before relocating to Jackson, and still visits often."

1737 Myers, Leslie R. "Morris' Friendship Pushed Groom Closer to 'Gump.'" *Clarion-Ledger*, 7 August 1994, sec. F, p. 1.

Observes that Morris was the first person to read the manuscript of Winston Groom's *Forrest Gump*. "'It's a very funny, unusual, truthful book,' Morris, 59, said.... 'I'm proud of Winston.'" Groom and Morris became friends in 1976 when they both worked for the *Washington Star* newspaper. "'Willie was actually the one who persuaded me to write my first book' [*Better Times Than These*], said Groom, who lives in Point Clear, Ala., in the land of his childhood on Mobile Bay. 'I held Willie in high esteem since he'd been editor of *Harper's*,' he said of their 18-year friendship. 'When someone like Willie says, "You not only can do it—you must do it," it was like orders from the captain.'"

1738 Myers, Leslie R. "'Southern Girls' Returns to Print to Remind Morris." *Clarion-Ledger*, 25 September 1994, sec. F, p. 1.

This month Louisiana State University Press is publishing Morris's *The Last of the Southern Girls* in its "Voices of the South" paperback series, "which brings volumes by top Southern writers back into print." Although Morris earned a great deal of money from the book, "He likes it the least. It was written at a low point in his life. That was after he resigned the august editorship of *Harper's* magazine. It's about a lover lost, 'kind of' at the same time, he said."

1739 Pettus, Gary. "An Uncommon Goal." *Clarion-Ledger*, 28 October 1994, sec. E, pp. 1–2.

A humorous article revealing that "a small, but devoted, band" of artists, writers, and professors sit in the south end zone of University of Mississippi home football games to cheer for their team. "Willie Morris started it all, they say. He says it, too. 'I started the south end zone,' he says." While living in Oxford, Morris enjoyed Ole Miss football, but he did not like sitting in the main section of the stadium. "'I got tired of socializing with people who were not there to see a football game,' said Morris, who now lives in Jackson." He and a friend noticed that the south end zone always held plenty of empty seats. "It was lust, at third or fourth sight. They spread the word, and a skeptical trickle of friends followed. 'They came to scoff,' Morris said, 'and they remained to pray.'"

1740 Yoder, Edwin M. "South May Be Headed for New Kind of Racial Separatism and Polarization." *Houston Chronicle*, 16 November 1994, sec. B, p. 11.

Morris's long-time friend visits him in Yazoo City three days after the midterm election gave the Republican party "a majority of Southern congressional seats for the first time in this century." As the two men drive around the Mississippi Delta, they review the election. "It is beginning to look as if the new political alignment in the Old Confederacy will feature two starkly different kinds of congressional seats: mostly conservative white Republican seats, with a sprinkling of black liberal Democratic seats, and little in the middle." An opinion piece.

1741 Myers, Leslie R. "Friends Turn Out for Good Old Boy, Writer Willie Morris." *Clarion-Ledger*, 4 December 1994, sec. F, p. 1.

Morris celebrated his sixtieth birthday with "about 300 of his closest friends" on November 29. The celebration, titled "The North (Jackson) Toward Home Birthday Bash" (named after Morris's memoir) included cocktails, "an elaborate skit," and dinner at a local restaurant. "Then the fest moved to Morris' northeast Jackson home for king-sized birthday cake and sing-a-longs around the piano." Some of the "absent admirers" who sent birthday wishes included Eudora Welty, William Styron, Winston Groom, Larry L. King, and Gloria Jones (widow of James Jones). Former Governor William Winter read a "warm happy birthday letter" from President Bill Clinton. See also item 1430.

1742 Martin, Philip. "Like Bourbon Through Silk: The Flowing Cadences of Willie Morris Reflect the South's Stubborn Persistence." *(Little Rock) Arkansas Democrat-Gazette*, 17 February 1995, sec. E, pp. 1, 8.

During an interview on the campus of the University of Arkansas at Monticello, the "courtly" Morris discusses his editorship of *Harper's Magazine*, his years in Oxford, Mississippi, and computers. "Morris sees technology as a great leveler of experience and, more depressingly, a silencer of conversation. Today's kids tend to be more impressionistic and less verbal, more solipsistic and less connected to the world at large. This worries him a little. Reconstruction couldn't dissolve the South, but the Cyber Age might." See also sidebar article: "Southern Author Making Comeback." *(Little Rock) Arkansas Democrat-Gazette*, 17 February 1995, sec. E, p. 8.

1743 Johnson, Rheta Grimsley. "All's Right with World in American Ireland." *Atlanta Journal / The Atlanta Constitution*, 26 March 1995, sec. C, p. 1.

A reporter flies to Jackson to interview Morris and reflects on what sets Mississippi apart from other states. She quotes Morris, who wrote that "Mississippi is truly our American Ireland, isolated and belligerent ... but one that has produced more than any subregion the best male and female writers of the Union." She praises Jackson's

Lemuria bookstore, "one of the finest bookstores in the nation, bar none. That's not just my opinion. Ask Miss [Eudora] Welty or Willie Morris or anyone who happens to know about bookstores."

1744 Johnson, Rheta Grimsley. "A Very 'Happy Puppy' Writes in Jackson, Miss." *Atlanta Journal / The Atlanta Constitution*, 2 April 1995, sec. B, p. 1.

Morris, happily married to his wife, JoAnne, and "as enthusiastic and emotional as a child," is content to live and write in Jackson, Mississippi. He is also excited about his latest book, *My Dog Skip*. "'I always loved Jack London dog stories,' Morris says. 'Forget "North Toward Home." Forget "New York Days." I'm more excited about this book than anything I've ever done.'"

1745 Kelley, Michael. "Morris Revisits His Miss. State of Mind." *(Memphis) Commercial Appeal*, 16 April 1995, sec. G, pp. 1, 5.

A somewhat confrontational question-and-answer interview with Morris, who is on a promotional tour for *My Dog Skip*. Kelley points out that many of the stories in the book originally appeared in *North Toward Home* and asks, "How much of [*My Dog Skip*] did you sit down and create from scratch?" Morris replies that his agent suggested he expand the "5,000-word section" about Skip in his first memoir and "knit it up to a book-length volume. I think I got it up to around 40,000 words." Kelley repeatedly questions Morris about the "sanitizing of the language" in *My Dog Skip*. For example, Morris uses the word "niggers" in a *North Toward Home* anecdote, but while rewriting the story for his later book changes it to "country folks." Morris tells Kelley: "I was just of a mood to do it.... I think subconsciously I wanted it to have the mood of growing up." When Kelley again asks why he altered the language, Morris replies: "I think I just wanted it to be more in the drift of those times." See also item 1746.

1746 Koeppel, Frederic. "South Toward Hokum: Morris Descends to Art of the Deal." *(Memphis) Commercial Appeal*, 16 April 1995, sec. G, p. 5.

A "commentary" on Morris's interview with Michael Kelley (item 1745) to illustrate "the cynicism of the book publishing industry." Koeppel quotes Morris's remark that his agent urged him to expand the section on his dog Skip in *North Toward Home* to book length "because he could assure me of a movie sale on this sooner or later." Although the arrangement is, Koeppel writes, "a pretty good deal" for Morris, "it's a bad deal for the reader. You will look in vain for any mention in *My Dog Skip* that the effort is an enhancement and expansion of a section of a book published in 1967 or that certain passages were lifted directly from *North Toward Home*." Koeppel further complains that unlike most authors, Morris did not have to sell his book. His agent "had an idea that would make money for agent, author and publisher alike.... First-time, second-time, even third-time authors should be so lucky."

1747 Pettus, Gary. "On a Swing and a Prayer." *Clarion-Ledger*, 21 April 1995, sec. E, pp. 1, 5.

Relates the circumstances that led to the writing and publishing of Morris's *A Prayer for the Opening of the Little League Season*. John Evans, owner of Lemuria bookstore in Jackson, Mississippi, and a Little League coach, "asked Morris to pen a prayer invoking the Lord's blessings on the kingdom of Little League." Months later, Morris, "just to get John off my back," wrote the prayer in one night. Evans read the invocation over the telephone to his friend, book illustrator Barry Moser, whose agent arranged for its publication with Moser as illustrator.

1748 Dart, Bob. "'Yaller Dog' Mississippi Democrat Writes Memoir About Old Canine Pal." *Atlanta Journal / The Atlanta Constitution*, 30 April 1995, sec. N, p. 3.

Morris talks about politics as well as *My Dog Skip* while in Washington, D.C., promoting his new book. "Race and all its complications continue to haunt the South, Morris reckons, speculating that these lingering issues helped propel the region's booming Republicanism. 'You saw the stirrings of it,' he said, when Lyndon Johnson signed the Voting Rights Act of 196[5]." Morris still misses Skip, "the remarkable canine who shared his 1940s boyhood." While growing up in Yazoo City, he recalls, "All of us had dogs, but my dog was better than their dogs, I always felt." This article, syndicated by the Cox News Service, also appeared in the *Houston Chronicle* of 23 April 1995.

1749 Kennedy, J. Michael. "It's a Dog's Life." *Los Angeles Times*, 29 June 1995, sec. E, pp. 1, 5.

Not only an interview with Morris, conducted during his *My Dog Skip* book tour, but also a detailed summary of his "career of ups and downs." Kennedy notes that "Willie Morris is having a fine old time of it these days in Mississippi, having rid himself of a devil or two from the past, having made peace with himself." He is now busy "peddling this little book that he did for the pure pleasure of it." *My Dog Skip* is a "charming reminiscence about life in a much simpler time in rural Yazoo City, Miss." It's also a "tribute" to Morris's favorite dog, and although the pet has been dead for forty years, he still talks about him: "Skip was like a brother to me and I still miss him."

1750 Myers, Leslie R. "If You Can't Map Out a Merry Christmas, It Still May Find You." *Clarion-Ledger*, 24 December 1995, sec. F, p. 1.

Discloses that Morris and his wife, JoAnne Prichard, "tried to usher in this Christmas, their fifth since marriage," by chopping down and decorating a "sprawling" cedar tree. About a week later, Prichard suffered an allergic reaction and twice "had to be rushed to a hospital emergency room for hives. 'We thought it was food,' Willie said. 'I thought it was me. But it turned out to be the cedar tree.'" They got rid of the cedar and she recovered. "Willie says, now with some joy, that this forever will be remembered as the year of 'the killer Christmas tree.'"

1751 Watkins, Billy. "Welcome to Winston's World." *Clarion-Ledger*, 11 January 1996, sec. D, p. 1.

Announces that Winston Groom, author of *Forrest Gump*, will speak tonight at Millsaps College as part of its Arts and Lecture Series. "Groom's mentor, the person he credits with giving him the courage to quit and write books, is Mississippi author Willie Morris." The two men became good friends while working for the *Washington Star* newspaper, and Morris will introduce Groom at this evening's program. "'Every time I see him, I thank him for encouraging me,' Groom says. 'Winston was a darn good writer and reporter, and I told him if he didn't quit and start writing books at that point, he may never do it,' Morris says. 'I felt he had the courage, the memory, the talent to be successful.'"

1752 Floyd, Nell Luter. "Whad' Ya Know, Jackson." *Clarion-Ledger*, 21 January 1996, sec. F, p. 1.

Michael Feldman, host of Public Radio's comedy/quiz radio show *Whad'Ya Know?*, is slated to broadcast his show live from Jackson's Thalia Mara Hall on January 27. "Local guests will include writer Willie Morris...." See also: Pinkston, Will. "More Than 2,000 Turn Out for Radio Show." *Clarion-Ledger*, 28 January 1996, sec. B, p. 1. See also item 1967.

1753 Kanengiser, Andy. "Grisham Highlights Khayat Inaugural Activities Set for April 11." *Clarion-Ledger*, 22 February 1996, sec. B, p. 1.

"University of Mississippi supporters and college leaders from about 40 states will salute Chancellor Robert Khayat during inaugural activities on the Oxford campus April 11." Author John Grisham "will head the lineup of speakers," while festivities during the inaugural week will include "readings by Mississippi writers Willie Morris, Barry Hannah, Ellen Douglas and Larry Brown." See also: Kanengiser, Andy. "Authors to Help Inaugurate Chancellor." *Clarion-Ledger*, 8 April 1996, sec. B, p. 3; Evans, Lynn. "You Can Tell the New Ole Miss Chancellor by the 'Company He Keeps.'" *Clarion-Ledger*, 18 April 1996, sec. A, p. 9.

1754 Capuzzo, Mike. "Story of Loving, Loyal Dog Teaches Life's Lessons." *Salt Lake Tribune*, 31 March 1996, sec. J, p. 3.

Morris, who is traveling around the country promoting the Vintage paperback of *My Dog Skip*, "is astonished at the reaction of dog and cat lovers to his lovely memoir of growing up in a small Southern town with a medium-sized fox terrier.... 'One woman asked me if I would sign the book to Cindy,' Morris said. 'So I asked her, "Are you Cindy?" And she said, "No, Cindy is my cocker spaniel." I've been signing books to dogs that are alive and dogs that are in heaven. I've even been signing them to cats.'" This interview, distributed by United Feature Syndicate, also appeared in the *(Denver) Rocky Mountain News* of 2 March 1996, the *(Raleigh, N.C.) News & Observer* of 8 March 1996, and *Newsday* of 16 March 1996.

1755 Holl, Shelley N. C. "The Write Way to See Mississippi." *(New Orleans) Times-Picayune*, 5 April 1996, sec. L, pp. 4–5.

Morris and a reporter take a "close-up look" at the author's hometown—"and favorite subject"—Yazoo City, Mississippi. "For Morris, every corner of Yazoo City has a story—or a tall tale—especially the cemetery where he used to play 'taps' at the funerals of servicemen killed in Korea. On that rising hillside with its scattered tombstones and trees, he told about the Witch of Yazoo who broke the chains surrounding her grave, rose from the dead and torched the town in 1904, fulfilling a curse made years earlier."

1756 "Festival Overcomes Heat, Humidity." *Yazoo Herald*, 22 May 1996, sec. A, pp. 1, 12.

Reports that despite high temperatures and humidity, hundreds of persons attended the

"Witch Way to Yazoo" festival on May 18 and 19. "Perhaps the portion of the two-day festival that showed the greatest increase in attendance was the Glenwood Cemetery tours...." The cemetery is home to the Witch of Yazoo, and during one evening's tour, Morris read from *Good Old Boy*, his book that chronicles the witch's story. A photograph of Morris reading before a group of people in the cemetery accompanies the article, while another photo shows a woman unveiling a newly erected monument at the grave of the witch. The stone marker reads (in all capital letters): "According to local legend ... On May 25, 1904, the Witch of Yazoo City broke out of these curious chain links surrounding her grave and burned down Yazoo City. Writer Willie Morris's classic 'Good Old Boy' brought national renown to this vengeful woman and her shameful deed." Below the inscription is this dedication (slashes indicate line breaks): "In honor of / Ray Rogers Sr. / Sexton 21 years / Jan. 7, 1974 to July 1, 1995 / Glenwood Cemetery / Yazoo City, Mississippi." See also item 1789.

1757 Cleveland, Rick. "Morris Leads off Olympic Program." *Clarion-Ledger*, 2 June 1996, sec. D, p. 1.

Morris has contributed an essay to the official souvenir program of Atlanta's Centennial Olympic Games. His essay, titled "A Prayer Before the Feast," is an "overview of the Centennial Olympics and the South, which serves as an Olympic host for the first time." Morris was pleased he was asked to contribute the article (item 898). "'I considered it a very important assignment and an honor,' Morris said. 'I put a lot of time and worked very hard on it. I didn't want one false word in it.'"

1758 Hood, Orley. "For Evers-Williams, There Were 2 Closure Points." *Clarion-Ledger*, 2 June 1996, sec. A, p. 1.

This evening in Natchez, Mississippi, Myrlie Evers-Williams, chairman of the board of the NAACP and widow of slain civil rights activist Medgar Evers, "will address several hundred patrons of the Natchez Literary Festival." Morris will introduce her to the audience.

1759 Bragg, Rick. "To Bind up a Nation's Wound with Celluloid." *New York Times*, 16 June 1996, sec. 2, pp. 1, 36.

Castle Rock Entertainment and director Rob Reiner are producing a motion picture about the murder of civil rights activist Medgar Evers and the trial and conviction of the man who killed him, white supremacist Byron De La Beckwith. Actor James Woods studied Beckwith's mannerisms in preparation for the filming, and Woods bears an uncanny resemblance to his real-life counterpart. "'It's spooky,' said Willie Morris, the Mississippian and Southern writer who serves as historical consultant for the movie, which is still untitled. It was Mr. Morris who encouraged Frederick Zollo, who is producing it with Mr. Reiner, to make the film in the first place."

1760 Hood, Orley. "Spotlight Shines on the People Who Played." *Clarion-Ledger*, 30 June 1996, sec. A, p. 1.

The new Mississippi Sports Hall of Fame and Museum is set to open on July 4. Among the 850 films is a feature that shows "Willie Morris reading from one of his stories, ruminating on the smell of freshly mown grass and baseball and Mississippi summertimes."

1761 "Generals Host Yazoo Night." *Yazoo Herald*, 3 July 1996, sec. A, p. 8.

A photograph of Morris, "who was given the honor of throwing out" the first pitch of a game hosted by the Jackson Generals baseball team.

1762 Gordon, Mac. "Group of Mississippi Writers Opposes Fordice Nominees." *Clarion-Ledger*, 10 July 1996, sec. A, p. 7.

Morris is among thirty-three "Mississippi-bred writers" who have issued a statement protesting Governor Kirk Fordice's "handling of College Board nominees.... Fordice's nomination of four white men to replace two white men, one black man and one white woman on the board was an act of 'retrograde,' the writers' statement reads."

1763 Myers, Leslie. "Morris Plans Book About Life, Death in Land of Hollywood." *Clarion-Ledger*, 11 August 1996, sec. F, p. 1.

Reports that Morris and his wife, JoAnne Prichard, have recently returned from Hollywood, where they viewed final filming of the motion picture *Ghosts of Mississippi*. "Morris is a consultant for the film, which recounts the conviction of Byron De La Beckwith for the 1963 Jackson murder of civil rights leader Medgar Evers." The author is planning a book that "will cover movie making and other personal observations."

1764 Myers, Leslie. "Morris, Mabus Among Speakers in Lecture Series." *Clarion-Ledger*, 1 September 1996, sec. F, p. 1.

Announces the schedule of speakers for the twenty-ninth season of Millsaps College's Arts and Lecture Series. Morris and *Ghosts of Mississippi* producer Fred Zollo will appear together on stage in December. "With the recent filming of three major movies in Mississippi—*Ghosts* [*of Mississippi*], *A Time to Kill* and *The Chamber*—*Ghosts* consultant/award-winning writer Morris of Jackson and Zollo discuss the impact on the state's image and economy." See also item 1767.

1765 "UM Library Acquires Willie Morris Papers." *Yazoo Herald*, 9 September 1996, sec. A, pp. 1, 3.

The University of Mississippi's Department of Archives and Special Collections has acquired Morris's letters, notes, postcards, clippings, and other personal papers. The collection numbers some seventeen thousand items, and "when read chronologically, they narrate the life of a man of letters. 'I'm delighted that the university has my papers,' said Morris, now a Jackson resident. 'I love Ole Miss and Mississippi and think it is appropriate that my papers remain in my native state.'" See also: "Ole Miss Acquires Morris Papers." *Clarion-Ledger*, 24 October 1996, sec. D, p. 1. See also item 1438.

1766 Dettro, Chris. "Writer Willie Morris to Pay Tribute to James Jones." *(Springfield, Ill.) State Journal-Register*, 1 November 1996, p. 21.

"Willie Morris, one of this century's most versatile Southern writers and editors, will pay tribute to his late friend James Jones as part of The Sixth Annual James Jones Symposium and simultaneous writers' workshop today and Saturday. 'I'll tell some stories about Jim, read some from my memoir,' Morris said in an interview." He will deliver the symposium's keynote address, "James Jones' Literary Legacy: Personal Perspectives from Three Decades," on Saturday, November 2. In his address he will discuss his relationship with Jones, which he recounted in his book *James Jones: A Friendship*. See also: Pokorski, Doug. "James Jones Remembered: Author's Legacy Continues During Two Springfield Events Nov. 1–2." *(Springfield, Ill.) State Journal-Register*, 20 October 1996, p. 54.

1767 "Ghost Story." *Clarion-Ledger*, 6 December 1996, sec. F, p. 1.

On December 11, the Millsaps College Arts and Lecture Series "will present *Ghosts of Mississippi* producer Frederick M. Zollo, author Willie Morris, state Film Commissioner Ward Emling and screenwriter Lewis Colick in a panel on 'Mississippi in Film: Impact, Image and Involvement.'" See also item 1764.

1768 Webb, John. "To Tell the Truth: Have Filmmakers Served History or Drama—or Both—with Ghosts of Mississippi?" *Clarion-Ledger*, 8 December 1996, sec. E, p. 1.

Questions Castle Rock Entertainment producers for not telling the story of Byron De La Beckwith's murder conviction "exactly as it happened" in the motion picture *Ghosts of Mississippi*. Hinds County District Attorney Ed Peters, who cross-examined a significant witness in the actual trial, insists that the filmmakers "played footloose and fancy-free with important events." Says screenwriter Lewis Colick: "It's not a documentary. It's a work of art.... You have to be faithful to history and basically tell it the way it happened, but you also have to help the story." Morris, who was a consultant on the movie, maintains that the film is "roughly 80 percent accurate but 100 percent true."

1769 Yardley, Jim. "A Prosecutor's Real Life Dramatics." *Atlanta Journal / The Atlanta Constitution*, 8 December 1996, sec. G, p. 1.

An interview with and profile of Bobby DeLaughter, the Hinds County, Mississippi, assistant district attorney who managed to convict Byron De La Beckwith, the white supremacist who murdered civil rights leader Medgar Evers in 1963. Beckwith was freed in 1964 after the all-white juries in two trials deadlocked. Twenty-five years later, DeLaughter reopened the case and won it in 1994. Castle Rock Entertainment will soon release *Ghosts of Mississippi*, a motion picture about the murder and Beckwith's eventual conviction. "'This movie,' says Mississippi author Willie Morris, a consultant on the film, 'will make people realize that Bobby DeLaughter is a national hero.'"

1770 Hood, Orley. "'Ghosts' Is Epic Evidence of Good Overcoming Evil." *Clarion-Ledger*, 15 December 1996, sec. B, p. 1.

Recalls that Byron De La Beckwith was tried twice for murder in 1964 but each time the all-white Mississippi juries failed to reach a verdict. Thirty years later, however, another Mississippi jury convicted the white supremacist of the 1963 murder of Medgar Evers, a black civil rights leader. "Willie Morris, the writer, and Fred Zollo, the movie producer, sat in the courtroom that morning, wrapped in gooseflesh, mesmerized witnesses to an extraordinary piece of history. Morris said, you know, Fred, there's a movie here, the means to preserve this moment, this triumph of humanity over evil, to share this victory with the rest of America and the world." After viewing the premiere of this motion picture, *Ghosts of Mississippi*, Hood proclaims that it is "a monument to vision, to integrity, to righteous stubbornness."

1771 "Thumbs Up: Director Thanks State on 'Today.'" *Clarion-Ledger*, 24 December 1996, sec. B, p. 1.

Notes that during his appearance on yesterday's *Today* show, *Ghosts of Mississippi* director Rob Reiner told co-host Katie Couric that numerous Mississippians deserve credit for their assistance with the motion picture. "Reiner mentioned he received help from Hinds County Assistant District Attorney Bobby DeLaughter, award-winning Mississippi writer Willie Morris of Jackson and Myrlie Evers-Williams, Medgar Evers' widow."

1772 Friedeman, Matt. "Can 'Ghosts' Help Us Lay Aside Misconceptions About Conservatives, Too?" *Clarion-Ledger*, 7 February 1997, sec. A, p. 13.

Disagrees with some of Morris's statements in his article on the motion picture *Ghosts of Mississippi* in *George* magazine (item 801). Morris contends that Hinds County Assistant District Attorney Bobby DeLaughter, who successfully prosecuted Byron De La Beckwith in a third murder trial, lost an election for a Court of Appeals seat to "a staunchly conservative white lawyer-politician" because he reopened the Beckwith case. Friedeman agrees that "the Beckwith trial cost DeLaughter the race" but argues that "Morris is the only one in this state I know who is willing to describe [DeLaughter's opponent, Frank Barber] as staunchly conservative." Barber, counters Friedeman in his opinion piece, is politically a liberal while DeLaughter is the one who is conservative. "Maybe in all the self-examination that a movie like *Ghosts* engenders some of the introspection should be that of political liberals. Is it time for the left-wing to admit its own pre-conceived prejudices and begin to appreciate the on-going, noble contributions of conservatives fighting for social and economic justice for *all* Mississippians?"

1773 Kelley, Mike. "Author Morris Recalls UT Time As His Intellectual Awakening." *Austin American-Statesman*, 27 February 1997, sec. B, p. 2.

During a speech at the University of Texas, Morris takes his audience "on an autobiographical stroll." Even though "he promised to 'try to avoid this being only a sentimental return to my beloved university,' he couldn't help recalling the shaping influence UT had on him." He quoted from *North Toward Home*, "saying that UT was where he first learned the 'acceptance of ideas themselves as something worth living by.'"

1774 Kanengiser, Andy. "Eagle Ridge Conference Center Site of National Civil War Seminar." *Clarion-Ledger*, 3 April 1997, sec. B, p. 3.

Announces that Morris and "Civil War scholars from across the nation" will participate in a seminar on the 1863 siege of Vicksburg, which is planned for April 26–29 at the Eagle Ridge Conference Center, Hinds Community College, in Raymond, Mississippi.

1775 Fowler, Ed. "Dierker Has Makings of Master Diplomat." *Houston Chronicle*, 7 April 1997, sec. B, p. 1.

When asked why he had a copy of Morris's *North Toward Home* on his office desk, Houston Astros manager Larry Dierker "said he had recalled a passage on Morris' relationship with the right-leaning pols he covered [for the *Texas Observer*] and brought the book in to bone up on media relations, and to show the relevant section to general manager Gerry Hunsicker." Dierker pointed out a section in which the liberal Morris told how he socialized with conservative politicians and came to like them. "The moral of the story is that it's hard to rip someone you like. If that seems a rather obvious tenet for anyone who deals with the media, you'd be amazed by how many in sports can't get their minds around it."

1776 Allen, Teddy. "The Best of the Southern Boys." *(Shreveport, La.) Times*, 21 April 1997, sec. D, p. 1.

An interview with Morris, who is scheduled to be the featured speaker at the annual "Authors in April" luncheon on April 26 at the Shreveport Country Club. "'I might give a speech on why I'm a writer,' he said last week from his home in Jackson, Miss. 'It's not likely to be especially literary; I hope it's universal.'" Morris is working on a "'very, very personal' work he finds hard to describe. It grew from his involvement in *Ghosts of Mississippi*, the recent movie recounting the 1994 retrial of Byron [D]e [L]a Beckwith for the 1963 murder of civil-rights leader Medgar Evers."

1777 Cleveland, Rick. "Rudy Has Made a Remarkable Career of Beating the Odds." *Clarion-Ledger*, 15 May 1997, sec. C, p. 1.

Morris, sportswriter Cleveland, and two others discuss their favorite sports movies. Morris, who "said he had watched *Hoosiers* 14 times," suggested that Cleveland and his son Tyler drop by for pizza one evening and they'll all watch the film *Rudy*. "So, we did. Tyler and I watched *Rudy* for the first time, Willie for the 12th.... It is the story of Rudy Ruettiger, who overcame truly incredible odds to realize his dream and play football for Notre Dame." Cleveland contacts the real-life Rudy Ruettiger, head of Rudy International, and discovers that he delivers more than 150 inspirational speeches a year around the world. "The message is simple: Never give up on your dreams."

1778 Getlin, Josh. "Texas Observer No More." *Los Angeles Times*, 18 May 1997, sec. E, pp. 1, 4.

A lengthy profile of Ronnie Dugger, who has left the *Texas Observer* after more than forty years as publisher "to build a national populist movement." Getlin notes that "Dugger is proud of those whose careers he has nourished through the Observer, including [Molly] Ivins, Willie Morris, Larry L. King and Robert Sherrill." Includes Morris's laudatory comments about Dugger from *North Toward Home*.

1779 Gregory, Ted. "Faulkner's Literary Legacy Revives Mississippi Town." *Richmond (Va.) Times Dispatch*, 29 June 1997, sec. J, p. 6.

An "artistic and cultural renaissance" has transformed the small southern town of Oxford, Mississippi, into a "surprisingly urbane and energetic place." Much of the creativity stems from William Faulkner "and the literary heritage he helped create," but the town boasts a large number of other writers as well. John Grisham heads the list, though "Larry Brown, Barry Hannah and Willie Morris, all acclaimed authors, live in and around Oxford as well." (Morris, however, left Oxford and moved to Jackson, Mississippi, in 1990 when he married JoAnne Prichard.)

1780 Hood, Orley. "Writer Sees Yazoo City with Eyes for Prose." *Clarion-Ledger*, 15 September 1997, sec. A, pp. 1, 5.

Morris takes Hood on what the author calls his "$10,000 tour" of Yazoo City, Mississippi, pointing out the homes of famous Yazooans and other sites both personal and historical. "Across Broadway we come to the Yazoo County Courthouse, the ancient magnolia tree that gave Morris a scar he still carries, and the Ricks Memorial Library, 'second oldest in the state,' he says, 'my favorite building.... Every house on every streetcorner has a memory for me,' he says."

1781 Baker, Donald P. "At 100, Novelist William Faulkner Gets a Sculpture in Yoknapatawpha County." *Washington Post*, 26 September 1997, sec. A, p. 3.

William Faulkner's one hundredth birthday is commemorated on September 25 in Oxford, Mississippi, with the unveiling of a bronze sculpture of the writer. "Leading the tributes to Faulkner today were fellow Mississippi writers [Willie] Morris and Shelby Foote, who told several hundred people sitting through a light rain that Faulkner will be remembered as America's greatest 20th century writer. 'This is Faulkner weather,' drawled Morris, 62, recalling Faulkner's words about 'the unhurried rain' sweeping across the Mississippi Delta, the locale of some of Faulkner's most memorable stories." Similar articles about the sculpture dedication were published in newspapers around the country. A large photograph of Morris and Foote standing next to the bronze figure is featured on the front page of the 26 September 1997 issue of the University of Mississippi's *Daily Mississippian*.

1782 Eck, Jeanne M. "The Shun Factor." *Washington Post*, 21 October 1997, sec. D, p. 5.

Declares that "when you separate from a powerful spouse, unless you are powerful in your own right, it comes as a shock that ... you find yourself being shunned socially." This occurred to Celia Morris, wife of Willie Morris. "'When Willie and I got a divorce, he was very powerful,' says the 61-year-old author of several books.... When they separated, she found herself dramatically and painfully excluded from their circle of friends."

1783 Lucas, Sherry. "Greeting the Season." *Clarion-Ledger*, 4 December 1997, sec. E, pp. 12–13.

Details the area's festivities planned for the holiday season, of which a principal attraction is the Jackson Christmas parade. "Out front, from the hometown corner, we have grand marshal, acclaimed author, Yazoo City native and Jackson resident Willie Morris. 'I've been out in the back yard, practicing throwing candy to the children,' and using his cat as a stand-in for the kids, Morris said." See also: Wagster, Emily. "Revelers Hit Streets As Holiday Parades Roll." *Clarion-Ledger*, 7 December 1997, sec. B, p. 1.

1784 Hood, Orley. "'Ghosts' Peers into Our Past for the Sake of the Future." *Clarion-Ledger*, 4 February 1998, sec. E, p. 1.

Remarks that Mississippi comprises numerous diverse individuals from widely varied geographic areas and economic levels. All persons are influenced by their ancestors, and each person's economic and social condition concerns his or her descendants. "'We are not makers of history,' Martin Luther King Jr. once observed. 'We are made by history.' In many ways and for many reasons, that's the point of Willie Morris' new book, *The Ghosts of Medgar Evers*. We can not exist outside the context of our history, and our circumstances powerfully affect the brushstrokes we provide for following generations."

1785 Watkins, Billy. "Murder, Mississippi and the Movies." *Clarion-Ledger*, 4 February 1998, sec. E, pp. 1, 3.

Morris, Robert Loomis (his editor at Random House), and others comment on the author's new book, *The Ghosts of Medgar Evers*. The volume chronicles the making of the 1996 motion picture *Ghosts of Mississippi*, which "bombed at the box office. 'It lost money.' Morris says. 'You can't make a civil rights movie today, minus pyrotechnics and naked women, and make any money. But this was an important story and relative to today's South.'" Loomis believes that one of the book's strengths is Morris's skillful blend of history and autobiography. "'Most writers trying to do this get too egotistical or get way out of perspective,' Loomis says. 'It's a natural talent with Willie, and I think it's unparalleled, really.'"

1786 Scanlon, John. "Morris to Read, Sign at Off Square Books." University of Mississippi *Daily Mississippian*, 5 February 1998, pp. 1, 7.

This evening Morris is slated to read from and sign copies of his new book, *The Ghosts of Medgar Evers*, at Off Square Books in Oxford. "'The organizing thread (of the book) is the movie,' Morris said. 'It's a good movie, but I always said it got caught up in political correctness.... There is a difference between accuracy and the truth. The movie is about 80 percent accurate and 100 percent truth.'" See also: Dees, Jim. "Morris Comes Home." *Oxford (Miss.) Eagle*, 6 February 1998.

1787 Grayson, Christy. "Skip Goes Hollywood: Morris Book Inspires Movie; Yazoo City Is Filming Site." *Yazoo Herald*, 14 March 1998, sec. A, pp. 1, 16.

Announces that a motion picture will be made of Morris's *My Dog Skip*, with filming to start in late April in the Mississippi localities of Yazoo City, Canton, and Jackson. Morris said in a telephone interview that several identical Jack Russell terriers will play Skip, as it would be difficult for one dog to withstand a grueling film schedule. "'They're trying to find a dog that can bark with a Southern accent—like "roof, y'all,"' Morris joked.... The movie, he said, 'will follow the spirit of the book.'"

1788 Pettus, Gary. "Filmmakers to Hold Child Casting Call." *Clarion-Ledger*, 21 March 1998, sec. B, p. 5.

The producers of the motion picture *My Dog Skip* are "holding a casting call for children" tomorrow in Jackson. Casting director Marshall Peck is looking for a boy and a girl to play the two lead characters. *My Dog Skip* is "based on Willie Morris' book about his childhood in Yazoo City" and should begin production late next month. It will be filmed in Jackson, Canton, and Yazoo City. See also: Baswell, Allen. "Yazooans Enjoy Casting Call for 'My Dog Skip.'" *Yazoo Herald*, 25 March 1998, pp. 1, 16; "Casting Call Set for Today in Canton." *Yazoo Herald*, 4 April 1998, p. 1.

1789 Deaton, Julia N. "It's Time to Bury the 'Witch of Yazoo' for Good." *Yazoo Herald*, 4 April 1998, p. 4.

A local resident and "guest columnist" complains about the monument in the town's Glenwood Cemetery that commemorates the Witch of Yazoo, the legendary character in Morris's *Good Old Boy*. "Yazoo City needs to wake up to the disgraceful promotion being executed by one pompous individual who thinks this community needs the legacy of some evil 'witch.'" Deaton summarizes the often-repeated tale about a witch, supposedly buried in the cemetery, who broke through the chains surrounding her grave and burned down the city in 1904. She adds that it is "ridiculous" that adults lead tours of children to the gravesite where they "hear this lie about a witch" and get this "sinister garbage ... instilled in their absorbing minds." She also accuses Morris of erecting the marker to himself in Glenwood Cemetery because he thought he was "important enough." See also item 1756. The *Yazoo Herald* published a number of responses to Deaton's column:

A Jones, Mary M. "Yazoo Should Embrace, Not Abandon, Legend." *Yazoo Herald*, 11 April 1998, p. 4.

Jones, a "contributing columnist," thinks it is "amazing" that she and Deaton "can have such different opinions" about the monument to the Witch of Yazoo and its "wonderful legend." Jones recalls the many people who regularly tour Yazoo City after reading Morris's *Good Old Boy*. A father and his son from Monroe, Louisiana, for example, had both read the book "and on this school holiday the father had taken a day of vacation so they could come look around Yazoo.... As for the marker which is now in Glenwood, Willie Morris had nothing to do with that except to gladly participate in the ceremony." An excellent, thoughtful column by a prominent business owner in Yazoo City.

B Morris, Willie. "Native Son Takes Issue with Writer's Comments on Marker." *Yazoo Herald*, 11 April 1998, p. 4.

Morris protests Deaton's "murky insinuation" that "I had the granite historical marker erected to myself at the witch's grave.... It was financed and erected by Discover Yazoo and dedicated to the longtime and respected sexton of Glenwood Cemetery, Ray Rogers, who guided numerous visitors to the grave over the years." (This letter to the editor is also documented as item 964.)

C Kuykendall, Harriet DeCell. "Legend of the Witch Parallels Yazoo's Recovery from Fire." *Yazoo Herald*, 15 April 1998, p. 4.

A retired Jackson teacher defends Glenwood Cemetery's Witch of Yazoo marker in a letter to the editor. She compares the witch story to the determination of local residents who "refused to be daunted" following the 1904 Yazoo City fire and managed to rebuild the town. "The legend demonstrates a parallel to the real experience of the fire. The witch refused to be bound but rose again." Kuykendall also writes that she enjoyed teaching *Good Old Boy* to the students in her classes. "Willie's interweaving of fact and fiction is masterfully done. The opening, which includes the witch legend, sets the tone for a work of the imagination with real-world trappings."

D Sikes, Vernon. "Spunky Writer Too Hard on Willie." *Yazoo Herald*, 15 April 1998, p. 4.

The *Yazoo Herald*'s managing editor disagrees with some of Deaton's statements, but acknowledges to her that "you've got spunk, and that can go a long way when it comes to column writing."

E Bales, Jack. "Morris Biographer Takes Issue with Critic." *Yazoo Herald*, 18 April 1998, p. 4.

A researcher of Morris's life and works and a "guest columnist" addresses Deaton's "rambling diatribe" against the author. "Mrs. Deaton's inference that the charming and often-visited monument to both the Witch of Yazoo and Willie Morris' popular book 'Good Old Boy' can 'desensitize' children and therefore directly lead to mass murder represents a leap in logic so wide that even famed motorcyclist Evel Knievel would not attempt to jump it." *Good Old Boy* "is a staple among young readers in Mississippi; indeed, I have learned of one teacher who presented a program at a school conference on how she uses the book in her classroom!" See also item 1789-F.

F Deaton, Julia N. "No Apologies for Her 'Rambling Diatribe.'" *Yazoo Herald*, 25 April 1998, sec. A, p. 4.

"Guest columnist" Deaton responds to Bales's column (item 1789-E), in which he referred to her article as a "rambling diatribe." She replies that "it probably was 'very rambling' to those who had their gorge rise and explode because of their callous attitude regarding respect and concern for others. It's sad that Bales couldn't understand the point of my article, which merely supports the principle of adults practicing respect and, in turn, instilling such in children."

G Bales, Jack. "Yazooans Should be Grateful for Native Son's Literary Legacy." *Yazoo Herald*, 6 May 1998, sec. A, p. 4.

A letter to the editor with "just a few more brief (and final) words on the 'Witch of Yazoo.'" Bales argues that *Good Old Boy* is "a timeless book," and he recollects that "on May 13, 1996, Willie Morris received a Resolution of Appreciation from his hometown, which proclaimed: 'Whereas through his colorful writings about his Yazoo City, Mississippi haunts and the imaginative portrayal of the witch's burning down the town, he has created folklore in our community.' Few writers have bequeathed such a legacy."

1790 Harden, Mike. "Mississippi Still Haunted by Specters of a Tainted Past." *Columbus Dispatch*, 10 April 1998, sec. C, p. 1.

Reports that numerous middle-class blacks are leaving the North and moving back to the Deep South. Some of them are retirees, while others, "in one of the towering ironies of our age, are returning to the small towns of states such as Mississippi to get away from the urban violence of northern cities." Mississippian Medgar Evers despised the state's "injustice, the inequality, and the hatred," and Harden wonders what the civil rights leader, had he not been murdered, would think about this "huge reverse migration." Morris, while analyzing "the long-standing 'collective inferiority complex' of his native ground," says that outsiders continually belittle Mississippi. "'How can you live there?' he was bluntly asked by former Texas Gov. Ann Richards. He shook his head. 'We have been America's Ireland, a violent pessimistic land of wonderful writers and poets; a brooding landscape. It's the way people talk and drink and tell stories—also the sense of defeat.'"

1791 Hood, Orley. "Author Invites Pearl Students to House for Cokes, Moon Pies." *Clarion-Ledger*, 16 April 1998, sec. B, p. 1.

Relates that after two high-school students were shot and killed in a Pearl, Mississippi, high school in October 1997, a ninth-grade English teacher at the school wondered how she could help her nervous students get their minds off the tragedy. As part of a class project, she had them read Morris's *Good Old Boy*, and they took a trip to Yazoo City to see the witch's grave that is featured in the book. The students enjoyed both the book and the trip so much their teacher, Sandy Davis, wrote the author and asked if he could come to the school to meet with the students. Morris telephoned her: "'Why don't y'all come over to my house? We'll have Coca-Colas and Moon Pies and talk about books.' So they did.... Morris told stories, asked questions and answered questions." The class project "has thrilled Davis, a teacher for 24 years, the last four in Pearl. She thinks it has helped close some of the wounds from last fall." See photo page 60.

1792 Hood, Orley. "Skip's Story Figures to Make a Doggone Fine Feature Film." *Clarion-Ledger*, 3 May 1998, sec. F, p. 1.

Discloses that four Jack Russell terriers will portray Morris's dog Skip in the upcoming motion picture, including the one who plays Eddie in the television comedy *Frasier*. "Ward Emling, director of the state film office, harbors high expectations for the movie version of *My Dog Skip*. 'This script is great,' he says. 'This writer, Gail Gilchri[e]st, did such a great job of creating a linear script and a really compelling story. It's going to make everyone love Willie as much as we do.'"

1793 "Morris to Sign Books at Festival." *Yazoo Herald*, 6 May 1998, sec. A, p. 1.

Morris is scheduled to sign copies of *The Ghosts of Medgar Evers* and *My Dog Skip* at Yazoo City's Discover Yazoo festival on May 23. "The signing coincides with filming of a motion picture based on 'My Dog Skip.' Filming begins this month, primarily in Canton [Mississippi], though some scenes will be shot in Yazoo City." See also item 1796.

1794 Grayson, Christy. "On Location: Canton Does Its Best Yazoo City Imitation for Filming of 'My Dog Skip,' the Movie." *Yazoo Herald*, 23 May 1998, pp. 1, 14.

Because Morris's hometown of Yazoo City has changed so much over the years, much of the screen version of the author's *My Dog Skip* is being filmed in less developed and more historic Canton, Mississippi. Canton, however, cannot offer everything the production company needs, and film crews have shot footage of Yazoo City cotton fields and the legendary witch's grave in Glenwood Cemetery. According to screenwriter Gail Gilchri[e]st, "Willie kind of made Yazoo City a romantic, misty place in his book. We wanted the town to be a subtle, invisible thing. Hopefully, you'll be able to feel the presence of the town in the movie."

1795 "'My Dog Skip' Cast Features Familiar Faces." *Yazoo Herald*, 23 May 1998, p. 14.

The movie adaptation of *My Dog Skip* features film veterans Kevin Bacon and Diane Lane, who portray "the parents of Willie Morris, on whose Yazoo City childhood the story is based." Among the several Jack Russell terriers who play Skip is Enzo, otherwise known as Eddie on the NBC situation comedy *Frasier*. "Less familiar is the name of up-and-coming 12-year-old Frankie Muniz of New York, who is portraying young Willie.... The real Willie Morris and his wife, JoAnne, showed the cast and crew what a true Mississippi welcome party is all about last weekend with a gala backyard party...." See also item 1798.

1796 Sikes, Vernon. [Photograph]. *Yazoo Herald*, 27 May 1998, p. 1.

A photograph of Morris signing a copy of *My Dog Skip* during the Discover Yazoo festival, held in Yazoo City on May 23. Morris's book signing was "one of the highlights" of the day's activities. See also item 1793.

1797 Long, Robert Lee. "Hollywood Gives Canton a 1940s Makeover." *Madison County (Miss.) Journal*, 28 May 1998, p. 16.

A behind-the-scenes look at the movie set of *My Dog Skip*. "To a novice, the filming of a feature film is certainly an eye-opener. The days are long and sometimes frustrating, often punctuated by hours of boredom and moments of chaotic frenzy.... Skip's antics on the ball field delighted the children the most as did the gracious and polite Frankie Muniz, who portrays 'Little Willie' in the movie. He patiently signed autographs in between takes and was quiet and unassuming, just like 'Big Willie.'" The striking photographs that accompany this lively, descriptive article illustrate how Hollywood transformed Canton, Mississippi, into "the sleepy little town of Yazoo City in the 1940s, a half-century, [i]f not a world away."

1798 "'My Dog Skip' Party." *Yazoo Herald*, 3 June 1998, p. 14.

Photographs of cast and crew members of the movie *My Dog Skip* taken during a party at Morris's home in Jackson. See also item 1795.

1799 Fraiser, Jim. "Movie Directors Work Their Magic in State." *Yazoo Herald*, 10 June 1998, p. 4.

A veteran actor of motion pictures filmed in Mississippi believes that "one of the most interesting aspects of Hollywood-come-to-town is observing the immensely talented feature film directors." While playing the veterinarian in *My Dog Skip*, the movie based on Morris's "fine" book, "I was amazed at how well [director] Jay Russell handled hundreds of crew members, extras and actors during a 20-hour work day in 95-plus-degree heat."

1800 Cleveland, Rick. "Yazoo Sports Legend Casts Long Shadow in 'My Dog Skip.'" *Clarion-Ledger*, 14 June 1998, sec. D, p. 1.

Morris reminisces about Kinsy Moore, a star athlete in several sports who played for "Yazoo No. 2" (Yazoo City's black high school) during Morris's childhood. "Kinsy Moore was Willie Morris's first hero. 'He walked by my house every morning on the way to Yazoo No. 2,' Morris says. 'Some mornings, I'd walk with him and we'd talk about the games.' They must have seemed an anomaly back in Yazoo City, Mississippi, back in the '40s, the 9-year-old white boy and his black teenaged hero." The casting director for the motion picture *My Dog Skip*, the screen version of Morris's book, auditioned numerous young athletes before he found the right one to play Moore in a baseball scene in the movie.

1801 Minor, Bill. "Doggone Ol' Skip Likes the Picture Show." *Clarion-Ledger*, 28 June 1998, sec. H, p. 3.

"In his book *My Dog Skip*, Willie Morris nostalgically recalls his happy times going to the kiddie matinee at the old Dixie Theater in his hometown of Yazoo City during the World War II years." Filmmakers producing a motion picture of Morris's book are re-creating those bygone days at the Star Theater in Mendenhall, Mississippi, "a mainstay of local entertainment for four decades after opening in 1936." As he watched some of the filming, "Morris called the experience 'spooky,' in how realistically it brought back the kiddie matinee in Yazoo City's Dixie Theater."

1802 Swartley, Ariel. "Of the South and Its Imprint on Literature." *New York Times*, 2 August 1998, sec. 2, pp. 25–26.

Addresses the influence of southern writers on American literature and acknowledges that "the very notion of a regional literature" raises widely differing viewpoints. "Does the convening of so many disparate voices under a single banner enhance or diminish the individuals involved? Or, more fundamentally, are writers born or made?" The "waves of opinion" concerning these questions are apparent in *Tell About the South*, "a documentary on Southern literature from 1920 to the 1940's that interviews or profiles more than two dozen writers, black and white." PBS will air the first segment of the three-part series on August 6. Morris, one of the writers interviewed, recounts that in 1960 while abroad as a Rhodes scholar at Oxford, he met the poet Robert Frost. When Morris told him he was from Mississippi, Frost replied, "'Hell, that's the worst state in the Union.' Well, it had produced some fine writers, a shaken Mr. Morris allowed. 'But can anyone there read them?' Mr. Frost returned."

1803 Grayson, Christy. "Hardcover Book Recaps Rich History." *Yazoo Herald*, 5 September 1998, pp. 1, 14.

Announces that Jo G. Prichard's *Making Things Grow*, a history of Yazoo City's Mississippi Chemical Corporation, will be published next month in conjunction with the company's fiftieth anniversary celebration. "Morris contributed four essays that help divide the book into four sections. Each essay is a review of the world outside MCC during the time frame that Prichard is writing about, giving current and former employees ... a chronological perspective on their efforts" (items 904 to 907).

1804 Cleveland, Rick. "Thank You, Mac, for a Night We'll Always Remember." *Clarion-Ledger*, 10 September 1998, sec. D, p. 1.

Morris, Cleveland, and "football's legendary Johnny Majors" are among those watching a baseball game on television at Morris's home. After St. Louis Cardinals player Mark McGwire breaks Roger Maris's home run record, they each telephone various family members. The author and his friends later discuss McGwire's achievement. "'I think,' said Morris, 'that this was baseball at its best and at its most traditional. That's why it's all enmeshed in family and community. That's why we wanted to share it with family and friends.'"

1805 Salter, Sid. "Even Billy Graham Couldn't Help Eagles." *Yazoo Herald*, 12 September 1998, sec. A, p. 4.

Looks back on "three really great college football road trips." On two of them, Morris, Salter, and some friends travel to see star athlete Marcus Dupree play. "These adventures were chronicled in Morris' 'The Courting of Marcus Dupree'—perhaps the best book ever written on the curious phenomenon of college football recruiting and set against the intense background of Neshoba County's difficult past."

1806 Myers, Donald P. "His Magic Days." *Newsday*, 24 September 1998, sec. B, p. 6.

Morris and James Jones's family reminisce about the late novelist, who is the subject of *A Solder's Daughter Never Cries*, a newly released motion picture based on a book by Jones's daughter, Kaylie Jones. Another film, *The Thin Red Line*, is modeled on Jones's novel and is due out later this year. "There was laughter and there were tears in the last two years of the life that surrounded James Jones in the Hamptons. 'Those were magic days, and I wish Jim could have lived longer to enjoy them,' said author Willie Morris, a former Sagaponack neighbor and the man Jones considered his best friend.... Morris, who now lives in Jackson, Miss., calls 'The Thin Red Line' the greatest combat novel ever written. He predicts that the two Jones movies this year will spur a resurgence of interest in his old friend's life and work."

1807 "Author Speaks at MWC." *(Fredericksburg, Va.) Free Lance-Star*, "Weekender" section, 5 November 1998, p. 4.

Morris is scheduled to speak at Mary Washington College in Fredericksburg, Virginia, on November 11. "Best known for his insightful comparisons of life in the deep South with the rest of America, Morris has had a long and distinguished career as a novelist and journalist." A large photograph of Morris at the monument by the "Witch's Grave" in Yazoo City's Glenwood Cemetery accompanies the article.

1808 Thornton, Carolyn. "Killing Time in Canton." *(New Orleans) Times-Picayune*, 22 November 1998, sec. D, p. 1.

Following the shooting of the motion pictures *A Time to Kill* and *My Dog Skip* in Canton, Mississippi, Wayni Terrill and other local residents have begun leading tours of film sets and displaying movie memorabilia. The "heart of Canton" is the antebellum Greek Revival courthouse on the town square. "Turn-of-the-century buildings with 1950s style angled parking flank all four sides of the courthouse square. It was against this backdrop that Wayni and the tourism staff watched a stuffed dog stand-in for Skip drive past the courthouse on several dry runs for the Willie Morris movie." As Thornton and a friend strolled around Canton, they "walked past a baseball dugout and a tomb from the witch's grave used in 'My Dog Skip.'"

1809 Hood, Orley. "State's History Comes to Life at Indianola School." *Clarion-Ledger*, 27 March 1999, sec. B, pp. 1, 5.

Brett Clanton, an English teacher at an Indianola, Mississippi, high school, arranges for Morris, Charles Evers (the civil rights activist whose brother Medgar was shot and killed by Byron De La Beckwith), and Bobby DeLaughter (the attorney who successfully prosecuted Beckwith) to speak to the school's students about the civil rights struggles of the 1960s. "Willie Morris, the writer, had the idea, says Clanton.... Do something on civil rights, on Medgar Evers. Kids need to know this stuff. They need to know about the blood that was spilled on their behalf. They need to hear the stories of the heroes."

1810 Mantell, Suzanne. "Writing Hollywood." *Los Angeles Times Book Review*, 28 March 1999, p. 4.

Jay Russell, director of the movie *My Dog Skip*, explains that he saw an early draft of Morris's book when he interviewed the author for the PBS documentary *Highway 61: Memphis to New Orleans*. A friend, John Lee Hancock, who wrote the screenplay of *Midnight in the Garden of Good and Evil*, "discovered the Morris book independently and suggested to Russell that they option it. 'It was a friendly option, not for a lot of money,' says Russell.... 'What we loved was the poetry of the writing, the reflection on childhood simplified to Willie's relationship to his dog. We all did it for the love of the project.'" See also: Wolfe, Ron, "A Man and His Dog: Arkansan Makes a Movie About a Boy's Best Friend." *(Little Rock) Arkansas Democrat-Gazette*, 5 March 2000, sec. E, pp. 1–2.

1811 Watkins, Billy. "Morris' Tribute to Welty in 'Vanity Fair.'" *Clarion-Ledger*, 13 April 1999, sec. E, p. 1.

Eudora Welty "turns 90 years old today," and to help celebrate the occasion, Morris has written an essay about her for the May issue of *Vanity Fair* magazine, now available on newsstands (item 803). "Morris calls it his 'toast to Eudora.'" Furthermore, "'I call her Eudora because she's been my friend since I was a little boy,' Morris says. 'I very strongly support the idea that she is the greatest living American writer. She's full of wackiness and humor and loyalty to her friends. She's just so generous. Always has been.'"

1812 Watkins, Billy. "Mississippi's Favorite Writers." *Clarion-Ledger*, 14 June 1999, sec. D, pp. 1–2.

In a poll sponsored by the *Clarion-Ledger*, readers have selected Morris as Mississippi's favorite nonfiction author of the millennium. Morris received sixty-two votes, followed by Shelby Foote with fifty-six. William Faulkner earned top honors as the favorite fiction author (eighty-one votes), with Eudora Welty and John Grisham tied for second place (forty-three). "Concerning his first-place finish in nonfiction, Morris said: 'I'm very gratified, considering that there are so many fine writers from Mississippi, where I believe the literary tradition is the strongest of any state. It's wonderful to be appreciated on your home ground where people know you best.'" Instructions for participating in this "Mississippi Poll of the Century" appeared in: Pettus, Gary. "Mississippi's Best & Worst." *Clarion-Ledger*, 12 April 1999, sec. D, p. 1.

1813 Hood, Orley. "JFK Jr.: Such Promise Lost, Says Willie Morris." *Clarion-Ledger*, 21 July 1999, sec. E, p. 1.

Morris, who is "on the road" with his wife, JoAnne Prichard, laments the tragic death of John F. Kennedy Jr. "'I thought the world of him,' Willie said Tuesday from Holly Springs. 'He had such tremendous promise.... I've been so saddened by this.'" Morris became acquainted with Kennedy when the magazine publisher telephoned to ask him if he would write an article on Senator Jesse Helms for *George* magazine. Morris was then a consultant on the movie set of *Ghosts of Mississippi* and could not undertake the project, but as the two talked about Medgar Evers and the film, "Willie told Jr. that JFK had given his most important civil rights speech on the night Medgar was assassinated by Byron De La Beckwith." Kennedy suggested that he write a piece on Evers and the motion picture, which he did (item 801).

1814 Travis, Neal. "'Dog' Has Its Day." *New York Post*, 27 July 1999, p. 9.

A New York gossip columnist avers that "everyone misses writer Willie Morris from the town's literary haunts since he went back to the Deep South...." Some of his friends, however, will be able to see an advance showing of *My Dog Skip*, the screen adaptation of his memoir. The motion picture is not due to be released until October, but the producers "want to get a buzz going. 'It's really strange to see our lives up there on the screen,' Morris tells me from his Mississippi home. 'My long-departed parents, the dog ... I got all teared up.'"

1815 Weaver, Teresa K. "Recommended Reading." *Atlanta Constitution*, 4 August 1999, sec. D, p. 1.

An annotated bibliography of recommended Morris books, published as a sidebar to Michael Skube's tribute (item 2023). The list includes *North Toward Home, The Courting of Marcus Dupree, Good Old Boy: A Delta Boyhood, The Ghosts of Medgar Evers, My Dog Skip*, and *My Cat Spit McGee.*

1816 Lampton, Lucius. "Writer Morris Had Deep Ties to Pike County." *Magnolia (Miss.) Gazette*, 5 August 1999, sec. A, pp. 1, 4.

An account of Morris's friendship with Dr. Verner Holmes, to whom the author dedicated his book *Homecomings*. A mutual friend introduced Holmes to Morris while the author was teaching at the University of Mississippi. Several years later, Morris mentioned to Holmes that he intended to take a leave of absence from Ole Miss to work on a novel. "The doctor invited him to come down to live and write at his three-decade-old pecky cypress house on the Bogue Chitto River, located on Highway 44 at Quin's Bridge, near Friendship Church.... Willie came down, got to work, and stayed a full two and a half years on the banks of the river in the 1980s." Morris primarily pored over his novel *Taps* during this period, but he also wrote *Good Old Boy and the*

Witch of Yazoo and began planning *My Dog Skip*. See also: Lampton, Lucius. "Verner S. Holmes Remembered for His Many Contributions to Mississippi." *Magnolia (Miss.) Gazette*, 25 May 2000, sec. A, pp. 1, 5, 10; Lampton, Lucius M. "Mississippi's Bridge Builder: Dr. Verner S. Holmes (1909–2000) Remembered." *Journal of the Mississippi State Medical Association* 41 (July 2000), pp. 671–77. See also items 1698 and 2078.

1817 Weatherly, Jack. "Autobiography of Morris Sheds Light on Our Past, Future." *Clarion-Ledger*, 8 August 1999, sec. C, p. 1.

The newspaper's business editor views *North Toward Home* as an "economic weathervane for Mississippi." Although Morris left his native state after graduating from high school, he eventually "started a slow turnaround and headed south toward home." Weatherly wonders if "our best and brightest" young people will stay in Mississippi or live elsewhere. "Experts, our prophets in the late 20th century,... tell us to strike now, take advantage of this economic opportunity by laying the groundwork of mutually beneficial cooperation."

1818 Soriano, Cesar G. "Gift of Sight Adds to Author's Legacy." *USA Today*, 18 August 1999, sec. D, p. 2.

Following Morris's death on August 2, his widow, JoAnne Prichard, and son, David Rae Morris, donated his corneas, which have now restored the sight of two Mississippians. The Morris family "originally donated the corneas anonymously. 'We decided to release the information in hopes that more people would donate their eyes,' Prichard said in a statement." Surgeon Connie S. McCaa, who performed both eye transplants, observed: "Willie loved Mississippi and the people of Mississippi. He's continued helping all of us." The Associated Press issued a news release on the donated corneas that appeared in a number of publications, including the *(Baton Rouge) Advocate* and *(Memphis) Commercial Appeal* of 17 August 1999 and the *Yazoo Herald* of 21 August 1999. See also: Baldwin, Gloria. "Author Lives on in Gift of Sight." *Clarion-Ledger*, 17 August 1999, sec. B, p. 1. See also items 1444 and 1832.

1819 Murray, Joe. "Searching for Willie Morris." *Tulsa World*, 4 November 1999, p. 15.

A senior writer for Cox Newspapers travels to Mississippi "to discover what memorials Yazoo City has bestowed on its recently departed, most famous man of letters." A "nice Southern lady" at the town Chamber of Commerce tells him that local "My Dog Skip" tours stop at various locations featured in Morris's books. "His cemetery plot is an attraction itself, buried as he is just 13 steps from the Witch's Grave, the occupant of which, local legend says, used her black magic to burn down the town."

1820 O'Briant, Don. "Out-of-Print Morris Memoir to Be Brought Back." *Atlanta Constitution*, 11 November 1999, sec. D, p. 2.

Most critics believe that Morris's best book is his memoir *North Toward Home*. "The University Press of Mississippi is issuing a hardcover edition on Nov. 29, which would have been Morris' 65th birthday." A brief notice. See also: "University Press to Honor Morris." *Yazoo Herald*, 24 November 1999, sec. A, p. 2. See also item 1446.

1821 Watkins, Billy. "Morris Lives on in Film, Books." *Clarion-Ledger*, 13 November 1999, sec. B, p. 1.

Several months after Morris's death, his new book, *My Cat Spit McGee*, is selling well, and the motion picture based on his book *My Dog Skip* is "scheduled for a series of nationwide press screenings.... 'All this is, of course, exhilarating,' says Morris' widow, JoAnne Prichard. 'But it also makes me sad that Willie isn't here to experience it. It's very bittersweet.'" A shorter version of this article appeared as: "Author's Widow Finds Book Sales 'Bittersweet.'" *(Baton Rouge) Sunday Advocate*, 14 November 1999, sec. B, p. 8.

1822 Hood, Orley. "Willie's 'Skip' Is a Study of the Secret Life of Boys, Dogs." *Clarion-Ledger*, 17 November 1999, sec. E, p. 1.

After viewing a special screening of *My Dog Skip*, Hood muses that growing up in Yazoo City in 1942 is not all that different from growing up in 1999. "All the important things are the same: family, friends, dogs, truth, standing up for what you believe." Kids back then had to cope with both puppy love and bullies just as they have to now. Morris, fortunately, had Skip to help him deal with the pressures of growing up, difficulties that transcend both time and place. "It's not a boy and dog from 1942, it's you and I wherever and whenever we grew up, with what was important to us, with whatever it was that we leaned on for comfort when the changes were coming too fast.... So when you read Willie's book, remember that's all of us, black and white, rich and poor, fighting the battle to grow up, to become who we became."

1823 Lucas, Sherry. "Mississippians Give 'My Dog Skip' Thumbs Up." *Clarion-Ledger*, 17 November 1999, sec. B, p. 1.

An "essentially hometown" group of movie viewers praise *My Dog Skip*, "the fictionalized account of Willie Morris' childhood memoir." At the Ridgeland, Mississippi, theater, "where many in the audience knew the acclaimed Mississippi writer and mourned his Aug. 2 death in Jackson, the movie brought back memories. 'It was extremely touching, of course, for anyone who was a friend of Willie's,' said Sam Olden of Yazoo City. 'It made it all too real. It made you think so much of him and home.'" The motion picture opens January 12 in Los Angeles and New York.

1824 Norquist, Jane. "'My Dog Skip' Earns Kudos at Screening." *Yazoo Herald*, 20 November 1999, pp. 1, 14.

My Dog Skip, the screen version of Morris's memoir, has been shown in Jackson, Mississippi, for the press and special friends of the author. "The verdict was unanimous: Fantastic!" JoAnne Prichard, Morris's widow, first saw the film with her husband in New York a few days before he died. She said that after it was over, "Willie was so very excited that he couldn't contain his exuberance. We returned to the hotel room and Willie called everyone he knew to tell them about the movie." Prichard added that she was pleased with Hollywood's adaptation of the book. Morris's son, David Rae, saw the motion picture in New Orleans. "'I had heard stories of my father's childhood and the role Skip played in his life so many times, but this film brought it all back to me on a highly emotional level,' he said."

1825 Sikes, Vernon. "Year in Review: Morris' Death Is Year's Top Story." *Yazoo Herald*, 1 January 2000, pp. 1–2.

"Hands down, the Aug. 2 death of native son Willie Morris attracted more attention — both national and international — than any other news event centering around Yazoo County in 1999. Hundreds of mourners filed into Yazoo City's First United Methodist Church and later to Glenwood Cemetery to say good-bye to one who had endeared the county to his many readers."

1826 Wagster, Emily. "Gubernatorial Inauguration: Musgrove Sets Goals High." *Clarion-Ledger*, 12 January 2000, sec. A, p. 1.

Reports on the inauguration of Ronnie Musgrove as Mississippi's sixty-second governor. During the ceremony, "Jack H. White, director of the Mississippi State University Honors Program, read selections from Mississippi authors Willie Morris and Eudora Welty."

1827 Lyman, Rick. "At the Movies: Tale of a Dog." *New York Times*, 21 January 2000, sec. E, p. 22.

A profile of Jay Russell, who directed the motion picture *My Dog Skip*. His first film led to some "Hollywood development deals," but when the projects fell through, he turned to documentaries, one of which was the five-part PBS miniseries *Great Drives*. He met Morris in 1996 while talking with people about Highway 61, the famous thoroughfare that runs through the Mississippi Delta. "'We went over to his house and interviewed him there, and he was one of these larger-than-life characters,' said Mr. Russell.... 'I immediately just fell for him.'"

1828 Watkins, Billy. "Coming Soon: My Dog Skip." *Clarion-Ledger*, 27 January 2000, sec. E, p. 1.

After the film *My Dog Skip* "produced solid box office numbers" in several test cities the last two weekends, "Warner Bros. has decided to open the film soon — probably sometime mid– to late February — in 1,800 theaters nationwide. Although an exact date hasn't been decided, film director and executive producer Jay Russell says it's 'just a matter of time now' before folks from Jackson to Seattle get a chance to see the film, based on the book by the late Mississippi author Willie Morris."

1829 Watkins, Billy. "'Malcolm in the Middle' Star Plays Willie Morris." *Clarion-Ledger*, 27 January 2000, sec. E, p. 1.

Narrates how fourteen-year-old Frankie Muniz, star of the new situation comedy *Malcolm in the Middle*, landed the part of young Willie Morris in the forthcoming motion picture *My Dog Skip*. Also reports that during the months of filmmaking, Morris and Muniz became good friends. "JoAnne Prichard, Morris' widow, recalls: 'When Frankie first got into town, Willie had him over to the house. Frankie got here before the rest of the cast so he could bond with the dog. Frankie and Willie sat out in the backyard and talked for a long time. He had him over several times after that. Willie thought he was great.'"

1830 Lucas, Sherry. "Century of Literature." *Clarion-Ledger*, 30 January 2000, sec. G, pp. 10–11.

To mark the new century and millennium, the Eudora Welty Library in Jackson has compiled its "Books of the Century" collection of 424 titles. "Questionnaires went out to more than 100 Mississippians prominent in the arts and humanities, asking which 20th century books meant the most to them, and which books had the greatest impact on the century and why." Forty-three people responded, including Jimmy Barksdale, Mary Ann Mobley, Morris, Eudora Welty, and Oprah Winfrey, and their selections form the nucleus of the collection. Morris's *North Toward Home* was among the titles frequently noted.

1831 "'My Dog Skip' Excitement Intensifies." *Yazoo Herald*, 12 February 2000, p. 1.

"With the soon-to-be-released film about the companion to one of Yazoo City's most acclaimed residents, the festivities surrounding the late Willie Morris' 'My Dog Skip' are beginning to intensify. The Yazoo Historical Society is contributing to the anticipation by loaning two Willie Morris artifacts to a Canton museum that will house memorabilia from the film...." These two objects are Morris's boyhood school desk and the white granite tombstone he made to mark Skip's grave in the back yard of the Morris family's Yazoo City house.

1832 Mitchell, Jerry. "'My Dog Skip' Keeps Memory of Morris Alive." *Clarion-Ledger*, 13 February 2000, sec. A, p. 1.

Reports that at a special showing of the motion picture *My Dog Skip* in Ridgeland, Mississippi, director Jay Russell said, "He [Morris] loved this movie, and he couldn't wait to show it to his fellow Mississippians." Morris died on August 2, and "at his last birthday party, the family joked that the author was 64 going on 9. 'Indeed, the 9-year-old is with us today,' said [his son] David Rae Morris...." Among those who watched the movie were the two men "who each received cornea transplants thanks to Willie Morris' posthumous donation." See also items 1444 and 1818.

1833 Morris, Anne. "Forget 'Skip' and Head to 'Celia's Place.'" *Austin American-Statesman*, 27 February 2000, sec. K, p. 6.

Celia Morris, Morris's "college sweetheart" from the University of Texas and first wife, recently "passed through" Austin while traveling from her home in Washington, D.C. "She's not seen 'My Dog Skip' ('I got sick of that dog 30 years ago') and says she feels some sadness Willie 'ended up writing about cats and dogs' instead of the subjects that engaged him in his early memoir, 'North Towards [sic] Home.'" Her own memoir, *Finding Celia's Place*, will be published later this year (item 1972).

1834 Grisham, John. "Love Off the Leash Leaves a Treasure: Skip Was No Ordinary Dog, Owned by No Ordinary Writer." *USA Today*, 2 March 2000, sec. D, p. 4.

Remembrances by the best-selling novelist, who first met Morris while a law student at the University of Mississippi. Morris read Grisham's first novel, wrote a blurb for it, and helped him get it published. "The friendship was born. He was genuinely thrilled when my books started selling. When I finished one, I would always send him a copy. And when he published a book, he'd make sure I received an early edition." Grisham had heard Morris mention his dog Skip in "several of his rambling, late-night stories," and after his friend sent him a copy of *My Dog Skip*, Grisham "read the book in two hours. The last chapter brought tears to my eyes, as it has many times since." Grisham also cried while viewing *My Dog Skip*, a film that "captures the spirit of Willie and Skip."

1835 Hood, Orley. "Museum Preserves Morris Memories from Life and Film." *Clarion-Ledger*, 3 March 2000, sec. B, p. 1.

Describes the Willie Morris / My Dog Skip museum in Canton, Mississippi, where much of the movie *My Dog Skip* was filmed. "There's the hat Little Willie's movie mom, Diane Lane, wore in the film.... In an alcove on the east side of the museum stands a desk displaying copies of notecards Morris used in the writing of *My Dog Skip*." Morris's widow, JoAnne Prichard, is touched by the tribute to her late husband. "'I just couldn't believe how wonderful the museum is,' Prichard says.... 'Willie would just be thrilled. He loved the people in Canton. By the time they finished making the movie there, Willie had just about decided he grew up there.'" See also: Sylvain, Metz. "Morris Exhibit Going in Museum." *Clarion-Ledger*, 29 January 2000, sec. B, p. 2.

1836 Bertram, Jack. "Morris Film Evokes Emotional Reaction." *Clarion-Ledger*, 4 March 2000, sec. B, p. 1.

Reaction to a showing of *My Dog Skip* yesterday "was all thumbs up.... Not surprisingly, many of the viewers had a personal connection to Willie Morris, the late Mississippi author upon whose book the movie is based. An obviously distraught Judi Hammons, of the Ross Barnett Reservoir area, said, 'I think it would call back anyone's childhood.'" Hammons grew up near the Morris family home in Yazoo City. "She said the movie 'demonstrates (Morris') ability to build love.'"

1837 Sikes, Vernon. "Skip Wows Movie-Goers." *Yazoo Herald*, 8 March 2000, p. 1.

After *My Dog Skip* was released nationwide on March 3, the film version of Morris's memoir ranks number three among the country's top-grossing motion pictures. "'They take a good many liberties with the book,' Morris' widow, JoAnne Prichard Morris, said.... 'They created a plot because "My Dog Skip" doesn't have [a] really drawn-out plot. They have created some things but I think they were all in the spirit of Willie.'" Despite the "liberties the movie studio took, she said Morris was satisfied because 'he understood the difference between a book, a memoir and a movie.'" See also: "Top 10 Movies." *San Francisco Chronicle*, 7 March 2000, sec. B, p. 5.

1838 Eller, Claudia, and James Bates. "FedEx Chief Banks on Film-Making Package." *Los Angeles Times*, 14 March 2000, sec. C, pp. 1, 20.

Discloses that billionaire Fred Smith, the founder of Federal Express, is the principal investor of Alcon Entertainment, the "little-known film company" that produced *My Dog Skip*. Last week, Alcon Entertainment "signed a five-year, 10-picture distribution deal with Warner Bros. on the heels of the surprisingly strong results from Alcon's family film 'My Dog Skip,' directed by Jay Russell. Through the weekend, the film, based on the late author Willie Morris' memoir,... grossed $14.1 million at the box office. While most movies lose business each week, 'Skip' was actually up 3% over last weekend." The motion picture cost seven million dollars. See also: Soriano, Cesar. "'Mars' an Astronomical Success," *USA Today*, 14 March 2000, sec. D, p. 1.

1839 Powell, Gene Harlan. "Remembering Willie from the My Dog Skip-Era." *Yazoo Herald*, 15 March 2000, p. 4.

A boyhood acquaintance of Morris's reflects on their years growing up together in Yazoo City. "When Yazoo got its first radio station (WAZF) in the late 40's, Willie got a job there as announcer. He sat in regularly to conduct Darkness On The Delta, spinning records of the big bands and a lot of Al Jolson.... He started writing for the Flashlight, Yazoo High's school paper, and the Yazoo Herald at about the same time. He was a sports reporter for the Herald."

1840 Bales, Jack. "My Friend Willie." *(Fredericksburg, Va.) Free Lance-Star*, "Town & County" section, 18 March 2000, pp. 3–4.

A Morris friend and admirer reminisces about the author after viewing *My Dog Skip*. "Throughout our visits, letters, and phone conversations, I discovered (as have countless others) that Willie had an unlimited capacity for kindness and generosity—his 'great sweetness' was how intimate friends privately described it." See also: Zitz, Michael. "Friends Remember Writer Willie Morris." *(Fredericksburg, Va.) Free Lance-Star*, 6 August 1999, sec. D, pp. 1, 3.

1841 Watkins, Billy. "Focus on Literature." *Clarion-Ledger*, 2 April 2000, sec. G, p. 15.

Announces that the seventh Oxford Conference for the Book will be held at the University of Mississippi from April 7 through 9. "The three-day conference will also include readings, panel discussions and a tribute Friday afternoon to the late Willie Morris, the author from Yazoo City. Morris' wife, JoAnne Prichard, is scheduled to speak." According to Ole Miss spokesman Michael Harrelson, she will "talk about his writing habits, how conscientious he was as a writer."

1842 Lohmann, Bill. "His Friend Willie." *Richmond (Va.) Times-Dispatch*, 23 April 2000, sec. G, pp. 1, 8.

Relates how a "special bond grew" between Morris and Jack Bales, editor of *Conversations with Willie Morris* (item 1945). After Bales read *My Dog Skip* in 1995, he wrote Morris a letter, asking questions about his books and literary career. Morris replied a few days later, and before his death in August 1999, the two men had exchanged hundreds of letters, numerous phone calls, and several visits. In their letters "they asked and answered each other's questions. The topics were wide-ranging: their respective work, their personal lives, current events, advice and encouragement." Lohmann's lengthy article includes remarks from Morris's widow, JoAnne Prichard, and his long-time friend and colleague Larry L. King. See also: Mitchell, H. Gregory. "Luckily, His Writing Is Left Behind." *(Fredericksburg Va.) Free Lance-Star*, 13 August 2000, sec. E, p. 4.

1843 Associated Press. "'New' Novel Will Tell Tales of Late Author's Teenage Years." *(Memphis) Commercial Appeal*, 10 June 2000, "DeSoto Appeal" section, p. 5.

Announces that Morris's novel *Taps* will be published next spring by Houghton Mifflin, the company that in 1967 brought out *North Toward Home*, which "propelled him into the national literary world." JoAnne Prichard Morris, the author's widow, "said the basic manuscript was completed in the late 1980s. She said Morris had 'revised it a couple of times, but he was never pleased with it.... People will recognize some familiar things; it's fiction and nonfiction,' she said.

'It's set during the Korean War when he was in Yazoo City.'" With the article is "'Taps,'" a few "selected passages" from the book. See also: "New Morris Novel Soon." *Houston Chronicle*, 11 June 2000, sec. A, p. 2.

1844 Moore, Matt. "Picnic Celebrates Morris's Special Ties to Miss. and N.Y." *(Memphis) Commercial Appeal*, 10 June 2000, "DeSoto Appeal" section, p. 5.

An Associated Press reporter writes that Mississippi's annual picnic in New York's Central Park has "taken on special meaning as the late Willie Morris is honored by his native state and the city he grew to love." Rachel McPherson, an organizer of the twenty-first "edition of the picnic," said that paying tribute to Morris "is the right thing to do" considering his ties to New York City. "'Willie, of all the writers from Mississippi, had a real understanding of New York and Mississippi,' McPherson said. 'He has something kindred to our souls.'"

1845 Sikes, Vernon. "Bales Signs His Tribute to Morris." *Yazoo Herald*, 10 June 2000, pp. 1–2.

In Yazoo City Jack Bales signs copies of his *Conversations with Willie Morris* (item 1945), a collection of Morris interviews and profiles that span some thirty years. During a summer 1997 research trip for his book, Bales interviewed the author and pored over most of the seventeen thousand items in the Morris collection at the University of Mississippi. "Commenting on one facet of Mr. Morris' appeal, Bales said, 'Whenever you were with Willie, he made you feel you were the most important person in his life at that time.'" See also: Baswell, Allen. "Virginia Writer Examines Morris." *Yazoo Herald*, 5 July 1997, p. 2.

1846 Kelley, Tina. "In Central Park, Another Sleepy Delta Day in June." *New York Times*, 11 June 2000, sec. 1, p. 45.

Reports that Mississippi Governor Ronnie Musgrove was among the four hundred people, "mostly Ole Miss graduates ... and others missing Mississippi," who attended the twenty-first annual Way Up North in Mississippi picnic in New York's Central Park yesterday. On a path, thirty watermelons, "offering up the promise of their wetness in the 92-degree heat, were arranged as if the honoree of the day, Willie Morris, the late magazine editor and author of 'My Dog Skip' and member of the Mississippi pantheon, right up with Faulkner and Welty, were there to describe them." See also: Blakney, Sonnie. "Mississippians 'Swap Tales' in Central Park," *Clarion-Ledger*, 11 June 2000, sec B, p. 1; "Big Apple Picnic Honors Willie Morris: Park Was Place to Meet, Greet." *(Memphis) Commercial Appeal*, 12 June 2000, "DeSoto Appeal" section, p. 6.

1847 Jennings, Doug. "Coffee Shop Perking As Movie Museum." *Clarion-Ledger*, 17 June 2000, sec. B, p. 2.

A building in Canton, Mississippi, that producers of the motion picture *A Time to Kill* used for a coffee shop and law office is now a movie museum. In the building "you can find props from *My Dog Skip*, an adaptation of the Willie Morris novel of the same name. Sharing the same room you can find the newest addition to the museum, also dedicated to Morris—and his memory. It contains a re-creation of his desk, complete with notes transcribed word-for-word from his own and a replica of Morris' favorite chair and table." Six movies have been filmed in Canton: *A Time to Kill, The Rising Place, My Dog Skip, A Worn Path, The Ponder Heart*, and *O Brother, Where Art Thou?*

1848 Bertram, Jack. "Books Pay Tribute to Morris." *Clarion-Ledger*, 2 July 2000, sec. G, p. 11.

The University Press of Mississippi has published two books about Morris. *Remembering Willie*, a compilation of twenty-seven tributes and eulogies, includes "memorials" by Rick Bragg, Bill Clinton, Winston Groom, David Halberstam, and William Styron (item 2081). *Conversations with Willie Morris*, edited by Jack Bales, "is a collection of 25 interviews and profiles that span more than 30 years and add up to a tribute in (mostly) Morris-the-writer's own eloquently-down-to-earth words" (item 1945).

1849 Lucas, Sherry. "Building a Winner." *Clarion-Ledger*, 2 July 2000, sec. F, p. 1.

The architect who designed the addition to the Jackson residence of JoAnne Prichard Morris and her late husband has won an honor citation at the annual convention of the American Institute of Architects' Mississippi chapter. A three-person jury, headed by *Architectural Record* editor Robert Ivy, selected four statewide winners of the prestigious awards, which "encourage excellence in design." The panel singled out architect Stan Wagnon's work on the Morris home "as a carefully crafted addition with a clear distinction between old and new.... 'Oh, it is all I imagined and more,' homeowner JoAnne Prichard Morris said, relishing particularly its modern feel, the intimate courtyard and the way various windows catch light at different times of the day."

1850 Wood, R[ichard] C. "The Writer Willie Morris: A Tribute." *Magnolia (Miss.) Gazette*, 6 July 2000, sec. B, p. 1.

An extensive evaluation of Morris's literary career, focusing on *North Toward Home*, *New York Days*, *The Last of the Southern Girls*, *The Courting of Marcus Dupree*, *Good Old Boy*, *Good Old Boy and the Witch of Yazoo*, and *My Dog Skip*. "Of course Willie Morris sentimentalizes his places and peoples, his dogs, his cat; he sings his successes and moans his failures. He hasn't the detachment that marks the fictions of Faulkner and Welty. He was too much the hot reporter on the one hand and the self-conscious memoirist on the other. But his contribution to Southern literature, which, by the way, is American literature in high degree, demands acknowledgment."

1851 Kiger, Christy. "Some Things Just Don't Ever Change As Return Home Reveals." *Yazoo Herald*, 5 August 2000, p. 4.

A Yazoo City native is inspired by Morris as she returns to her hometown and the newspaper on which she once worked. "I've always respected him as a writer but it wasn't until I had the opportunity to interview him about the production of the movie [*My Dog Skip*] that I came to know him personally. Mr. Morris was an inspiration to me as a writer as well as a native Yazooan.... Thanks to him, I may never stop writing."

1852 "Signed Copies of 'My Mississippi' Available." *Yazoo Herald*, 9 December 2000, sec. A, p. 2.

A brief write-up about Morris's *My Mississippi*, noting that although the author "wrote of New York City, Oxford, England, Texas and many other locales, [he] always returned to his favorite subject — his beloved home state, Mississippi."

1853 Cleveland, Rick. "The Rebellious Golden Tiger Dawgs? Willie, As Usual, Has an Idea." *Clarion-Ledger*, 13 January 2001, sec. D, p. 1.

Insists that Morris's *My Mississippi* "is a must for any Mississippians's bookshelf" for these reasons: "Willie Morris, the smartest, most caring, funniest, most eloquent man I have known, knew more about Mississippi than anyone. He loved Mississippi, all its virtues and despite its faults, as much as anyone. Willie saw things, including his beloved home state, clearly and with such depth and perspective."

1854 "Willie Morris Ming Dynasty Certificate." *Magnolia (Miss.) Gazette*, 1 March 2001, sec. B, p. 1.

A reproduction of the "certificate of membership" in the "Ming Dynasty Dining and Discussion Cotillion of Pike County, Mississippi." While Morris was living in McComb, Mississippi, in the 1980s, "he and his friends revelled in going to McComb's China Palace restaurant." They founded an informal social club and designed membership certificates. "Although the words [on the certificate] are brief, Willie's great gift with humor shines through."

1855 O'Briant, Don. "Mississippi Author Plays His 'Taps' from the Grave." *Atlanta Journal-Constitution*, 8 April 2001, sec. C, p. 1.

A formal question-and-answer interview with Morris's widow, JoAnne Prichard Morris, upon the publication of his novel *Taps*. She edited the book after he died in August 1999. When asked about her editorial changes, she replied: "I didn't have to add anything to the manuscript, and he had made notes about the cuts he wanted to make. I didn't write any new material unless it was a transition sentence."

1856 Watkins, Billy. "Finishing Willie's Work." *Clarion-Ledger*, 15 April 2001, sec. F, pp. 1–2.

As a teenager, Morris played "Taps" at the military funerals of local servicemen killed in Korea. JoAnne Prichard Morris, editor of her late husband's novel *Taps*, speculates on how this responsibility affected him. "When he played *Taps* at those funerals, it brought together so many things that mattered to him. It introduced him to so much — the land, the hill people, the Delta people, how geography affected people, how people were different.... I think that was when his eyes were opened to a lot of things such as race relations, cultural differences." Prichard Morris also describes her husband's research and writing routines.

1857 Eldredge, Richard L. "Remembering Willie." *Atlanta Journal-Constitution*, 30 April 2001, sec. D, p. 2.

At the Margaret Mitchell House in Atlanta, JoAnne Prichard Morris reads from *Taps* and answers questions about her late husband and his book. She spent about a year editing the recently published novel. "It ended up being therapeutic. Willie had all the edits he wanted written in the margins.... Once I got down into the manuscript, I discovered the whole experience became a conversation with Willie."

1858 Lucas, Sherry. "Day of Celebration Taps Threads of Friendship, Memory." *Clarion-Ledger*, 6 May 2001, sec. F, p. 1.

Lucas, a former University of Mississippi student, remembers Morris as "a challenging teacher and editor, and an irresistible raconteur. In class and out, he had a way of collecting people into his fold — a sort of centrifugal force that sucked listeners in and held them firm, captivated in the swirl." She adds that in Yazoo City on May 12, Morris's friends "will gather at the Triangle Cultural Center to pay tribute to the man and his words."

1859 Pettus, Gary. "Friends Gather to Remember Willie Morris in Yazoo City This Weekend." *Clarion-Ledger*, 11 May 2001, sec. E, p. 1.

Announces that Morris's "friends and colleagues" will honor the author, his life, and his works on May 12 in Yazoo City. "'Remembering Willie: A Yazoo Celebration,' will draw Pulitzer Prize–winning writers David Halberstam and Rick Bragg, a former governor, Morris' local friends and others to his hometown for discussions on such topics as a sense of place, the value of friendship, complex politics and the rush of social change." See also: Kennedy, Rick. "May 12 Brings Three Worthwhile Events to Yazoo City." *Yazoo Herald*, 2 May 2001, p. 4; Kiger, Christy G. "Remembering Willie: A Yazoo Celebration." *Yazoo Herald*, 9 May 2001, sec. B, p. 3; "Triangle Cultural Center Comes to Life with Authors' Memories of Morris." *Yazoo Herald*, 9 May 2001, sec. B, p. 4; Kiger, Christy G. "Friends of Willie to Celebrate — Yazoo Style." *Yazoo Herald*, 9 May 2001, sec. B, p. 5.

1860 Bertram, Jack. "Friends Celebrate Author's Life, Work." *Clarion-Ledger*, 13 May 2001, sec. A, pp. 1, 4.

Reports that more than three hundred persons recognized Morris and his literary legacy in Yazoo City on Saturday, May 12. "A wrenching, graveside rendition of *Taps* climaxed 'Remembering Willie,' but if there was an evolving theme to the day-long salute, it was a confidence by participants in the enduring quality of the works of an author who was termed by one 'Faulkner you can read.'" See also: Kennedy, Rick. "May 12, 2001 Was a Successful Day for Yazoo City." *Yazoo Herald*, 16 May 2001, p. 4; "Remembering Willie: A Yazoo Celebration." *Yazoo Herald*, 16 May 2001, p. 9.

1861 Yellin, Emily. "The Balm of Reminiscence, Small-Town Southern Style." *New York Times*, 15 May 2001, sec. B, p. 2.

Recounts the various tributes to Morris during the daylong "Remembering Willie" celebration on May 12 in Yazoo City, Mississippi. "Morris's humor and lack of restraint were affectionately lauded in each of the Willie stories the 30 or so friends shared with the audience.... But the talk also turned in earnest to the issues of racial injustice and Mississippi's past, themes that permeated most of Morris's 18 books."

1862 Metz, Sylvain. "Famous Natives Grace Wall." *Clarion-Ledger*, 18 May 2001, sec. B, p. 2.

Relates that eight years ago, Jackson high school art students painted twenty portraits of famous Mississippians that were hung in the school library. On May 17, sixteen additional student-painted portraits were unveiled, including one of Morris.

1863 Ramsey, Marshall. [Cartoon]. *Clarion-Ledger*, 24 July 2001, sec. A, p. 6.

A cartoon on the newspaper's editorial page published upon the death of beloved Mississippi writer Eudora Welty. William Faulkner, Margaret Walker Alexander, Welty, and Morris— all garbed in angel wings and robes— are standing together on clouds in front of an iron gate. As a banner in the background proclaims "Welcome Eudora," Morris tells the august group: "It's not Mississippi, but it's heaven just the same."

1864 Foster, Stephanie. "The Real Dink Jenkins Recalls Early Days and Former Neighbor, Literary Giant Willie Morris." *Yazoo Herald*, 29 August 2001, pp. 1, 8.

An interview with Bob Edwards, who lived next door to Morris in Yazoo City before enlisting in the army during World War II. While he was in France, Edwards sent Morris a German helmet and belt, German money, an iron cross, and postcards. In two of Morris's "endearing tales of life in Yazoo City," *Good Old Boy* and *My Dog Skip*, he "wrote fondly of his neighbor who went to war. In the movie, 'My Dog Skip,' the character Dink Jenkins is roughly based on Edwards."

1865 Sikes, Vernon. "Witch's Grave Is Subject of Documentary." *Yazoo Herald*, 5 September 2001, p. 1.

Representatives from TransAtlantic Films in London have filmed a story on the Witch's Grave in Yazoo City's Glenwood Cemetery "for a documentary that will be televised on the Discovery Channel somewhere around July 2002." The program will be titled "Living Legends" and according to TransAtlantic Films Director Andy Webb, "The theme running through it is famous people, generally speaking, who there is a story attached to them after they died." The grave of the Witch of Yazoo is featured in Morris's *Good Old Boy*.

1866 Pettus, Gary. "Art Contest Draws on State Writers." *Clarion-Ledger*, 9 January 2002, sec. E, p. 1.

Coverage of the Central Mississippi Regional Library System's calendar art contest for high school students. "The theme, 'Mississippi Reads,' embraces Mississippi writers," and three of the fourteen contest winners portrayed Morris and his books in their artwork.

1867 Pettus, Gary. "PBS Profiles 'Invisible Man's' Ellison." *Clarion-Ledger*, 19 February 2002, sec. D, p. 1.

Tonight PBS is airing a ninety-minute documentary on Ralph Ellison, the African-American writer. *Ralph Ellison: An American Journey* marks the fiftieth anniversary of Ellison's "influential novel" *Invisible Man*. In the late 1960s, Morris (then editor of *Harper's Magazine*) and Henry Wingate (now a U.S. district judge in Jackson but then a student at Grinnell College in Iowa) witnessed a "disturbing event" in Ellison's life, one that Morris wrote about in chapter 12 of *New York Days*. In "around 1968," Ellison and Morris spoke at a symposium sponsored by Grinnell. That evening the two men and Wingate, a moderator of the conference, attended an off-campus party. A "young radical" began to argue with Ellison about his book, berating him for the non-confrontational and non-violent ending. Although Ellison attempted to debate the issue, "he finally put his head on Wingate's shoulder and sobbed." Wingate and Morris's son, David Rae, were interviewed about the incident for the PBS program. "'Those of us who were present will always remember that,' Wingate said. 'Whenever I was with Willie (Morris) after that, he always went back to that occasion. He never got over it.'"

1868 Bertram, Jack. "Writing Project for 11th-Graders Honors Memory of Willie Morris." *Clarion-Ledger*, 20 February 2002, sec. E, p. 1.

The organizers of "Remembering Willie: A Yazoo Celebration," the literary festival held annually in Yazoo City in honor of Willie Morris, are sponsoring a writing contest. "The 2002 Willie Morris Prize and Project is open to all 11th graders in the state, who may submit an informal essay on or before April 15." The winner will receive a $2,000 college scholarship. Contest officials have mailed project information to Mississippi schools. See also item 1873.

1869 Maher, Marshall. "In Memory of Willie Morris." *Daily Texan*, 15 April 2002, p. 4.

Maher, the editor of the *Daily Texan* at the University of Texas, recalls the "legacy" Morris left for succeeding newspaper staffers and the "profound effect" the legendary editor had on him. Maher particularly honors "the spirit of Willie Morris" because on April 13 the author's widow, JoAnne Prichard Morris, "was present at the Delta Tau Delta house for the dedication of the Willie Morris room. It was a touching tribute as many of his pledge class members from across the country converged to the Delt house to remember a man who meant so much to them, the University and the *Texan*."

1870 "Second Willie Salute on Tap." *Yazoo Herald*, 18 May 2002, sec. A, p. 4.

Editorial thanking the "Remembering Willie" committee for organizing a popular attraction that has generated state and national publicity. "It would appear to us that the committee has done a good job in providing variety and relevance to each day of the event. In its own way, the Remembering Willie Celebration seems to be evolving and growing into yet another colorful tradition of Yazoo City. We congratulate the local committee for their hard work, and appreciate their dedication towards honoring Willie Morris."

1871 "Willie Celebration Gathering Momentum." *Yazoo Herald*, 18 May 2002, sec. A, pp. 1, 5.

The second "Remembering Willie" festival is scheduled for next weekend in Yazoo City. "'Willie would have loved last year's event — the stories read and told, the laughter and the good times and warm memories enjoyed by all,' said JoAnne Prichard Morris, his widow. 'This event is not to remember him in death but celebrate his life and the zest with which he lived it. And we want to bring together good writing and good writers because Willie truly loved both.'"

1872 Lucas, Sherry. "Festival Brings Writer and His Words Back Home." *Clarion-Ledger*, 21 May 2002, sec. E, p. 1.

"The second Remembering Willie festival, this weekend at the Triangle Cultural Center in Yazoo City, expands to three days this year and focuses on the importance of place." See also: "Remembering Willie Schedule of Events." *Clarion-*

Ledger, 21 May 2002, sec. E, p. 2; Koeppel, Frederic. "Yazoo City to Honor Writer This Weekend." *(Memphis) Commercial Appeal*, 23 May 2002, sec. E, p. 3.

1873 Grayson, Christy. "Manchester Academy Student Wins Willie Essay Contest." *Yazoo Herald*, 29 May 2002, p. 1.

Eleventh grader Nia Manard has won the first annual Willie Morris Writers' Prize, awarded during the "Remembering Willie" celebration in Yazoo City. She received a $2,000 college scholarship from the Friends of Willie Morris for her essay "City" about Philadelphia, Pennsylvania. "Out of 161 entries in the first essay contest bearing his name, Morris would have found it quite profound that Manard, the only African-American student enrolled at a private school in his childhood hometown, had captured the unbiased hearts of her readers with her essay." Photographs of the "Remembering Willie" festival appear on page 5. See also item 1868.

1874 Hood, Orley. "Willie's Still Winning Converts to the South." *Clarion-Ledger*, 20 September 2002, sec. E, p. 1.

Observes that non-southerners who read Morris's books often develop an appreciation for Mississippi and the South. "It happens all the time, Mary Jones says. Somebody from somewhere else will run across one of Willie's books, fall in love with it and with him, then call Yazoo City to find out more." Jones, a Yazoo City native and local historian, says that one elderly Morris fan from Indiana "'cries every time she thinks about Yazoo City and Mississippi.' It's easy to see why. Willie makes his childhood, his era, his South spring to life."

1875 Weeks, Linton. "Gone with the Wind: Has the Once-Towering Genre of Southern Literature Lost Its Compass?" *Washington Post*, 11 November 2002, sec. C, pp. 1–2.

Authors Lee Smith, Louis D. Rubin Jr., Shannon Ravenel, Fred Hobson, and Lucinda MacKethan discuss whether "there even is such a thing as Southern literature anymore." Morris is mentioned among other well-known deceased writers (such as William Faulkner, Eudora Welty, Thomas Wolfe, Katherine Anne Porter, Robert Penn Warren, and Flannery O'Connor) whose works are identifiable by a "common theme playing through most of the stories: the Defeated South." Their writings are also characterized by "a graceful prose style — in the fiction and the nonfiction — a gentility reflected in the culture. As the South has been swallowed up by America, all that has changed." There is no longer a mindfulness of the past nor a "sense of a shared history." The South has a "multicultural complexion" with writers from various areas of the world. As Fred Hobson affirms, "It's not just a black and white thing anymore."

1876 Hood, Orley. "Preserving Old Yazoo (Including the Witch)." *Clarion-Ledger*, 30 May 2003, sec. E, p. 1.

Yazoo City resident Mary Jones believes in the Witch of Yazoo, whose story appears in Morris's *Good Old Boy*. Yazooan Sam Olden, on the other hand, is a "determined though good-humored disbeliever," and "the very thought of Willie's book causes him to laugh." Both of them are committed to preserving the city's history, a heritage that too many local residents take for granted. The town's Preservation Day will be celebrated on May 31, which "will shed light on all manner of Yazoo history, pre-witch to post-witch."

1877 Hanrahan, Kathy. "Morris's Literary Cat, Spit McGee, Dies Following Dog Attack." *(Memphis) Commercial Appeal*, 13 August 2004, sec. B, p. 6.

Fourteen-year-old Spit McGee, a white cat with one gold eye and one blue eye and the "inspiration" for Morris's book *My Cat Spit McGee*, died on August 3 after being attacked by a dog near his home. "'He was just a presence and, like Willie, larger than life,' Morris's widow, JoAnne Prichard Morris, said Thursday." This article, syndicated by the Associated Press, also appeared in the *Clarion-Ledger* on August 13.

1878 Salter, Sid. "Sunday Morning with David Rae Morris." *Clarion-Ledger*, 7 November 2004, sec. G, p. 2.

An interview with Morris's son, David Rae. After the author left his native state in 1952 to go to college, he did not return to live until 1979. "He stayed away in part because he had opportunities elsewhere but also because he could no longer reconcile himself to the racial violence and the attitudes of his fellow Mississippians." In his memoir *North Toward Home*, Morris related what it was like growing up in the "segregated South. And he continued to write and explore the idiosyncrasies and contradictions of Mississippi and what he has referred to as the 'albatross of race.' I see his legacy as one of a boy from a small town in Mississippi who made a name for himself; yet in the process he challenged the very foundations of his own culture."

Books and Sections of Books

1879 Yazoo Historical Association. "William We[a]ks Morris." In *Yazoo County Story: A Pictorial History of Yazoo County, Mississippi, Covering Both the Old and the New.* Fort Worth, Tex.: University Supply and Equipment Co., 1958, p. 95.

Morris's senior class photo from the University of Texas and his biography appear in the "Some Famous Yazooians" section of a county history book. The paragraph notes his occupation as "scholar" and lists his accomplishments: "Public schooling in Yazoo City where graduated with distinction in 1952. Was member of National Honor Society and National Athletic Scholarship Society. Graduated Magna Cum Laude University of Texas, June, 1956." See page 36.

1880 Madden, David. *The Poetic Image in 6 Genres.* Carbondale: Southern Illinois University Press, 1969, pp. xxvii–xxix, 218, 219, 223–28.

A poetic image in a work of art, defines Madden, "focuses some element which in its prepared context is highly expressive, and is evocative of the work's important themes and experiences." He explores this concept in the genres of fiction (novels and short stories), lyrical essays, poetry, films, plays, and autobiographies. He analyzes *North Toward Home* in the latter study, noting that "the book depicts the 'Yankeefication' of a southerner who finally, though reluctantly, comes to regard North as home." Madden observes that Morris shares friendships with persons of various races, backgrounds, and religions. "In such relationships, with paradoxical, ironic, comic, and tragic roots in the cultural and geographical past, examined autobiographically, Americans are beginning to suspend bitterness to understand the past as it lives or languishes in the present. Willie Morris' testament is a major document in this process of understanding because its primary inspiration and motivation is not ideas, except as they inhabit images charged with human emotions and a sense of time and of place." Madden presents similar arguments in the *Survey of Contemporary Literature* (item 1882).

1881 Frost, David. "The South Is a Split Infinitive Trying to Get Together: Willie Morris." In *The Americans.* New York: Stein and Day, 1970, pp. 100–107.

A transcribed collection of Frost's television interviews includes a 1970 conversation with Morris, in which the author discusses racism and race relations. "We have to achieve some working, day-to-day form of racial harmony, if we're to live up to our greatest expectations as a mass multiracial democracy. If there ever is to be some meaningful, working, day-to-day racial harmony in this country, it'll come out of the deep South first.... It involves a common past, a common heritage, common suffering together." Near the end of the interview Morris makes the ludicrous statement that he met William Faulkner when "I was just a kid" and that "we went around in a sailboat" on a lake outside of Oxford, Mississippi.

1882 Madden, David. "North Toward Home." In *Survey of Contemporary Literature: Updated Reprints of 1500 Essay-Reviews from Masterplots Annuals, 1954–1969,* edited by Frank N. Magill. Vol. 5. New York: Salem Press, 1971, pp. 3293–96.

A synopsis of and commentary on Morris's autobiography, some of which originally appeared in Madden's *The Poetic Image in 6 Genres* (item 1880). The first section of Morris's memoir, covering the author's childhood in Yazoo City, Mississippi, "consists of a predictable recital of excruciatingly typical middle-class small town events." Too frequently, contends Madden, his memories and descriptions are "cutely condescending in tone, as when he describes fundamentalist religion, perennial target of sophomoric Southern liberal self-righteousness." Nevertheless, "the feel of *place* that the reader absorbs into his own consciousness forever" helps to transcend these and other flaws. The book's second part, devoted to Morris's years in Texas, shows that he has "an incredibly intimate knowledge of practical politics." As editor of both the *Daily Texan* at the University of Texas and the *Texas Observer,* "he fought cultural and political narrowmindedness and cruelty." In the New York City section of *North Toward Home,* "Morris' power lies in character study and story-telling, appropriate for a Southern liberal." Although Morris views many New Yorkers as mean-spirited and the city itself, which he calls "the Big Cave," as impersonal, he is "one of thousands of Southerners who yielded to the 'catastrophic wanderlust' of his generation and found a second home in the North."

1883 Carr, John. "Down Home: Willie Morris." In *Kite-Flying and Other Irrational Acts: Conversations with Twelve Southern Writers,* edited by John Carr. Baton Rouge: Louisiana State University Press, 1972, pp. 96–119.

A collection of formal, taped interviews with writers of fiction, nonfiction, and poetry. In Morris's interview, conducted in April 1970, he talks about growing up in the South, writing *North Toward Home*, racism and integration, editing the *Texas Observer* and *Harper's Magazine*, William Faulkner and other southern writers, and the New South. While discussing racism in Mississippi, he says: "It's in your bones, in your blood, in the whole atmosphere of the place. No matter how 'liberated' you might think you have become in later years, those old ingrained patterns will always be with you. And I think, without wishing to sound in the least bit self-righteous, I think it is a mark of civilization in a human being to come out of the sort of place we did and to fight hard within yourself against these almost glandular reactions to other human beings." See also item 1884.

1884 Carr, John. "Honkies, Editors, & Other Dirty Stories: Larry L. King." In *Kite-Flying and Other Irrational Acts*, pp. 120–48 (see item 1883).

The first part of this interview was conducted in April 1970. In the second part, taped in October 1971, King speaks about his and his colleagues' resignations from *Harper's Magazine* earlier that year. When asked if he and the other contributing editors might have stayed on "had certain compromises been made," King replied: "I doubt it. There are not many compromisers in the group. After John Cowles [Jr.] accepted Willie's resignation, the rest of us met with him to see if anything might be salvaged. But he walked in and coldly read us a 1200-word statement MacArthur might have hesitated to read to the Japanese on the U.S.S. *Missouri*.... He really left no room for negotiations."

1885 Berry, Jason. *Amazing Grace: With Charles Evers in Mississippi*. New York: Saturday Review Press, 1973, pp. 2, 49–50.

Berry, a white southerner, worked on the unsuccessful 1971 gubernatorial campaign of Charles Evers, a black southerner and older brother of civil rights leader Medgar Evers. In his account of his experiences, Berry mentions in a footnote that Morris's *Yazoo: Integration in a Deep-Southern Town*, "an impassioned and largely favorable report" detailing how the author's hometown addressed court-ordered integration, "embittered many people close to the situation. A Yazoo student told me, 'Integration's split our town terribly. We're not even havin' a prom this year. If [Morris] wanted to write about what it's really like, he ought to write about the success of the private academy and how those kids' parents don't get along with my folks cause I'm in a public school.'"

1886 Rouse, Sarah A. "Literature, 1890–1970." In *A History of Mississippi*, edited by Richard Aubrey McLemore. Vol. 2. Hattiesburg: University & College Press of Mississippi, 1973, pp. 446–476.

A historical survey that includes brief studies of individual authors. Rouse asserts that "during the second quarter of the twentieth century, Mississippi amazed the literary world by producing more writers who are read nationally and internationally than any other section of America." She devotes a paragraph in the "Mississippiana" section of her chapter to Morris and his *North Toward Home* and *Yazoo*, concluding that the books "are in essence social criticism." The two-volume *History of Mississippi* attempts "to present in an organized manner the scholarship of specialists in the different aspects of the history of the state."

1887 Genovese, Eugene D. *Roll, Jordan, Roll: The World the Slaves Made*. New York: Pantheon Books, 1974, pp. 93, 427–29, 540, 636.

Genovese quotes from Morris's *North Toward Home* as he supports his premise that "slaves made an indispensable contribution to the development of black culture and black national consciousness as well as to American nationality as a whole." While examining relationships among slaves, Genovese writes: "The pattern of slave behavior had its white counterpart; together they derived from and contributed to a regional culture that long survived its plantation, frontier, and folk origins. Willie Morris, writing of his boyhood in Mississippi, reflects: 'That curious Mississippi apposition — of courtliness and extraordinary kindliness on the one hand, and sudden violence on the other — was a phenomenon which never occurred to me.'"

1888 King, Larry L. "Looking Back on the Crime, or Rememberin' Willie and Them." In *The Old Man and Lesser Mortals*. New York: Viking Press, 1974, pp. 285–300.

King rounds out the articles in his anthology with a previously unpublished essay in which he reminisces about working with Morris, Robert Kotlowitz, David Halberstam, and his other colleagues at *Harper's Magazine*. He also describes the circumstances that led to the abrupt resignations of editor Morris and most of his staff. "A fair amount of nonsense has been written about what really happened at *Harper's* to bring about that mass resignation of spring 1971. Norman

Mailer's celebrated piece, 'The Prisoner of Sex,' was unfairly cited as a prime cause. If it was any factor it was a minor one, and then only because its publication coincided with larger problems then coming to a boil. It *is* basically true that the confrontation pitted the Literary Men against the Money Men, though, again, that's a simplification.... Willie Morris, never very patient with office politics and not excelling in the field, may have abdicated owner [John Cowles Jr.'s] ear to his in-house enemies at great expense; the rest of us, occupied with our own books and other out-of-house assignments, perhaps took too much for granted in failing to learn what transpired at all those tense Minneapolis meetings between Willie Morris, his detractors, and the harassed owners." See also items 1639, 1903, and 1943.

1889 Britton, Burt. "Willie Morris." In *Self-Portrait: Book People Picture Themselves.* New York: Random House, 1976, p. 167.

Since the early 1960s, Britton, a manager of New York's Strand bookstore, has asked writers, editors, critics, and other "book people" he admires to draw impromptu "self-portraits." More than seven hundred of the graphic images are reproduced in his book. Morris's picture, dated "Long Island, Summer '75," shows the torso of a man with "Y. C." [Yazoo City] on his chest, hat, and both upper sleeves. Surrounding him are five pennants, on which are written: "They endured"; "Miss. Champs, '52"; "Faulkner for Pres."; "Yazoo Indians"; and "Delta Valley Champs, '51." The figure is missing his right arm, and below the drawing Morris has quoted General Robert E. Lee's words upon hearing that General Thomas J. 'Stonewall' Jackson's left arm was amputated following his mistaken wounding by his own troops on the second evening of the Battle of Chancellorsville in May 1863: "He has lost his left arm. I have lost my right."

1890 Degler, Carl N. "The Distinctive South." In *Place Over Time: The Continuity of Southern Distinctiveness.* The Walter Lynwood Fleming Lectures in Southern History. Baton Rouge: Louisiana State University Press, 1977, pp. 1–25.

While discussing the distinctiveness of the South in a lecture delivered at Louisiana State University in April 1976, Degler states that although forty million immigrants settled in the United States during the nineteenth and twentieth centuries, "The South's share was disproportionately small." This absence of "diversified immigration into the South" contributed to a corresponding lack of diverse religions in the region, "thus further setting it apart from the rest of the nation." He quotes from Morris's *North Toward Home* to support his reasoning. "What relative absence of Jews, Catholics, Poles, Chinese, Italians, and Greeks might mean in the making of southern identity has been well suggested by the southern writer Willie Morris.... In his autobiography *North Toward Home*, Morris tells how impressed he was when reading books 'like Alfred Kazin's haunting poetic reminiscences of boyhood in an immigrant Jewish neighborhood in the East.'

Willie Morris's self-portrait, which he drew in the summer of 1975, is from Burt Britton's *Self-Portrait: Book People Picture Themselves.* See item 1889 (courtesy Burt Britton).

Morris could only marvel at the 'vast gulf that separates that kind of growing up and the childhood and adolescence of those of us who came out of the towns of the American South and Southwest a generation later.'"

1891 Podhoretz, Norman. *Breaking Ranks: A Political Memoir*. New York: Harper & Row, 1979, pp. 151–53, 160, 232, 249.

The editor of *Commentary* traces his "political development" from liberal to radical to neoconservative, comparing it to a "larger story about the political culture of this country." He became acquainted with Morris "almost from the moment" the Mississippian arrived in New York City. Morris's "air of fecklessness, combined with a deep southern accent that neither Oxford nor New York had moderated in the slightest degree and a 'shit-kicking' country-boy manner to go with it, all concealed the booster-rocket engine of ambition within which had carried him from Yazoo City to the 'red-hot center' of the New York literary world in record time and without as much as a minute deviation from the plotted course."

1892 King, Richard H. *A Southern Renaissance: The Cultural Awakening of the American South, 1930–1955*. New York: Oxford University Press, 1980, pp. 11, 195.

Morris is among the post–1920s southern writers and intellectuals who, King argues, attempted to "come to terms not only with the inherited values of the Southern tradition but also with a certain way of perceiving and dealing with the past." While Morris was working as an editor in New York City in the 1960s, "many émigré white Southerners found in *Harper's* an outlet for their writings, which offered a mixture of criticism and nostalgic good feelings toward the land they had left. There are several ironies in the title of Morris's autobiography *North Toward Home*."

1893 Garrett, George. "Southern Literature Here and Now." In *Why the South Will Survive*, by Fifteen Southerners. Athens: University of Georgia Press, 1981, p. 121–48.

Novelist and poet Garrett, one of the "fifteen southerners" who contributed essays to this "manifesto of Southern pride," believes that the South has a "reservoir of talent" among its many writers. He appears to have mixed feelings about Morris. "There are those, like Willie Morris and Larry King and Tom Wicker and Marshal[l] Frady, who have gone North and have actively joined the establishment, establishing their own impeccable liberal credentials by denouncing Southern life (often confirming stereotypical liberal suppositions in doing so) while managing to preserve something of the Southern style for themselves. This is, in effect, the ironic contemporary equivalent of the gesture called 'pulling wool' or 'pully woolly' (in some parts of the South), whereby certain sly black men ingratiated themselves with their oppressors by acting out with gusto and enthusiasm the part already assigned to them.... Of course, it can be justly argued that these writers are subtly 'working from within the System' even as they honestly criticize and call attention to the many faults and flaws of the South that they profess (as all of us do) to love."

1894 Mitchell, Frances. *Pete and Me: Twenty Poems*. University, Miss.: Pete's Press, 1981.

A collection of poems by Morris's neighbor in Oxford, Mississippi, who describes what she and Pete, his black Labrador, encounter on their many walks around the campus of Ole Miss. "There's a big black canine named Pete, / I've only partially adopted — / Because, actually, he belongs to another, But, he's mine too." Morris contributed an introduction to his friend's book (item 929). See also item 1651.

1895 "Willie Morris (1934–)." In *Mississippi Writers: A Portfolio of Portraits*. Jackson: University Press of Mississippi, 1981, n. pag.

Twenty Mississippi writers are featured in this folio-sized collection of photographs. The brief biographical paragraphs are "drawn largely" from *An Anthology of Mississippi Writers* (item 868). "Willie Morris is closely identified with Yazoo City, his boyhood hometown, and his writing, which is appreciated internationally, continues to draw from this rich resource of place."

1896 Mills, Hilary. *Mailer: A Biography*. New York: Empire Books, 1982, pp. 320–24, 332, 347, 361–62, 364–65.

A biography of author Norman Mailer examines his contributions to *Harper's Magazine* during Morris's editorship. "Morris had wanted to publish Mailer in *Harper's* ever since he had become an associate editor on the magazine in 1963. He had first met Mailer in Austin, Texas, in the early sixties through Harold and Barbara Probst Solomon, while he was still the editor-in-chief of the *Texas Observer*. 'Mailer and I hit it off,' recalls Morris. 'I always respected his writing and his courage as a human being.'" References to Morris appear in other works about Mailer, including Peter Manso's *Mailer: His Life and Times*

(1985) and Mary V. Dearborn's *Mailer: A Biography* (1999).

1897 O'Beirne, Frank. *The Harpers of Virginia, West Virginia, and Mississippi*. Arlington, Va.: privately printed, 1982, pp. 28, 37, 38, 53, 72, and folded leaf.

A genealogy and family history that covers Morris and his maternal ancestors. Morris's "autobiographical" *North Toward Home* "contains references to his parents and grandparents, and to his grandmother's sisters and brothers (who were the children of George William Harper and his wife Anna Lilly (Sims) Harper, of Raymond, Mississippi)."

1898 Yoder, Edwin M., Jr. Introduction to *North Toward Home*, by Willie Morris. Oxford, Miss.: Yoknapatawpha Press, 1982, pp. i–v.

Yoder became acquainted with Morris when both young men were studying at Oxford University. Fifteen years after the initial publication of *North Toward Home*, he still finds the book "compelling" reading and admires its "emotional honesty, its fidelity to the experiences of a young man with a genius for experience." He believes that Morris's "resistance," as a writer, to temptations in New York City (temptations, Morris says, "to be not merely careless, but dishonest"), represents the "ultimate theme" of his memoir. The various stages of Morris's life "tell a story of growth. And it is a growth of integrity: the integrity of seeing life steadily and seeing it whole. In a time too given to formulas, jargons, ideologies, systems, attitudes, stereotypes — all of them ways of evading human experience and guarding one against the task of coming to terms with it — Morris manages to be gloriously free of screens and poses and evasions."

1899 Hobson, Fred. *Tell About the South: The Southern Rage to Explain*. Baton Rouge: Louisiana State University Press, 1983, pp. 301, 304–306.

A scholar of southern literature and history includes Morris in his study of southern authors who have felt "the need to defend and to explain the American South." In *North Toward Home*, Morris "wrote in the tradition of those Southerners who have felt compelled to come to terms with the South and themselves as Southerners. His book, indeed, is perhaps illustrative of what happened to the Southern tradition of self-exploration as it moved into the post-civil rights era. A white Mississippian from the fringes of the Delta, Morris described in *North Toward Home* his journey from the Deep South to the University of Texas, where he had become editor of the campus newspaper, then to Oxford as a Rhodes scholar, and finally to the Northeast, where he found himself pondering the South."

1900 Jones, John Griffin. "Willie Morris." In *Mississippi Writers Talking*. Vol. 2. Jackson: University Press of Mississippi, 1983, pp. 75–118.

This second volume of a two-volume work "continues and concludes the series of interviews with Mississippi writers conducted by John Jones when he was oral historian with the Mississippi Department of Archives and History (1979–1981)." Jones, a knowledgeable scholar of southern literature, asks Morris incisive questions as the two men talk for almost two hours about the author's ancestors and family, his childhood and years in Yazoo City, race relations, politics, the craft of writing, and numerous aspects of his literary career. In response to Jones's question, "Will you go on writing?" Morris replies: "I don't know what else to do. I hate wearing a shirt and tie. They make my neck itch. I really do like to sleep till noon. I loathe committee meetings.... I can't tolerate office hours. I can't suffer the organized fools. I like sitting down on an afternoon and dwelling upon the things I care about, or remember with feeling, and then trying to give a little sense to them.... I don't have an alternative. I have no alternative to words." A detailed, wide-ranging interview, conducted in December 1980. Republished in *Conversations with Willie Morris* (item 1958).

1901 Garrett, George. *James Jones*. San Diego: Harcourt Brace Jovanovich, 1984, pp. xiii–xiv, 3–4, 43, 67, 69, 78, 80, 81, 84, 124–25, 129, 174–188 passim.

Garrett — a noted poet, novelist, story writer, editor, and essayist — relies on Morris's memoir *James Jones* for source material in his biography of Jones. Morris was one of Jones's closest friends and completed the novelist's *Whistle* after he died. "Willie Morris has written the definitive account of [Jones's] final months on Long Island. The last hundred pages or so of [*James Jones:*] *A Friendship* tell the story eloquently and thoroughly: the beauty of the place, which Jones rejoiced in (and Willie Morris claims is 'likely the most lovely terrain in America')...." Other works on Jones that mention Morris include James R. Giles's *James Jones* (1981), Frank MacShane's *Into Eternity: The Life of James Jones, American Writer* (1985), and

George Hendrick's *To Reach Eternity: The Letters of James Jones* (1989).

1902 Gray, Richard. *Writing the South: Ideas of an American Region*. Cambridge: Cambridge University Press, 1986, pp. 229, 273–74, 281–88.

Gray analyzes *North Toward Home* as he studies the "intellectual history" of the South and considers the ways in which southern people "have tried to forge the uncreated conscience of their region." Morris's book "is an act of self-exploration that hinges in particular on the relation between the writer's own personal story and what he sees as the story of his region. It is hardly surprising that the book borrows its epigraph from the greatest of all Southern novelists, William Faulkner, and alludes constantly to others, from Twain to Styron. For Morris is aware that what he is trying to do is what so many of them have tried to do before him: to write the South in the sense of struggling to disentangle the ties that bind — or, at least, once bound — him to the place where he was born."

1903 King, Larry L. *None but a Blockhead: On Being a Writer*. New York: Viking, 1986, pp. 20–22, 24, 31–32, 41, 43–45, 78, 81–86, 89–90, 92, 95, 102–107, 121–23, 127, 130, 132–33, 135, 139–47, 239, 241, 274.

Among the "ups and downs" of King's career that he describes in his anecdotal memoir is his tenure as a "contributing editor" for Morris and *Harper's* magazine. "In retrospect, *Harper's* as we knew it was doomed early on. The Nixon recession of 1970–71 caused losses larger than had been anticipated, and [publisher] Bill Blair was a bottom-line business type who cared no more for literary standards than a billygoat. Willie Morris, with only a small appreciation for office politics, had neglected to stroke [owner John Cowles Jr.] and Blair when it might have been helpful.... Today's *Harper's* is a thin, pale ghost compared to the magazine in its glory days under such talented editors as William Dean Howells, Bernard DeVoto and Willie Morris." See also items 1639, 1888, and 1943.

1904 Perkins, Barbara M. "Harper's Monthly Magazine." In *American Literary Magazines: The Eighteenth and Nineteenth Centuries*, edited by Edward E. Chielens. Historical Guides to the World's Periodicals and Newspapers. Westport, Conn.: Greenwood Press, 1986, pp. 166–71.

A profile of *Harper's* includes a four-page history, end notes, a bibliography, and a "publication history" that lists magazine title changes, volume and issue information, and names of publishers and editors. After Morris became editor in 1967, "He hired new staff and printed sections from controversial works like William Styron's *Confessions of Nat Turner* and Norman Mailer's *Armies of the Night*." At the time Morris resigned in 1971, "*Harper's* had lost ground to its arch-rival the *Atlantic* in both circulation and advertising revenue." Ninety-one other magazines are featured in this history of American literary periodicals founded before 1900.

1905 Horowitz, Helen Lefkowitz. *Campus Life: Undergraduate Cultures from the End of the Eighteenth Century to the Present*. New York: Alfred A. Knopf, 1987, pp. 17, 170–72, 223.

Horowitz maintains that undergraduates on American college campuses since colonial days have belonged to various "student subcultures," which were "created in particular historic moments, persist over time and that they still, at some level, inform the present." While examining the three principal groups—college men and women, outsiders, and rebels— she traces Morris's collegiate career as a political rebel. After he was elected editor of the University of Texas student newspaper, "Morris used his position to investigate and question critical areas of university life. At Columbia in 1932, these had been football and the administration of the dining halls. At the University of Texas in the late 1950s, Morris turned to the university's relation to Texas economic interests and racial segregation."

1906 Whitfield, Stephen J. *A Death in the Delta: The Story of Emmett Till*. New York: Free Press, 1988, pp. 12–13, 138.

A study of the 1955 grisly murder of black teenager Emmett Till in the Delta region of Mississippi, a crime that "spurred efforts to accelerate the tempo of civil rights advances for Southern blacks." The Delta is "the fertile wedge of land" between the Yazoo and Mississippi rivers. "One of its native sons, Willie Morris of Yazoo City, has eloquently testified to its 'pull ... its abiding mysteries and strengths.' ... The Delta dominated a state that has been like no other in the Union —'so eternally wild, so savagely unpredictable, so fraught with contradictory deceits and nobilities,' so divided in 'the gulf between its manners and morals, the extraordinary apposition of its violence and kindliness.'"

1907 Hannah, Barry. *Boomerang*. Boston: Houghton Mifflin / Seymour Lawrence, 1989, pp. 38–39, 54–55, 148–49.

Morris makes appearances in "Lost Pilots," "Modern," and "Furtherance," three of the vignettes in Hannah's novel. From "Modern": "I have been drunk some and Willie Morris has been drunk some, but Willie gave $140 [to an animal shelter] for the animals. Willie's heart has never been in doubt. He makes this little town swell with his dreams." Hannah, the writer-in-residence at the University of Mississippi in Oxford, does not include an introduction to his book, but the dust jacket flap reveals that *Boomerang* is a "weaving of novel and autobiography."

1908 Johnson, Rheta Grimsley. *Good Grief: The Story of Charles M. Schulz*. New York: Pharos Books, 1989, pp. 152–53.

In a biography of the creator of the *Peanuts* comic strip, Johnson compares the difficulties Schulz once had attempting to sell his cartoons in Chicago to the brush-offs Morris received when he first tried to find a job in New York City. "Things were getting tight by 1950, but it wasn't quite as brutal as now when Sparky Schulz pounded the Chicago sidewalks, carrying his cartoon portfolio. There were more syndicates, for one thing, and more newspapers and, paradoxically, fewer aspiring cartoonists.... In his book *North Toward Home*, Mississippi author Willie Morris describes the agonizing process of peddling one's creative wares to the people who are in charge."

1909 McLaurin, Melton. "Southern Autobiography and the Problem of Race." In *Looking South: Chapters in the Story of an American Region*," edited by Winfred B. Moore Jr. and Joseph F. Tripp. Contributions in American History, no. 136. Westport, Conn.: Greenwood Press, 1989, pp. 65–76.

The authors of the sixteen essays in *Looking South* "address the question of how the region copied with changes that challenged Southerners' dominant beliefs and institutions." McLaurin examines the autobiographies of Morris and other twentieth-century white southerners to understand how these authors—almost all "liberals of at least some variety"—view blacks as individuals. In their books, the majority of the writers show concern about segregation and the "problem of race," but they seldom reveal emotional or personal relationships with blacks. For instance, *North Toward Home* discloses little "of what its author thought and felt about blacks. Indeed, Morris's work is less an autobiography than an account of making it in America. Within this tale of success, blacks are seldom encountered as individuals," for the author fails to devote "a significant effort to explore his feelings about or reactions to individual blacks."

1910 Shnayerson, Michael. *Irwin Shaw: A Biography*. New York: G. P. Putnam's Sons, 1989, pp. 329, 345, 350, 351, 353–54, 360, 363, 370–72, 376, 386.

A sympathetic biography of the successful novelist (*Rich Man, Poor Man*), playwright (*Bury the Dead*), and short story writer ("The Girls in Their Summer Dresses"). Irwin Shaw became close friends with Morris when they both lived in the Hampton in the mid–1970s. "Despite their age difference, they shared passionate interests in both literature and sports. For Morris, a seminal experience had been reading [Shaw's football story] 'The Eighty-Yard Run' as a sixth grader in the Yazoo Public Library. 'It was on pulp paper, in some sports anthology,' he told Shaw, 'but I realized even then that this was a story different from all the others I was reading.... That story was probably my first true introduction to great writing.'"

1911 Yates, Gayle Graham. *Mississippi Mind: A Personal Cultural History of an American State*. Knoxville: University of Tennessee Press, 1990, pp. 227–28, 233–39.

Yates, who grew up in Mississippi during the 1940s and 1950s, returns to her native state and observes cultural changes "since the civil rights movement publicly began there in 1961." In her chapter "Gender and Sexuality," she discusses "man-of-letters Willie Morris," who is "prescient about men and race. He sees very clearly the breaking of the past power-grip of white male ascendancy based on race." For years this "power-grip" was particularly evident in football, and she reviews Morris's "fascinating" *The Courting of Marcus Dupree* to illustrate that white males no longer dominate the sport. "When he first heard about Marcus Dupree, Willie Morris knew that he had the symbol and the story of how that dominion has changed after the civil rights movement and after what was perhaps its most important accomplishment in Mississippi, the desegregation of the public schools."

1912 Bloom, Lynn Z. "Coming of Age in the Segregated South: Autobiographies of Twentieth-Century Childhoods, Black and White." In *Home Ground: Southern Auto-*

biography, edited by J. Bill Berry. Columbia: University of Missouri Press, 1991, pp. 110–122.

Bloom contends that southern childhood autobiographies emphasize both "*community*" (or its absence) and "the existence of this community in a specific *place*, highly significant to the child, with its particular customs and culture." The books also address the "pervasive experience" of segregation, and their authors "re-create the dawning and development of their own intellectual and moral consciousness, often at odds with the dominant values of white southern society." Although Bloom focuses most of her attention on Anne Moody's *Coming of Age in Mississippi* (1968) and Melton McLaurin's *Separate Pasts: Growing Up White in the Segregated South* (1987), she briefly surveys Morris's *North Toward Home*, noting that it "details, step-by-step, why and how he became a crusading young reporter." The thirteen essays in this volume were originally presented at the 1989 conference "Home Ground: Parents and Children in Southern Autobiography," held at Arkansas State University.

1913 Pearson, Michael. "The Sound of the Past: Faulkner's Mississippi." In *Imagined Places: Journeys into Literary America*. Jackson: University Press of Mississippi, 1991, pp. 65–124.

Pearson makes literary pilgrimages to six places where distinguished authors have "left a mythic imprint through their personalities or their writing." While visiting William Faulkner's Oxford, Mississippi, Morris acts as his "tour guide." Willie Morris "has written scores of essays on the land, the people, and the history of Mississippi, and recently a number of articles on Oxford itself, a town which 'lurks forever now in my heart.' His writing about Mississippi ... is always autobiographical. There is no way to separate the speaker and the place. For Morris, it is the landscape of the South and places like Oxford that give the acoustical range to his voice."

1914 Tebbel, John, and Mary Ellen Zuckerman. *The Magazine in America, 1741–1990*. New York: Oxford University Press, 1991, p. 319.

Tebbel, a leading historian of American publishing, and Zuckerman review *Harper's* in their detailed history of the magazine industry. They maintain that after editor John Fischer resigned in 1967, "The magazine drifted, for the first time in its long history. Willie Morris, the writer, was editor until 1971, without conspicuous success, and he was followed by Robert Shnayerson, from 1971 to 1976. As the youngest editor in the history of *Harper's*, Morris had made the magazine more topical, with David Halberstam and Larry King as contributing editors." Bill Moyers and Norman Mailer also wrote for the periodical. "*Harper's* was clearly becoming much more liberal, and Morris finally had to resign, along with seven staff members, after a dispute with management over policy."

1915 Cobb, James C. *The Most Southern Place on Earth: The Mississippi Delta and the Roots of Regional Identity*. New York: Oxford University Press, 1992, pp. 157, 160, 161–62, 163–64, 306, 312, 323.

Morris's observations in *North Toward Home* about blacks and his homeland are included in Cobb's comprehensive history of the Mississippi Delta. Cobb views the story of "the most southern place on earth" as "crucial to understanding the broad sweep of southern history." Morris's "recollection of his youth in Yazoo City was laced with references to blacks, whom he and his friends alternately pitied, imitated, and tormented."

1916 Manning, Robert. *The Swamp Root Chronicle: Adventures in the Word Trade*. New York: W. W. Norton & Co., 1992, pp. 313–14, 359–64.

In his reminiscences about his journalistic career, Manning, editor of the *Atlantic Monthly* from 1966 to 1980, notes that he and *Harper's* editor Morris were "friendly competitors." He reflects: "I have not met anyone who didn't like Willie Morris.... Willie's youth and country-boy fascination with the sophisticated big city made people want to help him. Small inquisitive eyes set like raisins in his plump boyish face, his soft Mississippi accent and courteous manner made him seem even younger and more vulnerable. This eased his entry into the Manhattan literary scene. Jack Fischer [the previous *Harper's* editor-in-chief], stern in manner and somewhat conservative in style, had been a formidable competitor, and so in a more unbuttoned and experimental way was Willie."

1917 Verich, Thomas M. "Willie Morris: The Last of the Southern Girls." In *English Magnolias: An Exhibition of Mississippi Fiction Printed in England*. University: Department of Archives and Special Collections, John Davis Williams Library, University of Mississippi, 1992, p. 18.

An exhibition devoted to British editions of Mississippi fiction was held at the University of

Mississippi's John Davis Williams Library from 6 August to 6 October 1992. The display included the 1974 André Deutsch edition of Morris's *The Last of the Southern Girls* (which features a dust jacket much more attractive than the uninspiring wrapper of the American edition). "An André Deutsch intra-office memo concerning the book's dust jacket directs the commission of 'a drawing or photo of the White House with the heroine in front of it—"a golden girl from the South," sexy and elegant.'" A photograph of the book's cover accompanies the entry in this exhibition catalog.

1918 Corry, John. *My Times: Adventures in the News Trade*. New York: G. P. Putnam's Sons, 1993, pp. 22, 28–32, 33, 42, 45, 55, 56, 60–70, 145, 162, 205, 212, 241, 243.

Corry spent some thirty years at the *New York Times*, pausing briefly in 1968 for a three-year stint at Morris's *Harper's*. "Willie's magazine," he writes in his memoir, "was *about* something; Willie cared, and late at night, when his cherubic look turned owlish, he would say that the magazine had to matter. He pronounced it 'mattuh,' but the meaning was clear, and to matter meant something important—life and death and American literature and the soul of the Great Republic." Corry was one of the magazine's staff writers who quit *Harper's* after Morris resigned in March 1971 (see item 1584).

1919 Wright, Lawrence. "Will Campbell: A Prophet in His Own Country." In *Saints & Sinners: Walker Railey, Jimmy Swaggart, Madalyn Murray O'Hair, Anton LaVey, Will Campbell, Matthew Fox*. New York: Alfred A. Knopf, 1993, pp. 157–202.

An essay on Southern Baptist minister and "legend in the civil rights movement" Will Campbell accompanies five other profiles of "religious leaders." In the spring of 1990, Campbell spoke at a fundraiser for the American Civil Liberties Union in Oxford, Mississippi. At a reception afterwards, Morris unsuccessfully tried to convince Campbell to perform a marriage ceremony for him and his friend. Morris "was in a feisty but maudlin mood, which seems to be the effect that liquor has on him." As Morris continued to drink, it occurred to him "that he and his companion ought to get married. As this thought unfolded and grew grander, he speculated that Campbell might marry them *right now*. 'Hell, Will, I know you don't require a license. All you need is a community of friends, and here—' Morris said, sweeping the room in an expansive gesture '—we are.'"

1920 Binswanger, Barbara, and Jim Charlton, eds. *On the Night the Hogs Ate Willie: And Other Quotations on All Things Southern*. New York: Dutton, 1994, pp. 10–11, 26, 29, 31, 105, 114, 131, 161–62.

Some of Morris's pithy comments are included in a quotations collection that embodies "the humor and passion that is the essence of the Southern experience." The "Willie" in the book's title comes from an observation by Pat Conroy: "My mother, Southern to the bone, once told me, 'All Southern literature can be summed up in these words: "On the night the hogs ate Willie, Mama died when she heard what Daddy did to Sister."' She raised me up to be a Southern writer, but it wasn't easy."

1921 Franklin, Jimmie Lewis. "Black Southerners, Shared Experience, and Place: A Reflection." In *The South As an American Problem*, edited by Larry J. Griffin and Don H. Doyle. Athens: University of Georgia Press, 1995, pp. 210–33.

A volume of essays on the American South that explores how the area has frequently been defined as being "at odds with the mainstream of American values or behavior" and therefore has been perceived as a "special problem." Franklin probes the "shared history" between southern whites and blacks and recounts Morris's reminiscence from *Homecomings* about the author's meeting with the black novelist Richard Wright in Paris. "The two quickly 'hit it off' as Mississippians. Although Morris probably overstates the case in maintaining that the intermingling of whites and blacks in the South made possible the ease with which the two met, he was nearer the truth in proclaiming that knowing the same things, eating the same kind of food, and being abused by the same weather gave them something in common that spoke to the issues of identity and place."

1922 Hollis, Daniel Webster, III. "*Harper's Monthly*." In *The ABC-CLIO Companion to the Media in America*. ABC-CLIO Companions to Key Issues in American History and Life. Santa Barbara, Calif.: ABC-CLIO, 1995, pp. 103–104.

An "encyclopedic media reference source that covers all areas related to multimedia history" contains a brief history of *Harper's*. Under Willie Morris's editorship of the magazine, "Lengthy articles dealing with contemporary politics or cultural developments became the norm. Morris fostered a personal brand of journalism without editorial direction for contributors.

David Halberstam contributed articles on the Vietnam War, and Joseph Kraft wrote a regular column of political commentary."

1923 Maraniss, David. *First in His Class: A Biography of Bill Clinton.* New York: Simon & Schuster, 1995, pp. 164, 170.

Mentions that in October 1968, the day before Bill Clinton left for England on a Rhodes scholarship, the future U.S. president "toured Manhattan in a taxi" with *Harper's* editor Morris. The two got together again the following June upon Clinton's return to America. "Morris had impressed Clinton with his charm and wit the first time they met, eight months earlier.... But their meeting this time left him disillusioned. Morris did not seem the same man. 'All the light is out of his eyes,' Clinton later wrote. 'All the life is out of his stories.'"

1924 Norman, Michael, and Beth Scott. "The Witch's Curse." In *Historic Haunted America.* New York: Tor, 1995, pp. 188–90.

The story of Yazoo City's legendary witch of Glenwood Cemetery is included in a compendium of "the most compelling *true* ghost stories" from across the United States and Canada. "Skeptics say that famed author Willie Morris made the whole thing up for his book, *Good Old Boy*, a remembrance of his youth in Yazoo City. The story of the witch is contained in its pages. Other longtime residents of the city are not so sure. One oldster said the story of the mysterious grave was known in the very early 1900s...."

1925 O'Connell, Shaun. *Remarkable, Unspeakable New York: A Literary History.* Boston: Beacon Press, 1995, pp. 300, 303–304.

A historical overview that examines the "various experiences of urban place" in the works of New York City writers. "Lost promise is ... the theme of Willie Morris's *New York Days*, a chronicle of his brief time of wine and roses in the City during the 1960s and 1970s." The memoir "stands as the latest and one of the best examples of a familiar American saga: yet again a young man from the provinces (Yazoo, Mississippi), on a wave of early successes ... comes to the Big Cave, as Morris calls it, where he is lifted beyond his wildest expectations and, after the good times, has a great fall."

1926 Applebome, Peter. *Dixie Rising: How the South Is Shaping American Values, Politics, and Culture.* New York: Times Books, 1996, pp. 298–300, 313.

A New York Times journalist argues that "the most striking aspect of American life at the century's end ... is how much the country looks like the South." The population is moving steadily southward, which in turn has greatly increased the South's influence, especially its "political clout." As Applebome travels around this region "to make sense of what the South's ascendance says about America and to figure out what kind of a place this South is, anyway," he interviews numerous persons, including Morris. "We got to talking about the persistence of Southern identity and what it was that made Southerners the dominant gene in the nation's cultural soup, a longtime Morris theme. He drew himself up like Stonewall Jackson at Chancellorsville ... and orated: 'I can answer in one word. Remembrance. Eudora Welty said we only have one thing as human beings and that is memory. The South today with all of its horrendous, damn near existentialist failings ... has one thing that distinguishes us as a culture within the great American commonwealth, and that is remembrance, memory and everything that is implied by it.'"

1927 Garber, Marjorie. *Dog Love.* New York: Simon & Schuster, 1996, pp. 21, 65, 199, 245–47, 250.

Garber analyzes Morris's "canine biography" *My Dog Skip* in her extensive study of the relationships between dogs and people. In the chapter "Dog Loss" she writes: "The death of the beloved dog of childhood is often quite naturally the occasion for a double grief, since what is lost is both the canine companion and a sense of one's own youth and innocence. Thus, for example, Willie Morris's memoir *My Dog Skip* is framed by deliberate and overt nostalgic gestures, from the first chapter, 'A Faded Photograph,' to the last, 'Going Away.'"

1928 Humphries, Jefferson, and John Lowe, eds. *The Future of Southern Letters.* New York: Oxford University Press, 1996, pp. 17, 34, 83–84, 90, 173.

Morris is referred to in several of the essays in this eclectic collection, the authors of which "address topics such as the past, humor, black autobiography, ethnicity, and female oral traditions in an attempt to define Southern culture today and ask who will be writing Southern literature tomorrow."

1929 Miller, Jim Wayne. "A Felt Linkage." In *Sacred Ground: Writings About Home*, edited by Barbara Bonner. Minneapolis, Minn.: Milkweed Editions, 1996, pp. 68–75.

In Miller's contribution to a collection of essays and stories on home and homelessness, he mentions Morris when he observes that people often find it difficult to go back to the places where they grew up. "The only other writer I know of who has recently written about leaving home and being unable to return who even remotely approaches [Thomas] Wolfe is Willie Morris, a former editor of *Harper's Magazine.* A Mississippian, Morris tells in his 196[7] book, *North Toward Home,* how he felt both alienated from the South and yet drawn to it. But the tension is slacker than what is found in Wolfe or [William] Faulkner. Morris's struggle, not particularly intense, is overcome and he is able to think of the American northeast as his home."

1930 Reed, John Shelton, and Dale Volberg Reed. *1001 Things Everyone Should Know About the South.* New York: Doubleday, 1996, pp. 131, 139, 254.

Morris is named in four of the 1001 paragraphs that examine the people, places, history, and traditions which "make the South different from the rest of America." While discussing why the region has produced so many authors, Reed and Reed conclude that "living outside the South often triggers writing." For instance, "Willie Morris realized that in New York 'the sensitive outlander might soon find himself in a subtle interior struggle with himself, over the most fundamental sense and meaning of his own origins.' Most Southern writers seem to have said something similar...."

1931 Brown, Fred, and Jeanne McDonald. "Willie Morris." In *Growing Up Southern: How the South Shapes Its Writers.* Greenville, S.C.: Blue Ridge Publishing, 1997, pp. 251–75.

The profiles of Morris and the twelve other southern writers in this volume reveal "common denominators that shaped their childhoods, and subsequently, their work." Brown and McDonald point out that with Morris's "special talent for description and his rich store of memories, [he] can reach back into the past and pull up his memories and breathe life into them again—for a while anyway, long enough to inspire the next story, the next reverie, a new link to the older South and America. 'People die and times change,' Willie Morris says with a soft break in his voice. 'But the memories do not die. They are forever.'" Revised as "Growing Up Southern—Willie Morris" for the web page *The Southerner* (item 1998).

1932 Cohodas, Nadine. *The Band Played Dixie: Race and the Liberal Conscience at Ole Miss.* New York: Free Press, 1997, pp. 2, 88, 113, 207, 212, 214, 216, 217, 226.

A study of race relations at the University of Mississippi includes passing references to Morris, such as his participation in Ole Miss's twenty-year anniversary observance of James Meredith's enrollment in 1962 as the school's first black student. "The twentieth anniversary was cause for rumination not just by outside parties but within the university as well, particularly in the [*Daily*] *Mississippian* and in a special issue of the Ole Miss magazine put out under the auspices of a journalism class taught by Willie Morris, the well-known native son who was writer-in-residence. Morris had written his own two-page essay to commemorate the event for *Time* magazine, reflecting on the university's transition and the changes in his 'beautiful and tragic and bewitched state'" (item 760).

1933 Linfield, Jordan L., and Joseph Krevisky, eds. *Words of Love: Romantic Quotations from Plato to Madonna.* New York: Random House, 1997, p. 229.

"Love will come again, but in circuitous paths," a sentence from Morris's *New York Days,* is included in a collection of thousands of categorized quotations that represent "some of the most sophisticated—and unconventional—writings on love down through the ages." Morris's words appear in *Words of Love*'s "Longing" section.

1934 Samway, Patrick H. *Walker Percy: A Life.* New York: Farrar, Straus and Giroux, 1997, pp. 235, 274, 291, 305.

A biography of Walker Percy, author of the novels *The Moviegoer, The Last Gentleman, Love in the Ruins,* as well as "Mississippi: The Fallen Paradise" in Morris's *The South Today.* In December 1968, Percy wrote a friend and chastised him for his poor review of *North Toward Home.* "Walker considered it unwarranted in its negative criticism. When he lived in Mississippi, he said, 'It took a lot of guts to buck the mainstream of good Christian racist businessmen and very few indeed did it, including my brother and Hodding Carter, and for their pains got obscene phone calls and garbage dumped in their driveway.'" About a year later, Percy wrote the friend again: "With your talents, intelligence, courage and integrity, and what with living in the South, you should not be attacking liberals like Willie Morris who, after all and whatever their faults, are on the right side of the big issue: race." Other works on Percy that make references to Morris include Jay Tolson's *Pilgrim in the Ruins: A Life of Walker Percy* (1992).

1935 Starr, William W. "Willie Morris." In *Southern Writers.* Photographs by David G. Spielman; text by William W. Starr. Columbia: University of South Carolina Press, 1997, pp. 106–107.

Morris is among the seventy-two leading writers of the South profiled and photographed for this album. Photographer Spielman tried to show the authors "in their houses or neighborhoods, at signings or book festivals, and, most of all, in their own work spaces." Morris is seated at his writing table, surrounded by note cards, paper, and pens. "His work has chronicled the timeless Southern issue of conflict between the insistence of memory and the need for change.... Photographed at his home in Jackson, Morris does most of his writing in the afternoon, shunning the computer, writing his words in longhand on a pair of long tables in an upstairs writing room."

1936 Milner, Jay Dunston. *Confessions of a Maddog: A Romp Through the High-Flying Texas Music and Literary Era of the Fifties to the Seventies.* Denton: University of North Texas Press, 1998, pp. 5–6, 59, 60, 66, 67–68, 69, 81, 82, 129, 142, 148, 176.

The Maddogs, according to Texas journalist Milner, were a "rabble of writers" and songwriters during the mid–1900s who worked hard and perhaps played even harder. "This group of merry pranksters who aspired to literary eminence" included Billie Lee Brammer, Gary Cartwright, Peter Gent, Dan Jenkins, Larry L. King, Edwin "Bud" Shrake, and Morris. "In the early and mid-sixties, it was Billie Lee and Willie Morris everybody wanted to hang out with. At least everyone of a certain liberal and perhaps intellectual turn of mind." See also item 1983.

1937 Rossinow, Doug. *The Politics of Authenticity: Liberalism, Christianity, and the New Left in America.* New York: Columbia University Press, 1998, pp. 28, 33, 38, 123.

Recounts Morris's activism on the campus of the University of Texas in this study that "traces the somewhat surprising emergence of a 'new' political left following the politically conservative era of the 1950s, the flowering of this left in the 1960s, and its frustration in the 1970s." In his senior year at the university, Morris edited the student newspaper, the *Daily Texan.* "When the in-house censor at the *Texan* refused to approve some of Morris's editorials, Morris sometimes ran a blank space instead, informing his readers, 'This Editorial Censored.'"

1938 West, James L. W., III. *William Styron: A Life.* New York: Random House, 1998, pp. 362–63, 422–23.

Morris is referred to several times in this biography of writer William Styron, one of his closest friends. In early November 1963, Morris wrote Styron asking if he would "contribute to a special issue of *Harper's* that Morris was planning, an issue on the contemporary American South" (see item 725). The two men met for the first time in historian C. Vann Woodward's office at Yale University, "and that meeting led to a friendship. Gregarious, bibulous, and prankish, Morris had a gift for fun and practical jokes that appealed to Styron. Morris also admired Styron's writing and told him so. Soon Morris and his wife, Celia, became members of the Styrons' social circle, and the two couples visited back and forth."

1939 Whitaker, Jack. *Preferred Lies and Other Tales: Skimming the Cream of a Life in Sports.* New York: Simon & Schuster, 1998, pp. 215–216.

Sports broadcaster Whitaker writes warmly of his friend Morris in his memoirs. During the mid–1970s, both men lived in Bridgehampton, New York, on eastern Long Island, and frequented a popular restaurant and bar called Bobby Van's. "The man who made Van's a Hampton's institution was Willie Morris, the writer/editor from Yazoo City, Mississippi, the University of Texas, and Oxford University. Among Willie's many talents was the capacity to bring together the townspeople who had been born and raised in the community and those of us who had moved there later in life.... Willie was also the playing manager of the softball team [Golden Nematodes] that played each Sunday in the field behind Bridgehampton High School, where Carl Yastrzemski had starred before ascending to the Red Sox."

1940 Black, Patti Carr. *The Southern Writers Quiz Book.* Jackson: University Press of Mississippi, 1999, pp. 12, 16, 17, 33, 37, 41, 75, 86, 87, 89, 90, 93.

Morris and his books are among the hundreds of twentieth-century southern writers and their works featured in Black's fifty-seven quizzes. The tests "suggest the staggering variety of fascinating characters, exotic locales (of the mind as well as of the landscape), and multilayered concerns found in southern literature."

1941 Bush, George. *All the Best, George Bush: My Life in Letters and Other Writings.* New York: Scribner, 1999, p. 408.

Former President George Bush includes a letter to Morris in his collection of letters, notes, memos, and diary entries. Bush wrote the message on 7 January 1989, soon after he won the 1988 presidential election. "Tough days ahead, but I am now getting excited about moving down the hall and getting to work. If it weren't for the damned deficit I'd be kicking up my heels and feeling like a Spring colt. I do feel that the potential out there for a more peaceful world is pretty good."

1942 Copp, Tara, and Robert L. Rogers. *The Daily Texan: The First 100 Years*. Austin: Eakin Press, 1999, pp. vi, vii, 3, 37, 58, 69–73, 82.

A centennial history of the University of Texas's campus newspaper surveys Morris's contributions and experiences as editor. "Although Morris supported school spirit, he began to feel *The Texan* wasn't fulfilling the promises he had made when he assumed the editorship.... So, much to the regents' chagrin, Morris swiftly changed his focus to a congressional proposal known as the Fulbright-Harris Natural Gas Bill, which had rivers of corrupt Texas money and influence dripping all over it. Regent Claude Voyles said in a February 7 interview, 'We feel *The Daily Texan* is going out of bounds to discuss the Fulbright-Harris gas bill when 66 percent of Texas tax money comes from oil and gas.'" Morris contributed the foreword to this story of the *Daily Texan* (item 943), and Copp and Rogers posthumously dedicated the book to him.

1943 King, Larry L. *Larry L. King: A Writer's Life in Letters, Or, Reflections in a Bloodshot Eye*, edited by Richard A. Holland. Fort Worth, Tex.: TCU Press, 1999, pp. 6, 14, 36, 57, 103–104, 105–110, 123–24, 126, 148–49, 150, 161, 166–67, 177, 184, 187–88, 190–94, 226–27, 318–19, 331–32, 395, 396.

A collection of King's correspondence, which spans the years 1954 to 1999, includes letters both to and about Morris. In March 1971, King vents his feelings about "the *Harper's* fiasco" to a friend. "Willie Morris— given all his giant warts and personality quirks— was simply the best at getting the best from the writer, and we worked with him — and each other — in a partnership of hot excitement over the potential to be reached.... Willie Morris just called, and though I am mad enough to kill the son of a bitch over his mishandling of the politics involved in the fiasco, there was a plaintive note that touched me and set me remembering the good in the sorry bastard.... The other day I took Willie about 3,000 letters and telegram that have come in supporting him, many of which said cancel their subscriptions if we all left, and I must admit that in our beery rancor they were pleasant to read." See also items 1639, 1888, and 1903.

1944 Leonard, John. "Editors Anonymous." In *When the Kissing Had to Stop: Cult Studs, Khmer Newts, Langley Spooks, Techno-Geeks, Video Drones, Author Gods, Serial Killers, Vampire Media, Alien Sperm-Suckers, Satanic Therapists, and Those of Us Who Hold a Left-Wing Grudge in the Post Toasties New World Hip-Hop*. New York: New Press, 1999, pp. 192–97.

Cultural critic Leonard's compilation of essays on contemporary books, television, and popular culture includes a commentary on *New York Days* and Paul Krassner's *Confessions of a Raving Unconfined Nut: Misadventures in the Counter-Culture* (1993). "Most of the reviews of Willie's book, like most of the book itself, were devoted to his days at *Harper's*. So be it. The only revenge a writer's got on the bean counters and back stabbers who buy and sell him like a yo-yo or a pork-belly future is to give us a book that pins them through their buggy little eyes down to a page of style, impales them on a consummate disdain. Even if Willie and his boys drank too much at Empire Chinese and ate too often at Elaine's, any magazine that in five years managed to publish Mailer on the armies of the night, Halberstam on the best and the brightest,... and Seymour Hersh on the My Lai massacre was doing wonderfully well, thank you, no matter what they thought in Minneapolis."

1945 Bales, Jack, ed. *Conversations with Willie Morris*. Literary Conversations Series. Jackson: University Press of Mississippi, 2000.

Spanning the years 1967 to 1998, virtually Morris's entire public career, these twenty-five interviews and profiles feature his candid views on his own life and literary career, sports, other authors, the 1960s, politics, the Civil War, dogs, the complexities of race relations, and of course the South and his beloved Mississippi. Morris assisted Bales with his research. "Literally up to the day of his untimely death, [Morris] generously (and characteristically, as countless writers will attest) offered his advice, cooperation, encouragement, and even his personal files. I am able to include several interviews in this book — including at least two previously unpublished ones— only because he gave them to me." The volume comprises the following literary conversations (items 1946 to 1970):

1946 Smith, Roger H. "Authors & Editors." In *Conversations with Willie Morris*, pp. 1–2 (see item 1945).

An interview and profile originally published in *Publishers' Weekly* (item 1377).

1947 Cross, Leslie. "Willie Morris, All-American." In *Conversations with Willie Morris*, pp. 3–4 (see item 1945).

An interview and profile originally published in the *Milwaukee Journal* (item 1546).

1948 Whittington, Mary Jayne Garrard. "Willie Morris." In *Conversations with Willie Morris*, pp. 5–7 (see item 1945).

An interview and profile originally published in *Delta Review* (item 1379).

1949 Cohen, Richard. "*Harper's* Willie Morris." In *Conversations with Willie Morris*, pp. 8–14 (see item 1945).

An interview and profile originally published in *Women's Wear Daily* (item 1573).

1950 Moore, Robert H. "The Last Months at *Harper's*: Willie Morris in Conversation." In *Conversations with Willie Morris*, pp. 15–22 (see item 1945).

An interview originally published in *Mississippi Review* (item 1398).

1951 Powell, Lew. "On Being the Famous Writer Willie Morris." In *Conversations with Willie Morris*, pp. 23–27 (see item 1945).

An interview originally published in the *(Greenville, Miss.) Delta Democrat-Times* (item 1591).

1952 Hoffman, Marjorie. "Willie Morris Comes Home Again." In *Conversations with Willie Morris*, pp. 28–29 (see item 1945).

An interview and profile originally published in the *Austin American* (item 1607).

1953 Delaney, William. "Willie Morris: Fiction Still Alive in U.S." In *Conversations with Willie Morris*, 30–34 (see item 1945).

An interview originally published in the *Washington Star* (item 1618).

1954 Dickerson, James. "Willie Morris Comes Home Again to the Delta." In *Conversations with Willie Morris*, pp. 35–40 (see item 1945).

An interview and profile originally published in the *Greenwood (Miss.) Commonwealth* (item 1623).

1955 Cummings, Mary. "*Hampton Life* Interviews Willie Morris." In *Conversations with Willie Morris*, pp. 41–45 (see item 1945).

An interview originally published in *Hampton Life* (item 1403).

1956 Baumann, Melissa. "Willie Morris: 'I Will Forever Consider This My Home.'" In *Conversations with Willie Morris*, pp. 46–49 (see item 1945).

An interview and profile originally published in the *Clarion-Ledger / Jackson Daily News* (item 1625).

1957 Thomas, William. "Willie Morris, Home Again." In *Conversations with Willie Morris*, pp. 50–56 (see item 1945).

An interview and profile originally published in the *(Memphis) Commercial Appeal* (item 1634).

1958 Jones, John Griffin. "Willie Morris." In *Conversations with Willie Morris*, pp. 57–90 (see item 1945).

An interview originally published in *Mississippi Writers Talking* (item 1900).

1959 Mullener, Elizabeth. "Like Other Mississippi Exiles, Writer Willie Morris Comes Home." In *Conversations with Willie Morris*, pp. 91–96 (see item 1945).

An interview and profile originally published in the *(New Orleans) Times-Picayune* (item 1645).

1960 Terkel, Studs. "An Interview with Willie Morris." In *Conversations with Willie Morris*, pp. 97–111 (see item 1945).

A previously unpublished interview originally broadcast in the fall of 1983 by WFMT in Chicago, Illinois. The two writers met on Terkel's radio show where they examined the complexities of race relations and racial changes while discussing Morris's *The Courting of Marcus Dupree*. Terkel tells Morris: "I think again and again of the experiences I've had of talking to southern whites and southern blacks in Chicago. Both came up here to make a living." Morris replies: "I would see that time and again when I was living in New York City: the mutuality of the southern blacks living in the great cities of the North and the Midwest with their white contemporaries. This is something that runs through Faulkner. I've always felt that this sense of community and a sense of a common past, despite so much of the anguish and pain of that past, would be one of the great salvations of the South."

1961 Bandler, Michael J. "The Good Old Boy's Taste in Books." In *Conversations with Willie Morris*, pp. 112–15 (see item 1945).

An interview originally published in the *Chicago Tribune Book World* (item 1661).

1962 Kotz, Mary Lynn. "Willie Morris Is Home Again at Ole Miss." In *Conversations with Willie Morris*, pp. 116–23 (see item 1945).

An interview and profile originally published in the *St. Petersburg (Fla.) Times* (item 1670).

1963 Polman, Dick. "A Son of the South: Author Willie Morris Speaks Out from the Land He Chronicled in the '60s on Life There in the '80s." In *Conversations with Willie Morris*, pp. 124–27 (see item 1945).

An interview and profile originally published in the *Philadelphia Inquirer* (item 1684).

1964 Rose, Charlie. "An Interview with Willie Morris." In *Conversations with Willie Morris*, pp. 128–35 (see item 1945).

A previously unpublished interview originally broadcast on 26 October 1993 on *The Charlie Rose Show* in New York City. Morris appeared on Rose's show to promote his recently released *New York Days*. When Rose asks him to "tell me what the story is" of the memoir, Morris replies: "This is a story of New York City in the sixties and the sense of community which we had: the interlocking worlds of literature, publishing, journalism, the arts, entertainment, politics, even sports.... And a provincial's coming to the great city. This is one of the sturdy chords in American literature — the provincial coming to New York and being immersed in its drama, its power, its glamour (and in my case the great old magazine in America) and trying to capture the intense pressures of the sixties and what was happening to the country.... Trying to get one's magazine to reflect the realities of our day." The two men also discuss what Rose calls "some criticisms of the book," though only cursorily.

1965 Pond, Wayne. "Praying for Baseball." In *Conversations with Willie Morris*, pp. 136–43 (see item 1945).

A previously unpublished interview with Morris and illustrator Barry Moser upon the publication of their *A Prayer for the Opening of the Little League Season*. The conversation was aired on the *Soundings* radio program during the week of 16 July 1995. When asked "how this book came about," Morris explains that one of his and Moser's good friends is John Evans, owner of Lemuria bookstore in Jackson, Mississippi, and a Little League coach. Evans had urged Morris for years to write a prayer for the opening of the Little League season, and for years Morris had begged off. One evening Morris told his wife, "'I'm going to get Johnny Evans off my back and I'm going to write that prayer.' I wrote the first draft (and stayed up all night doing it) and polished it a lot. Then I had the good fortune to hook up with, in my opinion, the greatest illustrator in the United States, Barry Moser."

1966 Rose, Charlie. "An Interview with Willie Morris." In *Conversations with Willie Morris*, pp. 144–47 (see item 1945).

A previously unpublished interview originally broadcast on 18 April 1995 on *The Charlie Rose Show* in New York City. Morris appeared on Rose's show to promote his new work *My Dog Skip*. During their discussion about Morris's book and his childhood, the writer tells him: "Skip, Charlie, was not my dog. He was my brother and I still miss him. When I recently walked into the Yazoo City Historical Museum and saw that Skip's tombstone was on display, I realized what a chord that our inseparable days together had been in that vanished era of World War II and beyond. We were, in every sense, brothers."

1967 Feldman, Michael. "An Interview with Willie Morris." In *Conversations with Willie Morris*, pp. 148–53 (see item 1945).

A previously unpublished interview originally recorded on 27 January 1996 before a studio audience on Public Radio International's *Whad'Ya Know?* Show. Morris banters with Michael Feldman, host of the comedy/quiz show, about sports, dogs, the South, and live radio shows. "I've heard about your legendary audiences, Michael. I look around this big auditorium in Jackson, Mississippi, totally packed, and it looks to me as if you have the most distinguished assemblage of people together under one roof since Elvis dined alone on catfish." See also item 1752.

1968 Bales, Jack. "A Conversation with Willie Morris." In *Conversations with Willie Morris*, pp. 154–82 (see item 1945).

Bales interviewed Morris on 8–9 June 1997 at the author's home in Jackson, Mississippi. During two lengthy, animated sessions, the men converse about Morris's formative years, his "New York days" at *Harper's Magazine*, sports, his writing career, and dozens of other topics. While the writer is discussing his controversial term as editor of the *Daily Texan* in college, Bales asks if he would "change anything" if he could go back and edit the newspaper "all over again." Morris answers: "I would not change anything in the totality of it, but I think I would use more humor in little things.... I think I would use the sharp edges of humor and satire more than I was able to do at the time. But back then I was young and a little frightened, for this was big-time stuff." See also item 440.

1969 Bain, Rebecca. "An Interview with Willie Morris." In *Conversations with Willie Morris*, pp. 183–92 (see item 1945).

A previously unpublished interview originally broadcast on 24 January 1998 on Nashville Public Radio's *The Fine Print*, WPLN-FM. During the session, Bain and Morris discuss an essay the author had written about growing older, "As the Years Go By, Do We Grow ... Crankier or More Tolerant?," which had just been reprinted in an anthology (item 899). Morris tells Bain that as he gets older, "I really do think I have mellowed." He adds that "a good marriage really helps. And spirited cats help. But also returning to one's roots as a southerner and a Mississippian; living on the banks of Purple Crane Creek, which overflows in the rains; renewing childhood friendships; and going back to my hometown Yazoo City a lot has kind of brought things together for me —certainly as a writer."

1970 Lopate, Leonard. "An Interview with Willie Morris." In *Conversations with Willie Morris*, pp. 193–200 (see item 1945).

A previously unpublished interview originally broadcast in February 1998 on New York Public Radio's New York and Company, WNYC. Morris appeared on Lopate's show during a promotional tour for his new book *The Ghosts of Medgar Evers*. During their discussion about Evers, who had been field secretary of the NAACP in Mississippi, Morris tells Lopate that "what I've always felt about Medgar was that he did not really reach any kind of national prominence until his death. After all, his early efforts for civil rights came before sit-ins, before Freedom Riders, before Rosa Parks and Montgomery, and before Dr. King in a place of abandoned repression — Mississippi. He only had his wife, Myrlie, and a handful of others who were wholly behind him.... To me, in writing this book, implicit in these circumstances were questions of greatness that transcend race, which are even more unimaginable because Medgar was black in Mississippi in the first half of the twentieth century and basically alone."

1971 Harvey, John H. *Give Sorrow Words: Perspectives on Loss and Trauma*. Philadelphia: Brunner/Mazel, 2000, pp. 71–72.

The author of a book on grief and sorrow uses a passage from Morris's "poignant" article "Here Lies My Heart" (item 777) to illustrate the anguish that victims of divorce often endure. "Morris hit upon many truths of loss in this article. But in the end, he has expressed a truth that we all should know about our major close relationships that end: Psychologically, close relationships never end."

1972 Morris, Celia. *Finding Celia's Place*. College Station: Texas A&M University Press, 2000, pp. 8, 68–69, 75–77, 84, 85–90, 93–97, 99, 101–104, 105–107, 109, 110, 112, 115–17, 119, 121–22, 124–25, 128–29, 131–55 passim.

A memoir by Morris's first wife in which she narrates "*my* version" of their relationship. "I was drawn to the idea of telling my own story because *both* my ex-husbands have had their say in print. Indeed, my first told what he took to be our saga *twice*— initially in an essay in *Esquire* that prompted people from all over the country to call and say it made them cry. When a second version appeared in a widely noticed book, virtually all the reviewers singled it out as the most moving chapter. And I too was moved, for these accounts read rather like an apology and a peace offering. Still, his version of reality and mine were as similar as the stork version of childbirth is to the natural process." See items 56, 777, and 1833.

1973 Richter, Curt. "Willie Morris." In *A Portrait of Southern Writers*. Athens, Ga.: Hill Street Press, 2000, n. pag.

Photographer Richter, whose works have been exhibited around the world, chose a close-up of Morris's face for his collection of ninety-six photographs of "contemporary Southern writers." The pictures are unaccompanied by text; the caption beneath Morris's portrait reads: "Willie Morris / Spring 1995 / Jackson, Mississippi."

1974 Wilkie, Curtis. *Dixie: A Personal Odyssey Through Events That Shaped the Modern South*. New York: Scribner, 2001, pp. 19, 20, 21, 24–25, 197, 244, 260, 262, 303, 304, 325, 330–336.

In this lively and engaging memoir, a journalist and native Mississippian revisits some of the major news stories he covered throughout his wide-ranging career, including James Meredith and the 1962 riots at the University of Mississippi, Mississippi's "Freedom Summer" of 1964, and the conviction of Medgar Evers's murderer in 1994.

During a "particularly hard period" at the height of the civil rights struggles in the late 1960s, Wilkie left his home state in despair. "I particularly related" to Morris's autobiography, *North Toward Home*, and "I was determined to join a band of expatriates on the East Coast." Like Morris, he returned to his roots decades later. When the author died suddenly in 1999, Wilkie was one of "Willie's eclectic circle of Mississippians" who came to Jackson to pay his respects. "For the better part of two days, we crowded the [Morris] yard, crying and laughing and recalling his pranks.... None of us felt embarrassed by our tears. Willie had made crying a legitimate emotion. Late in the evenings, after helping demolish several bottles of whiskey or wine, Willie tended to get sentimental."

1975 Bellows, Jim. *The Last Editor: How I Saved the "New York Times," the "Washington Post," and the "Los Angeles Times" from Dullness and Complacency*. Kansas City, Mo.: Andrews McMeel Publishing, 2002, pp. 174, 187, 224.

The memoirs of newspaper editor James G. Bellows contains tributes by many of his friends and colleagues, including Morris, who worked for him on the *Washington Star* newspaper. "Bellows is the kind of editor any writer would follow into battle.... I was attracted to the *Star* because it is after all in Washington, the most southern northern city, and it's the most powerful city in the world with the strangest social mores. But when Bellows made me the offer and I started writing the column, I realized how much I missed Washington and I think I did the best journalism of my life." See also item 1617.

1976 Black, Patti Carr, and Marion Barnwell. *Touring Literary Mississippi*. Jackson: University Press of Mississippi, 2002, pp. 13–14, 34, 35–41, 81, 86, 137, 138, 143.

Morris's house in Yazoo City, his grave in Glenwood Cemetery, the University of Mississippi, and other places identified with the author are pinpointed in this "helpful guide for travelers who ... want to see homes and other sites associated with Mississippi writers."

1977 Blow, Richard. *American Son: A Portrait of John F. Kennedy, Jr.* New York: Henry Holt and Co., 2002, pp. 82–85.

Blow, formerly a senior editor of *George* magazine, offers firsthand observations about John F. Kennedy Jr. and the brief time Kennedy served as the founder and editor-in-chief of *George* (1995 until his untimely death in 1999). In 1996 Blow asked Morris, a consultant on the motion picture *Ghosts of Mississippi*, to write an article about the film, and "the fabled southern writer" responded with a "moving piece" on civil rights leader Medgar Evers (item 801). "Willie Morris was old school, charming, gracious, and courtly, a natural storyteller who wouldn't let a phone call end without inviting me to come on down to Jackson. I felt fortunate to work with him."

1978 Flora, Joseph M., and Lucinda H. MacKethan, eds. *The Companion to Southern Literature: Themes, Genres, Places, People, Movements, and Motifs*. Baton Rouge: Louisiana State University Press, 2002, pp. 82, 83, 116, 120, 153, 155, 309–310, 325, 381, 392, 471, 499, 503, 505, 507, 615, 854, 855, 880, 918, 1008.

More than five hundred entries explore numerous aspects of the "southern experience as it is depicted in literature." The volume covers not only writers but "literary terms, genres (traditional and nontraditional), movements, motifs, types and stereotypes, schools and theories, both old-fashioned and newly minted." Morris's name appears in articles devoted to "Autobiographical Impulse," "Autobiography," "Border States," "Brown v. Board of Education," "Civil Rights Movement," "Good Old Boy," "Guilt," "Jackson, Mississippi," "Johnson, Lyndon Baines," "Manuscript Collections," "Mississippi, Literature of," "Mississippi, University of," "Mississippi Delta," "Oxford, Mississippi," "Sports Literature," "Telling About the South," "Twain, Mark," and "Yankee."

1979 Goldfield, David. *Still Fighting the Civil War: The American South and Southern History*. Baton Rouge: Louisiana State University Press, 2002, pp. 27, 59, 253.

Passages from Morris's works contribute to an explanation of why "southerners have remembered the Civil War and Reconstruction as they have, and how these perspectives shaped an American region." Goldfield writes that "when war and Reconstruction generations could no longer reach out to their children and grandchildren, the legacy of storytelling ... still surrounded their progeny.... Southerners growing up in the first half of the twentieth century found dating the war difficult because their elders often discussed the conflict as if it had happened yesterday or was still in progress. Writer Willie Morris recalled frightening his maiden aunts in the 1940s with fabricated radio reports that the Yankees were coming."

1980 Gollob, Herman. *Me and Shakespeare: Adventures with the Bard*. New York: Doubleday, 2002, pp. 146–51.

In a memoir narrating his post-retirement fascination with Shakespeare, Gollob reminisces about Morris and other authors whose works he had edited during his long career as a book editor. He describes Morris as "mercurial, dashing, quick-tempered, [and] charming.... He was irresistibly, incorrigibly boyish, boyishly handsome, with a hint of pudginess, and mischievously funny." Gollob met Morris in 1965. During a lunch together, "Willie proved to be an incomparable raconteur, spinning tales of his boyhood in Yazoo City, his newspaper days in Austin, his political advocacy, his time at Oxford."

1981 Hendrickson, Paul. *Sons of Mississippi: A Story of Race and Its Legacy*. New York: Alfred A. Knopf, 2003, pp. 132, 152, 166–67.

In October 1962, *Life* magazine published a photograph of seven Mississippi sheriffs, one of which is taking a practice swing with a billy club. These "seven faces of Deep South apartheid" had gathered on the campus of Ole Miss in Oxford to prevent James Meredith from becoming the first black student to enroll at "their sacrosanct state university." Former *Washington Post* reporter Hendrickson researches the lives of the sheriffs and their descendants as he examines both contemporary and current racial attitudes in the South. "From the start, I wanted to know: How did these seven white Southerners get to be this way, and how did it all end, or how is it still going on, and was there no eventual shame here...? He quotes from Morris's article in *Dissent* magazine, "Despair in Mississippi; Hope in Texas," written three months after Meredith "forcibly penetrated Ole Miss" (item 719).

1982 Clinton, Bill. *My Life*. New York: Alfred A. Knopf, 2004, p. 135.

Clinton devotes a paragraph in his presidential memoir to his friendship with Morris. In the fall of 1968, Clinton was in New York City "getting ready to sail for Oxford," where he would study as a Rhodes scholar. He and a friend "had a terrific lunch with Willie Morris, then the young editor of *Harper's Magazine*. In my senior year at Georgetown, I had read his wonderful memoir, *North Toward Home*, and had become a lifetime fan. After I won the Rhodes, I wrote Willie, asking if I could come to see him when I was in New York. In the spring he received me in his office on Park Avenue. I enjoyed the visit so much I asked to see him again before I left, and for some reason, maybe southern manners, he made the time." See also items 2052 and 2062.

1983 Davis, Steven L. *Texas Literary Outlaws: Six Writers in the Sixties and Beyond*. Fort Worth, Tex.: TCU Press, 2004, pp. 30, 33, 34, 41, 50, 75, 133–34, 136, 137–38, 151, 152, 154, 166, 183–87, 192, 194, 195, 197, 215, 216, 218, 223, 234, 239–42, 244, 247, 252, 254, 265, 266–67, 296, 315, 385, 418, 421, 431.

A fascinating and well-documented critical study of the lives and works of six Texas writers—Billie Lee Brammer, Gary Cartwright, Peter Gent, Dan Jenkins, Larry L. King, and Edwin "Bud" Shrake. Davis chronicles the friendship between King and Morris and details King's contributions to *Harper's Magazine*. "In truth, Morris' editorship was messy. He often overpromised himself to his staff writers, leading each of them to believe that their own article would be the magazine's cover story for an upcoming issue. His drinking, always pronounced, became even heavier after his wife, Celia, left him in 1968.... Still, his writers continued to support him, because Morris had exceptional editorial instincts, and he empowered them as writers." See also item 1936.

1984 Hotchner, A. E. *Everyone Comes to Elaine's: Forty Years of Movie Stars, All-Stars, Literary Lions, Financial Scions, Top Cops, Politicians, and Power Brokers at the Legendary Hot Spot*. New York: HarperEntertainment, 2004, pp. 64–65, 98–99, 103, 130–31, 135.

Hotchner, an author of numerous books and a regular at Elaine's in New York City, provides recollections and anecdotes about the restaurant and its owner, Elaine Kaufman. In one passage, journalist Bob Drury alludes to chapter 12 of *New York Days*, "Elaine's and Other American Peregrinations." Drury recalls that when he walked into Elaine's for the first time, "I spoke to no one until a stocky woman in a floral-print dress plunked down next to me.... She had a raspy voice and what Willie Morris, who devoted an entire chapter of his autobiography to the restaurant, described as a 'curly smile.'"

1985 Mailer, Norman. "To: Willie Morris." In *Norman Mailer's Letters on "An American Dream," 1963–1969*, edited by J. Michael Lennon. Limited edition of 110 numbered copies signed by Mailer and Lennon. Shavertown, Pa: Sligo Press, 2004, pp. 23–24.

A collection of seventy-six letters, dated 1963 to 1969, by author Norman Mailer to family members, friends and literary associates pertaining to his novel *An American Dream*. In his brief letter to Morris, dated 21 October 1963, he is obviously replying to his friend's request that he contribute an article to *Harper's Magazine*. Mailer tells him that "writing articles has a bit of drudgery to it for me, and now I'm free, for a year at least, to work on a novel, so I think I'll be keeping myself much to myself through this long winter." An editorial note preceding the letter states that Mailer "gives a hint of the lifelong tension in his writing life between his profound desire to write novels and the financial need to write shorter pieces of non-fiction."

1986 Yoder, Edwin M., Jr. *Telling Others What to Think: Recollections of a Pundit*. Baton Rouge: Louisiana State University Press, 2004, pp. 41, 65, 66, 72, 75, 76, 77, 80, 82, 89, 91, 92, 104, 191–207.

Yoder, a Pulitzer Prize–winning editorialist and a newspaper writer for forty years, states in his memoir that "Willie was, I believe, the largest figure it has been my fortune to know, large in every dimension, one of those people of whom we say, 'larger than life.'" His seventeen-page sketch, "Willie Morris," offers both a personal reminiscence and a thoughtful commentary. "As a writer, Willie was a rare combination of artistry and intellect. Behind the sometimes drowsy or passive-seeming exterior he was a polymath who knew a great deal about a great many important things, especially American and southern history and letters.... As a man, Willie was without detectable vanity or egotism. He was a wonderful listener, missing nothing, recalling everything, with an exquisitely sensitive emotional register." Parts of "Willie Morris" originally appeared in the *American Oxonian* (item 2077).

Theses and Dissertation

1987 Cole, Richard Ray. "A Journal of Free Voices: The History of *The Texas Observer*." Master's thesis, University of Texas at Austin, 1966.

Cole tells the "story of the only statewide political organ in Texas—*The Texas Observer*—and how it evolved from its forebears." Chapter 6 of his thesis, "The Second Idealist," details Morris's editorial work on the publication. "As editor, Morris made no great changes in the paper. He wrote much the same as Dugger—even to the incessant use of the 'editorial we'—and continued to probe the same type of political issues. The physical make-up stayed the same also. But Morris seared his own brand into the editorials."

1988 Walker, Carol Cavness. "Vision and Revision: *North Toward Home* and *Making It*." Master's thesis, Texas Tech University, 1971.

An analysis of Morris's *North Toward Home* and *Making It* by Norman Podhoretz, two memoirs published in 1967. Walker's thesis "will show that each author has undergone a critical revision of his self-image. By recounting various events recorded in the autobiography of each man, the thesis will explore the childhood, education, and other influences which helped to shape his youthful vision, and will trace the literary beginnings and full initiation into the power and politics of the harsh literary world of New York City."

1989 Bowen, M. Elizabeth. "A Small Affirmation of the Heart." Honors thesis, College of William and Mary, 1978.

Explores the careers of Morris and Larry L. King through personal interviews and studies of their writings. "This paper attempts to convey something of the personal charm and professional abilities of these two writers, to record their journeys and their lessons, and to discover what it is in the states that shaped them that continues to command their attention as writers and their loyalty as men."

1990 Fluitt, Lydia Wilson. "The Journalistic Career of Willie Morris: A Writer with a Strong Sense of Place." Master's thesis. Lamar University, 1983.

Traces Morris's years on the staffs of the *Daily Texan*, the *Texas Observer*, and *Harper's Magazine*. Fluitt reviews *North Toward Home*, *Good Old Boy*, *Yazoo*, and *Terrains of the Heart* and "point[s] out the strong sense of place that is evident in these works."

1991 Boxall, Michael. "Willie Morris at *Harper's*, 1967–1971." Master's thesis, University of Washington, 1988.

Surveys Morris's editorship of *Harper's Magazine*, a position he held from 1967 to 1971. "This thesis examines the tradition of literary journalism, of which *Harper's* felt itself a part, and also the editorial policies of the 117 years before Morris took over. It looks at the economic difficulties which all magazines faced after the end of World War II, and it tells how Morris responded to them; which was not to pay them as much attention as his employers felt he should."

1992 Watkins, James H. "Locating the Self: Southern Identity, White Masculinity, and the Autobiographical 'I.'" PhD diss., University of Florida, 1995.

Analyzes the "autobiographical discourse" of Morris and other white male writers in the South from the colonial era to the present. "The autobiographers I examine typically eschew autonomous individualism in favor of community-based honor and a more relational or organic conception of self and society. They rarely treat their 'whiteness' as transparent, obvious, or universal, and their masculinity is 'feminized' in regionally specific ways.... In the Civil Rights era, Willie Morris and other southern white liberals write confessional narratives which inscribe an individual conscience."

1993 Weldon, Susan M. "Pentimento: Willie Morris As an American in Mississippi." Honors thesis, University of Southern Mississippi, 2002.

A study of Morris's life and works as well as a commentary on his "double consciousness" of being both a southerner and an American. "Morris's brutally honest, emotionally charged writings about the southern–American experience carved out a different, liberalized, and introspective voice for what had traditionally been one of the most degenerate hyphenate groups in American society." In such books as *North Toward Home* and *Yazoo*, "examples abound of Morris's warring tendencies to be both southern and American. This double identity is riddled with complexities, paradoxes, and inner turmoil, propelling him toward national renown as a writer and editor but also serving as the genesis of his painful personal evolution."

Selected Web Pages

See also item 862.

1994 Bales, Jack. "Willie Morris." *The Mississippi Writers Page*, edited by John B. Padgett. University of Mississippi. http://www.olemiss.edu/depts/english/ms-writers/dir/morris_willie/ (accessed 12 November 2004).

Maintained by the Department of English at the University of Mississippi, *The Mississippi Writers Page* is "designed both as an introduction to the diversity of literary talent in Mississippi and (we hope) as a source of accurate and timely information for the serious literary scholar." The entry on Morris includes a biographical essay, lengthy primary and secondary bibliographies, annotated listings of "media adaptations" of Morris's works, and links to Internet resources. The article was last updated in August 2001 and appears in the "Famous Residents" section of *Yazoo: Gateway to the Delta*, the web page of the Yazoo County Convention & Visitors Bureau <http://www.yazoo.org/website/famous/famous_morris.htm> (see item 1999).

1995 "The Book." *My Dog Skip*. Warner Bros. http://mydogskip.warnerbros.com/cmp/book.html (accessed 23 November 2004).

This part of the website for the motion picture *My Dog Skip* includes a few paragraphs about Morris and his book. The site's "The Filmmakers" section provides another brief summary of the author's life and career <http://mydogskip.warnerbros.com/cmp/filme.html>.

1996 Morris, Willie. "Raymond: A Kaleidoscope of History." *Raymond, Mississippi*. http://www.raymondms.com/history/morris.htm (accessed 23 November 2004).

Morris's remarks at the dedication of the Raymond, Mississippi, Confederate Cemetery on 9 May 1987. "My great-grandfather, Major George W. Harper, was ineluctably linked to these dead. He migrated from Virginia to Raymond in 1843. He was the editor and publisher of *The Hinds County Gazette* from that year until 1881, to be succeeded by his son Samuel Dawson Harper." This page is part of the official website of Raymond, Mississippi. Another section, *Hinds County Gazette*, features a short biography of George W. Harper <http://www.raymondms.com/history/gazette.htm>. See also item 1680.

1997 "Willie Morris." *Mississippi Writers and Musicians*, Starkville High School, Starkville, Mississippi. http://shs.starkville.k12.ms.us/mswm/MSWritersAndMusicians/writers/Morris.html (accessed 24 November 2004).

A brief biography, primary and secondary bibliographies, book reviews, photographs, and links to "additional web sites." Starkville High School students participate in the school's Mississippi Writers and Musicians project by researching the lives and works of talented individuals who "have contributed to the literary and cultural heritage" of the state.

1998 "Willie Morris Tribute." *The Southerner* 1, no. 3 (1999). http://www.southerner.net/v1n3_99/ (accessed 18 November 2004).

The "first online magazine to embrace the full gamut of Southern journalism and literature" devotes a special issue in remembrance of Morris. "The main themes that emerge about Willie Morris in these pages are that he was a great writer and editor, a great helper of other writers, and an infamous practical joker, who had his quirks. Another recurring theme is that in spite of the homogenization of American culture in the age of interstate and Internet highways and television, there is still a distinct American South." Works written especially for this online tribute include: "Editor's Note" by Glynn Wilson, "Willie Morris: A Great Teacher" by Will Norton, "A Helper and a Joker" by Wayne Greenhaw, "Willie Morris Was a Happy Man" by Jack Bales, "Willie Had His Quirks" by Winston Groom, "The Greatest Editor I Ever Knew" by Larry L. King, "Willie Morris: The Prankster" by Curtis Wilkie, "Willie Morris Remembered" by Fred Brown, "The Day I Went North Toward Home" by Billy Field, "Gay Talese on Willie Morris," an interview with Talese by Glynn Wilson, and "William Styron: On Willie Morris and Southern Writing," an interview with Styron by Glynn Wilson. Previously published works on the web page include: "Does the South Still Exist?" by Linton Weeks (item 2026), "Is There a South Anymore?" by Morris (item 771), and "Growing Up Southern — Willie Morris" by Fred Brown and Jeanne McDonald (item 1931). A photograph of Morris at his writing desk, taken by Fred Brown, appears on the "back of the book." See page 57.

1999 "Witch's Grave." *Yazoo: Gateway to the Delta*. Yazoo County Convention & Visitors Bureau. http://www.yazoo.org/website/history/history_witchs_grave.htm (accessed 23 November 2004).

Observes that the legend surrounding the Witch's Grave in Yazoo's Glenwood Cemetery "became famous in Willie Morris' book, Good Old Boy, published in 1971. This story is an example of the unusual folklore surrounding Yazoo County." Includes "The Story of the Witch," an excerpt from chapter 1 of *Good Old Boy*. See also item 1994.

Obituaries and Memorial Tributes

2000 Dugan, Kieran. "Morris, Willie." In *Current Biography Yearbook, 1999*, edited by Clifford Thompson. New York: H. W. Wilson Co., 1999, p. 661.

"Writer; editor; a son of the old Deep South who brought to his literary journalism (along with some fiction) the complex sensibility of a man who had fought his way through the prejudices on which he was reared and whose liberalism was informed by a long historical memory...."

2001 Applebome, Peter. "Willie Morris, 64, Writer on the Southern Experience." *New York Times*, 3 August 1999, sec. A, p. 13.

Surveys Morris's life and literary career. "He wrote on subjects ranging from his childhood English fox terrier to Mississippi race relations; hunkered down in his favorite Mississippi haunts ... and delved into the interplay of past and present in the South." When Morris moved to Jackson he "spent his time evoking the clattering cacophony of warring emotions— love, hate, chauvinism, despair and, above all, a sense of something unshakable — that so many Southerners feel toward the region." Republished in *Remembering Willie* (item 2091).

2002 Associated Press. "Mississippi Author Willie Morris Dies of Apparent Heart Attack." University of Mississippi *Daily Mississippian*, 3 August 1999, p. 1.

"Willie Morris, a captivating storyteller who used his childhood adventures to spin stories of rural life in the Mississippi Delta and former writer in residence at Ole Miss, died Monday after suffering a heart attack. He was 64."

2003 Associated Press. "Willie Morris, Delta Memoirist and 'Good Old Boy,' Dies at 64." *(Memphis) Commercial Appeal*, 3 August 1999, sec. A, p. 8.

"Willie Morris, one of Mississippi's most treasured writers for his tales based on his childhood in the Delta and other personal experiences, died Monday night.... Six months after his birth in Jackson on Nov. 29, 1934, Morris's family moved to Yazoo City, the small town that would become the focal point for many of his stories. He also developed what he called a 'good old boy' love for the South and its people."

2004 Dees, Jim. "Oxford Remembers Willie Morris." *Oxford (Miss.) Eagle*, 3 August 1999, pp. 1, 8.

Morris "lived in Oxford from 1980 until 1990 and was fondly remembered in town today as [a] generous and undiscriminating friend with the heart of a good ole boy and the intellect of a

Rhodes scholar." At the core of all his books, "friends say, was a great friend, a great mind, and a mischievous practical joker." Remarked author Barry Hannah, who "was hired to teach writing at Ole Miss soon after Morris's arrival" on campus, "He was the most democratic person I ever met. Nobody was excluded. He made people feel good about themselves and this world."

2005 Lucas, Sherry. "Author Morris Dies at Age 64." *Clarion-Ledger*, 3 August 1999, sec. A, pp. 1, 5.

A page-1 headline in "Mississippi's Newspaper" informs readers of Morris's death. "Colleagues, friends and family praised Morris as a gifted writer and editor with an abiding sweetness and a boyish sense of humor. 'Willie Morris was part of the heart and soul of Mississippi,' said former Gov. William Winter, who was with Morris at St. Dominic/Jackson Memorial Hospital when the writer died. 'No one that I knew of radiated such sheer joy in the fellowship of his friends and the events of his life.'"

2006 Lucas, Sherry. "Friends Can't Imag[in]e State Without Morris." *Clarion-Ledger*, 3 August 1999, sec. A, p. 5.

Baptist minister Will D. Campbell, authors David Halberstam and William Styron, Mississippi journalists Rick Cleveland and Bill Minor, and former Mississippi Governor William Winter remember Morris. "Journalist Bill Minor, a friend since 1969, said, 'It is unthinkable to imagine Mississippi without Willie Morris—his Bohemian spirit, his brilliant mind and his deep and abiding affection for this often bewildering state from whose Delta soil his remarkable talent was nurtured and grew. He will be irreplaceable.'" Includes a list of "Major Works of Willie Morris."

2007 O'Briant, Don. "Obituaries: Willie Morris, 64, Noted Author, Editor." *Atlanta Constitution*, 3 August 1999, sec. B, p. 6.

Includes remarks by Morris's son and friends. "Mr. Morris and his old child, son David Rae, a freelance photojournalist living in New Orleans, were collaborating on a new book about Mississippi's past, present and future. He said his father had finished his part of the project. 'He was from a generation that had lived through a Mississippi that was at its worst, but he had come to peace with his homeland,' David Rae Morris said."

2008 Shows, Ronnie. "Willie Morris, Famed Mississippi Writer Passes Away." U.S. House. 106th Cong., 1st sess. *Congressional Record*, 145, no. 112, daily ed. (3 August 1999), p. E1734.

Congressman Shows (D-Miss.) eulogizes Morris in the U.S. House of Representatives. "One of our nation's greatest artists has passed away.... Willie lived in my district down in Jackson. Willie will always live, Mr. Speaker, in the hearts of thousands around our planet who have read his words discovering a world of penetrating wit, warm memories, and prose that can bring the angels to earth and soothe our longings to connect with our broader world."

2009 Thompson, Chris. "Farewell to Mississippi's 'Good Ole Boy.'" University of Mississippi *Daily Mississippian*, 3 August 1999, p. 2.

Eulogizes Morris as "the one person who helped me cope with change and growing up more than any other.... I love Willie Morris because he is the greatest Mississippian who has ever lived; his writing has taught me to love and appreciate the joy and pain of my home state in ways that no other human being could explain. His writings have sustained me during some of my life's hardest and most tragic periods." Republished in *Remembering Willie* (item 2105).

2010 Blair, Sam. "Willie Morris' Brilliance Proved in UT Days: Author and Editor Took on Regents, Earned Admiration at College Paper." *Dallas Morning News*, 4 August 1999, sec. A, p. 31.

A former staff member on the *Daily Texan* newspaper at the University of Texas reminisces about his colleague. "Everyone who enjoyed Willie's talent, wit and friendship through the years will miss him. As Austin writer Bud Shrake said Tuesday, 'Willie was so much fun to be around: a great storyteller and a true intellectual.' That's the Willie Morris I knew from the September day in 1952 when he first walked into the sports office of *The Daily Texan*, fresh from a 500-mile ride on a Southern Trailways bus."

2011 Gordon, Emily. "Literary Lion's LI Connection: Novelist Willie Morris, 64, Dies." *Newsday*, 4 August 1999, sec. A, pp. 7, 30.

Long Island's *Newsday* remembers Morris, who "spent nine years as a fixture of the East End, in the midst of an influential literary career that embraced and transcended the forces of North and South." While living in Bridgehampton, New York, Morris often "held court" in Bobby Van's, a restaurant and bar. Marina Van, the director of the East Hampton Chamber of Commerce, was then married to Bobby Van. She recalls that Morris "'loved everyone and he spoke to everyone ... he didn't care who you were, a celebrity or a waitress.'"

2012 Holland, Gina. "Southern Writer Willie Morris Dies." *Chicago Sun-Times*, 4 August 1999, p. 51.

Quotes from several of Morris's friends and his son in an obituary syndicated by the Associated Press. In 1963, Morris was appointed associate editor of *Harper's Magazine*, and four years later the 32-year-old writer "became the youngest editor in chief of the nation's oldest magazine. He left Harper's in 1971. 'He brought that magazine kicking and screaming into the present,' said writer David Halberstam, who was recruited by Mr. Morris to work at Harper's. 'With his love of words and very considerable charm, he'd taken an archaic magazine and made it an exciting magazine that was on the cutting edge.'"

2013 Hood, Orley. "Our Good Old Boy Always Stood Up for His Mississippi." *Clarion-Ledger*, 4 August 1999, sec. E, pp. 1, 3.

Part of Morris's charm, recalls one of his long-time friends, was that "he never grew up.... Till the day he died, which was Monday, Willie was still the kid who roamed the dusty streets of Yazoo City with his pals on sweaty summer afternoons.... He loved telling tales. When he'd get to the best parts, he'd whisper. Everyone would lean in to hear. Willie loved small conspiracies." Republished in *Remembering Willie* (item 2098).

2014 Husni, Diala S. "Ole Miss, Oxford Remember Morris." University of Mississippi *Daily Mississippian*, 4 August 1999, pp. 1, 8.

Members of the Oxford and Ole Miss communities share memories of their friend. "'Willie had a great effect on not only the bookstore, but on the general community of Oxford itself,' said Richard Howorth, owner of Square Books. 'He brought Oxford its reputation of being the "New South's Art Mecca."' ... David Sansing, professor emeritus of History at the University of Mississippi, said that 'the appointment of Willie Morris was a major turning point in the history of Oxford. He brought authors such as Barry Hannah to Oxford literature. He created a literary environment.'"

2015 Kelley, Mike, and Anne Morris. "Legendary Editor Took on the Texas Establishment: Willie Morris, 1934–1999." *Austin American-Statesman*, 4 August 1999, sec. A, pp. 1, 10.

Morris's first wife and others who knew him in Texas recount his years on the *Daily Texan* and *Texas Observer*. Mike Quinn, now a journalism professor at the University of Texas, was managing editor of the *Texan* the year of Morris's editorship. Quinn noted that the young editor "wrote columns that were well beyond his years in power and depth of feeling. He just had it. He had it from the get-go." Morris met Celia Buchan at the University of Texas and they married while he was at Oxford. She said: "Virtually everybody who knew him then (during the UT years) expected him to go far, far. And he did, though faster, perhaps, than turned out to be good for him."

2016 Lott, Trent. "Willie Morris, Honoring the Life of a Great Southern Writer." U.S. Senate. 106th Cong., 1st sess. *Congressional Record*, 145, no. 113, daily ed. (4 August 1999), p. S10214.

Senator Lott (R-Miss.) eulogizes Morris in the U.S. Senate. "Mr. Morris was a writer and editor who painted a vivid picture of the Southern way of life unlike any literary figure since William Faulkner. Mr. Morris had the heart of a good ole country boy who grew up in Yazoo City, and the intellect of a Rhodes Scholar."

2017 Minzesheimer, Bob. "Willie Morris, a Pure Product of Southern Soil." *USA Today*, 4 August 1999, sec. D, p. 3.

Morris "loved exploring the enduring contradictions of the South, defending it to outsiders, criticizing it to friends. 'I go back to the South,' he wrote in *Terrains of the Heart*,... 'physically and in my memories, to remind myself who I am, for the South keeps me going.'" Includes recollections from several of his friends, including President Bill Clinton. "Morris, Clinton said in a statement, 'was not only my friend, he was a national treasure.'"

2018 "Mississippi Deaths: Willie Morris, Writer." *Clarion-Ledger*, 4 August 1999, sec. B, p. 3.

Morris "will be remembered as a story teller, prankster and a lover of people."

2019 "Morris and 'Another Kind of Society.'" *Austin American-Statesman*, 4 August 1999, sec. A, p. 15.

The last three paragraphs of chapter 9 of the "New York" section of *North Toward Home* appear as an editorial commentary. "In October 1965, Willie Morris visited Austin to give a lecture about 'my generation of young Americans, and about the University of Texas in the 1950s.' He remembers the experience in 'North Toward Home.'"

2020 "Native Son Willie Morris Dies Monday." *Yazoo Herald*, 4 August 1999, pp. 1, 14.

A page-1 headlined obituary. "First came the news that Yazoo City native and author Willie Morris had been transported to a Jackson hospital after suffering what was thought to be a heart attack. Then, the worst. Mr. Morris, 64, died at 6:21 p.m. Monday at St. Dominic/Jackson Memorial Hospital of cardiomyopathy."

2021 Ramsey, Marshall. [Cartoon]. *Clarion-Ledger*, 4 August 1999, sec. A, p. 14.

A cartoon on the newspaper's editorial page depicts Morris, his dog Pete, and a black angel sitting on a hillside overlooking a small town. Morris points to the town and asks the angel, "Is this Yazoo City?" The angel replies, "No, Mr. Morris, this is heaven."

2022 Salter, Sid. "Up in 'Willie's Heaven,' Morris Will Be Telling Mississippi Stories That God Will Want to Hear." *Scott County (Miss.) Times*, 4 August 1999.

The newspaper's editor and publisher eulogizes his mentor and friend of twenty years. "Despite his generosity of spirit, his easy, self-deprecating nature or his willingness to indulge the claims of strangers on his time, his energy and his fame, Mississippi never produced a more ardent defender or a harsher social critic. That conflict — Willie's love of home, family and heritage tempered against his outrage at racism, hatred and injustice — would color the whole of his life and his work." Republished in the *Yazoo Herald* of 7 August 1999 and *Remembering Willie* (item 2102).

2023 Skube, Michael. "A Reverence for Writing: Once a Shining Star at Harper's, Troubled Life Ends on Happier Note." *Atlanta Constitution*, 4 August 1999, sec. D, pp. 1, 3.

Morris's friends recall that although the writer led a "troubled life" for years after he resigned from *Harper's Magazine*, his marriage to JoAnne Prichard and the success of *My Dog Skip* brought him happiness. "'What happened at Harper's hurt him. Everybody knew that,' [Winston] Groom says. Not only did he lose his job, but his marriage collapsed during his years at Harper's and his personal life went into a downward spiral that worried friends for years." In 1990 he married JoAnne Prichard, an editor at the University Press of Mississippi, and moved from Oxford to Jackson. "'Willie told me JoAnne saved his life,' Larry L. King says." Includes the first paragraph of *North Toward Home*. Republished in *Remembering Willie* (item 2103). See also item 1815.

2024 Watkins, Billy. "Willie Morris: A Few Last Words." *Clarion-Ledger*, 4 August 1999, sec. E, p. 1

Some of Morris's friends and admirers "comment on what author meant to them, state of Mississippi, South." The persons include author John Grisham, historian David Sansing, U.S. President Bill Clinton, bookstore owners Richard Howorth and John Evans, former Miss America Mary Ann Mobley, Jackson Mayor Harvey Johnson Jr., and reference librarian Jack Bales. "'Willie was Mississippi's voice,' Howorth said. 'He spoke for us and about us, and I think he was uniquely able to do that. It wasn't that he simply had a greater love of Mississippi or the South than others, although he had a deep love for both. It was more because of his knowledge about history and humanity in general. Because of his perspective, he was able to write about it and help us understand it better.'" Republished in *Remembering Willie* (item 2106).

2025 Watkins, Billy, and Sherry Lucas. "Willie Morris Memorial Services Scheduled for Thursday." *Clarion-Ledger*, 4 August 1999, sec. A, pp. 1, 4.

Announces that Morris will be buried on August 5 in his "beloved hometown of Yazoo City." President Bill Clinton, University of Mississippi Chancellor Robert Khayat, authors John Grisham and Josephine Haxton (pen name Ellen Douglas), and former next-door neighbor Helen Graeber reflect on their friend. "Flags at the University of Mississippi, where Morris became writer-in-residence in 1980, flew at half-staff Tuesday. 'Willie brought something special to the university,' Ole Miss Chancellor Robert Khayat said in a statement. 'When the heart of Willie Morris stopped beating on Monday evening, a voice was stilled which was quintessentially Mississippian, yet spoke to his state, his nation and indeed the world.'" See also: Associated Press. "Visitation for Morris to Be Held at Old Capitol Museum in Jackson." University of Mississippi *Daily Mississippian*, 4 August 1999, p. 8.

2026 Weeks, Linton. "Appreciation: Willie Morris, Heart of the South." *Washington Post*, 4 August 1999, sec. C, pp. 1–2.

A summary of Morris's life and writing career, with observations from some of his friends. "Playwright Larry L. King met Willie at the [Texas] Observer and they became lifelong buds. In fact, almost everyone who met Willie became a friend for life. 'I never knew Willie to do anybody harm or to want to,' King said yesterday. 'He was a helpful fellow to writers. That's unusual in this business.'" Republished in the *Yazoo Herald* of 7 August 1999 and *Remembering Willie* (item 2107). Revised as "Does the South Still Exist?" for the web page *The Southerner* (item 1998).

2027 "Willie Morris: Great Author Dead, Memory Lives On." *Clarion-Ledger*, 4 August 1999, sec. A, p. 14.

An editorial paying tribute to Morris and his writings. "His works delve deeply into his memory of places, people and things and give them a luster beyond comprehension of the average eye. It was his gift to us. And in our memory, through his books, he will eternally reside."

2028 "Willie Morris, 64, Dies; Was Renowned Writer." *Washington Post*, 4 August 1999, sec. B, p. 7.

A News Services syndicated obituary. Morris "served from 1980 to 1991 as writer in residence at the University of Mississippi. His writing courses proved hugely popular, and his own output — mostly autobiography or reflections on the South — established his name alongside such past or present residents as William Faulkner, Ellen Douglas, Barry Hannah and Richard Ford."

2029 "Yazooans Share Memories." *Yazoo Herald*, 4 August 1999, pp. 1, 14.

Residents of Yazoo City, Morris's hometown, recall their friend. Mrs. Helen Graeber lived next door to young Willie and his parents. "'Willie was a warm and loving child and adult,' she said. 'I remember his sitting on the glider on the front porch many afternoons with my husband as they watched the cars go up and down Grand Avenue. Willie would wave to anyone he knew, which included most of the cars going by.... And, of course, we all remember Willie playing with Skip, running around with him and throwing the stick to him. Skip and Willie were inseparable.'"

2030 Brown, Fred. "Willie Morris, Southern Author and Former Harper's Editor, Dead at 64." *Knoxville News-Sentinel*, 5 August 1999, sec. A, p. 3.

States that although Morris "wrote more than a dozen critically acclaimed books, he was best known as the editor of Harper's Magazine from 1967–71.... 'He was a towering figure,' said Michael Curtis, senior fiction editor of The Atlantic Monthly magazine, a colleague who competed against him in the days when Mr. Morris was at Harper's." Curtis added, "I must say he also scared the bejesus out of us. We never folded our hand, but he made us look at it closely."

2031 Cawthon, Raad. "Eloquent in Voicing His Roots, Humanity." *Philadelphia Inquirer*, 5 August 1999, sec. D, pp. 1, 3.

Cawthon, a staff writer for the *Inquirer*, remembers that he first met Morris in 1981 in Oxford, Mississippi. He and other reporters at that time, all "wishing to be the youngest Turks of Southern journalism, knew of Morris." In his memoir *North Toward Home*, Morris "gave voice to a generation fighting through the dense thicket of what it means to be a white Southerner in America, possessed by a land whose more benighted history repels us, casting us out only to be called home again." The author, Cawthon notes, wrote numerous "mostly good" words, and the stories about him are numerous "and mostly good" as well. In the end, however, "It is not about the stories or even, amazingly, about what he wrote. It is about what a good friend Willie was, not just to me, but to us, that community of humans, Southern and non–Southern alike, who struggle with the perilous nature of our humanity." Republished in *Remembering Willie* (item 2094).

2032 Greenberg, Paul. "Goin' Home: On the Death of Willie Morris." *(Little Rock) Arkansas Democrat-Gazette*, 5 August 1999, sec. B, p. 6.

A syndicated opinion piece that surveys Morris's career and "brim-full" life. "He was not just a mirror of the South but a mirror that talked back, one that was always about ready to jump out of the frame and run off. Not just a reflection, but a bourbon-drinking, storytelling response and, when necessary, rebuke. Over the years he somehow became an elder without losing the spirit of his youth." Also published in the *(Memphis) Commercial Appeal* of 6 August 1999 and the *New York Post* of 7 August 1999. Republished in *Remembering Willie* (item 2097).

2033 [Lampton, Lucius.] "Goodbye to Our Good Old Boy: Willie Morris." *Magnolia (Miss.) Gazette*, 5 August 1999, sec. A, p. 2.

An editorial applauding Morris as "a brilliant man who loved Mississippi. He has left us a beautiful written legacy we will enjoy and treasure for years to come."

2034 Lampton, Lucius. "Willie Morris, Acclaimed Writer and Contributing Editor of *Magnolia Gazette*, Dies Suddenly in Jackson." *Magnolia (Miss.) Gazette*, 5 August 1999, sec. A, pp. 1, 4.

Not only an obituary but a detailed summary of Morris's funeral. "The service, held at the First United Methodist Church in Yazoo City, was dubbed 'A Celebration of the Life of Willie Morris.' The building was packed an hour before the service began.... Summit [Mississippi] native Curtis Wilkie, a well-known journalist and author, told the *Gazette* at the funeral: 'Willie was never meant to grow old. He was always such a little boy at heart. We will certainly miss him.'" Includes photographs of Morris and copies of book inscriptions.

2035 Lucas, Sherry. "Willie Morris to Be Buried Near Witch's Grave." *Clarion-Ledger*, 5 August 1999, sec. A, pp. 1, 6.

Announces that Morris will be buried today in the old section of Yazoo City's Glenwood Cemetery, thirteen paces due south of the witch's grave that he immortalized in his book *Good Old Boy*. His friends "worked hard" to locate a lot in this area of the cemetery, which dates to the 1840s. "'Willie had always said to me that he wanted to be buried in the old part of the cemetery he loved so much,' said Sam Olden. When he told Morris' widow, JoAnne Prichard, about the lot, 'she gave a big smile,' he said."

2036 Pickering, Charles W. "Chip" "Tribute to Willie Morris." U.S. House. 106th Cong., 1st sess. *Congressional Record*, 145, no. 114, daily ed. (5 August 1999), p. E1784.

Congressman Pickering (R-Miss.) eulogizes Morris in the U.S. House of Representatives. "Willie Morris wrote about the little things that make small-town life special — like football games, dogs, and hole-in-the-wall restaurants. He also wrote about the big things— like faith, family and friendship. But Willie never shied away from putting these heart-warming descriptions in the context of the South's racial history, or revealing the challenges of laying down its burden.... As someone who lived through the transition from the Old South to the New South, he had seen dramatic change in his homeland. But one way or another, he always found a way to say: 'We must do better.'"

2037 "What They're Saying About Morris." *Clarion-Ledger*, 5 August 1999, sec. A, p. 6.

"A good old boy remembered: tributes from journalists." Quotations from obituaries and eulogies that have appeared on the World Wide Web and in publications around the country.

2038 Dees, Jim. "North Toward Last Call." *Oxford Town*, no. 312 (5–11 August 1999), p. 3.

Recalls how Morris helped trigger "Oxford's evolution into Litville: a town where people wrote books, actually read them, and would even pay for them.... Willie was Mississippi's mentor and Oxford in particular owes him a great debt for lighting the creative fires that still burn here late into the starry night." A photograph of Morris dominates the cover of this issue of *Oxford Town*, which is published by the *Oxford (Miss.) Eagle*.

2039 Associated Press. "Mississippi Remembers Morris at Memorial, Funeral." *Oxford (Miss.) Eagle*, 6 August 1999, sec. A, pp. 1, 12.

"From famous authors to hometown friends, they came from around the coun[t]ry to bid farewell to Willie Morris in the small Mississippi Delta town so dear to one of Mississippi's literary legends. Mourners filled the blond-brick First United Methodist Church Thursday afternoon to hear those close to the master storyteller recall their favorite Morris memories. Many who managed to get inside the church had to stand along the walls."

2040 Bragg, Rick. "To a Beloved Native Son, A Mississippi Farewell." *New York Times*, 6 August 1999, sec. A, p. 10.

A moving account of Morris's funeral. "Among the people who came to bid farewell today were literary types he had helped somehow along the way and perfect strangers who had read his words and just wanted to say goodbye. One of them, a house painter from Tuscaloosa, Ala., just shook his head when asked why he had come, and said, 'How could I not?'" Republished in *Remembering Willie* (item 2092).

2041 Harden, Mike. "However Brief Their Meeting, Willie Morris Made Impact." *Columbus Dispatch*, 6 August 1999, sec. H, p. 1.

An Ohio reporter remembers his brief visit with Morris. "To have known Morris is to understand that being truly Southern is not simply a geographic claim — any more than being truly Buddhist could be a mere religious preference. It is in the marrow, the viscera, every drawn breath.... Though I barely knew him, I liked him much and am saddened by his death."

2042 Lucas, Sherry. "'Power Crowd' Celebrates Author's Life." *Clarion-Ledger*, 6 August 1999, sec. A, pp. 1, 7.

"More than 400 writers, artists, judges, lawyers, politicians, movie people, musicians, businessmen, townsfolk, children and, always, readers, came to First United Methodist Church and the cemetery in Yazoo City to say goodbye and thanks to the man whose tales entertained and enlightened." The "power crowd," as one Yazoo resident called the assemblage, included authors David Halberstam, William Styron, John Grisham, Richard Ford, and Winston Groom. Also present were film producers Mark Johnson and Fred Zollo, Baptist minister and civil rights activist Will D. Campbell, former Mississippi Governor William Winter, and former U.S. Agriculture Secretary Mike Espy. During the funeral service, "Morris' sense of justice, struggle for equality, impish humor, keen intelligence, Southern charm and unshakable loyalty to his beloved home state were mentioned."

2043 "Morris Memories." *Clarion-Ledger*, 6 August 1999, sec. A, p. 7.

Artist William Dunlap, business executive Charles Henry, former Ole Miss basketball coach Ed Murphy, and authors Josephine Ayres Haxton (Ellen Douglas) and Rick Bragg remember Morris. Haxton, who writes under the pseudonym Ellen Douglas, compares Morris to Mark Twain's Huckleberry Finn and Tom Sawyer: "Willie had Huck's honor and toughness of spirit. He had Tom's love of a joke. And Mark Twain's incisive intelligence. And like Huck and Tom, I know he'd like to be here now, at his own funeral."

2044 Watkins, Billy. "'Good Old Boy' Goes Out Like a Statesman." *Clarion-Ledger*, 6 August 1999, sec, A, pp. 1, 7.

Reports that an estimated seven hundred persons walked by Morris's pecan casket to pay their respects as he lay in state in the Old Capitol in Jackson. He was the first Mississippian since Senator John C. Stennis in 1995 to be accorded this recognition. Said former Governor William Winter, a Morris neighbor: "There are certain Mississippians who have contributed so much to this state who are worthy of this special honor. Willie was without question one of those."

2045 "Willie Morris Goes Home." *San Antonio Express-News*, 6 August 1999, sec. B, p. 4.

Editorially pays tribute to Morris, recognizing him as "one of the most important writers and editors of his generation.... Not simply a Mississippi writer or Southern writer, Morris was an American writer who leaves an enduring stamp on his craft."

2046 Kalich, Tim. "Mississippi Loves Willie Morris." *Yazoo Herald*, 7 August 1999, p. 4.

An editorial contending that "Willie Morris embodied the soul of Mississippi and had the talent to put that complexity on paper. He will be missed, but his contributions will endure."

2047 Maddry, Larry. "Tribute: One of South's Most Eloquent Voices Lost in Morris' Death." *(Norfolk) Virginian-Pilot and The Ledger Star*, 7 August 1999, sec. E, p. 1.

Recalls meeting Morris in the 1970s in an old plantation house in Murfreesboro, North Carolina. "He wasn't impressive physically. Kinda double-jowled, face as round as a Moon Pie, with brown, curly hair sloping across his brow. But very polite to everybody: 'Yes, ma'am, I live in New York City now. That's what makes it so good to be down here. Kinda get back to your roots, you know.' ... All the guests later said how decent, unassuming and polite Willie Morris was."

2048 Sikes, Vernon. "Willie Makes Final Trip Home." *Yazoo Herald*, 7 August 1999, pp. 1, 14.

Coverage of Morris's funeral in a page-1 feature story with banner headline and both color and black-and-white photographs. "More than a time of mourning, Willie Morris' funeral was a celebration of his life. The Rev. Will D. Campbell said, 'His life was a speech for 64 years. A good speech deserves a good hand. Will you join me in a standing ovation?' And with that invitation, the hundreds of family, friends and admirers who had gathered at Yazoo City's First United Methodist Church on Thursday afternoon did just that. Exactly 28 seconds worth of rousing applause."

2049 Clanton, Chad. "The Magic of Morris: Southern Author Was Able to Speak to the Best Parts of Ourselves." *Austin American-Statesman*, 8 August 1999, sec. H, p. 3.

Reminisces about Morris in an op-ed article, declaring that "everything Willie did was magic. Because he made it magic. I'm not talking about something supernatural, although sometimes it seemed that way. Willie's magic was his unique ability [to] speak to the best parts of ourselves, both in his books and in person, and to make them better." Republished in *Remembering Willie* (item 2095).

2050 Johnson, Rheta Grimsley. "In Reality, Willie Morris Turned South Toward Home." *Atlanta Journal-Constitution*, 8 August 1999, sec. D, p. 3.

A syndicated columnist recounts her first

meeting with Morris and observes that "his charm lived up to reputation. We had dinner at a restaurant where everybody knew him, and it wasn't so much a meal as a love feast. Willie's admirers kept stopping by the table to compliment him on one piece of writing or another, quoting whole passages by rote as if they were taking oral exams. Willie beamed, obviously enjoying the sound of his own words come alive." Republished in *Remembering Willie* (item 2099).

2051 Mathis, Deborah. "Willie Morris: Life Not Always Fair, But He Relished It." *Clarion-Ledger*, 8 August 1999, sec. H, p. 5.

Asserts that although "there are new great writers in the wings who will inspire and educate and entertain," none will compete with Morris. "Willie Morris was one of my heroes, one of my role models. I admired his cellular understanding of human nature, his deep sweet love of the crazy, double-edged South, his mastery of words and his wisdom in putting them together." Heartfelt remarks by a syndicated columnist, which were also published in the *(Cocoa) Florida Today* of 11 August 1999 and the *(Boise) Idaho Statesman* of 12 August 1999. Republished in *Remembering Willie* (item 2100).

2052 Clinton, William J. "Statement on the Death of Willie Morris." *Weekly Compilation of Presidential Documents* 35 (9 August 1999), p. 1552.

In a press release and eulogy, President Clinton laments the passing of Morris. "Hillary and I were greatly saddened to learn of the death of our good friend Willie Morris. When I was a senior in college, I was captivated by his wonderful memoir, 'North Toward Home.'" Clinton met Morris in New York City when the author was editing *Harper's Magazine*. "In the 1980's, we became reacquainted, and I have enjoyed his wit, warmth, and wisdom ever since.... He will take his place beside Faulkner and Welty in the pantheon of the South's greatest writers." See also items 1982 and 2062.

2053 Cleveland, Rick. "Willie Really Was a Good Ol' Boy." *Clarion-Ledger*, 10 August 1999, sec. D, pp. 1, 4.

Shares "so many memories" about his friend Morris and provides details about the book the author was just beginning to write when he died, *One for My Daddy: A Baseball Memory*. "It would have been a personal memoir, the kind that brought out the best in Willie.... It would have been about how baseball links fathers and sons and creates continuity through the generations." His widow, JoAnne Prichard, said, "I've never seen Willie so excited about a book. This was one he had been thinking about for a long time. He was itching to get at it." Republished in *Remembering Willie* (item 2096).

2054 Wilkinson, Stephen H. "Thank You, Willie, for Touching My Life." *Clarion-Ledger*, 10 August 1999, sec. A, p. 6.

A letter to the editor by a former waiter at an Oxford, Mississippi, restaurant, who occasionally had served Morris and his friends. "He tipped good. But more important, it was a chance to hang out with Willie. Never mind he was an icon. He had an unassuming presence. All it took was to be around Willie one time, and he was your friend."

2055 Wills, Garry. "Morris Led a Writer's Life, Era." *(Albany) Times-Union*, 10 August 1999, sec. A, p. 11.

Features Morris's accomplishments as editor of *Harper's* in the 1960s, the "golden age for serious magazines." *Harper's* "made news of its own when it appointed a 32-year-old author as its editor in chief. Morris was a maverick, a hard-drinking, poetic soul not easily imagined in a managerial post. His appointment and early feats drew the kind of attention that Tina Brown gets now when she becomes the editor of another magazine."

2056 Sikes, Vernon. "City Officials Honor Morris with Resolution." *Yazoo Herald*, 11 August 1999, p. 1.

On August 9, the mayor and aldermen of Yazoo City "unanimously approved a resolution of remembrance in appreciation of Willie Morris and his many years of contributions to the city." In the resolution, the city officials said "Mr. Morris 'distinguished himself and Yazoo City through his unique ability to capture and convey the essence of the Southern spirit.' They also noted that during his early years of living in Yazoo City, he 'helped establish the reservoir of imagination and experience from which he created literature. Through his colorful writings about his Yazoo City friends, haunts and the imaginative portrayal of the Witch's burning of the town, he created folklore for our community.'" The concluding portion of the resolution stated that Morris should "be remembered for his everlasting contribution to our community, his distinguished literary career and for his love of Yazoo City, his hometown."

2057 Lampton, Lucius. "Farewell to Our Huckleberry Friend, Willie Morris." *Magnolia (Miss.) Gazette*, 12 August 1999, sec. A, p. 12.

Photographs of Morris's funeral in Yazoo City. "At the end of the service, taps with echo was performed. Morris had written of playing taps with echo in several of his books, and the buglers elegantly and emotionally closed a memorable salute to Mississippi's grand man of letters."

2058 Minor, Bill. "Some Say Willie Morris Was Mississippi's 2nd William Faulkner; I Called Him Friend." *Clarion-Ledger*, 12 August 1999, sec. A, p. 13.

A political columnist who knew Morris for thirty years reminisces about his friend. "There's no one left I can think of with his literary credentials and a smidgen of his network of friends who can — and will — explain this baffling state and win compassion and understanding of it nationally. It was so fitting that Willie, the quintessential good ole boy from Yazoo City, was the first Mississippi writer to lie in state in Mississippi's Old Capitol." Republished in *Remembering Willie* (item 2101).

2059 "More Tributes to Willie Morris Pour In." *Yazoo Herald*, 14 August 1999, sec. A, p. 4.

Excerpts from six letters to the editor. "The sudden and untimely death last week of Yazoo City's native son, Willie Morris, has stunned his friends, fans, and admirers around the country. We publish here excerpts from statements of affection and appreciation that have come across our editorial desk in the past few days."

2060 Buchholz, Brad. "Southern Comfort: Considering Willie Morris, 'North Toward Home,' and the Things That Last." *Austin American-Statesman*, 15 August 1999, sec. K, pp. 1, 10.

A lengthy, emotional paean to both Morris and his *North Toward Home*. Newspaper reporter Buchholz met Morris in the spring of 1982 in Philadelphia, Mississippi, while researching a story on football sensation Marcus Dupree. Buchholz did not share Morris's optimistic view that the athlete had brought black and white townspeople together, and he did not read the author's 1983 book *The Courting of Marcus Dupree*. "Instead, I turned to 'North Toward Home.' I'd heard so much about the masterpiece. I wondered: Was it really that good? Would I recognize the man in Philadelphia as its author? From the very first pages, I was captivated — inspired by the lyric nature of the prose, the confidence of the voice. Though I was certainly no child of the South — nor headed to New York — the book struck a chord within me with its sensitivity, its humanity, its idealism."

2061 Wilson, Charles Reagan. "Willie Morris' Southern Way of Death." *(Raleigh, N.C.) News & Observer*, 15 August 1999, sec. D, pp. 1, 5.

The director of The Center for the Study of Southern Culture at the University of Mississippi eulogizes Morris while exploring the "Southern way of death." He believes that Morris "would have enjoyed the ceremonies and storytelling" at his funeral, for he "was a writer whose work reflected a fascination with traditional Southern attitudes toward mortality.... Anyone who knew his tales of graveyards and ancestors and what he called his own 'melancholy Southern moods' understood that, for him, an awareness of death's brooding presence among the living was a part of his regional inheritance. The burden of the Southern past never seemed far from him, and his embrace of traditional ways made him a revealing example of how Southerners have thought about death." Wilson devotes the second half of his testimonial to a detailed description of Morris's funeral. He published similar remarks concerning the memorial service in the newsletter of The Center for the Study of Southern Culture: "Willie Morris, 1934–19[9]9." *Southern Register* (Fall 1999), pp. 11–12.

2062 Clinton, Bill. "Eulogy." *Time* 154 (16 August 1999), p. 21.

The President of the United States honors his friend Morris. "Willie's *North Toward Home* was a beautifully written, evocative portrait of one person's love for the South who had profound regret over the racial situation. It helped a lot of people like me who wanted to see the world and do well up north but also come home and live in the South." Republished in *Remembering Willie* (item 2093). See also items 1982 and 2052.

2063 Meacham, Jon. "Twilight South." *Newsweek* 134 (16 August 1999), p. 8.

A two-paragraph tribute that recognizes Morris's love for his beloved Mississippi. "Morris spent much of his life pondering — and evoking — the twilight world many Southerners inhabit, where manners and morals coexist with the enduring legacy of Jim Crow." *Newsweek* editor Meacham included an excerpt from *North Toward Home* in his *Voices in Our Blood* (item 918).

2064 "People in the News." *U.S. News & World Report* 127 (16–23 August 1999), p. 18.

A notice of Morris's death. "A few days before he died of a heart attack last week in Jackson, he was ... in New York at a private screening of an upcoming film based on his book *My Dog Skip*. Friends said he liked it a lot."

2065 Dugger, Ronnie. "South Toward Home." *Texas Observer*, 20 August 1999, pp. 3–4.

Dugger relates that when he was editing the *Texas Observer* in the mid–1950s, he met Morris, "the feisty young editor of the *Daily Texan*." Dugger recalls both fond memories and circumstances not nearly as pleasant. "He wrote carefully, editing his typewriter lines a lot, spinning out his lofted flowers of crafted and recrafted prose, working for rhythms and effects he felt before he knew them." Morris "after a while" returned home to Mississippi, "but things came to have a way of going wrong for him." Occasionally he would "get drunk and sound not just pompous, but too pompous—I saw him once like that among students at a university, and, not knowing what to do, quietly stole away."

2066 Hawtree, Christopher. "Obituary: Willie Morris." *(London) Independent*, 20 August 1999, p. 7.

Emphasizes Morris's contributions to *Harper's Magazine*, his memoir *North Toward Home*, and his years at Oxford University. "A taste for good prose—whether highly wrought or demotic—ran in Morris's blood, and he credited much of his education to his time in Oxford as a Rhodes Scholar, whose afternoons in the cinema with Dennis Potter were as stimulating as anything that New College had to offer (something overlooked by Humphrey Carpenter in his hefty 1998 biography of the dramatist)."

2067 Morris, JoAnne Prichard, and David Rae Morris. "A Loving 'Thank-You' from the Family of Willie Morris to His Hometown Folks." *Yazoo Herald*, 21 August 1999, sec. A, p. 4.

A lengthy letter to the editor in which Morris's widow and son thank residents of the author's hometown for their help and support during the burial preparations and funeral service. "Willie made his final journey home [to Yazoo City] on August 5, and we'll be forever grateful to all the many wonderful people in Yazoo City who worked so hard to welcome him back."

2068 Thomas, Bill. "Willie, Go Home to the South You Painted with Words." *(Memphis) Commercial Appeal*, 22 August 1999, sec. F, p. 1.

Thomas, who interviewed Morris for a newspaper profile in February 1980 (item 1634), looks back on the day in Oxford when he first met the man who would become "a valued friend over the years." Although he had planned to talk to the author in his faculty house on the University of Mississippi campus, Morris "suggested a trip to the cemetery where he could walk his dog, Pete, and visit the grave of William Faulkner, whose spirit still holds sway over Oxford town."

2069 Waddle, Ray. "As the South Seems to Reinvent Itself, One Southern Voice Is Silent." *(Nashville) Tennessean*, 25 August 1999, sec. A, p. 11.

Opines that the South has always been "a spiritual condition," and the death of Morris "throws it in doubt. His death, by heart attack, robs the South of a key shaper of identity in these giddy days of cyberspace and multiculturalism. Morris, 64, was a big-hearted Mississippian, a chronicler of regional contradictions and self-defeats, one of the South's great interpreters to the world."

2070 Younge, Gary. "Willie Morris: Editor and Chronicler of the American South." *(Manchester, Eng.) Guardian*, 27 August 1999, p. 28.

While summing up Morris's career, Younge notes that when the author returned to the South as writer-in-residence at the University of Mississippi, he was "something of a pioneer, one of the few southern scholars at the time who was interested not only in the south itself but in its developing relationship with the rest of America. Like others, he was keen to understand how the north had affected the south, particularly since the civil war.... But unlike others, Morris also had a keen interest in how the south had influenced the rest of the nation, giving it everybody from Elvis to BB King, from Clinton to Newt Gingrich."

2071 Graham, Don. "Don Graham's Texas Classics." *Texas Monthly* 27 (September 1999), p. 30.

Reexamines *North Toward Home*, Morris's "precocious autobiography," after the author's death. The center section, titled "Texas," stands as "one of the best accounts we have of what the state and its leading university were like during the supposedly torpid Eisenhower years." The book is "a fitting enough memorial to a lifetime spent in pursuit of Big Ideas: Race, Education, Politics, and Literature."

2072 Barrett, Dawn Dillon. "What's In a Name?: Memories of Willie Morris." *Magnolia (Miss.) Gazette*, 16 September 1999, sec. A, p. 12.

Barrett recollects that during a long-ago visit with Morris, she told him that she had co-authored a book but had failed to find a publisher. Morris admitted that this was a problem that most beginning writers faced. "'I'll tell you what,' he said. 'I know a guy from North Mississippi who's had the same problem, but I think he's finally found somebody. I don't think he'll mind if I give you his name and address. He may be able to advise you.'" The man's name was "completely unfamiliar" to Barrett, and she soon forgot about it. Years later she found the notebook in which Morris had written the name and address of John Grisham, "arguably the best-selling author in the world."

2073 Clay, Maude Schuyler. "Southern Scenes." *Oxford American*, no. 29 (September/October 1999), p. 112.

A full-page photograph of a pensive Morris, taken in Jackson, Mississippi, in 1993.

2074 Styron, William. "It Cannot Be Long: Remembering a Friend." *Oxford American*, no. 29 (September/October 1999), p. 111.

Styron's eulogy to Morris, given at his funeral on August 5 in Yazoo City, Mississippi. He recalls the day in the mid–1960s when he "first laid eyes on Willie," recounts several favorite stories about him, and details some of his distinguishing traits. "As I got to know Willie and became a close and devoted friend, I learned certain immutable things about him. I learned that he was unshakably loyal,... that he was wickedly funny, that his country-boy openheartedness and candor masked an encyclopedic knowledge and an elegantly furnished mind, that he was moody and had a streak of dark paranoia that usually evaporated on a comic note,... that his furiously driven literary imagination allowed him to produce several unostentatious masterworks; that in him, finally, there was an essential nobility of spirit — no one ever possessed such a ready and ungrudging heart." Also published in *Remembering Willie* (item 2083).

2075 Tartt, Donna. "Willie Morris, 1934–1999." *Oxford American*, no. 29 (September/October 1999), pp. 108–110.

Tartt, the best-selling author of *A Secret History*, first met Morris when she was seventeen and a freshman at the University of Mississippi, and he was a "great, mythical Mr. Micawber of a figure" in Oxford. She provides moving recollections of him and their friendship, remembering that he "was a boy in all the very best ways: quick to make friends, quick to take sides, quick to laughter and outrage and tears and mischief. Because of his unsuspicious good nature, he was not always so quick to defend himself, or to look out for his own best interests, but no one leapt more rapidly to the aid of a friend, and he mourned the disappointments of others as if they were his own." Republished in *Remembering Willie* (item 2104) and *Best of "The Oxford American": Ten Years from the Southern Magazine of Good Writing*, edited by Marc Smirnoff. Athens, Ga.: Hill Street Press, 2002, pp. 143–51. Republished as "My Friend, My Mentor, My Inspiration" in the *(Manchester, Eng.) Guardian* of 20 July 2002.

2076 Jones, Kaylie. "Willie Morris Remembered." *James Jones Literary Society [Newsletter]* 9 (Fall 1999), pp. 1, 4.

Jones, the daughter of novelist James Jones, looks back on her and her father's close ties to Morris. She attended Morris's funeral and noticed that all of the eulogists "touched upon his brilliance, his kindness, his generosity of spirit and his jokester's sense of humor. Which brought to my mind those first months when my family moved to Bridgehampton in 1975, when Willie would disguise his voice and pretend to be the dog catcher — he'd tell us he had our dogs but would give them back to us for a ransom.... Willie had been so kind and generous to me during the whole period of my father's illness and then after his death."

2077 Yoder, Ed. "Willie Morris, 1934–1999: A Personal Memoir." *American Oxonian* 86 (Fall 1999), pp. 286–93.

"A Personal Memoir" is a fitting subtitle of this moving essay, for as Yoder mentions on the first page, he and Morris "had been the best of friends for more than forty-three years— even before destiny put us on the same boat to Oxford in early October 1956." Because Morris's "distinctions, literary and civic, to say nothing of his good works, would require many pages to list," Yoder singles out three of his friend's "paramount accomplishments." Two are literary in nature: his editorship of *Harper's Magazine*, in which "he transformed a sedate magazine into the most vital and admired forum in the country," and his "precocious" and "immortal" autobiography *North Toward Home*. The third represents "an effort of will and integration" rather than a material achievement. After he returned to Mississippi following "two decades of exile," Morris "did more than any Mississippian of his generation to recall his troubled state from the brink of political terrorism, to hearten its better angels and to coax it towards the vibrant racial goodwill that prevails there today." Republished in *Remembering Willie* (item 2108). See also item 1986.

2078 Lampton, Lucius. "Goodbye to Mississippi's Good Old Boy: Willie Morris." *Journal of the Mississippi State Medical Association* 40 (October 1999), pp. 350–53.

A lengthy editorial celebrating Morris's literary career, especially his years in Pike County, Mississippi, where he lived and wrote in a house owned by his friend Dr. Verner Holmes. Vern, Dr. Holmes's son, "recalls that Morris's book *Good Old Boy and the Witch of Yazoo* was conceived and written in Pike County: 'When mother (Mrs. Emma Holmes) died, the Holmes family and Willie gathered around the kitchen table on Lissa Drive after the graveside service. It was there that the book *Good Old Boy and the Witch of Yazoo* was born. My niece Lyn Covington of McComb contributed the idea and Willie started the outline for the book there at the table.'" See also items 1698 and 1816.

2079 Clanton, Chad. "Remembering Willie." *Southern Living* 34 (December 1999), pp. 50–51.

In a tribute to Morris, "one of his great and many fans" recounts a trip he and the author spent along the back roads of the Mississippi Delta. "Willie Morris had shown me something along Mississippi's dirt roads and state highways. Even though under an impending book deadline, he had put down his pen and given me a chance to live in his books for a day. As the plane lifted off from Jackson and headed west toward my Texas home, I realized that Willie Morris had taught me as much about generosity and meaningfulness as he had his complex and beloved Mississippi."

2080 Hedblad, Alan, and Joyce Nakamura. "Morris, Willie 1934–1999." In *Contemporary Authors: A Bio-Bibliographical Guide to Current Writers in Fiction, General Nonfiction, Poetry, Journalism, Drama, Motion Pictures, Television, and Other Fields*, edited by Alan Hedblad and Joyce Nakamura. Vol. 183. Detroit: Gale Research Co., 2000, p. 270.

An obituary notice. "Author and journalist. Morris, the youngest editor-in-chief of *Harper's* magazine, grew up in the South and was so influenced by the region that it became the basis for much of his work."

2081 *Remembering Willie*. Jackson: University Press of Mississippi, 2000.

This "collection of tributes memorializing Willie Morris, the acclaimed southern author" comprises "the eulogies given at his funeral on 5 August [1999] in Yazoo City, Mississippi, and some of the many tributes published in the days following his death." The volume also includes Morris's "A Love That Transcends Sadness" from *Parade* magazine (item 752; see also item 914). The speakers' and authors' names represent the titles of the tributes in *Remembering Willie*; bibliographic details are recorded at the end of the volume. The nine eulogies appear first in the book (items 2082 to 2090), followed by the eighteen previously published testimonials (items 2091 to 2108):

2082 "Reverend Will D. Campbell." In *Remembering Willie*, pp. 11–12 (see item 2081).

A Baptist minister and social activist exhorts mourners to "softly speak [Morris's] name and move on." Campbell, who knew the author for many years, also encourages them to "let him go." And "as we let him go we ask of this sweet soul, this big man-little boy combo, this simple and complex genius, this literary giant whose likeness we are not apt to see again ... one last request. Save for us, at our last, old pal, some yarns to spin, some phrases to turn, new words to learn, a place at your table with a glass of something fine of the grape, and give us a big Willie Morris belly laugh to welcome us home."

2083 "William Styron." In *Remembering Willie*, pp. 13–16 (see item 2081).

A funeral eulogy first published in the *Oxford American* as "It Cannot Be Long: Remembering a Friend" (item 2074).

2084 "David Halberstam." In *Remembering Willie*, pp. 17–21 (see item 2081).

To illustrate how "the little boy in Willie always lived," Halberstam recalls two pranks Morris played on him when they were both working for *Harper's Magazine*. But "behind all the charm and all the jokes," Halberstam continues, was Morris's painful realization that his beloved Mississippi "could not be whole" until it addressed its long history of racial discrimination. "For he loved good writing and good books, but what he loved best was this region and this country. And he wanted the country to be made whole, and he knew that that could not happen until this most troubled part of the country entered a modern age."

2085 "Mike Espy." In *Remembering Willie*, pp. 22–23 (see item 2081).

Former U.S. Secretary of Agriculture Espy remembers that he last spoke with Morris soon after the "local screening" of the motion picture *Ghosts of Mississippi*. While the two friends were having dinner with film director Rob Reiner and actor Alec Baldwin, "I watched [Morris] talk and was reminded again of his abundant love of this place" [Mississippi]. As Espy listened, he began to realize that Morris wanted Reiner and Baldwin to know "that amiability does not necessarily make one less competitive.... In code that only colleagues can appreciate, he let them know that caricatures only go so far — that *this* South is changing — and can't forever be captured and encased within a celluloid frame."

2086 "Josephine Ayres Haxton (Ellen Douglas)." In *Remembering Willie*, pp. 24–25 (see item 2081).

Haxton, who writes under the pseudonym Ellen Douglas, recollects that she first met Morris while he was signing copies of *North Toward Home* in Greenville, Mississippi. "He was having a grand time and he made it an exciting time for everyone, and that's my overriding memory of him in his life — having a grand time and making it exciting for everyone.... Willie cared for everything and everyone. His passion for football produced that remarkable book, *The Courting of Marcus Dupree*. His love of dogs and cats, the playful histories of his pets.... He cared about his family, his friends, his colleagues, and he cared about the lives of the waiter at the Mayflower and the lady behind the cash register at the Jitney."

2087 "Governor William F. Winter." In *Remembering Willie*, pp. 26–27 (see item 2081).

The former governor of Mississippi relates that he first heard of Morris in the late 1960s "when I was looking desperately for some voices that would speak of what I thought the South was really about — of civility and courtesy and kindness and tolerance — not of rage and hate and bitterness and bigotry. I found in his writings the special insight of one whose affection for his home state was not only undiminished but reinforced by his recognition of our weaknesses as well as our strengths and especially of our need to reach out to more, indeed to all, of our neighbors and to erase the barriers that separated us from one another."

2088 "Harriet DeCell Kuykendall." In *Remembering Willie*, pp. 28–30 (see item 2081).

Morris's high school algebra teacher recounts some of her favorite memories of her pupil. In 1967, Morris was the "headliner" during Yazoo City's National Library Week festivities. "Willie insisted that he must talk at the all-black high school, ND Taylor, if he spoke at the all-white high school. I think such actions helped Yazoo get over the integration hurdle three years later.... The reaction of the Yazooans to *North Toward Home* was very interesting. A self-conscious disbelief was prevalent: 'Willie couldn't have done that, because I never did that.' As if all our experiences were cloned. Yazoo's 'tunnel vision' was opened a bit — the beginning of a much greater sophistication."

2089 "Jill Conner Browne." In *Remembering Willie*, pp. 31–32 (see item 2081).

Browne, author of *The Sweet Potato Queens' Book of Love*, declares that "Willie Morris had a remarkable effect on people. I first identified it by observing my daughter Bailey with him. She is very, very shy. But not with Willie. He brought out the best in her. It took about two seconds in that train of thought to see that he did the same thing for all of us. We knew — on a cellular level — how special he was.... Knowing how special he was made us feel better about ourselves, because he gave us his time and attention."

2090 "Winston F. Groom." In *Remembering Willie*, pp. 33–34 (see item 2081).

In 1976, ten years before he published *Forrest Gump*, Groom worked with Morris on the *Washington Star* newspaper. Morris inspired him to abandon journalism for novel writing, and in his graveside eulogy Groom expresses his gratitude to his friend. "And so, finally, and I hope it's not too late, Thank you, Willie, for all your generosity to all the younger writers you helped — some of us not so young anymore — for all the time and energy and genuine caring for the written word and encouragement and efforts to make the unworkable work. It is a debt that can never be repaid. Thank you."

2091 "Peter Applebome." In *Remembering Willie*, pp. 35–38 (see item 2081).

A tribute, "Willie Morris, 64, Writer on the Southern Experience," originally published in the *New York Times* (item 2001).

2092 "Rick Bragg." In *Remembering Willie*, pp. 39–42 (see item 2081).

A tribute, "To a Beloved Native Son, A Mississippi Farewell," originally published in the *New York Times* (item 2040).

2093 "President Bill Clinton." In *Remembering Willie*, p. 43 (see item 2081).

A tribute, "Eulogy," originally published in *Time* (item 2062).

2094 "Raad Cawthon." In *Remembering Willie*, pp. 44–49 (see item 2081).

A tribute, "Eloquent in Voicing His Roots, Humanity," originally published in the *Philadelphia Inquirer* (item 2031).

2095 "Chad Clanton." In *Remembering Willie*, pp. 50–52 (see item 2081).

A tribute, "The Magic of Morris: Southern Author Was Able to Speak to the Best Parts of Ourselves," originally published in the *Austin American-Statesman* (item 2049).

2096 "Rick Cleveland." In *Remembering Willie*, pp. 53–58 (see item 2081).

A tribute, "Willie Really Was a Good Ol' Boy," originally published in the *Clarion-Ledger* (item 2053).

2097 "Paul Greenberg." In *Remembering Willie*, pp. 59–62 (see item 2081).

A tribute, "Goin' Home: On the Death of Willie Morris," originally published in the *(Little Rock) Arkansas Democrat-Gazette* (item 2032).

2098 "Orley Hood." In *Remembering Willie*, pp. 63–64 (see item 2081).

A tribute, "Our Good Old Boy Always Stood Up for His Mississippi," originally published in the *Clarion-Ledger* (item 2013).

2099 "Rheta Grimsley Johnson." In *Remembering Willie*, pp. 65–67 (see item 2081).

A tribute, "In Reality, Willie Morris Turned South Toward Home," originally published in the *Atlanta Journal-Constitution* (item 2050).

2100 "Deborah Mathis." In *Remembering Willie*, pp. 68–70 (see item 2081).

A tribute, "Willie Morris: Life Not Always Fair, But He Relished It," originally published in the *Clarion-Ledger* (item 2051).

2101 "Bill Minor." In *Remembering Willie*, pp. 71–72 (see item 2081).

A tribute, "Some Say Willie Morris Was Mississippi's 2nd William Faulkner; I Called Him Friend," originally published in the *Clarion-Ledger* (item 2058).

2102 "Sid Salter." In *Remembering Willie*, pp. 73–75 (see item 2081).

A tribute, "Up in 'Willie's Heaven,' Morris Will Be Telling Mississippi Stories That God Will Want to Hear," originally published in the *Scott County (Miss.) Times* (item 2022).

2103 "Michael Skube." In *Remembering Willie*, pp. 76–79 (see item 2081).

A tribute, "A Reverence for Writing: Once a Shining Star at Harper's, Troubled Life Ends on Happier Note," originally published in the *Atlanta Constitution* (item 2023).

2104 "Donna Tartt." In *Remembering Willie*, pp. 80–88 (see item 2081).

A tribute, "Willie Morris, 1934–1999," originally published in the *Oxford American* (item 2075).

2105 "Chris Thompson." In *Remembering Willie*, pp. 89–92 (see item 2081).

A tribute, "Farewell to Mississippi's 'Good Ole Boy,'" originally published in the University of Mississippi *Daily Mississippian* (item 2009).

2106 "Billy Watkins." In *Remembering Willie*, pp. 93–95 (see item 2081).

A tribute, "Willie Morris: A Few Last Words," originally published in the *Clarion-Ledger* (item 2024).

2107 "Linton Weeks." In *Remembering Willie*, pp. 96–100 (see item 2081).

A tribute, "Appreciation: Willie Morris, Heart of the South," originally published in the *Washington Post* (item 2026).

2108 "Edwin M. Yoder, Jr." In *Remembering Willie*, pp. 101–110 (see item 2081).

A tribute, "Willie Morris, 1934–1999: A Personal Memoir," originally published in the *American Oxonian* (item 2077).

2109 Ford, Richard. "Southern Manners." *New York Times Magazine*, 2 January 2000, p. 45.

Novelist Ford remembers the kindness and "sweet ardor" of Morris. "Willie Morris was a man who knew how to act — a dying art in our day. Doing so required him not only to look for the good in others but also to search for it diligently in himself, and to put both into play.... He was a smart, decent, mirthful, valuable man, and in Mississippi, he was larger than life, though, persuasively, never better than life."

PART IV

A Sense of History: Tracing the Civil War with Willie Morris

In 1975, James Bellows, editor of the Washington Star, *inaugurated a "writer-in-residence" program in which writers would temporarily live in the Washington, D.C., area and contribute several columns a week to the newspaper on topics of their choice. Willie Morris's friend Edwin M. Yoder Jr. was then associate editor and editorial pages editor of the* Star, *and Bellows asked him to contact Morris to see if he might be interested in participating. Morris, at the time living in Bridgehampton, New York, joined the staff in January 1976, replacing the previous writer-in-residence, New York City journalist Jimmy Breslin. From January to March, Morris wrote twenty-two columns for the* Washington Star, *which represented, he remarked a few years later, "the best journalism of my life."**

Morris explains in James Jones: A Friendship *that in February 1976, Jones "wanted a break from his book, and he brought down his son Jamie and my son David, who were both then fifteen, for a two-week visit."† After sightseeing around Washington, the four set out in Jones's red pickup truck on a tour of several battlefields. The three columns that Morris wrote about their experiences (items 823 to 825) are reprinted here.*

In Morris's first article, he notes that they visited the Jefferson Memorial on George Washington's birthday. The column appeared in the Star *on February 17, so he undoubtedly meant Abraham Lincoln's birthday (February 12 as opposed to February 22). In the second piece, he mentions a "singer of masculine eminence." When Morris revised the article for publication in* Terrains of the Heart and Other Essays on Home, *he named Glen Campbell as the celebrity.*

Prelude to Setting Off in a Camper to History

Every time I live in Washington for a while, I find myself looking for the common things that hold Americans together. It's not even a conscious thing, and my mind never particularly worked that way when I served my stretch on Manhattan Island. But last night at sunset, going to look at the Jefferson Memorial on Washington's Birthday with my sixteen-year-old son David visiting from New York City and a friend who lives among the

*Jim Bellows, *The Last Editor: How I Saved the "New York Times," the "Washington Post," and the "Los Angeles Times" from Dullness and Complacency* (Kansas City: Andrews McMeel Publishing, 2002), p. 187.
†Willie Morris, *James Jones: A Friendship* (Garden City, N.Y.: Doubleday & Co., 1978), p. 224.

potato fields of Long Island and his fifteen-year-old boy whom we call Jamie, it was no surprise that the talk turned to that thin skein which holds the civilization together.

I suppose that's not a bad topic for fathers and sons to talk about around here at this time of the year.

My friend is a student of all this who just moved his family back to America after fifteen years on the Isle St. Louis in Paris. He smokes nauseating cigars and once wrote a book called *From Here to Eternity* and another called *The Thin Red Line*, and wherever he goes he carries several knives he got off the Japs at Guadalcanal. The four of us are about to take a red pick-up truck with a camper in the back down to Chancellorsville, Spotsylvania, and the Wilderness to listen to the rustlings of the ghosts of eighteen-year-old boys, and then on to Harpers Ferry and Antietam, from which the next report, God willing, will emanate, unless the writer vanishes into those terrible old echoes of the Sunken Road.

My friend and I discovered as we looked across the Potomac from our pick-up truck that Washington reminds us both of Rome — not that it's as old as ancient Rome or that it even looks much like Rome, but that it too may someday many years from now be ruins, and that some future scholar may conclude there probably was some kind of public meeting place here.

Not that we for a moment wished it, Lord knows, especially in that spectacular twilight and in the company of our two American boys, and I'm sure we would get down our knees and pray, if that could do it, that our hegemony will endure.

Surely it is the most beautiful edifice in Washington. The memorial to Kennedy has more activity inside, and the one to Lincoln is more solid, but this one more perfectly catches the spirit of the man and his age. One day last year, touring the rooms of Monticello with other visitors, under the guidance of one of those charming Virginia ladies who always call him "Mister Jefferson," David and I overheard a woman from the Bronx say to her husband, after we had borne witness to Mr. Jefferson's sixteenth invention: "He must have been some weird weirdo." Well, he was not, and as I watched Jamie and David go on ahead up the steps and start reading the words on the walls of his Memorial, I felt happy that he was around when he was, and even made a secret wish that he were here today, either here in this town right now or trampling about in the snows of New Hampshire if necessary.

Of the five quotations on the wall, Jamie said he liked the one that comes out against the commerce in human slavery best. I asked him why, and this fine boy who was born and raised in Paris and is also like a son to me, and who plays leftfield for a softball team we have on Long Island called the Golden Nematodes consisting of bartenders, potato farmers, writers, and boys (David plays centerfield), said because it makes such good sense.

I think David's favorite is the one which talks about the truths they held to be self-evident, although he says he hasn't made up his mind. Personally, I find myself partial to the promise he swore on the altar of God. My friend, who threw away his cigar before he went inside, likes every one of them, or I got that impression from the look on his face when he was reading them all, and by the fact that he dwelt on them for a very long time.

Later, the four of us went out on the steps and admired that majestic view you get from there against the burnt orange sky. Jamie said that once when he was a little boy he wandered around the forum at Rome at night time and got scared, and on top of that some scrawny stray cats who inhabit those pits came after him. That got David on the subject of a dismal afternoon we spent years ago at Stonehenge. My friend said he didn't have enough time to think of all that on Guadalcanal, but he did later when they shipped him back to the military hospital in Memphis, Tenn.

It was a good prelude to that country we are heading for, where all of this nearly washed away in blood. It was just a father-and-son sort of thing on Washington's Birthday.

Washington Star, 17 February 1976

Honeymoon and Stars at Harpers Ferry

Harpers Ferry—We saw the car parked outside the Civil War Museum in Chancellorsville, an undistinguished sedan of some years' vintage with District of Columbia plates and a faded George Washington University decal on the window. On the doors and the back were the faint contours of the words someone had tried to scrub away—"Just Married"—and inside, on the front seat, a few scattered grains of rice.

We sighted them for the first time several minutes later, gazing in the reverential semidarkness at a museum exhibit which outlined the casualty figures between the Rapidan and the Rappahannock in the spring and summer of 1864. They were both in their middle twenties—he a tall, gangling boy with a reddish beard wearing corduroys and a pullover sweater, she a small, pale figure with rather pretty features, wearing a blue dress which somehow seemed out of place in those circumstances, as if she were trying to please him beyond the measure of the moment and the surroundings.

She reached for his hand two or three times, and he would comply for a few seconds and then disengage himself and move on ahead of her to the next window. He seemed unhappy. Perhaps the horrendous new arrangement bothered him and made him insecure in the secret places of his heart and he wanted a little time to sort it out. Or perhaps it was that these old mementoes of death convinced him that he had made a cataclysmic error, so cataclysmic that nothing less than his manhood could be at stake, and that he should have borrowed the money and taken the honeymoon in Miami, or even New Orleans, or somewhere a long way from Washington.

We drifted outside at the same time, to the back of the building to visit the monument where Jackson fell to the volleys of his own men. They stood there wordlessly, examining the words carved in the stone, then briefly studied their maps and went back to their car. Soon they disappeared around a bend in the direction of Spotsylvania.

An hour or so later, we were at the Bloody Angle, walking over that ground where the forlorn shape of the trenches remains, and we saw the car turn and come toward us on Bloody Angle Drive, stopping just behind our pickup truck. The two of them emerged and paused before the enormous painting on the plaque there, at what had been the apex of that salient on the precise spot where we stood. Showing in close detail the hundreds of men who had killed each other there with bayonets, knives, rifle butts, and pistols. The birds sang all around us; the warm Virginia afternoon could have been springtime if the trees watering these fields had not been bare of leaves.

He stood with his hands in his pockets, absorbing the details of the painting, then looked up at a jetliner slowly descending toward Dulles or National with immaculate puffs of smoke in its wake, a gesture on his part so casual and mindless and yet so private that it seemed to evoke in the girl, who was standing to the side of him and had been observing him, there, an emotion of sorrow and bewilderment: she was trying so hard, and if she were displeasing him, so suddenly and without warning, then what could the sources be?

Now it was our turn to depart, leaving them to that haunted terrain, but I sensed that we would see them yet again, and more than once, much as I sensed such things in those years I was a student in Europe when the dollar lasted a long time and the green passport rode high—when you might see the same couple from Pennsylvania in a tour group on the Left Bank one day and at Versailles the next, then Avignon or Nimes, and never really speak, out of mutual embarrassment. That or the simple ennui of being with too many other Americans in Europe in 1959.

So it was no surprise that after we stopped for a while in the Wilderness, then ascended into the Blue Ridge to lose the taste of destruction, dipped into the Shenandoah and made a loop around the Massanutten before going north, we found ourselves at an adjacent table in the motel restaurant on the mountainside in Harpers Ferry the next morning.

That was when I discovered, eavesdropping as hard as I could on the strained, sparse fragments the honeymoon couple exchanged, that he works for one of the agencies, that he comes and goes in a carpool in the farthest of the suburbs and that they had best be getting back tomorrow. When she asked him why they should go back now, he said it was just the time, that was all.

Harpers Ferry is not the ghost town I once loved, not since the federal government more or less took it over, but it was quiet and lustrous on this day with so few visitors about and the rippling of the Potomac and the Shenandoah from their lonely banks was the evanescence of every lazy childhood. The couple had come there too, of course, to view the sight where Brevet-Colonel Lee and Lieutenant Stuart of the United States Marines had been dispatched to find John Brown, and in the small cluster of tourists the couple had noticed, as we had, the presence of a celebrity, a figure to be reckoned on the national talk shows, a singer of masculine eminence who also sings and plays the guitar and who at this moment was in the company of a lovely brunette whose silhouette bedazzled us. As we looked at the ruined outlines of John Brown's last stand, we heard the singer ask his companion if she had brought along their map of the village.

It was the most astonishingly perfect déjà vu from literature I have ever experienced. It was straight from Walker Percy's *The Moviegoer* when the young groom gives Bill Holden the light for his cigarette, so close to it that at first I watched as if it were a dream I had had a long time ago, or an old prescience of truth unfolding, as if Percy were a prophet of the human heart or a historian of the verities reenacting themselves as all good poets are. Here, in Harpers Ferry, the boy was at first more apprehensive. He withdrew his map and approached the celebrity, tapping him gently on the shoulder.

The man turned about, with that irritation of all such souls with well-known faces who have had their flesh touched too many times by strangers. But when he saw the boy was offering him what he had asked for, he smiled generously, and the two of them walked away a few steps to confer on the locale. And when the boy finally gave him the map, he smiled again and thanked him warmly, then with a gesture of farewell, left down the street with his companion.

The boy went back to his bride, and he too was smiling, the first we had seen in two days from him. The aura of recognition had seized on him. In his casual brush with greatness, in this village of blood and lost causes, of pillage and rapine, perhaps he felt he had performed well before her. Or he had a story to tell in the office. Or he had retrieved something in himself which profoundly mattered to him.

Who knows the true reason for such deep and human things? Surely it is enough that the two of them walked away benignly now, leaving us all the happier too as we turned once more to the ground where Brown, Lee, and Jeb Stuart's lives had briefly converged before departing in our pickup truck for Antietam.

Washington Star, 19 February 1976

The Fields of War Become a Cold Companion

Sharpsburg, Md.— One of the good things about Washington for me is the accessibility of honest countryside in such a short ride from the middle of town. After forty-five minutes or an hour from Manhattan, a man is still caught in the wastes of industrial New Jersey, or the horrendous sprawl of western Long Island. From the District you can whip along one of the big federal expressways, and the places immediately around them have a mood and a culture all their own, frenetic to themselves, but not many miles off one of these mass conveyors there is the older, more settled America, the America of our memories. Washington, D.C., the idea of it, the physical pale of it, is always close at hand in these places, and then again, in curious ways it is not.

I love the integrity of them, the way the people talk, the facades of buildings in shadow and sunlight along their streets, little boys in parks shooting baskets, the Potomac and the Shenandoah appearing suddenly as if from nowhere in their eternal twistings and turnings.

My three companions and I have driven on this day not from Washington but west from the battlefields of Chancellorsville, Spotsylvania, and the Wilderness. One of my friends is my neighbor James Jones, from Long Island, and the Civil War obsesses him. It sends reverberations through his head, he says. Among his books are *From Here to Eternity*, the great novel of World War II, and *The Thin Red Line*, perhaps the finest novel on combat in American literature, and most recently the non-fiction, illustrated best seller entitled *WW II*. With us are our two teenaged sons, the same two who had peregrinated around Washington with us the last few days to see the Jefferson Memorial at twilight, not to mention the Oval Room of the White House on a still weekday morning and the Washington Birthday Parade in good old Alexandria. During those battlefields between the Rapidan and the Rappahannock, my friend had been haunted, as any superior writer of fiction might be, by the knowledge that these armies in the spring of 1864 were fighting on the same terrain of battles of a year before, so that the boys who had survived that year and come back again to Virginia saw the old scenes of devastation, the skeletons of men and horses, the burnt-out woodlands, the makeshift graves. Wandering about these places in the warm sunlight, sometimes startling the illicit couples in parked cars who find their privacy in battlefields in the wintertime, he talked a lot about what that déjà vu must have done to the soldiers, as a man who knows.

We are headed now toward Antietam, north up the Blue Ridge to Harpers Ferry, then on a country road to Shepherdstown and Sharpsburg, and there it is before us, only a mile or so out of town, the very name itself—Antietam—resonant of something which matters.

It is a place linked closely to the Federal City some seventy miles away. Washington might be a different concept altogether if that fortuitous clash of two great armies on Sept. 17, 1862, had taken a different turn, and so also of course, might the nation. It was a draw, if such things can be called that, but it meant Lee had to call off his invasion of the North and return to Virginia; it also meant three more years of warfare. It enabled Lincoln to issue the Emancipation Proclamation, and all one has to do to perceive the effect of that is to look around him today from just about any street corner in the District of Columbia.

It was the bloodiest single day's combat in the Civil War. Shelby Foote in his monumental history says it was the bloodiest in the history of mankind up to then, with the possible exception of arcane goings-on in the interior of China earlier in the century. The boys on both sides were caught in outdated formations by the fire of deadly weaponry, new and old. They fell in rows. At Antietam they were firing cannons with chain-shot almost pointblank, two cannonballs attached together with a long chain, and when fired the chain would extend and cut men in half. More than 23,000 Americans fell that day; 6,608 fell on D-Day in France. And when it was over they took the wounded of both sides to a barn at the edge of the battlefield. "Screams, prayers, and curses made it a horrible place," Bruce Catton wrote, "with hundreds of anguished men packed together on the straw begging surgeons to attend them—surgeons barearmed and fearsomely streaked and spattered in blood, piles of severed arms and legs by the slippery operating tables."

It is a day of mists and unhurried rain, and as we pause for a long time at the Dunker Church there is an ominous rumble way off toward the skyline—it sounds very much like artillery. Was it D. H. Hill and his five brigades back to try again? We find out later it is some demolition work going on around Harpers Ferry, but it will give a draught of authenticity to the scenes we are to see in the Corn Field, where Hooker blasted the Southerners with cannon and Hood lost 80 percent of his Texas brigade; in the West Woods, where 2,200 of Sedgwick's men were killed by Jackson's sharpshooters in less than twenty minutes; at the Sunken Road and Burnside's Bridge.

My friend wears a slouch hat and is in

walking boots and in these places he tarries in the cold wind with a pair of binoculars. It is melancholy land with its hollows and ravines and knolls and rock outcroppings which snipers used, and they could hide a whole brigade in some of those places—"a general's paradise," my friend says, as he peers through the binoculars at the place Jackson hid his men, "but very hard on the legs of the troops. One of the things most people don't understand is the physical hardship a soldier goes through even when he's not being shot at. The average person couldn't climb that hill at Burnside's Bridge just to get there. And going downhill is sometimes even more draining than going uphill. If you've been a soldier you look at all that, I guess."

The ironies and juxtapositions are also a little insane. Here the federal government only owns strips and fragments of the land where the fighting took place, so all about us we see farm houses and even trailer houses with long television aerials and abandoned cars in back right next to some spot where hundreds of men died. Cows graze in fields which ran with blood, chickens and dogs go about their pleasures, and the farmers plant corn in those places where, as one witness described them, "Men, I cannot say fell; they were knocked out of the ranks by dozens." Far out in one cornfield, separated from us by the wire fence marking that this is the beginning of federal property, there is a lonely monument with a lion on top, with corn furrows going around it on each side. A visitor can not even get out to it unless he climbs the fence and walks several hundred yards over the corn stalks, but this, my friend and I surmise, is where Sedgwick's men were ambushed by Jackson. It reminds me at that moment of Tennyson's poem, I tell my friend:

The woods decay, the woods decay and fall,
The vapors weep their burthens to the ground,
Man comes and tills the fields and lies beneath,
And after many a summer dies the swan.

At the observation point in the West Woods we talk a little about the strategy, Lee with 40,000 men, McClellan with 90,000, how Lee continually moved men from one place to another; and the teen-aged boys are finally a little restless with this technical talk, and have gone off to dig up some earthworms. "Did you see that picture of Lee in the museum?" my friend says. "It's my favorite one of Lee. It's the one that shows that beneath the sweet, benign, religious facade, he was a very tough man. He knew that if you're a soldier settled into the mire, you don't know what's going on all around you. You get no notion of the whole picture. It's hard enough for the generals. They don't know themselves a lot of the time. Lee knew a hell of a lot more than the others and this is a perfect example right here."

In the guidebook we are using is a photograph of the burial details of both armies after the battle here, working together with the corpses under a flag of truce. They would sit and smoke together and talk. And my friend, looking at the picture, remembers the times he was assigned to such work on Guadalcanal, when a graves-registration officer would come by and ask for three or four men out of a company, and the First Sergeant would pick them. He once wrote a short story about that, called with irony, Greater Love ("Greater love hath no man than that he lay down his life for another"), about the smells rising from the temporary graves they dug up, about a boy from his company who was on one of those details and found his brother in a temporary grave, and about how they would laugh a lot to keep from cracking up.

The day wanes on in its mist and rain, and we have worked our way from Nicodemus Hill down the Smoketown Lane and past the Roulette Farmhouse, and now are at the Sunken Road, which at the time became known as Bloody Lane.

Here, along a line of a thousand yards, in a farm road worn down by the elements, the Confederate center took its stand, thousands of them firing at close quarter against the Federal troops charging across a series of ravines which slope southward across the crest of a ridge. It lasted three hours, and the dead Confederate soldiers lay so thick there that as far down the road as the eye could see, for a thousand yards, a man could walk upon them without once touching ground, and the bodies of the attackers lay strewn in piles across the whole ridge.

We have it all to ourselves, and the four of us walk down the road for a while, and peer out every so often from behind the wooden fences at the crest where the attackers came. The two boys are quiet now also, and for a moment they are looking silently at a monument only a few feet to the south of the road, dedicated to an Ohio brigade, and at the top of this is the stone silhouette of a boy who seems to be no more than eighteen raising his cap in one hand, holding a flag in the other.

To the right of the Sunken Road is an observation tower, evil-smelling with the reek of urine, and the four of us climb all the way to the top of it. The view from here is awesome, the Blue Mountains at the horizon, the sweeping sky, the tossing landscape below us in a diaphanous mist, the road itself sweeping almost to the opposite skyline. What had happened all around us here was difficult to comprehend, but except for a few monuments it all was exactly as it had been 114 years ago.

We have propped our elbows on the railing to linger for a bit, talking about what we have seen.

"The alacrity with which men went to die," my friend is saying, gazing down at the ridge where Richardson's men came. "It's incredibly sad. It breaks my heart. You wonder why it was necessary, why human beings have to do that to each other. This reminds me a little of Europe, where every blade of grass has twenty-one drops of human blood on it. That's why Europe's so goddamned green."

Well, why do men do it? One of the boys wanted to know. Why did they do it here?

"Well..." He pauses for an instant, to the patter of rain on the roof. "I think it's more because they didn't want to appear unmanly in front of their friends. On the average I think that counted more than any set of beliefs. Men don't like to be shot at. Take my word for it. They'd rather have been anywhere else than here. If you could just get men to expend the courage and energy on things that weren't destructive to other men, what a race we'd be." What was it Steinbeck said? He stopped to remember it. "Man has conquered every natural obstacle in the world except himself."

But the average run-of-the-mill of human experience is so full of sorrow and brutality anyway, I suggest.

"Without war," he replies. "You and I know that. We're writers. I honestly think people go to war to escape that kind of sorrow you and I have to live with. I honestly believe that. But these men would've had to be mystical to go farther than they did. I don't think men could go any farther than these men did in this battle and still be members of the planet."

At last we descend the tower, and the boys and I walk over to our car. Our companion has dallied somewhere, however, and we go looking for him. There he is, a solitary figure in a slouch hat, standing for a little while in the middle of the Sunken Road. When he returns, for the drive back to Washington, he says, with the faintest beginnings of a sigh: "I guess you really have to be alone in a place like this."

Washington Star, 22 February 1976

Index

A number preceded by a lower-case "p" refers to a page number. A number without a "p" denotes an item number in Parts II or III.